HISPANIC CATHOLIC CULTURE
IN THE U.S.

THE NOTRE DAME HISTORY
OF HISPANIC CATHOLICS IN THE U.S.
General Editor: Jay P. Dolan

Volume One
Mexican Americans and the Catholic Church, 1900–1965

Volume Two
Puerto Rican and Cuban Catholics in the U.S., 1900–1965

Volume Three
Hispanic Catholic Culture in the U.S.: Issues and Concerns

Hispanic Catholic Culture in the U.S.:

Issues and Concerns

Edited by

Jay P. Dolan

and

Allan Figueroa Deck, S.J.

UNIVERSITY OF NOTRE DAME PRESS

Notre Dame   London

Library of Congress Cataloging-in-Publication Data

Hispanic Catholic culture in the U.S. : issues and
  concerns / edited by Jay P. Dolan and Allan
  Figueroa Deck.
      p.   cm. — (The Notre Dame history of
Hispanic Catholics in the U.S.; v. 3)
      ISBN 0-268-01105-2 (alk. paper)
      1. Hispanic American Catholics—History—20th
century.   2. Catholic Church—United States—
Membership.   3. United States—Church history—
20th century.   I. Dolan, Jay P., 1936– .   II. Deck,
Allan Figueroa, 1945– .   III. Series.
BX1407.H55H56   1994   94-15464
282'.73'08968—dc20   CIP

CONTENTS

Acknowledgments

The Notre Dame History of Hispanic Catholics in the U.S. began in 1989 when the Cushwa Center for the Study of American Catholicism at the University of Notre Dame and its director, Jay P. Dolan, together with Mary Ewens, O.P., at that time the associate director of the Cushwa Center, began to design a plan for the study. An essential component of this phase of the project was an advisory committee made up of individuals who were engaged in various aspects of Hispanic studies. Allan Figueroa Deck, S.J., Gilberto M. Hinojosa, Michael J. McNally, Moisés Sandoval, Anthony M. Stevens-Arroyo, and Olga R. Villa Parra comprised this committee and have guided the study throughout the four years that it took to complete it. We are truly grateful for their assistance. Also making an important contribution to the study was Jaime R. Vidal, who replaced Mary Ewens at the Cushwa Center in 1990. He served as an important liaison between the Cushwa Center and the numerous scholars involved in the study. Another key person was the secretary of the Cushwa Center, Delores Dant Fain. She took care of a myriad of details and was mainly responsible for administering what proved to be a very complex project. We are very grateful for all her work on behalf of the study.

A special word of thanks must go to Jeanne Knoerle, S.P., and Fred L. Hofheinz of the Lilly Endowment. They continually encouraged us throughout the four years of the study; without their support the study would not have been possible.

Hispanic Catholic Culture in the U.S.: Issues and Concerns is only one part of the study. The other volumes in this history are *Mexican Americans and the Catholic Church 1900–1965* and *Puerto Rican and Cuban Catholics in the U.S., 1900–1965*. All of these books are available from the University of Notre Dame Press. Together they comprise the Notre Dame History of Hispanic Catholics in the U.S., a landmark study of a people too-long neglected by historians of American Catholicism.

INTRODUCTION

The dilemma facing contemporary students of U.S. Hispanic Catholic history is two-fold: 1) a lack of easy access to many of the primary sources such as parish and diocesan archives or the files of influential apostolic movements and organizations; and 2) a dearth of scholarly monographs on the vast range of topics relevant to the history of Hispanics in the United States Catholic Church. The advisory board that served in the elaboration of this study, the Notre Dame History of Hispanic Catholics in the U.S., was acutely aware of the need to take the scholarly discussion of Hispanic Catholic history to a new level of insight by laying out and arranging the field in a more extensive and coherent manner than ever before.

We were also convinced that one cannot do history by jumping to conclusions. We were aware of the fact that in an age of revisionism like ours, new, necessary, and compelling interests and perspectives are being taken to the understanding of the past. Enthusiasm for that timely task, however, cannot take the place of "doing one's homework." So the first two volumes consist of studies that identify and use the best primary and secondary sources and focus on manageable, discreet topics or themes. The intention is to face the dilemma mentioned above by moving beyond panoramic visions that in a new field like Hispanic Catholic history may have initially met the need but now no longer do so.

This volume, then, is an effort to assemble the material in new ways. No longer are the articles divided in terms of national origin—Mexican, Cuban, or Puerto Rican—as was done in the other two volumes of the study. Rather, the authors have identified key issues that cut across nationalities, regions, and generations and appear fundamental for a deeper understanding of U.S. Hispanic Catholics in the closing years of this century. Several articles in this volume address the delicate question of the interaction—not always smooth—among diverse Latino communities. This approach promises to result in a clearer conceptualization of the issues and in more substantial critical insights than were possible even a decade ago.

1

Joan Moore, a seasoned scholar of Latino social history, tackles the fascinating subject of the Hispanic social fabric. She does so with considerable depth and subtlety, respecting the growing diversity of the Latino communities in terms of national origin, generation, and social class. She finds in the concept of "fabric" an appropriate analogy for the astonishing complexity and interrelatedness of Latino social reality. She demonstrates the need to move beyond one-dimensional analyses of Latinos.

A young Latino scholar based in the Midwest, David A. Badillo, tells the story of midwestern Latinos. We are used to hearing about the California, Southwest, Texas, New York, or Florida Latino contexts. But we know little about the trends in mid-America where small and large Latino populations have thrived for two or three generations in places like Chicago, Kansas City, Detroit, and Lorraine, Ohio. Badillo contributes to a growing awareness of the diverse regional Latino contexts while helping establish the truly national character of the Hispanic presence.

Anthony M. Stevens-Arroyo, a leading Latino sociologist, provides a stimulating assessment of Latino Catholic social identity as it has emerged in the past forty years. He brings to this task insights from sociology and perspectives from his Puerto Rican and Neorican experiences. Stevens-Arroyo traces the events which helped shape the image of Latino Catholics in the United States. He shows how southwestern, Mexican-American voices tended to establish the agenda and define the issues. He discusses the inadequacy of this dynamic and the need to admit alternate Latino voices. Finally, Stevens-Arroyo critiques the Hispanic Catholic movement of the last twenty-five years for creating a "pastoralist" image of Hispanic Catholic identity by generally ignoring the issue of liberation, the socioeconomic and political dimensions of the Latino struggle. This has not contributed to the ability of Latinos to participate vigorously precisely as Latinos and Catholics in the public square.

The editor of *Maryknoll Magazine*, Moisés Sandoval, assembles the organizational puzzle of the Hispanic Catholic Church of the United States piece by piece. A life-long student of things Catholic and Latino, Sandoval authoritatively traces the development of today's Hispanic Church. Persons, places, institutions, and key moments are neatly woven together in an effort to document today's reality. Sandoval provides chronologies and periodizations that make a contribution to a more nuanced and substantive interpretation of events, trends, and possible future directions for Hispanic ministry.

The first United States Hispanic woman with a doctorate in theology, Marina Herrera describes the context and clarifies the sources for Hispanic Catholic leadership in the United States since the time of the Second Vatican Council. Trends in both the universal Church and in Latin America mightily contributed to the orientations, methods, and general spirit of U.S. Hispanic Catholic leadership. She carefully demonstrates the linkage between emerging concepts of Church, society, justice, and culture generated by the Second Vatican Council and the meetings of Latin American bishops at Medellín, Puebla, and Santo Domingo, along with the series of *encuentros* convoked under the auspices of the United States bishops. She takes us back to the initial gatherings of U.S. and Latin American Catholic leadership at the meetings of CICOP, the Inter-American Cooperation Program in the late 1960s. Herrera fills in a significant gap in knowledge regarding the actual sources of inspiration for many of today's Latino Catholic leaders. She names many key players, many of them women and until now perhaps forgotten, in the development of the first U.S. Hispanic Catholic leadership, listing the efforts in this direction into the 1990s.

Edmundo Rodríguez is a consultant on Latino leadership development with many years of experience in church and community organization. He highlights the crucial historical role of movements such as the Cursillo de Cristiandad, the Charismatic Renewal, Guadalupana societies or organizations such as HERMANAS or PADRES which have functioned as "schools of leadership." Rodríguez shows how these organizations have made significant contributions to the formation of some strong and enduring Latino leaders (clergy, religious women, and laity) throughout the country. Rodríguez's research and interpretation of events complements several other articles in this volume. He spends a considerable amount of time telling us about the apostolic movements as early players in the formation of U.S. Hispanic leadership, a topic that has not received the attention it rightly deserves.

Ana María Díaz-Stevens is an accomplished social scientist and professor at Union Theological Seminary. She adds two lucid articles to this collection. The first analyzes the complicated question of Latinas in the Catholic Church. Díaz-Stevens bridges the sensitivity of the Latin American women in Latin America, in this case Puerto

Rican, with the seasoned views of Latinas of the United States. She
explores the extraordinary role of Hispanic women in religion past
and present.

In a second article, Díaz-Stevens narrates the story of Hispanic
youth ministry efforts in the difficult urban context of New York.
The Hispanic communities of the United States are extraordinarily youthful. Insight into Hispanic ministry therefore can hardly
prescind from this basic issue. Yet reliable analyses of Hispanic
youth in the Catholic Church like this one are hard to find. She
cites chapter and verse in the Church's outreach to Hispanics using
material from her book *Oxcart Catholicism*, the most in-depth study
of Puerto Rican Catholicism in New York currently available. Her
method provides a paradigm for similar studies of Hispanic youth
outreach waiting to be done in other urban situations.

Many scholars of Hispanic Catholicism in the United States
have pointed to the central place of popular religiosity, the people's
religion, in the understanding of Hispanic Catholicism. Few are
more prepared to describe and explain the function of popular
religiosity than Hispanic theologian Orlando O. Espín. He brings
a great deal of learning—theological, historical, and anthropological—to this crucial question for Hispanic Catholicism. His article
establishes the terms of discourse for what is becoming a fascinating dialogue.

Since the time of the Second Vatican Council, change in the
Catholic Church has revolved around remarkable reforms of the
liturgy. Arturo J. Pérez, a leading Latino liturgist, tells the story
of liturgical renewal as it has been lived by Hispanics in the
United States. His article is one of the few efforts to develop this
theme. It provides many insights into the development of Hispanic
Catholicism in the United States as it unfolds in the people's life of
prayer and worship, perhaps the most graphic and revealing area
of their lives.

Allan Figueroa Deck, S.J., addresses the phenomenon of the
flight of Hispanic Catholics from the Catholic Church. He moves
beyond the anecdotal and attempts to get to the bottom of this
remarkable development. Using the most credible sources available for the interpretation of this trend, Deck juxtaposes several
approaches—Latin American and North American—that provide
a helpful and suggestive appraisal of what promises to be one of
the more dramatic and significant developments in the history of
Latinos. A vibrant, growing Hispanic Protestantism is here to stay.

The concluding article in this volume, by Jay P. Dolan, highlights the major points of all eleven essays. It seeks to present these conclusions in such a manner that the entire collection of essays may acquire a measure of coherence and significance not possible from a reading of any one essay.

These articles, then, are a fitting conclusion to the Notre Dame History of Hispanic Catholics in the U.S. While the surface of a fascinating history is still only being scratched, it can be said that a new plateau has been reached. Future researchers will have another map, one with clearer markings. If nothing else, this project is a significant step forward in the elaboration of a United States Catholic Church history that gives the remarkable Hispanic presence the recognition it rightly deserves.

Allan Figueroa Deck, S.J.
Jay P. Dolan

1

The Social Fabric of the
Hispanic Community since 1965

Joan Moore

Until very recently—well after World War II—most Latinos in the United States were defined as a regional minority, as both Mexican and southwestern. The rest of the country rarely gave them a thought; when it came to ethnicity, the major preoccupation was with the absorption of the children of immigrants from Europe. The nation was barely conscious even of the looming crisis in black-white race relations, and the Southwest was far away from the nation's political and cultural centers. It was recognized that there were Mexicans in the Chicago area, Cubans in Tampa, and Puerto Ricans in New York City, but Latinos were an unacknowledged and little-known population. Even the U.S. Census did not have a category for Hispanics until 1970.[1]

By the mid-1960s the situation had changed dramatically, and by 1990 more than 22 million Hispanics lived in the United States, approximately 9 percent of the total population. Latinos were among the fastest-growing segments of the population, increasing by 7.6 million, or 53 percent, between 1980 and 1990. There were predictions that Hispanics would outnumber blacks by the twenty-first century. In fact, if their immigration and birthrate continue at 1990 levels, the number of Hispanics will more than double by the year 2020. High birthrates also mean that Hispanics are generally very young, with a median age of twenty-six, compared to thirty-four for the non-Hispanic population.[2]

The population is very diverse, and no collective label ("Hispanic" or "Latino") should be allowed to evoke an image of uniformity. National origins differ: 61 percent of America's Hispanics are Mexican in origin; 12 percent, Puerto Rican; and 5 percent, Cuban. These three groups are the largest, but 13 percent of Hispanics are from other Caribbean, Central, and South American countries and another 9 percent were classified as "other Hispanics."[3] Most of this last group lived in New Mexico and were descendants of very early settlers and are often considered part of the Mexicano population of the Southwest.

Regional subcultural experiences further amplify the diversity that stems from differences in national origin. Not surprisingly, although Latinos are generally very heavily urbanized, they are unevenly dispersed around the country. States of the Southwest hold high proportions of Hispanics—largely Mexican. New York has many Hispanics who are predominantly Puerto Rican, although two-thirds of all Dominican Americans also live in New York. Florida has most of the nation's Cubans. Increasingly, the various subpopulations are beginning to disperse outside of their traditional regions. In some midwestern cities like Chicago, there are sizable numbers of Puerto Ricans as well as long-settled Mexicans. But in very many areas of the nation there are still very few Latinos, and the result is a tendency to dismiss their importance.

Much of this diversity among Latino subpopulations reflects the particular history of each group. Mexican Americans were initially incorporated into the United States when their settlements were conquered—first in 1836 by rebellious Texans, and later in a full-scale war with the United States that ended in 1848. Mexican Americans experienced a long history of discrimination and labor exploitation, but the colonial history means that the larger cities (and many rural areas) have always had a middle class. The many ebbs and flows in immigration reflect conditions in both Mexico and the U.S. (for example, such cataclysmic events as the Mexican Revolution, the Great Depression, and, more recently, changing economic conditions in both countries and shifts in American public policy). Immigrants usually settle in well-established Mexican-American communities, and even before they come they often, especially in border areas, can use personal networks based on kinship or on hometown friendships. However, many recent Mexican immigrants are undocumented and vulnerable to the threat of deportation; they are particularly easy prey for exploitative employers. By contrast, Puerto Ricans coming to the mainland arrive as citizens, and although economically exploited they are eligible for welfare benefits. Most came initially to New York; like Mexicans, later Puerto Rican in-migrants also tended to settle in established communities. When Cubans first arrived in Miami in large numbers in the early 1960s, they struggled hard to establish their communities. But once established, the community became a major resource for subsequent waves of refugees.[4] Very few immigrants

from the other Caribbean and Central American nations were able
to obtain the refugee status that had benefited Cuban immigrants.[5]
The efforts of Dominicans, Salvadorans, and other Central Americans in the 1980s to build viable and self-sufficient communities
have been hampered not only by their general struggle for survival but also by the fact that many are undocumented and are
consequently easy to exploit.[6]

Each subpopulation is very diverse racially. Mexico's Indian
legacy is so strong that in the 1990 census only 55 percent of Mexican Americans identified themselves as "white," while 38 percent
referred to themselves as "mestizo," "Chicano," "La Raza" or some
similar term—almost as a separate race. Similarly, though the racial
mix in Puerto Rico is mostly with Africans rather than with Indians,
only 48 percent of Puerto Ricans identified themselves as "white,"
and 43 percent chose some other designation that reflects the island's Afro-Caribbean heritage.[7] By contrast, the overwhelming
majority (84 percent) of Cubans chose the term "white."[8] Stepick
and Grenier[9] argue that Miami's Cubans have adopted and even
amplified American racism to "reconstruct Cuban and Latin society
as a peculiarly white society from which any blacks are implicitly
excluded." Strong evidence affirms that lighter-skinned Hispanics do better than darker,[10] and Hispanics generally are plagued
by discrimination based on racist stereotypes. Housing provides
a classic example: A careful study of housing discrimination (in
which matched pairs of Anglos and Hispanics applied for housing in twenty-five metropolitan areas) showed that 56 percent of
Hispanic would-be homebuyers and 46 percent of Hispanic would-
be renters were treated less favorably than Anglos. Discrimination
was particularly high in New York.[11]

Much variation of social class exists among Hispanics. Many
are members of the middle class; nevertheless, as a group Latinos
are more likely to live in poverty than other Americans. In 1991, 28
percent were poor as compared with 32 percent of blacks and 13
percent of all Americans.[12] Poverty had increased over the preceding decade: In 1981 only 24 percent of all Hispanic families were
classified as poor by the census. All Hispanic subgroups except
Cubans tended disproportionately to be poor, and Puerto Ricans
were particularly likely to be poor—41 percent. Even when there is
so much poverty across the board for Hispanics, deprivation wears
a different face for each subpopulation.

Two further common conditions affect Latino communities: immigration and economic restructuring. All Hispanic communities

have experienced substantial immigration within the past several generations. In fact, even though Hispanics have much higher birthrates than other Americans,[13] much of the rapid growth of the population—and perhaps some of the increase in poverty—is explained by immigration. Because there has been such a complex history and so much undocumented immigration from Mexico, it is difficult to trace Chicanos' recent immigration experience with much precision. However, even though most Mexican Americans (67 percent in 1990) were born in the United States, the late 1970s and 1980s have seen a significant increase in immigration from Mexico. The major surge in Puerto Rican migration to the mainland U.S. came earlier—shortly after World War II—in the Great Migration of 1946–1964. The population has been characterized by a "restless" movement of people back and forth from the island, with a steady accretion of the mainland population. The flood of Cuban migration started, of course, when Fidel Castro took power in 1959. Successive waves of refugees almost quintupled the number of Cubans, although recently the overall rate of growth decelerated. The 1970s and 1980s also witnessed a great increase in immigration from South and Central America, as well as from other Caribbean nations.

Economic restructuring has had a significant effect on most Hispanics, coinciding, in many cases, with increased immigration. Beginning in the late 1970s, jobs began to decline massively in some formerly prosperous parts of the country—and to grow quickly in other, formerly marginal, regions. Then the jobs moved overseas, and the nation as a whole was obviously losing "good" manufacturing jobs.[14] By the late 1980s, the geographical shift in the location of job growth manifested clearly the second and more important aspect of economic restructuring—the shift from a manufacturing to a service economy. This was deindustrialization and a major transformation.

A consensus holds that traditional manufacturing is not going to revive. Jobs in the new service and information economy are located disproportionately at either the high or the low end of wage and salary distributions. Many of the newer firms function without the internal differentiation of seniority and other markers of standing that might permit workers to move up within the company.[15] In the traditional unionized manufacturing firm, job ladders permit workers to climb from entry level jobs to more adequate employment. When these job ladders disappear—as they have—people with poor education are trapped in dead-end jobs, often for a lifetime of poverty. This kind of change in the workplace has major implications for poor communities, especially immigrant communities and minority communities with a history of discrimination and confinement in central city ghettos and barrios.[16] In the 1990s, restructuring began to affect white-collar employment as well, and the country saw massive layoffs of well-educated white-collar workers.

The concept of deindustrialization is especially useful in understanding the plight of Puerto Ricans (who are heavily concentrated in Rustbelt cities) and of Mexican Americans and Caribbeans and Central Americans in many cities. Even though some cities have not followed this same pattern, all American cities have undergone some form of economic restructuring that has deeply affected the material conditions of life.

Rustbelt manufacturing decline and Sunbelt growth demonstrate vividly what economic restructuring means. It is easy to assume that because Latinos are heavily concentrated in the Sunbelt, these economic shifts would be favorable. But in reality the economic adjustments have a more subtle effect. For example, many Sunbelt cities also experienced Rustbelt-style economic restructuring—in particular, the loss of industries. Los Angeles and Houston, for example, saw a major wave of plant closings in the late 1970s and early 1980s. These shifts put a fair number of Hispanics out of work.[17]

Neither the Rustbelt nor the Sunbelt has seen uniform economic change. In some of the deindustrialized cities throughout the nation there has been significant reindustrialization and many new jobs. But Latinos—especially the immigrants—are often at the bottom of the wage scale for such jobs.

Most of the expanding low-wage service and manufacturing industries, like electronics and garment manufacturing, employ Hispanics,[18] and some depend almost completely upon immigrant labor working at minimum wage.[19] Many larger cities have also seen the expansion of low-wage service jobs both to serve the corporate elite and to meet the demand for low-cost goods and services that is generated by Latino and other immigrant communities. The volume of immigration has been high enough to create its own new market, what Sassen calls a "Third World city . . . located in dense groupings spread all over the city."[20] Not only are the immigrant workers poorly paid but many must endure dangerous working conditions. Ironically, their desirability as cheap labor has generated some unpleasant side effects: One of the provisions of the 1986 Immigration Reform and Control Act was that employers would be sanctioned if they hired undocumented workers, and as a consequence about 20 percent of all employers choose to reject all job applicants who seem to be "foreign" in any way, even if only in, say, appearance or name. This study by the General Accounting Office points to a massive increase in discrimination against Hispanics in the workplace.[21]

Latinos also work in a wide variety of informal economic activities in large cities. These activities are usually small scale, informally organized, and by-pass government regulations.[22] They include new and exploitative arrangements in well-established industries (such as home work in the garment industry, as seamstresses take their work home with them). There are such individual activities as street vending, handy-man house repairs and alterations, and casual street-corner pick-up labor in construction and gardening. And, finally, the informal economy includes illicit activities—most notably, a burgeoning drug market in some cities.

These are common conditions that all Latinos share. But beyond these commonalities, each group is different and shows important variations in such critical elements as social class, family structure, and the degree of community viability (which is often related to the community's political strength), all of which are potentially important to the Church.

Mexican Americans

Most of the people in the largest Latino population—the Mexican Americans—were born in the United States. They have all of the characteristics of a minority population, and one that continues to be slighted. Even in the superficially prosperous Sunbelt, their problems are associated with economic restructuring and urban fiscal crises, as well as with the continuing neglect that stems from a long history of discrimination. Faltering school systems and declining government sector jobs add to the difficulties that face a population struggling to move into middle-class positions. How long this mobility remains blocked is an important question for the entire nation.

The Mexican-American population in the United States is so old and so diverse that it defies almost all generalities. The border cities of Texas, the global city of Los Angeles, and the old settlements of New Mexico offer three typical areas demonstrating the importance of local history and subregional economies.

The border cities

Mexican Americans are the dominant population in the long string of small towns, medium-sized cities, and agricultural developments that stretches along the Texas-Mexico border in one of the poorest parts of the United States. In the southernmost counties on the border, 80 percent of the population is Mexican American and many families maintain strong ties with kin across the border. Though there is a strongly entrenched elite and a solid middle class, in 1987 almost 40 percent of Mexican Americans were below the poverty line.[23] Wages are low, often below minimum wage levels, even though food and housing are as expensive as in other parts of the nation. Along the length of the border, an estimated quarter of a million people live in some 1,000 *colonias*—new rural slum communities that often lack basic utilities, water, and sewers; living conditions in the *colonias* pose a major health threat.[24]

There was much economic turbulence along the border in the 1970s and 1980s. Some towns became shopping meccas for northern Mexico; twin manufacturing plants were built on both sides of the border; "snowbird" tourism flourished. But the net result did not bring much economic improvement between 1960 and 1980. The median income for the four southernmost counties of Texas was 47 percent of the U.S. average in 1960 and it was 55 percent of the U.S. average in 1980. Poverty actually increased during the 1980s.[25] In 1983 a devastating freeze destroyed much of the local citrus industry for almost a decade, and the freeze coincided with the first of a series of Mexican peso devaluations that crushed most cross-border trade. The illicit economy, largely based on smuggling, flourished.

Los Angeles

Mexican Americans dominate the 40 percent of Los Angeles's 1990 population that is Latino. Vast areas of the metropolis are predominantly Mexican American. The global city has an expanded high-wage service industry and has undergone not only major expansion since 1965 but also many important economic changes. Los Angeles is suffering a little-publicized, serious deindustrialization. A low-wage reindustrialization is taking place in the garment industry and electronics, and low-wage service jobs are expanding. Along with other Latino immigrants, Mexican Americans are the mainstay both of the low-wage manufacturing industries and of the low-wage service industries. Many new arrivals are undocumented workers, adding to what may be "perhaps the largest pool of cheap, manipulable, and easily dischargeable labor of any advanced capitalist city."[26] The large influx of immigrants into barrios scattered throughout the metropolitan area has revitalized Mexican culture in those communities.[27] Commercial interests were quick to capitalize on this change, offering such cultural adjustments as a major grocery chain with several stores designed to resemble traditional Mexican markets. Beyond the barrios, the millions of Mexican Americans include many successful business people and professionals.

The old settlers

A third dramatically different lifestyle belongs to the so-called *manitos*, or Hispanos, of New Mexico and southern Colorado. This group is descended from Spanish settlers of the seventeenth and eighteenth centuries. Though in many respects manitos' culture closely resembles Mexican Americans', often they claim a distinctive identity.[28] Manitos are a strong presence at every level of New Mexico society and have been continuously visible in the state's political life, both in the countryside and in the cities. Nonetheless, in a poor state, many of the manitos are among the poorest.

Albuquerque, the state's largest city, is a regional hub and a center for military manufacturing. During the 1970s and 1980s low-paying garment and electronics factories also opened. The city engulfed several manito villages as it expanded and attracted many Chicano in-migrants from other small towns throughout the area (the number of immigrants from Mexico, however, remained relatively small). Among the poorer barrios, each type of community showed a different social structure: the former villages tended to retain strong informal resource networks, while interpersonal resources available in the newer settlements of immigrants tended to be far shallower.[29]

Social class

The border cities, Los Angeles, and the old settlements illustrate the wide variation in social class structure that exists in most Chicano communities. In most southwestern cities, a few Mexican Americans have been rich for generations, and some of them have been part of the elite: New Mexico has had several manito U.S. senators (including Dennis Chavez and Joseph Montoya), business leaders, and state politicians, and in the 1960s the Lower Rio Grande Valley produced the first federal judge of Mexican ancestry.

Most cities also have distinct middle class—primarily of small businesspeople and professionals—with a distinctive subculture.[30] After World War II, the Mexican-American middle class expanded as opportunities for education opened up, but the gains were not as substantial as one might have expected. Even as recently as 1991 only 9 percent of men of Mexican origin held managerial and professional positions, far less than the 28 percent of non-Hispanic men and women, and a smaller proportion than for any other Hispanic subgroup.[31] This figure shows a loss over the previous decade, a shortfall that demands an explanation.[32] Some portion of the loss can be explained by the increased immigration of poor Mexicans during the late 1970s and 1980s. Few Mexican immigrants were middle class, and the entire occupational distribution became more skewed toward the working class. But the disparities persist even when the figures omit the foreign born: For example, less than 8 percent of men of Mexican origin born in the U.S. held professional and semiprofessional jobs, compared with nearly 11 percent of U.S.-born Puerto Ricans and 14 percent of U.S.-born Cubans.[33] One might speculate that systematic barriers stand in the way of Mexican Americans' occupational attainment: The most obvious place to look is the educational system.

The educational achievement of Latinos in general lags behind that of other American populations, and the Mexican-origin population is the least well educated of all of the Latinos. Less than 6 percent of all Mexican Americans completed four years of college, and the median education was just a year or so above the eighth grade. Some of the low educational attainment can be explained by the entry of a large number of poorly educated Mexican immigrants, who in 1980 had a median of only six years of schooling (the lowest of all of the Latino immigrant populations). But even the U.S.-born lagged far behind other U.S.-born Hispanics. The U.S.-born have always lagged; racist school systems and inferior and segregated "Mexican" schools have deprived Mexican young people for generations. A voluminous literature on the educational concerns of Mexican Americans reflects generations of struggle with southwestern school systems as well as many significant educational innovations.[34] Today's Mexican-American population is better educated than at any time in the past, but severe problems remain, and even the youngest adults—those most recently out of school—are overrepresented among both the nation's dropouts and its illiterates.[35]

That the working class and the poor command most of the research interest on Mexican Americans in this country reflects the

fact that 28 percent of persons of Mexican origin fell below the
official poverty line in 1991 because of concentration in poorly paid
occupations.[36] This figure shows only part of the poverty, for there
is also substantial underemployment; in 1987, for example, more
than a quarter of the Mexican Americans were working well below
their capacity or motivation.[37] Another 14 percent of men and
19 percent of women were "working poor," i.e., were employed
full time but in jobs that paid wages that were lower than the
poverty level. The proportion that was underemployed increased
during the 1980s and was higher for Mexican Americans than for
non-Hispanic whites with comparable levels of schooling.[38] Recent
immigrants and workers in areas with low wages and high concentrations of Chicanos (like south Texas) also did relatively poorly.

Despite such discouragements, Mexican Americans continue to
be more attached to the labor force than any other Latino group—
in 1991, more than either blacks or non-Hispanic whites.[39] New
immigration probably enhanced this attachment. Immigrants generally are ineligible for welfare benefits, which is a significant factor
in their motivation. And in at least one city, Chicago, Mexican
immigrants were far more likely to work than were blacks, Puerto
Ricans, or non-Hispanic whites with similar characteristics.[40] But
even though the new immigration had a negligible effect on the
wages of non-Hispanics,[41] it may have lowered the wage levels of
native-born Chicanos who compete with immigrants in the same
job markets.

Political mobilization

Until the late 1960s, the problems and grievances of most southwestern Mexican-American communities went almost unnoticed
and unattended. Generally speaking, local Anglo politicians were
not responsive to their Mexican-American constituents: The system
was stacked against effective representation. In some places, like
south Texas, political bosses manipulated the Mexican-American
vote to enhance their own power, with little advantage to the
people.[42] In other areas, like Los Angeles, the population was simply ignored; districts were gerrymandered so cleverly that Mexican
Americans could not be elected to office. Small-town and rural
politicians were particularly insensitive to "across the tracks" Mexicans. Obstacles were placed in the way of voting; foreign-born
Mexicans distrusted the system and were slow to naturalize, and
this further diluted the voting strength of the population.[43] New
Mexico was an exception. The peculiarities of the local manito
social structure meant that some Hispano representatives were

always elected at all levels—local, state, and federal. Elsewhere in the Southwest, the Mexican-American elite and the small middle class continuously protested civil rights violations, occasionally winning some concessions and allies,[44] but by and large the vast Mexican-American population was politically ignored.

Veterans returning from World War II began to challenge and change the political status quo. But not until the Chicano movement of the mid-1960s did the long-delayed protests really have a noticeable political effect in particular local communities.[45] Backed by clergy, farm workers joined Cesar Chavez in a series of strikes and grape and lettuce boycotts that touched the hearts of Chicanos—and others—throughout the Southwest. Similarly, manitos in New Mexico joined in a militant effort to redress more than a century of grievances: These men and women believed that they had a legitimate claim to federal land that was being used for national parks and private profit. Young people in south Texas united when La Raza Unida party, a true alternative third party, came into being. A civic reform movement in Crystal City, Texas, produced a kind of model for small-scale "revolutions" that could replace corrupt and oppressive Anglo officials with Chicanos who would reorganize schools, police, and local government to respond to Chicano needs. In the Lower Rio Grande Valley the dissidents were supported by local religious organizations. In Los Angeles, young militant Chicanos placed particular emphasis on the schools, though police brutality and unresponsive county health organizations also received their share of attention. Strong grassroots support was mobilized.

This kind of grassroots efforts shaped the politics of a generation of Chicanos. The *movimiento* was highly controversial even inside Mexican-American communities, but it was a watershed in political activity. Even though La Raza Unida party vanished and the fervor generated by Caesar Chavez's United Farm Workers abated, political sophistication increased and promoted new electoral gains. Growing numbers of Chicanos came to sit on city councils, in state legislatures, and in congressional delegations.

More direct continuity could be seen in the organizing work of COPS (Communities Organized for Public Service) in San Antonio. Its founder Ernesto Cortes had worked with the United Farm Workers and was trained in Chicago's Industrial Areas Foundation. Getting under way in 1973, COPS was based in the city's parishes and community organizations, and its goal was empowerment: Fewer than ten years later the grassroots organization had won hundreds of millions of dollars of improvements from the city of San Antonio and had become established as a major political force.[46] Parallel organizations were developed in Los Angeles and in the Lower Rio Grande Valley. All of these Chicano organizations were consciously rooted in religious values, and priests took active leadership.[47]

The Chicano movement was also seminal in other respects. Many activists of the 1960s were college students, and institutional repercussions ensued as this well-trained generation moved into professional positions. School curricula began to reflect Chicano history; health and mental health workers found a rationale for the culturally sensitive delivery of services; lawyers organized the Mexican-American Legal Defense and Education Fund; Chicano priests became more vocal; and scholars began to develop a substantial literature reflecting the Chicano experience.

The family

By tradition and self-definition, Latinos are family oriented, perhaps none more so than the subpopulation of Mexican origin. At least as ideals, the family and extended kin group are highly valued. They are a source of emotional and material support, and their well-being takes priority over the advancement of individual aims. The Mexican family is generally viewed as patriarchal—a feature that has its positive elements but also generates images of irresponsible machismo and female oppression.

How valid are these images in late twentieth-century America? On the surface, families of Mexican origin are the most traditional of the Hispanic groups. More households are extended, that is, more likely than most other Americans' households to include other adults in addition to a husband and wife.[48] Most typically the other adults are young adult children who continue to live with their parents (this is also true of Puerto Ricans and of Central and South Americans). Immigrants from Mexico are particularly involved with, and often dependent on, extended family networks.[51] The manitos in New Mexican villages certainly followed traditional family patterns,[52] and, more recently, clusters of related households were found to serve mutual support functions for poor Chicanos in many cities, crossing the border in some parts of the Southwest.[53] The existence and importance of these household clusters elude analyses that are based on census data, which focus attention on a single household. Yet ethnographic studies make it clear that kinship remains a very important institution for Mexican Americans.

Compared to other Americans, more Mexican-American women also have more children, but decreases in the birthrate among more highly educated women and the use of contraceptives is quite common.[49] Mexican Americans generally have lower rates of divorce than either non-Hispanics or other Hispanic groups, although they (along with other Hispanics) are more likely to be separated from their spouses.[50]

Traditional norms are often breached, but there is also little question that they are observed among certain segments of the subpopulation, especially the Mexican born. Traditional norms of sexual behavior still appear to constrain Mexican-origin women—again, especially those born in Mexico; they tend to start sexual activity somewhat later in life and to marry and have children earlier.

Many vicissitudes can weaken a family's capacity and willingness to live up to its own ideals. Often, Mexican Americans who cannot afford to help their relatives feel ashamed because they have been taught that "normal" Hispanic families support kin, even though research shows that only a minority of Chicano families surveyed actually turn to their kin (Keefe, 1979). In addition, urbanization and social mobility tend to weaken ties within the extended family. In the late 1980s, research in south Texas, for example, showed that *compadrazgo* (godparenthood)—formerly an important way of strengthening bonds with "fictive kin"—had declined sharply in importance, especially for younger people and for the middle class. Among religious rituals, only funerals continued to reintegrate the entire extended kin group.[54] Failures of the patriarchy are also seen in the "broken" family. Female headship among Mexican Americans has always been slightly higher than among non-Hispanic whites, but lower than among other poverty-level populations; in 1991, 19 percent of families of Mexican origin were headed by a woman.[55] Mexican-American female-headed households are apparently more able to draw on kinship networks for emotional and material support than are similar black or Anglo households.[56] Kinship bonds are often complex and subtle and not easily measured by the instruments available to social science researchers; nevertheless, many people really do suffer from the gap between ethnic ideal and attainable reality.

What the traditional Mexican patriarchy really means is openly controversial. What are the patriarchal patterns, and how much do they persist in contemporary settings? Such questions usually focus on the male role. Though in general American discourse, the term *machismo* has been associated with crude male displays of physical and sexual prowess, the Mexican cultural complex implies that a macho is not only a good and loving provider for his family but also is one who commands respect by virtue of his steadfastness and moral strength. For example, traditional norms militate against wives working except in case of dire economic necessity. Indeed, in the 1960s Mexican-American women were less likely than Anglo, black, or other Hispanic women to be working outside the home in formal jobs. By 1990, however, the figure began to converge, and more than half of women of Mexican origin were employed in the labor force.[57] Male dominance is also a feature of the traditional family, even though it was probably exaggerated by some researchers of the 1960s.

Contemporary research finds a changing family structure among Latinos as well as among other Americans. Several studies report increasing egalitarianism—especially when wives are working.[58] But though traditional husbands may help at home when their wives work, they often are unhappy about it, and researchers caution against interpreting household help as egalitarianism.[59] In addition, changes within the family that tend toward egalitarianism may bring down opprobrium on the husband as having given in to a domineering wife. Mexican-American women (and especially women in the middle classes) seem to be carrying the brunt of change within the family, taking the lead in creating new roles and new relationships with their husbands.[60] Of course, within a population as large and as widely dispersed as the Mexican Americans, there are significant differences by region, generation, size of community, and class; and even in traditional households, mothers have strong situational authority. Some researchers find that the sharpest gap is between generations—with young adults differing sharply from both middle-aged and older people.[61]

Clearly, many changes in the Mexican-American family are associated with changes in the role and status of women and are often interpreted as related to women's work. Though there were Mexican-American women leaders and spokespersons through the earlier years,[62] Chicanas began to voice concerns about their subordination more loudly during the turmoil of the Chicano movement of the late 1960s and were particularly incensed about their subordinate role within the movimiento itself.[63] Particularly irksome is the double standard that provides males with a justification for sexual freedom and aggressiveness while it condemns women for similar behavior. The double standard undergirds the stereotypically

sharp distinction between "good" and "bad" women. The tendency
to condemn "bad" women even extends to victims of rape. In
San Antonio, Chicanas were more likely than Anglos and blacks
to blame rape victims as "inciters" and to follow other generally
outmoded stereotypes; rape and other sexual and domestic assaults
are probably seriously underreported among Chicanas because of
the stigma attached to victimization.[64] While it comes as no surprise
that many highly educated Mexican-American women academics
subscribe to feminist goals and principles (even though they are
very critical of mainstream feminism), many Chicana white-collar
workers also share this perspective: They experience discrimination
and sexual harassment at work, and they tend to press for more
egalitarianism at home.[65]

Here again, it is important to stress the many variations in
family structure and cultural response to Anglo society. Wide geographical dispersion, economic changes, heavy immigration (to say
nothing of a strong and well-remembered history) greatly condition
almost any generalization. Like all American families, Mexican-
American families respond to social pressures in a variety of ways.

PUERTO RICANS

Although Puerto Rican communities are found in Miami, Ha-
waii, and Los Angeles, most mainland Puerto Ricans live in Rustbelt states. New York has an especially large concentration, and life
in that one city has greatly shaped their history. In 1960, 72 percent
of all Puerto Ricans were living in New York City. By 1990, the
percentage living in New York State had dropped to only 40 percent, but other Middle Atlantic and New England states accounted
for an additional 32 percent, and a further 9 percent resided in the
industrial Midwest.[66] This regional concentration means that, more
than any other Hispanic population, the Puerto Ricans on the U.S.
mainland have been devastated by the economic restructuring that
has attended the decline of American manufacturing.

The deteriorating economic situation in New York has been
particularly well documented. The Great Migration from Puerto
Rico to New York was largely completed by the mid-1960s. At
that time, Puerto Rican in-migrants were more likely than other
New Yorkers to work in manufacturing, especially in the garment industry.[67] Not only did small plants lose some 441,000 jobs
between 1960 and 1980, but, after the mid-1960s, changed laws

permitted a wave of new immigrants—both Latino and Asian—to compete with Puerto Ricans for the remaining jobs. Since Puerto Ricans are citizens, they tend to be more assertive about their rights than are undocumented new immigrants and as a result often lose out in job competition. Their principal, continuing competition for work is with African Americans. Thus in New York Puerto Ricans lost twice as many jobs as blacks in manufacturing, and, while African Americans have developed a strong foothold in the public sector, Puerto Ricans have yet to do so.[68]

In 1980 Puerto Ricans were still more likely than other New Yorkers to work in factories, but there were far fewer factories. Puerto Ricans did not seem to be entering the new low-level service jobs, nor did government jobs open up for them, despite political pressure. Instead, they seemed to be dropping out of the labor market altogether.[69] By 1985 only 40 percent of Puerto Rican New Yorkers were in the labor market—a far lower figure than for whites, blacks, or other Hispanics—and many more Puerto Ricans were unemployed. By 1992, more than half (55 percent) of all Puerto Ricans in the city fell below the poverty line, compared with less than one-third of blacks and 12 percent of non-Hispanic whites.[70] Puerto Ricans were the poorest community in New York, a fact that was easily forgotten by policymakers.

What happened in New York was repeated in Puerto Rican communities throughout the Rustbelt, although less drastically. Between 1970 and 1980 the real family income of Puerto Ricans in the United States declined by 21 percent.[71] By contrast, family income rose for blacks, non-Hispanic whites, and all other Latino groups.[72] By 1991, the median income of Puerto Rican families was substantially below that of other Americans, including other Hispanics.[73] Puerto Ricans were also more likely than other groups to depend on public assistance for survival.[74] Outside New York—and especially in Sunbelt locations—Puerto Ricans were more likely to be working, so nationally almost two-thirds of all Puerto Ricans were in the labor force. This is certainly a higher proportion than in New York, but it is still well below the labor force participation of other subpopulations.

Poorly educated Puerto Ricans were especially likely to drop out of the labor force. Nationally, Puerto Ricans compete with Mexican Americans for the bottom of the educational attainment ladder. Puerto Ricans have a median education of only tenth grade, and less than 10 percent have completed college.

These gloomy statistics challenge sociological theories that would predict a better fate for such a large group of Hispanics. Economic restructuring explains a major part of their poverty, but not the fact that Puerto Ricans are on the bottom of the heap nationally. After all, Puerto Ricans are citizens of the United States. Even the migrants from Puerto Rico come from a system where English is taught in all schools. Why, then, do they fare worse than their Latino immigrant neighbors, many of whom are undocumented workers who speak only Spanish? Racial discrimination might be the answer, since Puerto Ricans are a racially mixed group: But why then are conditions worse for them than for their black neighbors?

Part of the answer may lie in patterns of movement between Puerto Rico and the mainland—again, focusing primarily on New York. One facile argument is that the frequent back-and-forth movement leads Puerto Ricans never to make a commitment to hard work on the mainland; that contention is vigorously contested and probably can be discounted.[75] Even if we dismiss this *va-y-ven* argument, the question still remains: What fraction of the crushing Puerto Rican poverty can be explained by selective migration? Is there a process whereby the poorest people leave the island and the middle class returns to the island? Apparently, yes. Some evidence suggests that in recent years Puerto Ricans who migrate to New York are less economically active and less capable of competing in the mainland labor market. Meanwhile, a lively migration to mainland locations outside of New York is taking place, and such sites attract the better-qualified Puerto Ricans.

The second—and perhaps more important—question is, Who leaves New York? In recent years the more stable and well educated leave New York, either for locations elsewhere on the mainland or to return to Puerto Rico.[76] In the 1980s, middle-class housing was extremely expensive in New York, well out of the reach of newly achieving middle-income residents and far more costly than in Puerto Rico. The departure of middle-income New York Puerto Ricans may well combine with the in-migration of the poor to concentrate their poverty in New York. It is extremely difficult to tease out the details of this pattern from statistical evidence, but it should not be forgotten that migrants have been continuously present in every mainland Puerto Rican community. The migration experience is very much a part of almost every family.

New York is also a hard place for the poor to live. Poverty in New York, as in other Rustbelt cities, often means an apartment in a seriously dilapidated apartment building, or perhaps life in one of the many fortress-like housing projects that dot the boroughs of the city. Many of these neighborhoods are dangerous, with crime a constant companion. Urban renewal funneled large numbers of Puerto Ricans away from Manhattan into outlying boroughs—especially Brooklyn and the Bronx—and the largely Puerto Rican South Bronx became a national symbol for urban disaster. Thousands of buildings were burned into rubble; amenities and services of the most basic kind were lost; drug dealing became common; neighborhoods collapsed. (New York houses the largest urban concentration of Hispanics with AIDS, most of whom acquired the disease through intravenous drug use.)[77] In the face of these problems, grassroots community groups have been very important in rehabilitation efforts in the South Bronx, and they include at least one that has long been run by an activist priest.[78]

What about the Puerto Rican middle class? From the census statistics since 1960, one might conclude that a substantial upgrading of social class has occurred—"success" within a generation. In 1960, Puerto Ricans were largely a lower working-class population. By 1991, however, only a small minority held such jobs.[79] At the other end of the spectrum, in 1960 only a tiny fraction held middle-class jobs, while by 1991 the figures had doubled.[80] But these figures are misleading: they refer only to those who were working at the time of the census. Those who might have been working at the lower-level blue-collar jobs in 1991 had not become middle class but actually had dropped out of the labor market. This reduction in the labor force produces a false image of success. Nevertheless, the figures remind us that a significant Puerto Rican middle class lives on the mainland.

The Puerto Rican middle class has helped make New York a significant center of Puerto Rican cultural activity, adding a Latino component to the city's enormous cultural resources. There are some Puerto Rican-owned businesses, but the real gains appear to have come in jobs in education and in social work. Outside of New York, the Puerto Rican middle class makes a less substantial impact: their numbers are relatively small and they tend to live in scattered, rather than concentrated, locations. But in New York, they have had not only a cultural but also a major political impact.

Political mobilization

Beginning in the 1950s, middle-class Puerto Ricans in New York initiated a series of civic organizations that rapidly became points

of focus for what might be called protopolitical activity. The Puerto
Rican Forum, Aspira, and the Puerto Rican Family Institute were
among the more prominent early groups.[81] These and other Puerto
Rican organizations also functioned as political springboards for
Puerto Rican leaders.[82] Although New York's political life is highly
ethnic and highly partisan, it did not particularly encourage Puerto
Ricans because they did not form a big enough voting bloc. Although they were citizens, many Puerto Ricans were barred from
voting before 1982, first by an English language literacy test and
then by a sixth-grade educational requirement. When these obstacles were overcome, only a third of eligible New York Latinos
were registered to vote. Then, too, Puerto Ricans were not concentrated in one community, but were dispersed in several settlements that were easily placed in competition with each other.[83]
Some political appointments of Puerto Ricans were made; significant electoral strength began when Herman Badillo was elected
Bronx borough president in 1965. In contrast to the generations
of political exclusion of Mexican Americans in the Southwest, this
is an extraordinarily quick rise to political representation. But a
succession of fiscal crises in New York beginning in 1975, followed
by a rollback in public services and more than a decade of racially
divisive politics, led to a feeling that the needs of the Puerto Rican
population were being neglected. Frustration generated a militant
response that was deeply rooted in the politics of Puerto Rico and
reminiscent of the Chicano and black movements of the late 1960s.
Protests brought some federal funds and some significant changes
in municipal services in New York City. Hostos Community College, for example, was established in 1969.

In Chicago, a violent riot in 1966 had a similar effect and was a
political watershed for Puerto Ricans. New grassroots leaders articulated the problems within the community, and a series of social
service agencies were developed. As the agencies became more
firmly established, they served less as a base for confrontational
politics, and Puerto Ricans began to push against the formidable
Chicago Democratic political machine. The machine, with its strong
tradition of ethnic voter mobilization, faltered seriously when it
came to Puerto Ricans. Districts were gerrymandered, and Puerto
Ricans were neglected in voter registration drives. After a decade
of "clientele politics," in which favored leaders received political appointments, the first Puerto Rican electoral victories came
in the early 1980s, with candidates promoted by the Democratic
machine.[84] Under the short regime of the black mayor Harold

Washington, Puerto Ricans began to establish a stronger role in the city's politics.

The nature of Rustbelt urban politics means that from the earliest years in New York Puerto Ricans have had to be sensitive to the politics of race. The first formal coalition between African-American and Latino elected officials was the Black and Puerto Rican Caucus in New York.[85] But relationships have not always been easy. The African-American mayors of three cities with large Puerto Rican concentrations—Chicago, Philadelphia, and New York—have had very different relationships to the local Puerto Rican communities. In Chicago, it is clear that Puerto Ricans became a power; in Philadelphia, they did not.[86] In addition, Puerto Ricans have had to be sensitive to the political presence of growing numbers of other Latino groups. Particularly in New York, they find themselves interacting with Dominicans, Colombians, and other, smaller populations. Electoral gains were made following the 1991 redistricting: City council members, state senators, and congressional representatives increased notably.

Puerto Rican civic life has been characterized by an unusually high visibility of women in major roles in both community based and nationally oriented civic associations. And that leads us to the role of women and the family.

The Puerto Rican family

By all statistical accounts, the Puerto Rican family has a lot of problems. Although Puerto Ricans, like other Hispanics, are more likely than other Americans to live in families, less than half of those families include both a husband and wife.[87] Even when education and age at marriage are controlled, Puerto Ricans experience notably more marital instability than other Hispanic groups and almost as much as African Americans.[88] Female headship is as common as it is among African-American families, and nearly half of all Puerto Rican children were raised in homes headed by a single parent.

Some authors have attributed the high incidence of female headship to a tradition of consensual unions among the poor in Puerto Rico.[89] However, this explanation seems less credible when we recognize that the proportion of mainland Puerto Rican families that were female headed rose dramatically in recent decades—particularly after 1970—well after the peak of migration. Others attribute the phenomenon to the nontraditional lifestyle of New Yorkers in general. Probably the most immediate cause, however, lies with the economic problems faced by young men in Rustbelt cities. Puerto Rican fathers who are employed are much more likely to marry the mothers of their children than are those who are not employed.[90] When jobs vanish it is reasonable to expect that marriage rates will drop and existing consensual unions will become more fragile.[91]

Puerto Ricans continue to have comparatively large numbers of children (more than most other subpopulations except Mexican Americans), and this despite draconian efforts at birth control on the island. According to some estimates, more than a third of all women in Puerto Rico have been sterilized; a careful survey of American Latinos shows a figure of 23 percent for Puerto Rican women living on the mainland.[92] The government of the Commonwealth concluded that the island was seriously overpopulated and its campaign to limit women's childbearing emphasized sterilization.[93]

Clearly, the statistics delineate a troubling picture, but Puerto Rican families share many of the values and structural strengths of Mexican-American families. Like Mexican-American clusters of related households, Puerto Rican families maintain complex reciprocal exchanges with other families in the extended kin group.[94] Although resources, already thin, are seriously strained by the economic hardships that so many Puerto Ricans face, the household clusters clearly function effectively in times of trouble. Female-headed or not, for example, families with access to extended kin were much less likely to have a heroin-addicted member than those who were cut off from kin.[95]

Puerto Ricans, too, tend to be traditional in attitudes about sex roles with norms that prescribe a sharp division of labor between males and females in the family. Mainland-born Puerto Ricans are less likely than in-migrants from the island to subscribe to such principles and more likely to share household tasks and decisions.[96] In general, the Puerto Rican family shows signs of change, with poor families of particular concern. Puerto Rican women have generally maintained a rather low level of participation in the labor force—lower, in recent years, than among other Latino women, and thus Puerto Ricans focus on family adjustment to working wives less than Mexican-American families do.[97] Clearly, however, many Puerto Rican women—especially among the poor and island born—are in conflict about their roles. The traditional division of labor by gender leaves women ill prepared for heading a family under the grim conditions found in poor Puerto Rican communities. Clinicians find that "parenting is conceived of almost exclusively in the context of a marital union," and when a single mother must take on what she defines as a paternal function, she feels strain.[98] Many of the women who report high levels of stress are thus under a double pressure,[99] from the heavy burden of poverty and the challenge of redefining gender roles.

CUBANS

Though sharing a similar cultural background, America's Cubans are quite different from other Latinos in terms of economic and social standing. They are older, better educated, and richer as a group, and more helped by various forms of government aid.[100] The percentage of female-headed households among Cubans is smaller than any other group of Hispanics. Cubans are highly concentrated in one area and are very clearly stratified by class and racial divisions.

Cuban Americans are heavily foreign born (72 percent in 1990), a consequence of three great waves of migration from Cuba immediately following the Cuban Revolution of 1959. In the first wave, the so-called Golden Exiles brought professional skills, investment capital, and the upper strata of an entire society that was undergoing revolutionary change. The refugees were overwhelmingly white, mature, and well educated. Two more waves of Cuban refugees with fewer resources entered the U.S. from 1966 to 1973. Then, again, the *marielitos* entered in 1980. This last group tended to be poorer, less white, and much younger. For all of the new immigrants and even the less advantaged marielitos, the federal government created a remarkable package of direct and indirect relief programs which were supplemented by city and county aid. In the end, nearly $1 billion was spent between 1965 and 1976.[101] Part of this welcoming attitude was the prevailing anticommunist and anti-Castro mood of the U.S. administration. Part was due to the easy access of Cuban exile leaders to power sources in Washington.

The results of this peculiar combination of political attitudes, human resources, and public aid are striking. First, the Cubans managed to create and maintain a strong enclave economy centered in Miami, the site of the largest concentration of emigres.[102] This economy not only provides Cuban goods and services but also includes Cuban-owned and staffed enterprises which serve the

larger Miami community. The enclave provides the kind of opportunity to new arrivals that is not available in most Mexican and
Puerto Rican communities. It is a Spanish-speaking world, which
protects fresh immigrants with few language skills and smooths
their integration into American life. (Figures from 1989 show that
over the course of a decade, the number of Miami Cubans who use
English at home actually declined. Over the same period, workplace Spanish increased.) And, at the top, Cubans have been able
to build Miami into the principal American financial center that
serves all of Latin America.[103]

Second, a relatively homogenous community decided soon after 1960 that it probably would not return soon to the homeland and began to take a serious interest in American political
life. Thus Cubans had one of the highest Hispanic naturalization
rates. Approximately 80 percent of the Cubans in Miami were
naturalized as against only 12 percent of a comparable group of
Mexican Americans. Cubans showed no interest in the kind of
militant protest that swept Chicano and Puerto Rican communities
during the nationwide ethnic disturbances of the 1970s. Cubans
were refugees from, and hostile to, a regime that used many of the
symbols so attractive to young Chicanos and Puerto Ricans; this
hatred of left-wing symbols accounted for an important part of the
community's sense of solidarity.

By the year 1980 approximately half of all Cuban Americans
lived in Miami, making Miami the second largest city of Cubans
in the world. (Many non-Cuban Hispanics also live there.) Cubans
held important political offices, including the mayor and city man-
ager, as well as state offices. Cubans in Miami vote as an ethnic
bloc and this solidarity appears to reflect accurately a strong sense
of community solidarity.[104] Miami's Cubans tend to define themselves as a white community (thereby reconstructing most of the
island's ethnic history), and substantial conflict with the city's black
population has occurred.[105] Some of this conflict is ideological and
political; much of it has to do with the relative success of Cubans
compared to the city's blacks.[106]

Cubans' economic and political achievements generally lead
most students of Hispanic life to consider them as something of
an immigrant success story.

Yet Cuban prosperity has its peculiar aspects. The median
Cuban family income in 1990 is nearly one-third higher than other
Hispanic families, but for 76 percent of working Cuban men, in-
dividual income was less than the U.S. average. What does this

mean? Some recent and careful studies tend to debunk anecdotes about individual rags-to-riches achievements in Cuban Miami. Cuban success seems to depend, rather, on a family unit that is mobilized for economic achievement. Cuban households tend to have more workers than other Hispanic households and considerably more than all U.S. households. Cuban women are more likely to enter the workforce, even when they are also mothers. A smaller proportion of Cuban families have young children. On the other end of the scale, a larger group of older citizens tends to free more married women for work outside the home.[107] Traditional Cuban values do not condone women working outside the home unless it is required by economic need. The high participation of Cuban women in the American labor force thus reflects a family income strategy.

Typically, enclave economies tend to exploit ethnic relationships, particularly those of new arrivals, and evidence suggests that Cubans in Miami tend to earn less money than those elsewhere in the nation (especially in the New York area).[108] Women tend to be particularly exploited, but, as interviews with garment workers indicate, they tolerate low wages for the convenience of being able to speak Spanish on the job and to take flexible hours that permit them to give priority to their responsibilities at home. In addition, many are willing to tolerate low wages because Cuban bosses have a reputation for helping their workers start their own small businesses—usually as subcontractors in the garment and construction industries.[109]

DOMINICANS, SALVADORANS, AND GUATEMALANS

Three nationalities dominate the Central American and Caribbean category that in 1990 made up about 8 percent of the total Hispanic population.[110] Salvadorans were the largest, with 30 percent of the category; followed closely by Dominicans, with 28 percent; and Guatemalans, with 15 percent.[111] The overwhelming majority—81 percent in 1990—are new immigrants.[112] Immigration from the Dominican Republic has continued for several decades, but the movement from El Salvador and Guatemala began to gain speed only in the late 1970s and early 1980s, as political violence swept both countries. Many of these new arrivals had witnessed terrorism at first hand, and the after-effects linger.[113]

The vast majority of Dominicans (69 percent in 1990) lives in New York. Most Salvadorans (60 percent) live in California—primarily in Los Angeles and in the San Francisco Bay Area. The majority (59 percent) of the Guatemalans is also in California; the remainder has settled in a number of different states.

The tiny trickle of traditional emigration from the Dominican Republic to the United States accelerated sharply during the political turmoil after the 1961 assassination of long-time dictator Rafael Trujillo. American foreign policy was deeply involved in Dominican affairs and viewed migration to the United States as a safety valve, and the government did its best to encourage such movement. Once established, the immigrant flow increased steadily, with an average annual flow of well over 20,000 persons. Perhaps as many as a third of these new arrivals enter the United States without the appropriate papers, some by overstaying tourist visas, some by passing as Puerto Ricans, some by paying exorbitant sums for transport and forged papers. In the late 1980s, economic conditions in the Dominican Republic were so precarious that the volume of undocumented emigration increased, and many of the undocumented workers were urban members of the middle class. Even though they often had better "qualifications" than their documented compatriots, they tended to work in firms that operate off the books, paying lower wages and fewer fringe benefits. But most undocumented Dominicans regularize their status in the United States within about 5 to 7 years, often entering into marriage in order to do so—or even in order to enter the U.S. in the first place.[114]

Most of the Dominicans in the United States live in New York City, and thus it should not come as a surprise that their occupational profile is similar to Puerto Ricans'. They (especially the women) are concentrated in garment and other low-skilled manufacturing and service jobs. Like Puerto Ricans, Dominicans are also involved in a thriving informal economy, and, in New York, there is a significant involvement in street-level drug trade. There are several contrasts with Puerto Ricans, however. First, New York is a union town, and marginal employers prefer Dominicans because they are less likely than Puerto Ricans to join unions or make demands. Undocumented workers are especially likely to work in nonunion shops. Second, Dominican men are more active in the labor market than Puerto Ricans.[115] In fact, this difference goes back to the very beginning: one set of researchers found that Dominican migrants appear to be more economically active than those left behind in the Dominican Republic while the opposite is true for Puerto Rican immigrants.[116]

Newly arrived non-English-speaking immigrants use their kinship and hometown networks to find Hispanic—and preferably Dominican—employers, who then tend to exploit them. These entrepreneurs are often in businesses that serve fellow Dominicans and also include small-scale garment subcontractors. Women are even more restricted in their job search than men, feeling that garment work is their only serious option, and they are generally paid even less than undocumented men; this is particularly unfortunate, given that female headship is almost as high among Dominicans—42 percent—as it is among Puerto Ricans in New York. Research in the early 1980s found that paid work, no matter how low paid, often gave a wife a much stronger position in her family. As a consequence, many women were reluctant to complain about a situation that gave them freedom both within the household and outside.[117]

Many Dominican families are transnational, with members living in both the Dominican Republic and in the United States. In the early 1980s Dominicans tended to regard their emigration as temporary. The late 1980s saw continual movement back and forth, with a residue of permanent settlement in the United States. Even men and women who return to the Dominican Republic for more or less permanent resettlement often go to extraordinary measures to maintain their hard-won American resident visas.[118] No matter how low the family income, by standards prevalent in the Dominican Republic many New York Dominicans can maintain what they consider to be a middle-class lifestyle. When they return to their homeland, however, they often fail to find jobs, and they cannot sustain that lifestyle. This reality makes the immigrants' "ideology of return" particularly poignant, and, in fact, few do return.[119]

The Dominican community in New York began to develop in a number of ways. First, by the early 1990s there was a significant number of people born—or at least brought up—in the United States. Second, community institutions began to form in the larger Dominican settlements in the United States. Dominican-owned businesses emerged, as did hometown associations (*clubes regionalistas*), social clubs, and political, professional, and cultural associations. Women were likely to join prayer groups, catechism classes, and other religious groups. Finally, the citywide consciousness of Dominicans began to grow. Latino newspapers began to feature news about Dominicans both in New York and in the

Dominican Republic, and citywide cultural and political organizations appeared. Though most of the Dominican associations had identifiable links with political ideologies in the Dominican Republic, a new Dominican ethnic identity began to take shape in New York. This was geared to American expectations of ethnicity, and coalitions were established both with Puerto Rican and with black politicians.[120] In 1992 the first Dominican was elected to a public body—the New York City Council. Finally, like the Puerto Rican communities in Manhattan and the Bronx, Dominican communities were not exempt from the violence and degradation associated with drug dealing.[121]

Fewer studies have been done of Salvadorans and Guatemalans. In California these immigrants have not formed ethnically homogeneous enclaves, as achieved by the Cubans. Instead, they live in general "Latino" neighborhoods—the Mission District in San Francisco and the Pico-Union/Westlake area in Los Angeles. This is also true in Washington, D.C., where the Latino community is dominated by Salvadorans.[122] In San Francisco, the businesses, churches, and community organizations all serve a mixed Central American clientele by providing a wide range of ethnic-specific goods and services.[123] Many Central Americans have been helped by the religious sanctuary movement and have been influenced by liberation theology as practiced in their homelands.[124]

In Los Angeles, in 1980 about half of the Central Americans were from El Salvador and about a third from Guatemala. A thriving Central American business community provides not only restaurants, street vendors, and food markets, but also specialized services, including travel agencies and courier express services which send money and consumer products back home. Several of these businesses support sports teams and ethnic festivals. Unlike the Cubans, however, the Central Americans lacked the resources to form a self-sustained enclave economy: instead, the businesses provide specialized services to these special populations.[125] In general, Central American workers maintain the same kinds of low-wage jobs that have traditionally been held by Mexican immigrant labor. Restaurants, hotels, cleaning services, garment factories, construction—all find their share of Salvadorans and Guatemalans side by side with other Latinos.[126] Most work in all-Latino environments. Street vending is common, especially among women who sell food, clothing, and other consumer products. Drug marketing is also common in Los Angeles, but many of the customers come from middle-class areas far from the barrios. The fact that Central

Americans and Mexican Americans find themselves in the same labor markets may contribute to some of the tensions between them; the usual explanation given by Central Americans, however, is that Mexicans simply take their preeminence for granted and fail to respect Central Americans.[127]

In contrast to the Mexican pattern of individual migration, many of the Central Americans immigrate as families.[128] They are deeply involved with their families beyond the common Latino pattern of depending on family networks for well-being. Many have left members of their family back home[129] and feel guilty at having escaped a bad situation in which their relatives are still embroiled.[130] This has further consequences: For adolescents, the American drive for individualistic achievement is alien. Motivation is high, but the emphasis is on helping the family. Adolescent aspirations are also dampened because many are undocumented and believe that their legal status bars them from college.[131]

Churches have been significant in California's Central American communities not only as sanctuaries but also as general sources of help, although the extent of the help may change rapidly with a change in parish leadership. The communities themselves have also generated a number of organizations specifically designed to meet the wide-ranging needs of these populations.

CONCLUSION

America's Hispanics are a diverse population that shares some very important common threads. They hold in common a similar cultural heritage, with variations. For example, Spanish is the dominant home language for all populations, immigrant and native born alike.[132] And even a superficial look at the family structure shows that in all groups, a traditional family structure is changing under economic pressures and particularly because of the changing role of women in American society. These changes can and do cause problems, but major features of the family structure persist and remain a resource to the people and their communities.

The common thread of immigration, by contrast, represents a series of significant problems for Hispanic community building. In most parts of the United States, and in most of the subpopulations, immigrants are a significant segment of community life. This means that most Hispanic communities include large numbers of people who face problems of adjustment to a new society.

No other large minority community has such a serious problem. The Cuban success story in Miami shows clearly that large-scale government help can make a major difference, but the message has not been generalized. The latest wave of Latino immigration coincides with serious fiscal problems in federal, state, and local governments; public help for Hispanic arrivals and their children will not be forthcoming. For their part, immigrants strain existing institutions, and in major centers of immigration (like Los Angeles and Houston) public schools and government-operated health facilities have occasionally done their best to reject their undocumented immigrant clients.[133] Even when some immigrants—like the Puerto Ricans—are eligible for public assistance, the economic crisis in cities like New York has caused such a cutback of government services that the Hispanic population finds itself at the very bottom of the economic pile. The community itself, and its fragile indigenous institutions, must take up the slack.

Immigration also has important implications for the functioning of the family. For populations like the Mexicans, with a longstanding pattern of circular migration, the resources of the extended kin group on both sides of the border are of major importance, but this strength should not distract attention from the concomitant stresses that migration places on families. The stresses imposed by family separation are most acute and most obvious among refugees, whether they be escaping from revolutions on the Left (as in Cuba and Nicaragua) or from terrorism on the Right (as in Guatemala and El Salvador), but they exist for all immigrants. In addition, the stresses of adjustment to new economic conditions often involve changes in the relationships between parents and children and between husband and wife, as the wife begins to assume responsibilities outside the home. The high rate of marital disruption and the very serious youth problems among some immigrant populations probably are directly related to the fact that few of these immigrants have access to resources that help to mediate and resolve family disputes. The shrinking pool of services provided by the government affects all Americans, of course, but it most particularly affects the poorer Latinos. The serious and increasingly desperate plight of America's newest immigrants highlights the issue in a most poignant fashion.

Immigration is just one source of population growth and change, and Hispanics continue to grow more rapidly than most other segments of the American population. This population growth places pressure on all institutions, including the Catholic Church. How the Church responds is open to debate: Will it be a simplistic reaction? Or will it be a more complex reply that deals with the community and family strengths and frailties? How can it deal with the many sources of diversity?

The importance of Hispanic cultural commonalities is somewhat diminished both by the diversity imposed by history and by the different economic situations. The Rustbelt location of most Puerto Ricans means that they have been devastated by poverty: The traditional family structure has withered, and community institutions are in constant struggle. By contrast, Cubans have created comparative comfort from their own resources combined with intensive government assistance. The result is a powerful community structure, with comparatively small and stable families. Even within subpopulations, the great variety of situations in which the Mexican-origin population lives means that the poor of the Lower Rio Grande Valley in Texas face much more difficult conditions than do the people of Los Angeles. Middle class Hispanos in New Mexico feel much more politically effective than do middle class Chicanos in San Francisco.

The cultural commonalities should not be misconstrued to mean that Latinos in the United States feel themselves to be a single population. Ethnic identity is intensely bound up with symbols of national origin and with the special experiences that each subpopulation has undergone. In cities like Chicago where, as a matter of political survival, weak communities of different kinds of Latinos cooperate, something like a collective "Latino" identity is beginning to emerge. However, it is still not the basis for a sense of community.[134] Los Angeles's Mexican Americans, by contrast, have struggled long and hard to gain a minimal political recognition in a city where they have been for many years the largest minority. They are not yet ready to take the small, embattled, and isolated Central American community under their wing, and Los Angeles's Cubans want little to do with what they perceive as "radical" Chicanos. Though Latinos of all national backgrounds have been involved in the Church's sanctuary movement for Central American refugees, they are less interested once the refugees are settled. Diversity within unity, deep needs—both chronic and critical— and important resources within family and community: these are some of the paradoxical features of the Hispanic population of the United States.

NOTES

1. In 1950 and 1960, the census counted "White Persons of Spanish Surname" in the five southwestern states where Mexican Americans were concentrated. In 1970, a self-identifier, "Spanish origin," was used for 5 percent of the sample, and Spanish language, Spanish heritage, and Spanish surname were asked of 15 percent of the sample. See Edward Telles and Edward Murguia, "Phenotypic Discrimination and Income Differentials among Mexican Americans," *Social Science Research* 14 (1977) pp. 142–168, for comparability issues. In 1980 and 1990, self-identification items probing Spanish/Hispanic origin or descent were used as the major identifier for the Hispanic population, asked of all respondents. See Frank Bean and Marta Tienda, *The Hispanic Population of the United States* (New York: Russell Sage Foundation, 1987), for details.

2. Cubans are an exception, with a median age of thirty-nine. These figures have implications for educational institutions: more than a third of all Mexican Americans and Puerto Ricans were under the age of sixteen, compared with less than a quarter of the non-Hispanic population. See U.S. Bureau of the Census, *The Hispanic Population of the United States: March 1991*, Current Population Reports Series P–20, no. 455 (Washington, D.C.: U.S. Government Printing Office, 1991).

3. These figures breaking down what is commonly known as the "other Hispanic population" are derived from tabulations of data from the 1990 U.S. Census and were released on June 5, 1992, by the Population Division of the Bureau of the Census. Other figures are derived from the U.S. Bureau of the Census, Summary Tape File 1C.

4. Seventy-two percent of the 672,123 immigrants from Cuba during the period 1961–1988 were labeled as refugees. The 1970s were the peak period for immigration, with the 1960s and 1980s following close behind. Guillermina Jasso and Mark Rosenzweig, *The New Chosen People: Immigrants in the United States* (New York: Russell Sage Foundation, 1990).

5. In El Salvador, death squad activity began to intensify in 1980; Nicaragua experienced a revolution in 1979, which accelerated immigration, and Guatemalan immigration accelerated in the early 1980s when government counterinsurgency efforts increased. During the 1980s there were 25,000 documented immigrants each year from Central America, and "undocumented . . . immigration was probably several times" that number. Steven Wallace, "The New Urban Latinos: Central Americans in a Mexican Immigrant Environment," *Urban Affairs Quarterly* 25 (1989), pp. 239–264.

6. Late in 1991, California's Governor Pete Wilson used the presence of welfare-dependent immigrants to argue that the state's AFDC payments be reduced so as to reduce the "magnet" effect. California received 35 percent of the nation's legal immigrants during the 1980s. *New York Times*, December 3, 1991.

7. Even though most Americans might consider many Puerto Ricans to be black, only 3.5 percent of Puerto Ricans chose the self-designation "black."

8. Nancy Denton and Douglas Massey, "Racial Identity among Caribbean Hispanics," *American Sociological Review* 54 (1989), pp. 790–808.

9. Alex Stepick and Guillermo Grenier, "Cubans in Miami," in Joan Moore and Raquel Pinderhughes, eds., *Beyond the Underclass Debate: Latino Communities in the United States* (New York: Russell Sage Foundation, 1993).

10. See Carlos Arce, Edward Murguia, and Parker Frisbie, "Phenotype and Life Chances among Chicanos," *Hispanic Journal of Behavioral Sciences* 9 (1987), pp. 19–32; Joe Hakken, *Discrimination against Chicanos in the Dallas Rental Housing Market* (Washington, D.C.: U.S. Department of Housing and Urban Development, 1979); Angela Jorge, "The Black Puerto Rican Woman in Contemporary American Society," in Edna Acosta-Belen, ed., *The Puerto Rican Woman* (New York: Praeger, 1979), pp. 124–141; and Telles and Murguia, "Phenotypic Discrimination."

11. Margery Austin Turner, Raymond Struyk, and John Yinger, *Housing Discrimination Study: Synthesis* (Washington, D.C.: Urban Institute, 1991).

12. U.S. Bureau of the Census, *Hispanic Population*.

13. In 1990, the birthrate for Hispanic women was 93.0 births per 1,000 women, and for non-Hispanic women it was 64.4 per 1000 women—a differential of about 30 percent. For blacks it was 78.4 births per 1000 women. U.S. Bureau of the Census, *Fertility of American Women: June 1990*, Current Population Reports Series P–20, no. 451 (Washington, D.C.: U.S. Government Printing Office, 1991).

14. Barry Bluestone and Bennett Harrison, *The Deindustrialization of America* (New York: Basic Books, 1982).

15. A shift to a service economy often entails a shift to underemployment (i.e., full-time employment that pays below poverty wages, part-time employment, and part-year employment). In 1980, this kind of underemployment was "most highly concentrated in the rapidly growing metropolitan areas of the South and West," with Albuquerque and Miami among the ten highest. Robert Sheets, Stephen Nord, and John Phelps, *The Impact of Service Industries on Underemployment in*

Metropolitan Economies (Lexington, Mass.: Lexington Books, 1987), p. 63.

16. John Kasarda, "Urban Change and Minority Opportunities," in Paul E. Peterson, ed., *The New Urban Reality* (Washington, D.C.: Brookings Institution, 1985), pp. 33–67.

17. Rebecca Morales, "Transitional Labor: Undocumented Workers in the Los Angeles Automobile Industry," *International Migration Review* 17 (1985), pp. 570–596; Edward Soja, Rebecca Morales, and Goetz Wolff, "Urban Restructuring: An Analysis of Social and Spatial Change in Los Angeles," *Economic Geography* 59 (1984), pp. 195–230.

18. Kevin McCarthy and Burciaga Valdez, *Current and Future Effects of Mexican Immigration in California* (Santa Monica: Rand Corporation, 1986); Thomas Muller and Thomas Espenshade, *The Fourth Wave* (Washington, D.C.: Urban Institute Press, 1986).

19. Patricia Fernandez-Kelly and Saskia Sassen, *A Collaborative Study of Hispanic Women in the Garment and Electronics Industries: Executive Summary* (New York: New York University, Center for Latin American and Caribbean Studies, 1991).

20. Saskia Sassen, "New Trends in the Sociospatial Organization of the New York City Economy," in Robert Beauregard, ed., *Economic Restructuring and Political Response* (Newbury Park, Cal.: Sage Publications, 1989), p. 70.

21. National Council of La Raza, "From the Editor," *Poverty Project Newsletter* 2 (1990), pp. 1, 3. Hispanic immigrants in Illinois, California, and New Jersey have serious injury rates that are up to three times higher than non-Hispanic workers in similar jobs (*New York Times*, February 18, 1992).

22. Alejandro Portes, Manuel Castells, and Lauren A. Benton, *The Informal Economy* (Baltimore: Johns Hopkins University Press, 1989).

23. Robert Lee Maril, *Poorest of Americans: The Mexican Americans of the Lower Rio Grande Valley of Texas* (Notre Dame, Ind.: University of Notre Dame Press, 1989).

24. Roberto Suro, "The Cholera Watch," *New York Times Magazine*, March 22, 1992, pp. 32–36.

25. Avelardo Valdez, "Persistent Poverty and Crime: The U.S./Mexico Border Region (Laredo, Texas)," in Moore and Pinderhughes, eds., *Beyond the Underclass Debate*.

26. Soja, Morales, and Wolff, "Urban Restructuring."

27. Joan Moore and Diego Vigil, "Barrios in Transition," in Moore and Pinderhughes, eds., *Beyond the Underclass Debate*.

28. They are culturally so distinctive that in the self-administered

census questionnaires many rejected the designation "Mexican origin" in favor of the designation "Other Hispanic."

29. Phillip Gonzales, "Historical Poverty and Restructuring Effects: Mexican American Neighborhoods in a Peripheral Sunbelt Economy," in Moore and Pinderhughes, eds., *Beyond the Underclass Debate.*

30. Richard Garcia, *Rise of the Mexican American Middle Class: San Antonio 1929–1941* (College Station: Texas A&M University Press, 1991).

31. U.S. Census Bureau, *Hispanic Population.*

32. The picture is different for women: In the 1980 census almost 12 percent of Mexican origin women were in upper white-collar occupations, and the proportion increased by 1991 to 14 percent. See Bean and Tienda, *Hispanic Population*; U.S. Bureau of the Census, *Hispanic Population.* It should be noted that most 1991 figures cited in this chapter are derived from a sample survey, the Current Population Survey, whereas figures for earlier years are derived from the census.

33. Bean and Tienda, *Hispanic Population.*

34. Thomas P. Carter and Roberto D. Segura, *Mexican Americans in School* (New York: College Entrance Examination Board, 1979), cite many works that attribute poor educational attainment to the "failure of the Chicano," e.g., to some aspect of Chicano culture, or language, or cognitive style, and also a large literature that sees the problem as "the default of the school." They also discuss efforts to adjust Chicano (and other Latino) children through such means as preschool programs, language training, etc., and also efforts at modifying the institution. Education continues to be one of the most widely analyzed aspects of Chicano life, and Carter and Segura's taxonomy continues to be very useful.

35. The 1980 census showed that 18.5 percent of Mexican Americans, 13.4 percent of Puerto Ricans, 7.8 percent of Cubans were illiterate. Mexican-American illiteracy was highest in Florida and Texas, where 2.5 percent were illiterate. See Bean and Tienda, *Hispanic Population*; Reynaldo Macias, *Latino Illiteracy in the United States: Summary of Results* (Claremont, Cal.: Tomas Rivera Policy Center, 1988).

36. In 1991, a total of 58 percent of Mexican origin males were in lower-status occupations: 32 percent were in lower blue collar jobs; 15 percent in service jobs; and 12 percent in farm jobs. The concentrations in the latter two occupations increased over the previous decade. A total of 44 percent of Mexican-origin women were in those occupations: 15 percent in lower blue collar jobs; 27 percent in service; and 2 percent in farm jobs (U.S. Bureau of the Census, *Hispanic Population.*

37. Almost 9 percent of Mexican American males and 11 percent of the women were working only part time whereas they wanted full-time jobs; another 6.5 percent of the men and 4 percent of the women were working only part of the year; and another 12.5 percent of the men and 13 percent of the women were unemployed.

38. Roberto De Anda, "Labor Force Inequality of Mexican-Origin Workers," in William Velez, ed., *Race and Ethnicity in the United States* (Dix Hills, N.Y.: General Hall, 1994). Analysis of 1980 census data also showed that returns to education were lower for Mexican Americans (and Cubans) than for Puerto Ricans or Central and South Americans (Beans and Tienda, *Hispanic Population*).

39. U.S. Census Bureau, *Hispanic Population*.

40. Robert Aponte, "Ethnicity and Male Employment: A Test of Two Theories," paper presented at the Chicago Urban Poverty and Family Life Conference, 1991.

41. See McCarthy and Valdez, *Current and Future Effects*; Frank Bean, B. L. Lowell, and L. Taylor, "Undocumented Mexican Immigrants and the Earnings of Other Workers in the United States," *Demography* 25 (1988), pp. 35–52. The controversy might be resolved by acknowledging, as Teresa Sullivan suggests, that each community has a different opportunity structure for Mexican Americans and a different mix of short-term undocumented immigrants and settled Chicanos. See her "Stratification of the Chicano Labor Market under Conditions of Continuing Mexican Immigration," in Harley Browning and Rodolfo de la Garza, eds., *Mexican Immigrants and Mexican Americans* (Austin: Center for Mexican American Studies, 1986). If the Chicano job ceiling is low, there may be fierce competition between immigrants and Chicanos, depressing the wage levels for Chicanos.

42. In a notorious instance, Lyndon Johnson obtained his first senatorial seat by virtue of vote manipulation in south Texas. See Robert Caro, *The Years of Lyndon Johnson: The Path to Power* (New York: Vintage, 1981).

43. This distrust persisted: As recently as 1981, for example, less than 5 percent of the 1971 entrants from Mexico had been naturalized. This contrasts with much higher rates for almost all other countries. Only Canada had lower naturalization rates (Jasso and Rosenzweig, *New Chosen People*). In the 1990 election, only 32.3 percent of Hispanics were registered, compared with 58.8 percent of blacks and 63.8 percent of whites. See U.S. Bureau of the Census, *Voting and Registration in the Election of November 1990*, Current Population Report, Series P–20, no. 453 (Washington, D.C.: U.S. Government Printing Office, 1991). For a general discussion of the effect of Mexican immigration on Chicano

politics, see Rodolfo de la Garza, "The Impact of Mexican Immigrants on the Political Behavior of Chicanos," in Browning and de la Garza, eds., *Mexican Immigrants and Mexican Americans*.

44. Maury Maverick, the liberal New Deal Democrat, made a point of working with the Mexican Americans in San Antonio during the 1930s. See Richard Garcia, *Rise of the Mexican American Middle Class: San Antonio, 1929–1941* (College Station: Texas A&M University Press, 1991).

45. Joan Moore and Harry Pachon, *Hispanics in the U.S.* (Englewood Cliffs, N.J.: Prentice-Hall, 1985).

46. Harry C. Boyte, *Community Is Possible* (New York: Harper and Row, 1984).

47. Valley Interfaith, organized in the early 1980s, is firmly based in south Texas parishes and like COPS was supported from the outset by the diocese. See Maril, *Poorest of Americans*. By the late 1980s there were a total of seven additional chapters under way in Texas. UNO, United Neighborhood Organizations of Los Angeles, is a similar organization but received less support from the diocese.

48. Specifically, 34 percent of Mexican-American husband-wife households have some other adult living with them, as compared with 20 percent of non-Hispanic white households, 31 percent of Puerto Rican households, and 33 percent of Cuban households (Bean and Tienda, *Hispanic Population*, p. 196).

49. Ibid. The proportion of Mexican-American women who were using oral contraceptives in the early 1980s was about the same as that of U.S. women as a whole, and was twice as high as any other Hispanic subgroup in the Hispanic HANES study. See C. A. Stroup-Benham and F. M. Trevino, "Reproductive Characteristics of Mexican-American, Mainland Puerto Rican, and Cuban-American Women," *Journal of the American Medical Association* 265 (1991), pp. 222–226. Abortion is also used, with Mexican-born women being more disapproving of the tactic. See Sandra Rosenhouse-Person and Georges Sabagh, "Attitudes toward Abortion among Catholic Mexican-American Women," *Demography* 20 (1983), pp. 87–89; and Maria Louisa Urdaneta, "Chicana Use of Abortion," in *Twice a Minority: Mexican American Women* (St. Louis: Mosby, 1980). Rates of neonatal mortality and low birth weight are quite low among Mexican Americans, despite poverty and poor health insurance coverage. This has been called a "public health enigma," and attributed to very low rates of alcohol, cigarette, and other drug consumption among Chicanas. It has also been attributed in part to the fact that high proportions of Mexican Americans are born outside of hospitals and death rates may

be underreported. See J. E. Becerra, C. J. R. Hogue, H. J. K. Atrash, and N. Perez, "Infant Mortality among Hispanics," *Journal of the American Medical Association* 265 (1991), pp.217–221.

50. Bean and Tienda, *Hispanic Population*.

51. See Leo Chavez, *Shadowed Lives* (Fort Worth: Harcourt Brace Jovanovich, 1992); and Nestor Rodriguez and R. T. Nunez, "An Exploration of Factors That Contribute to Differentiating between Chicanos and Indocumentados," in Browning and de la Garza, *Mexican Immigrants and Mexican Americans*.

52. See Clark Knowlton, "Changing Spanish American Villages of Northern New Mexico," *Sociology and Social Research* 53 (1969), pp. 455–474.

53. Carlos Velez-Ibanez, "U.S. Mexicans in the Borderland: Being Poor without the Underclass," in Moore and Pinderhughes, eds., in *Beyond the Underclass Debate*.

54. Norma Williams, *The Mexican American Family: Tradition and Change* (Dix Hills, N.Y.: General Hall, 1990).

55. U.S. Bureau of the Census, *Hispanic Population*.

56. Roland Wagner and Diane Shaffer, "Social Networks and Survival Strategies," in Margarita Melville, ed., *Twice a Minority* (St. Louis, Mo.: Mosby, 1980).

57. In 1960, 31.5 percent of Mexican-origin women worked, compared with 40.3 percent of Puerto Ricans, 47.2 percent of blacks, and 39.5 percent of Anglo whites. By 1980, however, 52 percent of Mexican-origin women worked, compared with 41.7 percent of Puerto Ricans, 61.1 percent of blacks, and 57.9 percent of Anglos (ibid.).

58. Lea Ybarra, "When Wives Work: The Impact on the Chicano Family," *Journal of Marriage and the Family* 44 (1982), pp. 169–189; Maxine Baca Zinn, "Employment and Education of Mexican-American Women: The Interplay of Modernity and Ethnicity in Eight Families," *Harvard Educational Review* 50 (1980), pp. 47–62.

59. Patricia Zavella, *Women's Work and Chicano Families* (Ithaca, N.Y.: Cornell University Press, 1987).

60. Williams, *Mexican American Family*.

61. Ibid.

62. Maria Cotera, "Feminism: The Chicana and Anglo Versions," in Melville, ed., *Twice a Minority*.

63. Marguerite Marin, *Social Protest in an Urban Barrio: A Study of the Chicano Movement, 1966–1974* (Lanham, Md.: University Press of America, 1991).

64. Joyce Williams and Karen Holmes, *The Second Assault: Rape and Public Attitudes* (Westport, Conn.: Greenwood Press, 1981).

65. Yvonne Pacheco Tevis, "Feminism and the Mexican American Woman," *UC Mexus News* 28 (1991), pp. 1, 4–7.

66. Data were provided by the U.S. Bureau of the Census, Population Division, in tabulations from the 1990 census released June 5, 1992. By "other Middle Atlantic and New England states" is meant New Jersey, Massachusetts, Pennsylvania, Connecticut, and Rhode Island. By "industrial Midwest" is meant the states of Illinois, Indiana, Michigan, Ohio, and Wisconsin.

67. Lois Gray, "The Jobs Puerto Ricans Hold in New York City," *Monthly Labor Review*, October, 1975, pp. 12–16. Twenty-one percent of all New York area male workers, but 32 percent of Puerto Rican males, were in manufacturing in 1970, and comparable figures for women were 21 and 42 percent (ibid.). By 1980, 28 percent of Puerto Ricans, compared with 16 percent of whites and 13 percent of blacks, were still in manufacturing. See Clara Rodriguez, *Puerto Ricans: Born in the U.S.A.* (Boston: Unwin Hyman, 1989).

68. In 1992, Latinos formed 24 percent of New York's population but only 12 percent of the city's government work force, while blacks formed 25 percent of the city's population and 37 percent of its municipal work force. Institute for Puerto Rican Policy, *Puerto Ricans and Other Latinos Today: A Statistical Profile* (New York: Institute for Puerto Rican Policy, 1992).

69. Luis Falcon and Douglas Gurak, "Features of the Hispanic Underclass: Puerto Ricans and Dominicans in New York" (unpublished manuscript); Rodriguez, *Puerto Ricans*.

70. Terry Rosenberg, *Poverty in New York City: 1980–1985* (New York: Community Service Society of New York, 1987); and Institute for Puerto Rican Policy, *Puerto Ricans and Other Latinos*.

71. Contrary to assimilationists' predictions, the decline was greater among mainland-born family heads than among those born in Puerto Rico.

72. Bean and Tienda, *Hispanic Population*.

73. The median income for Puerto Ricans was $16,169, slightly more than half of the non-Hispanic income of $30,513, and well below the $22,439 garnered by Mexican Americans—the next lowest Hispanic group (U.S. Bureau of the Census, *Hispanic Population*).

74. The figures were 9 percent for Puerto Ricans, 0.6 percent for non-Hispanic whites; 4.3 percent for blacks; 2.4 percent for Mexican Americans; and 2.0 percent for Cubans (Bean and Tienda, *Hispanic Population*).

75. The vast majority of mainland Puerto Ricans who were born on the island (about half of the total in 1980) had been living on

the mainland for more than five years (Bean and Tienda, *Hispanic Population*), and migration has not been a major contributor to Puerto Rican population growth in New York for some time.

76. Falcon and Gurak, "Features."

77. Samuel Friedman, Meryl Sufian, and Don Des Jarlais, "The AIDS Epidemic among Latino Intravenous Drug Users," in Ronald Glick and Joan Moore, eds., *Drugs in Hispanic Communities* (New Brunswick, N.J.: Rutgers University Press, 1990).

78. Nicholas Lemann, "The Other Underclass," *Atlantic Monthly*, December (1991), pp. 96–110.

79. Fifty-one percent of all Puerto Rican men and 69 percent of the women were working in lower-level blue-collar jobs in 1960. In 1991, 26 percent of the men and 12 percent of the women held such jobs.

80. In 1960, 6 percent of the men and 4 percent of all Puerto Rican women held professional and managerial jobs, compared with 12 and 22 percent, respectively in 1991 (Bean and Tienda, *Hispanic Population*, U.S. Bureau of the Census, *Hispanic Population*.

81. Joseph P. Fitzpatrick, *Puerto Rican Americans* (Englewood Cliffs, N.J.: Prentice-Hall, 1987).

82. George Martin, *Ethnic Political Leadership: The Case of the Puerto Ricans* (San Francisco: R and E Research Associates, 1977).

83. Institute for Puerto Rican Policy, *The Dinkins Administration and the Puerto Rican Community*, Proceedings (New York: Institute for Puerto Rican Policy, 1988).

84. Felix Padilla, *Puerto Rican Chicago* (Notre Dame, Ind.: University of Notre Dame Press, 1987).

85. Moore and Pachon, *Hispanics in the U.S.*

86. Institute for Puerto Rican Policy, *Dinkins Administration*.

87. In 1980, 20 percent were living alone or with nonrelatives, and 49 percent were in husband-wife families (Bean and Tienda, *Hispanic Population*). By 1991, 22 percent were living alone or with non-relatives, and only 41 percent were living in husband-wife families (U.S. Bureau of the Census, *Hispanic Population*).

88. W. Parker Frisbie, "Variation in Patterns of Marital Instability among Hispanics," *Journal of Marriage and the Family* 48 (1986), pp. 99–106.

89. Fitzpatrick, *Puerto Rican Americans*.

90. Mark Testa, Nan Astone, Marilyn Krogh, and Kathryn Neckerman, "Employment and Marriage among Inner-City Fathers," *Annals of the American Academy of Political and Social Science* 501, pp. 79–91.

91. In a study of a working-class community in Brooklyn, Mercer Sullivan found that many ostensibly female-headed households in fact

included a resident male. Several family ethnographies included a multi-generational history of consensual unions. On the other hand, premarital pregnancies were more likely in the Puerto Rican sample than in the black or Anglo sample to be handled by marriage. "Puerto Ricans in Sunset Park, Brooklyn: Poverty amidst Ethnic and Economic Diversity," in Moore and Pinderhughes, eds., *Beyond the Underclass Debate*.

92. Stroup-Benham and Trevino, "Reproductive Characteristics." Thirty percent of Puerto Rican women aged 15 to 49 living in New York had been sterilized. Most of those who were sterilized were island born and were older. Joseph J. Salvo, Mary G. Powers, and Rosemary Santana Cooney, "Contraceptive Use and Sterilization among Puerto Rican Women," *Family Planning Perspectives* 24 (September/October 1992), pp. 219–223.

93. Alfredo Lopez, *Dona Licha's Island* (Boston: South End Press, 1987).

94. Pablo Navarro Hernandez, "The Structure of Puerto Rican Families in a Context of Migration and Poverty: An Ethnographic Description of a Number of Residents in El Barrio, New York City" (diss., Columbia University, 1978).

95. Fitzpatrick, *Puerto Rican Americans*.

96. Lloyd Rogler and Rosemary Cooney, *Puerto Rican Families in New York City: Intergenerational Processes* (Maplewood, N.J.: Waterfront Press, 1984).

97. In 1980, for example, 42 percent of Puerto Rican women were in the labor force, compared with 52 percent of Mexican-origin women (1991 figures are about the same). In 1960, by contrast, 40 percent of Puerto Rican and 31 percent of Mexican-origin women were in the labor force (Bean and Tienda, *Hispanic Population*). Thus Puerto Rican levels have hovered around 40 percent for more than thirty years, while Mexican-origin women have changed. There is some controversy about why Puerto Rican women's labor force participation is so low. While the limited opportunities available to Puerto Rican women—particularly in New York—probably provide a good part of the explanation, there is some reason to believe that attitudes about appropriate gender behavior have some effect. As with other gender-related behaviors, there is a difference by birthplace: mainland-born women are distinctly more likely to work than those with similar characteristics who were born on the island. James Geschwender,

"Ethgender, Women's Waged Labor, and Economic Mobility," *Social Problems* 39 (1992), pp. 1–16.

98. Vickie Borras, "Dual Discipline Role of the Single Puerto Rican Head of Household," in Cynthia T. Garcia Coil and Maria de Lourdes Mattei, eds., *The Psychosocial Development of Puerto Rican Women* (New York: Praeger, 1989), pp. 201–213.

99. Alba Ambert and Clare Figler, "Puerto Ricans: Historical and Cultural Perspectives," in Alba Ambert and Maria Alvarez, eds., *Puerto Rican Children on the Mainland* (New York: Garland, 1992).

100. With a median age of 39.3 in 1991, Cubans are notably older than other Hispanics and even than non-Hispanics (whose median age was 33.8) (U.S. Bureau of the Census, *Hispanic Population*). This median age reflects both a greater number of old people (with 49 percent over 55, compared with only 39 percent of non-Hispanics and 16 percent of Mexican-origin people) and a smaller number of young children (with only 6 percent under 5 years of age, compared with 7 percent of non-Hispanics and 12 percent of Mexican-origin people).

101. Sylvia Pedraza-Bailey, *Political and Economic Migrants in America: Cubans and Mexicans* (Austin: University of Texas Press, 1985).

102. Alejandro Portes and Robert Bach, *Latin Journey* (Berkeley: University of California Press, 1985).

103. Stepick and Grenier, "Cubans in Miami," in Moore and Pinderhughes, eds., *Beyond the Underclass Debate.*

104. The Cuban community in West New York, New Jersey, was studied in the early 1970s, and again a strong sense of community solidarity seemed to compensate for economic difficulties. Eleanor Rogg, "The Influence of a Strong Refugee Community on the Economic Adjustment of Its Members," *International Migration Review* 5 (1971), pp. 474–481.

105. Stepick and Grenier, "Cubans in Miami," in Moore and Pinderhughes, eds., *Beyond the Underclass Debate.*

106. Harold Rose, "Blacks and Cubans in Metropolitan Miami's Changing Economy," in *Proceedings of the Conference on Comparative Ethnicity* (Los Angeles: UCLA Institute for Social Science Research, 1988).

107. Lisandro Perez, "Immigrant Economic Adjustment and Family Organization: The Cuban Success Story Re-examined," *International Migration Review* 20 (1986), pp. 4–20.

108. In 1970, Cubans in Florida earned an average of $8,100, compared with $10,140 in New York, $9,320 in New Jersey, and $10,430 in all other states. This is partly because many of the Floridians had lower educational levels and were in lower-status occupations, and

partly because of regional differences in salary levels. See A. J. Jaffe, Ruth Cullen, and Thomas Boswell, *The Changing Demography of Spanish Americans* (New York: Academic Press, 1980). Part of the difference may also be attributable to exploitation within the enclave. Jimy Sanders and Victor Nee examined the wage levels of immigrant employees in Miami and Hialeah, on the one hand, and elsewhere in Florida, on the other hand, and found that the former get a lower return for their educational and experiential assets than the latter. They argue that minority entrepreneurs benefit more from the enclave economy than do workers. "Limits of Ethnic Solidarity in the Enclave Economy," *American Sociological Review* 52 (1987), pp. 745–773.

109. Stepick and Grenier, "Cubans in Miami," in Moore and Pinderhughes, eds., *Beyond the Underclass Debate*.

110. Tabulations from the 1990 census released by the Population Division on June 5, 1992, show that Dominicans made up 2.4 percent of the total, and Central Americans made up 6.0 percent.

111. From tabulations of 1990 census data released by the Population Division of the U.S. Census on June 5, 1992.

112. Bean and Tienda, *Hispanic Population*.

113. Mario Suarez-Orozco, *Central American Refugees and U.S. High Schools* (Stanford, Cal.: Stanford University Press, 1989).

114. Eugenia Georges, *The Making of a Transnational Community* (New York: Columbia University Press, 1990); Sherri Grasmuck and Patricia Pessar, *Between Two Islands* (Berkeley: University of California Press, 1991).

115. Some 80 percent of the New York-based Dominican men and 50 percent of the women were in the labor market (Grasmuck and Pessar, *Between Two Islands*). Nationally, 79.1 percent of the Dominican and 73.8 percent of Puerto Rican men and 51.5 percent of Dominican and 52.0 percent of Puerto Rican women were in the labor market in 1980, compared with 84.6 percent of non-Hispanic white men and 57.9 percent of non-Hispanic white women (Bean and Tienda, *Hispanic Population*).

116. Falcon and Gurak, "Features."

117. Grasmuck and Pessar, *Between Two Islands*.

118. Georges, *Making*.

119. Like the Mexicans, Dominicans are slow to naturalize. Only 7.8 percent of the Dominicans admitted as permanent residents had naturalized by 1980 (Grasmuck and Pessar, *Between Two Islands*).

120. Eugenia Georges, "New Immigrants and the Political Process: Dominicans in New York," Occasional Paper no. 45 (New York: New York University Research Program in Inter-American Affairs, 1984);

"Political Participation of a New Hispanic Population: Dominicans in New York City" (unpublished manuscript, 1988).

121. Jeffrey Fagan, "Drug Selling and Licit Income in Distressed Neighborhoods: The Economic Lives of Street-Level Drug Users and Dealers" (unpublished manuscript, 1991).

122. Timothy Ready, *Latino Immigrant Youth* (New York: Garland, 1991).

123. Wallace, "The New Urban Latinos."

124. Suarez-Orozco, *Central American Refugees.*

125. Norma Chinchilla and Nora Hamilton, "Central American Enterprises in Los Angeles," report submitted to the Inter-University Program for Latino Research, 1988.

126. Wallace, "The New Urban Latinos" Norma Chinchilla, Nora Hamilton, and James Loucky, "Central Americans in Los Angeles: An Immigrant Community in Transition," in Moore and Pinderhughes, eds., *Beyond the Underclass Debate.*

127. Chinchilla et al., "Central Americans in Los Angeles."

128. Wallace, "The New Urban Latinos."

129. Chinchilla et al., "Central Americans in Los Angeles."

130. A survey of Central American workers in Los Angeles found that 60 percent of workers with children had left one or more of their children at home (Chinchilla et al., "Central Americans in Los Angeles"). This was a selected sample, not representative of the whole population.

131. Suarez-Orozco, *Central American Refugees.* Because so many of the Central Americans arrived after 1981, they are not benefited by the Immigration Reform and Control Act, which permitted many undocumented immigrants to regularize their status. In the late 1980s, as Los Angeles sank into a recession, there was some evidence that Central Americans were returning to their homelands (Chinchilla and Hamilton, "Central American Enterprises").

132. Bean and Tienda, *Hispanic Population.*

133. Hispanics in general have much lower rates of health insurance than other Americans. In 1989, 20 percent of all black Americans and 10 percent of non-Hispanic whites were uninsured. This contrasts with 37 percent of the Mexican Americans and 20 percent of the Cubans. Fifteen percent of Puerto Ricans were uninsured—a figure that indicates the importance of government insurance (provided through Medicaid) for which Puerto Ricans are more likely than Mexican Americans to be eligible. See Fernando Trevino, Eugene Moyer, Burciaga Valdez, and Christine Stroup-Benham, "Health Insurance Coverage and Utilization of Health Services by Mexican

Americans, Mainland Puerto Ricans, and Cuban Americans," *Journal of the American Medical Association* 265 (1991), pp. 233–237. The very high figures for Mexican Americans reflect not only the marginal jobs that many hold but also the fact that many are not citizens and hence not eligible for public health insurance.

134. Felix Padilla, *Latino Ethnic Consciousness* (Notre Dame, Ind.: University of Notre Dame Press, 1985).

2

Latino/Hispanic History since 1965: The Collective Transformation of Regional Minorities

David A. Badillo

Before 1965, regional and ethnic isolation characterized the Latino experience in distinct communities in the United States with distinct national, race, and class components. As their histories merged, diverged, and interacted in local as well as in global contexts, a newer collective identity gradually emerged. Nevertheless, one can legitimately question the existence of one Spanish-language or Latin American-origin community. However, the need for a term to describe persons tracing their ancestry to the Spanish-speaking countries of Latin American who reside or work primarily in the United States has become obvious to policy makers and citizens alike. The academic preference seems to lie with "Latino," as against "Hispanic," partly because of its Latin American, as against Spanish, or European, focus. Other reasons for the use of Latino have emerged in areas such as the Midwest, where several different Latin American-origin groups must share their space, resources, and to some extent their identity as they interact and sometimes intermarry. Despite the existence of a *lingua franca*, the dominance of Catholicism, and other similarities, the three largest groups maintain dual identities as Mexican Americans, Puerto Ricans, and Cubans (increasingly known as Cuban Americans), as well as members of the collective designation.[1]

In 1960 the Latino population residing in the United States stood at almost seven million; by 1990 it had increased to over twenty-two million, with about 63 percent Mexican in origin, 11 percent Puerto Rican, and 5 percent Cuban. Latino groups historically have clustered in distinct regions amid varied cultural landscapes, with Mexican Americans predominating in the Southwest, Puerto Ricans in the Northeast, and Cubans in Florida. Continued

50

immigration and high fertility rates have sustained Mexicans as the largest immigrant group from Latin America. California has the largest Latino population in the United States, followed by Texas. There and elsewhere in the Southwest the Mexican Americans—the overwhelming majority of whom, incidentally, are either native-born citizens or legal immigrants—overshadow all other Latinos. Proportionally fewer Puerto Ricans and Cubans currently settle in mainland communities, although these settlements are large and still growing.[2]

No restrictions on immigration from Western Hemisphere countries existed before 1965. The Immigration and Nationality Act Amendments of 1965 repealed the quota system that had been in effect since the 1920s, substituting ceilings that covered the countries of Latin America. One aim of the legislation was to treat all nations the same, while the inclusion of provisions for employment certification sought to protect the labor market for Americans and the U.S. economy. Thereafter, illegal migration increased, in part because it allowed employers to hire undocumented workers without penalty. More important, however, a worldwide pattern emerged during the 1960s of labor migration from less- to more-developed countries. Improvements in transportation and communication attracted people from throughout Latin America and the Caribbean and declining fares afforded even poor farmers in remote locations access to low-wage, unskilled labor in the United States.[3]

MEXICAN AMERICANS, PUERTO RICANS, AND CUBANS BEFORE 1965

In 1565, St. Augustine on the Florida peninsula became the first permanent settlement of Spaniards in what is now the United States. Another thrust of conquest entered northern Mexico and in the early 1600s the Spanish empire included the mountainous upper Rio Grande River Valley of New Mexico. During the eighteenth century, Spanish soldiers, clergy, and settlers established forts, missions, and cities around San Antonio, Los Angeles, San Francisco and a host of other locations from the Mississippi River to the Pacific Ocean. *Mestizaje*, the mixture of European and indigenous peoples, occurred on this northern frontier of New Spain, or Mexico. United States westward expansion ensued, culminating in the military conquests of the Mexican-American War of 1846–48 and the Treaty of Guadalupe Hidalgo, which resulted in the annexation of present-day Texas, New Mexico, Colorado, Arizona, California, and parts of adjoining territories. More than 80,000 Mexican inhabitants remained in the annexed regions, with the majority living in relatively populous New Mexico and the remainder in California and Texas. Overwhelming numbers of Anglo-European settlers arrived, forcing Mexicans to integrate into a foreign and often hostile political and economic system. They lost much of their previous autonomy, status, and property, often in violation of explicit treaty guarantees.[4]

Throughout the nineteenth century Mexican Americans remained isolated in southwestern cities, towns, and ranches. From 1910 to 1930, over one million Mexicans traveled north over the border, fleeing the devastating violence and economic dislocation of the Mexican Revolution. This unprecedented influx expanded the urban barrios of older settlements in Los Angeles, San Antonio, and El Paso and created new communities in southern California and along the Texas border. Mexican migrant workers boosted southwestern agriculture. With time they "settled out" from migrant streams into the cities and towns. Immigrants followed railroad lines running north from the Mexican interior, filling the labor vacuum during World War I. The imposition of restrictive quotas on Europeans in the 1920s prompted midwestern employers to recruit Mexican-American labor. Detroit automobile assembly plants, Chicago area steel mills, and Kansas City railroad shops all utilized Mexican workers, whose fortunes then hinged on the success of these industries. During the Depression, hundreds of thousands of newly arrived Mexicans returned home. Several localities deported thousands of unemployed immigrants to the border by rail.[5]

In 1942, because of an acute wartime labor shortage, the United States began contracting Mexican nationals to work in agriculture and, to a limited extent, in railroads and other depleted industries in the Southwest and West. Congress renewed this Bracero Program through 1964, appeasing agribusiness interests, who lobbied for the regular supply of "emergency" labor. Labor unions and many Mexican-American leaders, however, believed that imported labor undermined their efforts at organizing native-born workers while subjecting the contracted workers to exploitative living and working conditions. Braceros sent most of their earnings back home and often invested money in farming in Mexico. The increasing demand for contracts attracted potential workers to available jobs, boosting undocumented immigration. In 1954 the Immigration and Naturalization Service initiated Operation

Wetback, which rounded up and deported over a million undocumented Mexican workers. By the mid-1960s former braceros had developed relationships with employers that allowed them to seek work without going through the official recruitment mechanism of the binational agreement. Rather than diminishing with the termination of the Bracero Program, Mexican immigration to the United States flourished.[6]

This process made obvious the conflictual situation abiding in the labor needs of the United States and the availability of relatively inexpensive labor in nearby Latin America. During the late 1940s and 1950s border towns connected Mexican immigrants with employers, friends, and relatives in the United States and served as staging areas for border crossing. Since 1950 the Mexican-American population, once dependent largely on agriculture, has urbanized at a faster rate than the general population. Some 3.8 million Mexican Americans, or 4 percent of the U.S. population, lived in the United States in 1960; their numbers climbed to 9.1 million in 1970 and 14.6 million, or 6.4 percent, in 1980, a rise almost seven times greater than that of non-Latinos during the period.[7]

Puerto Rico, a Spanish colony since the fifteenth century, became a United States colonial possession after the Spanish-American War in 1898. Puerto Ricans were granted citizenship in 1917 under provisions of the Jones Act, and have since enjoyed unrestricted travel between island and mainland. Since 1952 Puerto Rico has been a commonwealth of the United States, but it enjoys neither representation in Congress nor voting privileges in presidential elections, although as citizens the islanders have served in the military since World War I. Despite incremental moves toward alternately, statehood and autonomy, the island's government remains an artifact of an awkward and unresolved colonial experiment.[8]

In an attempt to challenge the remnants of Spanish imperialism by asserting Antillean independence, Puerto Rican political exiles moved to New York City in the late nineteenth century. In the early 1900s, New York's cigar factories gave work to many émigré cigar makers, known as *tabaqueros*. The first large wave of migration from the island occurred during the 1920s aboard cargo ships following commercial routes. Emigrés took up residence in several working-class neighborhoods of New York City. Very little migration occurred during the Depression or the World War II era. However, beginning in the decade after 1945, Governor Luís Muñoz Marín attempted to transform the island's stagnant agrarian economy into an industrial one, attracting U.S. investment for a program known as Operation Bootstrap. Manufacturing failed to pick up the slack, although considerable progress toward modernization did occur. Employment rose in service industries and the public sector but the promised jobs never materialized. Meanwhile, about one-third of the island's labor force journeyed north, having been displaced from its land and its traditional way of life.[9]

Puerto Ricans came to the United States in most concentrated numbers during the 1950s, a time when the United States economy needed entry-level workers, especially in the industrial and manufacturing centers of the Northeast and Midwest. Puerto Rican immigration represented about half of the Latin American total during the 1950s, with movement in both directions. Poor, unskilled, migrants from the interior, known as *jíbaros*, arrived on inexpensive airplane flights from San Juan to New York City, whose Puerto Rican population rose from about 70,000 in 1940, to 246,000 in 1950, and to 613,000 in 1960. Around 1965 the Great Migration ended. By this time Puerto Ricans, along with incoming African Americans from the South, had become part of another wave of historic migration to New York City. However, the circumstances of their arrival and settlement, as well as the changed conditions in the metropolis, prevented their assimilation.[10]

The office of the Puerto Rican Migration Division served before 1965 as the only link with employment and governmental agencies on the mainland. Puerto Ricans built dozens of organizations devoted to advancing their interests on the mainland, especially in New York City where, beginning in the mid-1950s, hometown clubs organized the annual Puerto Rican Day parade. This celebration spread to Chicago and other cities with large numbers of migrants (especially in the Northeast). Puerto Ricans have inhabited Chicago's North Side since the late 1940s; it thereafter became the second city of the Puerto Rican diaspora. In Lorain, Ohio, Puerto Rican steel mill workers formed a middle-class community in the 1950s. Philadelphia's barrio grew after the early 1950s in response both to recruitment efforts by mainland companies and to informal family networks. Because migration between Puerto Rico and the U.S. mainland historically went predominantly to large cities, most of the rural migrants became metropolitan residents almost immediately after their arrival.[11]

Cuban communities in Florida grew as exiles reacted to the nineteenth-century independence movement. The first step came in 1869 when Vicente Ybor moved his cigar manufacturing business from Cuba to nearby Key West. A fire in 1886 caused the relocation of the factory to Ybor City in Tampa.[12] As in the case of Puerto Rico's economy, many tabaqueros followed. Patriot José Martí garnered support for the revolt against Spain there and in New York City, the two foreign nuclei of Cuba's independence movement. Many immigrants remained after the defeat of Spain and subsequently welcomed additional compatriots. During the early 1930s Miami, later a mecca for Cuban exiles, attracted political opponents of President Gerardo Machado.

A large number of Cuban exiles arrived in the United States only after Fidel Castro's successful overthrow of Fulgencio Batista's regime in January 1959. They came to escape what they perceived as economic harassment and an unconscionable political situation. Some 280,000 refugees left for the United States in the following three years, even though the Bay of Pigs invasion of April 1961 and the Cuban Missile Crisis of October 1962 strained diplomacy to the breaking point and the Cuban government increasingly imposed exit restrictions. During the early 1960s, more than 100,000 Cubans joined a small number of their compatriots, primarily those already residing in or near Miami's Little Havana neighborhood, an 800-square-block area centering on Southwest Eighth Street. For Cuban exiles and their offspring Miami has proved to be a good place because of distinct characteristics of the urban landscape as well as the immigration of a professional and middle class. The Union City–West New York region in Hudson County, New Jersey, became a northern counterpart of Dade County. The many refugees transferred there augmented a Cuban community that had arrived during the 1940s and 1950s to work in Union City's embroidery factories.[13]

At first Miami's relatively small Cuban community housed the newcomers, among whom they counted friends and relatives. Subsequently the weight of welfare assistance fell on outside agencies, including the diocese of Miami. In late 1960 Catholic Relief Services and the National Catholic Welfare Conference opened the Cuban Refugee Emergency Relief Center, which the federal government funded shortly thereafter. Some federal assistance, through the Refugee Center, went to training unskilled women to become self-supporting in Miami's garment industry. The pre-revolutionary social structure transplanted to Miami gradually gave way to a more representative cross section of Cuban society.[14]

Latino communities in the United States have varied experiences and cultures. Before 1965 no sense of a national Spanish-language group existed, although three large groups had a visible impact in their respective regions. Thereafter, increased immigration began to alter the ethnic composition of most major cities. Throughout the post-1965 period as increasingly diverse loci of settlement appeared, general patterns of movement have become evident, permitting a collective historical narrative going beyond the obvious facts of growth, immigration, and other demographic outcomes.

International Migration and Latino Nationalism, 1965–1980

Most nations in Latin America did not officially promote emigration or attempt to supervise the settlement of their nationals abroad. Potential migrant households developed deliberate strategies to work in the United States, based on chain migration. In these fluid—increasingly international, or "transnational"—settings, social networks replaced random movement. The greater numbers of women and children crossing the border signify a more long-term approach to migration. Remittances from the United States have had a strong impact on patterns of socioeconomic organization, especially in the rural towns, and especially on the ownership and quality of homes. International migration also permits rural households to enjoy modern consumer goods usually associated with urban life, as well as farm tools and machinery.[15]

By 1965, migration to the North had become an institutionalized method of survival for thousands of Mexican villagers. Mexico and the United States agreed to form a free trade zone along the border, borrowing from the Puerto Rico's Operation Bootstrap. Beginning in 1965 the Mexican government's Border Industrialization Program sought to attract U.S. capital to set up manufacturing firms, or *maquiladoras*, in an attempt to develop northern Mexico economically. Although the plan aimed at stemming migration by providing jobs, it attracted impoverished workers from the interior within striking distance of the United States. These developments, along with the rise of the "green card" commuters under temporary permits, made it easier for Mexicans to enter the United States and for many to remain.[16]

Before the Immigration Act of 1965 went into effect, Latin American immigrants to the United States represented less than 10 percent of the total legal U.S. immigration. Thereafter, Europe's share fell sharply while that from Asia and Latin America increased substantially. Rapid economic growth in the Southwest once again encouraged large-scale undocumented Mexican immigration. "Push" factors alone do not by themselves explain Mexican migration. Active recruitment by United States employers accompanied periods of extensive out-migration. Moreover, Mexico's wave of agricultural modernization in the late 1960s coincided with an intensification of labor demand on the U.S. side. With the expansion of migrant networks U.S. employment became easily accessible to virtually all segments of Mexican society.[17]

Throughout the 1970s Mexican immigration focused on California, the destination of about half all Mexican immigrants, and Texas, the destination of another 30 percent. Illinois expanded its role as a target of Mexican immigration, attracting about 10 percent of the total. However, the geographical distribution of Mexican immigration was remarkably stable during the decade. During the 1970s, Los Angeles received the most Mexican immigrants, followed by Chicago, El Paso, Houston, and San Antonio. Latinos ceased to fit conventional stereotypes of unskilled agricultural workers. Although Mexicans disproportionately worked in agriculture and manufacturing, only a small minority of all Latino immigrants came from farm backgrounds. About 50 to 60 percent of all those arriving in the 1970s worked in blue-collar occupations.[18]

La Lucha, as the Chicano movement of the 1960s and early 1970s became known, embodied the Mexican-American struggle for civil rights as well as its search for a distinct ethnic identity, neither fully Mexican nor American. The radicalism and nationalism of the Chicano movement emerged in different locations, attracting national attention in its attacks on traditional institutions and oppressive conditions. More than a campaign for higher wages and better working conditions, it sought an end to labor exploitation, racism, and inequality. Four individuals, César Chávez, Reies López Tijerina, Rodolfo "Corky" Gonzales, and José Ángel Gutiérrez, defined the issues, including organizing migrant farm workers; redressing historical violations of territorial rights guaranteed in the Treaty of Guadalupe Hidalgo; encouraging community activism; and taking a more active political stance in electing Mexican-American public officials.

Chávez, a one-time migrant worker from Arizona, blended nonviolent resistance and charismatic leadership in his campaign to bring stability and security to the lives of California migrants, relying on many organizing tools. The 1965 Delano Grape Strike of Mexican-American and Filipino farm workers, the ensuing boycott, and the 1966 march from Delano to the state capital brought Chávez and the farm workers to national prominence. A parallel movement in the Rio Grande Valley of Texas focused attention on the plight of agricultural workers along the border. Finally, after years of struggle, the United Farm Workers in 1970 signed the first of several labor contracts with major California growers. Luís Valdez, who later produced several important films on the Mexican-American experience, founded the Teatro Campesino in 1965 under the wing of César Chávez and La Causa. Teatro Campesino performed in fields alongside highways and sometimes even in parking lots and in factories, serving as a symbol of cultural solidarity. The California legislature in 1975 passed a landmark collective bargaining act for farm workers largely excluded from federal labor law coverage.[19]

A Texas Pentecostal preacher, Reies López Tijerina, carried the banner for a cause deeply rooted in the history of Mexican Americans in the Southwest. Tijerina protested the illegal seizure of Mexican lands by the United States government and its citizens during the annexation process. In 1963 he formed the Alianza Federal de Mercedes, a group that claimed several thousand members at its height, including the descendants of New Mexican settlers who received Spanish grants during the colonial era. For his role in the Alianza's forceable occupation of the Kit Carson National Forest, Tijerina served two years in a New Mexico penitentiary.[20]

"Corky" Gonzales rose to prominence as an organizer of Denver's Crusade for Justice. He encouraged local activism by Chicanos and pushed the concept of Aztlán, as the Southwest became known, after the mythical ancestral homeland of the Aztecs. Gonzales, also a poet, explored the mestizo background of the Chicano in his popular poem, "I Am Joaquin." He also participated in the 1970 Chicano Moratorium in Los Angeles, a counterpart of the anti-Vietnam War movement that protested the disproportionate number of Mexican Americans killed on the front lines. Like the other Chicano leaders, Gonzales fought to overcome political apathy and acquiescence in the status quo, while also helping to spur student strikes and walkouts protesting the indifference and lack of sensitivity of school administrators toward Mexican-American education.[21]

Mexican Americans have historically experienced much de facto segregation in schools and housing in Texas, southern California, and elsewhere in the Southwest, exacerbating widespread poverty. José Angel Gutiérrez, an organizer of the Mexican American Youth Organization as a student at St. Mary's College in San Antonio, adopted a novel approach. In the late 1960s he founded La Raza Unida party to harness the "Mexican vote" as an alternative to the Democrats and Republicans. This third party movement gained some strength statewide, electing in 1970 a predominantly Mexican American school board in Crystal City, Texas. It also made some gains in California, serving as a novel attempt at political empowerment and self-determination. Several years later another Texas leader of La Raza Unida party, Willie Velasquez, founded the Southwest Voter Registration and Education Project to boost registration among Mexican Americans and increase their participation in electoral politics.[22]

The War on Poverty programs of the 1960s included Latinos, whose participation in such initiatives as Model Cities contributed to the development of local leadership. With the decrease of federal funding, new neighborhood groups emerged, many with the backing of local churches. However, as Latino officials, Mexican-American and Puerto Rican, increasingly gained access to elective office, they lobbied for legislation to remove historical and structural barriers to a more open society. The 1975 amendment to the Voting Rights Act offered greater protection from measures that fragmented or diluted Latino voting strength, especially in Sunbelt cities, such as at-large voting, gerrymandering, and discriminatory annexations of contiguous areas. The use of the poll tax remained in force in Texas until 1965; other voter registration impediments effectively eliminated migrant workers and others from the election rolls. During the 1970s, court challenges by the Mexican-American Legal Defense and Education Fund in San Antonio modified political structures, allowing Latinos to summon majorities. Henry Cisneros, for example, won the 1981 mayoralty election in San Antonio, becoming that city's first Mexican-American mayor in over a century. Other modifications accelerated representation and helped overcome the reluctance of Latinos to engage in dialogue in the public sphere.[23]

Immigrants joined the homeland and the settled communities in interdependent economic, social, and political relationships. One linkage between Mexican immigration and Chicano activism in the United States developed in response to the media attention received, often stereotypically, by "illegal aliens" as a renewed threat in the 1970s. Bert Corona, a veteran labor organizer and founder of the Centro de Acción Social Autónomo (CASA) in Los Angeles, pushed the ideological struggle against nativism, popularizing the protection of the undocumented on humanitarian grounds. In the late 1960s and early 1970s he led CASA in organizing undocu- mented workers and discouraging unfounded fears of Mexican labor. Debate focused on how to draw boundaries and seek a bal- ance between well-established communities and new cultures, with a recognition of the changing nature of international migration.[24] The 1970 Census counted 7,850,000 Latinos, including 5,350,000 persons of Mexican origin located primarily in the southwestern states but increasingly in Illinois and the Midwest. The New York metropolitan area, Chicago, and Philadelphia contained most of the 1,500,000 mainland Puerto Ricans, while the Cuban community of 500,000 centered on Miami.[25]

Unlike the situation of Mexican Americans in the Southwest, Puerto Rican communities on the mainland emerged in neigh- borhoods previously dominated by European immigrant groups. One parallel, however, emerged in the ambiguous nationalistic voice of the second-generation "Nuyorican," born or raised in New York, alienated and searching for a mainland identity. This gen- eration had lost touch with its Caribbean roots and sometimes lamented the suppression of the *Boricua*, or Indian, heritage. Their mixed European, African, and native heritage as well as their en- counter with the indignities of barrio life shaped a struggle for civil rights, sometimes along the lines of African Americans, with whom Puerto Ricans shared highly segregated inner-city neighborhoods. The Young Lords, a militant Puerto Rican organization, sprang up in Chicago in 1969; its members brazenly occupied churches and seminaries and later opened a day-care center on the North Side. In the early 1970s, a New York Young Lords group took over a church in East Harlem and started free breakfast programs for children while drawing attention to the need for improving access to barrio health care.[26]

With declining economic opportunities in the manufacturing and apparel industries in the Northeast, reverse migration to Puerto Rico became dominant after 1965. It included some unemployed migrants but also consisted of professionals, business people, and other middle-class Puerto Ricans who might otherwise have moved to mainland suburbs but instead chose to work or retire on the island. They established themselves increasingly in urban areas, especially the San Juan metropolis, after 1970. New York, in- cluding adjacent portions of New Jersey and Connecticut, in 1970 contained more Puerto Ricans than did the San Juan metropolitan area—about 965,000 (out of a total of 1,400,000 living on the mainland) versus 851,000. However, better, less crowded, conditions existed outside New York. Boston's Puerto Rican community jumped dramatically during the 1970s by taking on agricultural workers from surrounding areas as well as incorporating migrants coming directly from the island and from other states. Other sizable communities emerged in Buffalo, Bridgeport, Jersey City, Miami, Milwaukee, and San Francisco.[27]

The South Bronx during the 1960s had become home of hundreds of thousands of Puerto Ricans who had followed subway lines from overcrowded barrios in Manhattan. The Puerto Rican population in the Bronx declined greatly after the mid-1970s with the widespread destruction of housing stock, mainly older apartment buildings, in a rash of deliberately set fires of mysterious origin, fueling the massive dispersal of Puerto Ricans throughout the metropolitan area and beyond. The city lost 600,000 unskilled and semiskilled jobs of the sort that many migrants had occupied. Fleeing residents, both Puerto Rican and non-Latino, left abandoned, often burned out, tenement hulks that remained as monuments to the dreadful time. Rebuilding efforts faltered after federal assistance for the area fell through. Although multipronged efforts have recently brought some improvements, this chilling episode created much disillusionment and considerable dispersal within barrios in the Northeast.[28]

The dire social, political, and economic circumstances following the 1965 civil war in the Dominican Republic led many islanders to emigrate from the island during the ensuing decades. During the early 1960s Dominicans from comparatively prosperous households moved from rural to urban areas—chiefly from the northern agricultural region of the Cibao to the Santo Domingo metropolis— and from there to the United States. Emigration also functioned as a way to accumulate funds to improve the land in the Dominican Republic, where government policies never emphasized agricultural reform and development, in order to purchase additional holdings and maintain the family's status in the community. International migration became essential to the economic stability of the country as remittances from emigrants financed many improvements. Increasing numbers of Dominicans sought to escape poverty during the 1970s by migrating to New York City, where they concentrated in Washington Heights in Upper Manhattan. Smaller communities arose in Queens, the Bronx, and Brooklyn. Other destinations included New Jersey and Puerto Rico.[29]

Many Dominicans presented themselves as Puerto Ricans, often after having crossed the perilous channel connecting the two islands by boat. There they then either entered the mainland "legally" from San Juan, a traditional Latino gateway to New York City, or searched for subsistence jobs in the depressed island economy. According to the 1980 census, 169,000 persons of Dominican birth resided in the United States, with 128,000 (about three-quarters of them) living in the New York metropolitan area. The community is especially hard to measure as it contains a large number of undocumented individuals. In 1980 city and state officials of New York filed a lawsuit against the Bureau of the Census, charging a massive undercount of anywhere from 500,000 to 1,000,000.[30]

Colombians accounted for the largest share of the Latino population originating in South America. They first entered during the 1950s to escape rural unrest and violence. Increasingly, they sought economic opportunities. Colombia's good, inexpensive universities graduated many professionals, especially doctors. Under a selective application process for emigration that favored those from professional and middle class backgrounds at the expense of the poor, many Colombians went to the United States and overstayed student, tourist, or other visas. New York City accounted for about 40 percent of the 64,000 Colombian immigrants legally admitted to the United States between 1966 and 1975, where they settled predominantly in Jackson Heights and neighboring communities in the borough of Queens. They soon dispersed throughout the New York–New Jersey metropolitan area, working in factories and at a wide assortment of jobs. Other settlements arose in Miami, Chicago, and Los Angeles. The proportion of immigrant Colombian females admitted to the United States between 1960 and 1980 consistently exceeded that of males, reflecting the emphasis of immigration legislation on the reunion of families as the basis for selection of immigrants and the structure of labor demand, among other factors.[31]

Cuban refugees became caught in the middle of United States–Cuba diplomacy. In September 1965, Castro permitted unrestricted departure of all dissatisfied Cubans whose exiled relatives came to transport them from the port of Camarioca to Florida. Despite a United States embargo, the Cuban government demonstrated longevity. In December 1965, under a binational "Memorandum of Understanding," the United States immediately initiated an airlift from Varadero Beach to Miami. These ongoing "freedom flights" lasted until 1973, bringing almost 300,000 Cubans to the United States, where they received special entrant status.

The early Cuban exodus consisted largely of the upper class, whose experience and access to financing provided avenues for accumulating capital. Initially, the refugees experienced difficulty in finding jobs. With time, they helped revitalize the Miami area, enjoying rapid socioeconomic mobility in the process. They opened a whole range of enterprises, from restaurants to banks, employing exiles arriving subsequently and frequently serving other Latino communities locally and elsewhere in Latin America. Ethnic solidarity and nationalism based on a strong anti-Castro ideology followed Cubans as they dispersed within Dade County, especially to the blue-collar suburb of Hialeah, taking advantage of garment industry jobs and the city's relatively inexpensive living arrangements.[32]

Meanwhile, between January 1961 and December 1972, the federal government resettled Cubans outside South Florida, hastening their economic independence while easing the housing and employment conditions of those remaining in Miami. It tended to isolate Cuban families from urban barrios. The resettlement program targeted professionals, providing language training, certification, and licensing for doctors, lawyers, university professors, and teachers. During the 1970s many Cubans returned from other areas of the country, joining their Miami compatriots in Dade County's southwestern suburbs and moving further north into Broward and Palm Beach counties.[33]

Germans and other European immigrant groups initiated programs of bilingual education in the nineteenth century. The visibility of Latinos during the 1960s and 1970s, however, resulted in novel programs of federal funding, beginning with a Ford Foundation grant to Miami's Coral Way Elementary School. This experiment, beginning in 1963 and lasting several years, allowed for social experimentation in a middle-class neighborhood among Cuban children and a group of volunteers representing the general populace. The Dade County public schools thereafter developed a pioneer program for helping children make the transition to English without holding back their academic progress. Other predominantly Latino school districts, including some in Texas, came to view the model, minus the teaching of Spanish to non-Latinos, as highly workable and desirable.[34]

The 1968 Bilingual Education Act viewed modified language instruction as a way of reversing low educational achievement and

high dropout rates, particularly among poor Mexican-American
enclaves in the Southwest. It appropriated $7.5 million for the
following year to support seventy-six pilot projects serving 27,000
children. In 1972 Aspira, an influential national educational organization known for encouraging Puerto Ricans to pursue higher
education and professional training, sued the New York City Board
of Education, claiming that tens of thousands of Latino students
received inadequate instruction in their native language, violating
federal guidelines. The United States Supreme Court, with the case
still pending, mandated in *Lau* v. *Nichols* in 1974 that school districts provide non-English-speaking students with special instruction, allowing districts to specify which linguistic approach best
suited their needs. A special "consent decree" mandated bilingual
education in such situations to supplement existing programs of
English as a Second Language. Expenditures increased steadily,
amounting to over $100 million by 1978, at which time state and
municipal matching funds supplanted dwindling federal appro-
priations. Most Latino groups have strongly supported the insti-
tutionalization and preservation of bilingual education as, at the
very least, a temporary tool for language transfer and often for the
more controversial purpose of cultural retention.[35]

LATINO DIVERSITY IN THE UNITED STATES SINCE 1980

Immigrants came to the United States during the 1970s and
1980s in numbers not seen since the turn of the century, including
some 500,000 legal migrants arriving annually. Because of family
reunification provisions, close relatives of adult citizens often entered the United States legally, maneuvering around often exces-
sively low numerical ceilings for Western Hemisphere countries
and other restrictions. Many immigrants during the 1970s and
1980s thereby obtained permanent resident status for their spouses
and children. Two other immigration laws, the Immigration Reform and Control Act of 1986 (IRCA) and the Immigration Act
of 1990 reflected compromise over unrestricted immigration, the
need for foreign labor in specific segments of the economy, and
the promise of equality and social justice in public policy. IRCA
resulted in the legalization of over one million previously undocumented individuals, primarily of Mexican origin, and subsequently
encouraged family reunification. Amnesty did not, however, erase
the hardships of many Latino immigrants, nor did it guarantee
smooth settlement and adjustment for the families affected.[36]

After forty years, international migration has become rooted in the social and economic structures of both Mexico and the United States. Immigration between sending areas and Latino communities increasingly becomes organized through social networks forged from kinship ties and shared local origins. Migrants fall under three general categories, depending on their strategy of entering and working in the United States. "Temporary workers" target specific jobs for discrete periods. "Recurrent migrants," typically married men who regularly travel back and forth between Mexico and the United States, support their families with remittances. "Settled" migrants live permanently in the United States, often with the benefit of legal residence documents, and usually work continually.[37]

Immigrants from the countries of Central America have lived in Latino communities in the United States for many years. However, unprecedented regional turmoil and upheaval followed the Sandinista victory in the Nicaraguan Revolution of 1979. The counterinsurgency tactics of the military regimes of El Salvador and Guatemala spurred a steady stream of refugees into Mexico and then the United States. This state of affairs first became public in 1980 with the death of over a dozen Salvadoran refugees in the Arizona desert and the arrest of the survivors by the Immigration and Naturalization Service. If forced to return, many refugees would face certain punishment from authorities back home. Catholic and Protestant clergy and laity banded together to carry out a sanctuary movement, designating their local churches as safe havens. Churches also contributed bond money and supported individual petitions for political asylum.[38]

Officials denied almost all such applications by Salvadorans and Guatemalans, whose countries received United States support, but more readily granted asylum to petitioners from Nicaragua and Eastern European countries. This policy relegated many persons from Central America, as illegal immigrants, to the status of economic refugees coming to the United States looking for jobs. Forced to enter surreptitiously, generally on foot along the California and Texas border, they then traveled to distant points, maintaining a low profile in cities, towns, and on farms throughout the United States.[39] San Francisco, Los Angeles, New York, and Chicago all attracted large numbers of Central American refugees during the 1980s. Salvadoran refugees have come to dominate Latino immigration in Washington, D.C., while Guatemalan Indians increasingly find their way into Florida agriculture. In the late 1980s large numbers of Nicaraguans settled in Miami's Little Havana; their community has since expanded outward within the city and metropolitan area.[40]

Latino population growth remained steady through recessions as well as booms, particularly in the Southwest. Mexican immigration to Houston continued through the eighties, but thousands of undocumented Salvadorans, Guatemalans, and Hondurans also entered the metropolis. For 1990 the total of 750,000 Latinos represented 28 percent of the total Houston population, twice the percentage of ten years earlier. Mexican Americans, who comprised two-thirds of the Latino total, have historically lived on the East Side, and other Latino newcomers joined them there. However, Central Americans also formed new settlements on the West Side, near service industry jobs and inexpensive rentals. Similar patterns of residential stratification developed elsewhere between new and old Latino groups. In Los Angeles, for example, Mexican Americans dominate the eastern portion of the city, while Salvadorans and Nicaraguans concentrate in the Pico-Union district west of downtown.[41]

Latino communities continued to spread outside the traditional Sunbelt receiving areas of Texas, California, and Florida into the Great Lakes states of Michigan, Illinois, and Wisconsin. Mexican immigrants in Chicago's Pilsen-Little Village area arrived in unprecedented numbers during the 1970s, giving that metropolis the largest Mexican-origin population other than Los Angeles. Newcomers overflowed into the traditionally Puerto Rican North Side areas, although West Town, Humboldt Park, and Logan Square remained Caribbean-American enclaves. Guatemalans recently replaced Cubans as the third largest Latino group in the city. Ecuadorians have also arrived, making Chicago a meeting place for Latinos as well as an urban laboratory revealing the dynamics of contemporary ethnicity.[42]

Few lasting rewards have flowed to Puerto Rico from its continued dependency as a commonwealth under United States rule. Meanwhile, on the mainland cycles of poverty and government assistance persist. Even though the labor migration abated, barrios remain arenas for segregation and racial discrimination. Meanwhile, the centuries-old popular culture of the island continues to lose its vitality. A recent trend of migration from Puerto Rico consists of a growing exodus of the middle class, particularly of college-educated professionals, to such mainland locations as Orlando, Florida. The number of Puerto Ricans on the mainland surpassed two million in 1980 and 2,700,000 in 1990, as against some 3,500,000 on the island in 1990.[43]

Dominican immigrants continue flooding New York City, where their children comprise a plurality in many public schools. As in the Puerto Rican experience, the path of settlement widened rapidly. Dominican communities exist in Miami, Boston, and Chicago, among other cities. The dream remains vague and sometimes unrealistic—to work and try to save enough money to return home someday, perhaps by establishing a business. The immigrant often represents the best hope for many relatives and feels responsible for contributing as much as possible. As with other Latino groups, the extended family network, including *compadrazgo* relations, helps Dominicans confront economic and other difficulties presented by their relocation.[44]

A major exodus from Cuba to Miami occurred in 1980 aboard vessels owned and piloted by Cubans living in South Florida. Between April and December of that year almost 125,000 persons departed from the port of Mariel, including more than 2,000 unaccompanied minors. After initial processing in military bases and other makeshift facilities, they faced relocation throughout the United States, although a large proportion ultimately settled in South Florida. No organized programs from governmental, religious, or social organizations responded to these "Marielitos." Federal officials assessed each entrance claim individually. No meaningful resettlement program existed to ease the burden on existing Cuban communities. This wave of exiles, consisting of many Afro-Cubans, represented the racial composition of Cuban society more accurately than ever before. Their ambivalent reception contrasted greatly with that given the predominantly white, upper- and middle-class émigrés who arrived after the Cuban Revolution.[45]

For refugees with few marketable skills, the Cuban-dominated Miami economy provided immediate jobs. However, the very size of the Mariel Boatlift resulted in problems inherently different from those posed by earlier refugee waves. Lack of preparation resulted in shortages of resources, space, and funding, forcing local communities to fend for themselves. School systems faced a crisis with little or no information on the new refugee student population. The appearance of crime dominated the Miami community's concern during the next several years.[46]

The national attention and general confusion following the influx of Marielitos exacerbated existing tensions in older Cuban settlements. Non-Latino resentment surfaced in South Florida, especially concerning the dominance of Spanish-language establishments, the difficulties for non-English speakers in negotiating Miami's cultural landscape, and the doctrinaire anti-Castroism of many exiles. In 1980 Dade County approved an anti-bilingual ordinance prohibiting the expenditure of county funds for the utilization of any language other than English or promoting any culture "other than that of the United States." All county government meetings, hearings, and publications would be in English only. A backlash had clearly developed, based on the perception of many Anglos that the exiles were dominating jobs, the schools, and even the government, with voter participation rates generally exceeding those of any other Miami group.[47]

Unlike Latino groups in other regions, South Florida Cubans became more concentrated during the 1970s after having returned from their original locations of resettlement. They now represent about one-half of metropolitan Miami's residents. Most mainland-born Cuban Americans have never been to the island and, significantly, they avoided the disruptive circular movements of Mexican immigrants and Puerto Rican migrants. Moreover, they hardly seem disadvantaged, having for many years compared favorably with native whites in most indices of education and income. In 1980 the Cuban median family income stood at $18,000, compared with $15,000 for Mexican Americans, $11,000 for Puerto Ricans, $16,000 for other Latinos, and $20,000 for the total United States population. The Cuban influx included large numbers of established professionals and well-educated middle-class individuals who quickly reestablished themselves politically as well as economically. Since the early 1980s the powerful Cuban American National Foundation has supported a hard line on maintaining the Cuban embargo and discouraging the reopening of diplomatic relations with Havana.[48]

Diversity among Latino communities often presents obstacles to effective social and political organization. Nationally, no monolithic identity has developed, making for tenuous and often transitory political bonds. Mexican Americans in Texas established the League of United Latin American Citizens (LULAC) in 1929 and it now serves Latino communities nationwide, with Puerto Ricans and Cubans having attained prominent leadership positions in some locations. Organizations such as the National Council of La Raza and the National Association of Latino Elected and Appointed Officials develop lobbying networks and seek to provide an underpinning for a common agenda. However, they have not

overcome deeply rooted patterns of nationalism or cultural and political differences among Latinos. Present patterns in Los Angeles
and New York, the largest and most visible Latino cities, indicate
continued heterogeneity and movement away from traditional patterns of bloc voting.[49]

Despite increased cooperation within and among constituent
groups since 1965, Latino unity remains largely a speculative concept, presenting a challenge to all Latinos to address mutual concerns. However, within the Latino experience, differences are great,
including socioeconomic disparities, means of self-identification,
levels of linguistic proficiency in both English and Spanish, and
historical trajectories. Pressures on Mexico from an expansionist
United States shaped contemporary southwestern institutions and
defined relations between incoming Anglos and Mexican Americans. Annexation in 1848 and the coming of the railroad in the
1880s brought new potential for societal change. Twentieth-century
immigration has continually revitalized Mexican-American settlements and solidified ties with Mexico. During the 1980s Latinos
in California constituted about 50 percent of the state's population growth; the proportion in Texas stood at about 40 percent.
Throughout Los Angeles and southern California, as well as in
the San Francisco Bay area, especially San Jose and Oakland, new
immigrants mix with older Mexican-American populations. Meanwhile, agricultural and other workers are moving in large numbers
to Oregon and Washington.

By contrast Spanish imperialism and United States colonial
policies have conditioned the Puerto Rican experience. The island
economy historically depended on the export of sugar, coffee, and
tobacco crops. Progress came about slowly during the nineteenth
century. After 1898 economic and demographic clashes accelerated internal migration to San Juan and other cities. Subsequently,
patterns of circular movement developed between the island and
mainland communities, foreshadowing transnational migration
from more distant parts of Latin America. Within the Caribbean
Basin, the Dominican Republic established strong linkages with
mainland communities after 1965. Hundreds of thousands of persons born in Central and South America live in areas of previous
Latino settlement. Poverty abroad has driven more women into
the work force, assuring that they will comprise a larger share
of the immigrant population. The high Latino birth rate clearly
presents challenges for the entire society, especially concerning
educational and other institutions. By any account, Latinos are

forcing a reevaluation and redefinition of United States culture, society, and laws.[50]

Notes

1. For an early attempt to analyze Latino constituent groups see A. J. Jaffe, Ruth M. Cullen, and Thomas D. Boswell, *The Changing Demography of Spanish Americans* (New York: Academic Press, 1980).

2. Frank D. Bean and Marta Tienda, *The Hispanic Population of the United States* (New York: Russell Sage Foundation, 1987), p. 59.

3. Saskia Sassen, *The Mobility of Labor and Capital: A Study in International Investment and Labor Flow* (New York: Cambridge University Press, 1988), pp. 1, 2; David M. Reimers, *Still the Golden Door: The Third World Comes to America* (New York: Columbia University Press, 1992), p. 134; Frank D. Bean, Jurgen Schmandt, and Sidney Weintraub, "Introduction," in Bean, Schmandt, and Weintraub, eds. *Mexican and Central American Populations and U.S. Immigration Policy* (Austin: University of Texas Press, 1989), pp. 1–3.

4. For Mexican American frontier history, see Carlos E. Castañeda, *Our Catholic Heritage in Texas, 1519–1930*, 7 vols. (Austin: Von Boeckmann-Jones, 1936–1958), Max L. Moorhead, *The Presidio: Bastion of the Spanish Borderlands* (Norman: University of Oklahoma Press, 1975), and John F. Bannon, ed., *Bolton and the Spanish Borderlands* (Norman: University of Oklahoma Press, 1964).

5. For new Mexican immigrants in old barrios, see Albert Camarillo, *Chicanos in a Changing Society* (Cambridge, Mass.: Harvard University Press, 1979). On migrant patterns, see Dennis N. Valdés, *Al Norte: Agricultural Workers in the Great Lakes Region, 1917–1970* (Austin: University of Texas Press, 1991).

6. Douglas S. Massey, Rafael Alarcón, Jorge Durand, and Humberto González, *Return to Aztlán: The Social Process of International Migration from Western Mexico* (Berkeley: University of California Press, 1987), pp. 55–57. For a good overview of Mexican Americans, see Carlos E. Cortés, "Mexicans," in Stephan Thernstrom, et al., *Harvard Encyclopedia of American Ethnic Groups* (Cambridge, Mass.: Belknap Press, 1980).

7. Leo Grebler, Joan W. Moore, and Ralph C. Guzmán, *The Mexican-American People: The Nation's Second Largest Minority* (New York: Free Press, 1970), pp. 106–107, 111.

8. For Puerto Rico in its regional context, see Gordon Lewis, *Puerto Rico: Freedom and Power in the Caribbean* (New York: Monthly Review Press, 1963); Center for Puerto Rican Studies, *Labor Migration under*

Capitalism: The Puerto Rican Experience (New York: Monthly Review Press, 1979); and Stanley Friedlander, *Labor Migration and Economic Growth: A Case Study of Puerto Rico* (Cambridge, Mass.: MIT Press, 1965).

9. On early migration and settlement, see Virginia Sánchez Korrol, *From Colonia to Community: The History of the Puerto Rican Community in New York City, 1917–1948* (Westport, Conn.: Greenwood Press, 1983); and Lawrence R. Chenault, *The Puerto Rican Migrant in New York City* (New York: Columbia University Press, 1938).

10. For the recruitment of Puerto Rican migrant workers on the mainland, see Edwin Maldonado, "Contract Labor and the Origins of Puerto Rican Communities in the United States," in James B. Lane and Edward J. Escobar, eds., *Forging a Community: The Latino Experience in Northwest Indiana, 1919–1975* (Chicago: Cattails Press, 1987).

11. Rosa Estades, "Symbolic Unity: The Puerto Rican Day Parade," in *The Puerto Rican Struggle: Essays on Survival in the U.S.* (New York: Puerto Rican Migration Research Consortium, 1980), eds. Clara E. Rodríguez, Virginia Sánchez Korrol, and José Oscar Alers, p. 87; Eugenio Rivera, "The Puerto Rican Colony of Lorain," *Centro de Estudios Puertorriqueños Bulletin* 2 (Spring 1987): 16.

12. For Cuban settlement in Tampa, see Gary R. Mormino and George E. Pozzetta, *The Immigrant World of Ybor City: Italians and Their Latin Neighbors in Tampa, 1885–1985* (Urbana: University of Illinois Press, 1987).

13. For the phases of departure of the early exiles, see Richard Fagen, Richard Brody, and Thomas O'Leary, *Cubans in Exile: Disaffection and the Revolution* (Stanford: Stanford University Press, 1968). For a general overview of Cuban Americans, see Thomas D. Boswell and James R. Curtis, *The Cuban-American Experience: Culture, Images, and Perspectives* (Totowa, N.J.: Rowman and Allanheld, 1983). On Miami, see Antonio Jorge, Jaime Suchlicki, and Adolfo Leyva de Varona, eds., *Cuban Exiles in Florida: Their Presence and Contributions* (Coral Gables: University of Miami, North-South Center, 1991). On New Jersey, see "For Union City and Miami: Sisterhood Rooted in Cuba," *New York Times*, November 30, 1992, p. A1.

14. *Resettlement Recap: A Periodic Report from the Cuban Refugee Center* [U.S. Department of Health, Education, and Welfare] November 1964, p. 3.

15. Massey et al., *Return to Aztlán*, pp. 169–171.

16. Robert L. Bach, "Immigration and U.S. Foreign Policy in Latin America and the Caribbean," in Robert W. Tucker, Charles B. Keely, and Linda Wrigley, eds. *Immigration and U.S. Foreign Policy* (Boulder:

Westview Press, 1990), p. 134; Massey, et al., *Return to Aztlán*, 175–179, 213–15.

17. Thomas Muller, *Immigrants and the American City* (New York: New York University Press, 1993), p. 49; *U.S. Select Commission on Immigration and Refugee Policy: 1952–1979* (Washington, D.C.: GPO, 1979), pp. 51, 53; Robert Warren, "Volume and Comparison of United States Immigration and Emigration," in Roy S. Bryce-Laporte, ed., *Sourcebook on the New Immigration: Implications for the United States and the International Community* (New Brunswick: Transaction Books, 1980), pp. 1–2.

18. Albert Camarillo, *Chicanos in California: A History of Mexican Americans in California* (San Francisco: Boyd and Fraser, 1984), pp. 104–108.

19. See Peter Matthiesen, *Sal Si Puedes: César Chávez and the New American Revolution* (New York: Random House, 1969).

20. Rodolfo Acuña, *Occupied America: A History of Chicanos* (New York: Harper Collins, 1988), pp. 340–341; Juan Gómez-Quiñones, *Chicano Politics: Reality and Promise 1940–1990* (Albuquerque: University of New Mexico Press, 1990), pp. 115–118.

21. Acuña, *Occupied America*, pp. 340–342; Gómez-Quiñones, *Chicano Politics*, pp. 112–114.

22. Cortes, "Mexicans," in Thernstrom, ed., *Harvard Encyclopedia of American Ethnic Groups*, p. 717.

23. Frances J. Woods, "The Model Cities Program in Perspective: The San Antonio, Texas, Experience" (Washington, D.C.: GPO, 1982), pp. 293–295; Peter Skerry, "Neighborhood COPS: The Resurrection of Saul Alinsky," *New Republic*, February 6, 1984, pp. 21–23. For the difficulties of creating Latino districts see Carlos Navarro and Richard Santillán, "The Latino Community and California Redistricting in the 1980s: Californios for Fair Representation," in Richard Santillán, ed., *The Hispanic Community and Redistricting*, vol. 2 (Claremont, Calif.: Rose Institute, 1984). See also David R. Johnson, John A. Booth, and Richard J. Harris, eds., *The Politics of San Antonio: Community, Progress, and Power* (Lincoln: University of Nebraska Press, 1983).

24. Acuña, *Occupied America*, p. 373; Gómez-Quiñones, *Chicano Politics*, pp. 150–152.

25. United States Bureau of the Census, "The Hispanic Population in the United States: March 1991," *Current Population Reports*, October 1991, p. 19; Bean and Tienda, *Hispanic Population of the U.S.*, pp. 146, 333.

26. Joseph P. Fitzpatrick, *Puerto Rican Americans: The Meaning of Migration to the Mainland* (New York: Prentice-Hall, 1987), pp. 108–111.

On Puerto Rican nationalism in mainland barrios, see Adalberto López and James Petras, eds., *Puerto Rico and Puerto Ricans* (Cambridge, Mass.: Schenkman, 1974) and Félix Padilla, *Puerto Rican Chicago* (Notre Dame, Ind.: University of Notre Dame Press, 1987).

27. José Hernández Alvarez, *Return Migration to Puerto Rico* (Berkeley: Institute of International Studies, 1967), pp. 57–63; New York City Department of City Planning, "The Puerto Rican New Yorkers: A Recent History of Their Distribution and Population and Household Characteristics" (New York: New York City Department of City Planning, 1982), pp. 8–11, 17, 90; George C. Myers and Clara G. Muschkin, "Demographic Consequences of Migration Trends in Puerto Rico: 1950–1980," *International Migration* 22 (1984): 217–221.

28. Bronx Museum of the Arts, *Devastation/Resurrection: The South Bronx* (Bronx, N.Y.: Bronx Museum of the Arts, 1979), pp. 45–50; Jill Jonnes, *We're Still Here: The Rise, Fall, and Resurrection of the South Bronx* (Boston: Atlantic Monthly Press, 1986), p. 317.

29. Glenn Hendricks, "Dominicans," in Thernstrom, *Harvard Encyclopedia of American Ethnic Groups*, pp. 282–284. See also Glenn Hendricks, *The Dominican Diaspora: From the Dominican Republic to New York City—Villagers in Transition* (New York: Teachers College Press, Columbia University, 1974).

30. Evelyn S. Mann and Joseph J. Salvo, "Characteristics of New Hispanic Immigrants to New York City: A Comparison of Puerto Rican and Non-Puerto Rican Hispanics" (New York: New York City Department of City Planning, 1984), pp. 24–27; Robert Warren, "Datos sobre legalización y otra información estadística acerca de la inmigracion dominicana a los Estados Unados," in Eugenia Georges, ed., *Dominicanos Ausentes: Cifras, Política, Condiciones Sociales* (Santo Domingo: Fundación Friedrich Ebert, 1989), pp. 39, 54–56; Eric M. Larson and Teresa A. Sullivan, "*Cifras convencionales* en las investigaciones sobre migración: el caso de los 'dominicanos desaparecidos,'" in Georges, *Dominicanos Ausentes*, pp. 67–70, 91. On the problems of estimates and the measurement of the mainland Dominican community see also Eric M. Larson and Teresa A. Sullivan, "'Conventional Numbers' in Immigration Research: The Case of the Missing Dominicans," *International Migration Review* 21 (Winter 1987).

31. Elsa M. Chaney, "Colombian Migration in the United States," in Wayne Cornelius, ed., *The Dynamics of Migration: International Migration* (Washington, D.C.: Smithsonian Institution, Interdisciplinary Communications Program, Occasional Monograph #5, 1976), pp. 117, 118.

32. On the residential dispersion of Cubans in South Florida, see University of Miami, *The Cuban Immigration 1959–1966 and Its Impact on Miami-Dade County, Florida* (Coral Gables: Research Institute for Cuba and the Caribbean, University of Miami, 1988); and Raymond A. Mohl, "Miami: The Ethnic Cauldron," in Richard Bernard and Bradley Rice, eds., *Sunbelt Cities: Growth and Politics since World War II* (Austin: University of Texas Press, 1981). For coverage of Cuban American entrepreneurship in Miami, see Alejandro Portes and Robert Bach, *Latin Journey: Cuban and Mexican Immigrants in the United States* (Berkeley: University of California Press, 1985).

33. *Resettlement Recap*, January 1967, p. 3. For an example of a dispersed community of Cubans resettled in Michigan, see Carol Berry, "A Survey of the Holland Spanish-Speaking Community" (East Lansing: Institute for Community Development, Michigan State University, 1970), pp. 1–4, 42–44.

34. See William F. Mackey and Von N. Beebe, *Bilingual Schooling and the Miami Experience* (Coral Gables: University of Miami, Institute of Interamerican Studies, 1990).

35. Isaura Santiago, "*Aspira* vs. *Board of Education of the City of New York*: A History and Policy Analysis" (Ph.D. diss., Fordham University, 1978), pp. 34–38. See also Alan Pifer, *Bilingual Education and the Hispanic Challenge* (New York: Carnegie Corporation of New York, 1979).

36. Dennis Gallagher, Susan Forbes, and Patricia Weiss Fagen, *Of Special Humanitarian Concern: U.S. Refugee Admissions Since Passage of the Refugee Act* (Washington, D.C.: Refugee Policy Group, 1985), pp. 3–7, 61–65.

37. Massey et al., *Return to Aztlán*, pp. 316–318, 320. See also "Temporary Worker Programs: Mechanisms, Conditions, Consequences," [Special Issue] *International Migration Review* 20 (Winter 1986).

38. Robin Lorentzen, *Women in the Sanctuary Movement* (Philadelphia: Temple University Press, 1991), pp. 3, 4, 26, 27.

39. Linda S. Peterson, "Central American Migration: Past and Present." [Washington, D.C., Center for International Research, CIR Staff Paper No. 25, November 1986], pp. vii–ix, 6–12, 20–22; National Immigration and Alien Rights Project, *Salvadorans in the United States: The Case of Extended Voluntary Departure* (Washington, D.C.: American Civil Liberties Union, 1984), pp. 1–6, 34–38, A29–A31.

40. See Sergio Aguayo and Patricia Weiss Fagen, *Central Americans in Mexico and the United States: Unilateral, Bilateral, and Regional Perspectives* (Washington, D.C.: Georgetown University, Center for Immigration Policy and Refugee Assistance, 1988); and Arturo J. Cruz and

Jaime Suchlicki, *The Impact of Nicaraguans in Miami: A Study for the City of Miami* (Coral Gables: University of Miami, Institute of Interamerican Studies, 1990).

41. Nestor P. Rodríguez "Undocumented Central Americans in Houston: Diverse Populations," *International Migration Review* 21 (Spring 1987), pp. 5–6, 14. For the history of Mexican American growth in Houston see Arnoldo De León, *Ethnicity in the Sunbelt: A History of Mexican Americans in Houston* (Houston: Mexican American Studies Monograph Series, University of Houston, 1989). See also Fernando Peñalosa, "Central Americans in Los Angeles: Background, Language, Education" [Occasional Paper No. 21] (Los Angeles: Spanish Speaking Mental Health Research Center, 1986); Steven P. Wallace, "Central American and Mexican Immigrant Characteristics and Economic Incorporation in California," *International Migration Review* 20 (Fall 1986); and Mike Davis, *City of Quartz: Excavating the Future in Los Angeles* (New York: Verso, 1990).

42. For an examination of Latino identity in the case of Chicago, see Félix Padilla, *Latino Ethnic Consciousness: The Case of Mexican Americans and Puerto Ricans in Chicago* (Notre Dame: University of Notre Dame Press, 1985). For patterns in the Chicago metropolis see "Hispanic Gains in Suburbs Found," *New York Times*, June 7, 1981, p. 36.

43. Douglas S. Massey and Nancy A. Denton, *American Apartheid: Segregation and the Making of the Underclass* (Cambridge, Mass.: Harvard University Press, 1993), pp. 12, 112–114, 144, 151. On problems of Puerto Rican poverty on the mainland, see Clara E. Rodríguez, *Puerto Ricans: Born in the U.S.A.* (Boulder: Westview Press, 1991). On the lingering status question, see Edwin Meléndez and Edgardo Meléndez, eds., *Colonial Dilemma: Critical Perspectives on Contemporary Puerto Rico* (Boston: South End Press, 1993).

44. Eugenia Georges, "New Immigrants and the Political Process: Dominicans in New York" (Occasional Paper No. 45] (New York: Center for Latin American and Caribbean Studies, New York University, April 1984), pp. 28–31. See also Jorge del Castillo, Eugenia Georges, David Bray, et al., *La Inmigración Dominicana en los Estados Unidos* (Santo Domingo: Editorial CENAPEC, 1987).

45. Everett M. Ressler, Neil Boothby, and Daniel J. Steinbock, *Unaccompanied Children: Care and Protection in Wars, Natural Disasters, and Refugee Movements* (New York: Oxford University Press, 1988), pp. 51, 52.

46. Helga Silva, *The Children of Mariel: Cuban Refugee Children in South Florida Schools* (Washington, D.C.: Cuban American National Foundation, 1985), pp. 25–27, 46–51.

47. See U.S. Commission on Civil Rights, *Confronting Racial Isolation in Miami* (Washington, D.C.: GPO, 1982). In May 1993 the Dade County Board of County Commissioners unanimously repealed the thirteen-year-old "English Only" ordinance. Although the vote led some Latino officials to proclaim a new era of tolerance and understanding, it could not obscure unresolved differences on the part of non-Latino whites (an estimated 250,000 of whom moved out of the county since 1980) and African Americans, who have long perceived favoritism toward Cubans in jobs and government contracts; see "As Hispanic Presence Grows, So Does Black Anger," *New York Times*, June 20, 1993, pp. 1, 11.

48. Metro-Dade County Planning Department, "Demographic Profile of Dade County, Florida, 1960–1980" (Miami: Metro-Dade County Planning Department, 1985), pp. 9–14; Metro-Dade County Planning Department, "Population Projections: Race and Hispanic Origin in Dade County, Florida, 1980–2000" (Miami: Metro-Dade County Planning Department, 1987), pp. 2, 5, 14–16; Metro-Dade County Planning Department, "Dade County Facts" (Miami: Metro-Dade County Planning Department, 1990), pp. 2, 6, 15; Lisandro Pérez, "The Cuban Population of the United States: The Results of the 1980 U.S. Census of Population" [Occasional Paper No. 40] (Miami: Latin American and Caribbean Center, Florida International University, 1984), pp. 13–15.

49. On the distinct elements of the Latino political landscape, see F. Chris García, ed., *Latinos and the Political System* (Notre Dame: University of Notre Dame Press, 1988). Diversity within the spheres of music, literature, and religion is equally characteristic. Concerning Latino literature see, for example, Marc Zimmerman, *U.S. Latino Literature: An Essay and Annotated Bibliography* (Chicago: March/Abrazo Press, 1992).

50 "Growth, But Not Power, for State's Minorities," *San Francisco Chronicle*, February 19, 1990, p. 1. For projections of Latino demographic growth and socioeconomic outcomes in California see David E. Hayes-Bautista, Werner O. Schink, and Jorge Chapa, *The Burden of Support: Young Latinos in an Aging Society* (Stanford: Stanford University Press, 1988). On the changing nature of ethnicity and pluralism in the United States see David A. Hollinger, "Postethnic America," *Contention* 2 (Fall 1992).

3

The Emergence of a Social Identity among Latino Catholics: An Appraisal

Anthony M. Stevens-Arroyo

"Who am I?" is an eternal question. Individuals are not the only ones to pose this question: Groups also utilize social and institutional processes to discover their identity within the events of human history. This chapter will trace how people of Latin American origin living in the United States have confronted this question of identity within the context of American Catholicism.

A few issues require definition. Individual assimilation is not the focus of this analysis. There have always been individuals who, for any number of reasons, exchange identification with another nation for complete assimilation of the culture of the United States. For such persons, the myriad characteristics associated with another culture are surrendered in order to become indistinguishable within United States society.[1] Such assimilation at the personal level has always occurred within ethnic groups and is often a conscious, individualized choice meriting respect.

My focus, however, is upon social expressions of Latino identity. I will study such expressions on the part of those who only partially surrender their Latino characteristics, those who refuse to surrender at all, and those who have surrendered, but who now attempt to recover and reclaim certain Latino characteristics. With a Latino identity come measurable values, customs, and behavioral patterns, which, however, are not rigid. Social identity changes with time, reflecting influences from the wider society as well as interactions within the group. Even the search for a name—Hispanics, Chicanos, Ricans, Boricuas, and Latinos—is part of a social process. [2]

Latinos did not invent the identity question within U.S. Catholicism. Dolan's studies of Irish and German Catholicism in the

77

nineteenth century have shown that cultural identification by immigrants within U.S. society had special religious results. For instance, the practice of Mass attendance and membership in Church societies increased patterns of church going over those that obtained in the homeland. This occurred, it is suggested, because the immigrant had scant familiarity with institutions in the big cities of the nineteenth-century United States, and Catholicism presented itself as part continuity with the old country and part accommodation to the new homeland.[3]

Tomasi has shown that an Italian national consciousness was particularly strong in the United States. While Italy became a unified national state only in the 1870s, in the United States all of the Lombards, Sicilians, Neapolitans, and other Italian-speaking groups were treated more or less the same by the United States and its Catholic Church. Since strength was found in numbers, these regional Italian groups quickly learned to find common ground in social, political, and institutional relations. In this process, the experiences learned in the context of Catholic life—organization, fund raising, leadership, publicity, political mobilization, and public relations—overflowed into the secular realm as well.[4]

Not surprisingly, religious practice in the United States produces similar results in Latino identity, but success is not automatic. Religious practice in the United States usually introduces special membership criteria—collection envelopes, bingo fund raising, parish schools, and the like—which have no exact counterpart in the homeland. At times the expectations that accompany these devices of parish maintenance appear more monetary than apostolic to Latinos. The Church may help Latinos economically and socially as it helped previous ethnic groups, but if Church assistance is lukewarm, paternalistic, or simply does not match expectations, Latinos may be alienated, sometimes leaving the Church. Catholicism in the United States has a long history of such accommodations, sometimes with success and sometimes with failure. A third area of Church experience in the United States touches the issue of identity more directly. Latino Catholics are more likely to encounter people of other cultures in parishes in the U.S. than in their homelands. Intensified contact with such groups may induce unity but may also inject conflict and competition for resources. Such interethnic battles also have antecedents in past struggles between ethnic groups within U.S. Catholicism.

But there are some characteristics of the Latino experience of Catholicism which have no direct parallels with other groups. The Spanish settlers founded the Catholic Church in the United States before there was a United States, arriving in Florida as early as 1521. Moreover, within Latinos are several different nationalities. When examining the sweep of more than a half-century in every part of the United States, contradictory patterns emerge which provide different material conditions for the expression of identity of each Latin American nationality group. Moreover, not only are Mexicans, Puerto Ricans, and Cubans different from each other, Mexicans in Texas may understand themselves differently from their compatriots in California. The same regional experiences affect Puerto Ricans, Cubans, and other Latin American groups. As a result, it is impossible to talk of a single Latino experience in this chapter. Instead, I hope to focus upon expressions of a cultural identity that transcend these differences of region and nationality to achieve a nationally inclusive term.

Social science has developed rigorous methods of measuring group behavior about aspects of social identity. Unfortunately, most social science data on Latino religious identity are focused upon monodimensional questions about religious practice and religious affiliation. Most of the survey data since 1950 are concerned about how many people consider themselves Catholics, how often they go to church, and how important religion is to them. Mills, Senior, and Goldsen, for instance, asked these types of questions in The Puerto Rican Journey, their 1950 study of New York Puerto Ricans. Forty years later, the 1990 political survey conducted nationwide by the Inter-University Program asked virtually the same questions.[5] Quantification about church affiliation and frequency of attendance are important issues, but they divorce religion from other aspects of social behavior and do not explore the ways in which religion shapes culture and the parameters of social interaction.

In the 1950s, Joseph P. Fitzpatrick provided perceptive probing of the sociological effect of religion among Puerto Ricans in his studies of family, marriage patterns, and cultural attitudes. Two decades of his commitment to analysis of the Puerto Rican community culminated in his now classic textbook on the meaning of migration.[6] Patrick McNamara researched the sociological process of Catholicism among Mexican Americans with his contribution to Leo Grebler's The Mexican-American People and in a subsequent study of clerical elites.[7] While neither scholar was a historian, their sociological approach to the questions of religious identity within institutional Catholicism included insightful appraisal of historical processes.[8]

Despite the value of these studies within their appropriate contexts, none of them adequately addressed a national identity for Latinos directly fostered by Catholicism. In the absence of more complete survey data, especially about the past, this chapter encounters formidable limitations. I have contented myself with use of a historical narrative to describe the context in which different notions of Latino identity have developed and how they have produced national impact. Because I do not pretend to judge how many Latino individuals adopted a particular identity at a given time, I believe I can show only that new definitions of Latino identity have emerged during the periods under study.

IDENTITY AND ASSIMILATION

The literature on identity, particularly within the social sciences, is too vast to be cited here, but many scholars have combined sociological approaches with historical analysis to review how various groups utilize Catholicism in order to achieve their social identity in this country. For much of this century, the core of studies about American Catholics usually treated the question of Catholic assimilation to United States society. In the post–Vatican Council II period, however, a growing number of scholars have dropped the "Church of the Immigrants" approach, considering it anachronistic.[9]

For Latinos the question of social identity has followed a different trajectory. The years since 1965, which marked a decline in ethnic consciousness for most Euro-American Catholics, have produced a much keener sense of ethnic Hispanic/Latino identity than had obtained before. Superficially understood, the Latino struggle for identity within Catholicism may appear as a belated attempt to imitate a process that Euro-Americans have already completed. I hope to show that the rise in Latino identity within the Church of the 1970s is a different phenomenon from the process that created an earlier "Immigrant Church" of European-origin groups.

One must ask why assimilation to the dominant society occurred so infrequently among Mexican Americans before the 1920s, despite their presence within the United States as an effect of the 1836 and 1848 wars with Mexico. Similarly, the U.S. takeover of Puerto Rico in 1898 did not result in the wholesale assimilation of the island natives to United States culture, and one is tempted to say that Puerto Ricans are more aware of their national identity today than in 1898.[10]

Since the 1970s, the assimilation premise has been rejected as an explanation of the Latino experience by a growing number of Latino scholars.[11] They highlight how different were the origins of Latinos in the United States compared to those of immigrants from Europe. Military conquest, rather than immigration, is the genesis of the Latino presence. While others *chose* to come to the United States, it is argued that for Mexican Americans and Puerto Ricans, the United States "came" to them. Thus, there is a larger measure of involuntary association with this country among the two largest groups of Latinos than with Euro-Americans. When contemporary scholars refer to the Latino colonial experience, they adopt this premise as central to the definition of Latino group identity. Subsequent waves of migration, particularly in the second half of the twentieth century, swelled Latino numbers, and there is a sizable number of foreign born lumped together with the descendants of Mexicans and Puerto Ricans in conquered America. But, in the opinion of those adhering to the colonial origin of Latino consciousness, the experience and consciousness of the first groups become normative for the more recently arrived.

In assessing this theory of colonialism and the status as conquered peoples of America, it is important to include the dimension of race. Sizable numbers of Latinos are black or Native American in race, and an even larger number are of mixed racial origin in various combinations. While both the 1980 and 1990 census recognize that "Hispanics may be of any race," there is a perceived inadequacy of the term *Latino* (or *Hispanic*) as a purely cultural term. In the 1980 census, nearly 40 percent of those who identified with one of the Hispanic identification terms also marked their racial category as "other," i.e., neither white, nor black, or Native American. Since upward social mobility in the United States is clearly tied to a measure of whiteness, the racial self-classification as "other" in racial terms merits further study by sociologists.[12]

I adopt here the general premises about colonialism and race from the Latino scholars, because I feel it is the perspective best suited to integrate studies of Latino identity within Catholicism to the existing literature. There are two basic questions to be asked. Why did the 1970s launch a conspicuous national movement within United States Catholicism that asserted and affirmed Latinos as a collectivity, and not before? And how does a Latino identity as conquered peoples of mixed race, rather than as immigrants like those of European origin, affect group behavior within institutional Catholicism?

In analyzing such questions, it must be borne in mind that identity is a subjective concept. While based on real situations and circumstances, identity is the result of human reflection and is subject to the same vagaries of behavior as any of our human experiences. In her succinct and precise article on Latino identity, Joan Moore points out that one conceptualizes identity within the group (endogenous) but may also have an identity imposed by others (exogenous).[13] I would call both of these the *relational dimension*. As she explains, these combine with the objective or *material dimension* for such identity, consisting of factors such as language, customs, and socioeconomic status. Thus, for instance, we get a glimpse of how people view themselves by evaluating how they use the Spanish language and in what contexts. This is the type of factor that can be measured and evaluated within Catholicism by examination of practices at the parish level. It becomes a tool to open a window on how much of the use of Spanish is motivated by personal preference and how often it defines Latinos over against an English-speaking majority.

The relational and material dimensions are not static. The outsiders' opinions and the group's conception of itself are in constant interaction. They may alternately reinforce or undermine each other. Moreover, as the material dimension changes—as the group gets more economically successful, for example—the relational dimensions are likely to be altered. Nor is it unusual for groups to have multiple identities, depending on the context. Thus, one may identify as a Catholic, as a woman, or as a Latina in different situations in which one or the other identity calls for adherence to a group. Moore calls these primary and secondary identities. Such prioritizing suggests logical control of identity. This is the positive side of ethnic awareness mobilization such as occurred for Latinos within the Catholic Church after 1967. But there may be an inability to manage multiple identities. When a group fails to identify itself logically, either internally to its own members or to the larger society, it becomes caught in collective cultural schizophrenia.

In understanding how a group consciousness is formed, some attention should be paid to the concept of *cultural crystallization* that has been developed in anthropology.[14] Without entering into technical definition, this is similar to a process of, as the name suggests, solidifying or hardening of group identity around a particular set of cultural characteristics. I find this concept useful in analyzing the history of Catholicism among Latinos because it connects certain expressions of Latino identity with the persons and institutions that respond to these expressions.[15] Specifically, there has been cultural crystallization for Latinos around the ethnic characteristics of 1) language; 2) religious faith; 3) shared traditions, values, and symbols; 4) literature, folklore, and music; and 5) special interest in certain political issues.

In this chapter, I compare conceptualization of a national or pan-Latino identity in four historical periods, posing questions about how Catholicism affected the identity in reference to these five characteristics. I have divided my treatment into four unequal sections on 1) the two decades leading to World War II; 2) the post-war period until the Second Vatican Council; 3) the church reforms and political radicalism of the 1960s; 4) the period of the Hispano Pastoral Encounter until the present.

Strangers in Our Own Land: 1926–1940

The first stirrings of a pan-Latino identity with a popular base in the U.S. came in the two decades before the Second World War. The Cristero Rebellion (1926–1938) and the Cárdenas presidency (1938–1944) in Mexico generated political divisions similar to those of the homeland among the Mexican-origin populations within the United States. Did one support the Cristeros in their opposition to the Mexican Revolution? Did one approve of the sweeping reforms of Cárdenas's nationalization policy? In the popular mind, these issues identified people as either pro-Mexican or pro-United States. And because Catholicism was part of the Cristero cause and socialism the political justification for Cárdenas's nationalizations, the Cold War dichotomy of Catholicism vs. socialism was a part of the Mexican experience even before there was a Cold War.

In Puerto Rico, Pedro Albizu Campos, president of the Nationalist party (1931–1965), defined his mission as the independence of the island from the United States *and* the restoration of Catholic civilization to Puerto Rico. Consciously patterned on the tactics of the Irish Rebellion of 1916, the Nationalist party's agenda was intended to force the concession of independence by the United States rather than enter the Second World War with a domestic revolt, much as the Easter Rebellion had a similar goal during

Britain's engagement in World War I. As in the case of the Mexican issues, agreement or dissent from the Nationalists became a defining issue for Puerto Ricans. Moreover, the strong support for Albizu Campos and the Nationalist cause by Vito Marcantonio, the New York congressman from Harlem, made Puerto Rican identity a significant issue within New York politics.[16]

U.S. intervention in Latin American countries, such as the campaign against Sandino in Nicaragua in the 1930s, served to awaken a group identity for Central Americans in the United States. The policies of the dictator Gerardo Machado did the same for Cubans. Machado introduced a populist nationalism into an otherwise corrupt military regime. His flirtation with a pro-Cuban nationalist agenda, such as repeal of the hated Platt amendment, tempted some to support him, despite his authoritarianism.[17]

But leaders in the different national communities resident in the U.S. were not content with rallying support of their countrymen alone. While Cubans enlisted other Cubans to bring down Machado—or keep him in power—they also tended to seek support among other Spanish-speaking people who were not from their own nationality group. In another example, support for the Republic during the Spanish Civil War was almost as important in New York's Spanish Harlem as specifically Puerto Rican and Cuban political issues.[18] Somewhat later, the rise to power of Peron in Argentina (1944–1954) and the ascent of the Dominican strongman Rafael Trujillo (1930–1961) fostered an intensive search for intergroup solidarity against these leaders among political exiles in the United States.

This generally anti-imperialist tone of pan-Americanism was strengthened by the development of the Good Neighbor Policy of Franklin Delano Roosevelt (1933–1945) that confessed to previous U.S. mistakes in foreign policy and sought to set out a new direction for relations with Latin America. The Roosevelt era also brought far-reaching domestic consequences for organized labor. Somewhat as an effect of militancy for Latin American political causes, most Latino leaders advocated socialism within what was to become the CIO. The official reward to these local labor leaders during the Roosevelt years was the formation of the Congreso de los Pueblos de Habla Española. This was a national umbrella group for the Spanish-speaking members of the labor movement and was intended to foster the continued organization of new immigrants and their education into the value of union membership along the general lines of syndicalist socialism.[19]

The creation of a pan-Latino awareness of political issues and a certain amount of cross-national solidarity on these important issues was immensely aided by the emergence of Latino newspapers and radio programs in such urban centers as New York, Los Angeles, Chicago, Tampa, and Philadelphia. This fledgling Spanish-language media allowed for various leaders in exile to communicate directly with a wide spectrum of Latinos in the United States. Because the writers were frequently leading political exiles, the quality and stature of those writing for the Spanish-language newspaper was often of the highest quality.

Politics was not the only seedbed for pan-Americanism. Popular culture provided a constant bombardment with pan-Latino concepts. Phonograph records and Spanish-language movies created experiences of commonality among different groups. Argentina produced its fair share of movies and records, and the tango helped project an image of Latinos that meshed with the Euro-American acceptance of Rudolf Valentino of silent movie fame. For a while, this Argentine persona as tango dancer became the popular cultural symbol of a pan-Latino identity. Later on, the Brazilian Carmen Miranda of the fruit basket head-dress performed a similar function. Mexicans in the United States listened to recordings of Colombian trios strumming the boleros of Cuban and Puerto Rican composers. By the 1950s, Cubans and Puerto Ricans watched film stars strut their stuff in slapstick comedies like those of the Mexican Mario Moreno, better known as Cantinflas. Thousands of tears were shed in soap-opera romances with the ever-suffering Argentine feminine icon, Libertad Lamarque.

This early form of asserting a national or even international meaning to the Latino identity was an advance over what had characterized the previous decades. Because specialized newspapers, radio programs, sound recordings, and films were increasingly common, larger and larger numbers of Latinos were in communication with each other across regional and national boundaries. There had been a cultural crystallization for a generic set of Latino symbols, aided in part by expectations from the larger English-speaking society. This new sense that the Latin American peoples constituted a significant social group stimulated diverse reactions. For some, Latin American culture was viewed through an optic focused upon the sensuous intimations of the tango or samba à la Hollywood. Latino peoples were associated with a pastiche of blaring music, dirty dancing, and vice. Others interpreted Latino differences from a paternalistic expectation that Latinos needed only Americanization to become successful, as had European immigrants before them. Alarmists feared that unless something were quickly done, Latinos would become radical revolutionaries within the United States.[20]

Catholicism exercised a role in shaping this initial move towards a pan-Latino identity. In some ways, a Catholic identity helped counteract the negative stereotypes of inferiority, sensuality, and revolution. Because the Catholic faith carried with it an affirmation of certain values and traditions of Latino experience since colonial days, it was already a part of the culture. Catholicism could be viewed as part of the Spanish patrimony, distinguishing Latin America from a Protestant United States.[21] Even if the individual had not visited a church in years, social identity included some element of Catholic religion. For believers, Catholic tradition involved the rites of passage, at the very least. But even for nonbelievers, the rejection of the faith was not passive religious indifference. Just as in Mexico and in Spain, rejection of Catholic identity brought anticlericalism as well.

For the majority of Latinos during the 1930s and 1940s, Catholicism was generally viewed as an institution opposed to Latin American nationalism. The role of the Church for Mexicans in the United States, for instance, was to rally support for the Cristeros and against the socialism of the Mexican government. For Puerto Ricans, the issue was more complicated. Albizu Campos was radically pro-Puerto Rican and Catholic, while the moderates were Protestants and pro-United States. Moreover, with a dearth of native clergy, most Puerto Rican Catholics were ministered to by Spanish clergy usually supportive of the dictator Francisco Franco. In proof that politics makes strange bedfellows, Albizu Campos and the Nationalist party had support from both the pro-Franco clergy (because Albizu was pro-Catholic) and from pro-Loyalist atheistic socialists (because he was anti-imperialist). It was not until the 1950 Jayuya revolt on the island and the attempted assassination of President Truman at the Blair House in Washington that the flirtation between the Nationalist party and the Catholic clergy was ended.[22]

In most cases, the ordinary Latino living in the United States identified Catholicism with the colonial heritage from Spanish sources. Opposed to the nationalist and anti-imperialist tone of pan-Americanism, Catholicism was a sentinel for tradition and a guardian of the purity of language and customs derived from the homeland. Through mechanisms as simple as baptism, marriage, and burial, parish clergy fostered the notion that all Latinos were Catholic in some residual sense. Church buildings also provided meeting places for Latinos, usually within communities too poor to maintain separate public facilities. The social functions of credit unions, neighborhood organization, and community education were often housed by a church. Nor were all of these activities dictated by the clergy. As had happened with previous Euro-American groups, there was a tendency for community-based activity to work semi-autonomously under a parish roof.[23]

Because the U.S. Catholic Church offered considerable prestige and social importance due to its membership in the tripartite civil religion of Protestant-Catholic-Jew, identification with Catholicism generally benefited the local Latino community by lending clout and social visibility. The parish usually could help in obtaining favors from the political establishment and this role was symbolically celebrated by a clerical presence at public parades, dedications, and festivals. Moreover, this mediating function worked to link the local Latino leadership to the Euro-American establishment.

In most ways, this mix of cultural Catholicism with a certain pan-Latino, pan-American feeling during the 1930s and 1940s was what contemporary Latino scholars call *cultural citizenship*.[24] There was no particular political agenda for those who identified themselves as "Spanish-American," "Latinoamericano," or "Spanish-speaking." They were more or less satisfied in *being* Latino, rather than in *doing* Latino things. Put another way, the mode of expressing cultural citizenship was membership within the Church.

THE CITY AS CURSE AND BLESSING: 1940–1964

The U.S. entry into the Second World War in 1941 presented a new set of social factors that shifted the focus of pan-Latino consciousness away from the politics of the homelands. The principal motor force for the new social factors was urban migration, which became the crucible for new material conditions. The outbreak of war sent much of the young adult white population to the armed services, and there was a need in U.S. factories for substitute workers. Among Mexican Americans this meant the move of a large number of rural people away from the farms and ranches of Colorado, New Mexico, Arizona, and southwest Texas towards cities like Los Angeles, Chicago, Houston, Denver, and Kansas City. The end of the war in 1945 intensified this migration, as Latino GIs tended to migrate to cities, rather than return to the small towns in the Southwest and Puerto Rico where they had been reared.

Moreover, even within the small-town structure of parts of Texas and California, where Mexican and Mexican-American farm labor had been a fixture since the end of the nineteenth century, there was a noticeable shift in residential patterns away from the previous isolation of the *ranchos* and the migrant camps into a more visible symbiotic relationship with the established towns. By the 1950s, Mexican and Mexican-American people were more likely to go to school in these towns and to use hospitals, restaurants, movie theaters, and churches than they had been previously. In many ways, this phenomenon paralleled the end of Jim Crow that was underway in the Deep South.[25]

The same urbanization trend also engendered the Puerto Rican Great Migration (1946–1964) that brought some 40 percent of the island's population to the United States in less than a generation. Because of Puerto Rico's unique political status and a 1917 law, the people were already U.S. citizens, even though they did not come from a state. Undeterred by immigration laws and responding to a desperate need for cheap labor in New York's immense manufacturing base, the migration was the largest and swiftest transfer of one country's population to the United States since the Irish migration during the nineteenth-century Irish Potato Famine.[26] Urbanization in twentieth-century Puerto Rico under Governor Luis Muñoz Marín (1948–1964) and his ambitious program of Operation Bootstrap literally emptied the countryside of its people. The mountain peasants or *jíbaros* were sent off to New York and other mainland cities because there were not enough manufacturing jobs on the island to satisfy the hunger for urban life and consumerism. Although there were Puerto Rican farm laborers, it was the urban experience of the majority of the migrants that produced the symbols of the Puerto Ricans in the United States—just the opposite of what happened with the Mexican Americans.

The urban migration increased the visibility of the Spanish speaking within new regions of the United States. Recognizing the need to address this new population, social service agencies and the public political establishment joined the Church in directing special attention to Latinos. In the 1950 census, for the first time,[27] the Spanish-speaking people were counted in an ethnic category.

Previously, the manner of counting Latinos in the census was through the classification, "foreign born." In other words, those Latinos born in Mexico (and before 1900, those born in Puerto Rico), Cuba, or any other Latin American country were distinguished by place of birth. But for those Mexican Americans born in the United States and for all Puerto Ricans after 1917, there was no national census category.

Although it was a significant advance, the 1950 census issued reports on the Spanish speaking only in the five states of the Southwest. Moreover, any Latino with a non-Spanish last name was omitted from the listing, even though persons with Spanish surnames who may not have considered themselves Latinos were included. Puerto Ricans in the New York metropolitan area were counted with a sample of 5 percent of the population. These numbers were extrapolated to profile the entire Puerto Rican population. For the 1960 census, two other categories were added to Spanish surname as identifiers: entries on "birth or parentage" and "mother tongue" were included. At best, these were imperfect conceptualizations of Latino identity, and the census data from the 1950s and 1960s suffer from these limitations.

The official recognition by the Census Bureau was an effect of a heightened official awareness of increasing numbers of Latinos migrating to urban centers. The unofficial reaction was laden with stereotypes, many of them negative. The high visibility of juvenile gangs in Pacific Coast cities gave rise to the Mexican *pachuco* or zootsuiter, with slicked-down hair and gangster mannerisms that fed anti-Mexican feelings. The future Nobel Prize winner, Octavio Paz, viewed the pachuco not as "Mexican" but as a tragic victim of the loss of Mexican identity. In a sense, the zootsuiter was the first "Latino," considered neither Mexican nor American. Moreover, the ugly incidents of the San Diego riots in 1943 that pitted Mexican Americans against U.S. sailors resulted in prejudiced trials that still serve as examples of racism against Latinos.[28]

The stereotype of New York Puerto Ricans in *West Side Story*, made into a long-running Broadway play by Leonard Bernstein and Jerome Robbins, bestowed upon Latinos a symbolic status like one of the feuding groups in Shakespeare's *Romeo and Juliet*. But in addressing racism against Latinos, *West Side Story* also reinforced the notion that Puerto Rican neighborhoods in the city were places of corruption, crime, and poverty. If you wanted to "live in America," the Latino had to leave behind the old and traditional society of the homeland. During his year of living on the West Side while attending Columbia University, the Puerto Rican playwrite, René Marqués, was inspired to write the play *La Carreta* (*The Oxcart*). His characters urge New York Puerto Ricans to return to the island in order to rediscover their identity.

During much of the 1950s, if the urbanized Latino managed to escape victimization as a juvenile delinquent, there was also the racism of white liberalism masked as paternalism lurking behind social programs. Despite a vast difference in ideology, both approaches stereotyped Latinos as needing to become Americanized. The decade was, after all, the height of the Pax Americana, wherein the prosperity of the American way of life, the righteousness of the fight against communism, and the nobility of the nation were scarcely questionable within the popular culture. For Latinos, this goal of middle-class existence was virtually unchallenged. Gradually, new organizations that were focused upon acceptance within an urbanized United States substituted for the anti-imperialist and homeland-oriented political groups of the pan-American pre-war years. Bolstered immensely by returning Latino veterans, the GI Forum, LULAC, Aspira, and the Puerto Rican Forum fostered the American Dream with programs of self-help in education and business development.[29] No longer was cultural distinctiveness within U.S. society dependent upon resolving faraway political issues. Instead, Latino identity now required a focus upon the dynamics of life in the United States.

The popularity of the *I Love Lucy* show, starring the Cuban-born Desi Arnaz, served as a paradigm for the upwardly mobile Latinos. The Lucy show broke new ground by making Arnaz play himself, transparently renamed "Ricky Ricardo," a Cuban band leader with a thick Spanish accent and the excitability of a Caribbean hurricane. But because he was treated in his middle-class surroundings as if he were just another immigrant to the United States, a message of gradual assimilation was transmitted. In a sense, Arnaz experienced artistic crossover and was able to play and sing his own music for an English-speaking audience. Caribbean music was "in," whether played by representative musicians like Xavier Cugat, Machito, Pérez Prado, or imitated by North American artists like Nat King Cole, Rosemary Clooney, or Dean Martin. Mambo and cha-cha-cha made the charts of the hit songs in the 1950s, and in the process the acceptability of Latino culture—if not Latinos themselves—was enhanced.

Ironically, it was somewhat easier to obtain a favorable image in United States popular opinion if one was directly from Latin

America rather than "just" a Latino, born and raised in the United States. Foreign policy in the postwar period stressed the exportation of the free enterprise system and North American investment to Latin America as a part of the growth of democracy and the extension of the Pax Americana. Even Walt Disney got into the act by producing a cartoon special in 1948 that let Donald Duck tour Latin America in a celebration of the rich cultures of Brazil and Mexico.

The contrast of the esteem for Latin America with the low opinion for the Latino in the United States was clear in the case of Puerto Ricans. While those in New York struggled against the stereotype of the juvenile delinquent and the welfare recipient, those in San Juan were afforded favorable publicity as industrious workers for Operation Bootstrap that brought rapid industrialization of the island through U.S. investment. Puerto Ricans on the island were pictured as willing apprentices to American teachers who helped lead them away from rural poverty and ignorance and toward a life of consumerism in an urban setting. The island was baptized with the names "Showplace of Democracy" and "The Bridge between Two Cultures." And as a reward for Puerto Rico's loyalty to this aspect of the American Dream, Theodore Moscoso, director of Operation Bootstrap, was named director of the Alliance for Progress by President John F. Kennedy. Moscoso was to preach that prosperity would come to Latin American nations if they followed Puerto Rico's example and strengthened economic and political ties to the United States.

Few stopped to ask why Puerto Ricans in the United States who were closer to economic and political absorption were so disadvantaged relative to the rest of the U.S. population. Moreover, Puerto Rico was projected by Washington as a Latin American country that had freely chosen in 1952 to adopt a commonwealth association with the United States that allowed the benefits of statehood but did not sacrifice Latin American culture. It is little wonder that surveys of Puerto Rican migrants to the United States during this period revealed a high level of interest in returning to Puerto Rico.[30]

It may be that cultural crystallization vis-à-vis U.S. culture had taken place in Puerto Rico *before* the Great Migration.[31] The island had been invaded in 1898, but the mass migration did not begin until nearly half a century later. During that time, Puerto Rico had hardened its sense of culture and self-identity, as for instance on the issue of language.[32] Moreover, this sense of Puerto Rican uniqueness over against a Protestant United States had developed its political expression in the Nationalist party under Pedro Albizu Campos.

These factors—a Puerto Rican majority on the island, the dominance of the Spanish language, and the viability of an independent political system outside the control of the Democratic and Republican parties—combine to make Puerto Rico function *culturally* for Puerto Ricans on the U.S. mainland like Mexico does for Mexican Americans. But because it is a colony under the U.S. flag, the island serves paradoxically as the same sort of base, *demographically* and *economically*, as Texas and New Mexico do for Mexican Americans.[33] Put another way, the overwhelming presence of U.S. businesses, of federal benefits like foodstamps and BEOG (Basic Educational Opportunity Grants), and the lack of a need for passport in migration makes Puerto Rico more akin to New Mexico or southwest Texas than to Jalisco or Nuevo León. But because the cultural crystallization of Puerto Rico had already taken place before the Great Migration (1946–1964), the island is cultural homeland for most Puerto Ricans the way Mexico is for Mexican immigrants.

This point is important because it helps define the different points of departure in the process of achieving an identity for the Mexican and Puerto Rican peoples, the two largest Latino groups in the United States today. Despite the similarities, there are significant differences between the two groups. Moreover, when the third group, the Cuban Americans, is added to the mix, the management of a single national Latino identity through the 1950s until 1964 can be better understood as a complex task.

As with the Mexican and Puerto Rican populations, there have been Cuban communities in the United States since the nineteenth century. The establishment of Ybor City near Tampa, Florida, is a social experiment that merits more attention than has been afforded by historians of Catholicism in the United States.[34] Moreover, Cubans lived and worked alongside other Latinos, particularly Puerto Ricans, in many East Coast cities. Cuban and Puerto Rican patriots forged alliances for the liberation of their islands from Spanish control, with New York as a headquarters for the exiles—hence the similarity between the flags of the two nations. But because of the unique political status that Puerto Rico has with the United States, migration from the U.S. colony out-stripped the migration of Cubans to the United States through much of the twentieth century.

The triumph of the Cuban Revolution in 1959, however, began a chain of events that rapidly increased the Cuban presence within the United States. Other scholars have examined the different segments of the Cuban migration since 1959 and to my understanding, they recognize the different segments of Cuban population.[35] The first Cubans to arrive in Miami in 1959—literally overnight—were members of the corrupt Batista regime. It had been the custom for ruling elites in the Republic of Cuba, including Batista himself, to establish a safe haven by purchasing property in Florida and opening accounts in Swiss banks. This group of Cubans were the political exiles, properly so-called, who claimed an initial influence beyond their numbers. Because these exiles willingly denounced the revolution as communist, they were allies to Washington in an attempt to undercut the independence of Cuba. The Batista supporters fully expected that as Cuban exiles in the United States they would return to the homeland as soon as the revolutionary government fell. Hence, their exile identity was focused on politics on the island, and their attention to domestic Latino issues in the United States was minimal. Consisting largely of office holders and political followers of Batista, this group was always small and shrunk into virtual nonexistence over time. The concept of Cuban identity as political exile, however, has been passed on and forms part of Cuban-American reality today.

A larger group of Cuban immigrants came from the economic and professional upper class. Although by U.S. standards these were upper middle-class urbanites rather than millionaires, in the Cuban class structure they represented an influential elite. Many worked for U.S. companies located in Cuba in 1959. These people often spoke English fluently and some had been educated in the United States. They were executives engaged in management, construction, and investment. Often, they had family ties to the Cuban professional class of doctors or lawyers and to native Cuban clergy and religious. While some of these Cubans may have disliked the Batista regime and may even have welcomed its overthrow by the 26th of July movement, they did not countenance extensive nationalization or ideological attacks on capitalism. Predictably conservative in any political context, they admired the wealth and size of the United States and identified Cuba as a client state in the Pax Americana.

At the time of the revolution's triumph, this second group was distinguishable from the Batista supporters. Hence, they were not political exiles in the narrow sense of the word. But because they were tied to capitalism as the source of their economic and social status, they were to interpret the installation of socialism in Cuba as political expulsion. It was from this group that opposition to the revolution first developed within Cuba, and it is this group that has nourished the stereotype of the Cuban American as well-to-do in comparison with other Latinos.

The third group of post-1960 immigrants is the largest of the nearly one million Cubans and their children who have come to the United States since 1959. These are working people and small business owners from the cities and towns of Cuba. As lower middle-class people, they enjoyed no special privileges under the Batista regime and were not a part of the economic elites who dominated prerevolutionary Cuba. A substantial number of these Cubans backed Fidel Castro as leader of the patriotic 26th of July movement. Even after the fall of Batista and the first populist reforms of the revolutionary government, many of these Cubans enthusiastically supported what they perceived as legitimate expressions of Cuban nationalism against the corruption of the previous regime. For these people it was not so much the triumph of the revolution in 1959 as the hostilities with the United States after 1961 that spurred flight.[36]

Cuban Catholics were most likely to be found among the members of the second and the third groups because the Batista followers, with a few exceptions, were not very religious. Among the educated middle class in Cuban society were Catholics who believed in the message of Catholic social justice and who committed themselves to Catholic Action. Since Catholicism in Cuba was a largely urban institution, these town and city dwellers were not as isolated from the institutional Church as most rural people. Even when their religious practice suffered from irregularity and lack of depth, they nonetheless practiced the tradition of religious rituals—baptism, marriage, and burial. Although there had been a low level of Catholic religious practice for Cubans overall, practice was highest among these urban groups. Hence, in the U.S. Cuban community practicing Catholics are a higher percentage of the population than in Cuba. Put another way, religious Cubans were more likely to leave Cuba than the nonreligious during the 1960s so that the composition of the Cuban community in the U.S. is weighted in favor of those practicing their religion. This premise is verified by the numbers of alumni of the prestigious Catholic schools and members of wealthy parishes that immigrated to the United States in the early 1960s.[37]

Added to the practicing Catholics who left Cuba for the United States were Cubans who started to practice after immigrating. Certainly, it was more acceptable to have left Cuba in search of religious freedom than in disgrace as part of the discredited Batista regime. In the context of anticommunism, even purely political exiles incorporated the symbols of Catholicism as props for a Cuban-American identity. In this conception, every person leaving the island was an exile, fleeing persecution on religious and ideological grounds, because the revolution tolerated neither Catholicism nor capitalism.

Life in the United States helped create a new identity of being Cuban and Catholic, awaiting the chance to return to the island as soon as Fidel could be toppled. Although political motives were never absent, this interweaving of politics and religion produced sincere conversions and undeniably strengthened Catholic practice, often beyond the levels of participation in Cuba. Despite pointing towards a return to Cuba, this Catholic-exile identity represented cultural crystallization around a new identity in the United States during the 1960s. The process was to wax stronger until the arrival of the 1980 immigrants, the *marielitos*.

Before concluding this section, it is necessary to turn to the unfolding of pastoral practice a decade earlier among Mexican Americans and Puerto Ricans. As Latino numbers grew in the post–World War II years, Church leaders addressed the Spanish speaking within the framework of existing national parishes and migrant ministry. But it soon became apparent to those who cared to notice that the national parishes or existing migrant chaplains would not be able to respond adequately to the new challenges. Since the financing of language chapels and migrant ministry usually came from a religious order or depended upon wealthy patrons, the massive migration soon overwhelmed these limited resources. Moreover, even within cities, Puerto Ricans and Mexican Americans were expanding from existing urban barrios to areas where there were no national parishes for the Spanish speaking.

These factors effectively forced institutional Catholicism in the United States to find new ways for understanding the Latino presence. With migration to cities, previous pastoral approaches fitted to a largely rural population were no longer adequate. The bishops addressed the migration of Mexican Americans in 1944 by authorizing a committee to coordinate migrant pastoral ministry at an interdiocesan level. Cardinal Stritch of Chicago helped mobilize support in 1946 for the project of the Bishops' Committee for the

Spanish Speaking in the United States. The committee wrote a pastoral plan that linked social services, religious instruction, and sacramental attentions. Key to this plan were missionary priests who lived among the migrants, and Archbishop Lucey of San Antonio became a major figure in this new type of coordinated pastoral outreach.[38] Lucey not only stressed that social concerns were vital to the success of the project, he also structured language and cultural training for non-Hispanic clergy so that the committee would not depend upon priests from Mexico for its operation. It was the great contribution of Lucey to have articulated for the bishops an identity for the Mexican American that was distinct from that of the Mexican. Ironically, the focus on the Mexican American as migrant worker tended to overshadow pastoral commitment towards permanent communities in New Mexico, Texas, and California.

In the New York archdiocese, Puerto Ricans not only brought to the city a new population requiring pastoral attentions, they also displaced Euro-American congregations. The scenario in many New York parishes was depleted Mass attendance and empty church buildings, while unchurched Puerto Ricans crowded into apartment houses, schools, and national language chapels. The entirely urban nature of the Puerto Rican Great Migration differentiated it from much of the Mexican-American experience.

One of the first decisions of Francis Spellman upon becoming the ordinary of the New York archdiocese in 1939 was to transfer the ministry of St. Cecilia's, a parish of the archdiocese in Spanish Harlem, to the Redemptorist congregation. Spellman had been much impressed by the success of the New York–based Redemptorists at transplanting U.S. Catholicism to the island. He expected that the missionaries would do the same for the Puerto Ricans in New York. Instead of new parishes, the archdiocese intended to use existing structures to serve both the English speaking and the Puerto Ricans, so that the facilities would be shared by two different language communities within the same parish.[39]

After the end of the war, recognizing that the number of Puerto Ricans in New York continued to grow, Cardinal Spellman decided to train archdiocesan priests in the Spanish language as the Redemptorists had prepared their missionaries destined for Puerto Rico. It was a pattern similar to the training of those ministering to the Mexican Americans through the Bishops' Committee for the Spanish Speaking. But the influx of Puerto Ricans overwhelmed even these efforts, and the reluctance of local pastors to admit the

Spanish speaking to their churches was a principal obstacle. Accordingly, in 1953, Spellman set in motion the process that created a chancery office to coordinate the apostolate within the boundaries of the archdiocese much as the Bishops' Committee was doing at a national level.

This Office of Spanish American Catholic Action also sponsored an interdiocesan conference in 1955 in Puerto Rico under the direction of the Jesuit Joseph P. Fitzpatrick and the Yugoslav Ivan Illich, a priest of the archdiocese. The result was the foundation of the Institute for Intercultural Communications at Ponce, Puerto Rico, which assumed a highly visible role in cultural and pastoral training for large numbers of clergy and religious who intended to work among the Puerto Ricans in the United States. Not only did these initiatives invite an immediate response from Puerto Ricans in the United States, hungry for pastoral attention, they also generated similar programs in other dioceses and archdioceses, including Chicago, which created special programs under the ordinary to coordinate pastoral care to increasing numbers of the Spanish speaking. As had already occurred for the Mexican Americans, Puerto Ricans in the United States had been recognized as a category related to, but distinct from, Puerto Ricans on the island.

Despite the timeliness of these and other pastoral measures taken by institutional Catholicism in the United States, it would be a mistake to interpret the ministry to the Spanish speaking as an unqualified success. For one thing, individual pastors could often escape the responsibility to minister to the Spanish speaking within their parish borders by inventing various excuses. Secondly, the commitment of resources and personnel was never completely adequate to the task. For instance, while the parishes offered themselves to the Latinos, they often did so only with the second-hand or inferior resources at their disposal. Thus, the Spanish-language Mass was typically celebrated in the basement church, far from the pomp and glory reserved for those in the upper, or official, parish building. Thirdly, the paternalism of the time was woven into the attitudes of those assisting the Church in its ministries. This paternalism, while more frequently displayed in an Anglo-to-Latino exchange, also had instances where one Latino looked down on others. Fourthly, these pastoral initiatives were clearly dependent upon the good will of the local ordinary for their funding and implementation. The foward-looking policies suggested for addressing the pastoral needs of Puerto Ricans also depended upon the pastors' ability to understand Puerto Rican identity with the insightfulness of those related to the chancery.

Friends of Latinos were at a disadvantage. Except in Chicago, Mexican Americans were one group and Puerto Ricans another, so that there was little actual cooperation between these ministries. The Bishops' Committee and the New York Office of Spanish American Catholic Action functioned separately. The negative public conception of Puerto Ricans in New York and Mexican-American migrant workers was stronger than the positive image promoted by the clergy interested in their welfare, and the negative stereotypes produced some recalcitrant pastors and antagonistic Euro-American parishioners. Progressive clerics remained isolated within their own regions, relating to local problems rather than to a national issue. Accordingly, much of the initial success in the Spanish-speaking ministry depended upon support from the local bishop.

Nor was there a sense of Latino self-determination or leadership. The Church was clerical and hierarchical both in theory and in fact. For instance, the only measure of self-determination for Puerto Rican Catholic organizations in the United States came with the Caballeros de San Juan, the Knights of St. John, during the 1950s in Chicago under the leadership of Father Leo Mahon. Clearly modeled on the Knights of Columbus, the Caballeros were intended as a mode of enlisting the aid of migrants into the works of the Church in Chicago. They were expected to represent the interests of Catholicism in the various lay and public agencies that had been created to serve the needs of the growing Puerto Rican population in the city. A similar effort under Monsignor James Wilson to bring the Caballeros to New York was less impressive. The Caballeros enjoyed initial success in Chicago, partially because of the prestige afforded them by institutional Catholicism, which had great influence in ward politics. But when Puerto Rican leadership demanded the articulation of a specifically Latino agenda, the Caballeros were unable to act independently of the clergy and came to be viewed as unrepresentative of the people.[40]

New York's major success in the Spanish-speaking apostolate came from the San Juan Fiesta, instituted in 1953 as a patron saint's day celebration in New York in the style of the village celebrations or *fiestas patronales* that characterize much of Mediterranean Catholicism. For the better part of a decade, the fiesta grew into the major celebration of a Puerto Rican identity within New York City as an acceptable ethnic group. The fiesta mobilized pious societies like the Legion of Mary, sodalities, and Holy Name organizations based in the myriad parishes with Spanish-speaking services and legitimized them before the cardinal and the public New York community with a series of massively attended ceremonies.[41]

Ana María Díaz-Stevens has shown that the mystique of Puerto Rican Catholicism in New York was largely derived from the adaptations made in the traditional practice of the faith in Puerto Rico.[42] On the island, the official Catholicism of the town existed side-by-side with a home-centered Catholicism in the rural areas. This home-centered Catholicism utilized custom for moral influence, empowered lay preachers and prayer leaders, dignified the role of women, and reflected the needs of a community. Yet without ever opposing the hierarchy or the clerical leaders of the church, this home-centered Catholicism preserved its autonomy by maintaining social distance from the official institution. Díaz-Stevens argues convincingly that this social distance role was repeated in the "basement church" of most parishes that invited the Puerto Ricans to use the lesser facilities of the established parishioners.

Among Mexican Americans, similar patterns obtained. By the 1960s, sympathetic Church leaders allowed and encouraged the public processions to Our Lady of Guadalupe in parishes that previously had not known of the Mexican devotion to this patroness of the homeland. But while these practices were observed with notable success, they did not constitute a general policy of any diocese. In fact, there was a conscious effort of some English speakers to separate the image of Catholicism from its Mexican roots in places like Santa Fe and Los Angeles.[43] Since Mexican Americans were economically poor and victims of discrimination, the Church often mirrored the attitudes of the dominant society and preferred to project itself as American and Americanizing.

Leading up to the Second Vatican Council, the identity of Latino Catholics was largely a regional one. Mexico and Puerto Rico were two different countries producing two different cultures, even in cities like Chicago where the two communities were close to each other. One's Catholic identity was traced back to the country of origin, not derived from a common experience of the United States.

The foundation of a Catholic agency to aid the Cuban exiles after 1960 did little to dispel these operative images. The notion was that with this help, Cubans would be bound more closely to the faith and more decided in their opposition to communism, foe of both Catholicism and the United States. There was little to tie the aid to Cubans with the Puerto Rican apostolate in New York or the Mexican-American apostolate in Los Angeles. The capacity of the large numbers of Cubans in the United State rapidly to achieve economic stability and even prosperity helped underline the differences between the generally poor Mexican Americans and Puerto Ricans with the upwardly mobile Cubans. In fact, an impression was generated that Cubans were more successful because they were more pro-American and that if all Latinos imitated the most recently arrived group, they too would achieve rapid assimilation into the middle class.

In Puerto Rico, some important changes took place that had an impact upon episcopal policy towards the Spanish speaking. Puerto Rico secured its first native bishop under U.S. rule when Luis Aponte Martínez was elevated to the episcopacy in 1959 as auxiliary in Ponce. He was the first U.S. born citizen of Latino heritage to be named a bishop. But in the election year of 1960, the non–Puerto Rican ordinaries of the island politicized Catholic teaching on birth control. In a decree of dubious canonical validity, the bishops excommunicated any Puerto Rican who voted for Governor Luis Muñoz Marín.[44] In the aftermath of this mixing of religion and politics, the bishops in Puerto Rico managed to antagonize Cardinal Cushing of Boston, who anticipated negative impact of the Puerto Rican predicament on the presidential candidacy of John F. Kennedy in that year. In Vatican actions after the election, Aponte Martínez was vaulted into the archbishopric of San Juan and a totally native Puerto Rican hierarchy was named in 1962. This indigenization of the episcopacy had been advocated by an association of progressive Puerto Rican Catholics, the indefatigable Arizmendi Society, that repeatedly urged the Holy See to appoint Puerto Rican bishops in Puerto Rico. The replaced archbishop of San Juan, James P. Davis, was named ordinary of Santa Fe, New Mexico, and he eventually achieved the unusual honor of being succeeded by native bishops, not once, but twice.

In the United States, the most positive contribution to the formulation of a new Latino Catholic identity during the period came with the establishment of the Cursillo movement, which was introduced to the United States from Spain in 1957. The Cursillo sowed seeds of change because in its affirmation of a specifically Spanish-rooted Catholicism it appealed directly to the Latinos in ways that other movements filtered through the existing Catholic structures did not.[45] The focus of the Cursillo in transforming cultural Catholicism into a practiced and informed faith was appropriate for most

Latinos. Moreover, the conversion experience that was woven into the Cursillo added a valuable personal dimension to the Catholic religious experience that was generally unattainable except through the pentecostal churches. In the Cursillo, the basement churches had leadership schools providing the migrants with a supportive religious community. Despite the hierarchical theology expounded in the Cursillo, the medium provided a liberating message: Latino leaders for Latino religion.

The naming of a totally native episcopate on the island of Puerto Rico was encouragement that the same could be done in the states for all Latinos. Ironically, the nineteenth-century mindset that had treated ecclesiastical Puerto Rico as if it were another New Mexico or California had now come full circle. The establishment of a native hierarchy in Puerto Rico was now to be repeated among Mexican Americans. But in both cases, the initial change in perception occurred largely because of a failure on the part of non-Latinos and not from any substantial success of Latinos in pressuring ecclesiastical authorities.

As the period ended, the universal Catholic Church was summoned to an ecumenical council. Prelates from the U.S. had only their Puerto Rican brothers as native Latino bishops, but some of the dioceses had more than a decade-long success in pastoral programs aimed directly at Latinos. The Bishops' Committee and the New York chancery-based office had helped fashion new instruments for pastoral ministry. The migration after 1960 had intensified the search for effective response. Chief among these responses was the Cursillo movement, which was relatively inexpensive in its operating expenses, was devoted to hierarchical authority, was parish based and supervised, and had produced increasing numbers of Latino Catholics intensely committed to the sacramental practice of Catholicism. The Cursillo also provided for grassroots leadership and coordinated its efforts through diocesan-wide councils, loyal to episcopal authority. There was even an emerging national role for the Cursillo movement to unify Latinos in different episcopal regions in one organization.

The Cursillo played a role in creating a Latino Catholic identity. In some places, such as New York, to be Catholic was virtually synonymous with being a cursillista. There was an expectation that every practicing Latino Catholic would eventually make the Cursillo. In the pre–Vatican Church, the Cursillo provided liturgies in Spanish, heavily influenced by folk music and cultural traditions. Sermons and instruction were provided in the Spanish that the people spoke and based on their daily experiences. The Cursillo movement and all the pastoral infrastructure necessary to make it effective provided a significant advance in Latino Catholic identity and laid the groundwork for much of what was to follow.

In the secular sphere, a similar trend towards local issues and organizations had replaced the homeland orientation of pan-Americanist political groups before the war. Self-help groups like Aspira and the GI Forum combated negative stereotypes, interceded before government, and provided native leadership in the secular sphere. But such mainstream organizations tended to be run by professionals. Their membership contrasted sharply with the grassroots cursillistas. Moreover, the image projected by most secular organizations was for professionalization, political representation, and upward mobility. The raison d'être was to improve Latinos and public perception of them. For the Church, on the other hand, the Cursillo focused upon acceptance of ordinary people as they faced daily problems, generally avoiding political entanglements.

POVERTY, POWER, AND REFORM: 1965–1972

In the decade of the 1960s, Latinos and their organizations were to undergo profound change. On many fronts, the premises for the middle-class dream of Latino upward mobility collided with new realities. The failure of the United States to subvert the Cuban Revolution by the 1961 invasion at the Bay of Pigs and the later accommodation to Soviet nuclear might in the Missile Crisis broke with the image of an omnipotent Yankee colossus and shattered the Pax Americana. Permanent poverty, poignantly described in Michael Harrington's *The Other America*, eroded the golden promise of upward mobility.[46] And the assassination of a popular Catholic president cast a pall over upbeat interpretations of an American character.

Several political changes altered forever the structures of Latino communities. President Lyndon Johnson announced an ambitious War on Poverty in 1964. The plan opened up direct federal grants to the poor—now classified racially as "minorities"—as long as these same people served leadership functions for the newly funded agencies intended to bypass the traditional urban political machines of the Democratic party. In 1965, the Civil Rights Bill was passed, and although centered upon African Americans and their struggle for justice, it allowed provisions to classify as illegal the imposition of the English language as a condition for voting rights. In 1965, the immigration laws were changed and new legislation allowed for dramatic increases in migration, not only of Mexicans, but also of other Latin Americans who previously had not established significant communities within the Unites States. Finally, in 1967 the first bilingual education program was funded in Dade County, Florida.[47]

The immigration provisions were dramatically to increase the numbers of the Spanish speaking in the United States, with the effect of blurring the differences between the newly arrived foreign born and the Spanish speaking who were born and raised within the fifty states. The availability of federal funds also shifted political and social interest away from the homelands and towards community needs within the United States. The new use of the term *minority groups* as a racial category also thrust Latino identity into a context wherein there was direct advantage in *not* being white; in taking pride in being born in the U.S. rather than south of the border.[48]

Bilingualism, always a reality within Latino communities, was now elevated to a desirable social goal in education. In seeking federal funds for this kind of education, school districts across the United States were also opened up to hiring bilingual teachers, who generally were Latinos. Moreover, bilingualism extended beyond the classroom and included civil servants, social workers, agency and personnel directors.

The shattering of the Pax Americana had also given rise to a defense of cultures and nations that were underdeveloped. The continents of Africa, Asia, and South America were lumped together as parts of the world that had not yet known prosperity or development as had the capitalist nations of the West or the socialist countries of the East. There was a Third World that needed to assert its own value systems, independently of meddling by the superpowers.

This mode of thinking became Third Worldism.[49] Spanish speakers had to be instructed in their native language, not only because it was the best way to learn English, but also because it was necessary to preserve their traditional values. Protection of language was a protection of culture. Bilingual education gradually became multicultural education, meant to prevent assimilation into the values of a middle-class America. Moreover, since it was perceived that culture was not transferable from one cultural group to another, it logically followed that only Latinos should teach Latinos, and that each of the cultures in the United States should remain distinct from the others. If it was imperialism to invade another country and impose an American economic and political system, so too was it cultural imperialism to force the Spanish speaking already in the United States to sacrifice any of their traditions in order to become assimilated.

This Third Worldism was mightily assisted both by a counterculture that developed in the United States in the middle of the decade and by opposition to the Vietnam War. In the fateful year of 1968, the assassinations of Robert F. Kennedy and Martin Luther King generated a sense that old, positive assumptions about the perfectibility of the American system were erroneous. Among African Americans the Ghandilike tactics of the civil rights movement were challenged by a militancy that advocated urban guerrilla warfare and the creation of a separate black American nation by secession of several southern states that would become a new black homeland.

Latinos, particularly college-age youth, were not slow in accepting these radical reformulations of ethnic/racial identity within the United States. Indeed, the figures of Che Guevara and Fidel Castro, two leaders of the Cuban Revolution, were prominently hailed as heralds for this Third Worldism. Thus Fidel Castro, reviled by the Cuban exiles as a dictator, was simultaneously a hero for Mexican Americans and Puerto Ricans in the United States. Leaders from the Mexican and Puerto Rican past who had also opposed Yankee imperialism were added to the new pantheon of Latino leaders. Pedro Albizu Campos, who had died in 1965 as a broken and demented leader, was resurrected as a Christlike precursor of Puerto Rican independence. Pancho Villa and Emiliano Zapata enjoyed similar reconstruction among young Mexican Americans who rejected the middle-class aspirations of an older generation. New heroes were also found among hitherto obscure personages who had lived or toiled within the United States, especially women, and in the case of the Mexican Americans the origin of Aztec society was placed within Atzlán, corresponding with what is now the American Southwest. Youth groups such as the Young Lords and El Comité for Puerto Ricans and MEChA, MAYO, and the Brown Berets achieved a high degree of visibility and influence in shaping a new identity for young Latinos.[50]

Third Worldism also recreated the pre-Columbian native reality as a near perfect society that bore striking resemblance to an advanced socialism. Countercultural values of feminism and tolerance for various expressions of sexual behavior were incorporated into this romanticized view of the Native American societies at the root of contemporary Latinos. Eventually even environmental concern was viewed as originating in the early Aztec or Taíno societies before the arrival of Europeans.

But although they molded history to their own vision, these efforts carried with them much energy and creative talent. Murals, modes of expression, clothing, haircuts, and jewelry were given new roles for distinguishing Latinos from the Euro-Americans. Eventually, new names were found for Latinos in the United States to distinguish them from people from the homeland. *Chicanos* became the new classification for Mexican Americans who sought Atzlán as a native homeland and *NiuRicans* described the children of the Puerto Rican migrants who longed for Boriquen. Only the young Cuban Americans seem generally to have escaped the revolt against existing norms that swept over the nation's youth. But even among the Cuban Americans there was a new curiosity about what really was taking place in Cuba and a melting down of the univocal opposition to everyone and everything associated with Fidel Castro.

These new identities did not completely replace the existing conceptions of what it meant to be a Mexican American or a Puerto Rican in the United States. In fact, the new identities seemed to be a generational affair: one could safely predict whether a person was Chicano or Mexican American by his or her age. The battleground for these competing notions of identity was every public meeting or event. As Estades showed in her treatment of the Puerto Rican Day Parade in New York, the need to compete against each other brought the rival camps onto the same stage.[51] Ironically, the more they fought each other, the clearer became their common bonds as two parts of the same experience. And while the Euro-American establishment sometimes tried to play one generation against the other, eventually the radicals became more pragmatic and the moderates became more challenging.

These tensions about Latino identities were transferred into the Church, which was undergoing its own identity crisis because of the reforms of Vatican II. The first session of the council had decreed the use of the vernacular language of the people in the hitherto all-Latin liturgy. True to this principle, it was now necessary to have two separate language liturgies in parishes where Latinos had achieved a basement church. Few of the initial efforts at special liturgy in the United States had the creative quality of the *Misa Jíbara*, which had been composed in Puerto Rico in 1964 by William Loperena, O.P., as a Latino version of the African *Misa*

Luba. Still, the experience of the Cursillo in adapting folk songs to a religious theme was now given a wider stage and became the basis for a more rapid liturgical development among Latinos.

The opening of the Latin liturgy to the vernacular paralleled the move towards bilingualism, and with the conciliar decree *Gaudium et Spes*, Catholicism gave its imprimatur to multiculturalism within the Church. To the conciliar feeling were added the progressive encyclicals of Pope John XXIII which seemed to distance Catholicism from its close identification with the West and the capitalist structure, placing more emphasis upon respect for developing countries and supporting the United Nations as a forum for addressing the legitimate needs of the Third World.

In New York, the enlightened liberal leadership of Monsignor Robert Fox moved the pragmatic administration of Spanish-speaking programs into a creative new apostolate to the urban poor. As described in detail by Díaz-Stevens, Fox changed the meaning of *Puerto Rican* in New York into a quasi-symbolic statement of all the urban poor.[52] Moreover, with his federally funded program, "Summer in the City," he addressed the social needs of the barrios independently of pastoral care. His laboratory for testing for these changes was the San Juan Fiesta which became no longer the celebration of Puerto Ricans alone but the statement of a progressive Church about its solidarity with the Third World and the poor of the other America. Instead of banners for the Sacred Heart, Our Lady of Providence, and St. John the Baptist, the new Hispanic Fiesta featured placards with the pictures of Martin Luther King, Robert F. Kennedy, and later César Chavez. Díaz-Stevens argues that this transfer met with limited success, largely because it was initiated from a progressive clergy without input from native Puerto Rican leaders. Still, she notes that without the Fox experience, Puerto Rican Catholics would have been less likely to become involved with the local politics of school boards and tenant groups.[53]

The mechanism that enabled Latinos to change Church thinking and organize a national movement within United States Catholicism was *cross-validation*. Cross-validation is the achievement of legitimacy from a source outside one's existing community, with the result that one gains power and influence because of a dual source of recognition. Within the Latino experience, cross-validation benefited young clergy and religious because the secular world bestowed on them a leadership function for Latinos beyond the authority that the Church allowed them. With Latinos increasingly restive in politics and neighborhood activism, it was assumed by people outside the Church that the Spanish-surnamed clergy or religious was more the leader of the people than the pastor or superior, who most likely was Euro-American. In concrete terms, it meant that the *New York Times* or the *Los Angeles Times* called the young Latino priest rather than a chancery official for comments about the Church's role with a Latino issue. This logic was based upon the principle derived from secular politics that only a member of a minority group could speak for that minority group.[54]

In this process, the institutional Church was at a disadvantage. If ecclesiastical officials sought to squelch the native Latino clergy, Church leaders were vulnerable to the charge of being racist. They had little choice other than publicly to support the Latino spokesperson as part of a Church anxious to serve the community. Church officials expected that the Latino leaders would remain loyal to the institutional Church but Latino clergy, who often were very young and had little if any previous claim upon Church policy, were thrust into a role as Catholic spokespersons, nonetheless. Moreover, the process worked not only for the clergy but also for women religious.

Thus, there was a transfer of a secular political norm into the ecclesiastical sphere because of the need of the institutional Church to include Latinos as leaders as well as faithful clients. But in this new identification of Latino leadership, institutional Catholicism did not control the bases of legitimacy. Society and the Latino people exercised a role in determining who was a leader and who was not. Title and rank within the Church were in themselves not sufficient to make a Latino religious leader.

The cause of the Mexican-American migrant farm workers during the Delano grape strike was a most important chapter in this process of new Catholic Latino leadership. César Chavez had unique credentials to merit the cross-validation he received to start this process at a national level. Chavez was both a Cursillista and a radical labor organizer. In another time, these two identities would have been contradictory. Labor organizing among Mexicans had largely been a function of anticlerical socialists during the 1930s. But the council reforms allowed Chavez to harmonize his piety and devotion to Catholic tradition with his radical labor agenda. His validation within the Church as a reliable Catholic was enhanced by his standing within the labor movement as a true leader of his people.[55] The attacks on him as a communist by the outspoken

Redemptorist Bishop Wallinger (former bishop of Ponce, Puerto Rico) rang hollow in the face of Chavez's Catholic piety. And when the Kennedy family took up the cause of the Delano strike, considerable national media attention made it impossible for Catholicism to ignore the justice of the cause.

Support for the Delano strikers was generalized throughout the Mexican-American community, particularly among those who had adopted the identity of Chicanos. In Los Angeles, some Catholics were distressed at the reluctance of the conservative Cardinal McIntyre to declare support for Chavez and his fledgling labor movement. Organized under the name, Católicos por la Raza, this group utilized the arguments of the secular Chicano community against the institutional Church. Just as Chicanos argued that the government had an obligation to apportion resources to the minority community to the same percentage as the population, Católicos por la Raza protested that the resources of the archdiocese of Los Angeles were not being devoted to the Chicanos in matching proportion. This was a key concept taken from the secular sphere and which became a rallying cry of a new kind of Latino Catholic. But it should also be stressed that there was a measure of sophistication in differentiating between the Church, i.e., institution—which was attacked—and faith, i.e., the gospel—which was defended.

The events that led to confrontation on Christmas Eve 1969 at St. Basil's Church also served as a symbol of an insensitive Catholic hierarchy.[56] A somewhat neglected aspect of the confrontation was the Mass celebrated defiantly in Los Angeles by the Puerto Rican bishop, Antulio Parrilla. Parrilla, a Jesuit, was in California at the time in solidarity with the Berrigans and to protest the war in Vietnam. He decided to demonstrate with Católicos immediately and to show that not all bishops agreed with the cardinal. It was a first glimpse at the way that an effort to reform the institutional Church would lead Latinos into solidarity across nationality lines.

The Delano strike served as catalyst not only for the confrontation at St. Basil's but also for the awakening Latino population. César Chavez became a symbol for a new kind of Latino—humble and rural in origin, but no longer docile before injustice. Even if Puerto Ricans could not claim Chavez as one of their own, the national recognition afforded the farm worker leader spurred Puerto Ricans towards expressions of solidarity. Mexican Americans everywhere rallied to support this struggle because it was connected to their own efforts at social justice. In February 1970, various priests from California and parts of the Southwest met in Tucson, Arizona, to discuss a way of coordinating support for Chavez among the Catholic communities of Mexican Americans that they served. From this meeting came PADRES, an organization for priests in the Mexican-American ministry, and later in similar fashion the association of Las Hermanas for religious women.

Both PADRES and Las Hermanas were the first attempts at national organizations of Latino Catholic leaders to articulate their special agenda. In the first definitions of their missions, both organizations stressed basic themes borrowed from the secular political scene. They argued for proportional representation in the leadership positions of the Church to match the demographic presence of Latinos; resources were demanded with the same formula; the need to defend and promote the Spanish language as a part of orthodoxy to conciliar decrees was explained; and it was generally understood that the underlying principle for each of these requests was the premise that only Latinos could understand Latinos.

Moreover, PADRES and Las Hermanas did not limit their attentions only to the Delano strike. Every Church interest now became a cause for the same set of reforms. Often enough these pleas for greater resources and Latino representation were backed by a wide spectrum of Euro-American leaders. This support sprang from the general agreement among many progressive Catholics that the Church should support the same principles of self-determination within the institution that had been adopted in the secular sphere.

In this recapitulation of the emergence of a native Latino leadership within Catholicism, several factors emerge as crucial to understanding the new meaning of Latino identity. The Latino clergy and religious had adopted many notions of a radical ethnic consciousness that had come from newly established Chicano and Puerto Rican studies departments within several universities. Moreover, the tactics of confrontation were joined to arguments about ethnic representation that were part of the political thinking of the time. In a sense, this early phase of Latino militancy was an ecclesiastical variation on the Latino movements that were generated by the War on Poverty and the radicalism of the late 1960s.

It is my opinion that PADRES and Las Hermanas were made possible by a process of cultural crystallization. During these years 1969–1972, a new sort of Latino Catholic identity had emerged. It accepted the premise of colonialism that had been developed by Latino scholars and applied to Catholicism the type of arguments in favor of ethnic representation that were common in the public sphere.[57] This new identity differed from the Latino image of the 1950s and early 1960s. No longer was the burden of change and adaptation laid exclusively on Latinos seeking to be Americanized: now, America itself was expected to change. Most importantly, the process of change required native Latinos to assume leadership for their own people.

Aware that the existing services to the Spanish speaking did not correspond to this new expectation, the United States Catholic Conference (USCC) decided to redefine the office established by the National Bishop's Committee for the Spanish Speaking. Located in Texas, better to serve the migrant workers, the office was now to be moved to Washington, where it became part of the Division of Social Services within the USCC.[58] A Mexican American from New Mexico, Pablo Sedillo was named director of the Washington office, and to bestow representation to Puerto Ricans, the USCC also named the New York–based Puerto Rican woman, Encarnación Padilla de Armas, as special associate.

The significance of this bureaucratic move reflected the new national identity that Latinos had assumed before the institutional Church. No longer could the national Church serve only migrant workers as Mexican Americans or urbanized Puerto Ricans as if these represented all the Latinos in the United States. Moreover, the move to Washington was intended to represent an upgrade in importance for Latino needs.

But instead of providing a buffer between the newly energized Latino leadership and the national offices of Catholicism, the new office repeated and supported a growing chorus of requests from Latino leaders for new Church priorities. The new militant identity for Latinos was repeated at various meetings, including the National Catechetical Conference and the Catholic Inter-American Cooperation Program (CICOP) that were sponsored by the Latin American Bureau of the USCC.

Matching the Third Worldism of the secular arena was the linkage of this new Latino identity with the theological innovations of the Latin American Church in the post-Medellín period. At first, the most popular notion was Freire's *conscientización*, but to this was quickly added new pastoral approaches such as *comunidades de base* and *pastoral de conjunto*. Importantly, the Chicano movement's concept of *mestizaje* was adapted to a theological purpose by Father Virgilio Elizondo, the head of the Mexican American Cultural Center (MACC) in San Antonio.[59] Elizondo wrote as a theologian, but he utilized some of the philosophical notions of José Vasconcelos to enrich his reflections. Puerto Ricans on the island engaged in similar theological reflection, but with more specificity upon the status question and with less impact on U.S. Catholicism.[60]

The genesis of the First National Hispano Pastoral Encounter (Encuentro), held in Washington in 1972 was very important.[61] It was a marvelously well-organized meeting, and considering that it was the first of its kind, its far-reaching effects surpassed the expectations even of many participants. The encounter documents charted new directions in virtually every significant aspect of pastoral life. At every turn the basic demands for representation and resources were repeated. Moreover, these agenda items were generally couched in theological language adapted from Latin American theology and were not easily dismissed.

The frictions among the Latino groups, which were addressed by the second encounter in 1977, did not abate and in some cases have been exacerbated within Latino Catholicism. But these issues, which will be analyzed below, ought not obscure the far-reaching effects of the 1972 encounter. That meeting in Washington crystallized a new identity for all Latinos within Catholicism. The new identity was rooted in a profound conviction—an ideology, if you will—that justice required a proportionate representation for Latinos within the power structures of U.S. Catholicism. Almost by definition, individuals were expected to claim identity as an American with Mexican, Puerto Rican, Cuban roots, an identity which was simultaneously interpreted as a declaration in favor of altered priorities in the dispensation of Church resources and advocacy for Church political involvement on behalf of Latinos. The shared commonality of language background, culture, and history as Latinos was considered sufficient to impart an ideology of change.[62] Because the focus was on gaining representation, not on what would happen after Latinos achieved representation, those without a radical ideology frequently cooperated with those with one.

Unity of purpose promoted the establishment of regional centers and programs to increase Latino leadership, both clerical and lay, within the United States Church. The encounter conclusions also articulated a pastoral formula of what could be expected within a parish, diocese, or region once Latinos were given recognition and resources. There were standard hymns and liturgies—given legitimacy when companies publishing parish missalettes began including special segments for Spanish-speaking parishioners. Spanish-speaking permanent deacons, movements, and pastoral

innovations like comunidades de base were linked at every level
with increasingly complex relationships that provided Latino Catholics with influence and organization usually superior to non-
Latino Catholics.

The stated priority of advancing the Mexican-American paradigm for pastoral care *in every region* can be viewed as a policy
based upon legitimation by the National Council of Catholic Bishops. Regional resentments arose because of the success of the first
encounter, not because of its failures. Thus, for instance, when
Encarnación Padilla de Armas retired from the secretariat office
in Washington, she was replaced, not by a Puerto Rican, but by
the late Frank Ponce, a Mexican-American priest from San Diego.
Since the national policy was to shape all regions in the model of
the Mexican-American paradigm, such a move made sense. But in
terms of the Latino identity, the Puerto Rican experience had lost
a symbol of its acceptance. Paradoxically, the very success of the
Mexican-American paradigm fed the distress of Puerto Ricans and
others in the Northeast who through no fault of their own could
not achieve the same measures of influence and power.

The paradigm promoted by Mexican Americans produced a
church-within-the-church. The Mexican American Cultural Center
in San Antonio was a combination of chancery, seminary, missionary training ground, community-organizing school, international
forum, publishing house, liturgical center, folklore and musical
museum specializing in Mexican-American issues. MACC replaced
the legitimacy of existing Church institutions to deal with any of
these concerns as they touched Mexican Americans. In a place like
San Antonio, this prominence for Mexican-American Catholics was
reinforced by demographics and history and was a change in identity for the city's Catholics that reflected an aura of inevitability.

But in other cities, such as New York and Chicago, it was
anomalous that people of the lower socioeconomic class would
have more institutional power in Catholicism than middle-class
whites, who had long identified the Church as theirs. Ana María
Díaz-Stevens has argued that in the archdiocese of New York it
represented a radical departure from established norms, equivalent
to the changes in Latin American Catholicism after Medellín.[63] Like
the radical preferential option for the poor that was part of the
articulated message of the Latin American bishops, importation of
the Mexican-American paradigm to some sees would have been
equivalent to preferring Latinos over other ethnic groups.

Outside regions where Mexican Americans dominated, the paradigm broke down because while it was legitimate to *increase* Latino representation, they were only one of many groups within the Church. Moreover, when there was more than one Latino group—as in virtually all of the Northeast and much of the Midwest—the Latino groups were divided into different nationalities and each merited equal representation.[64]

In sum, the creation of a Latino identity within Catholicism that was modeled after the Mexican-American experience in San Antonio provided many significant gains for Latinos but introduced serious problems nonetheless. Some other nationality groups of Latinos, especially Puerto Ricans in the Northeast, suffered a loss of influence as a result of the first encounter. The definition of "Latino/Hispanic" for the nation's Spanish-speaking Catholics was constrained to a Mexican-American experience that was not applicable everywhere. Ordinarily, such a limitation could be interpreted as growing pains, and remedies could be expected to emerge over time to resolve the tension. But other factors intervened to stall the normal evolution of a wider, more inclusive Latino identity.

During the five years after the first encounter, ideology emerged as a divisive factor within Latino Catholicism. The Mexican-American paradigm was identified by the nation's bishops with an understanding of the Latino Church defined as *pastoralist*.[65] It is a focus upon change within the Church and its structures as a more important sphere of activity than direct action for social change. In this model of Church, *symbolic* activity replaces direct political action. Utilizing the notion of *Church as sacrament*, the proper role of the believer is to inspire social change rather than collaborate in its management. In this same context, Latino culture is a symbolic category for poverty or victimization by racial prejudice. In a word, pastoralists define religion's role as one that alleviates the psychological effects of poverty and discrimination through a symbol system of faith that explains human social behavior with religious images.

Not all the leaders of Latino Catholicism agreed with this theological view that relativized poverty and the social condition. Some directly applied the goals of liberation theology to U.S. society so as to advocate a radical economic and political change in the direction of socialism. For such liberationists, the relevance of intra-Church struggles to the cause of social justice became doubtful. They understood the Church's role as an activist one in concert with secular groups that advocated Third Worldism, and the establishment of new agencies, programs, and departments in the Church was of secondary importance. These differences parallel in some ways the ideological differences in the secular sphere between *Chicanos* (Third World socialists, liberationists) and *Mexican Americans* (social justice reformers, pastoralists), or the Puerto Rican *independentistas* and the advocates of the existing Commonwealth.[66] Indicative of the pastoralist bent, the cultural center in San Antonio is Mexican American, not Chicano. This choice of title indicates its role to inspire and support reform rather than to organize specifically political activity.

While the pastoralists focused upon roles within the Church, the liberationists wanted Latino leaders to move directly into the secular community and political organizations as Catholic advocates of Third Worldism. To no one's surprise, the Catholic bishops preferred the pastoralist vision as closer to their own. The creation of new programs and agencies for Latinos drew almost continually from pastoralist leadership, placing persons with a moderate agenda in control of Latino Church institutions. Coincidentally, they became the arbiters of Latino Catholic identity. But as members of the establishment—albeit in a still inferior position—pastoralists found it increasingly difficult to maintain unity with the goals of the liberationists. In a previous decade when few had power or representation within the Church, all Latinos advocated change and shared in the feelings of a crusade. Now that pastoralists were inside positions of authority, while most liberationists remained outside, the ideological differences became more pronounced. Pastoralists like Virgilio Elizondo and bishops like Ricardo Ramírez, Roberto Sánchez, and Patricio Flores advocated the inclusion of Latinos in Church programs and structures. They viewed their task as reforms, meant to increase the efficiency of Church institutions. This put them at a distance from liberationists who considered radical change preferable to reform.

Gradually, in a process that accelerated after 1979, Catholics who embraced the liberationist agenda lost their influence on the national Church because the intermediaries placed in responsible positions held a different ideology. Eventually the marginalization of the liberationists extended to groups such as PADRES and Las Hermanas. These organizations, which once had made common cause with militant Chicanos and Puerto Rican independentistas, now retracted to an agenda focused upon internal Church reforms. When secular political goals were addressed, it was in terms of participation within the political and economic system, rather than upon radical subversion of ecclesiastical structures.[67]

The Latino liberationist leadership did not vanish from the face of the earth. They often found a more congenial arena for their struggle as the Latino representatives within Catholic groups advocating renewal through radical changes. Latino liberationists like William Loperena, Roberto Peña, Rosa Marta Zárate, and Carmen Villegas can be found today among Church groups advocating the ordination of women to the priesthood, new ministries to divorced Catholics, increased attention to gay and lesbian issues, the abandonment of obligatory celibacy for priests, a ministry of ecological concerns, and social justice based on racial harmony and economic justice. These leaders have moved away from the matters that affect only Latinos in the Church towards issues that concern all Catholics. The attrition of liberationists, however, has blunted the militancy that so strengthened Latinos of an earlier decade.

The divisions caused by the inter-Latino conflicts and growing ideological differences were magnified by changes in Catholicism occasioned by the ascension of Pope John Paul II. Moreover, the election of Ronald Reagan as president in 1980 began a political process that eventually undermined the ideological principles of ethnic representation upon which Latino militancy had been based. As had occurred in the social changes of previous decades, these factors had a heavy impact upon Latino identity.

The most important factor, I believe, was the diminished frequency of cross-validation of Latino Catholic leadership. There were various causes for the phenomenon. With the success of achieving leadership posts within the institutional Church, the issue of Latino representation lost some of its force. No longer able to criticize easily the programs they directed, some Latino leaders were forced to defend rather than attack the Church. Of course, including people with Spanish surnames within a bureaucracy or even within the hierarchy does not in itself ensure the adoption of an agenda favoring Latinos or a change in the priorities. But political institutions in the secular sphere engaged in tokenism—appointment of Latinos but without concession of power—and the Church was not immune to the same tactic. In a sense, it better served the institution to have a Latino who could or would do nothing for the community in an official post, than to have no representation at all. Persons who protested against the token power implicit in their position could easily be forced to resign since they held no real power.

Protests, demonstrations, and ethnic programs for proportional representation were classified negatively by an increasingly reactionary political atmosphere, as liberals took shelter everywhere.

Affirmative action, minority quotas, and political representation based on ethnic identification became negative terms, often equated with a form of injustice against the white majority. Reflecting such thinking, the media ceased to cross-validate Latino Church leaders on the basis of ethnicity. Thus Latinos without official rank in the Church lost the leverage of ethnic politics they had enjoyed during the 1970s.

No longer were institutions threatened by a lack of Latino representation because in the political arena such programs were now characterized as discrimination in reverse. By the time of the Third National Encounter in 1985, the U.S. bishops felt empowered to accept encounter proposals but not to finance them.[68] This presaged a general movement to consolidate Church agencies originally designated for Latino needs and merge them with general-purpose institutions. The argument is that this is "mainstreaming" Latinos and giving them equality as members of the Church. With some justification, Church officials could argue that they had financed programs specifically for Latinos from scarce general funds. It was time for Latinos to pay for their own programs from parish revenues. In all but a few places, special programs for Latinos were now considered a luxury that could not be afforded. The cuts in staff, diminution of authority, restrictions in budget during the late 1980s effectively halted the expansion of special offices and agencies for Latinos.

In 1991, Pablo Sedillo left the Secretariat for Hispanic Affairs that was a hollow shell of its former self, and this set a pattern repeated at diocesan levels nationwide. Such attrition also has a chronological component: the Latino leaders who were in their thirties at the time of the first encounter are now in their fifties. This "greying" of Latino leaders takes its toll on militancy. Moreover, the people who replace the older generation seldom have the same experiences of both militancy and unity of purpose that brought together diverse people in the 1960s.

If these problems were confined to the local levels, it would be bad enough: They are, however, also repeated at an international level. After the Puebla conference of 1979 the Vatican began to condemn and undermine the sociopolitical character of Latin American liberation theology. This deprived Latinos of a weapon that had been used earlier. It was no longer possible to cite the theological concepts of Latin America with the same authority. In fact, the Vatican under John Paul II actually censured leading Latin American theologians like Gustavo Gutiérrez and Leonardo

Boff. Coupled with an unstated policy of ordaining as bishops only those who adhered to a concept of Church closely aligned with the conservative organization Opus Dei, these policies of the papacy have effectively crippled the conciliar reforms of Catholicism. Even Latino Catholic theologians who support much of liberation theology are frequently at pains to distance themselves from simple identification with the Latin American thinkers. Thus, for instance, the Academy of Catholic Hispanic Theologians in the United States (ACHTUS) adopts the principles of Latin America's liberation theology but views its task as the development of another version more appropriate to life in the United States.[69]

Political discourse was far from the only change produced in U.S. society by the Reagan years (1981–1988). As has been shown in a comprehensive comparative study of the U.S. labor market, Latinos in general and Puerto Ricans in particular suffered a relative loss of economic participation since 1980 while African Americans and Euro-Americans generally did better.[70] With the redistribution of wealth that took place during this period, the gap between the very rich and the rest of U.S. society widened, leaving Latinos in a more disadvantaged position than in the 1960s when the movements for advancement had begun.

With the onset of recession (1991–1992), a severe contraction of the U.S. economy took place, the effects of which are still being felt. As usual in such times of economic woe, the poor suffer most. Moreover, as in the secular sphere, institutions trimmed their budgets and afforded less and less importance to programs specifically designed for Latinos as a group distinct from other Catholics. Hence, it is unlikely that the solutions of the 1970s can be applied in the 1990s to reinstitute the Catholic Church as an arena of Latino militancy.

In all of this, the identity of Latinos is altered. Without a strongly defined ideological component, Latino identity becomes a celebratory affair, somewhat like ethnic clothing that can be put on or off, depending on the occasion. Conservative Republicans deny that *Latino* means "poor" or carries a racial sense of "nonwhite."[71] Conservatives often assert that economic distress is tied to cultural or moral deficiency, thus opposing the view of the 1970s that they impugn as the liberalism of the Democratic party. The ideological cleavages among Latinos are exploited and the gap between the haves and the have-nots is exacerbated by a public discourse that sets one group against the other.

It is to their credit that Catholics argue with each other about these issues, although divisions of this kind may be factors in Latino adherence to fundamentalism and pentecostalism.[72] While the precise roots of the contemporary attraction of fundamentalism and pentecostalism need a more scientific clarification, they clearly have an impact upon Latino Catholic identity.

Paradoxically, the rise of the religious right has mobilized just about every one. Although both Catholics and Protestants are divided within their respective denominations by ideology as conservatives or progressives, a new sort of ecumenism has arisen. Progressives of various denominations, for instance, collaborate more readily and more extensively with their counterparts of another faith than with the conservatives within their own churches. Some Latino Protestants maintain that they have a Protestant faith but a Catholic cultural identity, and this more comfortable identity with cultural Catholicism may have far-reaching consequences within Protestantism.[73]

This essay on Catholic identity has tried to explain why the Latinos mobilized in the 1970s and not before. The phenomenon of urbanization after 1945 exercised a major influence because it put growing numbers of Latinos in contact with each other, forming the basis for concerted national strategies. With the War on Poverty, the militancy of the black civil rights movement, and the radicalism of protest against the Vietnam War, a new ideology for minority groups emerged. Secular society required minority representation within institutions. Together with other notions of anti-imperialism and anti-racism current at the time (I used the term, *Third Worldism*), identities as Latinos were wedded to an ideology of change.

Thus, secular movements which produced a more militant Latino identity played a large part in the emergence of similar changes for Latinos within Catholicism. The Church was particularly vulnerable to change because of the reforms of the Second Vatican Council. Enhanced by the interpretations of Latin American liberation theology, a new identity for Latino Catholics was crystallized by the 1972 First National Encounter.

These three factors explain the social, political, and ecclesiastical setting for Latino mobilization. I suspect a fourth factor is the self-doubt within Euro-American Catholicism during these two decades. The inability of most U.S. Catholics to fall back upon a paradigm of Catholic identity as strong as that of "immigrant Church," which had been left behind for Euro-Americans, helped the Latinos assume new influence within the Church. In other words, because Latinos were more sure of who they were and of what they wanted than Euro-American Catholics, the Latino Church was able to take gigantic strides of organization. Analogous to the laws of physics, a moving object has more force than a stationary one.

But while these secular and sociological factors spurred a new identity for Latino Catholics, the Church experience has particular characteristics. The believers mobilized by this new brand of Latino Catholicism were more representative of the general population than were most of the radical groups in the public sphere. While the latter were composed disproportionately of young people and university students, Church groups reflected a wide spectrum of grassroots communities. The Latino Church was never as radical as the Chicano movement, for example, but in the final analysis it continues to touch far more people with its message of empowerment and self-determination than the student groups do today.

It is also true that *Latino* continues to be a secondary identity for most people. They still prefer to be called Mexican American, Puerto Rican, or the exact name of their nationality.[74] Yet, it is a likely hypothesis that Church people will be among the most likely to use *Latino* when compared to other groups. It would require survey data to confirm this suspicion of mine, but I believe that the notion of solidarity and unity promoted among Latinos within parish churches provides a unique perspective on a pan-Latino identity.

Latino Catholic militancy has withered during the 1980s. The demographics of increasing urbanization have not changed, but factors, such as the political and ecclesiastical climate, have. Identity has been fragmented both ideologically and among various nationality groups and the rift between pastoralists and liberationists is a substantial one. Moreover, some influential Church leaders consider further attention to specifically Latino needs to be unnecessary. Bishop Roberto O. González, auxiliary of Boston, wrote to the organizers of this volume that the notion of a Hispanic Church is irreconcilable with the unity of Catholicism. The threat of such notions may help liberationists and pastoralists patch up their ideological differences in an effort to preserve past gains.

A more permanent problem has been a failure of Latino Catholicism to reconcile satisfactorily the different intra-Latino identities of Mexican American, Cuban American, Puerto Rican, and the Central Americans who are the "other Hispanics" of the census.

This last is the most rapidly growing group of all Latinos. Assuredly, in a given national context, the notion that Latinos have more in common with each other than with the Euro-American majority still functions. But the occasions for such coalitions have diminished as institutions are better able to manage the competing interests of minority groups. In areas such as Chicago, New York, and now Los Angeles, San Francisco, Washington, D.C., and Miami, the increasing diversity of the Latino population has altered previously fixed identification of all Latinos as Mexican American, Puerto Rican, or Cuban American.

Inasmuch as developments within the Church tend to parallel closely similar developments in the secular sphere, the coalition building and management of multiple identities currently underway in these multi-Latino settings may augur a more supple Latino Catholic identity. Southwest Texas and New Mexico, the most successful regions to date in articulating a Latino Catholic identity, may be penalized in this newer version of a pan-Latino reality because they are more isolated from other Latinos than the rest of the country. Ironically, what was an asset—a single cultural majority—may now be a liability.

There is no need to prophesy the future in these pages, but the solidification of neo-conservatism helps answer the second question posed in this chapter. How has institutional Catholicism received the notion that Latinos are a conquered peoples of mixed race, not to be compared with European immigrants? The answer is, Hardly at all. The facility with which Catholic agencies group Latin American immigrants together with Latinos is testimony that the official Church still is more comfortable with the image of immigrant than with that of a conquered people who have lived in this country for generations. Moreover, the use of the word *Hispanic* removes any taint of a nationalism or militancy to compete with Americanization. Like the neo-conservative public arena, the strongest tendency in the U.S. Church minimizes the need for special attention to Latinos.

This brief diagnosis does not discount the possibility that a new set of political and economic conditions will replace today's rightward tilt in politics and Church. What replaces discredited liberalism and doctrinaire Marxism may prove a more hardy specimen. Such an alternative may become the axis around which another cultural crystallization will take place. The increasing numbers of Central Americans within Latino Catholicism challenge Church believers once again to take initiatives before their secular counterparts. Since these Central Americans and their children born in this country increase the demographic importance and political clout of all Latinos, they will likely be included and demand representation in ways that will definitely break with the Mexican-American paradigm.

Because so many changes in Catholic identity have been linked to the secular sphere, I think the key battleground for Latino Catholicism's struggle is no longer representation within the institutional Church. More Latino bishops or Masses in Spanish scarcely serve as causes anymore. Religion is much more focused upon ultimate values. The breakdown of U.S. economic and political hegemony in a global economy has produced severe dislocations in society and a confusion about the future. Among Latino youth, in particular, there is a need to believe in something in order to survive the horrors of today's poverty long enough to function successfully in society. In some barrios, the only families not entangled with drugs are the church-goers. A new practical ecumenism is at work in claiming back the streets. The Catholic school is more likely than the public school to produce college-bound Latino students, which may prove significant in shaping a new generation of Latino leaders. And since much of the emphasis in all of education is upon moral values, religion may be considered to gain in importance, particularly among those trapped in poverty.[75]

The twenty-first century belongs to the children of the generation of the 1960s who constructed a Latino Catholic identity. Survival as Latinos requires this young generation to confront issues of language maintenance, bilingual and multicultural education, and an end to welfare dependency. In foreign affairs, recognition of the Cuban Revolution, the removal of economic barriers with Mexico and other parts of Latin America, the issue of Puerto Rico status, and the preservation of the ecology in Latin America loom as likely matters for social concern. If the young Latinos face these and other matters out of the conviction of their Catholic faith, they will not only affect social change but also alter much of U.S. Catholicism in the process. While such a process is uncertain, it is uniquely challenging.

NOTES

1. The *Harvard Encyclopedia of American Ethnic Groups* provides the basis for fourteen characteristics associated with culture: common geographic origins; migratory status; race; language or dialect;

122 ANTHONY M. STEVENS-ARROYO

religious faith or faiths; ties that transcend kinship; neighborhood or community barriers, shared traditions, values, and symbols; literature, folklore, and music; food preferences; settlement and employment patterns; special interests in regard to politics in the homeland and in the United States; institutions that specifically serve and maintain the group; internal sense of distinctiveness; and an external sense of distinctiveness. (See also Lionel A. Maldonado, "Latino Ethnicity: Increasing Diversity," *Latino Studies Journal* 2, no. 3 [Sept. 1991], pp. 49–57.)

2. This chapter employs *Latino* through much of the text because, as will be explained, it is the term of *self*, i.e., internal, identification. On this point, see Mario Garcia's biting essay, "The Hispanic in American History: Myth and Reality," *Latino Studies Journal* 2, no. 1 (Jan. 1991), pp. 75–85. But use of *Latino* in this article is a situational choice of this particular author and does not reflect any ontological or moral judgment about the utility of *Hispanic* or other terminology.

3. Jay P. Dolan, *The Immigrant Church: New York's Irish and German Catholics, 1815–1865* (Baltimore: Johns Hopkins Press, 1975), pp. 7–8, 102; Dolan, *Catholic Revivalism: The American Experience, 1830–1900* (Notre Dame, Ind.: University of Notre Dame Press, 1978), pp. 40–50, 181–183 and passim.

4. Silvano Tomasi, *Piety and Power: The Role of the Italian Parishes in the New York Metropolitan Area, 1880–1930* (Staten Island, N.Y.: Center for Migration Studies, 1975), pp. 1–9, 182–184 and passim.

5. C. Wright Mills, Clarence Senior, and Rose Kohn Goldsen, *The Puerto Rican Journey* (New York: Harper and Row, 1950), pp. 110–114; Rudolfo O. de la Garza and Angelo Falcón, "Identity, Policy Preferences, and Political Behavior: Preliminary Results from the Latino National Political Survey," Latino National Political Survey (New York: Institute for Puerto Rican Policy, 1992).

6. Joseph P. Fitzpatrick, S.J., *Puerto Rican Americans: The Meaning of Migration to the Mainland*, (Englewood Cliffs, N.J.: Prentice Hall, 1971).

7. Patrick H. McNamara, "Dynamics of the Catholic Church from Pastoral to Social Concerns, " in *The Mexican-American People*, ed. Leo Grebler et al. (New York: Free Press, 1970), pp. 449–485; and "Catholicism, Assimilation, and the Chicano Movement: Los Angeles as a Case Study," in *Chicanos and Native Americans*, ed. Rudolofo de la Garza et al. (Englewood Cliffs, N.J.: Prentice Hall, 1973).

8. As a point of contrast with the historical understanding in these works, compare the almost mechanical application of sociological theory in Poblete and O'Dea's interpretation of Pentecostalism among

Puerto Ricans as the product of anomie, that was predicted (incorrectly) to be waning in 1960 due to the achievement of a New York identity ("Anomie and the Quest for Community: The Formation of Sects among Puerto Ricans in New York," *American Catholic Sociological Review* 21 [Spring 1960], pp. 18–36). There have been various national surveys since the 1970s that ask questions about identity, the most notable of which attempts to prove that there is no separate Latino identity within Catholicism, merely a lack of assimilation into mainstream ways—a situation that can be remedied by education (Robert O. González and Michael La Velle, *The Hispanic Catholic in the U.S.: A Socio-Cultural and Religious Profile* [New York: Northeast Hispanic Pastoral Center, 1985]). Social science, like history, can be done either well or poorly. The judicious integration of the two seems to afford a measure of balance to serious scholarship.

9. On this point, see the summary in Joseph P. Fitzpatrick, *One Church, Many Cultures* (Kansas City: Sheed and Ward, 1987), where he traces a shift away from assimilation or even accommodation to the dominant culture on the part of the immigrants, to enculturation on the part of the institutional Church. Compare the opinion of David O'Brien in two works separated by nearly twenty years: *The Renewal of American Catholicism* (New York: Paulist Press, 1971); and "The Catholic Church and American Culture during Our Nation's Lifetime, 1787–1987," in *The Catholic Church and American Culture*, ed. Cassian Yuhas, C.P. (Mahwah, N.J.: Paulist Press, 1990), pp. 1–23. In the first (pp. 45–46) he lauded the importance of the immigrant perspective and in the latter (pp. 3–4), he minimized it. See also Philip Gleason, *Keeping the Faith: American Catholicism, Past and Present* (Notre Dame, Ind.: University of Notre Dame Press, 1987), p. 194 and passim. Despite these gains, it is not uncommon to see the Americanization ideal repeated as a goal of the Church. For example, in the Yuhas collection, alongside the essay by O'Brien, Carrier (pp. 90–108) treats assimilation as modernization.

10. As recently as 1991, Puerto Rico affirmed the primacy of Spanish as the official language of its people and merited the Prince of Asturias Award from the Spanish government for this singular adherence to the mother tongue despite repeated attempts from Washington to impose the English language. Ironically, with the change of government in 1992, English was put on an equal legal standing by a legislative decree.

11. Key texts that adopt this perspective for Chicanos are Rudolfo Acuña, *Occupied America* (San Francisco: Canfield Press, 1972); and

Mario Barrera, *Beyond Aztlán* (Notre Dame, Ind.: University of Notre Dame Press, 1988). For Puerto Ricans, see Centro de Estudios Puertorriqueños, *Labor Migration under Capitalism* (New York: Monthly Review Press, 1979); Manuel Maldonado Denis, *Puerto Rico y Estados Unidos: Emigración y colonialismo* (Mexico: Siglo XXI, 1976); and Alfredo Lopez, *The Puerto Rican Papers* (Indianapolis: Bobbs-Merrill, 1973).

12. Clara Rodríguez describes the Puerto Rican experience in New York (Rodríguez, Aida Castro, Oscar Garcia, and Analisa Torres, "Latino Racial Identity: In the Eye of the Beholder?" *Latino Studies Journal* 2, no. 3 (Sept. 1991); pp. 33–48. See the relationship of race to labor force participation in Clara Rodríguez, *Puerto Ricans Born in the U.S.A.* (Boston: Unwin Hyman, 1989). For general comments, see Joan Moore and Harry Pachon, *Hispanics in the United States* (Englewood Cliffs, N.J.: Prentice-Hall, 1985), p. 15.

13. Joan Moore, "'Hispanic/Latino' Imposed Label or Real Identity?" *Latino Studies Journal* 1, no. 2 (May 1990); pp. 33–47.

14. I utilized the notion of cultural crystallization in the context of Spanish culture in America in "The Radical Shift in the Spanish Approach to Intercivilizational Encounter," *Comparative Civilizations Review* 21, pp. 80–101. See also Thomas Glick, *Islamic and Christian Spain in the Early Middle Ages* (Princeton, N.J.: Princeton University Press, 1979), and George W. Foster, *Culture and Conquest: America's Spanish Heritage* (New York: Wenner-Gren Foundation, 1960), for other applications.

15. Among the studies on identity, those which carry a reference to Catholicism are the following: David Abalos, *Latinos in the United States: The Sacred and the Profane* (Notre Dame, Ind.: University of Notre Dame Press, 1986); David F. Gómez, *Somos Chicanos: Strangers in Our Own Land* (Boston: Beacon Press, 1973); see also the comparative essay on Chicanos and Puerto Ricans by Jorge Klor de Alva, "Aztlán, Borinquen, and Hispanic Nationalism in the United States," in *Aztlán: Essays on the Chicano Homeland*, ed. Francisco Anaya and Rodolfo Lomeli (Albuquerque: University of New Mexico Press, 1991). Charles A. Tatum offers a literary perspective on religious themes in his "Geographic Displacement as Spiritual Desolation in Puerto Rican and Chicano Prose Fiction," in *Images and Identities: The Puerto Rican in Two World Contexts*, ed. Asela R. De Laguna (New Brunswick, N.J.: Transaction, 1985). The best book on Puerto Rican identity within U.S. Catholicism is Ana María Díaz-Stevens, *Oxcart Catholicism on Fifth Avenue* (Notre Dame, Ind.: University of Notre Dame Press, 1993) although the various essays by Joseph P. Fitzpatrick, S.J., of Fordham University offer valuable insights, especially his *Puerto Rican Americans: The Meaning*

of Migration. For Cuba see Raúl Gómez Treto, *The Church and Socialism in Cuba*, trans. Phillip Berryman (Maryknoll, N.Y.: Orbis Books, 1988), although this book does not directly address Cuban Americans. For Cubans in this country, see the essay by Marcos Antonio Ramos and Agustín Román, "The Cubans, Religion, and South Florida," in *Cuban Exiles in Florida: Their Presence and Contribution*, ed. Antonio Jorge, Jaime Suchlicki, and Adolfo Leyva de Varona (Miami: University of Miami Press, 1991), and José Llanes, *Cuban Americans: Masters of Survival* (Cambridge, Mass.: Abt Books, 1982), which offers insights not based strictly on religion. This is an incomplete list on a subject that has not been systematically explored within social science and the series of which this volume is a part represents a significant advance in the study of Catholicism among Latinos.

16. See Stevens-Arroyo, "Catholic Ethos as Politics: The Puerto Rican Nationalists," in *Twentieth Century World Religious Movements in Neo-Weberian Perspective*, ed. William Swatos (Lewiston, N.Y.: Edwin Mellen Press, 1992), for the nature of the similarity with Irish independence. Information on support in New York is found in Gerald Meyer, *Vito Marcantonio: Radical Politician, 1902–1954* (Albany, N.Y.: SUNY Press, 1989).

17. The Platt Amendment was written into the Cuban constitution by the U.S. Congress before authorizing independence after the 1898 war. The amendment authorized unilateral military interference by the U.S. in Cuban affairs. See E. Bradford Burns, *Latin America: A Concise Interpretive History*, 5th ed. (Englewood Cliffs, N.J.: Prentice Hall, 1990).

18. Meyer, *Vito Marcantonio*, pp. 149–151 and passim. Lawrence R. Chenault, *The Puerto Rican Migrant in New York City* (New York: Columbia University Press, 1938).

19. Antonio M. Stevens-Arroyo and Ana María Días Ramírez, "Puerto Ricans in the United States,"in *The Minority Report*, ed. Gary Dworkin and Rosalind Dworkin, 2d ed. (New York: Holt Rinehart and Winston, 1982), p. 219; Meyer, *Vito Marcantonio*, pp. 150–151.

20. Information on such phenomena of politics and culture is found in a plethora of sources, both academic and popular. I have found very helpful the collections of "documentary histories" by Kal Wagenheim *(The Puerto Ricans: A Documentary History* [New York: Praeger, 1973]) and by Wayne Moquin *(A Documentary History of the Mexican Americans* [New York: Praeger, 1971]).

21. Excerpts from this philosophical understanding of national identity based upon Catholicism were resurrected during the 1970s; see Antonio M. Stevens-Arroyo, *Prophets Denied Honor* (Maryknoll, N.Y.: Orbis Books, 1980), pp. 25–63 and passim.

22. Antonio M. Stevens-Arroyo, "Catholicism as Civilization: Contemporary Reflections on the Political Philosophy of Pedro Albizu Campos," Working Paper #50 CISCLA, San German, Puerto Rico, 1992.

23. Dolan, *Immigrant Church*, pp. 73–82, 135–140; Tomasi, *Piety and Power*, pp. 128–142.

24. Rina Benmayor, Rosa M. Torruella, and Ana L. Jurabe, "Responses to Poverty among Puerto Rican Women, Identity, Community, and Cultural Citizenship," Centro de Estudios Puertorriqueños, Hunter College, New York, 1992.

25. Frances Fox Piven and Richard A. Cloward, *Poor People's Movements* (New York: Vintage Books, 1979), pp. 189–211.

26. For a statistical description of this migration with a political interpretation, see the work of the Centro de Estudios Puertorriqueños, *Labor Migration under Capitalism*; Maldonado Denis, *Puerto Rico y Estados Unidos*; and Rodríguez, *Puerto Ricans Born in the U.S.A.* For the term *The Great Migration*, which was coined by Stevens-Arroyo and Díaz-Ramírez, see their "Puerto Ricans in the United States," pp. 200–204.

27. The 1930 census used the term *Mexican* as a racial category alongside "white, Negro, Indian, Chinese, or Japanese," but this racial classification was discarded by 1940. (See U.S. Bureau of the Census, *Counting the Forgotten* [Washington, D.C.: Government Printing Office, 1974], pp. 5–6.)

28. For the Paz statement, see Stevens-Arroyo, *Prophets Denied Honor*, pp. 40–43. For a fuller treatment of the zootsuiter phenomenon and its impact on U.S. popular culture, see Mauricio Mazón, *The Zoot-Suit Riots: The Psychology of Symbolic Annihilation* (Austin, Tex.: University of Texas Press, 1984).

29. For the attitudes of Euro-American Catholics, see William M. Halsey, *The Survival of American Innocence: Catholics in an Era of Disillusionment, 1920–1940* (Notre Dame, Ind.: University of Notre Dame Press, 1980), pp. 169–175. Moore and Pachon, *Hispanics in the United States*, pp. 176–191 and passim, provide a summary of mainstream Latino organizations.

30. Eva Sandis, "Characteristics of Puerto Rican Migrants to and from the U.S.," in *The Puerto Rican Experience. A Sociological Handbook*, ed. Francesco Cordasco and Eugune Bucchioni (Totowa, N.J.: Littlefield and Adams, 1973); see Mills, Senior, and Goldsen, *Puerto Rican Journey*, pp. 100–105.

31. As early as the 1930s in Puerto Rico, Antonio S. Pedreira confronted cultural conflict in his celebrated *Insularismo*. Somewhat later, Tomás Blanco and Emilio Belaval confronted the meaning and

persistence of Puerto Rican culture in the face of Americanism of the island society. None of these authors used the term *cultural crystallization*, but I believe their observations may be interpreted in this light. The literature is mostly in Spanish and too vast for citation here. For summaries of these and other ideas, see Asela Rodríguez de Laguna, *Images and Identities: The Puerto Rican in Two World Contexts* (New Brunswick, N.J.: Transaction Books, 1987).

32. The issue of language is treated in Aida Negrón de Montilla, *Americanization in Puerto Rico and the Public School System, 1900–1930* (Río Piedras: Editorial Edil, 1970); Antonio M. Stevens-Arroyo and Ana María Díaz-Stevens, "Religious Faith and Institutions in the Forging of Latino Identities," in *Handbook for Hispanic Cultures in the United States*, ed. Felix Padilla (Houston: Arte Publico Press, 1993).

33. De la Garza and Falcón, "Identity, Policy Preferences, and Political Behavior."

34. For an explanation of how this lack has an impact upon scholarship, see Rodolfo J. Cortina, "Cubans in Miami: Ethnic Identity and Behavior," *Latino Studies Journal* 1, no 2 (May 1990), pp. 60–73. Gerald E. Poyo supplies a larger historical background in *With All and for the Good of All: The Rise of Popular Nationalism in the Cuban Emigré Communities, 1848–1898* (Durham, N.C.: Duke University Press, 1989).

35. Much of the early literature on Cuban Americans is heavily politicized. Thomas P. Boswell and James P. Curtis have provided *The Cuban-American Experience: Culture, Images, and Perspectives* (Totowa, N.J.: Rowman and Allanheld, 1983), which is helpful for its overview of the subject. Alejandro Portes and Robert L. Bach have used a comparative sociological approach in *Latin Journey: Cuban and Mexican Immigrants in the United States* (Berkeley: University of California Press, 1985). Both works distinguish between different types of Cuban immigrants and chronological "waves." With no intention of discounting these valuable studies, the synthesis provided here is my own.

36. Gómez Treto, *Church and Socialism in Cuba*, pp. 47–54; Llanes, *Cuban Americans: Masters of Survival*, pp. 27–28 and passim.

37. Ramos and Román, "Cubans, Religion, and South Florida"; for lists of persons and organizations, see *Anuario de la Iglesia Católica: Cuba, Isla-Diaspora, 1972* (Caracas: Unión de cubanos en el Exilio, 1972).

38. Albens Walsh, "The Work of the Catholic Bishops' Committee for the Spanish-speaking in the United States," Master's thesis, University of Texas, 1952. See Díaz-Stevens, *Oxcart Catholicism*; and Stephen A. Privett, S.J., *The United States Catholic Church and Its Hispanic Members: The Pastoral Vision of Archbishop Robert E. Lucey* (San Antonio, Tex.: Trinity University Press, 1988).

39. Fitzpatrick, *Puerto Rican Americans: The Meaning of Migration to the Mainland*, pp. 124–137; Díaz-Stevens, *Oxcart Catholicism*.

40. Felix Padilla, *Puerto Rican Chicago* (Notre Dame, Ind.: University of Notre Dame Press, 1987), pp. 125–137 and passim; for the fate of the New York group, see Díaz-Stevens, *Oxcart Catholicism*.

41. Ana María Díaz-Stevens, "From Puerto Rican to Hispanic: The Politics of the *Fiestas Patronales* in New York," *Latinos Studies Journal* 1, no. 1 (Jan. 1990), pp. 28–47.

42. Díaz-Stevens, *Oxcart Catholicism*.

43. See Jeffrey M. Burns, "Mexican Americans and the Catholic Church in California, 1910–1965," in the first volume of this collection, *The Mexican Americans* (Notre Dame, Ind.: University of Notre Dame Press, 1994).

44. Tarciscio Ocampo, *Puerto Rico: Partido Acción Cristiana, 1960–1962* (Cuernavaca: CIDOC, 1967), offers complete historical documentation.

45. Jaime Vidal, "Popular Religion among the Hispanics in the General Area of the Archdiocese of Newark," in *Nueva Presencia: Knowledge for Service and Hope* (Newark, N.J.; Office of Research and Planning, 1988), pp. 302–308.

46. Michael Harrington, *The Other America* (New York: Viking Penguin, 1971).

47. For a summary of these changes see Stevens-Arroyo and Díaz-Ramirez, "Puerto Ricans in the United States."

48. Juan Hurtado, *An Attitudinal Study of the Social Distance between the Mexican American and the Church* (San Antonio, Tex.: MACC, 1975); Alfredo López, *The Puerto Rican Papers* (Indianapolis: Bobbs Merrill, 1973).

49. See Klor de Alva, "Aztlán, Borinquen, and Hispanic Nationalism in the United States."

50. For an account of the Chicano movement, see Jack D. Forbes, *Aztecas del Norte: The Chicanos of Aztlán* (Greenwich, Conn.: Fawcett, 1973).

51. Rosa Estades, *Patrones de participación política de los puertorriqueños en la ciudad de Nueva York* (Río Piedras: Editorial Universitaria, 1978).

52. Díaz-Stevens, "From Puerto Rican to Hispanic"; and *Oxcart Catholicism*.

53. Ibid.

54. The process is described in Stevens-Arroyo, *Prophets Denied Honor*, pp. 117–118, 198–200.

55. John Gregory Dunne, *Delano: The Story of the California Grape Strike* (New York: Farrar, Straus, and Giroux, 1967).

56. A description of the events is cited in Stevens-Arroyo, *Prophets Denied Honor*, pp. 122–134.

57. For these trends see Robert H. Haveman, *A Decade of Federal Antipoverty Programs* (New York: Academic Press, 1977); and Adalberto López, *The Puerto Ricans and Their History* (Rochester, Vt.: Schenkman, 1990), pp. 323–341.

58. Moisés Sandoval, *On the Move* (Maryknoll, N.Y.: Orbis Books, 1990).

59. Virgil Elizondo, *Christianity and Culture* (Huntington, Ind.: Our Sunday Visitor Press, 1975).

60. For the Chicano notion of *mestizaje*, see Forbes, *Aztecas del Norte*; for an explanation of its philosophical origins, see Stevens-Arroyo, *Prophets Denied Honor*, pp. 32–39.

61. Sandoval, *On the Move*; Díaz-Stevens, *Oxcart Catholicism*.

62. Klor de Alva, "Aztlán, Borinquen, and Hispanic Nationalism in the United States," pp. 138–141 and passim.

63. Díaz-Stevens, *Oxcart Catholicism*.

64. Stevens-Arroyo, *Prophets Denied Honor*, pp. 197–201 and passim.

65. Ibid., pp. 175–179 and passim. Alan Figueroa Deck, S.J. *(Frontiers of Hispanic Theology in the United States* [Maryknoll, N.Y.: Orbis Books, 1992], pp. xix-xx and passim) uses the word *culturalist*.

66. Stevens-Arroyo, *Prophets Denied Honor*, pp. 209–305.

67. The difficulties of extending 1960s radicalism beyond the status of a counterestablishment movement can be seen by analyzing the *Raza Unida* Party which gained political control of Crystal City, Texas. See John Staples Shockley, *Chicano Revolt in a Texas Town* (Notre Dame, Ind.: University of Notre Dame Press, 1974).

68. Sandoval, *On the Move*, p. 83.

69. Deck, *Frontiers of Hispanic Theology*.

70. Martin Carnoy, Hugh Daley, and Raúl Hinojosa Ojeda, *Latinos in a Changing U.S. Economy: Comparative Perspectives on the U.S. Labor Market since 1939* (New York: Research Foundation of the City University of New York, 1990).

71. Garcia, "The Hispanic in American History: Myth and Reality."

72. Moore and Pachon, *Hispanics in the United States*, pp. 116–117.

73. Justo González, *Mañana: Christian Theology from a Hispanic Perspective* (Nashville, Tenn.: Abingdon Press, 1990).

74. De la Garza and Falcón, "Identity, Policy Preferences, and Political Behavior."

75. Antonio M. Stevens-Arroyo and Ana María Díaz-Stevens, "Latino Church and Schools as Urban Battlegrounds," in *Handbook of Schooling in Urban America*, ed. Stanley William Rothstein, (Westport, Conn.: Greenwood Press, 1993), pp. 245–270.

4

The Organization of a Hispanic Church

Moisés Sandoval

In the last twenty-five years, Hispanics have begun to place their own stamp on the Catholic Church in the United States.[1] They have ceased to be mere objects of ministry and have begun to exercise their own ministerial role. They have recovered religious traditions and put them into practice. They have developed new institutions and taken leadership in those created for them beginning in the mid-1940s. For the first time, native-born Hispanic bishops were ordained, and most of these shepherds brought to the Church an experience of the word of God that reflects the history of Hispanics in this country, the story of a people who have suffered conquest and discrimination. At the same time, some non-Hispanic bishops, clergy, and religious have made their own option to serve Hispanic people. One could say that a Hispanic Church is in the process of organizing, not just to serve the people of that culture but the Church and nation as a whole. This could not have occurred without a historic change in the way Hispanics perceived themselves.

Events in the 1960s indicated that Hispanics had finally found a secure identity as a people, without which they could not organize in the Church and preach their own unique message. That search had been going on throughout the twentieth century. Hispanics born in the United States knew who they were, but because of the unrelenting attack on their culture since the United States seized the Southwest from Mexico, many were prone to deny, even hate, their origins. Led by the League of United Latin American citizens, which organized in 1929 in Texas, they tried to gain acceptance in the larger society. Immigrants saw themselves as sojourners who would, one day soon, return to Mexico or other parts of Latin America. Gradually, Hispanics saw that the quest for assimilation was not only impossible but wrong. In the 1960s, they decided that their destiny was to remain distinct from mainstream society. They

131

realized as well that they had much to contribute because of their religiosity and values as Hispanic Catholics.

As part of coming to terms with their place in United States society, Hispanics began to treasure and recover the culture they had tried to reject in their unsuccessful efforts to enter the mainstream. Many began to relearn the Spanish they had tried to forget, to recover religious traditions that had been suppressed or abandoned. In the meantime, a steady inflow of Latin Americans continually reinforced and strengthened elements of Hispanic culture in the U.S. during the late 1940s, 1950s, and 1960s. They came from Mexico, from Puerto Rico, from Central and South America and, with the triumph of Fidel Castro in Cuba in 1959, from across the Florida straits. In 1950, according to Census Bureau estimates, Hispanics in the United States numbered 4 million; in 1960, 6.9 million; and in 1970, 10.5 million. In 1980, the first time a serious attempt was made to count them, the Census Bureau determined that they totaled 14.6 million, not counting the 3.5 million inhabitants of the Commonwealth of Puerto Rico. The Hispanic population grew by 53 percent between 1980 and 1990, when their numbers reached 22.4 million.

To be able to minister and, in a sense, become a Church, Hispanics in the United States had to reconstruct their society; a Church is by definition a community. Throughout the first half of the twentieth century the various peoples categorized as Hispanic were literally on the move. Native-born Hispanics underwent a vast migration to urban areas. In the 1920s, 75 percent were rural people; by the 1960s and 1970s, 85 percent lived in cities, the most urbanized ethnic group. Immigrants left their traditional societies behind in Mexico, Puerto Rico, Cuba, and other parts of Central and South America. The process of reconstructing a Hispanic society was well under way in the mid-1960s. The people were establishing social, political, and economic ties—that is, becoming a community, working for their common good.

Perhaps the most important sign that Hispanics were at last becoming a people was the commitment of those who were able to attain success. In previous decades, these fortunate ones, in the Church as well as in society, were all too glad to turn their backs on their own people. Now, in the 1960s, these leaders were coming back to struggle alongside their brothers and sisters. They led the civil rights movement of Hispanics in the 1960s, helping them to organize in politics, the economy, society, and even the Church.

A segment of the Church with a distinct Hispanic flavor emerged also because of factors external to the culture. Due to discrimination, the Church had created separate structures for Hispanics, though to a lesser degree than it did for blacks. In some parts of the Southwest, there were separate churches in the same parish for Anglos and Hispanics. Some of the separate churches endured until recent times. In parishes with only one church, Hispanics were welcome only for certain Masses. Parallel national directorates were established for the Marriage Encounter movement and the Cursillo. Protestant denominations also tended to establish separate Hispanic congregations rather than assimilate their Hispanic members. The division of Hispanics and Anglos by class, race, and culture was the path of least resistance.

What ultimately defined what might be called a Hispanic Church, however, was the ministry it could offer, first to its own members and then to the larger Church. That ministry, on a national scale, flowed from other than the usual sources—bishops, pastors, religious congregations, and orders. In the 1990s, Hispanics had only a token number of bishops, compared to their proportion of the Catholic population; two hundred native-born Hispanic priests and only fifteen hundred foreign-born Hispanic priests. Nuns were similarly underrepresented. Ministry in the Hispanic Church came, in large measure, from lay movements and laypersons, from groups and community organizations not part of Church structures, like the United Farm Workers and Communities Organized for Public Service, a federation of parishes in San Antonio, Texas. The Hispanic ministry's wellsprings were local but also international. Often, other Catholics were unaware that they were benefiting from it. Yet the Hispanic Church was having a decisive impact on their lives. Most of the recent significant movements or ideas in the American Church have been of Spanish or Latin American origin: the Cursillo, Marriage Encounter, basic Christian communities, liberation theology, and the preferential option for the poor.

SPECIAL STRUCTURES FOR THE HISPANIC CHURCH

In 1944, Archbishop Robert E. Lucey of San Antonio sponsored a seminar on the Spanish speaking, which was attended by about fifty delegates from western and southwestern states who met for three days to discuss aspects of the Church's work with Hispanic people. A second workshop was held later that year in Denver at the request of Archbishop Urban J. Vehr. Delegates came from California, Arizona, New Mexico, Wyoming, Oklahoma, Texas, and Colorado.[2] Those meetings led to the formation of Catholic councils for the Spanish speaking, which achieved official status the following year.

On Jan. 10–12, 1945, fourteen bishops met in Oklahoma City to establish the Bishops' Committee for the Spanish Speaking. The decisions they made defined Hispanic ministry for the rest of the century. The participants agreed to establish an intensive program of social and spiritual welfare in four episcopal provinces: Los Angeles, Santa Fe, Denver, and San Antonio. With funds from the American Board of Catholic Missions, the members of the committee decided that, as a first phase, they would construct clinics, settlement houses, community and catechetical centers. The second phase consisted of providing services for migrant workers, maternal and child care, and educational and recreational opportunities. The budget for the first year provided $15,000 to operate a regional office, based in Texas, and $180,000 for the construction of welfare centers.[3]

The bishops also directed that a Catholic council for the Spanish speaking be established in each diocese. The councils drew representatives from the chancery, the parishes, schools, the Confraternity for Christian Doctrine, and from a variety of Catholic organizations. They sought participation, according to an official statement, from both Anglos and Hispanos, for some, the first time they had had the opportunity to work together.[4] Whether the bishops' stated plan was a real design or only rhetoric, such contacts occurred as time went on. In fact, Hispanics eventually assumed the responsibility for some of the structures, and most of the leaders were laypersons.

The Catholic councils for the Spanish speaking soon spread far beyond the four episcopal provinces for which they had been created. They followed the migrant workers on their trek north, organizing in Missouri, the upper Pacific Coast, Montana, and the upper Midwest. By the early 1960s councils had been established in New York, Ohio, and Michigan. The councils' annual meeting in St. Louis, Mo., formerly a regional affair, was billed in 1960 as the first conference on a national level; Puerto Rican problems were to be discussed for the first time.

The ministry to migrant workers and their families, which dioceses in agricultural areas had developed over the years, did not reach the rapidly growing population of the permanently settled. New institutions were needed to serve these people. "We have noted a tendency on the part of agencies, organizations and the community at large to forget the Spanish-speaking once they have moved out of farm labor to become part of the urban community," said Joe Garcia, who founded the Hispanic apostolate office in the diocese of Saginaw.[5] Special offices for the Hispanic apostolate followed. By the early 1960s, representatives of 70 dioceses worked in liaison with the bishops' committee. The archdiocese of New York had the office for the Spanish Speaking; the archdiocese of Chicago, the Cardinal's Committee for the Spanish Speaking; the diocese of Miami, the Office for Latin American Affairs; the diocese of Cleveland, the Spanish Mission Office; the archdiocese of Denver, the Migrant Labor Project; the diocese of Madison, Wis., Our Lady of Guadalupe Center; the diocese of Baker, Ore., the Migrant Apostolate; and the cities of Norwalk and Bridgeport, Conn., the office for Spanish-speaking Missions. By 1982, the diocesan apostolates had grown to over 100. Eventually, about 60 percent of the country's 176 dioceses developed a Hispanic apostolate office.

In 1964, the bishops changed the scope of the Office for the Spanish Speaking, which they had established in 1945, from regional to national, though it remained in Texas, where it had rotated from diocese to diocese. The office was moved to Washington in 1970, the change coinciding with the naming of a new director, Pablo Sedillo, from New Mexico. The reorganization that created the national office deemphasized the regional and national role of the councils, though they continued to function in some dioceses until the 1970s.

By 1965, the policy of including Hispanics in the councils for the Spanish speaking had also evolved. The bishops' beginning to accept Hispanic leadership for the special offices meant appointing laypersons because the Church could hardly reassign the relatively few clergy or Sisters of Hispanic origin, native-born or immigrant. Fortunately, this change came at a time when Hispanics could respond to the challenge. Many had gone to college or gained other skills in the post–World War II period. More importantly, they were well disposed to work on behalf of their own people. Once known as the "silent minority," they now asked to be heard and served. They demanded better educational opportunities, justice in the workplace and in the streets, and response and commitment from the Church that claimed them as its sons and daughters. Their pressure earned them a small, but firmly established, place in the chanceries.

The change to Hispanic leadership occurred at all levels. By 1967, Father Patricio Flores, a dynamic young pastor in Houston, Texas, was state chair of the Bishops' Committee for the Spanish Speaking. The same year, the first Hispanic layman, Antonio Tinajero, was hired as director of the national office. Though he remained only three years, the precedent had been set; he was succeeded by Sedillo.

In the Midwest, the rise in Hispanic leaders was due, in large part, to the efforts of Ruben Alfaro, a former migrant worker who had become a barber in Michigan. When a new regional office for the Spanish speaking was established in the Midwest in 1967, he was named the director. As he helped organize diocesan apostolates, Alfaro urged that they be headed by laypersons who spoke Spanish. The same year, when a regional office for the Spanish speaking was organized on the West Coast, Salvador Alvarez, a young man with a master's degree in social work, was chosen to head it. He, too, lobbied for Hispanics to lead the diocesan apostolates. In the Southwest, where the regional office was reorganized in 1973, Lupe Anguiano, a former Sister, became the director. She wrote that the primary goal of the office was "to assist the dioceses in the region to involve the Spanish-speaking/surnamed layperson in the total mission of the Church."[6]

The initiative that placed Hispanics in charge of the apostolates often came from the laity. In the diocese of Toledo, Sylvester Duran developed a radio program that led him to form a community organization. Then he convinced the bishop to start a department for the Spanish speaking and to make him director. A similar process occurred in the diocese of Saginaw. Joe Garcia, hired as a Mexican-American specialist in the diocese's Community Affairs Department, found that his people were not getting the attention they needed. He persuaded the bishop to create the Department of Latin American Affairs.

The board of directors of the West Coast regional office consisted in the late 1960s of a priest and two members of the laity from each of the participating dioceses: Oakland, San Francisco, Santa Rosa, Sacramento, Fresno, and Stockton. Conspicuous by its absence was the huge archdiocese of Los Angeles, whose lack of interest was one of the reasons that the office closed in 1973 and did not reopen until the 1980s.

The concern for the involvement of the laity on the regional level continued. In 1989, the board of directors of the Midwest Catholic Commission consisted of fourteen persons—two bishops and two representatives from each of the five states, with the requirement that half of them be women.[7]

Regional offices were eventually established—reestablished on the West Coast, where the original office had been closed in 1973—in most of the Church's thirteen episcopal regions. Though priests or Sisters headed some of them, most of the directors were Hispanic laypersons, who also predominated among the staff. Several in the Midwest, Northeast, and Southeast also established pastoral centers. The West Coast office had a team that traveled from diocese to diocese for a few years, giving seminars and courses.

The Southeast office, headed by Cuban-born Father Mario Vizcaíno since it was founded in 1979, had one of the most ambitious programs. In 1992, its team of Vizcaíno and six laypersons served twenty-six dioceses in eight states. In thirteen years, the staff had logged more than 1 million miles giving courses in ministry, workshops, and retreats and organizing small Church communities. Fifteen professors of international renown gave courses in Miami that were videotaped and distributed throughout the region and beyond. A lenten program for youth utilized a textbook they had helped to prepare.

The Northeast regional office, based in New York, was not established until 1974, but, for a time, the Hispanic apostolate office of the archdiocese of New York had had regional scope. That office had been founded in 1953 by Cardinal Spellman to coordinate Spanish-American Catholic Action. Its spiritual and social action programs were based on research done by Jesuit Father Joseph Fitzpatrick, a sociologist at Fordham University. In the next few years, the annual San Juan Fiesta was inaugurated, the Cursillo was introduced, and the Institute for Intercultural Communication, directed by Father Ivan Illich, was begun in Ponce, Puerto Rico. Hundreds of priests, Sisters, and some laypeople learned Spanish and became acquainted with Puerto Rican culture at the institute.

Under the leadership of Monsignor Robert Fox, who became the director of the office in 1963, parishes started an outreach to Hispanics through a program called "Summer in the City." Fox urged the Church to become publicly involved in social change. He wanted to use the parish and its resources as a base for community organization. By naming Father Peter Ensenat, of Puerto Rican and Cuban descent, to head the summer session of the Institute of Intercultural Communication, he began the process of putting Hispanics in charge of some of the functions of the office.

That process was greatly expanded in scope and means by Father Robert Stern, who headed the office from 1969 to 1973. In the archdiocese, he started a series of pastoral encounters or workshops that presaged the First National Encuentro, a process that led to the creation of a national pastoral plan for Hispanic ministry in 1987. In the region, Stern organized the Interdiocesan Coordinating Committee for the Spanish-Speaking Apostolate in 1971; it had representatives from ten dioceses in four states.[8]

The Midwest Catholic Commission's office, directed for fifteen years by Olga Villa-Parra, a charismatic woman with roots as a migrant, had similar credentials. By 1989, the office had helped to create offices or coordinators for Hispanic ministry in twenty-seven of the twenty-nine dioceses in the five-state region of Michigan, Ohio, Indiana, Illinois, and Wisconsin. "We have had over 70,000 contacts with individuals in the last five years—for training and seminars, and other activities—and that does not include the phone calls, information, and coordination," Villa said.[9]

These successes, however, would come only after the regional offices came under local control. When first established in the 1960s, the Midwest and West Coast regional offices were run by the United States Catholic Conference (USCC) in Washington, specifically by the Department of Social Development and World Peace. The boards of directors selected by the dioceses could not make policy, set a budget, or hire or fire the staff. This led to conflicts not easily resolved, especially in the running of the West Coast office. The board of directors felt that the $20,000 allocated to run the office was insufficient to meet the needs of three million Hispanos scattered over fifteen dioceses. As a consequence, Alvarez resigned in the fall of 1969. The office was closed until a new director was hired nearly a year later. When that director resigned two years later, the office was closed again for months. Finally, in 1973, the USCC gave up control of the regional offices, and since then they have been administered by directors responsible to boards of directors appointed by the dioceses they serve.

The offices for Hispanics faced many problems. At the diocesan level, they had little leverage with other diocesan offices, which often ignored Hispanics, seeing them as the responsibility of the special offices. Yet, the latter could do little because of low budgets and lack of staff. The problem described by Lupe Anguiano in a letter to Bishop James Rausch, chair of the National Conference of Catholic Bishops' (NCCB) Committee for the Spanish Speaking was typical of other regional and diocesan offices: "In 1975 I made a serious attempt to operate on a $35,000 budget and found this impossible. I had no operational monies for December, not even for my salary. I have not had a secretary for seven months."[10] Similarly, Francisco Diana, the director of the Office for the Spanish Speaking of the Brooklyn diocese complained that with only one or two assistants he was expected to provide Hispanic ministry for all Hispanics, 40 percent of the diocesan population.

Similarly, when Sedillo arrived in Washington to take his post as director of the national office, he found he had neither staff nor budget. But after that challenge was met, he discovered that he had little chance of exerting any influence on other offices.

The national office was a division in the Department of Social Development and World Peace. Sedillo had no easy access to the top administrative units, the secretariats of the NCCB, whose policies were set by committees of the bishops' conference. It took four years of lobbying by Sedillo and pressure from many Hispanic leaders before the Division for the Spanish Speaking was finally elevated to the Secretariat for the Spanish Speaking in 1974.

Though the staffs of the Hispanic apostolate offices had no easy task in influencing the Church's bureaucracy, they still lobbied the bishops to hire more Hispanics for jobs in the chanceries and urged parishes to include more Hispanics on parish councils, to offer liturgies in Spanish, and to respect the religious traditions of the people. The directors were not afraid to hold the bishops accountable. A few years after the appointment of Robert F. Sanchez as the head of the archdiocese of Santa Fe, Lupe Anguiano made a survey that showed that pastors had been slow in carrying out the archbishop's wishes that Mass be celebrated in Spanish in parishes where there were large numbers of Spanish-speaking people. In the Southeast, Father Mario Vizcaíno often had to remind bishops that in their dioceses they had Hispanics who were not being served by the Church.

The Hispanic apostolate offices gave Hispanic laity in particular a place and role they had not had before. Dioceses, even those where the overwhelming majority of Church members were Hispanics, had been slow to recruit Hispanic employees. Thus in the beginning, the Hispanic apostolate office was the only one in which one could find them. From there, they were able to meet and gradually influence non-Hispanic leaders about their needs. The encounters, not always harmonious, nevertheless provided opportunities for mutual learning and understanding.

The Hispanic offices at every level generally shared the same priorities and concerns. In the social arena, they lobbied for social justice for immigrants, migrants, farmworkers, and the urban poor. They also sought to improve education for Hispanics. In the Church they sought to organize pastoral plans, develop leaders, train ministers, and establish basic Christian communities. They developed leaders in the parishes, dioceses, and in the community at large. They helped communities organize behind important issues: jobs, health, education, justice. They provided a steady flow of information on immigration and political, social, and economic issues, such as the struggle of farm workers.

The leaders were successful because they came forth, not from elites, but from the grassroots. Victory Noll Sister Carolina Lopez, who headed the Hispanic ministry office in the diocese of Tucson, had worked in the fields of the Coachella Valley in California until the day she left to enter religious life. Primitivo Romero, director of the Office of Hispanic Affairs for the diocese of Phoenix, had worked twelve years picking cotton and melons in Arizona before he could begin a slow climb toward a life of service helping his people.[11] While earning a living as a truck driver, he went to school at night, built his home with the help of his seven children, and still had time to volunteer in his parish. Olga Villa, the director of the office of the Midwest Catholic Commission, had been a migrant worker.

In New York, the most important lay leader was Encarnación Padilla de Armas, a well-educated Puerto Rican woman who had for decades fought for the welfare of her people in the Church and in society. For several years, she served as a consultant to the Bishop's Committee for the Spanish Speaking in Texas under Archbishop Robert Lucey of San Antonio. When the office was elevated from regional to national status and moved to Washington as the Division for the Spanish Speaking, she helped to organize the Northeast, working as a staff member from 1970 to 1973, when U.S. Catholic Conference policy forced her to retire because she had reached the age of 65. Pablo Sedillo, the director, credited her with helping him to understand the Puerto Rican community.[12]

These leaders, and many others like them, had not lost the common touch, the ability to lead and inspire their own people. Furthermore, they had the courage to speak out for them and, if necessary, to confront Church leaders on their behalf. At the same time, their achievements and dedication won the respect of non-Hispanic leaders in the Church.

Thus the Hispanic offices had developed leadership within the Church's structures and in the community which would not have otherwise developed. Yet a full appreciation of the good these leaders had accomplished was clearly lacking. In the late 1980s and early 1990s, some dioceses began to close their offices for the Hispanic apostolate. In part, this was motivated by financial problems; in part, by the growing appeal of the idea of lumping all minorities—Hispanics, blacks, and Asians—under one office for multicultural ministry. That pressure was felt also by the national office in Washington. Until the day, still far off, when Hispanics will be proportionally represented at all levels of the Church, these special offices will be necessary.

THE ENCUENTRO PROCESS

As Hispanics assumed leadership of the offices created for them by the bishops, they developed new processes to bring their agenda to the attention of the Church. The most effective of these initiatives was the *encuentro*, which some have defined as a movement, usually associated with a cause, charismatic leadership, and narrowly defined issues and goals. Though the encuentro at first had some of these characteristics, and had the same confrontational style of the civil rights movement, it evolved into a process that took Hispanics far beyond the goals originally envisioned. The encuentro began at the national level and, in time, came to involve Hispanic apostolate offices at all levels, all the other Church movements such as the Cursillo and Movimiento Familiar Cristiano, all the bishops, many of the clergy, religious, and laity working with Hispanics, and even many Catholics who had become alienated from the Church. The process remained in motion in the 1990s as dioceses continued to develop pastoral plans for Hispanic ministry.

The idea for the encuentro first surfaced in September, 1971. Father Robert Stern, director of the Hispanic Apostolate for the New York archdiocese, invited local leaders to meet with Father Edgard Beltrán, formerly with the staff of the Latin American Episcopal Conference (CELAM) and then on the staff of the USCC's Division for the Spanish Speaking. During the discussion of a plan for Hispanic ministry, Beltrán said there ought to be a national encuentro (encounter) for Spanish-speaking leaders of the Church of the United States. The participants liked the idea and turned it into a recommendation submitted to the Interdiocesan Coordinating Committee for the Spanish Speaking of the Northeast region. Working with Encarnación Padilla de Armas, Stern won the support of Sedillo, director of the Division for the Spanish Speaking. A month later, in October, more than one hundred Spanish-speaking delegates attending the meeting of the Congress of Religious Educators in Miami presented to the leadership and to the National Conference of Catholic Bishops a declaration in favor of the encuentro. In January, 1972, Bishop Joseph L. Bernardin, general secretary of the USCC, endorsed the First National Encuentro. Two workshops held in the New York archdiocese under Stern's direction provided the structural framework for the national meeting.

In Latin America, the word *encuentro* did not have the meaning that it acquired in the United States among Hispanics. There it referred to a meeting, a coming together for open discussion. Here it took on the meaning of confrontation, which appealed to Hispanics at the time. By then, the civil rights struggle—characterized by marches, manifestos, protests, and organizing—had peaked in society as a whole. But within the Church, the *movimiento*, the term that encompassed those activities, was just beginning. Archbishop Patrick Flores, speaking of that time, said there was much anger among Hispanics who felt the Church had not been a true shepherd. So the encuentro became a vehicle to confront the Church.

The First National Encuentro was held in June 1972 at Trinity College in Washington, D.C., and was attended by 250 persons, among whom one could count the bishops on the fingers of one hand. One of them was the imposing Cardinal John Krol, who tried to convince the audience that everyone was equal in the Church. The participants, however, would have none of it. Bishop Patricio Flores, elevated to the episcopacy barely two years before, charged that the Church had been silent while his people had been robbed of their lands, forced to live in conditions of semislavery, "in housing worse than that of monkeys in the zoo," and deprived even of their way of religious expression.[13]

The participants drew up seventy-eight conclusions and demands that they were making of the Church. They asked that the USCC Division for the Spanish Speaking be made a secretariat of the National Conference of Catholic Bishops (NCCB), that there be a bishops' committee for Hispanics, that more Hispanic bishops be ordained, and that diocesan newspapers have sections in Spanish. These demands were eventually met.

Other demands, much more radical, the bishops would not accept, for example, that basic Christian communities become a priority; that women be ordained deacons; that mature married men be considered for the priesthood; that the training of all candidates for the priesthood in all dioceses should include formation in spoken Spanish and Hispanic culture. By 1992, however, the last demand had become a requirement in dioceses where Hispanics are numerous.

The national encuentro led to a repetition of the process at the regional level and, in some cases, in dioceses too. "The whole idea is to create an awareness of where the Spanish speaking are in relation to the local church and to show that the Church has in many instances neglected the needs of the Spanish-speaking," Sedillo said. Though dioceses tried to avoid them, confrontations occurred. In Brooklyn, Hispanics rejected the agenda prepared by the diocese and drew up their own. In Denver, the news reports of the meeting so upset Anglo Catholics that Archbishop James V. Casey found it necessary to explain in the *Denver Catholic Register* that the archdiocese had not been pressured to hold the meeting:

> I want all of our people to understand that the questions raised at St. Thomas Seminary and the ensuing dialogue have happened because the Archdiocese of Denver issued the invitation for this to happen. . . .
> We were not besieged by the Chicano people nor were we forced in any way to have these two days of dialogue, but rather the Chicano people were there because we invited them to express openly, their ideas, thoughts and frustrations.[14]

Perhaps because of such difficulties, many other dioceses did not risk having such meetings. By 1974, only 15 of 156 dioceses and only three of twelve episcopal regions had held their own encuentro. One other regional meeting was held that year, in the Northeast, and it led to the founding of the Northeast regional office for Hispanics, with headquarters in New York.

Plans for the Second National Encuentro, held in Washington in August 1977, included several major changes that seemed designed to put an end to confrontation. First, while the First National Encuentro had been a meeting of Hispanic leaders, this one would at least represent the views of grassroots people. The committee preparing the meeting consulted 100,000 people, according to

Sedillo. They were people who had never before been surveyed about their views, their needs, and how the Church could meet them. Second, the meeting would feature no formal speeches, except for one by Archbishop Robert F. Sanchez and that only to explain the process to be carried out (Sanchez had been elevated to the episcopacy two years before). Third, and perhaps most significant, the language of the documents for the meeting would be Spanish. As a result, many of the Cubans and Puerto Ricans who spoke Spanish well dominated the meeting, diminishing the influence of some of the most radical participants—the Chicanos,[15] as the most militant Mexican Americans identified themselves. They had tried to no avail to make the documents bilingual. Lupe Anguiano wrote to the bishops of region 10: "Some of you have complained about the National Encuentro materials being only in Spanish and not bilingual. I just wanted you to know that I tried many times to get such materials bilingual but lost such motions."[16] What all this meant was that the institutional Church had appropriated the process of the encuentro; it could no longer be considered part of the movimiento, coming from and controlled by the people.

In contrast to the low episcopal presence in the First National Encuentro, thirty-four bishops came to the second one, and the number of delegates more than doubled, to five hundred, with another seven hundred attending as observers. Under the umbrella of evangelization, they discussed such topics as human rights, integral education, political responsibility, unity, and the challenge of pluralism.

Forty-five conclusions came from the Second National Encuentro. Father Frank Ponce, assistant director of the Secretariat for Hispanic Affairs, synthesized them into five points: The delegates, he said, made a commitment to continue a process of reflection and growth in Christ as a Hispanic community. They resolved to form basic Christian communities, seeing that "it is here that future leaders are born and fostered." They resolved to correct injustices both inside and outside the Church, especially those suffered by migrant farm workers and undocumented immigrants. "The delegates clearly gave notice that Hispano culture can no longer be ignored in teaching the Catholic faith," Ponce said. The delegates asked the Church to be poor in spirit, to seek unity in diversity rather than in homogeneity, and to help eliminate economic disadvantages. They committed themselves to convert persons and structures in the Church so as to return to the simplicity of the gospel message. Finally, as a common thread in all the documents, they emphasized that lay ministers must be encouraged and recognized by the Church.[17]

While the initiative in the previous encuentros had come from Hispanics, the bishops began the process leading to the Third National Encuentro, held in August 1985 in Washington. In 1983, they had approved a pastoral letter, *The Hispanic Presence: Challenge and Commitment*, which called for the meeting to take place. The bishops set a two-year period of preparation for the encuentro. During that time, a concerted effort would be made to reach the alienated. In Miami alone, the energetic Cuban-dominated Southeast regional office and the local apostolate visited 11,000 families no longer participating in the Church. Then the dioceses had their own encuentros, followed by the regions, and finally by the national meeting. The planning committee selected five themes for discussion: evangelization, integral education, social justice, youth, and leadership formation.

What had now become clear was that the planners were making what the Latin American bishops in their historic meeting at Medellín in 1968 called "the preferential option for the poor." In the selection of delegates, places were reserved for the farm workers and other marginal groups. At the same time, the delegation from each diocese was headed by the bishop. Again, like the Second National Encuentro, the proceedings were in Spanish, which again left out the Chicanos, though translators were available at the meeting for those who needed them. The documents were in both English and Spanish.

The 1,200 delegates from 130 dioceses who attended the Third National Encuentro approved the broad outlines of a national pastoral plan for Hispanic ministry. To assure that a consensus would be reached, the proceedings were facilitated by Brazilian Father José Marins, an expert in process who had played the same role at the meeting of Latin American bishops at Puebla in 1979. After the encuentro, a committee drawn from various regional and diocesan apostolate offices edited the plan for presentation to the bishops, who finally approved it in 1987, but without allocating any funds for its implementation.

While there was initial disappointment with the bishops' failure to commit funding, most Hispanics continued to work to put it into effect. "We have never had adequate funding, but I never equated money with the ability to do things," Olga Villa said. "Resources never equaled money for me because I never had any.

Resources for me have been people, energy, and faith."[18] She added that the national pastoral plan was being "digested locally."

As time went by, dioceses began to make their own pastoral plans for Hispanic ministry. Los Angeles Archbishop Roger Mahony, who liked to do things on a grand scale and ahead of other bishops, held a convocation in 1986 in Dodgers' Stadium where he promised about 50,000 people present that would improve Hispanic ministry. Among the steps he took to carry out that pledge, he invited the Guadalupana Missioners of the Holy Spirit, a Mexican congregation, to come to the archdiocese. These Sisters established a program for parish evangelization that was being implemented in many Hispanic parishes. Gradually, other dioceses also promulgated plans for Hispanic ministry. In early 1992, the archdiocese of Denver, with much fanfare, announced its own plan. Even in the Southeast, where Catholics of all ethnic roots are few, fifteen of the twenty-six dioceses had completed their own plan for Hispanic ministry early in 1992, and five others were working on theirs.[19] Thus the process was continuing seven years after the Third National Encuentro.

The results of the encuentros, and the national and diocesan pastoral plans that flowed from them, were mixed. In some dioceses money, energy, and creativity were invested, leading to significant improvements in Hispanic ministry. In others, the plans simply gathered dust.

Ultimately, the encuentros' most significant achievement may be that they taught Hispanics how to work together. Formerly, they had been many disparate groups vying against each other; they emerged from the Third National Encuentro with more mutual understanding and unity. The process identified and developed leaders who went back to their dioceses to assume important roles. In addition, the process made bishops more aware of the need to serve the Hispanic community.

The Bishops

Like the leaders of the encuentros, the bishops had felt the challenge of the poor as personified by the Hispanics. They had seen, perhaps for the first time, how Hispanics suffered in a society that discriminated and exploited them. But the programs they implemented dealt only with the effects of injustice, not with its causes. Robert E. Lucey, the strongest avocate of Hispanics, cultivated neutrality. In 1966, when farm worker organizing began in Texas and two of his priests went to the Rio Grande Valley to assist the workers and promptly stirred up the ire of the growers, he buckled to pressure and ordered them to stay out of the troubled area. When they persisted, he exiled them to New Mexico on a mandatory retreat and suspended four other priests who protested his action publicly.[20] Other bishops claimed that the Church's support for social justice did not allow it to align itself with "a particular union, owner organization or other secular enterprise."[21] San Francisco Archbishop John J. Mitty had abandoned that neutrality when he authorized the Mission Band in 1949. Eventually, however, when the powerful prelate was dying, other California bishops denounced the Mission Band. The 1960s and 1970s would push the bishops into a stronger commitment, in the fields as well as in the cities.

The historic event that forced the change occurred on September 16, 1965, when the National Farm Workers Association led by Cesar Chavez gathered in Guadalupe Church hall in Delano, California, and voted to go on strike. From the beginning, members of the Migrant Ministry of the National Council of Churches walked alongside the workers in the picket lines. Because of pressure from the growers, who threatened to stop contributing, parish priests did not stand with the strikers. The hapless priest who had allowed the farm workers to use the church hall was criticized so severely he had to take a long vacation in Spain. Chavez asked why Protestants, demanding nothing, came to serve the workers while parish priests remained in their churches. In response, Bishop Timothy Manning, of the diocese of Fresno, appointed Father Mark Day as chaplain of the farm workers.

Priests from religious orders or national organizations and women in religious congregations led the involvement of the Church. In December 1965, Father James L. Vizzard, S.J., executive secretary of the National Catholic Rural Life Conference came to Delano with a committee consisting of eleven prominent Catholic, Protestant, and Jewish clergy. The committee urged the farm workers to continue their struggle and criticized growers, local clergy, and community leaders who failed to appear at a scheduled meeting. Another influential priest who committed early to the farm workers' cause was Monsignor George Higgins, secretary of research of the U.S. Catholic Conference.

Chavez gradually won support by utilizing the symbols of his faith. In 1966, holding aloft a cross and a banner of Our Lady of Guadalupe, he and sixty strikers made a three-hundred-mile, twenty-five-day march to Sacramento. As they were nearing their destination, they won their first contract. In 1968, he undertook a twenty-five-day lenten fast which drew wide attention.

The following year, efforts were made to obtain the bishops' support for the farm workers' international grape boycott. But the bishops, prone to caution, voted instead to establish the Ad Hoc Committee on Farm Labor. The committee, led by Auxiliary Bishop Joseph F. Donnelly of Hartford, Conn., with Monsignor George Higgins of the USCC serving as consultant and Monsignor Roger Mahony of Fresno as its secretary, offered to mediate the dispute with the grape growers. Through their efforts, most of the grape growers signed three-year contracts and the strike came to an end. By then, Chavez's union had almost one hundred contracts.

In the next few years, however, the growers and the Teamsters Union reneged on agreements and conspired to defeat the farm workers union. The farm workers went on strike again. In 1973, representatives of the Conference of Major Superiors of Men and individual bishops walked the picket lines. Priests went to jail with workers for ignoring unconstitutional court injunctions.

Finally, in 1973, the bishops voted to support the farm workers' grape and lettuce boycotts and asked for secret, free elections in the farm dispute in California. Later they supported legislation in California to establish the Agricultural Labor Relations Board that would mediate disputes between the union and the growers. Mahony, by then the auxiliary bishop of Fresno, became the head of the board. Thinking the problems had been solved, the bishops disbanded their committee on farm labor in 1974. But the billion-dollar agricultural industry, in alliance with conservative politicians, was able to neutralize the board in a few years. By then, the bishops had moved on to other concerns. Though the struggle yielded some residual benefits, such as higher wages, the farm workers union had only 27,000 workers under contract in 1992. Chavez, who claimed the union still had 100,000 members, was trying to build support for another grape boycott.

Individual bishops made their own option for poor Hispanics, sometimes with regional or national support from the bishops' conference. That occurred after 1972, when the largely Mexican-American workers at the Farah Manufacturing Co. went on strike in El Paso. At the time, Farah was one of the largest manufacturers of men's slacks in the United States, with plants in Albuquerque and Las Cruces in New Mexico, and in El Paso, Victoria, and

San Antonio in Texas. Of its 10,400 employees, 85 percent were Mexican-American women who earned an average of $69 a week. The bishop of El Paso, Sidney Metzger, and Father Jesse Muñoz supported the strikers from the first day. Father Muñoz's parish, Our Lady of the Light, became the headquarters of the strike. Metzger wrote a letter to all his brother bishops to endorse a boycott of Farah products. The workers won their struggle to form a union after a judge of the National Labor Relations Board ruled that Farah was violating the rights of the employees and ordered the company to allow the union to operate freely.

Bishop John J. Fitzpatrick of the diocese of Brownsville made his own option for Hispanics, especially the tens of thousands of refugees from Central America who sojourned in his see on their way north during the 1980s. This quiet but courageous prelate faced down immigration authorities by supporting Casa Oscar Romero, a refugee center in Brownsville that sheltered as many as five hundred persons at one time. He also backed the hospitality of other groups and individuals who opened their doors to strangers fleeing war, persecution, and want in El Salvador, Guatemala, Nicaragua, and Honduras. He stood by pastoral workers who were jailed for violating immigration laws, and he reoriented all the structures of the diocese to serve the poor, those who live there as well as those coming across the border. At his invitation, hundreds of laypersons also became involved in ministry. Furthermore, he adopted a simple lifestyle worthy of emulation by other bishops. He sold the episcopal mansion, which had its own swimming pool, and moved to an apartment. During the years he was bishop, he took no salary.

In terms of organizing an institutional Hispanic Church, Archbishop Francis J. Furey was the pioneer. He did what no other prelate had ever done: name the first native-born Hispanic bishop. Shortly after being appointed the archbishop of San Antonio in 1969, Furey requested that Father Patricio Flores, a Mexican American, be named his auxiliary. When he was asked to submit two more names, he simply wrote in Flores's name two more times. "If I had three Mexican Americans who were equally qualified, I would write them all down," he explained.[22] He was determined that his auxiliary should be a Texan, and, in his mind, Flores had no rivals. Thus on May 5, 1970, Flores, a former migrant worker who had dropped out of school in the tenth grade, was ordained a bishop.

Symbolically, at least, the Hispanic Church was then complete; it had laity, women religious, Brothers, priests, and a bishop, a man

responsive to the needs of his times. During the first few years following his elevation, Flores functioned as the unofficial shepherd
of the Hispanic people in the United States. Once again as when
he was a boy, he followed the migrant trail to the Midwest and
Northwest, visiting squalid camps, celebrating Mass, and counsel-
ing the workers. When Cesar Chavez was jailed for ignoring an
unconstitutional court injunction, Flores went to visit him. When
he found himself in Los Angeles early in 1970 during a massive
march protesting the disproportionate Hispanic casualties in the
Vietnam war, he was the only bishop who met with the leaders of
the march, called the Vietnam War Moratorium, for which he was
rebuked by Cardinal Timothy Manning.

Flores spoke out against unprovoked or excessive police violence and defended persons unjustly accused of crimes. Once he
raffled off his episcopal ring for $2,200 to defend a twenty-one-
year-old man charged with a murder he did not commit. For years,
he was chair of the Texas Advisory Committee to the U.S. Commission on Civil Rights. He defended undocumented immigrants
and founded the first diocesan office in the Southwest to deal with
the problems of immigrants. In 1975, he established the National
Hispanic Scholarship Fund, which by 1992 had raised millions of
dollars in college scholarships. He persuaded Furey to support the
founding of Communities Organized for Public Service (COPS),
a community organization that became a model for a half-dozen
other cities in the Southwest.

All this activity occurred during the eight years that Flores was
an auxiliary to Furey. In 1978, Flores was made the bishop of El
Paso and, the following year, after the death of Furey, he became
the archbishop of San Antonio. His new responsibilities limited his
travels and reduced his involvement beyond his diocese, but by
then there were other Hispanic bishops who could fulfill that role.

Between 1970 and 1992, twenty-two other Hispanics were ordained bishops, almost half of them immigrants or from Puerto
Rico. Nine became ordinaries, all but two native born. In 1991,
however, Jesús Madera, the bishop of Fresno, had to give up his
post following an episcopal investigation of financial problems in
the diocese. He became part of the military ordinariate. One bishop,
Alphonse Gallegos, was killed in an auto accident in 1991.

Most of the Hispanic bishops have contributed in some way to
the organization of a Hispanic Church. Those who were ordinaries
hired Hispanics for important positions in the chanceries. Some
have spoken out courageously on social issues. Most, if not all, had

encouraged the retention or recovery of religiosity, language, and culture. Most won the respect of their own people. A few seemed unsure as to whether they had a special role vis-à-vis Hispanics. Consequently, they were never heard from on issues important to the community.

Some bishops have responded with great courage in times of crisis. One was Agustín Roman, auxiliary bishop of Miami. When Cubans rioted in federal prisons in Louisiana and Georgia in the late 1980s, he went to the prisons and negotiated a peaceful settlement. The inmates rebelled when they were told they would be deported to Cuba. He persuaded them to surrender their arms in return for a promise that their cases would get another hearing. Archbishop Robert Sanchez of Santa Fe tried with less success to mediate a state prison riot that left thirty-three inmates dead and ninety severely injured.

Efforts by others to speak for the poor were less successful. When ordained bishop, on June 21, 1974, Gilbert Chavez, auxiliary of the diocese of San Diego, said: "I have accepted the challenge to serve the poor, the Spanish speaking, the Indians, the blacks and other minorities." Unfortunately, he did not have an ordinary like Flores; in a few years he was effectively silenced, shunted off to serve as pastor of a border parish, though he continued to work quietly with Hispanic ministers throughout the diocese. A few others—notably Juan Arzube, auxiliary bishop of Los Angeles— also took prophetic stances that were criticized by their brother bishops, which may have dimmed their chances of promotion.

While Flores and a few others distinguished themselves for their stands on social justice, Sanchez made his mark for his work in the institutional Church. He reconciled the Penitentes, as the members of the Fraternidad Piadosa of Jesús Nazareno were known. A group of lay leaders who had done much to preserve the faith of the people during difficult times, they had been alienated from the church since the 1850s. He also revived many of the religious traditions of the people in isolated villages of the arch-diocese. He reversed the trend toward closing mission churches in small communities and reformed the seminary to make it more responsive to Spanish and Indian cultures. On a national level, he headed the Bishops' Ad Hoc Committee for Hispanic Affairs for fourteen years, giving strong support to the encuentro and other initiatives of the Secretariat for Hispanic Affairs.

Collectively, the Hispanic bishops had not organized effectively within the National Conference of Catholic Bishops. One of them said in the early 1990s that, far from forming an effective lobby, they had difficulty even in getting together for a meeting. Reflecting their varied backgrounds, they did not share the same views on culture, politics, the nation's policy towards Latin America, or the historic destiny of Hispanics in the United States. As Spaniards, Mexicans, Cubans, and Latin Americans, they did not think alike on many issues. The bishops were more successful in forming regional support groups. One consisted of bishops, both Anglo and Hispanic, in New Mexico, Colorado, part of Texas, and Arizona who met periodically. In the Northeast, the Hispanic bishops wrote joint pastoral letters to their people.

The Hispanic bishops, however, did come together to write a pastoral letter, *The Bishops Speak with the Virgin*, in 1982. Perhaps that example inspired the National Conference of Catholic Bishops to issue its own pastoral letter, *The Hispanic Presence: Challenge and Commitment*, in 1983. It was an historic document. In the past, the bishops, singly and collectively, had looked upon Hispanics as the cause of many problems; now they saw them in a completely different light.

"At this moment of grace we recognize the Hispanic community among us as a blessing from God," the pastoral began. "We call upon all persons of good faith to share our vision of the special gifts that Hispanics bring to the Body of Christ. . . . This Hispanic presence challenges us all to be more *catholic*, more open to the diversity of religious expression."[23] The bishops praised Hispanic Catholics for wanting to share their historical, cultural, and religious gifts and pledged to assist them in doing so.

The bishops urged all Catholics to respond "innovatively, flexibly and immediately"[24] to the Hispanic presence. They expressed their support for pastoral activity carried out in community, Spanish and bilingual worship according to the traditions and customs of the people being served, the proclamation of the word in "powerful, new, liberating images," and, among other creative possibilities, a catechesis that would be not only in Spanish but in "active dialogue with their culture and their needs."[25]

The pastoral signaled an end to the policy of assimilation or Americanization. From then on, Hispanics would have their own place in the Church. In the bishops' conference, for example, it became a given that the Bishops' Committee for the Church in Latin America should be headed by a Hispanic. The same policy applied to the Bishops' Committee for Hispanic Affairs, which had finally shed its ad hoc status and become a permanent committee in 1988.

By 1992, however, only one Hispanic, Sanchez, had served as an officer of the bishops' conference; he was elected secretary in 1991.

THE CLERGY AND RELIGIOUS

Historically, the experience of attending the seminary or of training to become a Sister or a Brother had deprived Hispanics of their culture. The experience of Father Ricardo Chavez, who became director of the West Coast regional office for Hispanics, was typical. The son of Mexican immigrants, Chavez grew up and went through the seminary in California. In the process, he said, he lost his identity as a Hispanic almost entirely. "When I was ordained I did not feel comfortable working with Hispanic people," he said. "I did not know how to work with them and, as a result, I did not want to. The process of losing my identity had not been a conscious decision. It was simply the result of the environment in which one lived."[26] Many others, though disposed to serve their people, were not allowed to do so. "In my first parish in Los Angeles I was not permitted to celebrate Mass or preach in Spanish in spite of the fact that 80 percent of the confessions I heard each week were in Spanish," said Father Juan Romero in discussing his service in East Los Angeles' St. Alphonsus parish.[27]

In the 1960s and 1970s, however, these Hispanic priests and Sisters rediscovered their roots and decided they ought to be serving their own people. But their superiors were often not sympathetic to their requests for reassignment. Cardinal John Cody of Chicago rejected the request of Servite Father Alberto Gallegos and of another priest to be reassigned to Hispanic ministry. Gallegos nevertheless eventually succeeded and ended up working in New Mexico. Sister Petra Chavez, who grew up in Ohio and was teaching in a Catholic school there, had to leave her congregation and join another, the Sisters of Mercy, who assigned her to work in California with Salvadoran refugees. Jerry Barnes, a Mexican American who became the auxiliary bishop of the diocese of San Bernardino in 1992, had been dismissed without any explanation from a religious order when he was a year short of ordination. He thought it was because of his insistence that he be assigned to work among Hispanics.[28] Accepted by Archbishop Flores, he was ordained a diocesan priest in San Antonio.

Those priests, Sisters, and Brothers who won reassignment created and staffed institutions and organizations to serve Hispanics and the Church as a whole, among them the Mexican-American Cultural Center, the regional pastoral centers, the Committee of Religious in Hispanic Ministry, and the National Advisory Committee for the Secretariat for Hispanics. They also constituted the core of the planning teams for the encuentros. The naming of Hispanic bishops was a result of their efforts, much more so than any urgency the Church may have felt. In Chicago, for example, a handful of Hispanic priests organized the Comité Guadalupano and made news in 1973 with their request to Cardinal Cody that a Hispanic bishop be named to serve the city's 500,000 Spanish-speaking people. Though the Cardinal curtly rejected their demand, Hispanics in that city got an auxiliary bishop in the 1980s, Claretian Plácido Rodríguez.

PADRES (an acronym for Padres Asociados para Derechos Religiosos, Educativos, y Sociales, Priests United for Religious, Economic, and Social Rights), was organized by fifty Mexican-American priests who met in San Antonio on October 7–9, 1969. At a press conference, they announced that their new national organization would transmit "the cry of our people to the decision makers of the Catholic Church in America." Voicing the option the encuentros would make later, PADRES emphasized it would be "the voice of the voiceless."[29] One of twenty-seven resolutions that its members submitted to the National Conference of Catholic Bishops later that fall asked that native Hispanic bishops be named in areas with heavy concentrations of Spanish-speaking people. Privately, they asked leaders of the hierarchy about the process of naming bishops and then began making nominations.

For a small organization, members of PADRES were ubiquitous. In August 1970, they ministered to the dying and wounded when police in Los Angeles attacked 30,000 people who marched in the Vietnam War Moratorium parade. They walked the picket lines with Cesar Chavez's United Farm Workers in the grape and lettuce fields of California. During the bishops' 1973 annual meeting in Washington, Father Juan Romero, the executive director, lobbied for Hispanic bishops. In New Mexico, they took part in the meetings of the Federal Alliance of Land Grants, led by Reies López Tijerina, then trying to recover land grants illegally taken from Hispanics.

Hispanic Sisters organized Las Hermanas on April 2–4, 1971, when fifty women religious from eight states gathered in Houston, Texas. Their stated purpose was to achieve "more effective and active service to the Hispanic people using the expertise, knowledge and experience of religious women in the fields of education, health, pastoral work and sociology."[30] The Sisters said they were greatly concerned "with the plight of La Raza and are determined to better our efforts to meet their needs."

Las Hermanas took up the cause of 1,000 Mexican nuns who worked in seminaries, retreat houses, and convents in the U.S. doing housekeeping, cooking, and other domestic service, earning as little as $50 a month. Their income was sent to Mexico to support their impoverished congregations. Even though, according to Las Hermanas, half of those Mexican nuns would rather have done catechetical work with Spanish-speaking people, they remained in domestic service. Las Hermanas also lobbied for Hispanic bishops, trained leaders in the barrios, served as faculty at the Mexican American Cultural Center, and gave leadership workshops in many parts of the country.

The activism of Hispanic clergy and religious men and women led to tensions and frustrations that caused some of the best people to leave active ministry, a major loss for the Church. Capable leaders who remained found that because they had challenged the Church they would not be elevated to the episcopacy.

In the Northeast and in Florida, Hispanic priests established the Association of Hispanic Priests (ASH). Unlike PADRES, whose members were native-born priests, many of the members of ASH were immigrants, particularly from Spain. Perhaps for that reason, ASH was much less activist than PADRES. ASH promoted the rights of its own members in the institutions of the Church rather than advocating for the Hispanic population as a whole.

Structures Founded by Hispanics

Training was necessary not only for new lay ministers but also for clergy, nuns, and Brothers reassigned to Hispanic ministry. Many of them had forgotten their culture and no longer spoke Spanish. Furthermore, the challenges could not be met by Hispanics alone. Other clergy and religious men and women had to be involved. That insight was not new. Since its founding in 1957, the Institute of Cultural Communication of the archdiocese of New York had sent priests to Puerto Rico, the Dominican Republic, and Colombia for a course on language and culture. By the end of the 1970s, about six hundred priests and two hundred Sisters knew at least some Spanish.[31] What was different was that the Mexican

American Cultural Center (MACC) and the other pastoral centers were founded by Hispanics themselves.

Father Virgilio Elizondo, son of a San Antonio storekeeper, said the thought of founding an institute for Hispanic ministry came to him while he was teaching at the Incarnate Word Pastoral Institute in San Antonio in 1970. When the idea was proposed at a PADRES retreat in Santa Fe, New Mexico, early in 1971, the members responded enthusiastically. In September of that year, the Texas Catholic Conference gave its unanimous approval. With Archbishop Furey heading the steering committee and Bishop Flores serving as chair of the board of directors, the center opened its doors in June 1972.

MACC became a national center for training in Hispanic ministry. It served as the entry point for Latin America's liberation theology; Gustavo Gutiérrez, its leading light, came regularly to give courses, as did many other scholars. In its first ten years, 9,000 persons, half of them Anglos—laypersons, clergy, and religious—took short or long courses in Hispanic ministry. These dealt with culture, pastoral service, preparation of missionaries for Latin America, pastoral Spanish, research and publications, leadership development, and media. Though funding difficulties had reduced both staff and input from Latin America, the center was still going strong as it celebrated its twentieth anniversary in 1992.

For Elizondo, president of MACC for fifteen years, what made the center special was that while Hispanics predominated, both among the staff and on the board of directors, it avoided being a ghetto by having Anglos working alongside them on the faculty. Hispanics set the agenda, gave the place its atmosphere, its values and culture. Clearly, this was their institution. At the same time, MACC had to be responsive to the bishops of Texas, who sent their pastoral ministers to study there, and to religious congregations, orders, societies, and foundations that provided about half the funds needed to run it. When Elizondo gave up the presidency, he was succeeded by Father Rosendo Urrabazo, at young Claretian and native of San Antonio who continued the same policies.

The other pastoral centers—in the Southeast, Northeast, Midwest, and West Coast—were more regional in scope, but a Hispanic presence prevailed among both the students and faculty. MACC and the other centers defined, for themselves and for the Church as a whole, the ministry their people would receive.

The concern for training also led to the founding of the Committee of Religious in Hispanic Ministry (CORHIM), which first appeared in 1981. Modeled on a process started by the Latin American Confederation of Religious (CLAR), consisting of members of women's congregations and men's religious orders, CORHIM offered an intensive three-week seminar of renewal for members of religious orders. The process began with an analysis of the reality of the participants, then constructed a frame of reference anchored on cultural, social, and religious life and concluded with a concrete plan by each participant to improve his or her ministry to Hispanics. Six such workshops had been held throughout the country by 1992.

CORHIM was started by three nuns who attended the CLAR workshop in Cuernavaca, Mexico, in 1979. As the project to which they committed themselves as part of the process, Consuelo Tovar, a Daughter of Charity, Corina Padilla, a Dominican, and Elisa Rodriguez, a Sister of Loretto, began organizing CORHIM and preparing the first seminar in the U.S. The following year, Carmelite Father Vicente Lopez attended the CLAR workshop in Paraguay and became an active member of the committee. Sister Carmen Aurora, a member of a Mexican congregation who was then teaching at the Mexican American Cultural Center and had been instrumental in starting the CLAR seminar in Latin America, played a central role in the early seminars. Passionist Father Clemente Barron, who joined the team about the same time, helped coordinate all of the seminars.

Religious orders established their own structures for Hispanic ministry, among the most notable being the Jesuits, the Claretians, and the Basilians. The Jesuits organized a Hispanic ministry conference that met every two years and drew participation from members who worked with Hispanics throughout the nation. Their ministries emphasized community organization, services to refugees from Central America, especially on the West Coast, and education. They also staffed important parishes in such cities as San Antonio, Los Angeles, Houston, and El Paso. Dioceses, religious orders, and congregations established special houses of formation for Hispanic vocations.

The Claretians dedicated themselves to Hispanic ministry in Chicago and Los Angeles, while the Basilians served Hispanics in Detroit, Houston, and other Texas cities. In the archdiocese of Denver, the Theatine Fathers, an Italian order, served the most important Hispanic parishes.

Some of the Hispanic bishops came from religious orders that made special commitments to Hispanic ministry. Ricardo Ramírez, the bishop of Las Cruces, is a Basilian; Plácido Rodriguez, auxiliary in the archdiocese of Chicago, is a Claretian; Enrique San Pedro, ordinary of Brownsville, Alvaro Corrada, auxiliary in the archdiocese of Washington, and Carlos A. Sevilla, auxiliary in the archdiocese of San Francisco, are Jesuits.

With a $10,000 grant from the Sisters of Mercy of the Americas, Joaquín Domínguez, a Salvadoran refugee layman, founded the Carecen centers, located in New York, Houston, Los Angeles, San Francisco, and Washington to serve refugees from Central America. Partially supported by the dioceses, these centers offer many social services. The Brownsville diocese's Casa Oscar Romero, which served thousands of refugees from Central America during the 1980s, was also founded by Hispanic laypersons and was later turned over to the diocese. Refugio del Rio Grande, a farm community for refugees outside of Harlingen, Texas, was founded by Pio Celestino, a Peruvian immigrant, and Lisa Brodiaga, an American immigration lawyer.

The charismatic movement received strong support from Hispanics. Hundreds of prayer groups were organized throughout the country. In the Los Angeles area alone, an estimated 60,000 people, most of Mexican origin, took part in the movement's activities in the 1980s. Many were associated with Charisma in Missions, led by Marilynn Kramar, an Assembly of God minister in South America before she became a convert to Catholicism. Its facilities, located in East Los Angeles, drew hundreds of Hispanics each weekend. Kramar said that Charisma in Missions touched the lives of 500,000 people each year.[32]

The Instituto de Liturgia Hispana, organized at the Mexican American Cultural Center in the late 1970s at the urging of Jesuit Father John Gallen, had a membership of about one hundred by 1989. It assisted the Bishops' Committee on Liturgy in its work. A committee headed by Bishop Ricardo Ramírez adapted many official texts for Spanish liturgy. The Northeast Pastoral Center produced a Spanish-language lectionary for use among the Spanish speaking in the United States.

In 1988, Jesuit Father Allan Figueroa Deck, then at the Jesuit School of Theology at Berkeley, California, organized the Academy of Hispanic Theologians. By mid-1989 it had identified eighty Hispanics with the doctoral degree required for membership, and half of them had joined the organization. A major objective of the academy was to develop an indigenous Hispanic theology in the United States.

Not all these organizations and institutes seem destined for a long life span. The refugee organizations will probably disappear when the civil wars end in Central America and the refugees stop coming. By the mid-1980s, PADRES appeared to have lost its raison d'être; by 1992, it has all but disappeared, with most of its remaining members becoming part of a new organization called Asociación Nacional de Sacerdotes Hispanos (ANSH, the National Association of Hispanic Priests). PADRES's historic moment of truth had come in 1981 when, at a meeting in El Paso, members had defeated by a single vote a proposal to admit laypersons. Las Hermanas, on the other hand, had voted to admit laywomen, but, ironically, they, too, seemed to have lost their way by 1992. Though the organization was alive and vital, it focused more on issues of feminism than on the goals of its founders.

In 1990, a group of Hispanic leaders took a step described as the coming of age of Hispanics in the Church.[33] They organized the National Catholic Council for Hispanic Ministry (NCCHM), a consortium of movements, organizations, institutes, regional offices for Hispanic ministry, and religious congregations. Eighteen regional and national groups founded the council. By 1992 membership had grown to thirty-three organizations. The council's first congress, held in Los Angeles in August 1992, drew about 750 participants from throughout the nation. Under the theme of the evangelization of cultures in the context of the fifth centenary, they focused on evangelization, education, political participation, medical care, and the family.

The leadership of NCCHM came from the national, regional, and diocesan offices for the Hispanic apostolate and particularly from the National Advisory Committee to the Secretariat for Hispanic Affairs. Deck, coordinator of the Hispanic program of the Center for Pastoral Studies of Loyola-Marymount University, Los Angeles, was elected president; Esther Lucero, director of the Multicultural Pastoral Office of the archdiocese of Seattle, vice president; Father Juan Díaz Vilar, S.J., of the Northeast Pastoral Center, secretary; and Father Mario Vizcaíno, Sch.P., director of the Southeast Pastoral Institute, treasurer.

The organization of NCCHM was considered historic because, for the first time, leaders in Church organizations took the initiative in organizing the council and its national meeting. Up to then, all their organizations, movements, and institutes had been established by Hispanics with episcopal approval, or founded by the Church at the request of Hispanics. Nevertheless, the organization welcomed episcopal participation at its first congress and invited dioceses to send delegates.

The organization of the council stirred concern in the Bishops' Committee for Hispanic Affairs. One member challenged the right of the founding groups to organize without episcopal permission. But such organization was sanctioned and encouraged by Vatican II in its document on the laity. One or more bishops in the committee were also unhappy that Archbishop Edward A. McCarthy of Miami had signed the Council's incorporation papers. Other bishops, Hispanic and non-Hispanic, saw positive benefits. Cardinal Roger Mahony, in particular, was enthusiastic, and his early support ensured the success of the congress.

The tensions in the Bishops' Committee for Hispanic Affairs arose in part because the organization of the council was seen as a reaction to an action the committee had taken. Some of the NCCHM organizers had been members of the National Advisory Committee (NAC), which had advised the Secretariat for Hispanic Affairs and the Bishops' Committee for Hispanic Affairs. NAC had become increasingly critical of the bishops' failure to allocate funds to implement the national pastoral plan for Hispanic ministry that they had approved in 1987. As a result, the Bishops' Committee for Hispanic Affairs, then headed by Bishop Raymundo Peña of El Paso, abolished NAC and replaced it with five consultants. But, though the abolishment of NAC may have been the immediate catalyst for the organization of NCCHM, it had been under discussion for years among leaders of Hispanic organizations.

CHANGE AT THE LOCAL LEVEL

The rapid growth of the Hispanic population since 1965 has created significant changes in many parts of the country. In a 1990 survey by the Secretariat for Hispanic Affairs, twelve dioceses disclosed that more than half of their members were Hispanic.[34] Several others in the same category did not respond to the survey, among them the archdiocese of Miami, which is 60 percent Hispanic. Another twenty-seven dioceses were more than one-fourth Hispanic.[35]

At the parish level, a less visible, but perhaps ultimately more important, organization, or reorganization, was taking place. Over the course of a few years many multi-ethnic parishes became almost exclusively Hispanic. In a sense, the historical clock was being turned back; melting-pot parishes were becoming national parishes. In New York City, for example, a Bronx parish where Mexicans predominated developed lively devotion to Our Lady of Guadalupe. In Manhattan, on the other hand, a parish where Dominicans were the majority had a strong devotion to Our Lady of Altagracia. Though the pastors of these parishes were not always Hispanics by ethnicity, they were *hispanos de corazón*—a distinction due not only to a better appreciation of what Hispanics had to offer the Church but also to the great emphasis given to Hispanic ministry.

In some areas, one could identify not only Hispanic parishes but an entire Church, with numerous pastors and chancery officials. One of these was the archdiocese of Santa Fe, which according to one bishop has more native-born Hispanic priests than any other diocese.[36] Another was the archdiocese of Miami, where 49 of the 135 priests who accompanied the Cuban exodus went to work. Two high schools for boys and one for girls, staffed by priests, Sisters, and Brothers from Cuba, were constructed in the early 1960s. Eleven new parishes were created for the refugees. Bilingual programs became an integral part of the curriculum of the Catholic schools, where 45 percent of the students were Spanish-speaking by 1975. Spanish-speaking associate directors and staff members were appointed to major departments of the chancery. Laypersons started more than a half-dozen apostolic movements. The archdiocesan seminary also became bilingual and bicultural, a model for the rest of the nation.[37]

Other areas had their special parishes that drew Hispanics from far beyond the parish boundaries. Our Lady Queen of the Angels, administered by Claretians in Los Angeles' historic district, drew attendance from all over the metropolitan region. Each Sunday there were eleven Masses, with a total attendance of 11,000. Two hundred baptisms and several dozen weddings took place each weekend. It was one of two parishes in the Los Angeles area, the other being Dolores Mission in Boyle Heights, that in the late 1980s declared themselves sanctuaries for both refugees and undocumented immigrants. In Denver, Our Lady of Guadalupe, administered by Theatine priests, served the same role, as did San Antonio's San Fernando Cathedral, whose rector was Father Virgilio Elizondo, a theologian and former president of the Mexican American Cultural Center.

In the late 1970s, St. Joseph parish in Saginaw, Michigan drew Hispanics from a large area. Eighty percent of the participants in worship and other activities were from outside the parish. Because of declining enrollment, the parish had closed its high school and then its grade school. The buildings were turned into an alternative school for dropouts, attended by five hundred students, and into a two-year extension college, with another five hundred enrolled. La Rondalla of St. Joseph, a group of musicians and dancers who performed at the Spanish liturgies, was famous for miles around. The parish's most important event each year was the novena to Our Lady of Guadalupe; Hispanics from surrounding communities gathered at the church for nine consecutive nights for Mass, plays, pageantry, fiestas, and talks by a visiting priest or bishop from Mexico or the Southwest. In 1992, the ethnic composition of the parish was 85 percent Mexican American, 10 percent African American, and five percent Euro-American.[38]

Unfortunately, shrinking resources were having an adverse impact on Hispanics. At St. Joseph parish in Saginaw, cutbacks in federal funding in the 1980s forced the closing of the alternative school and extension college. When financial difficulties forced the archdioceses of Chicago and Detroit to consolidate many inner city parishes in the late 1980s and early 1990s, Hispanic churches were often those that were closed.

In San Antonio, a barrio federation of local parishes and Protestant churches that called itself Communities Organized for Public Service (COPS) brought many improvements to parish life. Utilizing the tactics of Saul Alinsky's Industrial Areas Foundation, COPS gave political power to the poor. Its organizer, Ernie Cortez, built the organization by discovering and training the natural leaders in the parishes and churches; as a result, the parishes gained many benefits.

At St. Timothy's parish in San Antonio's impoverished West Side, Sunday Mass attendance went from 700 to 1,300 in five years. People came from all over the city and even from out of town. The catechetical program created by the parish staff was being used in four neighboring parishes. Volunteer lay leaders ran many of the activities of the parish. Instead of being a rubber stamp for the pastor, the parish council really administered the parish. Even the Mass was changed. "We devised a liturgy like a community meeting," Father Al Benavides, then the pastor, said. "Part of it is for people to come up and make announcements. The Mass becomes the way through which we communicate."[39]

Just as Cuban immigrants built a Hispanic Church in South Florida, Mexicans played an important role in the Southwest. On visits to Mexico, Archbishop Patricio Flores of San Antonio kept an eye open for potential vocations and over the years eighteen of these Mexicans were ordained to serve Hispanics in the United States. Besides the Guadalupana Missioners of the Holy Spirit, who work in Los Angeles, the Cordi-Marian Sisters established themselves in Chicago and San Antonio, and Mexican Carmelites in Houston. Individuals also made significant contributions. Sister Rosa Marta Zárate, for example, formed Christian base communities in the diocese of San Bernardino. Texan Carlos Rosas gained fame as a composer of music in popular Mexican-American style.

By the 1990s, Hispanics were making their presence felt in other ways. They were beginning to develop their own theology, a liturgy "unabashedly affective or emotive,"[40] and their own media. Los Angeles, Chicago, and Miami had established diocesan newspapers in Spanish, and many other dioceses had special sections or supplements in their newspapers. Books on history, theology, and ministry were appearing regularly by the 1990s.

In the quarter century beginning in 1965, Hispanics in the United States slowly but inexorably began assuming charge of their own destiny in the Church. Hispanics, no longer simply the objects of mission, were now contributing to ministry, both to their own people and to the larger Church. At the same time, the Church at large was latinizing—preparing itself better to serve the surging Hispanic population. In 1990, 40 percent of the dioceses required all priesthood candidates to study Spanish and some, like Los Angeles, made knowledge of Spanish a requirement for ordination. Dioceses, religious orders, and congregations were investing more resources and personnel in ministry to Hispanics. It was the time of *La Raza* in the Church, a time of growth, optimism, and opportunity.

NOTES

1. I am not suggesting the creation of a Church in a theological sense but, rather, that Hispanics have begun to put their own stamp on the Church, thus making it their own.

2. Bishop's Committee for the Spanish Speaking, "National Council for the Spanish-Speaking," *Progress Report*, 1962, p. 26.

3. Ibid.

4. Moisés Sandoval, ed., *Fronteras, a History of the Hispanic Church in the USA since 1513* (San Antonio: Mexican American Cultural Center,

1983), p. 418, citing Raymond McGowan, "History and Necessity of the Catholic Council for the Spanish-speaking," *Proceedings of the Tenth Annual Conference* (April 1960), p. 30.

5. Ibid., p. 422.

6. Southwest Regional Office for the Spanish Speaking, "Program Overview and Annual Report," March 27, 1976.

7. Moisés Sandoval, "Optimism Runneth Over," *Revista Maryknoll*, July 1989, p. 26.

8. Ana María Díaz-Stevens, *Oxcart Catholicism on Fifth Avenue: The Impact of the Puerto Rican Migration upon the Archdiocese of New York* (Notre Dame, Ind.: University of Notre Dame Press, 1993), p. 200. The dioceses, besides New York, were Bridgeport, Brooklyn, Newark, Paterson, Rockville Centre, Trenton, Boston, Camden, and Hartford.

9. Sandoval, "Optimism," p. 26.

10. Letter from Lupe Anguiano to Bishop James Rausch, January 9, 1976.

11. Moisés Sandoval, ed., *The Mexican American Experience in the Church* (New York: Sadlier Books, 1983), p. 25.

12. Sedillo, interview with author, July 1992.

13. Proceedings of the First National Encuentro, address by Bishop Patricio Flores, June 1972.

14. Sandoval, *Fronteras*, citing Archbishop James V. Casey, "Church Concerned," *Denver Catholic Register*, March 29, 1973.

15. The precise origin of the term *Chicano* is unknown, but it gained currency in the urban barrios after World War II and was used by activists to describe themselves and their colleagues.

16. Memo to bishops of region 10 from Lupe Anguiano, July 1, 1977.

17. Moisés Sandoval, *On the Move: A History of the Hispanic Church in the United States* (Maryknoll, N.Y.: Orbis, 1990), pp. 82–83.

18. Sandoval, "Optimism Runneth Over."

19. Father Mario Vizcaíno, interview with author, January 1992.

20. Sandoval, *Fronteras*, p. 383; Patrick H. McNamara, "Dynamics of the Catholic Church: From Pastoral to Social Concern," in Leo Grebler, Joan W. Moore, and Ralph C. Guzman, eds., *The Mexican American People: The Nation's Second Largest Minority* (New York: The Free Press, 1970), p. 465.

21. Ibid., p. 383.

22. Archbishop Francis J. Furey, interview with author.

23. National Conference of Catholic Bishops, *The Hispanic Presence: Challenge and Commitment*, Dec. 12, 1983 (Washington, D.C.: United States Catholic Conference, 1983), p. 3.

24. Ibid., p. 13.

25. Ibid., p. 14.

26. Moisés Sandoval, "The Long Road Back," *Revista Maryknoll*, September 1989.

27. Father Juan Romero, interview with author.

28. Father Jerry Barnes, interview with author.

29. Sandoval, *On the Move*, p. 66.

30. Sandoval, *On the Move*, p. 68.

31. Sandoval, *On the Move*, p. 95.

32. Marilynn Kramar, interview with author in 1986.

33. Araceli M. Cantero, "Católicos hispanos alcanzan 'mayoría de edad,'" *La voz católica*, January 31, 1991.

34. The twelve dioceses with a membership more than half Hispanic were Brooklyn, Yakima, Tucson, Las Cruces, El Paso, Lubbock, San Angelo, Brownsville, Amarillo, Los Angeles, San Antonio, and Santa Fe.

35. Laurie Hansen, "Hispanic Population Growing in Dioceses," *Denver Catholic Register*, November 14, 1990.

36. Bishop Ricardo Ramírez, conversation with author, April 1992.

37. Sandoval, *On the Move*, p. 107.

38. Leonard Armstrong, "St. Joseph Parish, Saginaw: The Hispanic Story," unpublished paper, Summer, 1992.

39. Moisés Sandoval, *Hispanic Challenges to the Church* (Washington, D.C.: Secretariat for Hispanic Affairs, 1978), p. 42.

40. Allan Figueroa Deck, "Proselytism and Hispanic Catholics: How Long Do We Cry Wolf?" *America*, December 10, 1988, pp. 485ff.

5

The Context and Development of
Hispanic Ecclesial Leadership

Marina Herrera

The decade of the 1960s brought momentous political, social, religious, and technological changes to this hemisphere and to the world. Many of these developments had a significant and immediate impact on the Hispanic community in the United States in its size, visibility, identity, and diversification. In the thirty-year period investigated in this study (1960–1990), the official number of Hispanics climbed from 6.9 million to 22.4 million, according to the reports from the Bureau of the Census. This increase, together with the rise in visible and prominent leadership—both within and outside the Church—and the diversification of the Hispanic community, has given impetus to an intense process of ecclesial examination of pastoral practices, search for new strategies, creation of new structures and models for serving Hispanics, and preparation of personnel to carry out the Church's mission among and through them.

The most obvious result of this scrutiny and creativity has been the birth, adolescence, and coming of age of Hispanic Catholic leadership. That leadership began toddling in 1945, held by the hand of some concerned bishops, none of whom were Hispanic.[1] That budding leadership has walked far and wide from its original Texas location, has made significant contributions to the religious landscape of this country, and has been on an intensive journey since the issuing of the *National Pastoral Plan for Hispanic Ministry* (1987), without peaking yet. If we can make projections about the future that are based on what has happened in the last thirty years, this coming of age of Hispanic Catholic leadership and of other Hispanic Christians will, in the next century, redefine the dynamics not only of the Catholic Church but of most Christian Churches in the United States. There are plenty of signs that this redefinition is already taking place in the many efforts that Hispanic and many

166

non-Hispanic Church leaders are making to reassess, readjust, and reshape all aspects of the Church's life in view of the growing Hispanic presence.

This essay's goal is to place the development of Hispanic ecclesial leadership in the U.S. within the context of the political, social, technological, and religious developments of the last thirty years and to indicate some of the key leaders, both individuals and institutions. Historical, sociological, and theological perspectives will aid in the process of identifying and characterizing Hispanic ecclesial leadership as it relates to the official Church's structures. We can see how Latin American and Hispanic ecclesial leadership has been an effective bridge between the Church and the peoples of North and South America as well as between non-Hispanic and Hispanic Catholics, and has brought Hispanics in the U.S. from the periphery to the heart of the Church. That leadership has given a face and a history to a group of Catholics that had been almost invisible prior to the late 1960s and has affirmed and nurtured the religious life of the people. In turn, the leadership has been strengthened and inspired by Hispanic faithfulness and devotion to Catholic spirituality, which have revitalized the Church in both innovative and traditional ways. I hope that this study will facilitate the search for ever-more appropriate responses to the pastoral care needs and aspirations of Hispanics as they find their rightful place within the Catholic Church and the society of the United States.

Political and Social Changes

In the political arena, several world events were crucial to the growth of the Hispanic community in the United States. Chief among these were

1. the establishment of the first communist regime in the American continent, led by Fidel Castro in Cuba, and the massive exodus of Cubans into Florida beginning in 1959, still in progress, but at a diminished pace;
2. the election, in 1960, of John F. Kennedy, the first Catholic president of this country, and his fresh and friendly overtures to the Latin American republics. His search for a new relationship with neighbors to the south changed the quota system of immigration to allow the western hemisphere 120,000

arrivals, without a per-country limit or preference system,
and advocating the reunification of families;

3. the 1961 condemnation of apartheid by the United Nations
that gave ethnic and racial minorities the world over a sense
of power and of the rightness of their cause, even in situations
where the unjust treatment of minorities was not as blatant
as in South Africa;

4. the worldwide spectacle of civil rights protesters in the southern states of this nation and their supporters of all races
who joined them, that ended in confrontations among whites,
police, and the marchers. Those confrontations were made
more tragic by the intervention of federal troops and brought
this undemocratic situation into the awareness of peoples of
other nations;

5. the "Freedom March" on Washington in 1963—the symbolic
beginning of a new era in racial relations and minority empowerment in the country—became the model to follow for
other protests here and abroad.

TECHNOLOGICAL ADVANCES

The communications revolution was set in motion when the
U.S. launched its first radio-reflector satellite in 1960 and both
Soviets and Americans sent men into orbit in 1961. These advances
in communications have brought the world to our living rooms,
and our living rooms to the world. The new technology immediately showed minority groups how to air their message beyond the
confines of a city, a state, or a nation. The wide publicity given to
the civil rights marchers and the impact on Americans of all races
of the "I Have a Dream" speech by Martin Luther King, Jr., made
apparent to other minorities and their leaders that raising one's
voice, preferably an eloquent one, could indeed bring attention
to situations of injustice and even bring about changes for the
better. Mexican Americans in the Southwest were awakened by
these events and began their search for "their day in the sun"
that would attain for them similar recognition, participation, and
sharing in political, social, and ecclesial power as that found by
the Afro-American community.

THE VATICAN COUNCIL: SEEDS OF CHANGE FOR HISPANICS

The Hispanic search for recognition, participation, and power found its biggest boost far from its original Texan birthing place, first, with the announcement by John XXIII, on January 25, 1959, of the convening of the first ecumenical council since 1870, and in 1968 with the Second Episcopal Conference of Latin America that met in Medellín.

The purpose of the ecumenical council was to look "to new conditions and forms of life [that have been] introduced into the modern world." Pope John believed that these new conditions within the world could open up new avenues for carrying out the Church's mission.[2] When he met with the council's preparatory commissions on November 14, 1960, he stated:

> We are expecting great things from this Council, which aims at bringing back a greater vigor to faith, to doctrine, to Church discipline and to religious and spiritual life. Furthermore, it aims at making a great contribution toward a reaffirmation of the principles of Christian law that serve as the basis and the framework for the developments of civil, economic, political and social life as well. The law of the Gospel must reach the point where it takes in and penetrates everything, even the things that come to us "from heaven's dew and from the earth's richness."[3]

When the council began, bishops from outside Europe, for the first time in the history of the Church's councils, outnumbered the Europeans. The Latin Americans were the most significant block of outsiders. Pope John's concern to revitalize the spiritual and internal dimensions of the Church had been incorporated in the Dogmatic Constitution on the Church, *Lumen Gentium* (LG), which was debated and approved during the first meetings of the council. The external and structural forms of the Church were still pending at the end of the first session. The need to shape this dimension of the Church was taken up by some influential European bishops—chief among them Cardinals Suenens, Lercaro, Montini, Doepfner, and Léger—and pleadingly affirmed by Bishop Helder Camara of Brazil in the request that the council Fathers deal with the relationship between the Church and the developed and underdeveloped worlds.[4] Those requests, clearly influenced by the concerns of Latin American bishops of which Helder Camara was an admired spokesman, were realized in the establishment of the commission that compiled the issues from which the Pastoral Constitution of the Church in the Modern World, *Gaudium et Spes* (GS), was created.

In its search to redefine the Church, the Second Vatican Council provided comprehensive statements on the Church's nature and mission in the many documents that it debated and approved.[5] When those documents and the spirit of dialogue, examination, and listening were applied and expanded by the bishops of Latin America when they gathered at Medellín, Colombia, they provided a solid base and extraordinarily rich source of inspiration for nurturing the nascent Hispanic leadership in the United States and for shaping the pastoral approach that Hispanic ministry would assume in the coming years. The seminal insights of the council which were fleshed out at Medellín and then transferred and adapted to the Hispanic community in the U.S. help us understand the growth and development of Hispanic ministry in the last thirty years.

Ecclesiological Shifts

1. The Church as mystery

The Church's own view of its mission in the world as expressed by the documents of the council underwent a major theological refocusing. The Church went from a perception of itself as mostly a human hierarchical organization to one which gave a central place to the notion of the Church as a spiritual reality that is not easily contained or explained by its external organizational structure. The Church as presented in *Lumen Gentium* is, first and foremost, mystery; second, people of God; and third, a hierarchical organization. The document intended to show that what all Catholic believers have in common rests on their human dignity prior to any distinction among them due to role or a specific state in life.[6] In this light, the Church's mission is perceived as the vehicle of people's salvation, through Christ and through faith in him carried out by announcing to the world by word and action the message of Christ.[7]

This ecclesiological shift would enable Hispanics to see themselves as legitimate ministers of the gospel without the need to surrender either their attachment to family or their rejection of celibacy as demanded for participation in the ordained ministry.

When the order of deacons was restored after the council, Hispanic men in the U.S. flocked to the preparation programs that were initiated. Today in the U.S., Hispanic men constitute 12 percent of the total number of ordained deacons—1,300 out of 10,400, with some 400 enrolled in diaconate programs in 1992.[8] The significance of this proportion is surprising when considering that Hispanic priests constitute 2 percent of the total number of Catholic priests.

2. The Church as listener

Ecclesiological shifts were also apparent in the Pastoral Constitution of the Church in the Modern World (GS), when, breaking with tradition, the Fathers addressed not only the Church's members but also "all who invoke the name of Christ . . . [and] the whole of humanity" in an attempt to explain to everyone how the Church conceives its presence and activity in the world.[9] More importantly, the Church's relation to the world is defined not in terms of juridical norms that regulate everyday situations but instead in light of gospel principles, the circumstances in which the Church finds itself. There were no ready-made solutions, but the Church wished "to respond to the perennial questions which [people] ask about the present life and the life to come, and about the relationship of the one to the other" (GS, no. 4). At the local level, this shift from a Church which asked the questions and provided the answers to a Church interested in the questions and concerns of the people called for a different type of ecclesial leadership as well as a different relationship with the people on the part of those leaders.

There was a willingness to hear, relate, and converse earnestly with the world and its people in the unique circumstances of the present. This dialogical thrust of the Church appealed to Hispanics, who love to talk and tell their stories. It provided new channels of communication which immediately began to alter the content of the input that the Church had been receiving about who Hispanics were. Hispanics began telling who they were to anyone who cared to listen; they would no longer depend upon persons of good will within the Church for telling their stories. The importance of having ministers who were capable of speaking in the language of the people was highlighted by the approval of vernacular languages for the liturgy. Soon priests in areas with large, recently arrived Hispanic populations saw the need to offer liturgies in Spanish, and many dioceses began to send priests and even bishops to Mexico and the Caribbean to learn Spanish. New patterns of relationships were being established which would significantly alter pastoral services to Hispanics.

3. Rediscovery of biblical roots

The concept of the Church as mystery and other prominent ecclesiological trends of Vatican II rest on the return to a biblical orientation and a movement away from the juridical conceptions based on Aristotelian categories that had characterized post-Tridentine theology.[10] In perceiving the world as created by God's hands and in the process of becoming—not as a static, complete, and hierarchical reality, as seen by classical philosophers— the Church's relation to the world was affected radically. Moving away from an attitude of dogmatic, authoritarian paternalism and condescension towards the world and towards its members, the Church seeks to foster relations, dialogue, service, and collaboration and sets out to rediscover the poetic and artistic dimensions of human creativity it once held in high esteem. Instead of definitions of itself, the Church at the Second Vatican Council provided manifold biblical images to clarify and explain its spiritual and material dimensions. Thus, the Church is a sheepfold, a tract of land to be cultivated, the edifice of God, mother, body of Christ, people of God (LG, 6,7).

The Church as people of God in pilgrimage had a natural appeal for Hispanics. A song with that theme, "Somos un pueblo que camina" ("We Are a Journeying People"), by Emilio Vicente Matéu, although originating in Spain, has become the hymn of Hispanics in the United States.[11]

The Church as people of God, *Pueblo de Dios*, echoed easily and powerfully within the Hispanic soul in its pilgrim condition in this country. A pilgrimage implies a conscious decision to follow the call, or the urge to journey, and is not possible without the communitarian solidarity that enables pilgrims to survive the struggles of the journey. Hispanics did not need to look far to see reflected in their lives—touched by discrimination, injustice, and the difficulties of their pilgrimage—abundant signs of that solidarity. This firsthand experience of one of the ecclesial images put forth by the council has placed Hispanics in a unique position for convincingly proclaiming the link between communitarian solidarity and Jesus' command to love one another. The call, or election, in the biblical sense, always implied a mission, or the realization of God's plan, which is beyond the person alone. These elements of call, solidarity, and mission would be repeated again and again in the deliberations set in motion by the three Hispanic *encuentros* held in the U.S. between 1972 and 1985.

4. Human dignity and openness to the world

While the Dogmatic Constitution on the Church (LG) emphasized the centrality of Christ in the life of the Church, the Pastoral Constitution of the Church in the Modern World (GS) chose to center its message on the human person. The cornerstone of *Gaudium et Spes* was the unambivalent and unequivocal assertion of the dignity of the human person, a creature made in the image and likeness of God; the importance of engaging the human family in dialogue; and the need to see the human task of building the earth as a joint venture in which all humans, regardless of race, culture, and creed, must participate. *Gaudium et Spes* also abandoned the categories of natural law which had always dominated ecclesial writings and considered human existence in the world as a vocation or a task to be accomplished through culture, rather than as the predetermined outcome of one's place in the ordered, Aristotelian scheme of things.[12] This document, the most influential in shaping the Church in Latin America, and through it the Hispanic community in the U.S., does not define the relation of the Church to the world but sees it as being linked to the "joys and hopes, the griefs and the anxieties of the people of this age" (GS, no. 1). The Church's relation to the world was to be worked out in actually relating to the world and not decided through preordained fiat. To accomplish this end, the Church affirmed its desire to engage in conversation with the world, which necessarily takes place in conversation with its people.

Giving importance to the value of all human work and action as elements towards the completion of the saving acts of Jesus in history brought Hispanics to feel closer to the mission of the Church; that mission was no longer perceived as the sole domain of ordained ministers. Hispanics' seeing their own work, often menial and ill-paid, as related to the saving mission of Christ gave them a new sense of pride and of the value of their human dignity.

5. The Church as eschatological sign

Another important departure from past ecclesiology was the emphasis on the eschatological dimension of the Church. After three centuries of emphasis on the Church as primarily a worshiping community and a compendium of moral precepts, we had "lost the sense that Christianity implies hope. This reasonable religion had allowed the secularization of its eschatology."[13] The eschatological dimension restored the realization that the Church's fullness will come only at the end of time, when all things will be fulfilled in Christ (LG, no. 48). In fact, in order to underline the importance of human beings and their activity, the document places Christ at the end of time as "the goal of human history, the focal point of the longings of history and of civilization, the center of the human race, the joy of every heart, and the answer to all its yearnings" (GS, no. 45). The theology of liberation and the anthropocentric spiritualities of the present have been inspired by this eschatological emphasis.[14]

This affirmation found an echo within the Hispanic spirit because of their well-documented tendency to place many of their pressing concerns in God's hand, as illustrated in their frequent use of the phrase, *Si Dios quiere* ("God willing"). The emphasis of the culture on trust in God, abandonment to the divine will, and hope in the midst of difficulties—all three validated by the eschatological thrust of *Gaudium et Spes*—did not deter Hispanics from tackling the urgent questions that the situation posed. Hispanics also heeded the council's call not to allow the expectations of a new earth to downplay the importance of human work within the present one: "For here grows the body of the new human family, a body which even now is able to give some kind of foreshadowing of the new age" (GS, no. 39). This affirmation gave impetus to U.S. Hispanic activists who could now see their search for social and political reform fall and be integrated within the scope of their religious activity.

The Church was seeking to make its stance towards the world one of trust and cooperation rather than of suspicion and antagonism, as had characterized the post-Enlightenment era. Having risen above the total identification between the world and the Church, as in the Constantinian age, with all its abuses of power, and the alienation of the post-Tridentine era, with its fragmentation of the Christian community, the council Fathers opened the door to allow the riches and insights from other cultures and traditions to enter the life of the Church and end its total reliance on European modes of thought and spirituality.

Pope Paul VI's encyclical from 1964, *Ecclesiam Suam* (ES), which called for a new relationship with the world, gave much of its spirit to *Gaudium et Spes*. To convert the world, one has to relate to it and approach it (ES, no. 3).[15] Gone are the injunctions to flee the world and the anathemas of the nineteenth century that repudiated all the "heretical" philosophies of the world. While still holding on to some of the dichotomous tensions that are found even in Scripture, i.e., "Do not love the world or the things of the world" (1 John 2:15), the emphasis was on reconciliation and on admiration for the progress of the world accomplished by human hands. In the same spirit, the council called for humanity to "increasingly consolidate its control over creation," for the aim of "serving individuals as well as groups to affirm and develop the dignity proper to them" (GS, no. 9). By exalting the responsibility of Christians to participate in the affairs of the world and to govern it "with justice and holiness," the Church declared that "by subjection of all things to man [sic], the name of God would be wonderful in all the earth" (GS, no. 34).

In the ample considerations given to culture—the composite of all that human beings have created to give meaning to their existence—the council made its most fruitful overtures to the world. This approach has been of great value in attempting to express and develop the legitimacy of cultural variables in the religious life of different human groups and has provided the foundation for Hispanics to reclaim their religious heritage and to pursue its development without first being assimilated into the dominant ecclesial structures and practices.

6. *Culture as vehicle and pilot.*

For the biblical perspective to be complemented and brought to immediate application, the council wrestled with the "enigmatic and polyvalent"[16] reality of the phenomenon of human culture. This was, for many of those who were closely associated with the council, the central point of interest of the Pastoral Constitution of the Church in the Modern World.

Culture as defined by the documents of the council includes two types of human activities: the objective ones, such as art, architecture, language, and music; and the subjective ones, such as the development of the person's intellectual potential, moral attitudes, and physical prowess.[17] The diverse human communities that have emerged have dignity and worth that is determined not by their technological or literary achievements but by their being creatures of God; those communities which are also Christian, because they are in continuity with the chosen people of God.

The far-reaching implications of those insights were brought to bear on the Decree on the Church's Missionary Activity, *Ad Gentes Divinitus* (AG). "The young churches," the document states, "*borrow* from the customs, traditions, wisdom, teaching, arts and sciences of their people *everything* which could be used to praise the glory of the Creator, manifest the grace of the saviour or contribute to the right ordering of Christian life" (AG, no. 22; emphasis added). In the Declaration on the Relation of the Church to Non-Christian Religions, *Nostra Aetate* (NA), the Fathers declared that "the Catholic Church rejects nothing of what is true and holy in these [non-Christian] religions"; and, they continued, all Christians are urged to "acknowledge, preserve and encourage the spiritual and moral truths found among non-Christians, also their social life and culture" (NA, no. 2). It is easy to see, then, why Virgil Elizondo, in one of the first books to appear in the U.S. that attempted to explain Hispanics' identity, their history, practices, and unique style of being Catholics, exclaimed: "If the Church can speak in this way of customs, traditions, and ways of life of the non-Christian, how much more must this apply to customs, traditions, and ways of life of peoples who are already Christians, even though to the outsider they may not seem too Christian."[18]

Hispanic's search for recognition and appreciation by the dominant ecclesial culture of their religious gifts and wisdom, art, and music, as well as the legitimation of their style and practices, would come to the forefront of all the debates on Church policy beginning in the late 1970s. When the National Conference of Catholic Bishops met in Chicago in March of 1978, they dedicated an entire day to considering the meaning and implication of the Hispanic presence for the Church in the United States.

The council documents, especially those which treat of the church and its relation to other religions and other cultures, recognize that all good things are not necessarily European. Similarly, God's action in history on behalf of the people has in no way been limited in time, place, manner, or culture to the history of Europe and the Middle East; we require new categories of thought and different evaluative criteria from those used to measure the cultures of pre-Christian Europe. The acceptance that God's action in history, made specific in the person of Jesus at one particular time and place, may not have been restricted to the part of the world that was first under Jewish-Christian influence had deep repercussions within the Church of Latin America and the Hispanic community.

Giving validity to the riches of other cultures opened the door for a new look at the reality of *mestizaje,* or mixture of blood of Europeans and natives, natives and Africans, Africans and Europeans, that had transformed the genetic pool of the world in ways that had been first noticed by the Mexican philosopher José de Vasconcelos and sung about in the poetry of *The Aleph* by Jorge Luis Borges. Many Hispanics would begin to recognize the positive contribution of the European encounter with the Americas and consider the legitimacy of mestizaje at the level of ideas and religious insights, spirituality, and even ritual. Carlos Fuentes recently elevated mestizaje to new heights in his commemorative book of the quincentenary of the arrival of Columbus in the New World. Hispanics, he insinuates, presage "the perfect instant in time and space where all the places in the world can be seen at the same moment without confusion, from every angle, in perfect, simultaneous existence."[19] In the Spanish American world of belief and practice we would see "the Indian sense of sacredness, communality, and the will to survive, the Mediterranean legacy of law, philosophy, and the Christian, Jewish, and Arab strains" all present to produce the variegated reality that falls outside the categories and criteria from which outsiders try to understand us.

THE CHURCH REESTABLISHES CONTINUITY WITH THE PRE-REFORMATION ERA

Gaudium et Spes and many contributions to other council documents were the brain children of avant-garde theologians such as Henri de Lubac, Marie-Dominique Chenu, Yves Congar, and Edward Schillebeeckx who took and made the property of the Church the theological insights that had evolved in Europe, mainly at Louvain, after the horror of two world wars. No one would have guessed that the documents would find so fertile a soil in the Americas, especially in Spanish-speaking communities. This was further proof of the continuity between Latin American and European thought.

Without perhaps being conscious of it, the Church of Vatican II was reconnecting with some positive ecclesial outlooks that had been relinquished after the rupture caused by the Protestant Reformation and the overzealous reaction generated by the inquisitorial fever of the Counter-Reformation. Because the Reformation did not affect Spain as it did other countries of Europe, the Church of Spain which came to the Americas possessed and preserved some of the qualities that the council was now trying to foster: the emphasis on the local church; rituals for and by the people; the cultivation of artistic creativity and personal and communal piety that nurtures the soul in the daily routine of life.

The Church that came to the Americas in the fifteenth century had brought the legacy of Stoic philosophy and interiority from Seneca to the Christian mystical heights of Juan de la Cruz and Teresa de Avila.[20] It was an individualistic Church with a great sense of regional uniqueness, and it did not think kindly of invaders or of far-removed chieftains. It was also a Church that loved rituals and engaged in all sorts of processions and celebrations of local saintly heroes that have endured to this day and have been strengthened by the vitality of the Vatican council's liturgical reforms. It was also a Church engaged in all aspects of public life, shaping not only the spiritual world of its members but all other human activities, from cooking to music, clothing to law.

The Church of Spain was more tolerant of cultural differences, being as it was an institution in a nation that had been invaded by Iberians and Celts, Greeks and Phoenicians, Carthaginians, Romans, Goths, Arabs, and Jews; and being a Church that prepared clerics to be mediators between the human and the divine realms and not just administrators, counselors, teachers, and moral arbiters, as in the church of North America. That was the Church in Spain, on the eve of Columbus's journey, as it had emerged from the medieval period and whose identity had been forged in the constant give-and-take with Moslems and Jews with whom, prior to their expulsion in 1492, it had coexisted in the first pluralistic religious society of Europe.[21] Those were the characteristics of the Church that the Spanish missionaries brought to the Americas in the sixteenth century and that remained with little variance due to the difficulties of communication over the extensive Spanish empire, the scarcity of priests, and the array of other issues that the Church faced in trying to determine how best to bring the gospel to the inhabitants of this continent.

The questions raised by the presence of scores of peoples who did not fit into the categories of the known cultures of Europe, Asia, and North Africa had theologians, canon lawyers, philosophers, and all wise men of the time locked in fierce ideological and political battles that, as we know, were won by the power of cannons, the unquenchable greed of conquerors, and the unmitigated scourge of disease. While the debates did not have any significant impact on stemming the tide of death in the first fifty years of Christianity in the Americas, the *Leyes Nuevas* protecting the Indians were passed in 1542, and little by little the Church embraced them and their culture, not wholeheartedly perhaps, but with sufficient dedication and creativity that, by 1570, the Church was beginning to show the first indications that ideas were being exchanged in both directions. One of the first clear manifestations of the cultural symbiosis which was beginning to occur can be found in the Christian art of the New World in Mexico, where Our Lady of Guadalupe's attire is in the style and bears the symbolisms of the native culture; in hymns and Masses composed by native musicians and that appeared as early as 1540;[22] in Peru, where angels were depicted with feathered wings, a native ornamentation seen for the first time on those heavenly creatures.[23]

Today, anyone with the opportunity to travel throughout Latin America and Spanish North America and see the high cathedrals, the adobe churches, and the *ermitas* in remote villages with access only by jeep or mules cannot miss the underlying similarity in the religious practices of the people; their respectful disposition before what they consider holy; their devotion to Mary, to the Passion and Crucifixion of Jesus; their sense of familiarity and comfort before the mystery and reality of death; and their strong sense of family. These similarities cut across socioeconomic status, nearness or remoteness to Native American ancestors, or little or no contacts with African cultures. What they all have in common are the flowerings, over five hundred years, of the hybrid religious seeds planted by the Spanish missionaries on the religiously receptive soil of the indigenous cultures of the Americas.

LATIN AMERICA AND HISPANICS WAKE TO NEW POSSIBILITIES

In spite of the many threads present in the council documents that appealed to the Latin American mind and heart and style of Church life, the speed with which the Latin American bishops set out to take those documents and make them alive may seem spectacular in terms of the usual pacing of Catholic Church agendas. The fact that their work even surpassed in clarity and power those of the Vatican could be perceived as almost miraculous. How did Medellín, so tarnished by its reputation as drug capital of Latin America, come to be forever identified as the birthplace of the post-Vatican Catholic Church in Latin America and from there, and quite directly, of the Hispanic Church in the U.S.?

Latin America was fertile soil for the new vision presented by the Vatican because some important links with the European centers of learning, where many of the Vatican theologians had come from, had been fostering developments in Latin America for ten years prior to the closing of the council. Rome had turned its attention towards Latin America with the publication of an alarming report on the growth of Protestant groups, published in 1955 by Prudencio Damboriena, S.J., of the Gregorian University and entitled "Le péril protestant en Amérique Latine."[24] The Vatican heeded the alarm, and its ears and pockets were turned towards Latin America. An army of European sociologists, mostly trained in Louvain, began arriving in 1958, when Monsignor L. G. Ligutti, the Vatican observer to the Food and Agricultural Organization of the United Nations, entrusted to FERES (International Federation of Institutes for Socio-Religious and Social Research), housed in Louvain, the taking of a census of the Latin American Church to determine its resources and capabilities. Father François Houtart was appointed director of the research. By 1962 there were research centers in Colombia, Chile, Brazil, and Argentina; by 1967, in Mexico, Venezuela, Peru, Bolivia, Ecuador; and then Guatemala and Uruguay soon followed. The centers were concerned with looking at the image of the Church in Latin America, the state of liturgy, catechesis as a means of religious socialization, popular piety, the role of religious, and some historical studies.[25] At the urging of the centers, many noted Latin Americans, both religious and lay, including Eduardo Frei of Chile on the political and social front and Bishop Marcos McGrath of Panama, began calling for a new religious vision and spirituality to offset the impoverished conditions in which millions lived. Even before the Second Vatican Council, some bishops had donated their residences to be used as schools or training centers for labor leaders, as did Archbishop Tulio Botero of Medellín in 1962.[26]

LATIN AMERICA IS READY FOR CHANGE

The ecclesiological shift expressed by the council was easier to implement, and its effect quicker to discern, in Latin America because the Church there was not burdened by a long history of self-definitions and mission shaped by the dynamics of its dialogue with the breakaway churches of Europe, with Eastern Christians, with the ancient religions of Asia, or with the rationalism of European intellectuals. The Church in Europe had forged its identity in the constant battle to define and redefine itself and its mission in

relationship to Churches that emerged after the Protestant Reformation, in the intellectual anticlericalism of the Enlightenment, and
in the continuing political realignment of hostile powers. In that
adverse environment the burden of the Catholic Church was to express its truth, mission, and uniqueness in terms of clarity of dogma
and teachings. As a result, the principles on which the Church had
come to rest were in large part responses to questions arising from
the political, religious, social, and technological changes in Europe
and had, naturally, been shaped by the tools of "classic" philosophy, theology, and ethics. Those conceptual frameworks and their
categories provided a certain style of leadership, the tenor of its
worship, the images, colors, and sounds of its artistic expressions,
and the structures for its service and educational enterprises.

After the period of persecution and discrimination that Catholics had endured in this country during the nineteenth century and
the first decades of the 1900s, the close link through culture and
language of North American society and its Catholic prelates, even
those born here, to the leading countries of Europe had imbued the
Church in the U.S. with similar concerns and style. The churches
of Europe and North America had slowly moved away from the
leadership style, language, and structures close to the agrarian life
that had been present at the Church's inception in Palestine.

At the time of the council, the Churches of Latin America,
Africa, and Asia were the poorest in the world, and some of those
Churches, as in Latin America, had been in the fold for nearly
five hundred years without showing much native leadership but
having a distinctive life of their own. By contrast, the Churches of
Europe and North America, in the aftermath of two devastating
world wars, the erection of the Iron Curtain, and the violent end
of millions of Jews and Christians caught in the power struggles of
the first half of the century, had lost their religious innocence, entered an era of secularization, and failed to bring about heaven on
earth that had been promised by the industrial and technological
revolutions.

Latin Americans and Hispanics, for the most part, were still
living closer to the agrarian life, had only been shaken by the
power struggles of local dictators and well-contained revolutions
that failed to catch on. There, and in the absence of the bombing
raids or gas chambers that held most of Europe in fear and later
moved it to concerted reconstructive action, the vast majority of
the people plodded along, content with a religious vision of life
that promised heaven only after a life of self-denial and patient

cross-carrying. In that setting, the Catholic Church, not in the habit of contending with other Christian groups vying for the deep-rooted allegiance of the racially, religiously, and culturally mixed populations of the continent acted as master of ceremonies for elaborate religious celebrations, led the educational institutions that prepared many countries' leaders in the style of European nobility, and provided a measure of compassion to the deprived masses in the absence of governmental social services.

The Church in Latin America had, more often than not, failed to bring its action for justice into harmony with its words because it had grown complacent in the belief that the Catholic ethos was the dominant force in the society. But the reality was different. Latin American mestizos, mulattos, and natives, in some countries constituting 90 percent of the population, had increasingly been cut off from access to the means of production and the benefits of education and health care available in urban centers. As a result, their quest for meaning and dignity could not easily be pursued in the halls of theological schools that were still shaped by the European cultures of the secularized postwar period. The Church's teachings had become increasingly unintelligible to the majority of believers, but the Second Vatican Council and the theological ferment created by its ecclesiological shift would soon provide the opening for a new Church, new workers, new hopes, and, best of all, the open use of the languages of the people in its liturgy.

In the U.S., Hispanics who were concentrated in areas that had become part of the country by conquest or war with neighboring Mexico had been mostly ignored or discriminated against by influential Church leaders. After the council, Hispanics could remind leaders that the message of salvation had not always been proclaimed in an understandable language, nor in actions that could be perceived as welcoming or accepting of the inalienable dignity inherent in their humanity.

With the newly perceived need for the Church to act in accordance with its best proclamations on the equality and dignity of all human beings, the message of Paul VI acquired new meaning: "Modern man listens more willingly to witnesses than to teachers, and if he does listen to teachers, it is because they are witnesses."[27] Hispanic leadership would set the Church in search of a new agenda.

CHANGES SET IN MOTION

The Latin American bishops came back from the Second Vatican Council ready to implement its new vision of the Church for the world. Barely a year after the conclusion of the council, an extraordinary assembly of the bishops took place at Mar del Plata, on October 9–16, 1966,[28] which was attended by the representatives from each national episcopal conference and some *periti* to prepare the way for a general assembly that would translate the Vatican council into Latin American terms. Among the speakers on that occasion were bishops, sociologists, educators, politicians; Father José Marins, pastoralist, subdirector of the Department for Ministry of Brazil's episcopal conference; and Father Pedro Velázquez, director of the Inter-American Conference for Catholic Social Action of Mexico. These two priests, tremendously influential in Latin America, became equally influential among Hispanics in the U.S.

The new social awareness of the Latin American bishops was evident at Mar del Plata, and the speakers did not need to use much rhetoric to convince the participants of the urgency, demanding action, of the social and religious privation of the continent.[29] All the talks made use of *Gaudium et Spes* and a letter written by Paul VI on the tenth anniversary of the Latin American Episcopal Conference (CELAM), portions of which were quoted in the final document of the assembly and which freshly reflect this new relationship among priests, religious, laypersons, and the world:

> The pastor must never cease to study the world for many reasons: because our concern and vigilance for the Gospel must go on; and because the world changes and it is necessary to know how to satisfy its growing demands and interpret its new needs. The pastor will know how to avail himself of the help of specialists, theologians and sociologists in order to prepare capable leaders among the clergy as well as the laity; he will promote frequent courses of pastoral "aggiornamento," inviting priests, religious and laity, in a spirit of fraternal comprehension, and teaching them the solid principles of genuine pastoral spirituality whose development must be rooted in the faith.[30]

The trumpet had been sounded, and it would reverberate throughout the continent. A search for a fresh approach to earthly realities was begun; the inclusion of Pope Paul's statement in the document of Mar del Plata helped to convert the skeptics who still viewed the involvement of the Church in temporal matters with suspicion. The Latin American bishops wanted to drive home the point that human beings are the artisans of culture and that the possibility of changing the reality of the continent was in their hands.

Norms for involvement were issued that called for two qualities in those who wished to enter into the process of transformation: 1) a genuine interest and sufficient grasp of the circumstances in which this action is to be carried out; 2) a solid theological understanding of the Christian vocation as it should be worked out in today's world. The methodology born of those premises would be summarized in the model for mission adapted by most religious after Medellín: observe; judge; act.

The Mar del Plata assembly contained the first declaration in favor of justice made by the Latin American Church, as well as its recognition that it had sometimes abandoned the poor. The document was widely read—supported by many, harshly criticized by others. It marked the turning point for the Church from its identification with the powerful to the beginning of its reaching out to the dispossessed, no matter where they found themselves. It could be said that this was the remote preparation for the theologians of liberation while Medellín provided its most immediate inspiration. At Mar del Plata, development and integration had been the motto; at Medellín they were joined into one word: liberation.

The Medellín CELAM Conference

At Medellín, the anthropocentric emphasis of the Pastoral Constitution of the Church in the Modern World (GS) and the responsibility of human beings to transform their situation took center stage and were examined from every angle. The conclusions of the assembly represented the Latin American appropriation of the great social encyclicals of their century. Following the tone of those encyclicals, the bishops chose to be prophetic spokesmen by denouncing injustice and clarifying moral priorities and normative principles that would direct the unfolding of society in ways that would benefit those suffering abject poverty.

It did not take long before observers, analysts, and people in positions of leadership within the U.S. National Conference of Catholic Bishops took notice of what was happening South of the Rio Grande and began to feel the need to share in the exciting happenings there. At the same time, ecclesial leaders in Latin America could neither contain their enthusiasm nor refrain from sharing it with their cousins and sometimes actual brothers and sisters in the North. The exchange of ideas and resources, both human and material, began in earnest and will necessarily grow as consideration is given to the invitation made by Pope John Paul II at the opening of CELAM IV in Santo Domingo, on October 12, 1992, to hold an extraordinary gathering of the bishops of the hemisphere in the not-too-distant future. Such a gathering would bring together bishops and theologians who have already been engaged in dialogue and fruitful exchanges, although sometimes shortlived, in the course of the years since Medellín.

LATIN AMERICANS IN DIALOGUE WITH U.S. LEADERS

In 1964, John Considine, a Maryknoll priest who headed the office for Latin American Affairs of the U.S. bishops, created CICOP, the Catholic Inter-American Cooperation Program, for the purpose of educating North Americans about Latin America and its needs. This was two years after Cardinal Cushing had proposed the establishment of a national collection to aid Latin America. The first meeting of CICOP was held in Chicago, and the office functioned out of Davenport, Iowa, until 1968, when it moved to Washington, D.C. The presentations from the meeting were compiled in a volume, edited by Considine and published by Fides Press of Notre Dame in 1964 with the title *The Church in the New Latin America*. Among the presenters were Bishop Marcos McGrath and Marina Bandera; they would become regular visitors to the North in subsequent years. By 1968, under the leadership of Father Louis Michael Colonnese, CICOP became an ecumenical forum for Latin American bishops, theologians, pastoral agents, and lay persons who would speak before North American audiences to share their insights.[31] CICOP only lasted until 1973; its funding was suspended because of complaints from conservative and reactionary groups both from within and outside the hierarchy who saw Latin Americans as using CICOP for attacking American policies towards their countries and who were certain that anyone who spoke about social justice had to be communist.

The organization, however, left a lasting imprint on those who were able to participate in those encounters. Among the Latin Americans who enriched the Church in the U.S. and made Hispanics and others turn their eyes and ears to what was happening there were Gustavo Gutiérrez, from Perú, the father of the theology of liberation; Pepe Alvarez y Casas, head of the Christian Family movement in Mexico City; Paulo Freire, from Brazil, one of the greatest educators of all times; Jorge Mejía, Jorge Lagos, Jon Sobrino, S.J.; and Hugo Assman, among others.

Some Latin Americans, such as Fathers Edgard Beltrán and José Marins, both of whom were key Latin American *periti* at the council and crucial players in the education process of bishops, clergy, religious, and the laity in South America, began to come on a regular basis to this country to share with the Spanish speaking. Beltrán, with a team from CELAM, had been responsible for the design and facilitation of a course for South American bishops held in Medellín and later in Guatemala. Their enthusiasm for the transformation of the Church in Latin America was experienced by anyone who participated in their workshops and lectures and was the source of inspiration for many of their listeners who decided to join the ranks of those who, hearing the call of the council, wanted to be counted among the reshapers of the Church on this continent. The preferential option for the poor, *pastoral de conjunto* (joint pastoral planning), and small faith communities gave courage and inspiration to many among those who attended the workshops to prepare themselves to carry out the tasks the Latin American Church had laid out before them.

After two years of periodic visits to the United States, Beltrán was invited to join the staff of the National Conference of Catholic Bishops' Secretariat for Hispanic Affairs in Washington after a course he taught in New York, where the idea of the encuentros was born. He was responsible for setting the encuentros in motion, and he also helped in the deliberations for the formation of the Mexican American Cultural Center, for the style and scope of the Secretariat for Hispanic Affairs, and for the ecclesiological and anthropological principles underlying the *Pastoral Plan for Hispanic Ministry*. Other prominent Latin Americans who have been actively engaged in the formation of Hispanic leaders in the U.S. through their writings, retreats, courses, and lectures are, among others: Gustavo Gutiérrez, Segundo Galilea, Amparo Beltrán, Enrique Dussel, Samuel Ruíz, Ricardo Antoncich, Jorge Julio Mejía, Jesús Andres Vela, and Jesús García. Not a Latin American but very influential among Hispanics in the U.S. has been Casiano Floristán of the University of Salamanca, Spain. Through his leadership many Hispanics have been admitted to Salamanca to pursue theological degrees.

From those early promotional efforts on behalf of Hispanic leaders much progress has been made. According to the most recent survey of diocesan offices conducted in 1971 by the Secretariat for Hispanic Affairs showed that over 70 percent of dioceses reporting (93 out of 140) have some form of Hispanic pastoral plan; more than 80 percent have an office for Hispanic affairs, and of those, 52 have been established since 1970. A large portion, 71 percent, promote small faith communities; nearly 70 percent offer courses for Hispanic ministry; more than 60 percent have *escuelas de ministerio*; a little over 50 percent have *escuelas de evangelización*; and 65 percent sponsor diocesan encuentros. When Monsignor Arturo Bañuelas, in El Paso, Texas, announced a class to prepare laypeople in the Church's ministries, he expected forty or fifty participants, but twelve hundred showed up. He began the Tepeyac Institute, with courses for lectors, leaders of song, hospitality ministers, ministers for prisons and hospitals, and catechists for sacramental preparation. More than four thousand persons have passed through the institute in three years.[32] In addition, almost 60 percent of dioceses promote Hispanic vocations through youth retreats, vocation days, information dissemination, and youth and family career days, among other activities.

Nearly 80 percent of the diocesan directors responded that their diocese has specific priorities for ministering to Hispanics. The priorities most often mentioned included children and youth ministry, migrant ministry, sacramental preparation, lay leadership formation, Spanish liturgies, radio ministry, recruitment of Spanish-speaking personnel, evangelization, social services, promotion of apostolic movements, Spanish language and cultural awareness classes for priests, and adult education.[33]

Many Hispanics who experienced the energy and enthusiasm of Latin Americans began to participate in a center for the preparation of pastoral agents that had emerged in South America, IPLA (Instituto de Pastoral Latinoamericana), in Quito, Ecuador, and in courses and seminars offered in Colombia. Among the first participants were Arturo Tafolla, now bishop of Pueblo, Colorado, and Lonnie Reyes, vicar general of the diocese of Austin, Texas.

Hispanic Women in Leadership Roles

Hispanic women religious were the pioneers in waking up the people of God to all that was happening in the Church and in this hemisphere. Among the first to return to the U.S., armed with skills for social analysis and liberating and integrative education were Carmelita Espinosa and María de Jesús Ibarra, who, while working for the diocese of Yakima, Washington, began to create catechetical materials for Hispanics in the Northwest. Other Hispanic women whose leadership has given great impulse to Hispanic ministry throughout the country are Elisa Martínez, in Boise, Idaho; Dolorita Martinez, in Omaha, Nebraska; Rosa Marta Zarate, in southern California and in Minnesota; Mario Barrón, in northern California and Texas; Sarita Mendieta in San Diego, California; María Iglesias, now with the national office of Renew; and Margarita Castañeda, in the Northeast; Consuelo Covarrubias, in Minnesota; Yolanda Tarango, in Texas and Illinois; Dominga Zapata in Chicago, South Bend, and Hartford. These women have been key figures in diocesan offices and state and national organizations, especially Las Hermanas, the Leadership Conference of Women Religious, and the Secretariat for Hispanic Affairs, in raising their voices among non-Hispanics to become aware of Hispanic identity, needs, and gifts. They have also been deeply involved in serving the religious education needs of Hispanics in their dioceses, communities, and parishes by creating programs and materials and by preparing other Hispanics for leadership while constantly renewing their own education.

Another group of Hispanic women who had a head start on working with Hispanics were the Missionary Catechists of Divine Providence (M.C.D.P.) who were founded in 1933 and approved in 1946 as a branch of the Sisters of Divine Providence for Mexican Americans. Never a large group, but at any given time in the last thirty years between fifteen and twenty of their Sisters can be found in key diocesan positions. Concentrated in the Southwest, they influence policies and in many instances direct diocesan offices of Hispanic ministry to insure that the needs of Hispanics are heard and heeded.

Looking at the ecclesial landscape at the national and diocesan levels, more than a token number of Hispanic women head important posts: In 1992, Sister Anita de Luna, M.C.D.P., was the first Mexican-American woman religious to be elected president of the Leadership Conference of Women Religious. A Hispanic (Cuban) woman, Lucy Vazquez, is the current president of the Canon Law Society of America and the director of the marriage tribunal in the diocese of Orlando, Florida. Helen Alvaré, a Spanish-Cuban lawyer is the director of planning and formation for the Pro-Life

Secretariat, and María Luisa Gastón, a Cuban American served as national coordinator of the Committee for the Fifth Centenary, both offices of the National Conference of Catholic Bishops (NCCB). Hermelinda B. Pompa, Mexican American, was the program coordinator for the National Catholic Conference for Interracial Justice. In the spring of 1992, María Cantón, also of Cuban descent, became the first layperson, woman, and Hispanic to be given the Pope Paul VI Award for Leadership in Evangelization by the National Council for Catholic Evangelization. She started the storefront Catholic Evangelization Center in Miami shortly after her arrival here from Cuba among the *marielitos*.[34]

Hispanic women have also attained prominence outside ecclesial roles. Outstanding examples are Elsa Gomez (Dominico-Puerto Rican) who on assuming the presidency of Kean College, New Jersey, became the first Hispanic woman president of a four-year public college; and Antonia Novello (Puerto Rican), who held the post of surgeon general during the Bush administration.

Today, several communities of Hispanic religious women hold important positions of ministry throughout the country. The Carmelite Sisters of Charity, a Spanish order founded in 1826 by a widowed mother of nine children, has fifteen sisters in Washington and eight in New York who work with the Hispanic communities in those cities. The community attracts both Hispanic and non-Hispanic members who engage in a variety of ministries: shelters for homeless women, Hispanic Catholic centers, health clinics, parish administration, youth groups, prison ministry, religious education in parishes, adult education programs that include literacy, English, and citizenship classes. They also sponsor groups of women domestic workers and advise them on their rights, fair job practices, and acquiring skills that enable them to pursue better working contracts.

The Teresian Sisters (Compañía de Santa Teresa de Jesús), also founded in Spain (1876), have a province in the United States with its headquarters in Covington, Louisiana. The Sisters, who come from various Hispanic, as well as non-Hispanic, backgrounds, occupy diocesan posts in education, vocation, and social welfare and minister as school principals, teachers, and nurses in Texas, Florida, and Louisiana.

RELIGIOUS EDUCATORS IN LEADERSHIP

One group of Hispanics that has quietly and without much fanfare exercised very fruitful leadership in the Church and in the Hispanic community has been Hispanic women religious educators. Lay and religious women from all over the country and accompanied by one layman, four supportive Hispanic clerics, and Bishop Gilberto Chávez met in Corona, California, December 13–20, 1977.[35] This gathering, the first national meeting of Hispanic catechists, was sponsored by a grant from the American Board of Catholic Missions made to the Department of Education of the U.S. Catholic Conference to launch the first national effort to identify the catechetical needs of the Hispanic community and to plan, create, and promote both the preparation of suitable educational materials for Hispanic children and youth and the development of alternate training models for the preparation of Hispanic catechists.

The deliberations of the Corona meeting were gathered in a publication of the Department of Education with the title *Methodology and Themes for Hispanic Catechesis.* This was the basis for the elaboration of a training model for Hispanic catechists which adhered to the guidelines that had emerged from Medellín and were affirmed at the Second National Encuentro in August of 1977, in which most of the catechists at Corona had participated. The group called the methodology that they created *evangelizing catechesis.* It was expanded by catechists from each of the regional offices of Hispanic ministry which were already in place by the late 1970s. It was used with more than five hundred Hispanics who joined for nine full days, symbolic of the nine-month gestation cycle of new human life, and made a novena of prayer, study, and Christian praxis between June of 1979 and November of 1980, in California, New Jersey, Notre Dame, Denver, and Kansas City, Kansas.[36] Participants in those training sessions were also helped to develop their leadership potential. Through these sessions many Hispanics found their call to serve as religious, deacons, or parish coordinators of religious programs.

Catechetical efforts for and by Hispanics have not operated as a movement or a highly visible organization. The heir to the first groups of catechists that met at Corona is a national group known as NOCH (National Organization of Catechists for Hispanics), led until April of 1993 by Carmen Cervantes, from the diocese of Oakland, California, and now by Sister Mary Lou Barba, M.C.D.P., from the diocese of Austin, Texas. Under Cervantes' leadership, this organization has developed a model for catechesis and evangelization entitled "Semilla del Reino" ("Seed for the Kingdom"), initially used by the diocese of Oakland, which is now being edited for wider distribution for the sacramental preparation of adult Hispanics.

NOCH members have also been involved in a catechetical project sponsored by the episcopal commission of Alta/Baja California and being tested in California and Arizona to be used on both sides of the U.S.-Mexico border. This effort is directed by Sister Maria de la Cruz Aymes and is entitled "Sin Fronteras: Lineamientos para una catequesis evangelizadora" ("Without Borders: Guidelines for an Evangelizing Catechesis"). Sister Maria has brought together bishops, peoples and many catechists from both countries who are concerned with the specific needs and circumstances of Hispanics in one of the most volatile and fastest-growing areas of the country. The catechetical initiatives of Sister de la Cruz were deeply felt by the Catholic community at large in the textbooks she prepared in the 1970s for William H. Sadlier, Inc.—the largest publisher of religious education materials in the U.S. In those textbooks she brought the theological and educational guidelines from the Second Vatican Council documents to bear on the catechetical formation of an entire generation. Her efforts will now be felt by the Hispanic community as well.

Since 1989 NOCH has been publishing *Voz catequetica*, a biannual catechetical journal for the continuing education of Hispanic catechists. NOCH has working relations with the National Association of Parish Coordinator/Directors of Religious Education (NPCD); the National Catholic Council for Hispanic Ministry (NCCHM); and the National Conference of Catechetical Leadership (NCCL), the successor to the National Conference of Diocesan Directors (NCDD).

The Department of Education of the U.S. Catholic Conference also has an official group, the National Advisory Committee for Catechesis with Hispanics (NACCH), that serves as a resource group for the department on issues related to the formation of catechists, textbooks, and the inclusion of the Hispanic dimension in all aspects of the work of the department.

A new chapter in the awareness of religious educators began when the National Conference of Diocesan Directors (now the National Conference of Catechetical Leadership), with the advocacy of those members who were convinced of the growing importance of Hispanic ministry, approved a resolution at their annual conference

(New Orleans, 1978), to be included in all their programs presentations, that would highlight the particular religious education needs
of Hispanics, African Americans, and Native Americans and would
offer models for the preparation of catechetical ministers to serve
those needs. From that time, with only one Hispanic (acting as a
consultant) to the present, the growth of Hispanic leadership on
this key ministry of the Church can be most fully appreciated. Their
present treasurer is Sister Mary Lou Barba, M.C.D.P. (Mexican
American), from the diocese of Austin, Texas; they have a Hispanic
representative from among the diocesan directors, a position being
filled by Carmen de la Vega Neafsey, diocesan director from San
Francisco; and a diocesan office staff representative, a position
being filled by Maruja Sedano, of the Los Angeles archdiocese.
There are twelve dioceses whose diocesan director was an Hispanic person in 1992, and in other diocesan positions in religious
education there are over fifty Hispanics.

The impact of that resolution filtered immediately to the diocesan and local levels through the inclusion, for the first time, of presentations by Hispanic religious educators on many of the issues
that flowed from the growing Hispanic presence in almost every
diocese of the country. From Sacramento to New York, Portland
to Boston, passing through Toledo and Chicago, religious education congresses would have Hispanics as keynote speakers and
also include practical workshops on teaching religion to Hispanic
children and cultivating relations with the parents.

HISPANIC LAITY BEGINS TO PARTICIPATE

The expansion of Hispanic ecclesial leadership began in the
late sixties with the entrance of the first Hispanics into graduate theological programs in this country. The first U.S. doctorate
in theology to be earned by an Hispanic was conferred on me
in 1974 by Fordham University. While at first the ones pursuing
academic degrees were chiefly priests and religious, laypersons
soon followed with graduate degrees in theological and religious
education. Fordham, Catholic University, Notre Dame, Marquette,
Harvard, Berkeley, Union Theological, St. Mary's University, and
Princeton have nurtured the academic development of Hispanic
ecclesial leaders in the U.S. for the last twenty years. Abroad, Hispanic scholars from the U.S. pursued their academic studies at the
Institut Catholique in France, Salamanca in Spain, the Gregorian

University in Italy, the Pontifical Catholic University of Rio de Janeiro in Brazil, and the Titus Brandsma Institute of Nijmegen University in Holland.[37]

Starting in the 1980s many seminaries in the country began to include as a requirement for their seminarians Spanish as a second language. In the archdiocese of Miami, the need to prepare Hispanic priests for the explosion of the Spanish-speaking Catholic population that had begun with the Cubans' arrival in 1960 saw the birth of the first bilingual, multicultural seminary in the country at St. Vincent de Paul Seminary in Boynton Beach, Florida. The seminary, which had opened its doors in 1963 with one Hispanic in its first class, was led in 1980 by Father Felipe J. Estevez, the first Hispanic (Cuban) rector in the U.S. The holistic program was coordinated by Sister Pilar Arensanz, a Teresian Sister from Spain. It included language preparation both for Hispanics who needed English and for non-Hispanics who needed Spanish. Prayers, core courses, electives, and field placements were provided in both languages.

Among those ordained at St. Vincent between 1968 and 1979, 23 percent were Hispanics. After the bilingual, multicultural program was in place, from 1980 to 1992, 36 percent were Hispanics. There have been students from Cuba, Puerto Rico, Colombia, Nicaragua, the Dominican Republic, Mexico, Ecuador, and Peru. Presently, almost 50 percent of the students are Hispanic.[38]

Another seminary with Hispanic (Mexican) rectors—Father Rafael Luévano (college level) and Monsignor Gabino Zavala (theologate)—is St. John's Seminary in Camarillo, California. In the year 1992–1993, Hispanic seminarians at the undergraduate level totaled 40 percent (45 of 113 students) in the Fall semester, 42 percent (52 of 121) in the Spring. Vietnamese and Koreans constituted the other significant minorities, with 25 percent in the Fall and 24 percent in the Spring. The faculty is 13 percent Hispanic: there are 2 Hispanic members in the resident faculty, and 2 in the academic faculty. The dean of students in the seminary college is a Sulpician with a doctorate in Spanish literature. The college seminary fosters its Hispanic dimension through clubs for the different Hispanic groups; a major is offered in Spanish (others are theology and philosophy); and every Wednesday all the activities of the college are conducted in Spanish, including meals, liturgy, and prayers. In the 1993–1994 academic year the seminary at the theologate level will begin to focus on a bilingual approach to theology in cooperation with some religious orders, the Piarists and Holy Trinity Missionaries. A core of courses will be offered in Spanish and English but not on a dual track as at St. Vincent. All students now are required to have a second language. While many study Spanish, the students' diocese selects the language that it requires for its specific population needs.

The Encuentros: Schools of Leadership

While a small number of Hispanics was busy "hitting the books," many more were busy knocking on doors of diocesan chancery offices and, above all, dialing phone numbers to gather the momentum and support that led to the encuentros. From the beginning, the encuentros were perceived as a training school for leadership. This is one of the four goals mentioned, beginning with the First National Encuentro in 1972 and repeated again for the second (1977) and third (1985) encuentros.

This leadership goal was promoted through the formation of diocesan coordinating teams, which, under the aegis of the Secretariat for Hispanic Affairs, were created in the 125 dioceses who accepted participation in the encuentro process. The teams were composed of priests, religious, and laypersons who were already active in the Church's ministry through their participation in the more popular movements: Cursillo, Christian Family, and charismatic. Now they had to learn to develop teamwork skills as well as to enlarge the scope of their own concerns. They also received training in planning, organization, advocacy, door-to-door promotion, leading prayer and reflection groups, and evaluation. It is estimated that for the Third National Encuentro some 2500 Hispanics were prepared as leaders for the diocesan and regional encuentro process, and they in turn led some 200,000 Hispanics in reflection, study, and participation in the encuentros.[39] These leaders are found as *animadores* of small Christian communities, Renew programs, and in the many ministerial volunteer services that parishes require.

THE PERILS OF HISPANIC LEADERSHIP

The encuentros also provided a forum for Hispanics to express ideas about the kind of leadership they felt was required to bring about the changes in the Church that they were beginning to envision. Identifying and forming leadership would require a continuing process of dialogue and discernment that had not been customary for the Hispanic groups that were, for the first time, just beginning to be in touch with one another and that were acquiring new contours as members of different nationalities begin to share in the political clout and preeminence that had been possible, prior to the 1960s, only for the Mexican Americans. Exercising leadership in the Hispanic community is a difficult and perilous task that requires understanding of the unique issues Hispanics face in identifying and accepting leaders.

The Mexican-American leadership that emerged in the 1960s—even in the Church—focused on political, economic, and social issues that had been festering for decades and had come to light with the civil rights movement. Hispanic leadership in the Church was a different matter since entrance into positions with true clout are so restricted by sex, education, and selection. There were very few Mexican-American priests. For its ministry to Hispanics the Church relied, for all practical purposes, on diehard missionaries, some of whom were from Spain, whose emphasis was along the paternalistic, colonialist, and ethnocentric lines that characterized the mission efforts of the Church before the Second Vatican Council. The preconciliar Church, with its other-wordly stance and its aloofness from the concerns of the people, had been more welcoming to women than to Hispanic men. In the quiet churches they could say their well-loved and comforting prayers handed down for generations while very few Hispanic men seemed to be invited by or attracted to the clerical ranks.

The possibility of Mexican Americans having significant impact on ecclesial and pastoral affairs was out of the question until the ordination of Bishop Flores to the episcopal ranks in 1970. Until then, those paying attention to the pastoral needs of Hispanics were non-Hispanics whose missionary zeal and personal sensitivity had alerted the Church as a whole, starting with the councils for the Spanish speaking in the 1940s. For the most part, priests formed in U.S. seminaries and religious houses who have no connection to Mediterranean or monastic spirituality have been at a loss to understand, accept, or celebrate the religious traditions that link Latin

American and Hispanic Catholics to fifteenth-century Spain. They continue to belittle Hispanic practice and spirituality and often put it in the same category as magic, witchcraft, and superstition. Even the more positive label, *popular piety*, or *popular religiosity*, that academicians and contemporary theologians use do not guarantee the respect that the religious expressions of Hispanics deserve, nor do they insure that the people, creators, and sustainers of those expressions will be allowed to have them unfold from within their own particular dynamics without the influence of outsiders whose own spiritual depth has not been proved and often lacks historical foundations.

The number of Mexicans in the U.S. was boosted by the immigration laws of 1965, which called for the reunification of families and a generous quota for other categories. In the 1970s, Mexican immigration topped, for the first time, all other national categories of immigrants since 1821 and outpaced even that of Germans, the dominant category since the years prior to World War II. By their sheer numbers alone, Hispanics of Mexican descent were a presence to contend with. It was natural, then, for the seeds of Hispanic leadership in the Church to be planted in Texas; the first Catholic Council for the Spanish Speaking was established by the Catholic bishops when they met in Oklahoma City in 1945. The situation would change drastically and require new structures fewer than twenty years later.

New and Varied Hispanic Faces: An Imposed Identity

When throngs of Puerto Ricans, Cubans, and Dominicans found their way to the eastern seaboard, the scope of the councils for the Spanish speaking was enlarged and the offices for the Spanish speaking apostolate began their work. When the Secretariat for Hispanic Affairs was established in 1970, the issues of Hispanics and their social and pastoral needs were placed on the agenda at the administrative heart of the Catholic Church, but maybe not yet at its living heart. That would have to wait until the bishops declared the Hispanic presence "a blessing" in their pastoral letter of 1983.

Many a meeting of the National Conference of Catholic Bishops and of countless diocesan staffs began to wrestle then (1983) with issues relating to the growing Hispanic presence—a presence that could no longer be considered a seasonal phenomenon resulting from the migrant streams that cultivated fields from California to

Alaska, Michigan to Texas, Maine to Florida. The false assumption that the Spanish speaking were migrant workers and that their needs were of no concern to the dioceses where they passed through did not disappear quickly. This widely held belief was still evident at the end of 1978 in the answers given by some diocesan offices of religious education to a study conducted by the Department of Education of the U.S. Catholic Conference that inquired about diocesan services for the Spanish speaking. At least four dioceses indicated that the only Spanish speaking they had were migrant workers who resided in the area only during the summer months; since there were no summer programs available for any group, there was nothing for Hispanics.[40]

The widening scope of the Spanish-speaking community brought about the redefinition of this most varied of ethnic groups from *Spanish speaking* to *Hispanic*, an umbrella term that was thought to describe them better. The development of settled communities of migrants in the Midwest, as shown by the 1970 census, coupled with the massive arrival of Cubans to Dade County in Florida and the continued immigration of Puerto Ricans, Dominicans, and Colombians into New York in the first years of the 1960s, changed the location and composition of the Spanish-speaking community and forced the redefinition. The Bureau of the Census, for example, adopted the use of the word *Hispanic* over *Spanish speaking* for the 1970 census. This label which is now, at least in academic sociological circles, understood as a cultural, not as a racial, descriptor has not been widely accepted by Hispanics. As many Hispanics see it, *Hispanic* is a term made in the U.S., and since so many Spanish speaking were not born here, they do not feel at all included in the term—hence the persistence of such terms as *Latinos, Chicanos, browns*, and *La Raza*.

The preferred descriptors are more specific and identify national origin—Mexican, Mexican American, Cuban, Puerto Rican, etc.—as shown in the Latino National Political Survey of December 1992, the first study national in scope to ask specifically: "What do you prefer to be called?" Considering these findings, the *Economist* tries to allay the fears of those outside the United States who believe that "the growth and increased political power of Hispanics would make America either more like the third world, or more like the Balkans." To them, the weekly magazine that calls itself a newspaper says:

> This [fear] is risible. It is risible, first, because only in the minds of
> ignorant Europeans or patronizing politically correct Americans can

24m Hispanics be lumped together and told that they all believe in the same things. . . . It is a long way, in more than miles, from the quiet mountain villages on the High Road from Santa Fe to Taos to the Dominican enclave in Manhattan, where *merengue* blasts from the tape-decks.[41]

The stance of fear and the misunderstanding about who Hispanics are is more widespread than simply among ignorant Europeans and patronizing Americans. It is quite generalized in academic and ecclesial settings, where generalizations influence policy and have uncertain and negative results.

It is extremely difficult and even perilous to speak, for the sake of academic purity, religious unity, or expediency, of Hispanics as one ethnic group with one voice. It is difficult because if one finds broad enough parameters that encompass the variety of communities that comprise the Hispanic population, then most policies are rendered inoperative and next to useless in the programming of services and programs to serve them. All Hispanics are not Spanish speaking, all are not Catholic, all are not of a particular racial makeup, all are not poor, all are not outside the mainstream culture, all are not without the best education, all are not politically powerless, all have not experienced racial or cultural discrimination at the hands of the dominant society. It is perilous also because false expectations of unity from both Hispanics and non-Hispanic leaders causes serious divisions and unnecessary hostilities in communities where Hispanics are struggling to make inroads into the controlling structures, discovering who they are and the contributions they can make.

The experiences of Mexican Americans or Chicanos as conquered people are very different from those of Cubans as welcomed ones. A similar contrast obtains between Puerto Ricans, many of whom are unhappy with their Commonwealth status in relation to this country, and Dominicans, who give anything to come to the U.S. While Puerto Rican animosity towards this country flourishes periodically in political protests and even violence, Dominicans dream of the day when they can come here, if not as Major League baseball players then to work hard and earn some money so they can exhibit all the signs of a successful American connection. The Dominican attitude to this country is best exemplified in a graffito that appeared in 1964, at the height of the American occupation of Santo Domingo ordered by President Lyndon B. Johnson: "Yankee, go home *y llévame contigo*" (and take me with you!).

The political diversity shown by Hispanics and linking them with the United States in different ways is only one of the variables which hampers efforts to unify Hispanics in the U.S. on a national scale. There is also the question of education and social class. The archdiocese of Washington, for example, has three distinct Hispanic communities: the struggling Central American community, composed mostly of Salvadoran and Guatemalan natives who are seen taking on menial jobs in shopping malls and hotels, gardens and homes; the professional community, which works in banks, radio stations, and international businesses, such as the World Bank and the Inter-American Bank; and the diplomatic community, with representatives to the White House as well as the Organization of American States, who host parties and balls that attract high-ranking officials of both the U.S. government and others. The national parish in Washington that serves the Hispanic community, located in the Kalorama section of the city, one of the wealthiest in the metropolitan area, attracts Hispanics who reside in that area because they fulfill the domestic work that had been performed there in the past by the black community. One can visit churches in Bethesda, a prosperous suburb just outside the District of Columbia, and see no "Hispanic-looking" people but hear, as the celebrant begins to process out of the Church, many groups of Hispanics exchanging greetings, saying "Hola, Señor Embajador" (Hello, Mr. Ambassador). These parishes' only concession to their Hispanic constituents is to offer to hear confessions in Spanish at Easter and Christmas. The religious needs of grandmothers, nannies, and domestic workers who labor in the homes of diplomats and foreign officials in those affluent suburban neighborhoods, who as a rule do not speak English, are not given any other attention. It is not unusual to see the elderly and the domestic workers saying their rosaries, their stations of the cross, and their private prayers all during the English liturgy which goes on without them. From among those ranks and from among Hispanic migrants, the storefront churches and evangelicals are drawing their greatest admirers and converts.

UNIFYING POINTS OF RESISTANCE

The observation by John Higham, in the introduction to a collection of papers presented at Johns Hopkins University in 1976, is quite accurate regarding Hispanics:

The American ethnic group . . . is an amorphous entity, difficult to define and in the great majority of cases very incompletely separable from other elements in the population. Except for unusual instances of great internal discipline or external resistance, ethnic boundaries are vague, fluid, and indeterminate. An ethnic group fades out—like a magnetic field—as the distance from its center increases. Its history is one of the energy it generates and the direction in which it moves.[42]

We can see instances of "internal discipline and external resistance" in some Hispanic organizations that emerged from the protests of the 1960s, as in the farm workers' boycotts; in the unifying goals of COPS; among Cubans and their Cuban-American Alliance to bring about the fall of Fidel Castro; and Puerto Ricans and their pro-statehood or *independentista* movements. But the resistance that characterizes those movements and motivated those leaders are irrelevant in defining the group when you speak to the Mexican Americans or Puerto Ricans who climbed the ladder of success, went to Congress, occupied cabinet posts and were elected mayors, college presidents, or rose to the top of the artistic charts or the sports world with their successes. Right now, the Cubans have the strongest unifying resistance point of all Hispanic groups—bringing an end to Fidel Castro's stranglehold on their land.

There are, however, some unifying resistance points that cut across all Hispanic groups and that consistently appear in national surveys. These may offer rallying points for would-be Hispanic leaders in every sphere of human activity: Hispanics overwhelmingly support bilingual education; think that residents of the United States should learn English; are proud of being in the United States; are confident that their economic condition would be better in the future; and consistently express stronger religious beliefs and feelings than other groups while at the same time being less inclined to participate in religious events.

While these resistance points may not seem to be too closely linked to the religious dimension of the lives of Hispanics, ecclesial leaders may look to what those common characteristics reveal about Hispanics' "hopes, joys and anxieties," as *Gaudium et Spes* suggests (GS, no. 2). These points of agreement together with the broadest statement of consensus achieved by Hispanics are found in the conclusions of the Third National Encuentro[43] and are made explicit in the National Plan for Hispanic Ministry;[44] and they constitute the Hispanic ecclesial leaders' agenda for the next decade.

Here they can find clear signposts on the road to build Hispanic faith communities that are guided by "incarnated and committed leaders."[45]

RISKS, CHALLENGES, AND ACCOMPLISHMENTS
OF HISPANIC ECCLESIAL LEADERSHIP

The stated objective of Hispanic ecclesial leadership is summarized well in the *National Pastoral Plan*, which echoes in every line the ecclesiological tenets of Vatican II and the Medellín conclusions as examined earlier in this chapter:

> To live and promote . . . by means of *Pastoral de Conjunto* a model of church that is: communitarian, evangelizing, and missionary, incarnate in the reality of the Hispanic people and open to the diversity of cultures, a promoter and example of justice . . . that develops leadership through integral education . . . *that* is leaven for the kingdom of God in society. (p. 7)

There is, however, one particular risk that ecclesial leaders need to be very careful to avoid in nurturing Hispanic communities—separation and aloofness from one's national Hispanic origin. "In configurations of leadership distinctness and clarity disappear when we look at the group as a whole."[46] Leadership that has been learned in the rough-and-tumble of the mainstream Church acquires peculiar traits that cannot be said to exist in the ethnic group they represent. Having acquired the jargon of the academy, the corporation, or the diocesan office and the survival mechanisms that minorities have evolved in those settings, many Hispanics in Church leadership are often removed from the people that give them their identity and provide their particular dynamism.

The key accomplishment of ecclesial Hispanic leadership has been to place Hispanics, and many of the issues that concern them, on the agenda of the Church at all levels. However, agreement on the details of what the agenda should be has been sporadic, and the goals have not been clearly formulated either, in spite of the encuentro documents. New Hispanic leaders have tended to proceed in an ahistorical context without reference to the road that has been traveled in the last thirty years. These volumes produced by the Cushwa Center could become the required textbooks for Hispanic leadership formation programs.

The greatest challenge that Hispanic ecclesial leaders face goes hand in hand with the risk of aloofness from their group. It is to discover ways for preserving their links to their particular cultural identity within the group from which they come while developing a positive, collaborative, and dynamic relationship with the dominant Church leadership. This challenge also demands that leaders learn to relate to and promote the legitimate aspirations of other Hispanic groups within the Church and to collaborate with them in all issues that promote the common good.

Hispanic ecclesial leaders will be effective in the years to come only in the measure that they rise above individualistic, sexist (on the part of both men and women), and nationalistic tendencies so that as a unified group they can reshape and participate in guiding from the center the Catholic Church of the twenty-first century.

"May Mary, mother of the new Adam, be the midwife who assists at the birth of this new Christianity."[47]

NOTES

1. For details of these developments, consult the essay in this volume by Moisés Sandoval, "The Organization of a Hispanic Church."

2. Gregory Baum, ed., *The Teachings of the Second Vatican Council* (Westminster, Md.: Newman Press, 1966), p. 6.

3. *The Pope Speaks*, vol. 6, pp. 383–384.

4. *La Documentation Catholique* 59 (1962), col. 1613.

5. The Constitution on the Liturgy (*Sacrosanctum Concilium* [SC]), the Decree on Ecumenism (*Unitatis Redintegratio* [UR]), the Decree on the Apostolate of the Laity (*Apostolicam Actuositatem* [AA]), the Decree on the Church's Missionary Activity (*Ad Gentes Divinitus* [AG]), Declaration on the Relation of the Church to Non-Christian Religions (*Nostra Aetate* [NA]), the Pastoral Constitution of the Church in the Modern World (*Gaudium et Spes* [GS]), and the Dogmatic Constitution on the Church (*Lumen Gentium* [LG]).

6. Yves Congar, "La Iglesia como Pueblo de Dios," in *Selecciones de Teología*, vol. 31, no. 121, pp. 45–50.

7. *Apostolicam Actuositatem*, p. 6.

8. These figures were provided by Ramón Lima, president of the National Association of Hispanic Deacons, based on figures collected in 1991.

9. M. Useros, *La Iglesia Novedad Contemporánea* (Bilbao: Mensajero, 1967), p. 32.

10. Ibid., p. 33.

11. This image had first appeared in the writings of Yves Congar in 1937 and was fleshed out in the following decades ("La Iglesia," p. 46).

12. Edward Schillebeeckx, *The Real Achievement of Vatican II* (New York: Herder and Herder, 1967), pp. 47–48.

13. Ibid., p. 47.

14. Much of Cardinal Ratzinger's disquiet over the theology of liberation and the more anthropocentric spiritualities of the present has its root in what he perceives as a crude Teilhardianism which debases human hope and equates it with theological progress. See J. Ratzinger, *Theological Highlights of Vatican II* (New York: Paulist Press, 1966), p. 158.

15. *The Pope Speaks*, vol. 10, pp. 3, 275.

16. B. Lambert, "La problematique generale de la Constitutione," in *Vatican II, l'Eglise dans le monde de ce temps* (Paris: Editions du Beaf, 1967), vol. 2, p. 133.

17. P. Riga, *The Church Made Relevant: A Commentary on the Pastoral Constitution of Vatican II* (Notre Dame: Fides Press, 1967), p. 233.

18. Virgilio Elizondo, *Christianity and Culture* (Huntington, Ind.: Our Sunday Visitor, 1975), p. 102.

19. Carlos Fuentes, *The Buried Mirror: Reflections on Spain and the New World* (Boston: Houghton Mifflin, 1992), pp. 348–349.

20. See ibid., p. 40.

21. See Jane S. Gerber, *The Jews of Spain: A History of the Sephardic Experience* (New York: Free Press, 1992).

22. John McAndrew, *The Open Air Churches of Sixteenth Century Mexico* (Cambridge: Harvard University Press, 1965), p. 361.

23. Notes from a lecture on Latin American religious art in the sixteenth century, by Barbara von Barghahan, in a course sponsored by the Smithsonian Associates Program, Spring, 1989.

24. In *Documentation Catholique*, vol. 52 (Nov. 13, 1955), cols. 1457–1469.

25. David E. Mutchler, *The Church as a Political Factor in Latin America with Particular Reference to Colombia and Chile* (New York: Praeger, 1971), pp. 29–30.

26. *NCWC Bulletin*, June 18, 1962. NCWC, the National Catholic Welfare Conference, became the United States Catholic Conference and carries out the programs of the National Conference of Catholic Bishops.

27. The statement first appeared in a speech to the Concilium de Laicis and was enlarged in his *Apostolic Exhortation on Evangelization in the Modern World* (*Evangelii Nuntiandi* [EN], p. 28).

28. This conference has not been known to Catholics in the North. I was able to obtain copies of speeches and names of participants from notes and mimeographs found in the archives of Maryknoll Seminary in New York when I was writing my doctoral dissertation.

29. The main presenters were Bishops Brandao Vilela of Teresiña, Brazil, and Marcos McGrath from Santiago de Veragua, Panama, and the French Jesuit Pierre Bigó, ex-director of Action Populaire in Paris and then director of the Latin American Institute for Doctrine and Social Sciences (ILADES) in Santiago, Chile.

30. Letter of Pope Paul VI to CELAM, November 24, 1965, as cited in the final document of the Mar del Plata Assembly.

31. Father Colonnese was responsible for the publication of the English version of the Medellín documents and acted as editor of the two-volume set published in 1970 by the Latin American Bureau of the Department of International Affairs of the USCC and the General Secretariat of CELAM.

32. "Deseo ferviente de servir," in *Revista Maryknoll*, December 1992, 20–23.

33. The outcome of this survey was made available by the NCCB/USCC Secretariat for Hispanic Affairs through a press release dated 1991.

34. *National Catholic Reporter*, June 19, 1992, p. 3.

35. Present at that meeting were Mr. Franklin Abréu, Brooklyn; Mrs. Elena Almanza, Burley, Idaho; Sr. Maria Teresa Banderas, Coachella, Cal.; Bishop Gilberto Chávez, San Bernardino; Sr. Gabriela Covi-Maffei, Salinas, Cal.; Sr. Angela Erevia, San Antonio; Mrs. Victoria Espinosa, Browley, Cal.; Sr. Santos María Fernandez, Othello, Wash.; Sr. Gloria Galván, Holtville, Cal.; Sr. María Luisa Gastón, Baltimore, Md.; Mrs. María P. Gonzales, Escondido, Cal.; Fr. Patricio Guilléen, Corona, who together with Sr. Rosa Marta Zarate hosted the event; Sr. María López, Milwaukee; Fr. Andrés Martinez; Fr. Ricardo Mejía from Calexico, Cal.; Sr. Elvira Ríos, Sacramento; Sr. Louisa María Rodriguez, Philadelphia; Sr. Eva María Sánchez, San Bernardino; Sr. Maruja Sedano, Los Angeles; Ms. Imelda Valades, Corona; Sr. María de Jesús Ybarra, Granger, Wash.; Sr. Dominga Zapata, Chicago; and this author, who facilitated the sessions.

36. These workshops were featured in *Retrato de Evangelización Hispana: Entrenamiento de Evangelizadores*, booklet no. 6 of the series prepared by Cecilio Morales for the Committee on Evangelization of NCCB (Washington, D.C.: United States Catholic Conference, 1980).

37. Data gathered from ACHTUS (Academy of Catholic Hispanic Theologians of the U.S.), Membership Directory, 1991.

38. The data about St. Vincent was provided by Father Michael J. McNally, faculty member of the seminary and member of the advisory committee to the Cushwa Center. This information was gathered in June of 1992.

39. See Maria L. Gastón, "Leadership Development in the Hispanic Community," in *Faith and Culture: A Multicultural Catechetical Resource* (Washington, D.C.: Department of Education, United States Catholic Conference, 1987). The figures were obtained in an interview with Gastón, who was a member of the coordinating team of the Third National Encuentro.

40. Documents from the Office of Multicultural Catechesis, 1978.

41. "Columbus's Children," in the *Economist*, December 26, 1992–January 8, 1993, p. 32.

42. John Higham, ed., *Ethnic Leadership in America*, Johns Hopkins Symposia in Comparative History, no. 9 (Baltimore: Johns Hopkins University Press, 1978), p. 1.

43. *Prophetic Voices: The Document on the Process of the III Encuentro Nacional Hispano de Pastoral* (Washington, D.C.: United States Catholic Conference, 1986).

44. National Conference of Catholic Bishops, *National Pastoral Plan for Hispanic Ministry*, bilingual ed. (Washington, D.C.: United States Catholic Conference, November, 1987).

45. *Prophetic Voices*, p. 6.

46. Higham, p. 2.

47. From a prayer I wrote in the year of the Quincentenary of the arrival of Christianity in the New World.

6

The Hispanic Community and Church Movements: Schools of Leadership

Edmundo Rodríguez, S.J.

This chapter attempts to describe how Catholic Hispanics in the United States exercised leadership through organizations and regularly scheduled repeating events before 1965, the decline of these forms because of the changes brought into the Roman Catholic Church as a consequence of both the Second Vatican Council and the awakening of the Church of the poor in Latin America, and some of the Church movements and organizations which arose after 1965 that have provided new schools of leadership. Since other chapters analyze the reasons for the changed paradigms and models of Church operative after the Second Vatican Council and as a consequence of the Latin American developments, I concentrate on the concrete ways in which the changes showed themselves in predominantly Hispanic parishes and communities.

Now, lest there be a misunderstanding, I want to emphasize that although the organizations and events which predate 1965 have declined in their influence as organizational tools and leadership schools, they have by no means disappeared. In many places they continue to exist and to be useful as a means of involving parishioners in the life of parishes. Clearly, however, many have simply disappeared, and others involve a much smaller membership than, say, in the 1950s. In the meantime, many of the post-1965 organizations and movements have grown in membership and influence.

A word about what is meant by leadership and schools of leadership. . . . The opposite of being a leader is not to be a follower but rather to be passive and inactive. Leadership is the ability to influence other people to act in concert either for good or for ill. A Christian leader is one whose influence is permeated by the values of the gospel and who is helping to form Church, that is, a believing community of faith, by his or her actions. Leaders are knowledgeable about the goals they are pursuing, the methods and means to reach those goals, and the relationships that must exist if others are to be motivated to action. Leaders not only have some skills at planning and problem solving, but also have a vision which calls them forward.

This does not mean that leaders are always fully aware of all the elements that go into leadership in an explicit way. Effective leaders, however, exercise their skills in one way or another. Some people are natural leaders; they have an instinctive way of relating, motivating, negotiating, and providing direction. But even natural leaders do not get far unless there is some stable place where they can exercise their leadership skills, receive feedback, and get training to enhance those skills. For many Hispanics in the United States, who have often been cut out of the political processes, business networks and other institutional opportunities, Church organizations, movements, and events have provided that stable place for exercising and developing leadership skills.

Furthermore, an identifiable community of people, particularly one which is struggling with all the problems related to immigration, assimilation into a different culture, discrimination, and with overcoming all the centrifugal forces which pull a community apart, needs leadership to pull together and to be able to face community issues. This is the reason why it is important to examine the Catholic Church and its various expressions as a key factor in the development of leadership for the Hispanic communities of the United States. While a large number of Hispanics have moved from Catholicism to various kinds of Protestantism, a majority still identify themselves as Roman Catholic. Those who move from Catholicism to Protestantism seem to fall into two camps: the smaller camp is comprised of those with strong leadership potential who move up socially, economically, and educationally but identify Catholicism with a poorer and less enlightened life. Those in this camp often join the mainline Protestant churches.

The larger camp is made up of those who have been at the margins of formal Catholic Church life and find themselves more comfortable in fundamentalist congregations. Often they have not followed or understood the changes which have taken place in the Catholic Church and feel betrayed by them, or they are motivated to change by their individual or family need for simple, clear, and Scripture-based solutions to their human problems. There is no doubt that fundamentalist congregations tend to provide what looks like a more disciplined form of life. They seem to respond better to a more authoritarian kind of leadership than that offered currently at grassroots Catholic parishes. Since the Second Vatican Council, most parishes have developed a more participatory style of leadership, which can be confusing for those seeking clear directions for their lives.

So, what does this mean? It means that many of the Hispanics who remain in the Catholic Church are those who have been involved in the "political" life of the Church, understand the changes which have taken place, and look for leadership from within their own ranks. This makes the work of the schools of leadership of Church movements and organizations critical for the advancement of the Hispanic communities, whether these be the new immigrant communities or the more rooted communities of Cuban, Mexican, Puerto Rican Americans.

In my judgment, on the whole, the various Church movements and organizations have done a credible job of developing leaders, but there continues to be some discontinuity between the official Church leaders in the United States and those movements and organizations which serve and are directed mostly by Hispanics. South Florida, south Texas, and southern California have been notable exceptions. The reasons for this discontinuity seem to be these: 1) Hispanics have for so long been seen by the dominant Church as the targets of missionary activity rather than as a people who have something significant to contribute to the development of the Church. 2) Hispanics themselves have been uncomfortable with the liturgical and governance styles of the dominant Church. The words *cold* and *legalistic* are often associated with these styles in the thinking of Hispanics. And 3) The American Catholic Church has only recently begun to see the importance of sharing power with the laity and with minority peoples.

This chapter explores the phenomenon of *cofradías* (confraternities) and other regular organized activities by which Hispanic laity in the Church have exercised leadership. While the cofradías reach all the way back to the Middle Ages and predate the movements and organizations that came after 1965, many of the leaders of these relatively new movements were shaped by participation in the older forms. Furthermore, these older forms still exist in many predominantly Hispanic communities, and a growing desire among Hispanics to preserve their heritage has motivated many to try to revive some of the traditions like the *pastorelas* (shepherds' plays). These forms also illustrate some important characteristics of Hispanic religiosity: its love of pageantry, its concentration on the struggle between good and evil, its appreciation of suffering as redemptive, and its respect for traditions which have weathered the centuries.

The early 1960s saw the diminishment of the old parish organizations in predominantly Hispanic churches. From the turn of the century until the beginning of the Second Vatican Council, many active Hispanic Catholic parishioners exercised leadership through the activities of organizations known as cofradías (confraternities). The cofradías were a traditional form of organizing local parish and mission churches since the days of the Spanish missionaries and can be found all over Latin America. The cofradías were organizations of men or women, rarely of both, which served many purposes. They had a code of conduct, a rule of life, prescriptions for pious practices including participation in sacramental life, with conditions for membership, and a well-defined governance structure. The explicit purpose of the cofradías was primarily a religious one, as, for example, to obtain the grace of final perseverance and a peaceful death (one can imagine how important this was to a people who had often had to deal with both political and family violence). But the cofradías also had other very important purposes. They were a means of socializing and communicating, not just through meetings and liturgies, but through the *jamaicas, kermeses* (carnivals, festivals), and other festivals which the cofradías organized. They were also a way that churches, which with the advent of urbanization were growing beyond human scale, provided a sense of belonging to human-size communities. The cofradías also functioned as insurance societies for the poor who could not afford regular life insurance policies. By paying a few pennies each month into the treasury of the cofradía, members could be assured that their family would be given some help for their burial expenses upon their death. The members themselves could count on an impressive send-off by their cofradía: a Mass complete with procession and banners and a special graveside eulogy. Furthermore, the cofradías served as mutual aid societies by which members helped each other in times of financial distress.

The cofradía parish organizations covered the whole family. There were cofradías for adult women, for adult men, for boys, and for girls. So, for example, the Inecitas (named after the child martyr St. Agnes) was for preteenage girls; the Hijas de María for unmarried young women; the Luises (named after St. Aloysius Gonzaga) for teenage young men; the Damas del Sagrado Corazón de Jesús (Ladies of the Sacred Heart) and the Guadalupanas for mature women; and the Santo Nombre (Holy Name) and the Caballeros de San Juan (Knights of St. John) for mature men. There was even a cofradía for older men and women, La Sociedad de San José y de la Buena Muerte (Association of St. Joseph and a Peaceful Death), to help them prepare for death.

The cofradías were both schools of leadership and places where ordinary parishioners could exercise ministry. In their heyday many of their activities were the works of mercy: visiting the sick, consoling the bereaved, feeding the hungry. The cofradías were also the vehicles for fund raising for parish and school. Membership in these cofradías was large and enthusiastic, and members took pride in their work and in their contribution to their parish and their community.

LAS TRADICIONES: INFORMAL ORGANIZING BASED ON THE LITURGICAL YEAR

Other ways in which Hispanic parishes were organized was through *las tradiciones* of *parrandas* (house parties), *aguinaldos* (gifts), *pastorelas* (shepherds' plays), *los apostoles del jueves santo* (Reenactment of the Washing of the Feet), *el pésame* (Condolences), *la vigilia* (The Holy Thursday Watch), and *las posadas* (Looking for Lodging). Although these events happened only once a year, many families prepared costumes, rehearsed parts, and recruited helpers during a good part of the year. The tradiciones also included *procesiones* and *peregrinaciones* (processions and pilgrimages) which brought together people from many different churches.

The pastorela is a play about the shepherds' journey to Bethlehem to adore the *niño Jesús*. The story is performed in costume with long theological reflections in poetry and song about evil, redemption, the incarnation, and the response of human beings to God's saving initiative. While the heroes are characters like St. Michael the Archangel and the Holy Hermit, the more interesting characters are the legion of devils who symbolize the capital sins. Pastorelas were performed in Europe since the Middle Ages. Franciscan friars brought these poetic dramas to the Americas as a way to help the ordinary people reflect on the drama of the incarnation. The texts and music of these four- and five-hour dramatizations were handed on through oral tradition, and the parts were handwritten into family books which often also contained family histories. The roles of the various characters of the pastorelas passed from person to person within families and the rehearsals and performances were vehicles by which many families came together to do a service for their community, to pray, and to enjoy themselves. The principal performance of a pastorela was just before the Christmas midnight Mass and was accompanied by tamales and chocolate.

Pastorelas have by and large disappeared from Hispanic communities, with rare exceptions (as in Our Lady of Guadalupe Church in San Antonio, Texas, which has printed the text of *Los Pastores*, brought from Mexico by Leandro Granados in 1908),[1] though some Hispanic communities around the United States are trying to revive this tradition.

The posadas is still a familiar tradition in many Hispanic parishes, especially those which are predominantly Mexican or Mexican American. This practice represents the journey of Mary the mother of Jesus and her husband Joseph about the village of Bethlehem seeking shelter. This tradition has been especially popular with immigrant Hispanics who can identify with a family seeking shelter in a strange land. Posadas are often done not in the parish church but in the neighborhoods. People lend their homes for the various stations. A piñata party usually concludes the evening at the last station. This again is a Christmas tradition which provides a structure by which many families are able to celebrate together.

Very popular in the Puerto Rican community were and still are the parrandas which begin in late November and end in January, when the Nativity cycle ends. The parrandas are something like the posadas but have less a religious than a family feast character. *Parranda* does not signify the same thing in Puerto Rico as it does in Mexico, where the word connotes a drunken spree. Rather it means that a family makes a promise to take the Magi (*santos reyes*) on a house-by-house journey asking for *aguinaldo* at each house. *Aguinaldo* usually means asking for an offering of money which is used at the end of the Nativity cycle for a party to be given at the home of the originating family. In more traditional times in Puerto Rico, an entire village community was invited to this feast. At other times, the offering was used to help persons who might be suffering from hard times or else given to the local church for the poor or to have Masses said for someone who had died recently in the community. The Magi were made by the village *santero*, who carved wooden statues of *los santos reyes* who were always sitting on horses. The Magi represent three races: white, black, and Asian. The white and the Asian magi rode on black horses and the black, Melchior, always the most popular of the Magi, always rode astride a white horse. The popularity of Melchlor is consonant with the fact that the most popular image of Mary is that of the Virgin of Montserrat which depicts Mary as a black madonna.

The parranda is usually dedicated to the magi, but on occasion they may also be dedicated to one or another of the patron saints of the family which promotes the parranda. The families who take part in a parranda move from house to house, singing *aguinaldos*, also the name of the songs used for this occasion, which are improvised in part by a person who is a specialist at making up verses. Families who are visited by the parranda join the journey to the remaining houses. The parranda usually begins at nightfall and goes on for several hours. In places where the faith is strong, the parranda may end at the church for an early morning Mass (*misa de alba*), especially during the nine days immediately before Christmas. Out in the countryside, the people of the parranda light their way with torches, thus giving plenty of warning, both by the torches and by the music of their guitars, that they are approaching the next dwelling. The parranda brings the community together—people who had perhaps not seen much of each other all year—and gives them a chance to party together.

In cities like New York, the Puerto Rican community continues to celebrate the *parrandas* with many adaptations to take account of the urban environment. Where possible, parrandas are held within a *barriada* or neighborhood. At other times, people organize parrandas among families that are related by marriage or friendship rather than by neighborhoods. Interestingly, urban parrandas have developed into short surprise visits by a family or group of families and these visits are called *asaltos* (assaults)!

People become so enamored of the parrandas that many times they do not end with the feast of the Magi in January. Rather they continue for the *octava* (eight days after the feast) and even for the *octavita* (sixteen days after the feast).

Just as Christmas had its traditions so did Holy Week, the time when the Church remembers the passion, death, and resurrection of Jesus Christ. On Holy Thursday night, a group of twelve men, dressed as apostles, had their feet washed by the priest as part of the solemn liturgy. The apostles' roles belonged to and stayed within certain families. Later on Holy Thursday night there was a vigil before the Blessed Sacrament; the vigil lasted all night to commemorate the time when Jesus was arrested and imprisoned to await his trial. Again, some parishioners took turns keeping vigil while others prepared food and drink for those who came to spend the night watching and praying.

On Good Friday night, after commemoration of the passion and death of Jesus by a three-hour series of seven sermons combined with music to commemorate the seven last words of Jesus from the cross, the people returned for the ceremony of *el pésame* which means "condolences." Several women, dressed in mourning black, stood by a statue of Mary which was also dressed in black. Dirges were sung and a series of reflections on Mary's seven sorrows was delivered by a preacher. Then at the end of the ceremony, the people came up to venerate the instruments of the passion: the nails, the whip, the crown of thorns, and a representation of the heart of Mary pierced by seven daggers. The women of the pésame then handed each person a flower which was a symbol of hope in the resurrection to come. The pésame was a visually moving ceremony which was followed by the ritual burying of Jesus beneath the high altar. This pretty much closed Holy Week as far as the ordinary people were concerned. Interestingly, there were almost no popular traditions surrounding Easter.

Good Friday is considered by Puerto Rican Catholics to be the most sacred day of the most sacred week of the year. In earlier times, especially in the rural areas of Puerto Rico, all preparations of food for Good Friday had to be done the day before, there was to be no work, and silence was the order of the day. After the *trae horae* (a three-hour sermon on the passion and death of Christ), the men and women went out in procession. The men circled the church to one side carrying the statue of the dead Christ in a coffin, and the women circled in the opposite direction dressed in black and carrying a statue of Mary with the seven daggers in her heart. The two processions would meet in the plaza in front of the church where the women kneel as the Christ figure passes, then both processions enter the church and the services are concluded.

In New York City, the Puerto Rican community presents a dramatization of the *via crucis* which generally ends at St. Joseph's Church in the Bronx, in an area that is afflicted with drugs and crime. Yet on Good Friday the whole community emerges to reclaim their religious traditions and the streets around their church. The same thing is done in the Lower East Side. It takes courage and leadership to organize people to take the streets where danger lurks everywhere. Keeping alive the tradition of the via crucis continues to remind people that the victims of crime and drugs and poverty and injustice are intimately connected with the death of Jesus on the cross. It is a reminder that he is one of *los de abajo* (the poor) and that his fate was not so different from the poor of today.

Holy Saturday for the Puerto Ricans becomes a time for mostly secular celebrations like dances (*bailes del sábado de gloria!*), a kind of release after the solemnity of Holy Week and especially after the severity of Good Friday.

Of course, the via crucis is done in many other Hispanic communities throughout the United States. Most communities use very graphic techniques to represent the crucifixion itself. Unfortunately, in some communities the biblical texts used sound anti-Semitic and there is no opportunity to interpret the events being witnessed by the public. Still, the impact of such representations is very powerful in connecting life experiences with the death of Jesus.

Another one of the traditions which brought and still brings the Hispanic community together in a prayerful way are the pilgrimages, the peregrinaciones. This is especially true in west Texas and New Mexico where the custom of doing peregrinaciones goes back more than two centuries. The church at Chimayo, New Mexico, just north of Santa Fe is the focus of an annual peregrinación by people of the surrounding towns who make *promesas* to walk to the church which has a "well" of dirt which is considered curative. The shrine is adorned with the crutches of those who have come on them to the shrine and left without them; the crutches date all the way to the last century. Another popular place of pilgrimage is the shrine of San Lorenzo, Mártir. People walk from Ysleta, Socorro, Fabens, and San Elizario to Clint, Texas, near El Paso, on the saint's feast day to fulfill *promesas y mandas* (promises and vows). The Indians from nearby Tigua come to do a ritual dance as well. Many of the pilgrims join in their all-day dancing as a way to fulfill the promises they have made to the saint. The ritual dancing of the *matachines* (ritual dancers), usually children and young people who portray the indigenous strain of Mexican identity, is coming back more and more for various feast days, particularly for the feast of Our Lady of Guadalupe.

The cofradías and the tradiciones served Catholic Hispanics very well until the changes in the Church and society during the mid-1960s began to erode them. After the Second Vatican Council the Catholic Church began to forge a new definition of itself and the old organizations, and traditions did not fit the renewed parishes very well. Why not? Beginning with the clergy and religious, the sense of what was important and to be pursued changed and thus the purposes of parish activities changed. As insurance became more accessible to a greater number of Hispanics, one of the main purposes of the cofradías was no longer operative. Then there was the emphasis on activities which did not separate men and women but rather helped them work together in parish activities. Parish councils, liturgy committees, and school boards were formed with both men and women serving. The principal liturgical celebration pushed out the many novenas and even some of the other traditions. But the most important change that took place was that people began to feel that they were part and parcel of the Church and not clients only. It was no longer so important that they join subsidiary organizations to have a sense of belonging in the Church. The Church no longer belonged only to the clergy. It belonged to the people.

Furthermore, the smaller, more compact Hispanic communities began to swell with new immigrants as economic conditions worsened in Latin America, especially in Mexico and Puerto Rico. The barrios became places not just of poverty, but of substandard overcrowded housing, high unemployment, and even worse underemployment. The old sense of neighborhood broke down as marijuana and heroin made their destructive way into the barrios. Thus, many Hispanic parishes began to experience the pain and depression which comes from watching a beloved family member die a slow death. Priests and people alike found themselves searching for new ways to be Church, for another way to exercise leadership, for another way to organize through the churches. At the same time, a growing number of immigrant communities were developing throughout the cities and the countryside in places where they and their Hispanic-style Catholicism were regarded with suspicion. It was in this context that new Church movements and organizations came to influence Hispanic Catholics in the United States.

THE CURSILLO AND THE CHILDREN OF CURSILLO

The Cursillo was the first of the powerful renewal movements to give Hispanic Catholics a new-found sense of purpose and involvement in the Church. The Cursillo movement began on the island of Mallorca (Majorca) a few years after the end of World War II. It grew out of a training course for those who were to be leaders on a pilgrimage to the tomb of Apostle St. James in Santiago de Campostella. Acción Católica, Catholic Action, the movement which arose as a result of Leo XIII's social justice Magna Charta, *Rerum Novarum*, created the climate in which the Cursillo came to be, for it was the young men's branch of Acción Católica, which in 1932 decided to hold their Second National Congress in Santiago de Campostella. Their plans were interrupted first by the Spanish Civil War which erupted in 1936 and then by World War II which followed on the heels of the Spanish Civil War. After the great War, Acción Católica was reconstructed in Spain and reorganized around the parishes. As a preparation for the still-pending pilgrimage to Santiago de Campostella, the young men of Mallorca developed training courses for those whom they expected to be leaders at Santiago. The courses, called *cursillos de Cristiandad*, short courses on Christianity, were so well received that they were soon happening in Madrid and other Spanish cities. A young energetic layman provided the dynamic leadership which gave rise to the schools of leadership. That young man was Eduardo Bonnin who is revered as the founder of the Cursillo movement.[2]

In 1957, a pair of Spanish air cadets were in Waco, Texas, for training. On May 27 of that year, they held a Cursillo for a group of Hispanic men. The Cursillo responded to a felt need of Catholic Hispanics to find a way to exercise leadership in the Church and to find ideals which would reenergize them. Many of the early cursillistas were men and women who had belonged to the diminishing cofradías and other traditional parish organizations. In the Cursillos, Hispanics found a new sense of purpose and belonging. Lay men and women could minister to each other through the process of recruitment, by delivering the *rollos*, key talks, of the Cursillo, and by helping with the follow-up, interparochial *ultreyas*, supportive reflection meetings, for those who had already experienced the intensive Cursillo experience.

Because many bishops, first in Spain but also in the other countries where the Cursillo quickly became established, including the United States, saw the response of the lay people to the gospel ideals, the community-building process, and conversions undergone by those who made the Cursillo, they supported the movement. Still, there were some bishops and many pastors who opposed it because they were suspicious that the movement might drain their parishes of their best and most committed workers. In the early stages, the Cursillo coexisted with the cofradías which struggled to continue in existence even as the Cursillo began to make itself felt. But it soon became clear that the real excitement for Hispanic Catholics was in the Cursillo and the other *movimientos*, movements, which were attracting them.

Although the Cursillo among Hispanics in the United States was presented as a religious rather than a social action movement, it nevertheless motivated many Hispanic leaders who have made important contributions in the struggle for justice. Among these was Archbishop Patricio Fernandez Flores of San Antonio.[3] Another cursillista was Cesar Chavez, the president of the United Farm Workers Union. Besides these well-known leaders, there were many other men and women who developed a deeper social consciousness through the Cursillo movement and committed themselves to social action. Genaro Garcia of San Antonio, who was president of FAMA (Federation for Action by Mexican Americans) in the turbulent late 1960s and early 1970s says that the Cursillo helped him to recover his language and his cultural heritage. The methodology of the Cursillo, which gave him a way of looking at issues and immersed him in a community of people who could share both aspirations and the concerns of their lives, helped him to develop an awareness of social issues affecting the Mexican-American people of San Antonio's Westside. The result was a commitment on his part to work on specific issues like the need to remove the welfare assistance ceiling set by the Texas State Constitution, job discrimination, school-funding disparities, and the selection of Mexican Americans on grand juries, among others.[4]

Verónica Méndez, R.C.B., a woman religious from New York, now on the formation staff of Mundelein Seminary in Chicago, speaks about the power of the cursillo movement in the New York metropolitan area where she worked for many years:

> If one does not know and is not willing to get involved with movimientos up here, a person will not be effective in Hispanic ministry. Why? Because that's where *el pueblo* is. That's where the people go. Many parishes don't respond to the needs of the people, be it faith, or cultural expression, or support of the people as Hispanics, or as Catholics as the movimientos do. . . . In the movimientos you cry, you clap, you sing, you dance, you tell salty jokes—all of which are part of our culture and our culture is very much part of our religion as our religion is also part of our culture.

To Verónica, it is clear that Hispanics prefer the style of the Cursillo or the *renovación carismática* which touch the heart while providing nourishment for the mind to the more staid approaches to worship found in many parishes.[5]

Father Antonio González, who directed the Cursillo movement in the Lubbock, Texas, area for many years, says that the movement opened the doors for Hispanics to be able to access the power structures of the Church. Many of the cursillistas developed a sense of confidence which made them become assertive both at the parish and at the diocesan levels. The cursillistas of the Lubbock area worked to put Hispanics in public office for the first time and organized *huelgas* and *marchas* (strikes and marches) to protest conditions of injustice. The Cursillo movement served as a motivating instrument, a networking vehicle, and a leadership training school for Hispanics of the Lubbock area, who until the 1960s had no political or economic power and little voice in either Church or society.[6]

Bishop Agustín Román, auxiliary of the archdiocese of Miami, calls the Cursillo the motor for all the movements which vivify the Church in the Miami archdiocese. He says that the Cursillo was instrumental in helping the Catholic Church maintain the allegiance of the Cuban exiles in the 1960s. Without the Cursillo the Masons would have been very attractive to the Cuban exiles.[7]

The Miami archdiocese appointed Bishop Román as vicar for Hispanics in 1976 and one of his prime duties was to stay on top of the developing movimientos to make sure that they were coordinated and that the kind of jealous feuding which has sometimes marred their work in other places did not take place. Each month he holds a meeting with all those who are in charge of the various movements. At these meetings there is discussion of a pastoral theme which Archbishop Edward McCarthy issues each year. For example, the theme for 1980 was "The Family"; in 1981, it was "The Parish"; in 1982, it was "Faith"; in 1983, it was "Prayer"; in 1984, it was "Charity"; in 1985, it was "Vocations," etc. Once the archbishop issues his pastoral letter announcing the theme for the year, each of the movements meditates on the theme and then decides how to respond to the theme within their structure. For this reason they are usually more in tune with the pastoral plan of the diocese than the parishes which depend more directly on the thinking of the pastors.

Bishop Román contends that Catholics are still not very clear about the difference between a movement and a parish. Parishes generally reject movimientos or try to adapt them to parish patterns. The parishes tend to be places for the settled Catholics who often do not have a missionary spirit. They do not reach out to many Catholics who are not churchgoers. These are Catholics who only show up at church for the great feasts like Christmas and Easter or for weddings and funerals and are not, for the most part, reached by the parish. The movimientos, on the other hand, give the Church a way to respond to these Catholics. But since they are a fairly new phenomenon in the Church, there is still much suspicion about them. "There is a reluctance to talk about them because they are like a hurricane. They stir things up."[8]

In the Miami archdiocese, the movimientos have centered around the family. The first thing that began to develop seriously in the Miami archdiocese was the Movimiento Familiar Cristiano (MFC, Christian Family movement). But then the Church saw the necessity of helping parents deal with adolescent children because of the huge generation gap which arose between the first generation of Cuban immigrants and their children. From this concern arose El Encuentro Familiar, which brings together parents and their adolescent or young adult children. The purpose is to help the family understand that what has happened to them is not unique to that family and can be remedied through dialogue. Then was seen the need to have a movement which would take younger children into account. Thus, was *Impactos* born for families whose children are ten years old and under.

Then it was noted that the problems began even earlier than when a family had children. There was a need to do something for those preparing to be married which was more than the pre-Cana conferences. The movimiento which was developed for engaged couples and others dating seriously is called Camino del Matrimonio. Camino is a process by which people who are seriously contemplating marriage are helped to develop friendship with each other and thus to move beyond sexual attraction as a basis for marriage. There is still another nascent movimiento called Amor en el Principio for those who are just deciding to begin dating on a steady basis but are not yet sure where it might lead.

There is need now to develop a movimiento for those recently married who undergo many crises of adjustment within the first five years of marriage. There is a ministry to these persons which is developing and will also become a movimiento with time. These newlyweds, who had so much support before they were married, are left without support until they start having children and by that time they are already experiencing many difficulties.

As far as the leadership of the movements goes, they each have a spiritual director who can be either a priest or a permanent (married) deacon. But their real power stems from their being a peer ministry of laypeople to each other. They are schools of leadership through ministry which is based on life experiences and reflection on the demands of the gospel. Thus the movimientos in Miami have done things which neither the archdiocese nor any of the parishes could have done. For example, they are funding and producing six daily hours of religious media programming in Spanish. The radio station which carries these programs from six A.M. until noon has seen its ratings increase consistently. The prison ministry is done by some 150 members of the various movimientos. These committed laypeople conduct prayer services and provide religious instruction inside the walls of the jails and prisons. The movimientos can focus on a project and motivate large numbers of people to take on that project in a way that no parish or diocese can do, simply because these latter are so burdened by administrative and management issues and must serve such a variety of publics. The movimientos, on the other hand, are more able to concentrate their resources and their forces on a few projects because so many different services are not expected from them.

The Cursillo and the other movements have indeed been schools of leadership for Hispanics, imparting conversion experiences, social awareness, ways of networking, and spiritual insight. They continue strong in many places though many other renewal programs and community organizations have entered the competition for the attention and loyalty of Hispanic Catholics.

Encuentros Matrimoniales

The original Marriage Encounter weekends started in Spain and were later modified and adapted for English-speaking couples. Marriage Encounter weekends became very popular and helped to heal many marriages throughout the United States, but, ironically, they were not available to Hispanics unless they made them in English. Then in 1976 Roberto and Rosie Piña of San Antonio were recruited to make the encounter. For Roberto and Rosie the experience was not just one of renewing their marriage but of rediscovering their ethnic and cultural roots. They became convinced that a program like Marriage Encounter was needed in the Hispanic community of San Antonio and in other places, so they began agitating for the leadership of Marriage Encounter to attend to Hispanics. The leadership in turn challenged Roberto and Rosie to develop a version of Marriage Encounter which would work for Hispanics. They took up the challenge and before long they were traveling not just all over the United States, but to Mexico and other Latin American countries to bring to them Los Encuentros Matrimoniales.

Roberto himself testifies that Hispanic men are by and large quite resistant to participating in the encounters. The cultural conditioning of many generations does not generally provide Hispanic men with models of mutuality in marriage. The model has been of a male who is in control of his household, meaning his wife and children. Men often make each other feel guilty if it seems that the wife is seeking a greater role in the marriage, or at least a greater explicit role. The philosophy of the encounter, which promotes dialogue rather than simply the obedience of wife and children, can be threatening to those who grew up with a different model of being husband. Thus, the encounters are not just renewing individual marriages but even creating a new paradigm for Hispanic married life.[9]

Pastoral Youth Programs

One of the most startling demographic facts about Hispanics in the United States is the high percentage of those who are under twenty-five years of age. Moreover, Hispanic youth are experiencing the highest school drop-out rate of any racial or ethnic group. It is no surprise that gang membership and activity is an area of acute concern for political leaders, pastoral agents, and families. Another associated concern is the poor self-concept which afflicts many Hispanic youth. Thus, there is always much anxiety among those who serve Hispanic youth to develop effective programs which will help reverse the effects of exclusion and discrimination and create a sense of pride and confidence in them.

The Encuentros Juveniles, Youth Encounters, of the Cursillo movement have produced much fruit in the Dallas–Fort Worth area, according to Andres Aranda, who directs the youth ministry office for the diocese of Fort Worth.[10] Verónica Méndez, who worked with youth for many years in the New York area, also testifies to the power of the Youth Encounters. Bishop Román talks about their value in the Miami area as well. This is important since the largest percentage of the Hispanic population is under twenty-five years of age. In fact, only 9 percent of the Hispanic community is forty-five years or older.[11] *Búsqueda*, the Spanish-language version of SEARCH, has also been successful with younger Hispanic youth. The Southeast Pastoral Institute (SEPI) has a powerful youth program which is designed to help young people build a positive self-image. The program is based on the work of Jesuit Alejandro Londoño of Bolivia, who generally comes each year to participate in the SEPI youth programs.[12] The youth movements are beginning to produce a number of religious and priestly vocations, especially in the Southwest, where many of the participating youths are directly from Mexico or Central America.

The impact of the youth movements is being seen more and more both in the number of young people who are expressing an interest in the seminary and religious life and in those who are dedicating themselves to the service of the Church as laypersons. The youth movements do something which Hispanics appreciate very much: they encourage a sense of close-knit community, family, and they use the kind of lively music which appeals to the young. These movements also hand over the leadership for planning and speaking and directing to the young people themselves, making them responsible, under the guidance of adults who have a renewed vision of the Church, for carrying out the recruitment and the processes. The secret of their appeal to the young is full and serious participation. These Church movements for the young are a great sign of hope for the Hispanic community, particularly for new immigrants.

The one great drawback of these youth programs seems to be that they do not appeal very much to those young people who have been affected more deeply by the dominant culture of the United States. These young people are simply harder to reach. They either do not live in barrios anymore or are not comfortable with Spanish or do not relate well with the new immigrants. Some have pretty much dropped out of any of the socializing institutions, like churches and schools. One of the real challenges facing the Church in the Hispanic communities is how to reach the young people who have dropped out.

RENOVACIÓN CARISMÁTICA: ENERGÍA DEL ESPÍRITU

A flourishing and ever-expanding charismatic renewal took the Catholic Church in the United States by surprise in the early 1970s. Unlike some of the earlier enthusiasm movements which had stirred the lower middle-income American classes in the nine-teenth century, the charismatic revival, in the Anglo-American community, has attracted fairly affluent Catholics. It hit quite force-fully in the Anglo community where emotional expression in wor-ship and prayer had long been tamed so that there was little room for outbursts of spiritual enthusiasm.[13]

In the Hispanic community the renovación carismática, charis-matic renewal, also started among the middle-income Catholic population but soon attracted many low-income people as well. Because the Hispanics tend to be religiously conservative, many, especially those who had been used to the ways of the more staid cofradías, found the outward expressions of emotion, the praying in tongues, the slaying in the Spirit, and the other manifestations of the renovación, quite disturbing. Many traditional Hispanic Catho-lics viewed those who became Spirit filled as having turned *protes-tantes*. Many parish communities experienced tension and division as the renovación began to make inroads into the congregations.

During the decade of the 1970s, however, the charismatic re-newal did attract a large number of Hispanic adherents and was a means of genuine conversion for many. There were some features of the renewal which resonated with Hispanic piety and popular religiosity: the expression of emotion in the prayer echoed back to the religious processions of yesteryear; the emphasis on prayer and on God's action to bring about changes in the person, in the family, and in the world, reflected the si Dios es servido dependence on God; and the inclusion of the children in the prayer meetings was very much in tune with the value which Hispanics put on family unity. But as there were very positive aspects to the movement, so there were negative ones. Just at a time when the bishops were encouraging Catholics to engage more directly on social issues, those Hispanics involved in the renovación showed a marked ten-dency to substitute prayer for social involvement and to do so out of the apparent conviction that only God can change society and that what is needed is not so much action but prayer. Many in the movement seemed to feel that too many Catholics had fallen into a sort of activism and this needed correction. Then, too, a strong emphasis on a kind of biblical subordination of women reinforced a tendency toward patriarchy already present in Hispanic soci-ety. The governance system by which leaders "emerge" from the members of the prayer groups seemed to cause a special problem among Hispanics. In many prayer groups there developed a fierce infighting among the leaders for control of the group.

Notwithstanding the problems, many Hispanics came to enjoy participating in prayer groups and made such participation a central feature of their spiritual life. The charismatic renewal brought many people back to the practice of the faith and to reinvolve themselves in the Church.

PADRES ASOCIADOS PARA DERECHOS
EDUCATIVOS, RELIGIOSOS, Y SOCIALES

The PADRES organization was born when its members walked out of the national convention which they had convoked and reorganized themselves on February 4, 1970, in Tucson, Arizona. According to a press release issued by the organization on February 9, the dramatic step was considered necessary to ensure the survival of PADRES as the voice of Mexican-American priests.[14]

The organization began in the barrios of San Antonio, Texas, where a number of priests working among Mexican Americans began meeting to discuss problems which were affecting the Mexican Americans of San Antonio's Westside: hunger, malnutrition, unemployment, and underschooling as well as problems of the Catholic Church's relationship to the people these priests were serving. The leaders who promoted this series of meetings were Rafael Ruiz, Balthasar Janacek, and Lawrence Matula, priests of the archdiocese of San Antonio; Franciscan Manuel Martinez; and Jesuit Edmundo Rodríguez, among others. Rafael Ruiz in particular, who was director of the archdiocesan inner city apostolate and had appeared in a CBS television documentary illustrating conditions of hunger among Americans, had high visibility. The Westside of San Antonio provided numerous examples of families and elderly persons who because of poverty were experiencing hunger and malnutrition. Ruiz's vision and energy made him a natural to lead PADRES once it began to take shape.

In 1969, the San Antonio priests invited priests working with Mexican Americans from around Texas to come to a meeting in San Antonio. The result was unexpected. The meeting turned out to be more than a Texas meeting. Priests came from Colorado, Arizona, and New Mexico as well as Texas. Among those who came to that early regional meeting of PADRES was Patricio Fernandez Flores who would become the first native-born Hispanic bishop of the United States in 1970. The enthusiasm of the San Antonio meeting issued into the first national meeting of the PADRES organization in Tucson, the convention which was marked by the walk-out of the Mexican-American priests.

PADRES had a powerful impact on the Catholic Church in the United States. By the time of its 1975 national convention in San Antonio, four Hispanic bishops were in attendance: Bishop Juan Arzube of Los Angeles; Bishop Gilbert Chávez of San Bernardino; Bishop Patricio F. Flores of San Antonio; and Archbishop Roberto Sánchez of Santa Fe. Other attending priests would later become bishops: Raymond Peña of Corpus Christi and Ricardo Ramírez of Tehuacan, Puebla, Mexico. PADRES was the organization leading the fight to have the Catholic Church open its hierarchical doors to Hispanics. The 1975 convention also called for 1) a revision of the seminary system in which Hispanic candidates were said to experience "deculturalization and alienation . . . from (their) cultural patrimony"; 2) "redistribution of the human and material resources of the Church itself to promote justice and integral liberation and development for all men and women but especially for the poor"; 3) the support of local churches for community-organizing efforts to address "neglect of public works by local governments, redlining by financial institutions, and the unequal distribution of school finances"; 4) a rejection of "the notion that we all need to be reduced to the lowest common denominator . . . a melting pot"; 5) Hispanic women to be prepared for priestly ordination; 6) the governments of the United States and Mexico to recognize "the right of individuals to migrate in order to improve their state of life as affirmed by Pope Paul VI in *Cura Migratorum* of 1969"; and 7) strong support by all PADRES members for the United Farm Workers in their struggle for better living and working conditions, just wages, and protection under the law.[15]

In some ways the 1975 PADRES national convention represented the organization at its peak. In 1976 the national convention was held in New York City. Notwithstanding a heroic effort by Antonio Stevens-Arroyo to enlist the predominantly Spanish priests of the New York area into PADRES, the latter did not think it advantageous to join. After that time, many of the members of PADRES became involved in community organizing efforts, diocesan Hispanic ministry offices, or became pastors of parishes. Later conventions simply did not have the spirit and involvement of the early years, so the organization all but disappeared by the mid-1980s and some of the priests who had belonged to PADRES joined

ANSH, the Asociación Nacional de Sacerdotes Hispanos. Moisés
Sandoval is of the opinion that if PADRES had been transmuted
into "PUEBLO" at its El Paso meeting in 1981 by admitting not
only Hispanic deacons and religious brothers as full members,
as it did, but also lay men and women, it would have survived
the way Las Hermanas has.[16] Juan Romero, a priest of the archdiocese of Los Angeles, who was executive director of PADRES
during its heyday, believes that many of the organization's goals
had become reality and so the energy created by the challenge
to achieve those goals began to dissipate. In the mid-1980s, the
PADRES leadership, under president Ramón Gaitán, reopened serious discussions with ASH, Asociación de Sacerdotes Hispanos,
an organization of mostly Spanish priests based in New York which
had viewed PADRES as a powerful Chicano organization. The
contact resulted in ANSH, Asociación Nacional de Sacerdotes Hispanos, which became formalized in 1990 under the presidency of
Eduardo Salazar, S.J., an active PADRES member.[17]

ANSH: Asociación National de Sacerdotes Hispanos, EE.UU.

When PADRES fell apart, many Hispanic priests continued to
feel the need to belong to a national organization which would
carry their agendas forward in the American Church. In October
1990, ANSH held its first annual convention in Albuquerque, at
which it adopted a constitution and elected Eduardo Salazar, S.J.,
as president; Joachim S. Beaumont as vice-president; Enrique J.
Sera as secretary; and Einer Ochoa as treasurer. According to the
constitution and by-laws, the purposes of ANSH are 1) to promote
unity and fraternity among Hispanic priests of the United States;
2) to be the official voice of Hispanic priests belonging to the association before the National Conference of Catholic Bishops; 3) to
serve as support to priestly ministry and pastoral activities aimed
at the promotion and development of the Hispanic community;
4) to provide a national forum of Hispanic priests in which personal
and pastoral experiences are shared and focused toward a common
vision which will help understand and resolve the problems that
arise in different communities and among the priests; 5) to develop the priestly identity of Hispanic priests, to advocate for their
rights as persons and pastoral agents and support these priests
in their responsibilities and needs; 6) to take a position in regard

to problems that affect priests and their Hispanic communities in the United States; 7) to participate in the development of the Catholic Church in the United States without losing the broader perspective for the universal Church; 8) to promote and encourage a genuine spirituality for Hispanic priests; 9) to promote and encourage continuing education, such that Hispanic priests might achieve an integral education; 10) to promote and encourage the integration of the Hispanic priests in the American environment, in terms of language and culture; 11) to encourage solidarity and fraternity within the diversity of the nationalities and cultures of the Hispanic priests; 12) to cooperate in the implementation of the *National Pastoral Plan for Hispanic Ministry*; and 13) to promote vocations within the Hispanic community to the priesthood, diaconate, religious life, and lay ministries.[18]

The theme of the 1990 national convention was "The Role of the Priest in Evangelization, Yesterday, Today, and Tomorrow." Unlike PADRES, to which belonged mostly Mexican American and other priests working among Mexican Americans, the priests who have joined ANSH represent a broader spectrum of the Hispanic community. The presence of priests from Spain who are working in the United States is especially noteworthy since there had been rare instances of Spanish priests working alongside of Mexicans, Mexican Americans, Cubans, Cuban Americans, and Puerto Ricans before ANSH came along.

As becomes clear from the statement of purpose in the constitution and by-laws, ANSH directs its attention mostly to Church intramural concerns and to issues which directly affect the priests themselves. Social and political issues tend to be divisive, so the organization seems intent on avoiding them. But in doing so, ANSH will not earn the privilege of speaking for Hispanics from within the Church structure. This is unfortunate because since the demise of PADRES, no Hispanic Church organization has directly addressed the social and political issues affecting Hispanic communities. Perhaps it is impossible for any national Church organization to attempt to address controversial issues and maintain a broad membership.

ANSH illustrates that organizations create different kinds of leaders. The development of Hispanic priests who exercise leadership in the wider community is now limited to the work of community organizers, while Church organizations tend to develop leaders for more directly ecclesial concerns.

LAS HERMANAS: A STEP TOWARD PUEBLO

About the same time that the Mexican-American and other priests were organizing PADRES, Mexican-American religious women were also organizing themselves. It is important to note that the two religious most immediately involved with the early organizational efforts of Las Hermanas, Gloria Gallardo, S.H.G., and Gregoria Ortega, O.L.V.N., were both working in San Antonio's Westside and connected with the archdiocesan inner-city apostolate. So, like PADRES, Las Hermanas was born from the poverty and suffering of the Mexican-American people. The first meeting of the organization was in Houston in 1971. Some fifty Hispanic women religious attended. Gloria Gallardo became the first president of the organization.

Almost from the beginning, Las Hermanas began to include laywomen. At first, the laywomen were the Hispanic women who had joined Hermanas as religious and opted to stay as part of Hermanas even after they left their religious communities.[19] Other Hispanic women were soon invited to join and so the organization was transformed into a powerful vehicle for the aspirations of Hispanic Church women.[20] A principal purpose which emerged early on for Las Hermanas was mutual support and affirmation of their identity as Hispanic women. Many of the Hispanic women who entered religious communities in the United States had practically been forced to abandon their cultural identity. One of the important tasks of Las Hermanas was to help each other find that identity again.

Las Hermanas took on some of the women's issues, especially as they affect the Church. Thus, many of them saw the women religious from Mexico who work in seminary and retreat house kitchens around the United States as another form of the oppression of women in the Church. The position of these Mexican religious seemed to say that women belonged in the kitchens but not on the faculties of seminaries. So Hermanas took on the task of contacting these women and convincing them that they were capable of doing important pastoral work among Hispanics in the United States. The effort caused some deep disagreements among the Hermanas members. Some of them heard the Mexican religious plead not only financial need to support their communities in Mexico, but, more importantly, that they saw their work as an apostolate of prayer and service which they identified as their charism. The effort was eventually abandoned but not before raising many issues about women in the Church.

On other fronts, however, Hermanas has continued to support the efforts of the Women's Ordination Conference to press for the ordination of women in the Catholic Church. The organization has also been working with the National Association of Religious Women on issues like the use of inclusive language and with the Leadership Conference of Women Religious (LCWR) on vocations and other questions from the perspective of Hispanic women. Many Hermanas are doing work on the cutting edge: Verónica Méndez and Marina Herrera are on seminary faculties; Silvia Sedillo is director of the Women's Spirituality Center in Santa Fe; Yolanda Tarango became one of the general councillors for the Sisters of the Charity of the Incarnate Word; Olga Villa-Parra is a key staff person for the Lily Endowment; Anita de Luna is superior general of the Missionary Congregation of Divine Providence (M.C.D.P.) and current president of LCWR; Rosa Maria Elías is director of the Spanish Apostolate in Hartford, Connecticut; Elisa Rodríguez does cultural awareness workshops with many dioceses and works with CORHIM, the Committee on Religious Hispanics in Ministry, which runs workshops for Hispanic religious men and women to help them reflect on their roles as Hispanics within religious congregations, a work closely modeled on seminars developed by the Latin American Conference for Religious (CLAR); Marta Zárate and Ninfa Garza are among the experts in the practical implementation of the concept of *comunidades eclesiales de base* in the United States; and the list goes on.

Las Hermanas as a religious-lay Church organization of Hispanic women highlights the strengths of Hispanic women: the depth of their commitment to issues of justice; their willingness to get involved with issues even at the risk of failing; their organizational skills; and the deeply religious motivation which informs their activities. The choice of Las Hermanas to open their membership to laywomen in the Church has been a significant step toward the dream that many Hispanics have that one day all the different pieces will come together and there will be a significant Church organization/movement called PUEBLO (PEOPLE), which will see laypeople and priests and religious, men and women, young and old, organized into a powerful network which will not only address ecclesial, social, and political issues, but will impart to the Catholic Church in the United States significant gifts from Hispanic-American Catholicism.

The Mexican American Cultural Center (MACC)

The moving spirit and founding president of MACC, Virgilio Elizondo, a priest of the archdiocese of San Antonio, puts the birth of MACC at the first PADRES retreat in Albuquerque, which was directed by John Linskens, C.I.C.M. who at that time had been teaching in the East Asian Pastoral Institute in Manila. Fifty members of PADRES came to the 1972 retreat, the first retreat under the sponsorship of the nascent organization. Its theme was justice in the Gospel according to St. Luke.

During the course of the week the participants took time to discuss an issue which had already been part of a heated discussion among members of PADRES in San Antonio. The question was whether or not the organization ought to advocate the establishment of a national seminary wholly dedicated to the formation of Mexican-American candidates for the priesthood. While some PADRES members strongly supported the idea on the premise that young Mexican Americans rarely survived in seminaries such as they were in 1972, others vehemently opposed the idea as creating a structure whose graduates would be considered to be second-class priests. Yet, everyone was in agreement that something needed to be done both to support young Mexican-American candidates for the priesthood and to sensitize and help provide cultural formation for those priests who were already working among the Mexican-American people. The result of the discussion was the ideal which soon became MACC, the Mexican American Cultural Center.[21]

Virgilio Elizondo presented the idea to Francis Furey, archbishop of San Antonio, who advocated the idea of the center with other bishops and offered the use of vacant buildings on the grounds of Assumption Seminary on San Antonio's Northwest Side. Through Archbishop Furey's advocacy, the Texas Catholic Conference appointed a steering committee which included Archbishop Furey; Archbishop James P. Davis of Santa Fe; Bishop Lawrence de Falco of Amarillo; Bishop Thomas Tschoepe of Dallas; Auxiliary Bishop Patricio Flores; Sister James Elizabeth González; Sister Gloria Gallardo, president of Las Hermanas; Jorge Lara-Braud, director of the Hispanic American Institute in Austin; Leonard Mestas; historian Richard Santos; and Fathers Virgilio Elizondo, Peter Kellerman, Joseph Montoya, Ron Anderson, Ed Bily, and Roberto Flores, who was executive director of PADRES.

Virgilio Elizondo was appointed as the first director of MACC. Elizondo had been the driving spirit behind the founding of MACC and was already acquiring a reputation as the leading Mexican-American theologian in the United States. The center was greatly helped by Elizondo's reputation as a public speaker. He was much in demand by both Catholic and Protestant organizations for participation at various high-level conferences. In 1992 Elizondo received the President's Award from the National Federation of Priests' Councils. The award recognizes a priest's leadership which enhances the ministry of others. Elizondo's leadership of the center has certainly done that. Elizondo is at present pastor of San Fernando Cathedral in San Antonio but remains on the center's staff as a professor of theology.

The center was similar to other pastoral and language institutes already established in San Juan, Puerto Rico; Cuernavaca, Mexico; and Quito, Ecuador, but its scope was broader. An important difference from those other centers was that MACC was run by the Mexican Americans themselves and not by others.[22] At MACC, the participants not only studied language—English and Spanish were taught simultaneously—but could study and explore the history, culture, problems, and needs of the Mexican-American people. San Antonio provided an excellent locale for this because the participants experienced a religiously renewed and politically active Mexican-American population. For this reason, one of the programs developed at MACC was the United Parcel Service Internship Program, which provided potential managers with six weeks of living, working, and learning among the poor of San Antonio to sensitize them to the needs of the workers whom they would be managing. James McLaughlin, president of UPS, joined the MACC board of directors in 1977.

The connection between Latin American and Spanish liberation theologians and the Hispanic Catholic community in the United States was made primarily through MACC in the early 1970s. Although resident faculty included people like Angela Erevia, M.C.D.P.; Marcine Klemp, O.P.; Juan Alfaro, O.S.B.; John Linskens, C.I.C.M.; Edmundo Rodríguez, S.J.; and Leonard Anguiano, the center brought in distinguished theologians and scholars such as Gustavo Gutiérrez, the founder of liberation theology; Edgar Beltrán, one of the *periti* at Vatican II and an influential tactician at the Latin American bishops' conference of Medellín in 1968; Enrique Dussel, the liberation theologian and historian; Casiano Floristán of Spain; Alfonso Nebreda of the Philippines; Johannes Hoffinger, the expert on catechetics; Juan Mateos and Alonso Schokel, who translated the New Testament from the original Greek and Hebrew into a contemporary Spanish version; and many others. Others who have spoken or taught at the center include Lionel Castillo, former commissioner of the U.S. Department of Immigration and Naturalization; Father Pedro Arrupe, the late superior general of the Jesuits; Rosa Guerrero, whose course on cultures through a series of dances called "Tapestry" has become known throughout the United States; Thomas Rivera, eminent scholar on Hispanic culture and lecturer on Chicano literature; and many others.

In 1972 MACC arranged for seven San Antonio parishes to serve as parochial laboratories for comunidades eclesiales de base (CEBs, Christian base communities) for a course taught by a team led by José Maríns of Brazil. Many if not most of the efforts to redefine parishes according to the CEBs' concepts among Hispanics in the United States grew out of the courses which were originally taught by the Maríns team and now by Ninfa Garza, who directs the small communities in the diocese of Brownsville, Texas. In 1974 a new formation program for Latin American missionaries began. The program coordinators were Carmen Aurora Gómez, S.S., and George Dwyer, O.P. The program also debriefs returning missionaries. The same year, Leonard Anguiano organized the "Flor y Canto" Literary Festival at the center. More than a hundred Chicano poets, essayists, dramatists, musicians, and painters participated, and *El Quetzal Emplumece: An Anthology of Chicano Literature* was published by the center as a result.

From its inception, there was always a team from the center, which at various times included Leonard Anguiano, Gary Tijerina, Sister Mario Barrón, Gregoria McCumber, Brother Trino Sánchez, and Fathers Juan Romero, Edmundo Rodríguez, and Juan Alfaro, which did leadership formation workshops for Hispanics in towns and cities throughout the United States. The workshops mostly targeted the poor—parishioners in low-income churches, migrant workers, and politically disenfranchised Hispanics in small towns—and were sponsored by both Catholic and Protestant churches, and by civic and social organizations. These leadership development workshops created a bond between the center staff and the people in those communities who were struggling to overcome the effects of discrimination and exclusion. The workshops were based on Paulo Freire's pedagogy of the oppressed and had the effect of creating energy for change in many communities. The workshops opened the door to successful voter registration drives and political organizing in many communities which had up to then had little or no political involvement by Hispanics.

In the summer of 1992, as part of the twenty-year anniversary celebration, the center brought together some forty alumni and staff members to reflect on the present state of the Hispanic community, to tell the stories of their pastoral ministry and experience, and to look at where such ministry should be moving in the near future. Rosendo Urrabazo, C.M.F., the president of MACC, provided the group with demographic data about the economic, health, and housing situation of Hispanics in the United States, generally the ethnic group at the bottom of the economic charts. To the participants it was a moving and sobering look at the fact that not much has changed in the last twenty years. The hope that came with federally funded job training, health care, and housing programs during the 1970s was dashed when these programs were gutted or disappeared altogether during the 1980s. In the past decade, the number of new immigrants from different Latin American countries and especially from Central America has increased dramatically and has made the task of addressing the needs of Hispanics much more complex.

Among the many suggestions made to MACC by the participants at the 1992 conference were the following:

1. Continue leadership formation work with a strong emphasis on *conscientización*.
2. Find ways of evangelizing the Hispanic middle class who now can effect social changes in the political sphere.
3. Continue to bring Hispanics together to reflect on ecclesiology, symbols, culture, and other items which help Hispanics uncover the elements which create an environment in which Hispanics feel at home in the Catholic Church.
4. Develop formation programs for parish and diocesan staffs which work with Hispanics so that they may understand the concept of and practice the *pastoral de conjunto*.
5. Become a resource center for archival documentation, research, and writing on Hispanics in the Church.
6. Develop a think-tank satellite on the United States border with Mexico to encourage both reflection on that reality and action by the Church.
7. Continue to prepare Hispanics to work in the barrios. It is not those with doctorates who will come there but rather those who themselves are coming from the barrios and colonias.

One of the many new projects suggested for MACC was to bring together annually Hispanic church, civic, and other leaders to dialogue with each other about issues important to the whole

community. This is especially important because many of the organizations which used to bring leaders together, like PADRES, have
nearly gone out of existence.

MACC remains an important national resource for language
studies and pastoral courses in Hispanic ministries. The clientele
of the center is changing, however. In the 1970s, women religious,
priests, and seminarians came to the center in large numbers. Many
"professional" church people still come for the Spanish language
program, but few are coming for the programs in pastoral ministry
while the number of laypeople has increased. Consequently, the
center has had an income shortfall because laypeople either have
to be sponsored by their parishes or diocesan offices or from their
own pockets, making them less able to attend MACC without
scholarships. The Church has not generally made funds available
for the formation of lay ministers who serve Hispanics. It is clear
that the continuance of MACC and other centers like it will depend
very much on a change in the funding priorities of the Church in
regard to Hispanic ministry.

THE NATIONAL SECRETARIAT:
AN INFRASTRUCTURE FOR HISPANIC MINISTRY

The first national office for the Spanish speaking was established in 1945 under Archbishop Robert E. Lucey of San Antonio,
and while it originally was based in San Antonio, it eventually
moved to Washington, D. C. Then in 1971, the U.S. bishops responded to the pressure from PADRES and other Hispanic groups
for a more visible advocacy office for Hispanics within the structures of the National Conference of Catholic Bishops–United States
Catholic Conference (NCCB-USCC) structure, and established the
USCC Secretariat for Hispanic Affairs. Pablo Sedillo was its first
director, followed in 1992 by Ron Cruz.[23]

The United States was then going through great social and political upheaval, with a growing protest movement against the war
in Vietnam, an intensified struggle on civil and human rights, and
the turmoil caused by the continuing problems of inner-city poverty which plagued the nation. In part from new consciousness and
in part as an attempt to respond both to the ferment outside and to
the tensions within the Church itself, the bishops established two
new offices; one was the Campaign for Human Development and
the other was the Secretariat for Hispanic Affairs. The Campaign

for Human Development affected Hispanics directly inasmuch as it provided initial funding for what would become a nationwide network of community organizations: Communities Organized for Public Service (COPS) in San Antonio; the Metropolitan Organization (TMO) in Houston; United Neighborhood Organizations (UNO) in Los Angeles; the Interfaith Project in Dallas; and others.

The secretariat was established as an office which would be an advocate for Hispanic issues among the bishops. Among these issues were the civil rights of Hispanics throughout the country, the promotion of voter registration, and helping the Church at the national level to understand Hispanics, their traditions and their culture. It also established an infrastructure for Hispanic ministry. Beginning in the early 1970s, the secretariat worked to help establish diocesan offices for Hispanic ministry throughout the Church in the United States. There are now 140 such offices. Regional offices were also established in the Midwest, the Northeast, the Southwest, the Southeast, the West, and in the other episcopal regions. (For a more extensive treatment of these organizations, see the chapter by Moisés Sandoval in this work.)

In 1972, the secretariat organized the Primer Encuentro Nacional Hispano de Pastoral in Washington, D.C. The participating Hispanics in the First National Encuentro were primarily clergy and women religious with only a few laypeople and only one Hispanic bishop in the country, Bishop Patricio F. Flores, then auxiliary of San Antonio. By the second encuentro in 1977, the participation of laypeople had increased to about 50 percent and a number of other Hispanic bishops had been appointed. By the same token, more lay leaders had become directors of the regional and diocesan offices.

On the feast of Our Lady of Guadalupe, December 12, 1983, the bishops of the United States issued the first pastoral letter on Hispanics, *The Hispanic Presence: Challenge and Commitment*, urging the Church to see the presence of Hispanics as a gift and not as a problem to be solved. This led to the Third Encuentro in 1985 which involved the participation of thousands of Hispanics at the parish and diocesan as well as the regional level who gave input to what eventually was translated into the *Plan National Hispano de Pastoral* which was approved by the U.S. bishops in 1987. The process used for listening and getting input from the grassroots has been highly praised in many quarters for its effectiveness and as a sign of a Church renewed and putting in practice a more participatory manner of planning. It was the secretariat in concert with national Hispanic leadership which was responsible for designing and developing the process used by the Third Encuentro.

Issues that the secretariat has dealt with over the years have included assisting with the 1990 U.S. Census so that Hispanics would not be so grossly undercounted as they had been in the past. The secretariat has also been involved in researching and sounding out reactions for the bishops on questions like immigration policy. Along with other organizations, it has worked on human rights cases like that of the three young Mexicans imprisoned and tortured by ranchers in Arizona in the early 1980s. The secretariat has been involved with many national Hispanic organizations which have also tried to influence federal legislation on issues affecting Hispanics. The secretariat makes sure that in whatever work the lobbying offices of the NCCB-USCC are doing on Capitol Hill, the Hispanic perspective is included. It works with national Church organizations, like the National Association of Catholic Family Life Ministries, to help develop Hispanic components within these organizations. The secretariat also produces Spanish-language materials, such as a pamphlet on political responsibility, for distribution and use in predominantly Hispanic parishes throughout the United States.

In the 1990s, a serious problem looms for Hispanics in the U.S. Catholic Church. The Church is beginning to set up offices of multicultural affairs rather than for specific ethnic groups, and there is a danger that the Secretariat for Hispanic Affairs will be subsumed into another less specifically focused office. Many Hispanics feel that this would be a serious mistake just at the time when the percentage of Hispanic Catholics in the United States is growing significantly and their needs are more pressing than ever. Either to water down or to amalgamate the work of the secretariat will be to weaken the infrastructure which has been built for Hispanic ministry. If the national office and the regional and diocesan offices begin to disappear, the dialogue which has been taking place between Hispanics and the mainline Church may simply disappear as well, leaving Hispanics at the margins once again.

COMUNIDADES ECLESIALES DE BASE

Christian base communities are not a movement or an organization; rather they are a different ecclesiology, a different way of thinking and of being Church which resurrects an intimate sense of community, trims the modern urban neighborhoods down to size, and affords ordinary people an opportunity to do ministry. The idea of Christian base communities was born among the struggling poor of Latin America but has been taking root in many Hispanic communities around the United States. In the Midwest, Edgar Beltrán and his wife are using CEBs to unify and develop ministry among Hispanics under the sponsorship of the diocese of Rockford. Beltrán was one of the earliest and strongest proponents of the use of CEBs among Hispanics in the United States.[24] Beltrán had been a *peritus* at the 1968 Latin American episcopal conference in Medellín, Colombia. He was an excellent teacher of the concepts and practices of the progressive Latin American theologians for Hispanic Church leaders in the United States. Before going to the Rockford diocese to do grassroots work, Beltrán had been hired by Pablo Sedillo as a pastoral theologian for the USCC Secretariat for Hispanic Affairs.[25]

A good example of the CEBs in action is the work of Ninfa Garza, a Missionary of Jesus, who has created over five hundred communities in the diocese of Brownsville, Texas. Ninfa is a native of Brownsville herself and knows the people in the urban barrios and rural colonias intimately. Her methodology is simple: a three-day mission on the Holy Trinity done in someone's home, with neighbors invited to attend. On the third day, the topic is the Holy Spirit and the birth of the Church. On that day, she brings a cake and celebrates with the people the birth of the Church in their neighborhood. Leaders are chosen and a new basic ecclesial community is begun. After that it is a question of nurturing the leaders, firing up their religious imagination, and helping them get in touch with the reality around them. As people begin to know their neighbors, pray with them, plan with them, and respond to the needs around them with them, the face of the barrio changes. The members of the community develop a renewed sense of their own self-worth. Police officers in the areas where CEBs have been established have reported that the crime rate has gone down. Isolated, lonely older people have found companionship. Young people's needs are better served. All this is done by the people themselves reflecting on their reality and judging it in the light of the gospel.

Ninfa says that the Brownsville CEBs are especially blessed because they can connect closely with Valley Interfaith, an Industrial Areas Foundation organizing project put together by the genius of

Ernie Cortés. The communities and Valley Interfaith have joined hands to fight real estate fraud and to work for better schools. The members of the communities also attend to many forms of direct neighborly service like refurbishing an older person's home.[26]

It should appear by now that there are many different church-related schools of leadership in the Hispanic community. This chapter has provided a description of a few, but there are many more that cannot be covered here, such as RENOVACIÓN, the Spanish version of RENEW, which has been ably promoted throughout the United States by Ken Davis, O.F.M.; the Tepeyac Institute of El Paso which does lay ministry formation under the direction of Arturo Bañuelas, priest of the diocese of El Paso; the National Catholic Council for Hispanic Ministry; the Midwest Institute for Hispanic Ministry; and many other such "schools."

Organizations like PADRES, Las Hermanas, MACC, and movements like the Cursillo have sought a working relationship with the bishops but not official sponsorship from them. Hispanics have been quite deliberate about maintaining control of their schools of leadership, in part because they feel that the official Church has not always known how to respond to the needs of Hispanics, and in part because many of the church movements and organizations that were developed or used by Hispanic men and women who were shaped by the struggle for justice found themselves at odds with more established institution, including the official Church. The challenges of the 1990s and beyond for all these movements and organizations is to maintain their prophetic freshness and to be open to an ever-increasing diversity in the Hispanic community. If they cannot rise to this challenge, then the movimientos will surely suffer the same decline as the cofradías.

NOTES

1. From the foreword to the 1949 edition of *Los Pastores* by Father Carmelo Tranchese, S.J. (San Antonio: Treviño Printing).

2. Information on the history of the Cursillo was provided by the National Center of the Cursillo Movement, Dallas, in June 1992.

3. Moisés Sandoval, *On the Move* (Maryknoll, N.Y.: Orbis Books, 1990), pp. 84–85.

4. Genaro García, interview with Edmundo Rodríguez, S.J., July 20, 1991, at the Mexican American Cultural Center in San Antonio.

5. Verónica Méndez, R.B.S., interview with Edmundo Rodríguez, S.J., June 26, 1992.

6. Monsignor Antonio González, interview with Edmundo Rodríguez, S.J., June 5, 1991, at the Mercy Retreat Center in Slaton, Tex.

7. Bishop Agustín Román, auxiliary bishop of the archdiocese of Miami, interview with Edmundo Rodríguez, S.J., November 28, 1992.

8. Ibid.

9. Roberto and Rosie Piña, interview with Edmundo Rodríguez, S.J., June 27, 1992.

10. Andrés Aranda, interview with Edmundo Rodríguez, S.J., July 9, 1992.

11. Verónica Méndez interview.

12. Mario Viscaíno, presentation made at a conference on the Hispanic presence in the south, Spring Hill College, Mobile, Ala., June 3, 1992.

13. Joseph H. Fichter, S.J., "How It Looks to a Social Scientist," *New Catholic World*, November/December 1974, pp. 244-245.

14. Edmundo Rodríguez, S.J., "P.A.D.R.E.S. as a Distinct Voice," news release of February 9, 1970.

15. "Conclusions of the PADRES National Congress," February 2–5, 1975, San Antonio, pp. 78ff.

16. Moisés Sandoval, taped interview of June 23, 1991, sent to Edmundo Rodríguez, S.J.

17. Juan Romero, "Charism and Power: An essay on the history of PADRES," *U.S. Catholic Historian* 9 (winter/spring 1990), pp. 161-162.

18. *Constitution and By-Laws of Asociacion National de Sacerdotes Hispanos, EE.UU.*, Article II, numbers 1 through 13, October 1990.

19. Verónica Méndez interview.

20. María Carolina Flores, C.D.P., interview with Edmundo Rodríguez, S.J., June 22, 1992, in San Antonio.

21. Virgil Elizondo, interview with Edmundo Rodríguez, S.J., June 25, 1992, at the Mexican American Cultural Center in San Antonio.

22. Antonio M. Stevens-Arroyo and Ana María Díaz-Ramirez, "The *Hispano* Model of Church: A People on the March," *New Catholic World*, July/August 1980, p. 156.

23. Ron Cruz, director of the USCC Secretariat for Hispanic Affairs, interview with Edmundo Rodríguez, S.J., June 25, 1992.

24. Stevens-Arroyo and Díaz-Ramirez, "*Hispano* Model," p. 157.

25. Romero, "Charism and Power," p. 156.

26. Ninfa Garza, Interview with Edmundo Rodríguez, S.J., June 26, 1992.

7

Latinas and the Church

Ana María Díaz-Stevens

With more than 54 million persons, the Catholic Church in the United States is a rich quilt of diverse racial, ethnic, and socio-economic backgrounds. Unfortunately, this diversity is not always recognized in studies of "the American Catholic"[1] that focus upon an institutional U.S. Catholicism. For the purpose of this chapter, however, Catholics are defined as those baptized within the Catholic Church and who profess the faith, thus meriting rights to the institution's care. In this definition, the burden of inclusion falls upon the institution. It has the responsibility to reach out and meet the pastoral needs of all who identify themselves as Catholics.

Viewed in this way, even when the institutional Church lacks a clear policy or generous outreach to Latinos, the people of Latin American heritage resident in the United States are a force within Catholicism in this country. Not only are Latinos affected by the Catholic Church here, they also are changing U.S. Catholicism. Besides taking the size of the Latino population into account, the specific mode of religion practiced among Latino Catholics must be given careful consideration in order to understand adequately its nature and impact upon the wider religious community.

THE WOMAN'S UNIQUE PRESENCE IN RELIGION

The Latino or Hispanic population in the United States sur-passes 24 million persons. Despite increasing conversions to main-line Protestant denominations, pentecostalism, and other groups such as Jehovah's Witnesses and the Unification Church, this pop-ulation continues to identify itself as Catholic, making Latinos the largest ethnic group within U.S. Catholicism today. More than half of the Latino Catholic population comprises women. However, the importance of Latinas within Catholicism is not just a question of numbers but of the role they have traditionally played in the maintenance and creation of a religious production. This is an important role, whether exercised in their country of origin or in the U. S., whether from within or from without the institutional structures.

Through military and/or economic invasions of their lands, Latinos were forced to make adaptations to a North American presence among them. The ensuing process of (im)migration and the need for adaptation to a new society has had a deep effect upon the roles of women in their communities and in the general society. A commentary on a radio documentary entitled *"Nosotras trabajamos en la costura*/Puerto Rican Women in the Garment Industry," summarizes in part the contribution that Puerto Rican women in migration have made as they strove not only to survive but to provide a better life for their families:

> These are the women who raised us. They were not only our mothers and grandmothers, but our cousins, aunts, neighbors, friends. They went to the factories early in the morning and sat in front of those machines day after day. They confronted the difficulties of migration, poverty, low pay, discrimination, and unstable jobs. In spite of that, they raised us and kept our families together. They fought for our education, organized in the communities and on the job, and they gave us a legacy of struggle.[2]

The adaptation that Latinas must undergo in this country, however, does not require the casting aside of Latino traditional values for North American ones. It is, nonetheless, a transformative process which touches all areas of their lives and which requires the careful evaluation of old and new modes.

Thanks in great measure to the sacrifices of earlier generations of Latinas, their daughters and granddaughters have been able to secure important positions at different levels of the political, economic, educational, and general social structure of U.S. society, in parallel with the rise of women's status over the past two decades. These positions present the opportunity to exert a certain influence not only upon Latino communities but upon general society as well. Yet, the sphere of religion has been generally neglected by scholars of the Latino community. This is unfortunate, because beyond affording women the opportunity for influence, religion has oftentimes given Latinas affirmation as leaders, especially at the grassroots level. Even the contradictions inherent in a religious system which purports to accept everyone on an equal basis while reserving its positions of authority and decision making to males only have proved incapable of destroying or negating the legitimacy of women's role in the religious sphere.

In an unpublished survey conducted during a thirty-day period in New York City in 1980 along with other research on youth employment for the Puerto Rican Migration Research Consortium,[3] thirty young people, ages fifteen to twenty-five, were asked who was the person they most respected in the community aside from their parents. In most cases (66.6 percent) the person mentioned was an elderly woman in the community known for her piety and her role as the leader of nonecclesiastical religious communal rituals and prayer. Such a role has been a constant in Latin American and Caribbean communities for centuries and carries the respectful title of *rezadora*, literally meaning "the prayerful one." In the community studied in New York, she ranked higher than priests and teachers. An insignificant number reported that they would confide in a teacher, and only 30 percent would approach a priest. When asked why they would go to these elderly women instead of a priest, the response was "because she is like a mother; she knows how to listen." To the question, "Would you tell her things you would not tell other people?" 50 percent said they had and another 25 percent that they would. Some said they would follow her advice unquestionably. Others said they would not dismiss it right away but take it into serious consideration.

In the majority of cases the reason these young people gave for seeking and following an elderly woman's advice was because "she is wise" and because "she is holy." When confronted with the idea that perhaps they should instead go to the local priest, a good number (one-half) said that going to her was different because she was one of their own; she understood their feelings and what they were trying to say. While Latinos are probably not the only ethnic group to value mothers, grandmothers, and wise old women in their communities, the substitution of such women for clerical religious authority does represent a special role for women within U.S. Catholicism.

A second phenomenon was the frequency of home altars. The two homes where the field researcher stayed for the duration of the investigation were headed by females. One was Dominican and the other Puerto Rican, but each maintained a home altar in her apartment. Besides the difference in national origin there were differences in socioeconomic status: one woman was a working-class immigrant, with limited command of English; the other a professional (graduate of Columbia University), who had been raised in New York City. But in these, as in many of the other apartments, the home altar was an important place in the dwelling. In all, 155 families were visited, and 88 (56.7 percent) were headed by women. In many others, the women worked outside the home, sharing financial responsibility with men. Over one-third of the 155 apartments had home altars, with the majority found in the female-headed households. The home altar, of course, is a religious and ritual symbol. It is logical to presume that the prevalence of these altars was tied to other religious attitudes and behavior.

Three salient pieces of information emerged from this research. Firstly, it revealed that customs long associated with a rural popular religiosity have been carried into this urban center of Latino migration. Certainly, some traditions have been lost while others have been adapted to new circumstances (home altars fall within the latter category). Secondly, in all the cases encountered in this investigation, these traditions were related to women's roles. While men participated in these rituals of religion in an urban context, women assumed the major responsibilities of religious leadership. Thirdly, and significantly, the rituals and women's religious endeavors seem to have been targeted towards family, children, and immediate community.

If the relationship of family and religion is evident among ethnic groups in general, it is no less true of people of Spanish and Latino origin. Given the pervasive role that religion and the Church had in the colonization of Latin America and the Caribbean, it could be argued that the impact that religion had upon other institutions such as the family was even greater than what it may have been elsewhere. As an instrument of domination or as defender of the natives' rights, the Catholic Church was one of the strongest institutions planted in the New World. To determine what the impact of religion upon the family and community life may have been, one must look not only at the Church's universal teachings but also at the various historical events and processes in its development in this new setting. But rather than look at these as static episodes particularized by time and space, an interlocking, spiral movement through time seems a more appropriate perception. Therefore, an attempt will be made in this chapter to interpret the role of religion and the development of a Latino reality as part of an ongoing historical process in which past and present experiences are regarded as indispensable for the existence of the present and the construction of the future. Such a sociohistorical interpretation will provide a focus upon the interaction of Church and social norms, taking into account the rapid social changes among Latinos that have occurred during the second part of this century.

From the onset, it is recognized that the information available on Latinas within Catholicism is scattered, some of it anecdotal, and some based on theological rather than sociological analysis.[4] Furthermore, there is no published history of organizations of Catholic Latinas. Much archival work needs to be done to identify incidental reports that have historical value. An attempt must also be made to correct historical and analytical biases. Clearly, this brief analysis begins with some significant obstacles. Even in survey data on attitudes, the focus upon the attitudes of Latinas is scarce. Yet despite these limitations, the story of Latinas in Catholicism is important and deserves attention, no matter the difficulties in making the analysis comprehensive.

There is also the difficulty and confusion that may come of grouping the diverse national and Latino ethnic groups in one population. Each Latino subgroup's initial contact with the U.S. and the migration process responds to their country of origin's particular political relationship with the U.S. as it responds to the particular causes for, and time of, migration. Moreover, there are also differences in terms of official classification among Latinos in the United States: undocumented as opposed to documented aliens; citizenship by naturalization or by birth; membership in first, second, or further generations. Their integration process into North American society and their relationship to other Latino groups in the U.S. may be affected not only by their particular regional origin in the Caribbean and Latin America but by place of settlement in this country. Lastly, their own perception of themselves as Latinos, as members of this society, or as members of their particular Latino subgroup may vary.[5]

The available data on Latinos, both historical and social, generally emphasizes one of three major Latino groups; i.e., Mexican Americans, Puerto Ricans, and Cubans. In some regions, such as the Northeast, two other important groups, the Dominicans and Colombians, are identified, while all other Central Americans are grouped together.[6] In this chapter, therefore, the focus will be upon these three major groups and upon the similarities among all groups even when differences exist.

THE HISTORICAL ORIGINS OF RELIGIOUS ROLES FOR LATINA WOMEN

Since the Middle Ages, women in convent life and in congregations of religious Sisters have held the most clearly recognized roles for women within the Catholic Church. It must be remembered, however, that in the hierarchy of values, women's roles were always seen as less important than those of men because the power to govern the institution derives from Holy Orders, which is a sacrament reserved to men. Based on that tradition, institutional power within Catholicism resides chiefly with men. Thus, Catholicism can be considered a patriarchy par excellence.[7]

But this is no reason to conclude that women have no power within the Catholic religion. Nor should it be assumed that once women are made part of the ordained clergy, they will automatically influence and have power equal to men within the structures of the institution. It is not even known if ordained ministry will continue to carry the prestige and power it has traditionally enjoyed. Patriarchy is a relative and culturally conditioned concept. It implies that men appropriate to themselves positions they consider to be dominant and allow lesser functions for women. But that does not preclude the coexistence of patriarchy with matriarchy. If men have clearly defined roles within religion, what is not assigned to them falls to women. As social conditions change, what may have been once the powerful and the powerless of social roles may invert. Eventually, the segregation of women to a particular sphere, such as religious influence, may become a power function supplanting male roles. This is what is referred to in this chapter as the matriarchal core of Latino religion that is, by definition, a function of power.

The matriarchal core lies at the heart of most Latino religious practice and it is women's sphere of influence. In pragmatic terms, the core refers to all those practices and rituals that have survived the test of time mainly because of women's role in them. It also applies to the values undergirding these practices and rituals as well as to the specific mode and character imparted to them by women's active and creative participation. It should be understood that not all that is positive in religion has survived merely on account of women. But there is a particular religious production which is tied to popular religiosity bearing the distinctive imprint of women's genius and psychology. This is particularly true of Latino religion, and it merits attention.

While the term *matriarchal core* may be new, the reanalysis of the role of women in religion is not. Some modern feminist scholars find in the convents of medieval Christianity subsocieties in which women had autonomous power to shape and interpret their own values. Electa Arenal and Stacey Schlau write of various nuns—

many of them until recently unknown—who wrote, advocated for, and defended women's rights to a formal education and greater participation in religion. Among them, María de San José, Teresa of Avila's contemporary, lamented how this lack of opportunity for education and rampant "clerical stupidity . . . hindered women's fuller, reasoned participation in religion." She pleaded "for the recording of women's history," and made use of "highly elaborated structures and controlled modes of expression" in her own writings, "to affirm, through religious symbol and history and against all opposition, the primacy of female lineage."[8]

Since the formal institutions of the Catholic Church in Spain were brought to Latin America's colonial society, early women religious enjoyed the same autonomy in the New World as their sisters in Europe. Following a tradition already established by their sisters in Spain, they pressed on, not so much for recognition as for legitimation and independence of action. "The women of colonial convents took on greater symbolic and political importance than their peninsular Sisters," declare Arenal and Stacey. And their "convents being generally . . . closer to centers of power in the colonies than in Spain, their social function was also more significant." Adapting architectural design, language, and social styles to the new circumstances, "they contributed to the establishment of new structures on the ruins and distortions of the old ones."[9]

The most famous of these Latin American women who demonstrated autonomy from a male-dominated church is the Mexican Hieronymite nun, Sor Juana Inés de la Cruz. But it is important to recognize that while she may be the most famous, she is not the only Latin American religious woman to achieve a distinct role in the development of Catholicism.

Sor Juana and other Hispanic women in the religious life used the literary resources at their disposal to relate new perspectives on Catholicism and religious feeling. For the first three centuries their writings were almost exclusively the only writings produced by women in the New World.[10] Often, they also challenged an all-male monopoly over Catholic values. Sor Juana's letter on the role of women in the Church is a classic of Christian spirituality that has been slow in achieving the study it richly deserves.[11]

However, it would be a mistake to believe that the autonomy women ultimately enjoyed was given to them eagerly and freely, just as it would be to consider that convent life automatically bestowed on these women the ability to think critically and creatively about themselves and the Catholic religion. Yet, while of itself convent life in the Spanish colonies did not confer upon them the capacity for achieving theological and pastoral insights into Latin American Catholicism, it provided a favorable atmosphere to foster the interpersonal relationships, rituals, writings, and devotions that ultimately contributed to a particular Latin American way of being Catholic.

A separation between male and female spheres of religious behavior was not the unique domain of monastic or consecrated religious life; it was the norm in and out of convents walls. This separation provided women with both the need and the opportunity to develop their own religious expression. For people in the hinterland, and especially for peasant women, the distance between them and the centers of male-centered ecclesiastical and political power served a function similar to that of the cloister, allowing the matriarchal core to flourish in the guise of folklore— or, as is recognized by contemporary theology, as popular religiosity. Since until recently most of the Spanish-speaking Caribbean and Latin America remained rural, the Catholicism that has been passed down from generation to generation has been heavily endowed with a decidedly female legacy.

Emphasis upon the development of urban centers and a general lack of resources did not allow for the erection of parish churches in rural settlements in Spanish colonial times. Sometimes, in the major haciendas there were chapels and, in exceptional cases, even a resident chaplain. As a rule, however, the most common practice was to have some scattered *ermitas*, or shrines, which featured a cross, a statue, or an altar. Cared for by laypersons who attended to simple duties such as cleaning and the placing of fresh flowers, the ermitas were the place for an occasional eucharistic liturgy. Neglected by the institutional church and devoid of the leadership of an ordained clergy, the ermitas became the center of communal prayer and devotion.

Amidst the lack of institutional resources, the people proved to be very creative in meeting their religious needs whether for thanksgiving or to ask special favors and blessings. Where there were no ermitas, oftentimes one of the homes would allow for a similar shrine, or home altar, that created sacred space for prayer.[12] But whether it was in the hacienda chapel, in the ermita, or before the home altar, ultimately rural Latin American Catholicism fashioned a religious expression around the two things central to the people's existence: land and family. Due to the tradition of extending family membership to anyone related by blood, marriage, adoption, or *compadrazgo* (a quasi-fraternal relationship entered into by parents and godparents of a child upon baptism), the family was often synonymous with the whole community. Even if we have little written proof that the native land and the extended family were afforded the same measure of sacrality as the urban church building or the ordained clergy, the practice of the people's religion clearly depended on the appropriation of religious importance to the symbols and practices that they controlled in the absence of clergy.

WOMEN'S ROLES IN TRADITIONAL RURAL CATHOLICISM

In the rural outreaches of the mountains and plains of Latin America, distanced from clerical control, women, more often than men, assumed religious roles. The prevailing attitude that "only men who wore skirts" should be overtly involved in religion helped in this process. Although the literature available has to be re-assessed from a Latino perspective, thus far it reveals that like the *machismo* of peasant Spain, the machismo of Latin America, although not exclusively, is nonetheless focused among lower-class males who cannot aspire to upward social mobility.[13] As a means of achieving rank among their male peers, they choose to boast about their sexual exploits with women and domination over those under their charge. The main audience of the typical macho, then, is his male counterparts whom he seeks to impress with his manly prowess. The approval of this group through their belief of his exploits and acceptance of his position in the male hierarchy they have established among themselves is much more important than actually being successful as a Don Juan.

This machismo of the lower classes (whether rural or urban) is very different from the chivalric norms of honor, dedication to knightly ideals, and sacrifice for God, church, country, and lady. These upper-class conventions are the source of what has been called *marianismo*, or the elevation of women to a higher moral standard than that used for men. The price women had to pay for this "privileged" position was strict adherence to a social and moral code that restricted their center of activity to the home and family and kept them socially and economically dependent upon the menfolk. While many accepted these conventions, others either overtly cast aside or covertly subverted them. It is an often-repeated mistake of some scholars to relate machismo to marianismo as if they were opposite sides of the same social behavior, and in the process to overlook a crucial social class difference.[14] Moreover, it is an equally grave mistake to believe that attitudes consonant with marianismo and machismo are the unique domain of Hispanics or Latinos. The recent study entitled "The Latino National Political Survey" indicates that gender bias may be more pronounced among Euro-Americans than among Latinos.[15]

Among the more pragmatic urban lower social classes and in the rural areas, the practices of the upper urban class were not easily attainable. Less pretentious and with limited social and economic power, the rural dwellers and lower social class were more concerned with survival than with image making or social prestige.

The question of gender bias, however, is important because it frames an understanding of the role of women in rural Latin American communities. The existence of a machista attitude among peasant men was gender bias, but at times it benefited women. The macho abandoned control over important social functions associated with religion and gave women a sphere of power.

This bestowal of power to women in peasant society is very different from marianismo, the phenomenon more clearly a part of upper-class urban Catholicism in Latin America. For men in the upper strata of social power, the Catholic religion in Latin America was often perceived as exacting too much compliance while allowing relatively little room for personal power and free expression. Accordingly, the submission to religious norms was more appropriate to their wives and daughters, who as upper-class urban women had little social identity apart from their husbands and fathers.

The peasant women who assumed the tasks of religious leadership were not infected with a marianismo that shirked the pragmatic dimensions of everyday life.[16] Rather, they achieved in the rural settings an influence and immediacy with symbols of the supernatural that were reserved to male clerics in the cities. Nor were these roles restricted for each woman to her own immediate family. With the passage of time, those called to lead the people in prayer and religious celebrations came to be recognized for their virtue and wisdom. Often women—especially older women—were assigned these tasks by the community.

These rural women can be said to have exercised an autonomous role analogous to the nuns of institutional Catholicism. From Teresa of Avila and Sor Juana Inés de la Cruz to the lowly rezadora (leader of communal prayer) and *comadrona* (midwife) of the hinterlands, women were capable of understanding, analyzing, and producing a genuine religious expression. Moreover, the community of believers selected such persons for sustained roles of familial and communal ritual leadership. For example, still today in most of our countries of origin, a woman is frequently afforded the task of leading the community in prayer and preparing the celebration of feastdays in accordance with a liturgical calendar and an agricultural cycle. La rezadora, as she continues to be called, is often asked to lead the petitions or thanksgiving prayers for a good crop, just as her prayerful guidance is sought in times of drought or floods, at weddings, baptisms, in the commemoration of the final departure of a friend or relative, and for special feastdays, such as the patron saint of the nation, region, or town.

In the typical rural community, the comadrona, or *partera* (midwife),[17] was relied upon to look after the well-being of the expectant mother and to give advice on how to nurture and protect the life of the unborn child. Just as the midwife was asked to pray over the expectant mother, she was asked to bless the unborn child in a ritual called *santiguo*, where the imposition of hands, massages, and the aspersion of holy water, accompanied by prayers specifically designed to protect the individual from all kinds of physical, emotional, and spiritual harm, is common. No matter the time of day or night, when a child was to come into this world, the comadrona was always willing to give of her expertise and care. The distance and the inconvenience of travel through mountain paths did not deter her professional drive and personal commitment. Often she had been witness to the birth of two or three generations. For all her troubles, she would usually receive the gift of a chicken, some fruits and vegetables, perhaps a few coins, and the deep gratitude of the parents, who often also had come to this life attended by the same old woman who seemed as ageless as the hills. The other privilege she claimed for herself was the immediate baptism of the child after birth. She had also been witness to many deaths. Due to a high infant mortality, the church had granted this privilege and responsibility to the community.

It was common for a reputable midwife to be sought after by neighboring communities in very difficult cases when the life of the unborn child and/or mother were in danger. And, it was equally common for this role of midwife to be handed down from generation to generation within the same family just as the role of *santero* (the art of crafting statues of saints out of wood) was commonly reserved and propagated by the male folk of a selected group of families. These roles were within the reach of many, but it was believed that to be successful at them a special calling and commitment was required.

The constant contact with matters of life and death frequently afforded the midwives and leaders of communal prayer an appreciation for life and a value system far deeper than that of the ordinary person. The midwife was oftentimes a very respected and spiritual person. In many cases, her position was strengthened by her role not only of rezadora but that of *curandera* (faith healer) as well. When these three roles—comadrona, rezadora, and curandera— were joined, not even the occasional missionary visits from the priest would challenge or detract from her position of respect and influence in the community. As such, she could also claim the role of centralizer and counselor, often hearing more confessions and intimate details of the life of community than the priest. As far as absolution was concerned, for the ordinary person, the acceptance of a saintly and wise person in the community who knew of their struggles and pains was just as, or more, comforting than the absolution by a virtually unknown priest.

When called upon to help a terminally ill person prepare for a good death (*ayudar a alcanzar una buena muerte*), she was also made responsible for *el perdón y el ajuste de cuentas*. Literally, what this meant was that she was to decide when to send for those with whom the dying person wanted to settle accounts—to forgive, to ask forgiveness, or just to ask for a special favor or promise to be fulfilled, usually after his or her earthly departure. This holy woman led in prayer the members of the family and friends who had gathered to bid farewell to the dying person. And upon death she helped bathe and prepare the body for interment, along with directing the traditional prayers and the blessing with holy water. While *la despedida del duelo* (last parting words at the cemetery) was usually reserved to a male relative, the rezadora was the central communal and religious leader at the *velorio* (wake) and the *novenario*, or nine consecutive days of prayer and celebration after the departure.

The rosary, the devotion par excellence of the peasant people, was the most commonly used prayer in the novena. Among a people where Bible reading and contact with the institutional Church was at a minimum, the novena with its recitation of the rosary provided an excellent didactic opportunity. Not only was a space created where they could demonstrate Christian solidarity and kindness towards the deceased members of the community and their families, but the practice also created a ritual where communal prayer and reflection upon the main mysteries of the life of Christ and the Church were shared. In other words, the novenas and the rosary were occasions for open Christian witnessing and the strengthening of communal and religious bonds.

Incorporating fifteen important events taken from the New Testament and Catholic dogma, the proclamation of the various articles of faith in the Apostles' Creed, the archangel's salutation in the Hail Marys, the praise to a triune God in the doxology, and the recognition of dependence upon God's fatherly love in the Lord's Prayer, the rosary can be considered the oral Bible of the rural dwellers and lower social classes. By dwelling upon Mary's example, the rosary also emphasizes women's and the lowly's capacity for participation in the redemptive work of Christ. This was a devotion with which the Latinas and the rural classes could closely identify. In Puerto Rico, for example, Iñigo Abbad y Lasierra testified that

> These islanders are very devoted to our Lady. Every one of them wears the rosary around his neck, they recite it at least twice a day. Every family begins the day with this holy exercise, some of them repeat it at noon without omitting it at night.[18]

In many areas of Latin America and the Caribbean this and many other practices where the role of women is paramount are commonplace even today.

Among these peasant women, moreover, some were able to assume significant historical roles as preachers and founders of religious movements. For these tasks official approval was a secondary consideration. The matriarchal core allowed women to mesh their perspectives with Christian doctrine: Claiming an infusion of power by the Holy Spirit was sufficient for their calling.

Clear examples of peasant women rising to such influence in Latino religion can be found in Texas and Puerto Rico. Two such women are still remembered for their unselfish commitment and influence in the community: the Mexican curandera, Teresa Urrea (1873–1906), and the turn-of-the-century Puerto Rican Catholic lay preacher, Madre Elena. Their prophetic voices caused consternation and anger among some but brought peace and hope to many others. Sometimes because of the period of history in which they lived, even in spite of themselves, their religious role spilled over into the secular—political—realm.

Urrea, better known as "Santa Teresita de Cabora," was a Yaqui mestiza who inspired her people to revolt against the abuses of the dictatorship of Porfirio Díaz in Mexico. Exiled to parts of Arizona and El Paso, Texas, she gained great prominence for her curing skills.[19] Madre Elena began her preaching in the northeastern part of Puerto Rico as a means of counteracting the Protestants' efforts when the island was taken over by the U.S. in 1898. These women were influential because they fulfilled deep religious expectations of the people, otherwise unattended by ecclesiastical institutions.

THE EFFECTS OF MIGRATION

Of course, not all elements of traditional rural Catholicism are transferable to an urban situation. The centrality of the family, the well-defined roles of each one of its members, and the importance of the local community are not as clear in the great metropolitan centers where many Latinos live today. In this setting, women's roles in traditional religion are challenged by social change, by rapid technological developments which often are out of kilter with the people's needs, and by accelerated demographic shifts. People do not live in a historical vacuum, however. And, while challenged, what through the centuries has come to constitute the tradition of a people seldom disappears completely.

Among Latinos, a persistent element is the centrality of women's endeavors in the religious sphere. Thus, rather than diminish, the persistence of the matriarchal core gives Latinas legitimacy in their role, making the maintenance and transformation of religion possible among Latinos in the United States. Besides being a creative force, the matriarchal core is also a repository of moral and family values, and for this reason it takes on added importance as a stabilizing element in a community in transition.

It is, however, the double-faceted nature of the matriarchal core—maintenance/transformation—that has allowed it to survive even in the face of a harsh migration experience. Perhaps this anchor more than any other helps many a Latina to adapt to new surroundings. The contemporary Latina has proved quite capable of casting aside those values which hamper her personal development as a fully mature social being. But she also expresses a need to hold on to roles and traditions which in part determined her identity. Furthermore, provided with opportunity, she is able to distinguish the good from the bad in making the necessary adjustments. The experiences of Latina Catholics in the U.S. have been determined in great measure by the Church's capacity and willingness to afford them the opportunity to maintain the positive values of the matriarchal core of traditional religion as they adapt to the modern urban condition.

It is important to make a distinction between Latin American women who were not born under the United States' flag but now live here, and Latina women who were born as U.S. citizens and have witnessed the world change around them. Among the latter, Mexican-American (or Chicana) and Puerto Rican women are the majority. Unlike their sisters who have migrated to the United States, for the women of former Mexican lands and the island of Puerto Rico, it was the United States that "migrated" to their homelands via military conquests.[20] Some of these women have migrated to large U.S. cities, of course. But even if they remained in Texas, California, or Puerto Rico, they have seen a rural way of life give way to a highly modern, urban, and technological society that has profound impact on traditional women's roles.

While women all over the world face similar challenges, the rootedness of Latina women's religious identity in the rural setting presents special problems of adjustment. And while there are differences between those Latin American women born and raised elsewhere and those who have always been U.S. citizens, no matter the place of origin Latinas as a group have a great deal more in common with each other than with women from other cultural and religious backgrounds.

PRECONCILIAR RELIGION FOR LATINAS IN THE U. S.

Before the Second Vatican Council, the principal roles afforded Latinas in the U.S. were through membership in *cofradías* (confraternities) and sodalities. These were lay Catholic organizations that segregated women from men within the Church while still affording them some useful function of assistance to the parish. The cofradías did not foster the autonomy found in the rural settings because the organizations were very much controlled by the clergy. The societies often sought membership according to a woman's state in life.

For instance, among Puerto Ricans, sodalities like Hijas de María (Children or Daughters of Mary) were principally for unmarried women, while Damas del Sagrado Corazón (Ladies of the

Sacred Heart) was for married women. Among Mexican-Americans, Las Guadalupanas asked women to prepare celebrations for the parish, presuming upon their roles as homemakers. Sometimes, questions of social status entered into membership because the women were expected to provide certain resources voluntarily as part of their service to the parish. For instance, the Damas del Sagrado Corazón were frequently given charge of altar linens and flowers, which were expected to come from their own resources.

There were also organizations where both men and women, married and single, were admitted and even allowed to collaborate, such as the Third Order of St. Francis (*las tercera órdenes* or *terciarias*) and the Legion of Mary. Because of their numbers, commitment, and constancy, women often had greater visibility and leadership roles than men.

Such functions were important and even indispensable to the Catholic parish for the Spanish speaking but seldom produced clout within the institution's all-male hierarchy. But the matriarchal core implicit in these traditional and apparently powerless lay societies nonetheless contained an inner energy and potential within the Church that could be unleashed with a change in social and political conditions.

With the massive migration of Puerto Ricans and Latinos to the Northeast U.S., the Catholic Church was, like the U.S. during World War II, in a crisis.[21] It was forced into ceding to Latino laity, in general, and to Latina women, in particular, a greater participation in the ministry than was ordinarily extended to Euro-American women in parishes where priests were abundant. Perhaps inadvertently, the Church in this process also left itself open to a heavy dose of religious production which was specifically Latino/female influenced.

A role frequently assigned to Latinas in the changing urban parish was that of catechist. Consonant with the primarily female role of religious education of the rural family, it was women who generally sought the authorization of the clergy for instructing children. In many cases, the religious instruction needed no legitimation; rather, what members of the Legion of Mary and Las Hijas de María sought was to have the parish accept the children they had prepared as candidates for the sacraments of eucharist, reconciliation (then called penance or confession), and confirmation. Some pastors recognized that because no other Spanish-speaking persons were available for this task, they had to accept these Latinas or allow hundreds of people living within their parish to go unattended.[22] This is only one example of how woman's role of transmitter of religious values based on a rural Catholicism was successfully transformed to suit an urban parish made Latino by migration.

Because some pastors of New York parishes that were changing to Puerto Rican faithful refused to recognize the need for catechetical attention to the Spanish speaking, the only Catholic churches open to many Spanish-speaking people were a handful of relatively small national chapels staffed by religious priests often of Spanish origin. Two of the better-known national parishes which continue to serve Spanish-speaking congregations until the present day are La Milagrosa in Lower Manhattan and La Esperanza in the Upper West Side.

THE APPEAL OF PROTESTANTISM AND PENTECOSTALISM

As the cultural niche upon which traditional peasant roles depended was eroded so too was the religious autonomy peasant women had enjoyed. Culturally and geographically uprooted, they were presented with Protestantism or pentecostalism both as religious alternatives and as tools for adaptation in an urban setting. Historically, both in the Northern Mexican territory and in the Caribbean Island, Protestantism was introduced with the invading army. The new religion was the religion of those in power. Acceptance of Protestantism brought benefits that the new system offered to the family's well-being.[23] In Puerto Rico after 1898, for instance, civil service jobs, preferential housing, and handouts of food and clothing were liberally provided by Protestant churches as inducements for native Puerto Ricans to join their congregations.

The Protestant evangelizing effort was reinforced by the school system, whose carefully chosen personnel had, alongside the responsibility of teaching English, the mission of rescuing the future generations of Latinos from what North American Protestant Church and government officials considered the "obscurantist" hold of the Catholic Church.[24] In 1898 Commander George G. Groff saw this as a civil and divine commitment, calling upon "good men, who can see in others, and understand even Latins . . . to spy out the land and to establish pioneer churches, and specially schools."[25] This sentiment was echoed in 1906 by David W. Creane when the cornerstone of the George O. Robinson Orphanage building at San Juan was being laid:

It is no slight task laid upon our Government by Divine Providence to bring the people of Porto Rico to the highest standard of American citizenship—and nothing short of that will satisfy God. . . . We stand professed witness of Gospel power to save, regenerate and inspire men to godly service.[26]

This was no personal view or private inclination. The 1906 annual report of the Board of Missions of the Presbyterian Church in the U.S.A. indicates that in fact it was considered a mandate.

Under the influence of our commerce and schools and religious philanthropic agencies the character of the people is being transformed. But if the great masses of these are to be lifted out of darkness into the light and prepared for the exercise of the prerogatives and privileges of American citizenship, then must the work of education and Christian evangelization not only be maintained, but enlarged and pursued with new vigor and earnestness.[27]

Finally, summarizing the low esteem in which Catholicism was held and the goal that had been set for Protestantism on the island, the Protestant newspaper, El defensor cristiano, published an article in 1903 that warned that while Catholicism "is opposed to the general education [of the people], Protestantism accepts it; the former flees from it, the latter seeks it; the former looks upon public schools as its enemies, the latter looks upon them as their friends." "Romanism," it concludes, is a hindrance to any democratic system and those who seek freedom but continue to support the Romanist system are only seeking an unrealizable dream."[28]

Such a mentality and a similar pattern of action are found both in the encounter with Protestantism in Puerto Rico and in much of the Southwest, in Texas and in California. In these areas, as in Latin America and the Caribbean, many of the Latino conversions from Catholicism to Protestantism were wrought by Latino couples who visited the homes and were successful in evangelizing the housewives and through them, their children. The religious conversion of the husband was often attained later through the example, commitment, and patience of the wife.[29]

For some Latinas, an attraction to Protestantism continues to be the fact that it offers them greater institutionalized leadership roles, including the ordained ministry. Thus, as Catholic women convert to Protestantism, as well as continue to nurture and transmit Christian values in the family and community in the way to which they have been accustomed, they assume other roles more closely related to the institution. Though these women have not yet achieved the same level of power within the institution as men have, through their newly attained roles in the ministry they share greater participation in policy making for their congregations than women in the Catholic Church. Policy making, along with the ordained ministry, is something that even today Catholicism does not allow women.

When Latinos began to move in significant numbers from rural areas to cities of the United States after the First World War, this proselytizing pattern continued. It was notably successful, especially in terms of pentecostalism. New York City experienced the rapid spread of Puerto Rican and Latino Protestant congregations served through storefront churches by native and Spanish-speaking pastors, while in the Catholic Church Latinos were shunted either to underfunded national parishes or to the so-called integrated parish which for the Latinos usually amounted to a basement church served mostly by a member of the North American clergy who had learned Spanish. Because this curate was usually the youngest or the last one assigned to the particular parish, his decision making power was very much limited. In those cases where the "Spanish priest" was also an extern (that is, a priest incardinated or legally bound to another diocese, usually in Spain or Latin America), virtually no decision making power was afforded him. In all cases, the priest assigned to minister to the Latinos often not only had to assume responsibility for the Latino community but also had to accept other general tasks in the parish. This included officiating at English liturgies during the week, imparting the sacraments to members of the general community, visiting the sick in hospitals and at home, and being on call for any other parish need or emergency generally known as "parish duty." In a sense, this basement church served as an antidote to pentecostalism. It provided access and immediate attention for Latinos. What it lacked was true native leadership.

Within the Protestant tradition, the layperson's call to missionary work is not only accepted but encouraged. As members of their Church, every person is responsible for spreading the gospel and bringing others to their fold. Institutional and personal resources are committed to a well-delineated proselytizing effort in each community where churches are established. In most cases, if not in all, the effort is ongoing and comprehensive in that it tries to meet the various social and spiritual needs of the community over a long period of time. The participation of husband-and-wife teams and of the women within the families and local communities are of great importance and in many cases can be the reason for success or failure.

In contrast, in the archdiocese of New York as in other dioceses, a chancery-based office operating under the instructions of the cardinal was necessary in order to force reluctant pastors to permit catechetical instruction and other services in Spanish. This was a way of combating the loss of Puerto Ricans to other churches. Simultaneously, programs to train the volunteer catechists in doctrine and method were begun, and, since in keeping with the Latino tradition Latinas had continued to accept responsibility for this role, they were the first to be trained.

LATINA WOMEN AS CHURCH LEADERS

The experiences of Latinas who entered religious life before the council are only now being given scholarly attention. Often it was involvement with catechetical education that brought a young woman into prolonged association with religious Sisters, some of whom were native English speakers who had learned Spanish. A frequent dilemma for aspirant Latina religious was a conflict between an apostolate dedicated only to her own people and loyalty to the religious congregation that had other ministries such as teaching in parish schools or service in hospitals where ministry to the Spanish speaking was incidental. Others, while having a serious missionary outreach to Latin America, ignored the presence of Latinos in the U.S. Unfortunately, integration into the religious life sometimes implied abandonment of a deep identification with one's own traditions.

By the eve of the council in 1962, however, Latina women had significant roles in Catholicism. Through perseverance and commitment, Latinas' lay organization had more numbers, resources, and thrust than that of Latinos or English-speaking women's groups. There were occasions when members of the English-speaking congregations who knew Spanish would join the Latinas' groups because they judged the spirit and the organization of the Latinas' ministry as superior to their own. As part of their ministry, the Latinas visited the sick in hospitals and homes, counseled families, catechized children, instructed adults, gathered clothing and food for the poor, conducted prayer meetings at church and in the homes, directed and were members of the choir, conducted fund-raising activities for the purchase of organs, music books, and general renovations of basement chapels, took care of altar linens, put on theatrical performances and provided other enter-tainment for the members of the parish, and even provided food for the "Spanish priest" who sometimes was unaccustomed to a North American diet. Without trespassing into the male clergy domain, Latina women were frequently viewed as reliable and indispensable leaders within the parish communities. Occasionally, the prominence of a particular woman in society, either through politics or (more frequently) because her husband was wealthy or powerful, had an impact upon the church.

A prototype of this kind of Latina is the late Encarnación Padilla de Armas (d. 1992). Born in Puerto Rico to a wealthy family, doña Encarnación was educated in private schools in Cuba, where she obtained her bachelor's degree in liberal arts. She married a Cuban man and migrated to the United States for his business reasons. Upon his death, she was forced to seek employment to maintain herself and family. The twin passions of doña Encar-nación were advocacy for Puerto Rican independence and service to the Church. She combined both aspirations by administering social work in Spanish-speaking communities.

What other women had been doing at the local parish level, doña Encarnación was able to do at the diocesan, regional, and national levels. In her career, she worked in the Bishop's Office for the Spanish Speaking in San Antonio; she helped Monsignor Ivan Illich set up the Institute of Intercultural Communication in Ponce, Puerto Rico, to train New York diocesan priests in the Span-ish language and Puerto Rican culture; confronted and counseled Cardinal Spellman on his responsibilities to the Puerto Ricans; and assumed a leading role in the initial stages of what was to become the National Secretariat for the Spanish Speaking in Wash-ington. It is known that she was the key organizer of the First National Hispanic Encounter. But because doña Encarnación rose to leadership when women were still expected to be subordinate to men, she did not receive all the credit due to her. Still, because she served not only Puerto Ricans, Cubans, and Dominicans, but also Mexican Americans, and Latin Americans, she may be con-sidered the first Latina who achieved leadership within national Catholicism.[30]

WOMEN'S CONSCIOUSNESS OF RELIGION
AND MINISTRY SINCE THE REFORMS

Although the Cursillo was brought to the Latinos of the United States before the Second Vatican Council, the movement did not achieve its wide membership until the time of the first session of the council in 1962. By 1965, the Cursillo had been established in many of the regions of the United States where Latinos had a presence.[31] And although many English-speaking Cursillos had been held alongside the Spanish-speaking ones, Euro-American Catholics became less and less involved in the national movement of Cursillos as the conciliar reforms displaced the Cursillo as a focus for revitalizing Catholicism.

True to its preconciliar roots in Spain,[32] the Cursillo was initially targeted for men. There was a certain presumption that women were already religious and had little need for the Cursillo. Some of the Spanish clergy who inherited supervision of the Cursillo among Latinos in the United States perpetuated this conception. But women could not easily be excluded, especially in an industrial society like the United States. When the Cursillo movement was introduced in New York in 1960, there was a series of restrictions on women's participation that gradually eroded over time. At first, women could not make the Cursillo until their husbands had already done so. Nor could unmarried women participate, since they were still "children" and were unprepared for consideration of the segments of the Cursillo focused upon married life.[33]

Despite such limitations, women developed their own teams to conduct the Cursillo among Latina women. In the patriarchal-matriarchal separation of tasks, these female cursillistas gained an autonomous space from control by men. In some ways, the woman's Cursillo was a lay religious order concerned about recruitment, apostolate, and training. During the four days of the Cursillo, it functioned like a medieval convent with its own version of abbess and nuns, postulants, and novices. The clergy was allowed into the temporary cloister of the Cursillo for the instruction on the sacraments, to hear confessions, and to celebrate the liturgies under circumscribed conditions.

In effect, the Cursillo allowed for the traditions of rezadora to become formalized, adapted, and improved. And while at a local level the man was usually in charge of representing the parish group at the interparish meetings or *ultreya*, in fact women often had a more effective role in mobilizing resources and organizing

the community. Moreover, as the scope and direction of the conciliar reforms filtered down to the parish level, the roles of leadership
afforded to women by the Cursillo provided transition into the new
roles such as lector at the Mass and member of the parish council.
Looked at theologically, the Cursillo was a preconciliar movement;
but in pastoral terms, it was precursor of the sweeping reforms of
Vatican II.

Although the Cursillo provided Latina women nationwide with
an autonomous ministry within Catholicism, it remained a limited
vehicle for advancing the notion of a specifically women's role. The
Latina woman in the Cursillo gained her influence precisely because the Cursillo did not allow men and women to make the four-
day retreat together. As soon as men and women were convened
together, the Cursillo had a built-in preference for male authority.
In an analogous way, the Catholic charismatic movement has always had a membership in which women figured significantly. Yet
the focus of this movement upon prayer and support groups has
not lent any special importance to a ministry specific to women.

LAS HERMANAS: LATINA WOMEN IN RELIGIOUS LIFE

In April of 1971 in Houston, Texas, the idea of a Catholic organization for women and women's ministry took shape through the
organizing efforts of Sister Gloria Gallardo of the Holy Spirit Sisters
and Sister Gregoria Ortega of Victory Knoll, who later became an
organizer for the United Farm Workers and had been a close ally
of Robert Kennedy and Andrew Young in their outreach to the
Chicano community. These two religious were stationed at the
time in San Antonio, Texas, and were aware of the initiative of
Mexican-American priests who had started PADRES a year before.
Recognizing that a similar effort for women was needed to advance
the cause of the Spanish-speaking apostolate, Sisters Gregoria and
Gloria summoned about fifty Latina religious women to a meeting
to discuss the establishment of such an organization. In November,
a meeting was held in Santa Fe, New Mexico, and Las Hermanas
was established as an organization of Catholic Latina women in
that region.[34]

Part of the dynamism of Las Hermanas, like that of PADRES,
depended on the validation that the members received both from
the Latino people as well as from the society at large. The people in the barrios looked up to Las Hermanas because they were

Sisters, and the society at large saw Las Hermanas as religious leaders of the Latino people because the Sisters were Latinas. In different ways and with different immediate effects, the superiors of religious women and Church hierarchy came to recognize that any apostolate with the Spanish speaking for religious women would have to be mediated by Las Hermanas. This perception was mightily aided by Las Hermanas' valuable participation in the national Hispanic pastoral encounters, which began in June of 1972.

Soon after the First National Encounter, Las Hermanas expanded its membership to include not only Mexican Americans but also Puerto Ricans, Cubans, and other Latin American–origin sisters. Among the Puerto Ricans invited to coordinate their outreach in the Northeast were Sister Rosamaría Elías, a Trinitarian who worked in Brooklyn, and Sister María Iglesias, a Sister of Charity of Cuban and Puerto Rican extraction. To Sister Rosamaría belongs the distinction of being named, years later, head of the Spanish-Speaking Apostolate Office for the diocese of Hartford, Connecticut, a position she held until recently, while Sister María Iglesias distinguished herself as a member of Las Hermanas' National Coordinating Team as well one of the few Puerto Rican women, religious or otherwise, to be invited to represent Latinas at the Women's Ordination Conference.

Following the 1972 encounter, Las Hermanas decided to allow former religious who had returned to the lay state, often to be married, to remain as full members of the organization. Eventually, no restrictions on active membership were imposed upon women, except that of commitment to the ministry. The inclusive approach that Las Hermanas attempted was echoed in a statement that Lupe Anguiano, then director of the Southwest Regional Office for the Spanish Speaking, made before the Call to Action Conference held in Detroit, Michigan, in October 1976. In it she points to the suffering of women in "a society and church much prone to false male superiority" where their capabilities in and out of the home are not recognized or respected.

> We hunger for Hispanic lay leadership . . . for recognition of the leadership talents of many men and women in dioceses and parishes. Hispanic lay persons hunger for the opportunity to be ministers of the Word in the structured parish. Instead they are confronted with a strong clerical attitude, which asks them to cut the grass, cook a fiesta meal, run a Bingo, sell tickets, clean the church,

wash altar cloths, etc. This attitude is contrary to the teachings of the church.[35]

Recognizing Las Hermanas' efforts to be inclusive is in no way an attempt to ignore that they often fell short of their mark or that their organization was free of conflict. By the time of the Second National Encounter in 1977, some twenty regional encounters had been held. The role of Las Hermanas in organizing the people for these encounters had helped organize Las Hermanas as a truly national organization, but not without encountering certain conflict in the proccess. Even when laywomen were welcomed into the organization, a certain preference for the religious Sisters spilled over at times into a sort of condescension to Latina laywomen.[36] Furthermore, the inclusion of laywomen seems only partially successful. Thus, while overall this approach of Las Hermanas was commendable, at least in the Northeast, lay participation does not appear to have been a decisive factor in their continuance. Despite the organization's efforts at inclusiveness, laywomen continue to perceive it as one too closely tied to the religious life and the institutional Church. In fact, Las Hermanas never became a grassroots mass organization, even if members did focus upon the needs of the grassroots communities in their work. In some instances they have been viewed with a certain resentment and mistrust. Such a view finds echo in the words of Haydée Borges, a laywoman who has worked for at least thirty years in various capacities in the archdiocese of New York, and who found objectionable the mode of organization of Las Hermanas and other religious leaders. Lamenting that laypersons from New York had been excluded in the planning of a conference for women in the Northeast, she wrote:

> Here can be clearly seen the third-class role that is given to the woman who is not a member of any religious order. We are discriminated against, first because we are Hispanas, second for being women, and third for being lay persons who do not belong to any religious orders. [The religious don't have] the right to speak for all women in the church, since they have to recognize that we nonreligious women live a very different reality. As a laywoman and as a leader, I ask that the voice of all the women in the church be heard. . . . We women of the grassroots serve God by a divine vocation through our baptism, without any limitations or bonds to the structures which oppress and stifle the spirit. I, as a single laywoman committed completely to the service of the church, wish to publicly raise my voice . . . since they don't pay any attention

when you speak privately. . . . As a free woman in Jesus, I speak out loud for the equality of rights of women in the church, and as a Christian I ask and demand that our dignity as daughters of God be respected in our diverse states—single women, married, widows, divorcées. We serve the total church—without pay—by vocation and love for God and neighbor, and as laywomen we carry the royal priesthood of Christ, consecrating our femininity day after day on the altars of service to the People of God.[37]

A second area of conflict for Las Hermanas was related to their Latino rather than Latin American roots. When the organization reached out to the Mexican and Latin American Sisters in the United States, they encountered some difficulties in translating the demands of the ministry among Latinos in the United States. A good number of the women in Latin American congregations were contracted for domestic duties such as cooking and cleaning within seminaries and hospitals. The ministry for these religious was within the narrow confines of such institutions. For reasons as much cultural as theological, these Sisters did not view the need for an autonomous ministry with the same urgency as did the members of Las Hermanas.

On the one hand, Las Hermanas argued that such domestic work in kitchens and laundries was demeaning and oppressive; on the other, the Latin American women engaged in these tasks preferred them to full-time pastoral ministries in the parishes. At issue was a perception of the role of women. The mostly Latina women of Las Hermanas and the Latin American religious who had been prepared for pastoral ministries desired an elevation in importance of women in the Church that would correspond to the growing visibility of women in society in general. On the other hand, the Latin American Sisters who had embraced menial domestic work as a definition of their vocation generally viewed such upward mobility as worldly and more North American than Latin American. Ultimately, Las Hermanas proposed the Mexico Project, an educational program for those religious who were involved in domestic work but who had expressed a desire to take part in an apostolate related to the local parishes or the dioceses. As means of continuing the conscientization effort they also established an orientation center that would offer programs of renewal for religious involved in the Spanish-speaking apostolate and to provide orientation to candidates or postulants to the religious life interested in ministering to the Hispanic community.

Las Hermanas has been very effective in mobilizing the Church for greater respect for the equality of women. In parallel with various aspects of the women's movement in the society at large, Las Hermanas has translated certain causes into concrete recommendations for implementation within Catholicism. Chief among the positive results of Las Hermanas' work has been the increased representation of women in most pastoral agencies. Las Hermanas' members have themselves been named directors of regional and diocesan offices for the Spanish speaking as well as members of seminary faculties, heads of diocesan Catholic charities, and as superiors of their religious congregations.

Lupe Anguiano's words at the Call to Action Conference proved partially prophetic. They are also an example of how a member of Las Hermanas used the norms of the women's movement to advance the cause of Latinas in the Church. But what is of interest in terms of the underlying premise of this presentation is that at that national convocation of Catholicism in the United States Anguiano summed up the premise of a matriarchal core and presented it with the urgency of woman's liberation: "The gift of faith given to our forefathers so embedded in our history and in our culture has been preserved and shared through our families, especially through the woman—the mother."[38] Yet, beyond a mere proclamation of the matriarchal core of Latino Catholicism, her presentation challenged the official Church to accept this mode of religiosity and to support programs of literacy, training, and assistance to married and single mothers as practical ways to sustain this essential transmission of religious values through the Latina women.

By 1977, despite all the difficulties it encountered and many growing pains, Las Hermanas, which had originated in the Southwest among religious Sisters working with the Mexican-American community, had managed to become a national organization that strove to include the needs, visions, and aspirations of a more diverse group of Latina lay and religious women from different areas of the country and representative of many Latin American backgrounds. Strengthened by successes and learning from failures, this everwidening outreach helped move the Latinas' leadership further away from the ranks of Church personnel and for a considerable period of time kept them closer to the people. Lately, however, there has been talk of a tendency toward a more inward type of movement.

Evolving Roles of Women's Ministry

Las Hermanas provides examples of how the matriarchal core continues to be modified and adapted to a changing religious situation. What Las Hermanas has not been able to achieve is ordination for women. In the Catholic Church, the issue of the priesthood for women remains a point of contention and even theological debate, meriting from time to time pastoral pronouncements. These have called for "a consistent policy within the Church to acknowledge in word and practice the equality of women before God and to affirm their giftedness." Priests and bishops have been reminded that "patronizing, condescending" attitudes toward women, that is, "sexist attitudes or an inability to deal with women as equal should be considered an indication that a seminarian is unfit for ordination to the priesthood." And yet the 1976 Vatican declaration that the hierarchy does not consider itself authorized to admit women to priestly ordination is upheld. Presently, the best that can be done to answer to the hope of this portion of the Catholic population is to call "for expanded church programs to train women to take up leadership roles open to them within the church."[39]

What these programs and the nature of their expansion are, is difficult to ascertain. One thing these pronouncements do, however, is to put additional stress on an already stressful situation. Women are told to turn a deaf ear to their calling to the ordained ministry or to interpret such a calling as not coming from God. Men are told to respect women, to treat them as equals but not equal enough to be ordained priests like them. They are told to accept and respect a woman's gifts and role in the Church except if she should be called to a position of leadership in the priestly life.

As discussed above, one of the efforts within the Church community that has helped underscore the importance of the Latina has been the organization of Las Hermanas. Begun as an organization for religious women working among the Latino community, the role of the Latina laywomen in the final outcome of this organization cannot be ignored.

In the process of ministering to their Latino communities, perhaps one of the most important lessons that the initial members of Las Hermanas learned was that indeed the people had much to teach them. Having left their Latino communities to become members of non-Latino religious orders and congregations, these women had been removed from their culture of origin and from Latino religious practices. Their formal religious and ministerial training had taken place in an environment foreign to the world they had come from and to which they would someday return. After the Second Vatican Council, when thousands of members of women religious left the classroom and traditional convent life to insert themselves in community work, the Latina religious women found themselves back whence they had started. Their work in the local communities was a constant reminder of the cultural and religious roots they had forsaken for the sake of an institutionalized religious state. Once again, they came face to face with women without formal religious training who had preserved the faith through a ministry based on a lay, female, centuries-old religious tradition oriented towards the family and community. The rezadoras, the curanderas, the venerable old grandmothers, always ready to nurture, teach, and give advice, were still there. The sacred space and activity they had created was as relevant then as ever before. The Latina women religious returning to their community found that before they could be true leaders, they had to be accepted as such by their people. True leadership and acceptance was merited when the individual could identify with the needs and aspirations of the community rather than on the basis of formal knowledge or official titles. In other words, one would receive acceptance and respect when one demonstrated acceptance and respect. Thus, by accepting the religious role that laywomen had played in the community and by extending membership within the organization to both former religious and laywomen, Las Hermanas assured themselves of a more diversified membership and legitimacy within the community. Diversity and legitimacy were also gained by incorporating members from all regions of the nation. Thus, despite its shortcomings, Las Hermanas represents, to date, the most creative and successful effort for solidarity in a diverse U.S. Latino reality.

Of great significance is their contribution in forming *comunidades eclesiales de base* and in trying to foster a theological understanding consonant with the needs and experiences of Latino/Latina reality in this country. Without abandoning important roles in catechetics and education among the Spanish speaking, Las Hermanas has produced significant leadership in adapting the Latin American model of these grassroots communities to the conditions of the United States. Besides the personal contact with their communities in the U.S., the affinity for and training in Latin American pastoral institutes offered many Hermanas members a special insight into the workings of these communities. Moreover, as Madeline Adriance has demonstrated,[40] it can be argued that *comunidades de base* is a ministry that keeps its advocates close to the people with the autonomous space characteristic of the matri-archal core.

With Las Hermanas as a vital organization, when the Women's Ordination Conference was held in 1974, it was expected that La-tina lay and religious women would be well represented. This, in fact, was not the case. Of approximately 1,300 persons attending the conference, there could not have been more than a dozen Lati-nas. The number is statistically insignificant when one takes into account that by that time Latinos constituted approximately 25 per-cent of the Catholic population in the United States. In other words, Latinas constituted at least 12.5 percent, if not more, of the na-tional Catholic population, but they represented less than 1 percent of those attending. Furthermore, other minority women and lay-women as such (both Latina and non-Latina) were also underrep-resented. Although allowed to voice some opinions, the scope and importance of their interests and concerns were not given the time and attention they merited, nor was an agenda which answered to the Latinas' presence and contributions within the Church fur-thered. From the lay, minority, and Latina women's position, then, the Women's Ordination Conference structurally reflected a Euro-centric national church and religious elitism which seems to have continued until the present time, although the formation of some smaller groups has improved the situation somewhat.[41] There is little evidence that those advocating for the ordination of women are eager to advocate equally for adequate representation of Latinas and other minority groups in this endeavor. With very few excep-tions, the literature produced on women in the ministerial work of the Church gives strong indication that it has been "business as usual" as relates to the role of Latinas. In most cases it has been one of benign neglect if not almost total exclusion.[42]

CONCLUSION

Before the Second Vatican Council, if a Latina wanted to serve the Church in the religious state, in most cases she had to remove herself not only from the so-called secular world but also from her cultural-religious world as well. More recently, Latinas have expe-rienced greater cultural sensitivity in the religious life. However, institutionalized religious life continues to have little appeal for the Latina.

Latinas have always known that they have a role as women that is not identical with those for Euro-American women. Without abandoning solidarity with the goals of women's liberation, Latinas in and out of the church have defined several differences between themselves and women of other ethnic backgrounds in the United States. Those among them who have undertaken the task of doing theology see this endeavor as a communal process which goes beyond attaining doctoral degrees in theology or gaining good insights into matters of religion. It requires conversation in order to deepen understanding and to set the basis for an ongoing conversion experience. But the conversation must come from a "clear identification of the day-to-day life of those engaged in doing this theology, their needs and their struggles . . . [even if it is not] objective but rather [endeavors] to state clearly its subjectivity at the levels of analysis and strategy."[43] Equally important is for such an understanding to be the driving force upon which the community becomes an active agent of its own history. "As a culture within another culture, Hispanics need to establish a clear sense of 'us' distinguishable from Anglos, blacks, and all other ethnic/cultural groups in the United States."[44]

Using the term *mujerista* rather than feminist theology, Ada María Isasi-Díaz and Yolanda Tarango have attempted to dramatize the Latinas' desire to distinguish themselves and their needs from those of their male counterparts as well as from the general female population in the United States, while recognizing that the term itself and the ideas embodied in its definition fail to include the variety of opinions within the Latina community. Because of the sexism, ethnic prejudice, and classism inherent in this society, Latinas understand that in the forging of the identity for all the Latino people in Catholicism, there is an evident need to include a Latina woman's perspective.[45]

> Hispanic Women have come to understand that they have a very important contribution to make. The particularity of their oppression has led them to understand that the solution to their oppression has to be liberation and not equality.
>
> Concretely, this last point means that Hispanic Women do not seek greater participation within the present oppressive patriarchal structures of both church and society. Because these structures are patriarchal, they are based on dualistic and hierarchical understandings. Thus, by their very nature they will oppress someone. Out of the particularity of their situation Hispanic Women have come to

understand that a radical change in these structures is the only possible solution to oppression. Though differing in ways of doing it, they seek a shift in paradigm; it is not a matter of changing positions with males and with Anglos or sharing equally with them. It is a matter of bringing about a new reality; Hispanic Women believe that they have a distinct and valuable contribution to make to such a task.[46]

Casting aside institutional protocol, historically Latinas have absorbed and appropriated priestly roles within their traditional ministry in the home and community. If today the issue of women's ordination to the clerical state fails to spark their enthusiasm it may be that, as Isasi-Díaz and Tarango point out, their understanding of their religious commitment precludes acceptance of a system which is inherently oppressive of both men and women. Ultimately it is liberation, not equality, which is being sought.

Las Hermanas, as an inclusive organization, purported to offer Latinas a measure of equality and a certain amount of freedom in defining their ministry among their communities. But as successful and influential as Las Hermanas may have been in promoting a woman's perspective in Latino ministry, they did not invent it nor did they explore it to the fullest. There are many other organizations, especially at the local level, which have been crucial in maintaining a Latina presence in the Church an in constructing Latino Catholicism in the United States, each one offering specific opportunities and limitations. The role that movements, such as the Cursillo, Movimiento Familiar Cristiano, and Movimiento Carismático, have played cannot be denied. Traditional sodalities and associations such as terciarias, Hijas de María, Guadalupana, Damas del Sagrado Corazón, and Legión de María have been important to this process. And lastly, the traditional roles Latina women appropriated to themselves as leaders of communal and familial prayer, as spiritual advisers, as catechists, and as nurturers of the faith have never waned. They continue to gain strength and visibility especially in a Church community with decreasing membership and decreasing clergy.

Ironically, under the guise of "new" ministry, Latina women today are regaining much of the influence they once wielded in a clergy-poor rural setting. And because the shortage of male celibate clergy is likely to continue in the United States, the importance of the Latina lay or religious women in the Church ministry will grow rather than diminish in the future. Thus, the priestly and prophetic role Latinas are accustomed to exercise will strengthen not only Latino Catholicism but the Church as a whole. Because the Latinos are the fastest-growing and youngest population in the nation and in the Church, and because women traditionally have assumed such important roles in the maintenance and transformation of religion, the survival of the Catholic Church in the United States may, in considerable measure, be in the capable and creative hands of Latinas.

NOTES

1. Two such studies are Andrew Greeley, *American Catholic* (New York: Basic Books, 1977); and William D'Antonio et al., *American Catholic Laity in a Changing Church* (Kansas City, Mo.: Sheed and Ward, 1989). Both omit data on Hispanics from their analysis.

2. Quoted from "Handout #6b: Our Mother's Struggle Has Shown Us the Way," excerpts from a radio documentary, "*Nosotras trabajamos en la costura*/Puerto Rican Women in the Garment Industry," produced by Rina Benmayor, Ana Juarbe, Kimberly Safford, and Blanca Vázquez Erazo, Centro de Estudios Puertorriqueños, Hunter College, 1985, in *Ibero-American Heritage Curriculum—Latinos in the Making of the United States of America: Yesterday, Today and Tommorrow: Teacher Guide*, sponsored by the New York State Education Department et al., 1993), p. 1240.

3. Parts of the Puerto Rican Migration Research Consortium's survey were published by José Hernández Alvarez in *Youth Employment* (Maplewood, N.J.: Waterfront Press, 1983). I conducted the unpublished research on religion.

4. See Ada María Isasi-Díaz and Yolanda Tarango, "Construyendo nuestra esperanza," newsletter, St. Mary's Press, Winona, Minn.; and *Hispanic Women: Prophetic Voice in the Church* (New York: Harper and Row, 1988).

5. The 1991 study, "Latino National Political Survey," conducted by Rudy de la Garza and Angelo Falcón, recorded a preference for the specific nationality label as opposed to a generic *Latino* or *Hispanic* designation. A summary of the data can be obtained from the Puerto Rican Policy Institute in New York.

6. There have been two national surveys of Latinos in religion: *A Gallup Study of Religious and Social Attitudes of Hispanic-Americans* (Princeton, N. J.: Gallup Organization, Inc., August 1978); and Roberto O. González and Michael La Velle, *The Hispanic Catholic in the U.S.:*

A Socio-Cultural and Religious Profile (New York: Northeast Hispanic Pastoral Center, 1985).

7. See Ana María Díaz-Stevens, "Assessing the Matriarchal Core of Latino Popular Religion," paper presented at the annual meeting of the Association for the Sociology of Religion, Pittsburgh, Pa., August 18, 1992.

8. Electa Arenal and Stacey Schlau, *Untold Sisters: Hispanic Nuns in Their Own Works* (Albuquerque: University of New Mexico Press, 1989), pp. 37, 41.

9. Ibid., pp. 293, 294.

10. Ibid., p. 294.

11. Octavio Paz, *Sor Juana: Her Life and Her World* (Cambridge, Mass.: Harvard University Press, 1988). Also see George H. Tavard, *Juana Inés de la Cruz and the Theology of Beauty: The First Mexican Theology* (Notre Dame: University of Notre Dame Press, 1991).

12. See Anthony M. Stevens-Arroyo and Ana María Díaz-Stevens in *Handbook of Hispanic Cultures in the United States*, ed. Félix Padilla, Spanish ed. (Madrid: ICI), English ed. (Houston: Arte Público Press, in press).

13. In much of English literature the three concepts of *donjuanismo*, *machismo*, and *hombrismo* seem to be thoroughly confused. Briefly put, the Don Juan goes around chasing women, the macho boasts about his sexual exploits while making fun of other men and their inability to be successful as he is in the lovemaking game, and the *hombre cabal* is the noble caballero who is always ready to risk even life for honor of his name, his lady love, and his beliefs. But, it seems as if the supposed Spanish male obsession with his manliness has given rise to another obsession on the part of non-Hispanic scholars. Eager to find its roots and analyze them, some have looked at religion for a possible explanation, and others even at Spanish sports such as *la corrida de toros*. Sometimes they have "discovered" in their coexistence a possible correlation. In this author's view, this intense preoccupation with the "dark" side of the Spanish psyche represents a continuation of the Black Legend perpetuated by Anglo non-Catholics. An interesting analysis of the Spanish sport of bullfighting and a Spanish machista mentality is offered by Timothy Mitchell, *Blood Sport* (Philadelphia: University of Pennsylvania Press, 1991). Interestingly, when he encounters literature describing Hemingway's obsession with la corrida as exhibiting the same "pathological" attitudes that are ascribed to Spanish men, he concludes "they ought to be taken with a grain of salt" (p. 5). From a Spanish perspective, if not a machista attitude, such an assessment may convey at least a rather chauvinistic one, since it

seems to imply that only men of Spanish background or those who "assimilate the Spanish worldview completely" (p. 5) can behave in such a manner.

14. Evelyn P. Stevens, among others, presents machismo and marianismo as two sides of the same coin. Unfortunately her analysis of the Mexican people has been used to perpetuate a negative image of male-female relationship in all of the Spanish-speaking world. Furthermore, her generalizations often convey cultural chauvinism and condescension. For Stevens' treatment of machismo-marianismo, see her works, *Protest and Responses in Mexico* (Cambridge, Mass.: The MIT Press, 1974), and *"Marianismo*: The Other Face of *Machismo* in Latin America," in *Female and Male in Latin America*, ed. Ann Pescatello (Pittsburgh: University of Pittsburgh Press, 1973).

15. See Rudy de la Garza et al., "Latino Policy Survey."

16. This is the experience recorded by North American missionaries to the inhabitants of New Mexico as analyzed in Sarah Deutsch, *No Separate Refuge: Culture, Class and Gender on an Anglo-Hispanic Frontier in the American Southwest, 1880–1940* (New York and Oxford: Oxford University Press, 1987). Based on my own research, I would conclude that, if anything, the peasant women were more inclined towards *madonismo* or *sentido de maternidad*; that is, reverence for a type of relationship often transcending physical motherhood. Thus, the widow, the physically barren, the woman who had lost her offspring to sickness and natural catastrophes, and even the virgin could all aspire and claim motherhood through the care of the orphaned, the underprivileged, the sick, and other members of the immediate family and community in need of nurturing.

17. See ibid.

18. Iñigo Abbad y Lasierra, *Historia geográfica, civil y natural de la Isla de San Juan Bautista de Puerto Rico* (1789) (Río Piedras, Puerto Rico: Editorial Universitaria, 1959), p. 193 (my translation).

19. Richard and Gloria L. Rodríguez, "Teresa Urrea, Her Life, as It Affected the Mexican-U.S. Frontier," in *Voices*, ed. Octavio Ignacio Rodríguez (Berkeley, Calif.: Quinto Sol Publications, 1973), pp. 179–199.

20. Anthony M. Stevens-Arroyo and Ana María Díaz Ramírez, "Puerto Ricans in the States: A Struggle for Identity," in *Minority Report*, ed. Anthony G. Dworkin and Rosalind J. Dworkin (New York: Holt, Rinehart, and Winston, 1982), pp. 196–222.

21. Ana María Díaz-Stevens, *Oxcart Catholicism on Fifth Avenue: The Impact of the Puerto Rican Migration upon the Catholic Archdiocese of New York* (Notre Dame, Ind.: University of Notre Dame Press, 1993).

22. Ibid.

23. Deutsch, *No Separate Refuge*.

24. Emilio Pantojas García, *La iglesia protestante y la americanización de Puerto Rico* (San Juan de Puerto Rico: PRISA, n.d.). Aida Negrón de Montilla, *Americanization, Puerto Rico, and the Public School System, 1900–1930)* (Río Piedras, Puerto Rico: Editorial Universitaria, 1975).

25. Quoted by Pantojas García, p. 14.

26. Quoted by Pantojas García, p. 18.

27. Quoted by Pantojas García, p. 23.

28. Quoted by Pantojas García, pp. 21, 22.

29. Dan Wakefield, *Island in the Sun: The World of Spanish Harlem* (Boston: Houghton Mifflin, 1959).

30. In the Puerto Rican community, there is an impressive list of women who have excelled in all professions. Among these are the late Marta Valle, director of New York Youth Services; Luisa Quintero, Spanish-language journalist; Pura Belpré, librarian-educator; Evelina Antonetty, community services, educator. Famous Puerto Rican women today include Rita Moreno and Miriam Colón, actresses in cinema and theater; Nicholasa Mohr, writer-artist and educator; Nydia Velázquez from Brooklyn, the first Puerto Rican congresswoman in the U.S. House of Representatives; Olga Méndez from Manhattan, a N.Y. State senator; María del Carmen Alicia Ramírez, director of N.Y. State bilingual education; Isaura Santiago, president, Hostos Community College; and Elsa Gómez, president of Kean College in New Jersey. Equally impressive are the lists of Mexican-American and Cuban-American women.

31. Anthony M. Stevens-Arroyo, "Puerto Rican Struggles in the Catholic Church," in *The Puerto Rican Struggle: Essays on Survival in the U.S.*, ed. Clara E. Rodríguez, Virginia Sánchez-Korrol, and José Oscar Alers (New York: Puerto Rican Migration Research Consortium, Inc., 1980), pp. 133, 134. According to this source, the Cursillo was brought from Spain in 1960; in December of 1962 the movement was introduced in the Brooklyn diocese; in 1964 the Cursillo began both in Newark and in Philadelphia.

32. See Jaime Vidal, "Popular Religion among the Hispanics in the General Area of the Archdiocese of Newark, Part IV," in *Nueva Presencia: Knowledge for Service and Hope—A Study of Hispanics in the Archdiocese of Newark* (Newark, N.J.: Office of Research and Planning, Archdiocese of Newark, 1988).

33. Interviews with Haydée Borges of New York archdiocese (December 1992) and Alicia Salinas, St. Rose of Lima Parish, New York City (November 1992).

34. Antonio M. Stevens-Arroyo, *Prophets Denied Honor* (Maryknoll, N.Y.: Orbis Books, 1980), p. 136.

35. Quoted in ibid., p. 309.

36. See Haydée Borges, "The Voice of the Laywoman in the Church of the Northeast of the United States of America," in Stevens-Arroyo, *Prophets Denied Honor*, pp. 289–291.

37. See Borges, in Stevens-Arroyo, *Prophets Denied Honor*, pp. 290, 291.

38. See Lupe Anguiano, "Statement for Call to Action Conference, Detroit, Michigan, October 1976 (excerpt)," in Stevens-Arroyo, *Prophets Denied Honor*, p. 307.

39. Draft of the U.S. bishops' pastoral letter, April 1988.

40. See Madeline Adriance, "Agents of Change: The Roles of Priests, Sisters, and Lay Workers in the Grassroots Catholic Church in Brazil," *Journal for the Scientific Study of Religion* 30, no. 3 (September 1991), pp. 292–305. Adriance states that "Women religious are the largest group of pastoral agents involved with CEBs, outnumbering priests by three-to-one. They are the ones who carry out most of the actual day-by-day work of organizing and supporting the base communities. Sisters who work at the grassroots level are almost always directly involved in some aspect of CEB work: for example, community organizing, youth groups, women's groups, child health work, political education, and leadership training. The role of the lay pastoral agents, who are relatively few in number, is similar. The work of the priests, however, is restricted by their sacramental and administrative functions. . . . Although there are some clergy who manage to be effective, even charismatic, community organizers in spite of their work load, it is clear that women religious and laypeople have an advantage in this task." She quotes priests working in the CEBs as saying: "Those who work at the level of the community, those who accompany it, and those who give the most to this work are the women. . . . They work better than a priest in the community. . . . Animating the people. Getting to know the people. Preparing the people to live their faith. . . . If that community had ten priests, maybe these priests could do the work that those three sisters are doing" (pp. 299, 300).

41. See Mary Jo Weaver, *New Catholic Women: A Contemporary Challenge to Traditional Religious Authority* (Harper and Row: New York, 1985), pp. 110–115 and passim, who reflects the neglect of Latina women that was general until recently.

42. Isasi-Díaz and Tarango, as two Latina theologians, are among the few who are articulating a Latina agenda in this regard. Virtually

all literature produced by non-Latinas ignores and therefore omits the Latina experience and agenda. At a scholarly conference where Ruth Wallace was presenting the findings for her book *They Call Her Pastor: A New Role for Catholic Women* (Albany: State University of New York Press, 1992), I asked her what percentage of the women interviewed were Latinas. She said she thought there were two included. Early in 1993 at a scholarly conference when I suggested the need for cultural awareness both in the ministry and in the research involving the role of women in religion, Wallace did not recognize me, but remembered that "there was a Latina woman who had a similar concern when I first presented my findings," and suggested that I might be interested in doing research into that particular issue. *Sociology of Religion* dedicated its Spring 1992 edition entirely to the question of women in religion. As I scan through it I find not one article, not one quote, not even one cited source on the question of Latinas and their religious experience. In the eyes of certain sectors of the institutional church and of academia, we either simply do not exist or are not interesting enough to be studied.

43. Ada María Isasi-Díaz and Yolanda Tarango, *Hispanic Women: Prophetic Voice in the Church* (San Francisco and New York: Harper and Row, 1988).

44. Ibid., p. 3.

45. Ibid.

46. Ibid., pp. 3, 4.

8

Latino Youth and the Church

Ana María Díaz-Stevens

"A church without youth is by definition committed to mortality," wrote Lincoln and Mamiya in their study on the black church in North America.[1] Scholarly journals, newspapers, books, and even sermons from the pulpit warn of the alarming statistics of the decline in religious and priestly vocations in the Roman Catholic Church. The only rising numbers in the vocation picture are the ages of the average priest or religious. Even the most optimistic of Catholic Church leaders have cause for concern. The lack of new blood is evident not only among the ranks of institutionalized and ordained ministries but in the membership of the overall congregation. This phenomenon is too complex to be adequately analyzed in a chapter whose main concern is the role of Latino youth in the Church. But there is an admitted lack of success in the incorporation of Latino young adults to the ordained clerical and religious life. Thus, in addition to a structure which keeps married men and women from the ordained priesthood, the graying of the Catholic clergy and religious communities in the United States may be attributed to an inability to attract Latinos.

Various reasons have been given for the distance between Latino youth and the religious and priestly vocations. A common assumption is that people of Hispanic and Latin American background value family and children to the detriment of priestly and religious life. Others, looking at particular historical periods in some regions of Latin America, conclude that all Latinos are anarchic and anticlerical.[2] Such assumptions lead to erroneous conclusions.

The survey of the history of Latino communities in this country reveals that the response given by the Latino people to the institutional Church is usually conditioned by the type of reception extended by the clergy and other ministers. Do Latinos, young and old, perceive the Catholic Church in the U.S. as "home" or, as in colonial Spanish America, as an institutional apparatus which

278

has remained alien to their particular cultural and religious needs? The Catholic Church in the U.S. has traditionally played a vital role as an agent of integration in the immigration process of other ethnic groups to this country. What has been the role it has played in the integration of all Latinos, especially the young?

This chapter begins with a brief sociohistorical interpretation of the traditional role of children and youth in a Hispanic setting and the changes brought about by migration. It includes information on the educational and socioeconomic condition and the obstacles faced by this segment of the population as they seek integration into U.S. society. An analysis of their relationship with the Catholic Church in the U.S. is made by highlighting specific examples of responses initiated either by members of this community or by the Church.

As in other chapters, mention must be made here of the difficulties of grouping all members of the diverse Hispanic or Latino subgroups into one category. I will join information drawn from census data and official documents with analytical studies. The personal experiences and observations of the author and other persons involved in the processes described in this chapter will no doubt color the analysis. But this should counterbalance much of the literature on Latino youth that has emphasized a pathological perspective, viewing the subject as a problem to be solved (or contained), rather than as a reality to be studied.

THE MINISTRY TOWARDS LATINO YOUTH
BEFORE THE CONCILIAR REFORMS

The traditional Latino understanding of youth derives from the rural culture of their countries of origin. In the countryside, persons were children until they married and moved out of their parents' house. Until then, they were expected to assume without question the authority of the father, to contribute with their work to the family, and to uphold its good name.[3] Even after marriage, they were not to forsake a family member in need, especially younger siblings who were not yet able to care for themselves, elderly parents, and grandparents. Marriage and courtship took place in a communal context and had to be approved by the families of the couple. Many scholars have concluded that marriage often was more of a family affair than a romance. Marriage, furthermore, did not sever the close relationship between parents and their offspring.

Respect, honor of the family name, filial devotion, and deference to parents and elders were expected from all children, single or married, young or adult. Even as Latinos became more urban by migration and modernization, many of these views persisted.

The idea of teenagers—no longer children, but still only young adults—did not fit a pre-1960 Latino society. A relatively early age for marriage and the virtual end of educational opportunity with high school graduation deprived most Latinos of the teenage experiences of the dominant U.S. society. Even the relatively well-to-do among Latinos frequently chose to ignore the model of U.S. teenagers, preferring instead a Latin American conception. Thus, puberty marked the entrance directly into adulthood, as rites of passages such as *quinceañera* or *debutante* indicate.

Migration to the cities affected the culture of all Latinos[4] but fell especially hard on teenagers. Schooling turned Latinos against the values and the world of their parents by offering education and upward social mobility as the fruits of assimilation. At a time when bilingual education and multiculturalism are familiar, it is hard to imagine the overt depreciation for Latin America, its values, and its people that permeated the classrooms of North America before 1960.[5] Celia Alvarez, a member of a research team that conducted an oral history project for the Centro de Estudios Puertorriqueños of CUNY in the fall of 1988 remembers what it was like to be a Puerto Rican growing up in New York in the 1950s and 1960s. She recalls that the only formal mention of Puerto Rico in the first twelve years of her school had been in a geography class in which mineral resources had been discussed. Even the family became part of the conspiracy of silence, not out of shame, but to spare its young members the suffering that went along with the telling: "No one wanted to talk about the poverty and pain, the family truces and secrets which clouded the tremendous upheaval from Ponce to San Juan to New York."[6] She goes on to outline that poverty and pain the children felt nonetheless—the pain of being caught between two cultures, with their corresponding competing values, both of which were only partially known to them.

> I grew up speaking Spanish, dancing *la pachanga, merengue,* and *mambo,* eating *arroz con habichuelas* and drinking *malta y café.* I was smart, and learned to play the chords of the bureaucratic machinery of housing, education, and welfare very well at a very young age. . . .
>
> I never told my parents about the racist slurs—never had the heart. They were breaking their backs to send me to school; my

father kept his job at a city hospital for thirty years and took on a
second job at the docks. We would all go help him clean offices at
night and on weekends after our day outings together. My mother
went back to work in a paper factory down the street. Prior to that,
she had taken care of the children of women in the neighborhood
who worked. I've also worked since about the time I was fourteen.[7]

But being exposed to this reality did not mean that Puerto Rican
and other Latino children growing up in the United States could
understand the magnitude and complexity of the life they had to
live. For Alvarez as for so many others, survival meant being on
the alert and keeping one's eyes open at all times.

It was hard to understand it all, to try to make sense of what I was
as a Puerto Rican in New York, so I read everything I could get my
hands on; watched the games the government would play between
Afro-Americans and Puerto Ricans with social service monies; heard
the poverty pimps tell their lies; watched the kids die of dope or
heard about them getting killed down elevator chutes in the middle
of a burglary; noted the high overpriced tags on old food being sold
in the only supermarket in the neighborhood; knew of kids being
raped and thrown off the roof. And I asked, "Why?"[8]

While some Latino youth opted for assimilation into the dominant U.S. society, many others rejected its values and created their
own versions of an urbanized Latino society that was recognizably
their own. But this often also meant that added to the responsibilities they had traditionally fulfilled in their native lands, such
as caring for younger siblings, Latino youth in migration were
expected by their parents to take on other roles which were neither
present in their native lands nor ordinarily imposed upon young
people in the United States. Among these was that of translator, a
role for children found frequently in the ethnographical studies of
urban Latinos in the 1950s: "I translated for everyone—my mother,
her friends, our neighbors, as well as my teachers. My parents
kept us close to home and it was my responsibility to keep my
brother and sister in tow."[9] So, while in the adult world of their
country of origin, children were virtually voiceless, in the U.S.,
eight- and nine-year-olds served as intermediaries between social
agencies and their parents by translating even highly confidential
exchanges for both government and family. Because they generally
spoke English, young Latinos often accompanied their parents to
stores where they helped transact family business.[10] In some cases,
young Latinos worked as cashiers or salespersons in their parents'

shop to handle the occasional English-speaking client and negotiate with suppliers. These and other factors, such as an expected
early marriage, gave Latino children and young adults a voice and
influence in family matters far beyond that of other urban youth
in the United States.

It is not clear if the new roles migration thrust upon Latino
youth in the 1960s were recognized by official institutions like
schools and social services in large U.S. cities. Although power was
being given to Latino young people along with responsibility, there
was seldom a corresponding institutional mechanism to prepare
young Latinos for the added burden imposed by these new roles.

The Catholic Church was not prepared to address these matters
adequately, either. Perhaps because they still were not sure how
to deal with the parents, typical Catholic Church organizations
paid scant attention to these and other special needs of Latino
teenagers in an urban environment far removed from their own
culture.[11] As in the sending societies, sodalities such as Las Hijas
de María (the Children of Mary) continued in the U.S. to provide
segregation of young unmarried women not only from men of
all ages but also from married women. A young woman who
married was expected to curtail her relationship with unmarried
ones and to become promptly a member of Las Damas del Sagrado
Corazón (Ladies of the Sacred Heart) or any other organization for
married women. In a sense, such organizations served the purpose
of insulating and keeping young women "innocent." They also
served as the chaperone system of Mediterranean culture in which
young men and women were never left alone without supervision
of an adult.[12] While allowing and even sponsoring social events,
these Catholic organizations emphasized strict adherence to such
Christian virtues as chastity and the reception of the sacraments
of penance (now reconciliation) and the eucharist. The local parish
profited from women's organizations such as Las Hijas de María,
since in many instances they were the ones called upon to instruct
a younger generation of children into the faith and the reception of the sacraments. In general, these programs were helpful
in maintaining the young Latino's loyalty to the doctrines of the
Church and keeping them partly in touch with old, family-based
traditions, but they did not do as much to prepare them for their
newly attained responsibilities in a new country and culture.

Most Catholic teenagers are expected to join the Catholic Youth
Organization (CYO), which accepts both male and female participants. Race and class have often been related to level of educational

and economic attainments in the U.S., and economic conditions determine the particular parish community in which people can afford to live. Due to these circumstances, many young Catholics, along with their parents, have been segregated along ethnic, linguistic, and racial lines. Like neighborhoods, parishes become "tipped," gaining a predominantly Latino representation. In the archdiocese of New York, for instance, in some such parishes, the CYO membership was predominantly Latino. When this happened, the parishes within the CYO districts for the Bronx were regrouped so that the Latino and non-Latino CYO members were segregated. In some areas, however, no amount of such shifting of district areas could keep some level of necessary integration from taking place. Despite their limitations, the CYO organizations of some local parish churches provided support, sharing, and learning, as Celia Alvarez describes.

> The socially active local parish church became my refuge. It was there that I began to make connections with the poor whites, Afro-Americans, and Asians in my community, and said there had to be a better way for us all. I participated in a variety of activities including youth programs, the local food coop, and newsletter, which basically involved me in community organizing, although I didn't know you called it grassroots work then.[13]

Although at the practical level the Catholic Youth Organization seemed to have emphasized programs to coordinate the leisure activity of youth, in fact its stated purpose was fourfold: spiritual, cultural, social, and athletic. Furthermore, the cultural, social, and athletic components were all geared to bring about and enhance the first one, "that end to which all other must be subservient, the service and praise of the Creator."[14] As explained by John F. O'Hara, C.S.C., archbishop of Philadelphia in the foreword to the *Catholic Youth Organization Handbook*:

> The final objective of all Catholic youth work is, of course, the salvation of souls. All activities, recreational, social, cultural, are directed to the honor and glory of God; the whole program should keep its subject close to the sources of grace, the Sacraments and Prayer.[15]

Therefore, although the expenditure of parish resources—gyms, team uniforms, practice fields, coaches, etc.—was much greater in the CYO programs, the ultimate purpose was similar to other, more traditional youth and young adults organizations to which

Latino youths were accustomed: to provide a controlled and safe environment where young people could channel youthful energies towards the maintenance of Catholic moral values so that they could give Christian witness before the world.[16] Unfortunately, however, the segregation that was sometimes imposed through the shifting and redistricting of parishes within the CYO network gave its own witness, conveying a message other than the one being proclaimed.

Another movement among young Catholic adults was the Newman clubs. In the college and university campuses of the U.S., the Newman clubs attempted to bring Catholic students together for religious and social action. But very few Latinos made it to college and, therefore, the Newman clubs were not accessible to them.

Based on the concepts "observe, judge, and act" developed by the Belgian priest, Canon Joseph Cardijn, the Catholic Action movement, Young Christian Workers (YCW), was important to young people from the middle of 1930s until the 1960s.[17] Paul McGuire, who introduced the Catholic Action movements from Europe to the U.S. in 1938, made a distinction between Catholic Action and Catholic Social Action. He perceived Catholic Action as dealing with personal and religious issues while Catholic Social Action was related to social problems.[18]

This distinction, along with others,[19] made the movement in the U. S. different from its more popular expression in Europe and Latin America. The inability to focus upon the special needs of groups such as Latinos and blacks may in fact have come from such a dichotomized understanding of Catholic Action in the U.S. The focus upon like-to-like apostolate also proved problematic because this U.S. approach effectively segregated the movement along the lines of the dominant society. "Minority workers in the black communities were not easily reached by white organizers. This is not surprising in view of the movement's emphasis on a like-to-like apostolate, and it did sometimes complicate matters for the blacks who did join."[20]

Hispanic parishes in California in places like El Cajón, Hanford, Los Angeles, and in Arizona in Winslow had established the movement back in 1953. At first, these groups were concerned with local problems but two decades later became very much involved in César Chavez's struggles on behalf of migrant workers.[21] In Detroit, Tomás Gonzáles recruited many Latinos to the Young Christian Workers before he left his position at General Motors to continue his efforts among farm workers at the San Joaquín

Valley of California.[22] But these were areas long settled by Latinos and where a sizable proportion, if not the majority, of the parish congregation was in fact Latino, mostly Mexican in origin.

In the northeastern United States, the Latino population was less established. Only in the twentieth century did New York acquire its large Puerto Rican population that according to census reports became the city's largest ethnic group in 1990. During the 1950s, Puerto Rican migrants were more likely to have had experience with Catholic Action groups because of the emergence of an urban middle class on the island. The familiarity of New York's Spanish-speaking young people with Latin American forms of Catholic Action was intensified by the Cuban exiles who entered this country as an immediate consequence of the 1959 Cuban revolution and an even greater influx of Dominicans and Central Americans after the 1965 change in the immigration laws. Unfortunately, the U.S. Catholic Action leaders viewed the Spanish language as a barrier to full participation in the movement.

> However, language problems were a serious deterrent to the recruitment of Hispanics in many cities, especially in the Northeast and Midwest where many were recent immigrants. In Chicago in the late fifties and early sixties, there were a number of Spanish-speaking sections, but they were out of the mainstream of the Chicago federation because of the language barrier. They used the inquiry method to work on local problems they encountered in their communities, but they were unable to use the prescribed national inquiry program. It was not until the sixties that the YCW published materials in Spanish.[23]

But, "the language barrier" which seems to be equated with an inability "to use the prescribed national inquiry program" may have been a conscious decision on the part of the Latinos. Latinos had learned to be Catholic in their countries of origin, where English was not required for Church membership. Moreover, Catholic Action groups for youth were highly visible in most Latin American countries, often exceeding the U.S. YCW both in numbers and influence. Young people with positive experiences of Catholic Action groups were likely to bring to the movement the same traditional approach of their relationship to the institutional Church in their ancestral homelands. In fact, rupture with the U.S. policies may account for the relative success of the Latino groups.[24] A more fluid structure had proved successful not only among Latino groups in the U.S. but also in Latin America, something the

YCW found out in their efforts at international networking of the movement with Latin America.[25]

An interesting fact is that the original name given to the New York archdiocesan office that ministers to the Puerto Ricans and other Latinos was Spanish Catholic Action Office. Its name was changed to Spanish Community Action in the 1960s at a time when the North American Catholic Action seems to have been on the decline. Robert Fox, the young priest heading the office, had been trained in the Catholic Action approach in Uruguay.

The Catholic Action movement in Latin America, as in Europe, made a distinction between workers and students. There was the JOC—Juventud Obrera Católica—whose members were commonly known as *jocistas*. The JOC was designed for unmarried full-time working youth while university students were grouped in the JEC—Juventud Estudiantil Católica. Wherever Catholic Action groups for young people existed, they were generally focused upon labor struggles, political voting rights, and ideological advancement of papal teachings for social justice. Their approach seemed to have focused more on learning by doing than in learning to do. Their overall structure seemed more fluid than that of the movements in the U.S., and their efforts more localized.

Fox, however, did not totally break away from the U.S. tendency to divide Catholic Actions from Catholic Social Action. He did subjectivize the apostolate, emphasizing an understanding of self and one's reality over overtly political action. Fox trusted that such an understanding would propel the individual into action in his or her own setting. Success was not measured by results in attacking the problems that affected the Latino urban poor through deep-rooted structural changes. Moreover, in his desire to bridge the gap between urban and suburban, priest/religious and laity, working class and professionals, white, black, and Latino, Fox ignored the growing call for nationalist consciousness among young Puerto Ricans during the 1960s.

ESTABLISHMENT OF A LATINO YOUTH MINISTRY

Specialized programs were important especially at a time when young Latinos were facing a hostile and often dangerous environment. Unfortunately for some, they saw in the popularized subculture of the youth gangs and drug cult a place of acceptance and group identity. In fact, as Piri Thomas clearly describes in his book,

Down These Mean Streets, the price of peer pressure and acceptance into this world was alienation from one's own family, traditional culture, and society. For a number of Latino youth, as for the youth of many other ethnic groups, involvement in gangs and drugs had more than a passing effect upon their lives.[26] At local levels, Latino groups competed for influence and turf with Euro-American youth, sometimes even losing their lives in the process. The media did its share to accentuate the differences among ethnic groups, to emphasize negative characteristics and behavioral patterns, and in the process did much to reinforce existing stereotypes.

Notwithstanding that Latinos have not been the only ones involved in and affected by gang activity and that the actual number of Latino youths belonging to these gangs may have been relatively small, there is no denying the deleterious effects upon individuals, family, and the overall Latino community. Tied more to drug commerce than to mere addiction and made fatal because of the escalation of violence brought about by the easy acquisition of handguns, today juvenile gangs' activities go well beyond the traditional struggle for local turf.[27] The bad image generated by the activity of a few and reinforced by a mass media goes a long way towards the perpetuation of mistreatment of and discrimination against the total community. Even within the Catholic community, these negative stereotypes of Latinos as delinquents and welfare cheaters have been repeated.

Despite overwhelming social problems in the cities, a strong factor in the process of identification for Latino youth continued to be religion. And for the majority of Latino young people religion remained a family affair. As Alvarez pointed out, parents tried to keep their children "close to home." Family rituals, including prayers before the home altar, infant baptism in the home, puberty rituals such as quinceañera celebrations, special traditions tied to Holy Week and Christmas, the quasi-religious observance of Mothers' Day, and even wakes followed by novenas for the deceased members of the family provided space and opportunity for identification as members of a family and as Catholics. Latino youths may have felt somewhat uncomfortable explaining the traditional *bendición* or blessings that they asked of their parents upon leaving or coming back home, but they knew what family traditions expected of them. Seldom did they seek to omit asking for the blessing, and seldom did the parents refrain from imparting it. In fact, la bendición is one of the traditions that has persisted to the present and remains tied to the concept of respect and deference to elders. But not all practices persisted. As the contact with the outside world took on greater importance and roles within the family began to shift so did the understanding of the role of religion, religious traditions, and the relationship to religious institutions.

The most predictable contact with Catholicism outside the home was through the catechetical programs of the local church. Often enrollment in such supplemental education was the price to be paid in order to receive the rites of passage: baptism, first holy communion, and eventually matrimony. While such efforts were limited by a lack of resources and effective teaching techniques, they served to transmit the faith to a generation that otherwise would have been lost to institutional Catholicism before the council.

Moreover, by the middle 1960s certain pioneer programs for a Spanish-speaking apostolate had produced vital parish groups of Latino young people. In New York City, for example, clergy who had received special training for the Spanish-speaking ministry expressed their preference to assignment to Puerto Rican parishes because of the opportunities for a youth apostolate. Puerto Ricans had become the majority of the local CYO teams, and the Puerto Rican members of "establishment" sodalities such as Hijas de María (Children of Mary) and the Legion of Mary gradually gained acceptance as participants in archdiocesan-wide councils. Similar success stories can be found in California and Texas for Mexican Americans and in Chicago for both Puerto Ricans and Mexican Americans.

Perhaps most importantly for Latino youth by 1964, the modest prosperity afforded their parents in an urban economy had opened the doors to the Catholic schools. While statistics from the period are virtually impossible to construct, oral histories among Latinos indicate that the children were sent to parochial schools in increasing numbers during the 1960s. As their numbers increased, Latino enrollment often provided the margin of difference for solvency in the parish school. Moreover, parents and family were included in the general activities of the school, thus providing an integration in parish affairs that membership in Spanish-speaking societies did not afford.[28]

Despite some relatively modest gains, however, Latino youth receive far less attention with specialized programs within the Catholic Church than they do from public society. The Puerto Rican self-help group, Aspira, focuses attention and resources upon help-ing Latinos obtain a college education. Mexican-American groups such as LULAC and the GI Forum place a high priority upon youth-oriented programs. The plethora of bilingual education pro-grams as well as remedial and recreational programs funded with public money also recognize Latino youth as a target population with special needs and a high priority.

YOUTH CONSCIOUSNESS OF RELIGION
AND MINISTRY SINCE THE REFORMS

In the early years after the Second Vatican Council, the young people from Mexico, the Spanish-speaking Caribbean, and Cen-tral America who had belonged to organizations using a Catho-lic Action approach often sought to continue the movement after migration to the United States. They expected local parishes to provide a meeting place where Latino and Latina youth could come together as members of an ethnic group and as Catholics. But there was no national policy established within the U.S. Church to institutionalize these existing groupings of members of the JOC, JEC, etc. When Latinos organized themselves, no effective effort was made to combine them with existing Euro-American Catholic Action groups nationwide.

Following conciliar reforms, in the early 1970s, the Latino Youth Ministry instituted by the archdiocese of New York was put under the direction of the Spanish Community Action Office (renamed Office of the Spanish-speaking Apostolate). Under the direction of two Puerto Rican priests, José McCarthy González, O.F.M., and Antonio M. Stevens-Arroyo, C.P., a conscious effort was made to follow the Latin American Catholic Action approach with adapta-tions to the New York City and migration experiences. Mr. Bibiano Pizarro, a JOC leader from Puerto Rico, was employed as orga-nizer, and Dominican JOC and JEC leaders residing in the U.S. were invited to form a New York organization affiliated with the archdiocese. In some local parishes, clergy from Latin America or Europe, either members of religious congregations or secular priests who were on loan to the archdiocese, sought to continue programs utilizing the Catholic Action approach, sometimes seek-ing diocesan linkages and other times totally unconnected. Written materials came directly from Puerto Rico or other Spanish-speaking countries or were produced by the groups themselves.

This effort coincided with the organization of the First National Hispanic Encounter in 1972. That Washington meeting is historically very important for Latinos in the Catholic Church, but unfortunately it did not specifically addressed the needs of young people. While not neglecting Catholic parochial schools as a valued resource that should be opened up more widely to Latino participation, the encounter documents stressed leadership formation. This term more or less corresponds to what might be called in the secular world adult or continuing education.

Through a host of programs which imitated the Cursillo movement but bear different names—Crusade for Youth, Jornada, youth retreats—the churches have attempted to create a conversion experience for Latino youth. Targeting the troubles of young adults in urban centers, the commitment to Christ involves renunciation of drug use, gang membership, and adherence to a moral life consonant with the teachings of the Church.

Such strategies are easier to install within a denomination that has a tradition of conversion as integral to Church membership. On the face of it, this would seem to favor pentecostals and evangelicals over Catholics, since the former have a theology based upon adult conversion, while membership in the Catholic Church usually is imparted through infant baptism. But the Cursillo movement and the youth programs patterned after it have provided Catholicism with a pastoral vehicle that utilized an emotional commitment to religion for young people.

Usually the Jornada or youth retreat involves leaving the neighborhood and spending a weekend in a rural or suburban setting that provides individual sleeping arrangements and communal dining. Directed by youth already initiated into the group, each stage of the retreat invites self-revelation and structured activities that inculcate trust in one's peers. Of course, there are limitations to emotion-based conversion experiences, but it seems appropriate here to stress their effectiveness.

As previously stated, in 1971, New York City, which includes the New York archdiocese and the Brooklyn diocese, each had a youth movement specifically for Latino youth. A short history of how they came to cooperate in the context of the Second National Hispanic Pastoral Encounter illustrates the emergence of a national awareness of Latino youth. Funded by the Catholic Bishops' Campaign for Human Development, the New York archdiocese had established a youth project called, "Equipos Unidos" (United Cells or Teams). Its leaders were young people, mostly in their twenties, from the Dominican Republic and Puerto Rico who had extensive experience in the Catholic Action movements of those island nations. The idea of the project was to institute training sessions, or workshops, so that young Latinos could assess their own life goals within a support group of peers. But there was a deemphasis of the role of emotion and a focus upon follow up in the local groups, or *equipos*. Imbued with a sense of social mission that derived from liberation theology, Equipos Unidos added the dimension of social justice to the moral training. At its peak in 1973, there were some thirteen local parish equipos of some fifty to seventy members each, in areas of Manhattan and the Bronx, each cooperating with the central committee in coordinated leadership training and social justice projects.[29]

In Brooklyn, there was an even larger youth movement called the Jornada (the Spanish word for a day's work or journey). Based on the Cursillo, it was directed by one of the priests on the Cursillo staff in Brooklyn. The Jornada conducted eight to ten retreats each year, drawing participants from the members of the local parish groups and other interested individuals. When they were not engaged in staging the jornada, local jornadistas planned activities such as raffles, car washes, clothing drives, and dances. Social justice issues, political education, and self-assessment for developing leadership abilities were virtually nonexistent.

In 1973, the New York archdiocese disassociated itself from Equipos Unidos, depriving the group of its central office and salaried priest director. This rejection by the archdiocese was only one of several reactionary measures taken in reprisal for Latino Catholic militancy.[30] When the expulsion came, Equipos Unidos found itself internally divided along national lines. On the one hand were the Spanish-speaking, first generation migrant youth from the Dominican Republic: on the other, were the Puerto Rican youth born and raised in the city who were less likely to prefer Spanish over English. Additionally, they had developed a teenage Latino culture that differed significantly from most of the Dominicans.

This dynamic of intra-Latino rivalry is characteristic of multiple nationality urban centers and seriously divides many Latino youth efforts. Moreover, among Mexican-origin people, there is a profound difference between those who have been born and raised in the U.S. (the Chicanos and the Mexican Americans)[31] and those who have migrated here (Mexicans). These differences are highly pronounced among adolescent youth who are at an

age most sensitive to questions of group identity and who lack
previous experience to guide themselves. Thus in everything from
dress, choice of music, sense of humor, food preference, types
and forms of social activities, the social distance between Latinos
born here and those who have migrated from Latin America is
considerable.

NABORÍ: A UNIQUE LATINO YOUTH RESPONSE

The First National Hispano Pastoral Encounter of 1972 in Washington paid little attention to youth, preferring instead to speak
about Latinos in general. But since youth movements already existed before the first encounter, the stipulation that all Latinos
prepare for a second encounter by review of their goals necessarily included these movements as well. In 1974, in the parish
of St. Joseph in the Bronx, New York, a unique youth group was
founded that eventually became a catalyst in placing Latino youth
organizations on the agenda of the Catholic Church. Called Naborí,
after the native Taíno Indians of Puerto Rico, this group of a dozen
university-age youth was organized as a grassroots community.[32]
Using cultural identity as the matrix for organization, Naborí's
members viewed their Puerto Rican identity as interwoven with
a Catholic religious tradition. The experience of a weekend retreat
helped in this process, but as with Equipos Unidos, weekly meetings and self-assessment were intended to continue the process
begun by the retreat experience by enhancing self-development
without undue emphasis upon the emotional dimension.

Naborí was successful with this notion of cultural identity as
a window to both Church loyalty and social commitment, largely
because the City University of New York, which most members
attended, offered courses in Puerto Rican studies that cast Puerto
Rican identity as a commitment to work for radical social change
and for the independence of Puerto Rico.

Naborí's members prepared themselves after nearly a year's
work to launch the idea of cultural awareness retreats for a wider
audience of Latino youth who had not yet considered the issues of
social identity. The retreat was so successful in instilling in the participants a sense of urgency and personal responsibility for the local
youth ministry that the pastor, alarmed by their articulation and
assertiveness, declare Naborí "communist." Consequently, both the
priest leader and the group were expelled from the parish!

The group was forced to widen their scope to focus upon not just a particular parish but upon the larger Catholic community. Securing participation in the Northeast Regional Pastoral Encounter of November 1974, Naborí resolved to introduce a youth panel into the agenda for a second national encounter. At the regional encounter, Naborí made a presentation in a workshop on youth that proved the first step in uniting movements from various cities of the Northeast. Rapidly, the different local movements joined the Consejo Pastoral Juvenil (the Youth Pastoral Council) and obtained legitimation from the adult committee of the northeastern dioceses. The CPJ, as the council was commonly called, managed to inherit the remaining funds of the now-defunct Equipos Unidos and, over the summer of 1975, sponsored three weeks of the cultural awareness retreats at Holy Family Youth Center in West Hartford, Connecticut.

The cultural awareness retreats, named Operation Understanding, offered a week of university-style study of history and culture of Latino groups with a focus upon the role of Catholic values and required a week's apprenticeship to a social justice cause, the Asociación de Trabajadores Agrícolas or ATA, founded to organize migrant Puerto Rican agricultural workers. Subsequent programs followed the same model and were held at St. Joseph's College in Hartford, Connecticut, in 1977 and 1978. These other workshops recruited Mexican-American youth from the Midwest, Southwest, and California. Thus, what started out as a specifically Puerto Rican program in the Northeast had become truly national and Latino.

The superior vision, organizing skills, and personal gifts of the Naborí members gave them wide influence over youth groups that generally followed the Jornada model, wherein a narrow Church focus and once-in-a-lifetime emotional experience was the basis for organization. Yet, Naborí members had made a conscious decision to generally avoid roles as president or chair of the youth committees they helped organize. In fact Naborí itself had no president and no dues. They were not interested in the day-to-day tasks involved in running or administering groups. Their goal was not control but *conscientización* among the leaders of larger groups. In other words, their time and energy was devoted to empower youth with a better understanding of their ethnic culture and history, the structures of the society in which they lived, their role in that society, and ways to improve themselves in order to be of service to others in the community. Among the lessons learned and passed down to others were those of strategizing, the difference between short- and long-range planning, and networking.

Conservative Church leaders found it difficult to halt the cultural awareness approach to youth ministry because if they themselves opposed the young Naborí organizers they would be viewed as authoritarian. When they let the young people sort out their own affairs, more often than not Naborí members played a vital role in shaping the discussion. Usually, such discussion would revolve on the reciprocal responsibilities that the Church and its members—in this case the young people—had to assume for an effective youth ministry. On more than one occasion the young people pointed out their dissatisfaction with the leadership of some members of the clergy and adult lay leaders who rather than empowering the young people to think and act for themselves offered bingo and basketball games as apostolic work or, even worse, pitted one youth group against another in order to insure their own power over all. They asked for acceptance, adequate resources, and above all respect for what they had to say and contribute.

> Once we asked help from a parish and it was denied us. Instead they offered us basketball games and participation in bingo as the apostolic programs of the parish. . . .
> Youth is the hope of the future. But if this youth does not return to the church, what church will be left for us tomorrow? For example, in the City of New York, half of the Puerto Rican population is nineteen years old or less. But, brothers and sisters, does our church dedicate half of its attention and its resources to us? Are our Hispano children, let alone half of them, admitted to Catholic schools, or to Catholic high schools? The answer to these questions is a firm "No!"[33]

They reminded the adult leadership that if in fact they were serious about *pastoral de conjunto*, the young people could not be excluded. To the claims made by adults that the young people were inexperienced in Church matters, the youth responded that the struggles they had to face in their relatively short yet difficult lives had taught them lessons which perhaps many of the adults had never had to face when they were young.

> Some of us are university students and, as such, we know the problems of youth—our problems—by their scientific names. We suffer from social disintegration, from alienation, from exploitation, from a family structure which has been destroyed, etc. But we also

know these sad realities because we have felt them in our own flesh. And so we prefer to speak of them in terminology common to everyone; we want to speak *tú a tú* of our personal experiences.[34]

The general consensus was that if more experience was needed, then the Church had to do its share in making the proper accommodations and providing adequate opportunities for it to take place. More than a few of the older clergy and older lay leaders seemed to have been threatened by these pronouncements and by the attitude the young people took before their authority.

Although Naborí readily surrendered official positions of directorship to the other movements, they worked as a collective and always produced a document or an agenda that bound the elected leader to implement the decisions of the group rather than arbitrarily impose a leadership style from the top down. Any plan of action agreed upon, then, had Naborí's imprint and the endorsement of all other groups as well. In this way loyalty from the elected leaders and seriousness of intent from Church officials were more likely to be secured.

The Eucharistic Congress held in Philadelphia in the summer of 1976 provided the opportunity for the Concilio Pastoral Juvenil (CPJ) of the Northeast to introduce the issue of a youth panel at the forthcoming Second National Pastoral Encounter. Because the Eucharistic Congress provided funds to include CYO members from all over the nation, the CPJ in the Northeast argued that similar funds should be provided for Latino youth to participate as equal members of the Church. The Washington-based secretariat office provided for a planning session in San Antonio, Texas, previous to the congress, and the CPJ was represented by a member of Naborí and a member of the Brooklyn Jornada. The planning session in San Antonio helped assure a significant youth representation from regions where Cubans and Mexicans predominated. However, when the Encounter organizers proposed eliminating a special workshop on the Latino youth and its needs, preferring to scatter the young people into a dozen or more adult-dominated sessions on other issues, this divide-and-conquer strategy was squelched by the personal intervention of Cardinal Terence Cooke of New York, who viewed the CPJ as the Latino youth movement of the Northeast.

With this birthright, the National Hispanic Youth Task Force was formed as a result of the 1977 encounter, and Latino youth achieved a national presence. The members of Naborí, however, never came to enjoy the fruits of their labor. Although one member was named to the first national task force,[35] Naborí had seen its organizers graduate, go on to professional schools, get married, and start families. Naborí had more or less stayed with the original organizers and was content to disband in 1978, considering that it had completed its mission. They left to the National Task Force the task of elaborating and advocating for a youth agenda within the Church. But ultimately the absence within the National Task Force of Naborí or similar Mexican youth groups diluted the political vision of Latino youth nationwide. Without the leadership that these groups had provided, the remaining groups represented in the National Youth Task Force seemed to have been caught up in the shift from justice to morality that both the Church and general society were experiencing. It was not only that the challenges that groups such as Naborí had presented had become less important and less central to the agenda of Church but without Naborí's presence the National Youth Task Force lacked the thrust and voice it once had had. And when budgetary constraints shrunk the activities of the Washington secretariat office, the National Youth Task Force was an early victim. But the legacy of this struggle has combined concepts of cultural awareness and political involvement with the more traditional moral training focus of the youth apostolate.

CATHOLIC SCHOOLS AND LATINOS

The first organized school in lands now under the United States flag was founded by the Spanish Dominican Friars in San Juan, Puerto Rico, in 1521.[36] Other such institutions of learning were later established throughout the Spanish colonies. There students were taught not only the basics in education but also philosophy and theology as preparation for the ministry. Yet, as late as the 1950s, Latinos—principally Mexicans, Puerto Ricans, and Cubans—were treated as if they were immigrants and recent arrivals not only to the United States but to Catholicism as well.

The subterfuge used to turn the original inhabitants of Texas, New Mexico, Arizona, Colorado, and California into immigrants was to lump third- and fourth-generation natives with Mexican immigrants on the basis of language, so that speaking Spanish made a person "foreign." The U.S. Catholic Church followed this pattern by building new parishes for the English-speaking who poured into Texas, the Southwest, and California. These churches segregated themselves and their financial resources from the already existing Spanish-speaking parishes that had been founded under Spanish and Mexican rule. The mission churches did not follow the patterns of urban Catholicism that sought to build a Catholic school in every parish. Even the increased migration of Mexicans to Texas and California during the upheavals of the revolution (1910–1917) and during the Cristero revolt (1922–1927) did not significantly alter the pattern of assigning the Spanish–speaking to inferior facilities on the basis of language.

In urban centers like New York and Chicago, national parishes for the Spanish speaking were organized; by the post–World War II period, however, it was argued that new parishes in the cities would be counterproductive. The white, Euro-American Catholic population was on the move out of the cities and towards the suburbs. Latinos (along with African-Americans from the U.S. South) were pouring into urban centers for manufacturing jobs. Rather than build new national parishes for the Spanish speaking alongside almost empty churches, several bishops like Spellman in New York realized that if the Catholic Church was to remain a viable institution in these urban areas and continue to maximize available resources, the Spanish speaking had to be incorporated somehow into the existing structures. Thus the emergence of the so-called integrated parish.[37]

This integrated parish approach did not guarantee equal accessibility of time and resources to the members of the Latino community. The parochial schools, for instance, continued to draw their enrollment almost exclusively from the non-Latino population even as the Latinos showed significant increase within the local parish community. Even upon entering the 1990s, the number of Latino children in Catholic schools is comparatively small, representing only 10 percent of the entire Latino population of school age.[38]

Catholic schools in the 1950s were relatively affordable for most working-class families. Because the teaching faculty was composed mostly of religious who worked with only minimal compensation, parish members were able to finance an entire year's education, both grammar and high school, for as little as $300 tuition per child. Through investment portfolios, real estate holdings, and centralized banking, many costs of education were subsidized at a regional level by bishops. In some parochial schools the only expenses for which parents were responsible were the cost for school uniforms, books, and occasional activities such as school outings and Christmas shows.

Added to the fact that in the 1950s and 1960s a $30- or $40-a-month tuition per child may have presented a real economic burden in a Latino family with two or more children of school age, failure on the part of the schools to include the Latino experience in their curriculum may in part account for the low numbers of Latino children in Catholic schools. The cultural and religious values that the Catholic schools promoted more often than not reflected the prejudices of the larger society.[39] Also, the common practice of requiring grade repetition for Latino students coming from Latin America, the Caribbean, or even from public schools in the U.S. discouraged Latinos from even seeking admission. Furthermore, there is no evidence that the Catholic schools tried aggressively to attract or recruit representative numbers from this growing population of Catholics. As irony would have it, with an insignificant number of Latino students, the Catholic schools did not feel compelled to give serious consideration to a curriculum inclusive of the Latino reality. And thus the cycle of exclusion continued. Certainly in the 1950s and well into the 1960s Latinos were virtually invisible in the parochial schools of this prosperous and complacent urban Catholicism.[40]

Yet when the notion of a separate Catholic society with its own institutions and school system withered after the Second Vatican Council, urban Catholic schools were forced out of their cozy niche. With the rise in school costs for faculty salaries and the demographic changes that swept Euro-American Catholics to the suburbs, tuitions rose dramatically. Thus many Latino families who inherited the parish were prevented from inheriting the parish school. And in the dictates of capitalist economics, the fewer the students, the higher the tuition; the higher the tuition, the fewer the students. From 1970–1985, more Catholic schools were closed than were opened. And although there has been a leveling off, and even slight gain, in enrollments since 1985, the nature of Catholic parochial schools has been irrevocably altered.[41]

But while the overwhelming number of Catholic Latino youth are in the public school system, Catholic schools are important to Latinos. Despite the barriers of cost it is not uncommon today for the parochial school in many Latino neighborhoods to have a nearly 100 percent enrollment of Latino and African-American children. Faced with an educationally bankrupt public school system operating in an often volatile environment, Latino and African-American parents often sacrifice other basic necessities in order to give their children the benefit of a Catholic education in a relatively secure atmosphere. Thus, while the Catholic school system as a whole can be criticized for not being open to more Latinos, it must be recognized that through the combined efforts of parents and Catholic school officials there are at present a number of Catholic schools virtually dedicated to Latino youth at the local level. As with European immigrant groups, a Catholic education for Latinos often means upper mobility. Certainly it has proved to be a positive factor in the ability and desire to pursue a college education. For example, approximately 59 percent of graduates from Cardinal Hayes High School in New York are Latinos, and 90 percent of Hayes graduates go on to colleges and universities. The rate of New York public school graduates pursuing a college education is 10 percent. Furthermore, it appears that once in college, the Catholic high school graduate is five times more likely to graduate with a four-year degree than is the public school graduate.[42] Doctors, lawyers, successful business and community leaders are much influenced by the value system of their education, even if they cease to practice their religion in a regular way. Thus, the question of the availability of Catholic education for the Latino community is a very important issue not only for the Latino community but for the general Catholic community as a whole since, hopefully, many of the future leaders for these communities will come from this pool of Catholic educated Latinos.

The moral training, the discipline, and the parental involvement at every level are compelling characteristics of the Catholic schools. Despite their low wages, Catholic school teachers generally exhibit a high degree of commitment. Often lacking adequate resources in such areas as computer training, art, dance, recreation, and science, Catholic schools usually concentrate on the basic skills of education and generally achieve high grades in the periodic standardized testing within education today. Most importantly, the parochial school is a community school, where teachers and parents strive to implement plans based on shared educational and religious values.

Several of these elements of Catholic school education are now entering the realm of public school education. Faced with low performance levels, high absenteeism, increased drop-out rates, and lack of discipline, some public schools are now adopting policies long associated with parochial schools. In New York City, uniforms, dress, and haircut codes are now standard in a growing number of public schools, as is the direct involvement of parents.

A matter that still needs to be addressed, however, is the introduction into the Catholic school system of school curricula which show awareness of the multi-faceted and multi-cultural reality of the Catholic community in the United States. Often, Latino students are able to form extracurricular clubs and associations to provide some minimal source of cultural identity within the larger community. But it remains to be seen how, or if, Catholic educators will provide civic or history texts that enhance the kind of cultural awareness so successfully utilized by Naborí simultaneously to develop personal pride in one's heritage and to stimulate a progressive sense of commitment to Catholic values.

CONCLUSIONS

Within the Latino youth movements in the U.S, notions of cultural identity, group loyalty, linguistic preference, and social consciousness have often competed for acceptance. Despite attempts to bring first and subsequent generations together in the same groups, unity has often proved illusive. Ironically, as first-generation Latin Americans in the U.S. marry and have children, their offspring come to resemble culturally the Latinos whom their parents had found difficult to understand. In other words, a second-generation Dominican in New York often finds him- or herself holding more in common with second- or third-generation Puerto Ricans than with his or her parents. The frequent intermarriage of Puerto Ricans with Dominicans in New York[43] may produce a generation of true Latinos who are a mixture of Puerto Rican and Dominican and who experience little or none of the intra-Latino conflicts of earlier generations. The same may hold true of Puerto Ricans and Cubans in Miami, or Puerto Ricans and Chicanos in Chicago.

During the 1980s, the CYO in the Northeast moved to a less sports-oriented format. This more serious direction for the CYO came from its own leadership and is not directly attributable to Latino youth. Nonetheless, at a regional level, the superior vision of the meaning of a youth movement that is frequently found among the Latinos has served as a stimulus to Euro-American groups to do the same. Ironically, at the end of two decades, the roles of the pacesetter and the follower have been inverted, with Latinos leading the way in the 1990s where before they were expected to follow the example of the Euro-Americans in the Church.

The programs highlighted in this chapter were attempts, some very deliberate and others less so, to respond to the needs of Latino youths in a complex and rapidly changing urban situation. In some cases the institution took the initiative while in other cases people from the grassroots created programs suited to the youth at the local level. And finally, some were more successful than others. Admittedly, there were many other attempts by the churches at the local level as they struggled with their immediate realities and their need to keep the loyalty of the so-called newcomers. An essay such as this is not able to document all of these attempts or their success. But if the maintenance of traditional family values is a measure of loyalty to Catholicism, then there has been a measure of success. A 1992 census report shows that Latinos are the most likely of all Catholic groups to have households constituted by the traditional family of husband and wife with children under the same roof.[44] This persistence of family values continues among Latinos, despite more than four decades of disruptive social and cultural changes for the majority of Latinos who are among the poorest inhabitants of the major U.S. cities. While more extensive survey analysis will be needed to analyze fully the causes and effects of the persistence of family structures among Latinos against such high odds, it would appear that religious values should be considered as a major factor in shaping Latino families today.

The rate of apparent success of the traditional family among Latino Catholics as a whole notwithstanding, there are many factors that threaten the stability of the Latino community. Further, we cannot ignore the fact that in some Latino subgroups there is a disproportionate rate of households for which young females are solely responsible. In these cases, whether practicing Catholic or not, support systems bridging the family, religion, and the community are an imperative. Community organizations not affiliated with the Church have come to realize that certain moral and cultural values reinforced by Latino Catholicism and the Latino family are indeed invaluable resources in the development of Latino youth into mature and responsible adults. Based on a cultural-religious concept, community efforts such as the New York–based Madrinas have attempted to provide counsel and emotional support to teenage Latinas who are actual or expectant mothers. There is some evidence that Catholic Charities and other such Church-based agencies have recognized Latinos as a target population. Yet it would be premature to identify these as Latino organizations.

The level of support the Church is willing to give these efforts and other programs geared to the Latino youth of today may in great measure decide its own future. For certain, it will decide the answer to the questions asked at the beginning of this essay: Is the Catholic Church the "home" of the Latino community in this country, or are the Latinos to remain foreigners in an immigrant Church which in the past was widely successful in incorporating other ethnic groups into its fold? Put another way, is the Catholic Church in the U.S. ready to be challenged and revitalized by the aspirations, richness, and experiences of Latino Catholicism or is it to continue business as usual with its diminishing resources?

Ultimately, religion and the Church may hold the answer to many of the problems affecting Latino youth today, but Latino youth may also hold the answer to many of the existing needs within the Catholic Church. Unfortunately, the Church will not be able to claim the loyalty of this important segment of its population if the Church itself is not ready to undertake a process of reassessment and transformation. Short of this, the Church will fail Latino youth and in doing so, will fail itself. As Lincoln and Mamiya indicated, in youth rests the answer to a more fruitful and successful future, and without them, the Church, or for that matter any other institution in this or any other society, is doomed to extinction.

The Church must approach Latino youth with the respect, openness, and sense of discovery that is proposed by Puerto Rican poet, Sandra María Esteves.

> . . . So when you come to me, don't assume
> That you know me so well as that
> Don't come with preconceptions
> Or expect me to fit the mold you have created
> Because we fit no molds
> We have no limitations
> And when you do come, bring me your hopes
> Describe for me your visions, your dreams
> Bring me your support and your inspiration
> Your guidance and your faith
> Your belief in possibilities
> Bring me the best that you can
>
> Give me the chance to be
> Myself and create symphonies like

The pastel dawn or the empty canvas
Before the first stroke of color is released

Come in a dialogue of we
You and me reacting; responding
Being, something new
Discovering.[45]

Such a challenging response by the Church to the Latino youth of today holds the promise of revelation and the Church's own salvation.

NOTES

1. C. Eric Lincoln and Lawrence H. Mamiya, *The Black Church in the African American Experience* (Durham: Duke University Press, 1990).

2. See Robert Sam Anson, "The Irish Connection," *New Times*, May 17, 1974, pp. 29–33.

3. David Landy, *Tropical Childhood* (New York: Harper Torchbooks, 1965); also Julian Steward, *The People of Puerto Rico* (Urbana: University of Illinois Press, 1972); and Leo Grebler, Joan Moore, et al., *The Mexican-American People* (New York: Free Press, 1970).

4. Jesús Colón, for instance, writes about his misgivings about helping a young white mother in a subway station for fear that his good intentions and sense of what in Puerto Rico was common courtesy may be misunderstood simply because he was a Puerto Rican black man. See Jesús Colón, *A Puerto Rican in New York and Other Sketches* (New York: Mainstream Publishers, 1961).

5. For another account of what it was for Puerto Ricans to live in the Northeast part of the United States, see César Andreu Iglesias, ed., *Memoirs of Bernardo Vega: A Contribution to the History of the Puerto Rican Community in New York* (New York and London: Monthly Review Press, 1984).

6. Celia Alvarez, "Stories to Live By: Continuity and Change in Three Generations of Puerto Rican Women," excerpts from "Oral History Review Project," conducted by Rina Benmayor, Ana Juarbe, Blanca Várquez Erazo, and Celia Alvarez, pp. 1–46. Reprinted as Handout #6c in *Ibero-American Heritage Curriculum—Latinos in the Making of the United States of America: Yesterday, Today and Tomorrow: Teacher Guide*, sponsored by the New York State Department of Education et al. (Albany, 1993), p. 1242.

7. Alvarez, reprinted in *Ibero-American Heritage Curriculum: Teacher Guide*, p. 1241.

8. Ibid., p. 1241.

9. Ibid., p. 1241.

10. See Elena Padilla, *Up from Puerto Rico* (New York: Columbia University Press, 1958).

11. See Anthony M. Stevens-Arroyo, "Puerto Rican Struggles in the Catholic Church," In *The Puerto Rican Struggle: Essays on Survival in the U.S.*, ed. Clara E. Rodríguez, Virginia Sánchez-Korrol, and José Oscar Alers (New York: Puerto Rican Migration Research Consortium, Inc., 1989), p. 130.

12. This is not exclusive to Latino Catholics. It is also found in Protestantism and pentecostalism. Piri Thomas makes reference to "how to court a girl in the best tradition of Puerto Rican style" in *Savior, Savior, Hold My Hand* (Garden City, New York: Doubleday, 1972), pp. 99–101 and passim. Interestingly, when parents are asked why they adhere to the chaperone system, oftentimes the reason given is not lack of trust in the female children but on the male counterpart. "I trust my daughter; but I am not so sure I trust someone else's son," is a frequent reply.

13. Alvarez, reprinted in *Ibero-American Heritage Curriculum: Teacher Guide*, p. 1242.

14. See *Catholic Youth Organization Handbook* (Philadelphia: Archdiocese of Philadelphia: August, 1953), p. 3.

15. See ibid., forward; see also pp. 3–6.

16. See ibid., p. 15. In summary fashion, "Article II—Purpose–Section 2, No. 6." reads: "To encourage the members to carry into their everyday lives the true principles of Christian living, whether it be the home, in the classroom, on the field of competitive sport, or at a social function.

17. Mary Irene Zotti, *A Time of Awakening: The Young Christian Worker Story in the U.S., 1938-1970* (Chicago: Loyola University Press, 1991).

18. Ibid., p. 13.

19. Introduced in the U.S. in the late 1930s as the Young Catholic Workers, it broke with the practice of keeping the young people separated by gender. More than ideological conviction, the idea of mixed groups was a means of solving the male recruitment problem. But there was a catch to the adoption of mixed groupings. In the words of Monsignor Hillendbrand, the national director, "There is only one simple rule: as many or more fellows than girls." Young women leaders within the movement were not to be "too mannish," or "aggressive" but instead to stay "one step behind" the male leaders.

20. Zotti, *Time of Awakening*, p. 141.

21. Ibid., p. 142.

22. Ibid., p. 255.

23. Ibid., p. 142.

24. Zotti, p. 230, states: "The success of Spanish-speaking sections doing their own programming on local problems was seen as evidence that members could be formed in Christian action without the national program."

25. Ibid., pp. 211–215, 231.

26. See Piri Thomas' personal account in *Down These Mean Streets* (New York: New American Library, 1967).

27. Besides being amply exploited by the mass media, youth gangs' activities have been a subject of much scholarly study and controversy for many years. Among the latest literature on Latino youth gangs there are two very illuminating articles in *Latino Studies Journal*, 3, no. 3 (September, 1992): "Chicano Urban Youth Gangs: A Critical Analysis of a Social Problem?" (pp. 15–28), by Alfredo Mirandé and José López; and "California's Chicano Gang Subculture: The Journey from Pachuco 'Sadistic Clowns' to a Norteño 'Society of Houses'" (pp. 29–44), by John Donovan.

28. Interview with Alicia Salinas, presently an educator with the New York public school system and member of St. Rose of Lima parish school council in the 1970s.

29. For the role of the Dominican leadership, see Glenn Hendricks, *The Dominican Diaspora* (New York: Teachers College Press; 1974), pp. 110, 118–119.

30. See Ana María Díaz-Stevens, *Oxcart Catholicism on Fifth Avenue: The Impact of the Puerto Rican Migration upon the Archdiocese of New York* (Notre Dame, Ind.: Notre Dame Press, 1993), pp. 204–218. See also Hendricks, *Dominican Diaspora*, p. 110.

31. For the difference between these two terms, see Anthony M. Stevens-Arroyo, *Prophets Denied Honor* (Maryknoll, N.Y.: Orbis, 1980), pp. 1–32, 155, 256, 287, 349–351, 361.

32. The history of this group remains untold. The original members included the author of this article. For one of the documents from Naborí, see Lala Torres, Edna Zallas, Annette Ramos, "Presentation by Naborí, Youth Workshop, First Northeast Regional Pastoral Encounter, November 30, 1974," in Stevens-Arroyo, *Prophets Denied Honor*, pp. 341–343.

33. Torres, Zallas, and Ramos, "Presentation by Naborí," in Stevens-Arroyo, *Prophets Denied Honor*, p. 342.

34. Ibid., p. 342.

35. See Ibid., pp. 314–343.

36. These were certainly schools and certainly Catholic. Yet, the term *Catholic schools* is not applied here since that term has a unique connotation in the United States. In comparison the Spanish colonial *institutos de enseñanza* probably had a much more rigorous curriculum than the U.S. Catholic schools of the present, and they were for the most part dedicated to the education of young men with the intention of building a pool of candidates for the priesthood.

37. Díaz-Stevens, *Oxcart Catholicism*, pp. 91–116.

38. Suzanne Hall, S.N.D. and Carleen Reck, S.S.N.D., eds., *Integral Education: A Response to the Hispanic Presence* (Washington, D.C.: National Catholic Educational Association, 1987).

39. See Anthony M. Stevens-Arroyo and Ana María Díaz-Stevens, "Religion and Faith among Latinos," in *Handbook of Hispanic Cultures in the United States*, ed. Felix Padilla (Houston: Arte Publico Press, forthcoming).

40. A relatively small number of Puerto Ricans were enrolled in the Catholic school system. Often the Catholic school was seen as the domain of the white community. To be among the first to be admitted to Catholic school was both a privilege and a challenge. It often required not only that one be an excellent student but a staunch defender of one's ethnic and cultural identity. Alvarez recalls that when she went to a Catholic high school in the heart of Flatbush in the 1960s it was predominantly white school. "I found myself desegregating the Catholic school system, one of five or six Latinos and Afro-Americans in my class. I was known as one of the girls from the ghetto downtown and was constantly called upon to defend my race. One day it went too far. Someone said my father didn't work and that their parents supported my coming to their school. I 'went off'! You just didn't talk about my family!" Alvarez also recalls how when she graduated with honors from this school she went to the guidance counselor to inquire about government grants programs for college only to be told, "Well, you're not the only one who needs money to go to school, dear." See Alvarez, reprinted in *Ibero-American Heritage Curriculum: Teacher Guide*, p. 1242. Also see Díaz-Stevens and Stevens-Arroyo, "Religion and Faith."

41. Robert J. Yeager, Peter Benson, Michael J. Guerra, and Bruno V. Manno, *The Catholic High School: A National Portrait* (Washington, D.C.: National Catholic Educational Association, 1985).

42. The American Council on Education (1990) reported that high school completion rates for Hispanics, ages eighteen to twenty-four, dropped from 62.8 percent in 1985 to 56 percent in 1989. See also Hugh L. Carey and Seymour P. Lachman, et al., "Roman Catholic

Schools in New York State: A Comprehensive Report" (Albany, N.Y.: State Educational Department, 1993), pp. 16–19 and passim.

43. See Joseph P. Fitzpatrick and Douglas T. Gurak, *Hispanic Intermarriage in New York City: 1975* Monograph no. 2 (Bronx, N.Y.: Hispanic Research Center at Fordham University, 1979).

44. American Demographics, U.S. Census Bureau, cited in the *New York Times*, August 23, 1992.

45. Sandra María Esteves, "Transference," in *Tropical Rains: A Bilingual Downpour* (Bronx, N.Y.: African Caribbean Poetry Theater, 1984), reprinted in *Ibero-American Heritage Curriculum: Teacher Guide*, p. 1244.

9

Popular Catholicism among Latinos

Orlando O. Espín

Popular religion seems to be an omnipresent phenomenon among U.S. Latinos.[1] It is difficult to understand any of the Hispanic cultural communities without somehow explaining and dealing with popular beliefs and rites.[2]

In this chapter I will attempt to introduce the reader to U.S. Hispanic popular Catholicism.[3] The brevity of these pages should make clear that no complete introduction can or will be attempted. My intent is solely to point to the salient features of popular Catholicism among Latinos, particularly emphasizing the history of this religious universe, while offering some suggestions for an adequate interpretation of this very complex religion. I hope that the bibliography included in the notes (necessarily selective) will lead the reader to further study.

Some clarifications are necessary at the start of this chapter. Hispanics in the United States are very diverse, and their diversity must be taken seriously. However, they also share some basic cultural elements that allow for their common study. The fundamental structures and roles of popular religion stand out as very important in all Latino cultures.

Our study refers only to U.S. Hispanics. Although many of them came to this country as immigrants, many others were born here. The nineteenth-century annexations of Florida and the Southwest included not just land but also populations, and the borders have since remained very porous. This evident fact should also explain why a study of U.S. Latino popular Catholicism cannot start with the Mexican-American War or the Florida Purchase. To disregard the Spanish and Latin American past of the people's religion would deprive the reader (and the people themselves) of some very important elements for an adequate interpretation of this religion. Hispanic popular Catholicism in the United States, as it now exists, cannot explain itself without its earlier history.

One final clarification. Although I will insist on the importance of popular religion for understanding Latinos, the reader should realize that not all Hispanic Catholics participate in the rites or hold the beliefs of this religious universe. However, an argument can be made on the enduring cultural importance of the symbols of popular Catholicism for all Latinos (including Protestant and agnostic ones).

POPULAR RELIGION

To understand popular Catholicism one should first set it within the more general context of popular religion.

Popular and Official Religion

Every major religion, to the degree that it has a well-defined normative core of beliefs and liturgy, has aided in the development of a popular version of itself.

Groups of "religious virtuosi"[4] seem to have developed in most religions, thereby becoming responsible for defining what is and what is not normative within the religions. Most believers, however, either do not have or cannot have access to the training required for or the doctrinal arguments proposed by the virtuosi, and hence the majority are placed in the role of following the symbolic production and doctrinal decisions of the specialists.

History shows, nevertheless, that among the majority of believers alternative paths are created to circumvent the exclusive definitory power of the virtuosi. These paths can and do lead to the formation of what could be called a *popular* version of the religion, parallel to the pretended *official* doctrinal and liturgical norm set up and controlled by the specialists, but somehow still connected with the normative version of the religion.[5]

This connection appears to be one of selectively shared symbols and ethos, and an appeal to common foundational figures or events. Similarly, there is a rereading of the doctrines and rites of the official religion whereby a set of different emphases is given to them. Furthermore, this rereading can interpret the religion to the point of altogether disregarding some elements that the virtuosi might consider essential, while inversely considering fundamental certain beliefs, rites, or behaviors that the specialists would not emphasize at all.

Let us take Catholicism as an example. It is evident that its
virtuosi are the theologians and the clergy (especially bishops and
popes). It is the role of these specialists to define and set the limits
as to what is or is not acceptable and normative in the Church.
For most people, however, theological work and episcopal/papal
ministry are not the common ways of participating in the religion. Most Catholics play the role of recipients of the doctrinal
and liturgical production of the specialists. Nevertheless, the long
history of Catholicism (in many culturally shaped ways) has witnessed the birth of parallel paths that attempt to bring the religion
close to the people's needs and circumstances. Often enough these
paths have reread official Catholicism in the ways indicated above,
and thereby produced the people's own version of the religion.
This is popular Catholicism. It claims to be authentically Catholic,
and yet it has reinterpreted the normative as set forth by the
Church's virtuosi.[6]

Apparently, popular Catholicism came into being very early
in the history of the religion.[7] The reactions to it, on the part of
the specialists, have historically run the gamut from cooptation to
outright persecution. The wide variety of official reactions throughout the centuries seem to have depended on how far the popular
rereading of the normative had gone, and on how the virtuosi perceived the importance of maintaining the links to popular religion
in each historical context. All too often, political and other social
reasons were more determining of the official reactions to popular
Catholicism than strictly doctrinal considerations.

Other Popular Religions among Hispanics

We will devote most of this chapter to the study of popular
Catholicism. So at this point I will not enter into the discussion
of its origins, development, and contents. However, I do want to
point out that the Latino popular version of Catholicism is not the
only popular religion present among U.S. Hispanics, nor the only
one with some links to it.[8]

Any acquaintance with the Latino communities of Florida and
the Northeast (and of some areas of the Midwest and southern
California) will indicate the presence of Santería and probably Palo,
for example. It would be highly inaccurate to claim that either one
of these religions is a type of popular Catholicism. It would also
be unacceptable, given the solid research to the contrary, to view

either of them as mainly (or solely) the result of mixing Antillean Catholicism with African religions.

These two Afro-Latino religions have indeed included some symbols of colonial Antillean Catholicism, but only peripherally and almost exclusively for self-preservation purposes. The great syncretic process did not fundamentally occur with Catholicism but among the several African religions (mainly Yoruba, Fon, and Kongo) that came to the Spanish Antilles during the slave trade. It was among these religions that doctrinal and ritual sharing occurred, resulting this century in Santería and Palo. To some degree the same can be said of both the Haitian and Dominican forms of *Vodou*.

Many Hispanics, mostly of Cuban ancestry, brought Santería and Palo to the United States. But today these two religions have spread (and continue to spread) well beyond the Cuban-American communities, reaching into other Latino groups (for example, Puerto Ricans) as well as African Americans and even Anglos.

Can these religions be called *popular*, in the sense expressed earlier? I think so, and for several reasons. First of all, when studied vis-á-vis their African roots, the Antillean versions display the same processes and adaptation that I have pointed out in reference to popular religions in general. They have certainly reread the religions of origin (whether Yoruba, Kongo, or Fon) and did create other paths in order to bring the older African specialists' normative core close to a people now enslaved in the Caribbean. These resulting paths, interestingly enough, in turn became the new norm in the Antilles.[9] New virtuosi came to define the religion in Cuba, simplifying it and adapting it to the new circumstances. With immigration, new parallel paths (now in the United States) have begun to appear, further separating present-day Santería and Palo from their original counterparts as the former popularly adapt and reread (in the American context) the norms handed-down by their virtuosi.

Another reason for believing that these two religions are indeed popular is the content resulting from their rereading of the norm of the root religions. As I said above, they simplified and adapted to new circumstances. However, the way they have gone about it and, especially, some of the doctrines and rituals that have resulted from these processes are not quite in agreement with what a present-day Yoruba (or Fon, or Kongo) religious specialist would hold as fully orthodox, if that category were used.[10]

Besides Santería and Palo, which are the most widespread of the other Hispanic popular religions, there are others. For example, among U.S. Latinos with roots in the Dominican Republic there are varieties of beliefs and rituals that can be identified as popular adaptations of the Dominican strand of Vodou. Among Dominican Americans other religious forms of lesser importance appear as well.[11]

Puerto Ricans have created an interesting version of Kardecian spiritism, with strong and lasting appeal among many. There is a growing bibliography on this type of spiritism, showing it in turn to be a popular adaptation of the Kardec canon.[12] In some quarters Puerto Rican spiritism has begun a process of mixing with Santería, the results of which are still unpredictable.

Among the Mexican and Mexican-American populations there does not seem to be (as compared with Hispanics of Antillean ancestry) a wealth of popular religions apart from popular Catholicism. However, some vestiges of ancient native religious practices and beliefs are discernable, though more frequently at the hermeneutic level, and well mixed with current popular Catholicism. I return to this later.

Distinct popular religions, apart from popular Catholicism, do not seem to be in evidence among Mexicans or Mexican Americans in the United States. I wonder, however, if research were done on some types of southwestern rural *curanderismo* whether we might not indeed discover more than just traces of ancient religions. Nevertheless, as far as the data presently allow us to conclude, non-Christian popular religions appear mostly in the U.S. Latino contexts of marked Antillean influence.

The Study of Popular Catholicism

There is no doubt that the most frequent religion among U.S. Hispanics is popular Catholicism. This is the case among all the different cultural communities (Mexican and Mexican American, Puerto Rican, Cuban American, etc.). Certainly, many Latinos participate in the official type of Catholicism, but both numerically and culturally the symbolic universe of the popular version of the religion is by far the more widespread and commanding of the two.

It might seem, after only a superficial glance, that the different Hispanic cultural communities have their own style of popular Catholicism. And that is indeed the case. The influences that came together to forge this religious universe were quite distinct. Though the Spaniards imposed the same Iberian religion on their American colonies, here it was received and interpreted by diverse groups of native Amerindians or Africans. Hence, the resulting Catholicism of the Mexican American, for example, is not identical to that of the Cuban American or of the Puerto Rican. However, a closer look would clearly indicate a basic similarity in the fundamental structures and functions of the popular religious universe in all three communities.[13]

It can be argued that, first of all, popular Catholicism is the manner in and through which most U.S. Latinos are Catholic; and secondly, that this popular Catholicism is a key matrix of all Hispanic cultures. If this is the case, and I believe it is, then the importance of the study of this religion is crucial for an adequate understanding of all Hispanics, whether they currently participate in this type of Catholicism or not. I need not point out the obvious consequences for historical, pastoral, and theological studies.[14]

In the growing body of literature on Hispanic religion, both in Latin America and in this country, the approaches taken in studies of this religious universe are extraordinarily diverse.[15] One can find works that run from the merely descriptive and panoramic to those that attempt a most detailed analysis of very minute pieces of the religious puzzle. There are studies that concentrate on the social implications while others look at the symbolics. Some have emphasized the political consequences without regard to the faith contents of the religion, and yet others have done the exact opposite.

The methodologies used vary from the Marxist (orthodox, humanist, etc.) to the naively pious, with every other possible interpretive school represented in between. The motives for studying popular Catholicism are as diverse as the methods employed, running the gamut from entrenched defense to utter disdain. And although most serious works have left their contribution to the field, it has become evident that the days are past when a single author, alone, could dream of understanding or explaining Hispanic popular Catholicism in a sufficiently adequate and complete way. Indeed, no single discipline could ever accomplish this feat.

I bring this up because it is important for the reader to realize that I am not claiming, or could claim, that what follows is a single, definitive presentation or interpretation of popular Catholicism among Latinos in the United States. This chapter, much more modest and realistic, is a quick synthesis of my own and other people's research, requiring further study, nuance, and contextualization.

POPULAR CATHOLICISM: A BRIEF HISTORY

Latino popular Catholicism is popular in the sense described earlier in this chapter. It is the religious universe that Hispanics created in order to bring closer to them what they interpreted to be the foundational and other key elements of normative Catholicism.

This creation occurred through a centuries-long process of re-reading and adaptation of what the Church's virtuosi presented as normative. It happened within the specific contexts of vanquishment and depredation resulting from the Spanish conquest of the Americas and later from the second-class status imposed on Latinos after the Euro-American annexations. In other words, very strong components of suffering and abuse have acted as historical matrix for the religious universe of Hispanics and still show themselves, for example, in iconography and ritual.[16]

How did contemporary U.S. Latino popular Catholicism come about? To answer this question adequately, no matter how synthetically, one must first turn to medieval Spain, then to its religious encounter with the native Amerindian and African worlds during the early and the late colonial periods. This section will summarily cover the history of popular religion, from Iberia to the dawn of the nineteenth century. Without the story of the formation and development of popular Catholicism, no matter how briefly it is told, we cannot expect to understand the religious present of Latinos.

Medieval Spanish Catholicism

There is no need here to describe the beliefs, rituals, and other religious practices of the Spanish Middle Ages. However, some general understanding of the religious world of the *conquistadores* is necessary because, after all, it was their religion that was brought to, imposed on, ultimately interpreted by Amerindians and Africans in this hemisphere and unfortunately was used to justify the conquest of these lands. Hispanic Catholicism, normative or popular, cannot be understood without recourse to the Iberian world.

Roman Catholicism, as we know and describe it today, did not exist before the Council of Trent (1545–1563). What existed before Trent and the Reformation was simply western Christianity.[17] That distinction might seem surprising or meaningless to some readers, but I think it is very important because the religion brought to the Americas by the Spaniards was not Roman Catholicism, but western Christianity in its Iberian form. It was not the Church of anti-Protestant polemics but the religion that had sustained the seven centuries of the Spanish *Reconquista*.[18] This Christianity, therefore, was medieval and pre-Tridentine, and it was planted in the Americas approximately two generations before Trent's opening session.

The Reconquista period

Iberian Christianity had a long history prior to 1492.[19] It was one of the oldest organized Churches in the West, its roots firmly planted in the patristic period. Leander and Isidore had been two of its great theological stars, profoundly influencing the later Middle Ages in the rest of Europe. Some of its regional councils and synods contributed decisively to settle doctrinal and disciplinary questions, with ramifications even today. The Iberian Visigothic Church, however, was to be tested by the crises begun in 711 C.E.

That year saw the start of the Muslim conquest and occupation of most of the Iberian peninsula. While the rest of Europe was confronting the so-called Dark Ages and then attempting to grow beyond them, Muslim Spain was creating a major civilization, the synthesis of Islamic, Christian, and Jewish contributions. Arguably, the most advanced and sophisticated society in the medieval West was to be found in Spain during this period. Geography and historical circumstance had forced Muslims and Christians to live next to each other. Jointly they had created great centers of learning, the envy of the rest of the continent. Through medieval Spain, for example, the wisdom and writings of the ancient Greeks were preserved, copied, and shared with Europe. In Spain, as opposed to the rest of the continent, Christians had to deal with the "infidel" for centuries, not merely or mainly in battle, but in everyday trade, family ties, and in religious dialogue.

For a number of political, economic, ethnic, and religious reasons, the sole remaining Christian land in the Iberian peninsula (the kingdom of Asturias) began the long process called the Reconquista. It took over seven hundred years, and in 1492 it brought final victory to the Christians, by then led by the crowns of Aragon and Castille. During this entire period, in the lands held by the Muslims as well as in those controlled by Christian kings, the new Spanish national character was being forged.

A unique mixture (perhaps difficult to comprehend in modern either/or categories), the Spanish character that resulted from seven centuries of Muslim occupation and Christian Reconquista became notorious for outstanding feats of heroism, for profound religious commitment and reflection, for sincere love and promotion of the arts and of learning, and for great cooperation with and tolerance of those who were different. And yet, somehow, this same resulting Spanish character was equally capable of incredible acts of cruelty, of militant religious bigotry, of great intolerance, and of sometimes despising even simple gestures of human compassion. Apparently the Reconquista, with its multisecular demands of co-operation with the enemy even as one engaged in war against him, forged these contradictory national traits. Two powerful church-men, both of the same fifteenth-century Spanish Church, stand out as telling symbols of this double-sided national character: Jiménez de Cisneros (the great reformer and humanist) and Torquemada (of inquisitorial fame).

As can be expected, this entire period had its impact on Iberian Christianity.[20] The increasingly victorious Spanish monarchies jus-tified their military successes through religious categories. It was evident, as far as they were concerned, that the God of Chris-tians was the only true God, and therefore they—defenders of the true faith against the errors of the Muslim "infidels"—were being blessed by God with victory over the enemies of true religion. In typical medieval fashion, religion was called upon to legitimize the spoils of the victors. So in 1492, after the defeat of the last Islamic ruler, the attention of the monarchy and the Church was turned to cleansing Spain of all who might otherwise contaminate the faith and land of Christians.

But just as this view of victorious Christianity was being pro-moted, another and quite different thread was also being woven into the Spanish religious fabric. There was, during the same pe-riod, a renaissance of piety and devotion, of monasticism, and of theological learning. Both at the universities and in the villages, re-ligious interests and fervor seem to have shown a marked increase. In the rural areas of Spain, especially in the south, the numbers of hermits and penitents swelled considerably. The period of the Reconquista had indeed shaped Iberian Christianity in ways that paralleled the national character.

The year 1492 saw the final consolidation of Christian con-trol over the Iberian peninsula. That same year brought to the Spaniards the news of a vast and very different world on the other side of the ocean. With this news the Spanish character engaged in the task of conquering that other world, therein displaying its dual capacity for heroic generosity and for brutal bigotry.

Medieval and pre-Tridentine Christianity

I said earlier that it was important to distinguish between modern Roman Catholicism, the fruit of Trent and the polemics since the Reformation, and the Christianity that came to the Americas in the fifteenth and sixteenth centuries. Iberian Christianity was medieval and pre-Tridentine. In that religious world, every dimension of daily life participated (or could participate) in the transmission and sustenance of Christianity. To some degree, the patristic notion of *traditio* remained very much the norm.

Traditio cannot be simply translated today as "tradition."[21] *Traditio*, during the Iberian Middle Ages, included the beliefs held by Christians as part of revelation and as part of the ancient credal definitions. It involved the liturgical and sacramental practices of one's local and regional Church. But *traditio* also implied the behavior that was expected of Christians, the pious devotions of one's community, many other religious beliefs and demands held to be important for Christian living, the (canonical and consuetudinal) discipline of the local and western Church, and just about every customary facet of daily life in which religion was involved. As can be deduced from this description, the medieval Iberian concept of *traditio* was practically coextensive with what Christians believed, how they worshiped, and how they lived.

With this view of *traditio* in mind, we can understand why pre-Tridentine Spaniards communicated their faith through symbol and rite, through devotions and liturgical practices, and why the *autos sacramentales*[22] became so popular and important. We can see that the cycles and components of village life became fundamental transmitters of the Christian message. The teaching of the gospel did not usually occur through the spoken, magisterial word, but through the symbolic, performative word. Even the great preaching crusades caused great celebrations and, indeed, took place as part of local communal celebration.

There were synods and great universities where bishops and theologians would explain and theorize. But the vast majority of people did not participate in this official, doctrinal world. For "common folk" (and for much of the clergy), essential doctrine was embedded in the ordinary.[23]

It would be naive to think that distinctions were not made in medieval Spain between what was essential to Christianity and what was not.[24] The people did have, after all, the Bible and the creeds. But their religious world, in spite of all the distinctions, did not divorce doctrine from the other aspects of Christian living and did not teach doctrine except through all other dimensions of Christian living. One was a Christian not by merely or mainly holding to correct doctrine (though this too was necessary), but

by also living accordingly. Medieval *traditio* for all its evident
shortcomings and abuses, was not as naive or farfetched a notion as
today's Catholics might think. Within the Iberian sacral worldview,
all of reality could sacramentally speak the message of religion.

At this point in our study I want to recall one crucial moment in the history of western Christian theology.[25] During one
of the sessions of the Council of Trent (in 1546), Jesuit theologian
Claude LeJay made a distinction between *traditiones quae ad fidem
pertinent* ("traditions that pertain to the faith") and the *traditiones
ecclesiae* ("traditions of the church," which closely resemble what
Luther had called "human sentences"). LeJay was probably not
aware of the consequences his contribution was going to have.
Incorporated into post-Tridentine theology, the separation between
received, unchanging doctrine (*Traditio*, now with capital *T*) and
other (equally received) reformable traditions (*traditiones*, now with
lower-case *t*) was to have an enormous impact on modern Roman
Catholicism. As the decades progressed, revelation came to be
viewed as "doctrinal," and the rest of Christian living (spirituality,
worship, the ethical life of communities and individuals) became
dangerously demoted to reformable traditions. LeJay, Trent, and
their successors in Catholicism seem to have responded to the
reformers' arguments by assuming as valid many of the latter's
premises. This was certainly not medieval western Christianity.

The Colonial (Re)birth of Popular Catholicism

Most of the Spaniards that came to the Americas in the fifteenth and sixteenth centuries were people from the villages. They
were often enough from southern Spain (especially Andalucia and
Extremadura). Even the official missionaries, though trained in
theology, were sent to the newly conquered lands not because of
their profound theological expertise but because of their ability to
communicate with "common folk." In other words, the Christianity
brought to the Americas had to be—given the people who did the
evangelizing—the "village" *traditio* and not the highly doctrinal
and elaborate "university" or "magisterial" version. Later attempts
at implanting a more doctrinally oriented and sophisticated, post-
Tridentine Catholicism tended to remain largely at the level of the
colonial elites.

There is no question that the majority of friars and other religious that came to the Americas did so with the sincere intention of
proclaiming the gospel to the native and slave populations.[26] Most

missionaries worked very hard and were very creative in developing catechetical methods for the conversion of the Amerindians and Africans. But they were children of their time and culture, thereby transposing to the new lands the national traits and religious universe of fifteenth- and sixteenth-century Spain.

The colonial evangelization of the Americas did not happen as the result of the religious dialogue between equals. The interlocutors engaged in this evangelistic process because they were definitively not equal.[27] The Christian missionaries arrived on this continent and had the possibility of making themselves heard only because other Christians had first violently conquered lands and peoples, forcing them to submit to the new religion. Evangelization was made possible by conquest, that is, by first vanquishing the potential hearers of the gospel. This irrefutable historical fact has colored and shaped Latino popular Catholicism.

It is of no lesser importance that the original justification offered to the native populations (and later to the African slaves) for their conquest and vanquishment was, precisely, that the Christian God had sent the Spaniards to them. It was argued by many of the missionaries that Christianity showed its superiority over the native religions in that victory had been given to the Spanish conquistadores over the Amerindians and Africans. It was evident, they claimed, that the Christian God had proved to have far greater power than all the native divinities. The consequence of this line of argumentation was clear to the conquered people—they had to submit to the new God and accept this divine power and will, as expressed by the missionaries and the Spanish colonial authorities.

Much has been said, and rightly so, on the frequent brutality that the Spaniards displayed against Amerindians and Africans. Even during the early colonial period a number of powerful Spanish voices were raised (very often without much success) against the atrocities being committed. One of the worst and bloodiest genocides in human history was perpetrated against the native populations of the Americas by the Spanish. And though many missionaries attempted to defend the victims, their defense proved quite insufficient.[28] In regard to the African slaves, the historical reality was even worse because there were no great voices ever raised on their behalf, and their slavery lasted well into the nineteenth century.[29]

It was in this context of conquest, brutality, and vanquishment that the Christian gospel was first announced in the Americas. Unfortunately, the subsequent colonial and postcolonial history did not substantially change the structures of domination planted by the original conquest. Many of the blatant atrocities were either stopped or covered up in the later period, but violence and depredation continued in and through the new institutions (often well into the present).

Conversions and sacral worldviews

When confronted with the colonial history of the Americas, one might well ask, Why didn't the Amerindian and African populations rebel against the Spaniards? And, more to our point, Why did they accept Christianity? There were, indeed, many well-documented cases of rebellion on the part of natives and slaves.[30] There also were instances of refusal to accept the religion of the conquerors. But these attempts, remarkable as some were, ended in failure. Why?

In the specific area of our study (i.e., the religion of the people), it seems at least misleading or naive to claim that natives and slaves did not really accept Christianity but had it forced onto them. Although there is some truth to that claim, historical facts nevertheless point to a widespread acceptance of the new religion.[31] Even though some African religions have survived and are still very much alive among Latinos, they do not erase the great success of colonial Catholicism's evangelizing efforts. Once again, why was Christianity accepted?

I would argue that, in a horrible twist of coincidences, Spanish Christianity had in its favor the very religious arguments used to justify the conquest, and that Amerindian and African religions had against them their own sacral worldviews. Let me explain.

We have already seen that the Spanish believed theirs to be the only true religion and the only true God. Furthermore, they sincerely thought that this God had given them victory over the Iberian Muslim kingdoms precisely because they (the Spanish Christians) were defending truth against the errors of the infidels. We have also seen how these Christians held that it was their God who had made them overcome all odds and conquer the vast American lands. In their mind this divine favor only indicated that they were right, and consequently it was their privilege to subjugate the conquered ("infidel") peoples and impose Christianity on them. What we often forget nowadays is that the Amerindian and African sacral worldviews assumed as basically true the same premises held by the Spanish.

The Nahuatl-speaking peoples of Mesoamerica and the native Arawak (Taínos and Caribs) of the Antilles,[32] as well as the

later African slaves (especially Yorubas, Fon, and Kongos), had
inherited worldviews that explained human success and failure in
explicitly religious terms. These peoples assumed that divine favor
rested upon the victors and not upon the vanquished. They further
believed that it was important to take on the worship (and the
accompanying beliefs associated with this worship) of the gods of
the victorious. Within their sacral worldviews, the refusal to adopt
the new divinities was an invitation to more cosmic calamities and
earthly punishment.

Evidently, these assumptions did not necessarily imply the
abandonment of their religion on the part of the conquered, but
they certainly can help us understand today why those who lost
in fifteenth- and sixteenth-century America could accept the beliefs
and worship of the winners, without our having to appeal to
arguments of religious imposition, as if these were the only or best
possible explanation. Nevertheless, one must also keep in mind
that this acceptance of the victorious God happened in Mexico
and the Antilles from the cultural perspective of Amerindians and
Africans. Therefore, one can wonder if the conversions were so in
fact (in the common western sense of the term), or whether they
were only part of the process of rereading and interpreting normative Christianity. This process would eventually lead to today's
popular Catholicism.

Public ritual as religious communication

One interesting cultural detail is very germane to our discussion. It is well known that Amerindians (in Mesoamerica especially, but also in the Antilles) and Africans (particularly the
Yoruba) engaged in religious pageantry at key moments in their
ritual cycle.[33] Sacred space—often in front of temples or shrines—
were reserved, at least at some point in the yearly calendar, for
these elaborate public (and popular) ceremonies. It is no insignificant fact, for example, that the great Tenochtitlan included the
great ceremonial avenues and causeways that led to its impressive
temple complex.

These ceremonies appear to have been highly complex, involving the participation of large numbers of people. Preparation for
the rite was almost as important as the ritual action itself. And
through it all the holy stories of divinities and ancestors, the doctrinal contents of the religion and its ethical demands, were communicated to the participants. These elaborate ceremonies, therefore,
acted as an indispensable catechetical moment in the religious life
of the people.

Everyday life, however, was not as religiously elaborate. Nevertheless, there were small family and clan shrines, and frequent rites celebrated in them (on a daily basis in some places). And here again we seem to find ritual action used as a main channel for religious instruction. It is not insignificant that all ritual celebration, massive or familial, is necessarily symbolic.

The reader might recall the importance of the Iberian autos sacramentales, their popularity and use in catechesis. Religious ritual (symbolic, massive ceremonies, or familial rites) were well known and liked in medieval Christianity. The coincidental similarity with the Amerindian and African liturgical universes proved to be indispensable when the missionaries attempted to communicate Catholicism to natives and slaves.[34]

Colonial normative Christianity

In their culturally possible (and probably culturally expected) acceptance of Christianity, and in their subsequent interpretation of the latter, Amerindians and Africans had no way of knowing that what they were assuming to be normative, official Catholicism was in fact Iberian and pre-Tridentine Christianity. This fact is of utmost importance and consequence. The religion presented to natives and slaves by the Spaniards and their missionaries was the medieval traditio, the village type of Catholicism that I mentioned earlier. Furthermore, the religion that the new colonial Christians passed on to their mestizo[35] (and native and Afro) descendants was this pre-Tridentine Christianity—it was, after all, the only Christianity that was preached to them for centuries.

When, almost a century later, the theology and reforms of Trent finally arrived in the Americas,[36] they were often used (by royal and Church authorities) to keep Lutheran and Calvinist ideas out of the continent, thereby preserving pre-Tridentine Christianity on this side of the Atlantic (since no urgent reason other than anti-Protestant polemics was then found to systematically carry out what the council had mandated). Even though seminaries were established and other disciplinary reforms implemented, these benefited the Spanish and criollo[37] elites and seldom affected the vast majority of people. Perhaps the reformed liturgy, celebrated in a language (Latin) and through symbols doubly foreign to Amerindians and Africans, was the only popularly accessible Tridentine innovation—when and if priests were available. Furthermore, given that for quite a long period of time, during the colonial centuries, only Spaniards and their criollo sons could be admitted to the ordained ministry, even priests and bishops were not often inclined to work for any implementation or spread of Trent's teaching among Amerindians, Africans, and the new mestizos. In the clergy's view, this would at best be unnecessary for the people's religious well-being. Thus the medieval *traditio* remained, by and large, normative Christianity for the majority.

Interpretations of the Normative during the Colony

There are not many studies on colonial Amerindian and African interpretations of pre-Tridentine Catholicism in Mesoamerica and the Antilles.[38] One important reason for this dearth of material is that natives and slaves were not allowed to preserve in writing much of what they thought of Christianity. After all, they confronted almost certain danger if they dared to express (especially in writing) any unauthorized understanding of or misgivings about the new religion. However, a few priceless pieces of evidence have survived. Other texts—written, visual, or performed—have also been preserved and through them we can surmise what the conquered thought of the new religion.

The evidence (written or otherwise) from the late colonial period is more plentiful because by then some of the legal prescriptions against mestizos had been removed or had become obsolete. For most of the three to four centuries of colonial rule, however, the mestizos shared (both as actors and as victims) in most of the prejudice against natives and slaves. Although a number of these mixed-race people were able in time to move up the social ladder, both bigotry and law kept the vast majority of them (and not a few of those who seemed to have succeeded in life) in second-class status vis-à-vis the Spaniards and white criollos. Much of today's popular Catholicism survived the late colonial period thanks in part to the mestizos who appropriated it in their search for a distinct national, ethnic, and cultural identity.

Evidence available today

Let me very briefly summarize the main types of evidence we have available to us today and through which we can surmise the people's rereading of colonial, normative Christianity.

Some of the early pictographic catechisms used in evangelization have been preserved.[39] Their particular importance in tracing what the native populations understood is based on the fact that most of these catechisms were drawn by *tlacuilos*,[40] interpreting what the missionaries taught. The contents of these catechisms, though basically orthodox in doctrine, do evidence an emphasis on the devotional and the symbolic as the proper means of evangelizing. Needless to say that in this they closely resemble the methods of medieval *traditio*. But more importantly, these catechisms include some explanations of Christian beliefs and practices that could not possibly have come from the missionaries' preaching. Some of these pictographs reinterpreted terms and meanings turning them into critiques (albeit mild) of the new religion, while other drawings indicate the beginnings of a rereading of colonial Christianity in ways easily identifiable with today's popular Catholicism.[41]

Parallel to these pictographic catechisms drawn by natives are a number of other religious education texts directly written (seldom painted) by the Spanish missionaries themselves.[42] These other catechisms can indicate to us what, in the intended native listeners' or readers' understanding, was considered—in Spanish eyes—inadequate, unacceptable, or in need for further catechesis. As the colonial period progressed, fewer specialized catechisms appeared and more imitations (or outright copies) of imported Spanish models became common. Needless to say that this latter approach reinforced the perceived and actual distance between official Catholicism and the people's religion.

Other texts written by missionaries and other colonial authors also contribute to our contemporary understanding of the natives' and slaves' interpretation of and reaction to Christianity. These writings run the gamut from very detailed and descriptive chronicles to private letters sent to superiors or friends.[43]

In some rural areas of Mexico and of the Antilles one can still find today interpretations of Christianity performed in popular liturgical rites, in songs, and in annual religious plays that date back to the colonial period. Many U.S. Latino communities have preserved (and somewhat modified) a number of these songs, rites, and dramas, and thus they can still be witnessed and heard.[44] The emphases and the explanations communicated through these performed texts of popular Catholicism often coincide with the normative Christianity of the colonial Church; but, once again, there are enough variations that indicate the presence of popular interpretations of the religion. And evidently, the very existence of these liturgical and catechetical performances recalls the evangelizing methods of pre-Tridentine Catholicism.

The pious, artistic styles of religious imagery (crucifixes, santos de palo, etc.) that originated in the Spanish period and that have been actively preserved until today repeat the same pattern of substantial agreement with what was considered to be the Catholic norm, while at the same time displaying emphases that would point to an interpretive effort on the part of the popular artists.[45] The symbolic catechetical vehicle, so typical of medieval Spain, continues to be successfully used and displayed in the present.

Also preserved for us are a few writings by early Amerindian and later Afro-Antillean authors that clearly show the painful recognition of their peoples' plight and, with decreasing vehemence, incisively critique the religion of Spaniards and criollos.[46] As the colonial period progressed (i.e., into the eighteenth and early nineteenth centuries), more of these writings appeared and often fueled the aspirations for independence of later criollo and mestizo generations. These texts are not necessarily attempts at religious interpretation, but what they assume to be integral parts of Catholicism (whether to accept them, ignore them, or critique them) does indicate the manner and content of the popular rereading of Christianity at the time of their writing.

Interpretation of the normative

What do these pieces of evidence, taken together, seem to say about what natives, slaves, and mestizos thought was "normative" in Christianity—as it was presented to them during the colonial period? What reinterpretation(s) of this religion does the evidence indicate?

Since later in this study I will present an overview of the religious contents of contemporary Hispanic popular Catholicism in the United States, at this point it seems best to limit the presentation of the rereading to the Spanish colonial period (which ended early in the nineteenth century in Mexico, the American Southwest, and Florida, or very late in the same century in Cuba and Puerto Rico).[47]

Native, slave, and mestizo religious interpretation during the colonial age—a veritable popular reinterpretation of what was considered to be normative Catholicism—is very important. Postindependence and postannexation developments in popular Hispanic Catholicism, which are with us today, occurred from the doctrinal, ethical, and liturgical premises assumed as true and normative in Christianity by the colony's conquered peoples and their descendants.

It is equally important to keep in mind that the medieval Iberian village, which was the socioeconomic and political microcontext for the shaping of Spanish Catholicism and of Spain's daily life, was sufficiently transplanted to and inculturated in Mesoamerica and the Antilles. It survives today (and not just architecturally).[48] The sacral worldview of the village was very much alive in the shaping of colonial popular Catholicism and its more contemporary descendant.

For the sake of brevity, I point to one key area (the doctrines on the trinitarian nature of the one God) in which a popular reinterpretation of religion took place.[49] Evidently, the ideal introduction to Hispanic popular Catholicism would include sections on the ecclesiology, ethics, liturgy, etc., implicit in colonial popular religion. Unfortunately, we do not live or write in an ideal world.

What did natives and slaves hear and understand about the Trinity? The question is not irrelevant, and it certainly does not refer to some obscure or esoteric fine point of Christian theology. In mainstream, orthodox Catholicism, belief in the one and triune God is absolutely indispensable. Hence, no evangelization could possibly claim to be acceptable without clearly communicating the trinitarian doctrines. One thing, however, is to try to communicate, and another is to be successful in the attempt. Though other elements of Catholicism might seem more interesting, it can be argued that no other teaching has deeper consequences than the one on the Trinity.

Iberian Christians believed, certainly in the fifteenth century and later, in the traditional trinitarian doctrines. They were familiar with the creedal formulations of Christian antiquity. After all, these doctrinal statements were repeated every Sunday at the Eucharist, included in the baptismal rite, and repeated often enough in other devotional and liturgical contexts. Every prayer and every major activity of the day began with the *En el nombre del Padre, y del Hijo, y del Espíritu Santo* ("In the name of the Father, and of the Son, and of the Holy Spirit").

Familiar with the doctrines and terms they were. But what did the people in the villages of Spain understand and believe about the Trinity? I am afraid that one can only guess (based on the few medieval indications we have) that most Christians in rural Spain simply did not worry about understanding or explaining trinitarian doctrines. They believed, or so they liturgically repeated and claimed, that there was only one God, and that there were three Persons in that one God: Father, Son, and Holy Spirit. In this the Iberian villagers were in agreement with doctrinally orthodox Christianity. But I would argue that this coincidence with orthodoxy was mostly at the terminological level. It seems that what they in fact held to be true was a strict monotheism that would leave little or no room for the trinitarian relations. And given this type of monotheism, their Christology had to run the gamut from Arian to Docetist.[50]

The mendicant friars who were first responsible for the evangelization of the Americas, the Spanish villagers who came as the original conquerors, and all those who followed them, were convinced of their doctrinal orthodoxy. The missionary effort that ultimately succeeded in converting first the natives and then the Africans, was based on this conviction.

What did natives and slaves hear and understand about the Trinity? What could they? I have shown elsewhere why the probable doctrinal outcome of colonial evangelization on the Trinity was either strict monotheism (with concomitant Arian or Docetist Christologies), or practical tritheism (frequently disguised by using the trinitarian language of the liturgy).[51] Clearly, the theological terms I am employing here would never have been accessible to the natives or the slaves, but the doctrinal contents expressed through these terms seem to have been there.

It is my belief, given the Hellenic background and European cultural settings of mainstream Christian doctrines and terms on the Trinity, that no evangelization on the one and triune God could have been successful in the fifteenth, sixteenth, or even later centuries. It is only today, with our growing awareness of the depth of culture's impact on human thought and on perceptions of truth, that new possibilities are slowly opening for authentically inculturated mediations of the Christian trinitarian doctrines among the non-European or non-Europeanized.

There can be little doubt that the very idea of monotheism would have been extraordinarily foreign to natives and slaves.[52] Culturally, historically, religiously, all of Mesoamerican and Antillean reality defied the monotheistic doctrine of Christianity. Though it might be possible to argue theoretically that natives and slaves were somehow capable of understanding what the missionaries were teaching on the Trinity, in real life this understanding was not very likely—not because of lack of intelligence but because of the sheer alien and culturally outlandish nature of the concepts. More importantly, the massive "conversions" of peoples could not possibly have facilitated any kind of real native understanding of or reflection on what Christian monotheism was all about.

Monotheism, however, was being preached by people who must have culturally and religiously confused the natives and the slaves. Most of the Christians with whom Amerindians and Africans came in contact,—during the foundational period of the colonial Church— were pre-Tridentine Christians. And we already saw how nominal (even if sincere) was the trinitarian belief of these Iberian Christians of the fifteenth and sixteenth centuries.

These Christians were claiming that there was only one God, in three Persons. Native and African mythologies had also claimed that the one high god was capable of being in more than one form.[53] But the divine form, in these mythologies, had always been masculine, feminine, or both. So it was only a matter of time before these ancient and culturally reasonable categories came to the aid of natives and slaves as they attempted to make sense of Christian teaching on God.

It is well known that the missionaries did try to explain as best they could something about the three Persons of the Trinity, especially what each meant and did in a Christian's life. The missionaries, however, could not have prevented (or perhaps foreseen) their listeners' understanding these explanations from a dramatically different cultural perspective. A strong argument can be made to show that the trinitarian doctrine was probably heard and interpreted through the categories of the masculine/feminine forms of the one supreme god. The results of this highly plausible interpretation of Christianity are impressive, indeed.

Briefly presented, the early native interpretation seems to have concluded that the Christian high god, in his masculine form, was the so-called Father, or just plain "God." This was the conquering, majestic, and frequently authoritarian divinity that had handed victory to the Spaniards. This God was to be feared, placated, and obeyed. He could be capricious but could be convinced (through prayer and sacrifice) to be fair and just.

On the other hand, another early native interpretation of the Christian God seems to have occurred. The Mexican version is the most notable (but not the only) example. Catholic missionaries would have been shocked to know that their listeners had also interpreted the Christian high god in a feminine form. The Iberian devotion to Mary does not seem to have come across to the newly converted with all the important doctrinal explanations and nuances that the missionaries presented. What was heard by the natives (I would argue) was the feminine form of the Christian high god.[54]

This culturally acceptable, feminine form of the supreme divinity, however, was not to be called *divine* by the vanquished peoples. They soon learned the *ortholalia*[55] necessary for survival in an adverse environment. Nevertheless, the symbols employed and the manner of the devotion do indicate a link with the ancient forms of the divine. The short period of time that elapsed from first evangelization to apparitions (1523 to 1531 in the case of Guadalupe) could not have allowed for the thorough reshaping of cultural religious categories among the Amerindian populations. This reshaping of deeply held categories would have been required for a strictly orthodox Christian understanding of Mary or of Guadalupe.

The Virgin of Guadalupe cannot be simply identified with Tonantzin—not even at the very beginning. But I do not see either how the natives could have simply identified Guadalupe with the Catholic Mary. From the start it seems that there was an effort (on the part of the Amerindians) at speaking a religious language, through culturally understandable religious categories, that would interpret for them the Christian message about God. And just as there had been much said to the natives about the conquering might of God, much had also been said to them about the compassionate mercy and care of that same God. These latter attributes or dimensions of the divine are the ones that were interpreted as the feminine form of the Christian high god, symbolized through the acceptable Catholic imagery of Mary.

Perhaps modern theologies of the Holy Spirit can explain, as indeed they have begun to, that marian symbols have been used in the past to speak of the Holy Spirit.[57] After all, the symbols of a dove or a flame do not seem to have any more claim to doctrinal accuracy than the feminine symbols connected with Mary.

One difficulty remains as one attempts to understand the early Amerindian and African interpretations of the Christian doctrines on God. What of the Son, in European Trinitarian terms? It seems that the overall message of the missionaries was profoundly Christocentric. The emphasis was placed on Jesus as the crucified, innocent, eternal Son of God. The missionaries presented Jesus both as fully human (and his suffering was the most important sign of humanness) and as fully divine (his power to work miracles—his own resurrection included—was the great sign).[58]

The native and slave populations seem to have accepted the message but, once again, as they were able to understand it through their cultural, religious categories. Their own sacred stories reminded them of divinities who were solidarious with the victimized, and who were willing to share in human suffering as a sign of their sincere concern and care for humans. Some myths recalled the tragic end or the punishment endured by innocent gods. Indeed, some of the most popular and sincerely venerated divinities of both the Mesoamerican and Yoruba mythologies had experienced this kind of treatment or defeat.[59]

It was, therefore, very possible for natives and slaves to interpret Jesus and his story through the prism of their own traditional sacred stories. He could be accepted as both fully human and fully divine. And his power and caring solidarity could indeed move the newly converted to sincere commitment and devotion. But this does not solve, however, the trinitarian doctrinal question.

The traditional high god had been responsible, according to the mythologies, for the birth of other deities. What could the Amerindians and Africans of the early colonial period have understood, from a doctrinal perspective, when they were also told that this crucified God had also been born of a woman thanks to the activity of the high god? I think that an argument can be made to the effect that the conquered peoples accepted and believed in the humanity and divinity of Jesus, but that they did so only in the manner that their traditional religious categories would have made possible. These religious categories could not have interpreted Jesus as Son in a trinitarian, orthodox way.

It soon became apparent, after the initial period of colonial evangelization, that the missionary task was far from complete. New lands were still being opened to the new religion by the advancing Spanish occupation forces. More importantly, however, there grew an awareness—as the colonial centuries progressed—that the Catholicism of the native, slaves, and mestizos was not quite like the religion of Spaniards and criollos. The differences were not merely in emphases, devotional or liturgical. There were, from the official point of view, serious doctrinal shortcomings (if not blatant error) in the Catholicism of the people. A new effort at re-evangelization seems to have been started.[60]

Notice, however, that this new missionary effort was directed not mainly at "pagans" (as in the early colonial period) but at baptized Christians. Secondly, this reevangelization was more explicitly for the correction of error (potential or otherwise) and for the more proper religious education of natives, slaves, and mestizos. It assumed that the religious worldview that had to be addressed now was the one born from the original evangelization of the fifteenth and sixteenth centuries. The original Amerindian and African interpretation of the Christian message became the focus of concern during the later part of the colonial centuries.[61]

But there was more. If I could continue using the doctrines on the Trinity as illustrative example, it could be shown that as the decades of Spanish rule continued, other influences came to play a part on the people's doctrinal understanding. The most important of these influences was the family.

The family structures had begun to shift. New family roles and relationships, by now profoundly influenced by colonial legislation and mores, came to be projected onto the popular interpretation of the Trinity. God as father, Mary as mother, Jesus as older brother, and the many saints as members of the extended family and community networks—a sufficiently elaborate (and seldom explicit) ecclesiology was put forth, founded on and reflective of earlier trinitarian interpretations.

The revived missionary effort of the late colonial period also saw the publication of new catechisms, the creation of new approaches, and even new devotions were introduced in order to catechize the baptized masses. Whenever inevitable, colonial authorities relaxed legislation against mestizo participation in the ordained ministries, thereby establishing a more responsive link between popular and official Catholicisms. As a result, some success at reevangelization began to appear and consolidate itself.

The most important result of this late colonial catechetical process, in my estimation, was (and still is) the slowly growing identification of the Virgin of Guadalupe with Mary. However, the connection seems to have happened between the Mary of Catholic popular devotions and the Virgin of Guadalupe, and not between the latter and the historical person Mary of Nazareth.[62]

Another very important outcome of late colonial reevangelization was the increased religious influence of the mestizo. Both in the cities and in the villages, in lay and clerical contexts, the mestizos frequently managed to bridge the worlds of the victorious and the vanquished. Later generations owe the definitions of nationhood and, to a great degree, of cultural identity to the mestizos. Much of contemporary popular Christianity, in Latin America and among U.S. Hispanics, is the mestizos' Catholicism.

The mestizos were, in the late colonial period, mainly responsible for the (often grudging and only partial) acceptance of many popular religious symbols by the ecclesiastical elites. Although through the mestizos bits of the reevangelizing effort reached natives and slaves, most of it was addressed directly at them. In a strange twist of circumstances, mixed-race people were the most frequent vehicles of late colonial catechesis, thereby (and inevitably, in cultural terms) filtering the intentions, symbols and doctrines of the ecclesiastical authorities through mestizo prisms.

The mixed-race were fast becoming the majority population. Aware of the Spanish and white criollo civil and ecclesiastical world, and to some degree its heirs too, the mestizo population soon began to have national and religious importance, still denied the Amerindians and Africans.

The reevangelization of the late colonial period, so briefly described here, set the stage for today's U.S. Latino popular Catholicism. It is important to note that mestizos who were mainly responsible for that catechetical process, were building their religious interpretations and symbolic syntheses on premises—considered normative—that were (still) pre-Tridentine. The doctrines and worldview born of Trent were only peripherally present in late colonial Catholicism, even when the ecclesiastical elites made themselves believe that the Tridentine decrees were being implemented.[63]

POPULAR CATHOLICISM IN THE NINETEENTH CENTURY

The early nineteenth century saw the flowering of a new nationalism all over Spanish America. Most countries in Latin America won their independence at that time. This century was also cataclysmic for the Hispanic populations already present on the lands that were annexed by the United States.[64]

I will not attempt to give a history of Hispanic Catholicism since the annexations. I will instead very briefly focus on the main outline of how Latino popular Catholicism seems to have developed and reacted to the history immediately after independence in Mexico and during the last colonial century in Cuba and Puerto Rico.[65] The approach I have chosen will stress the responses of Hispanic popular Christianity and the different elements that forced it to confront the modern world. The influences on the current status of this religious universe will become evident through this brief discussion.

The First Confrontation with the Modern World: Nationalism

We have seen that the religion taken to be normative Christianity, in the early colonial period, was Catholicism as *traditio* (in its medieval, Iberian, pre-Tridentine version). It was this religion that was interpreted by the native and slave populations in their attempt to make cultural and religious sense out of their conquest and vanquishment.

We have also seen how this interpreted Catholicism was perceived, late in colonial times, to be in need of reevangelization. Mestizos were by then fast becoming the majority of the population, and it was through and to them that the new catechetical efforts were channeled. This allowed for some elements of reevangelization to reach Amerindians and Africans, but their religion remained basically as it had been.

The late colonial reevangelization mainly reached the mestizos. This allowed them to interpret the new messages being presented through the prism of their inherited popular Catholicism (which was still seen by them as normative). This latest interpretation slowly became the Catholic norm for the mixed-race majority. It was this religion, for all practical purposes, which was the only Catholicism acceptable by most people during the independence movement.

A split can be clearly detected at the start of the nineteenth century, bound to widen since. The official Christianity of the bishops and of the social elites, presenting itself as the sole valid norm, was quite distinct from the Christianity of the vast majority of the population. This popular religion also claimed to be the valid norm, though acknowledging the existence of the clerical version.[66]

By the time proindependence movements broke out last century, the bearers of official Catholicism had usually become the main pillars of Spain's colonial rule (and therefore, inimical to the anticolonial forces). The other strand of Catholicism, the popular version that the ecclesiastical and social elites so deplored, was the religion of the independentists (or at least openly allied with them).[67]

It became commonplace to find the symbols of popular Catholicism used as gathering banners for the people against Spain. The ecclesiastics that collaborated with the colonial rulers invoked all sorts of religious arguments to condemn the independentists as enemies of Christianity and of legitimate authority. On the other hand, the people and other lesser clergy fighting Spain appealed to God, to the Virgin, to the faith, and to religious symbols of the majority in order to demonstrate that God was indeed on their side.

The mestizos and criollos created the independence movements. What had been official colonial Catholicism soon identified itself with criollo interests (after independence in the case of Mexico and Cuba, and after American occupation in the case of Puerto Rico), while most mestizos still claimed popular religion as theirs. Therefore, even after Spain's defeat, the dual-level Catholicism of the late colonial period was preserved. And the link between the two versions of the religion was maintained thanks to the mestizos' gift for cultural reinterpretation. Some mestizos had finally entered the clergy and risen through its ranks, allowing popular Catholicism to receive partial acceptability from the postindependence ecclesiastical hierarchy. This belated acceptability, however, had its price.

Nineteenth-Century Uses of Popular Catholicism

During most of the postindependence period in Mexico, and during the colonial nineteenth century in Puerto Rico and in Cuba, the Church hierarchy started participating in some key rites of popular Catholicism. Whether the bishops (and other clergy) suspected these rites of syncretic, superstitious, or other elements did not seem as important as the fact that these rituals were, indeed, Catholic. They were a sacred, public link between the hierarchy and the people, recognized as such by all.

The maintenance of this sacred and public link became very important during the nineteenth century. The institutions of the Church came increasingly under attack by a growing intellectual elite, criolla and mestiza, that were influenced by the European currents of modern thought. The Enlightenment had arrived in the Americas with an anti-Church zeal. The ecclesiastical hierarchy, apparently sensing the danger, saw in popular Catholicism an ally and tool in the Church's defense strategy. The natives, slaves, and mestizos, for centuries marginalized from the official institutions of the Catholicism, were now courted and their religion blest.

On the other hand, the intellectual elites—in typical nineteenth-century rationalist style—had no use for the Church and its economic and political power, while also condemning popular Catholicism as obscurantist ignorance. They thought that popular religion prevented the people from achieving higher levels of educational and material development. Intellectuals of the last century, in Mexico and the Antilles, in their disdain for Church and ignorance, actually fomented a strategic alliance (necessarily clothed in acceptable theological and pastoral language) between the ecclesiastical hierarchy and the masses of people.

Nineteenth-century official and popular Catholicisms confronted the same enemy in Mexico and the Antilles, and they joined forces. But by then the official brand was itself far too imbued with the mentality of the post-Reformation and the Enlightenment. It was only a matter of time before the rationalist intellectuals and the Church establishment would discover a sufficiently comfortable dialogue, and then turn their sights and disdain onto popular Catholicism.

The intellectual elites of the nineteenth century have—one hundred years later—either lost their influence or have (most probably) transformed themselves into other ideological or political shapes and adopted new names. Much of modern-day education, business, politics, etc., in Mexico and in the Antilles, depend on the new versions of the rationalist mentality. Curiously enough, the powerful elites of the Right as well as many of the revolutionaries of the Left share the same basic worldview that sees the people's religion as an unfortunate (or at best, folkloric) vestige of the past. In their common view, the best use of popular religious symbol is its instrumentalization.[68]

For the ecclesiastical hierarchy, still dialoguing with but not fully trusting the modern world represented by the rationalism of either Right or Left, popular Catholicism remains a necessary buffer in cases of crisis and confrontation. The Church, since the nineteenth century, seems to have learned to tolerate popular religion (at best an ill-catechized form of pious devotionalism, in the official view). This tolerance, it is hoped, will not lose the masses of people that justify (and potentially defend) the Church's institutional importance in the larger society. This instrumentalization of popular Catholicism has produced mixed results.

Popular Catholicism in the Annexed Lands

I have been discussing popular religion mainly in Mexico and in the Antilles during the nineteenth century. I have done so because of the great influence that events in both geographic areas have had on present-day U.S. Hispanic popular Catholicism. Immigrants from Cuba and Mexico, clearly, did not leave their religious history behind. But the nineteenth century is also the time of the American purchase of Florida and of the U.S. military conquest and annexation of Mexico's northern half.

Florida's Hispanic Catholics,[69] mostly gathered in the cities of St. Augustine and Pensacola, chose either of two paths when their purchase from Spain occurred—few decided to stay in the new American territory,[70] but most elected to leave Florida and settle in Spanish Cuba. Not until several decades later (in the mid-nineteenth century) did large communities of Hispanic Catholics settle again in the peninsula, fleeing the increasingly repressive Spanish colonial authorities in Cuba. The new settlers, however, this time established themselves in Tampa and Key West. Smaller groups of Cubans went to Philadelphia and New York.

Did these Cubans bring their popular Catholicism to the U.S. last century? There are some indications that Tampa and Key West, where few of the independentist elites settled, did see forms of popular religion. But one must be very careful on this point, because of the religious apathy that accompanied much of the Cuban nineteenth century.[71]

The Southwest, however, had a different story from Florida. The lands from Texas to California were annexed by the United States after military intervention, and with the lands came towns and villages. Many of these had been founded at least two centuries before, and the presence of Catholicism in them was as old.[72]

The dual-level Christianity of Mexico had also become part of the religious life of the Southwest (these lands were still, after all, part of Mexico). Here, however, popular Catholicism seems to have had so heavy an influence that even the local ecclesiastical establishment—too weak to claim power on its own—had to promote it actively, thereby publicly linking it to the clergy. The same fundamental reasons of defense and buffer, evident in the rest of Mexico at the time, were operative in the northern frontier as the clergy allied itself here with the symbols of popular religion.

The new American Southwest had been Mexico's remote northern border outposts. Not many of the Mexican enlightened elites of the period would have chosen to leave the big cities in the south and come to settle in the frontier. Even the few residents that pretended to belong to these elites were numerically insignificant and ultimately powerless.

Popular Catholicism remained the de facto religion of the vast majority of the population. Its shape, functions, and sociodoctrinal developmental process parallel the ones we have indicated for the

rest of Mexico. In other words, the popular Christianity that preceded the American annexations was at its core the pre-Tridentine
traditio.[73] It was mestizo, but in this case because mestizos were the
ones who mainly settled here. This religion assumed as normative
the Catholicism that had been interpreted by earlier popular generations in southern Mexico. However, the reevangelization efforts,
so important during much of the late colonial period, had barely
any effect in the lands from Texas to California.

But then came the American military conquest and subsequent
annexations. For the first time Hispanic American Catholicism was
going to confront the Reformation.

The confrontation was going to be between, on one side, a
militant Protestant nation, increasingly aware of its military might
and apparently convinced of its moral superiority (its Manifest
Destiny). On the other side there was a conquered people, suddenly and violently deprived of right and land, whose religion had
long roots in the medieval past that the new conquerors loathed
as obscurantist. The Catholicism of the people was not the post-
Tridentine version, by now common enough in Catholic Europe
and in the eastern American states. It had assumed as self-evident
that the truth was Catholic. It seemed to be no intellectual match
for the Protestantism of the occupiers.

The religion of the people, however, was also going to face
another confrontation—the arrival, with the annexation, of post-
Tridentine Catholics.

The Confrontations With Trent, The Reformation, and Modernity

I believe that Hispanic popular Catholicism in the U.S. is now,
at the end of the twentieth century, displaying the effects and consequences of its first century of confrontation with post-Tridentine
Roman Christianity, with the heirs of the Protestant Reformation,
and with the modern world (initiated and disseminated mainly by
the Calvinist and Roman theological traditions).

Confrontation with Post-Tridentine Catholicism after the Annexation

The implementation of the decrees and doctrines of Trent had
been very selective in Spanish America. Tridentine Catholicism,

arriving at least a century after the conquest, became identified mostly with the Spaniards and criollos. There were so few Protestants in Spain's colonies that the European urgency of reform seemed foreign here. The result, as we have seen, was the preservation of pre-Tridentine Christianity in the western hemisphere.

The reevangelization of the late colonial period attempted to bring Tridentine Catholicism to the people, but only with limited success. By then even the official religion was undergoing a profound change that would eventually lead to the centralizing Romanization started by Pius IX. Latin American Catholics first confronted Tridentine Catholicism, in an inescapable way, with the dawn of the twentieth century.[74]

However, U.S. Latinos were forced to deal with the Church of Trent immediately after the American annexation. Their popular Catholicism, fundamentally untouched by the reforming council, suddenly confronted a new type of Church that seemed always on the defensive, that emphasized doctrinal knowledge (and guilt) over experience and affect, and that devalued lay participation. Worst of all, this new Church supported the American conquest of the Southwest.

Today we can understand why the Catholicism of the American eastern states appeared to be on the defensive. It was. And perhaps this in turn led to American Catholics' perceiving public, popular Hispanic Catholicism as superstition in need of correction and catechesis. Compounding this perception, however, was the growing influence and control of the Irish in the U.S. Church; many among them became fierce opponents of the Mexicans in the annexed lands.[75] I am assuming that the American (specifically Irish) Catholics' need for acceptance and respect in the wider U.S. society led many to conceive of Hispanic religion as an added weight they did not want to carry and as a source of embarrassment to their reformed, Tridentine Church.

Some of the public, social celebrations of popular Catholicism were soon transformed into more private, family expressions.[76] The new Church organized itself basically according to the ecclesiastical patterns developed in the eastern states. Although most Catholics in the Southwest were Hispanic, their participation and leadership in the institutions of religion were drastically diminished. The people's alternative seems to have been the withdrawal into the universe of popular Catholicism—it was theirs, and it made familiar sense of God and Christianity. By taking refuge in this religious world Latinos were also preserving one of the most important roots of their cultural identity.

However, for the new Euro-American ecclesiastical establishment in the Southwest, Hispanic flight into traditional religion implied that the new Catholic elites could ignore Latino Christianity and further emphasize to the Protestant majority that popular Hispanic Catholicism was not really Catholic—only a marginal anachronism from the past, in need of instruction. Euro-American Catholics had, thereby, assumed as true and valid the Protestant Reformation's premise that pre-Tridentine Christianity was deviant.

Confrontations with Contemporary Post-Tridentine Catholicism

As long as the Church in the Southwest doctrinally and pastorally ignored Latinos, and as long as the Latinos maintained the ritual link with the Roman clergy (thereby identifying themselves as Catholics), Hispanics could keep their popular Catholicism with only occasional hierarchical interference. Some local Latinos joined the ranks of the clergy, but their meager numbers and lack of real institutional influence did not alter the fundamentally ritual (i.e., devotional) relationship that existed between priests and people since the colonial days.

But this uneasy truce between the official Euro-American (mostly Irish) Church and Hispanic popular Catholicism started to unravel in the middle of the twentieth century, and more specifically after Vatican II. Let us, therefore, look at the present situation.

The contemporary Church's approach and alternatives

Several elements of the contemporary world came together to force the current confrontation.[77] There is, for example, the influence that decades of access to Euro-American mass media have had on the sacral worldview underlying and sustaining much of Hispanic popular Catholicism. There too are the efforts of public education (no matter how otherwise ineffectual and insufficient) in communicating the values and worldview of modernity. It is difficult to see how the long exposure to Euro-American society (heir to the Calvinist religious tradition, imbued of individualism, and increasingly secularized) could not have affected the very foundations and premises of the Hispanic religious and communal universe. The growth of urbanization and of a city-based job market after World War II began to have a deep impact on the stable, traditional family and community relationships so fundamental to Latino religion. Finally, the upsurge of immigration (to American cities) from Mexico and the Antilles added huge concentrations of Hispanics. This immigrant wave (which has not ended) brings to the U.S. people who are not accustomed to being treated as foreigners in their societies or Church.

Finally, and more importantly, the poverty and discrimination (and consequences thereof) suffered by so many Latinos seem to have socially justified, in the eyes of the larger society, the perpetuation of the "subaltern" role of the Hispanic populations. [78] The dominant ideology has long attempted to explain and "prove" the supposed reasons for this subaltern status. Needless to say, precisely as a symptom of their social vulnerability, many Latinos internalized the "proofs" put forth by the dominant ideology. Unfortunately, the Euro-American Catholic Church all too frequently uncritically assumed these ideological justifications, thereby reaffirming the "validity" of the arguments of prejudice within its ecclesiastical milieu. It also became an active accomplice in the Latino internalization of the dominant ideology.

Demographics (and probably not the long-standing pastoral need) finally made the Euro-American Church take notice. It is also true that many were moved to action by the new vision of Vatican II. But whatever the motive, the alternatives offered by official Catholicism (progressive or conservative) to U.S. Latinos seem clear and are certainly not new—either leave the pre-Tridentine style of Catholicism behind by becoming religiously Euro-Americanized, or face the continued onslaught of accusations of ignorance and superstition, followed by pastoral activity geared to educate "correctly" in "real" Roman Christianity. The American Church's attempts at understanding Hispanic popular Catholicism seem all too frequently motivated by the hope for the latter's early and definitive demise.[79]

The current trend at multiculturalizing the American Church seems to me to be concealing the obvious (and not surprising) fact that those who really set the pastoral agendas, determine the doctrinal parameters, and direct the implementation strategies for the multicultural dioceses and parishes of the future, are still the Euro-American Catholics. Therefore, even this well-intentioned effort at cultural diversity does not question the unspoken premise that Hispanic popular Catholicism must be left behind.

Latino Catholic responses to the Church's alternatives

The U.S. Latino responses to the alternatives offered by the Euro-American Church are creative attempts at religious and cultural survival. There is still, for example, the learned pattern of flight into the traditional religious universe. Some Hispanics (perhaps the majority among a certain age group, or even many recent immigrants) do choose to perpetuate the forms and vision of pre-Tridentine Catholicism. They are probably not aware of its having been the official religion centuries ago, nor are they familiar with the long history of the western Christianity that preceded the Reformation. For them this is their Catholicism, their way of being Christian, and that reason suffices.

But there are other responses to the official Church's alternatives. These alternatives have been, in different ways and to varying degrees, culturally optimizing paths for preserving traditional religion and its sustaining worldview vis-à-vis the always encroaching world of modernity and post-Tridentine Catholicism. These newer responses are compromises with a Euro-American reality perceived as (at best) overwhelming or (at worst) dangerously invasive.

I would argue that nonparochial lay movements and associations, such as the Cursillos de Cristiandad or even the more traditional *cofradías* have allowed for the formation of an alternative Hispanic Church within the broader community of Catholicism. This Latino Church has acted, for all practical purposes, as parallel parish and diocese, permitting a high degree of participation and leadership to Hispanics otherwise marginalized from the Euro-American controlled parishes and dioceses. Through the acceptance of varying degrees of institutional links to the hierarchy, Latinos managed to preserve a considerable degree of autonomy within the lay movements.

A close examination of the latter would show how deep, indeed, is the influence of the symbols and the worldview of popular Catholicism on the movements. Acts of public piety, for example, are consistently encouraged, praised, and performed. Some of the associations have been specifically established for the purpose of preserving traditional forms of devotion and communal prayer. Through this lay-led, parallel Catholicism, Hispanics have managed to preserve and reinterpret significant elements of their shared worldview, together with their emphasis on family and community. The movements have also served as important vehicles for the dissemination of many of the doctrinal contents of popular Catholicism, though sufficiently adapted (and concealed) in forms acceptable to the modern ecclesiastical realities. It is important to note also how emphatically Christianity is presented by these movements and associations as a *traditio*, thereby affirming the very traditional foundation of pre-Tridentine Catholicism.

The Euro-American Church's reaction to the Hispanic lay movements and associations has been frequently adverse, demanding that local (Euro-American) parishes and dioceses exercise control over the people's alterative Catholic spaces. Not perceived by most Latinos as the institution's sociological need to control, the Church's reactions have often been understood by the people as one more battle in the American clergy's continuing attempt to dismantle Hispanic religion. Of course, this religion could now only be the popularly interpreted pre-Tridentine version, since official Latino Catholicism either no longer exists in the United States or it has become an extension of the Euro-American, post-Tridentine Church's vision and interests.

Some developments within popular Catholicism

It is important to note that as Latino popular religion attempts to survive by (somewhat) adapting to post-Tridentine Roman Catholicism, it has begun to modify and reinterpret the doctrinal contents and symbols that have traditionally distinguished it. For example, the connection between the Virgin of Guadalupe and the Mary of Catholic devotion is (apparently) progressing. There is, too, a growing sense of social protagonism as part of the discerned will of God, thereby beginning the transformation of the mostly fatalistic past image of divine providence. Symbols of popular Catholicism have prominently appeared in and been associated with some important social and political movements among U.S. Hispanics.[80]

The most telling example of the contemporary reinterpretation of symbols and contents refers to the Bible. It seems highly inaccurate (indeed, arrogant) to think that western Christianity did not know the Bible before Trent and the Reformation. In the Iberian villages, where people did not usually know how to read and where medieval culture was still very much alive, the Bible's contents were presented graphically through art, autos sacramentales, story telling, and preaching. The same, as we saw, held true of pre-Tridentine colonial Christianity in the Americas. The Bible was known at the popular level, but through enacted or visual symbol and the spoken word, not through reading the printed page.

Currently, however, with the ever-increasing literacy rate, the direct reading of the text of the Bible has become widespread. There is no doubt that, after Vatican II, the official Roman Catholic insistence on biblical reading was heeded by Hispanics. The growing numbers of Latino Protestants have also been a strong influence.

Whatever the reasons for this scriptural awakening, there is no
question that the written text of the Bible has been taken out of the
hands (and potential control) of the ecclesiastical institution and
is now being interpreted by the people themselves. Interestingly,
this increase in familiarity with the sacred texts of Christians does
not seem to have decidedly contributed to the massive exodus
of Hispanic Catholics from the Roman Church. It seems, in fact,
to be strengthening the symbols and fundamental worldview of
popular Catholicism through another process of reinterpretation,
this time biblical.

Popular Catholicism, pentecostalism, and the Reformation

There is another common Hispanic response to the either/or alternatives offered to popular Catholicism. This is pentecostalism. I
have elsewhere argued that Latino pentecostalism has shown itself
as an important culturally acceptable vehicle for the preservation of
the pre-Tridentine (and premodern) religious worldview.[81] Though
obviously (and consciously) rejecting many medieval and colonial Catholic symbols and practices, pentecostalism has managed
to hold on to the very sacramental, symbolic ethos and worldview that made pre-Reformation Christianity possible. More importantly, it seems to view Christianity in the manner of *traditio*, so
essential to pre-Tridentine religion. Many symbols have been "reformed," some modern ones added, but the fundamental structures
and premises of the traditionally religious Hispanic worldview
have basically remained. I do not think that one can understand the
current popularity of the Catholic charismatic movement among
U.S. Latinos, or the ever-increasing number of Protestant pentecostal churches within the Hispanic religious universe, without
realizing the seemingly crucial role of cultural (and religious) preservation that the pentecostal movement (in its Catholic or Protestant versions) is playing.

It is well documented that the growth of the charismatic, pentecostal communities is in direct relation to people's perceived sense
of threat or invasion at the hands of modernity.[82] In these studies,
the Christian Churches (of any denomination) that appear allied
to the modern worldview and against the traditional religious and
communal relations, will suffer considerable numerical losses. It
is, therefore, highly ironic that the Roman Catholic Church, which
engaged in the ideological battles that followed the Reformation
on the side of tradition, should now be an uncritical bearer of the

Reformation's own theological premises vis-à-vis pre-Tridentine Hispanic Catholicism.

The contemporary confrontation of Hispanic popular Catholicism with the Euro-American Roman Catholic Church, I would argue, is the modern version of the sixteenth-century Reformation that Latino religion never had to face. This time, however, it is official Roman Catholicism that has taken the side of the Protestant reformers, arguing through similar logic and with surprisingly similar doctrinal assumptions. Unfortunately, popular pre-Tridentine Catholicism had earlier been robbed (by the consequences of annexation, prejudice, and poverty) of most theological and institutional means of defense and self-affirmation needed in this new Reformation.

Popular Catholicism among U.S. Latinos has a long history and is bearer of an old tradition. Its roots are planted in the medieval type of Christianity that preceded Trent and the Reformation, and in the Iberian Reconquista process that formed the Spanish character. However, it is not understandable without the sacral worldview and histories of the Amerindian, African, and mestizo peoples of Mesoamerica and the Antilles.

We have seen how this popular Christianity preserved the pre-Tridentine *traditio*, and how it has attempted to adapt itself to the realities of today's Euro-American Roman Catholic Church. Unfortunately, this Church has all too frequently been Hispanic popular Catholicism's worst foe.

I have tried to bring out the several strata of traditions, adaptation techniques, and historical moments of interpretation throughout the story of popular religion among U.S. Latino Catholics. The reader must realize by now that the full, complete history of this religious universe is extraordinarily complex and yet to be written. No easy formula of understanding can be applied to this religion of millions. Perhaps that is very good.

What does the future hold for Hispanic popular Catholicism in this country? No one knows for sure. There are some indications from the past, however, that would question prophecies of its early demise at the hands of modernity and its religious messengers.

Popular Christianity has been around for too many centuries. It has proved to be very resilient and adaptable, and it has all too frequently frustrated the modern penchant for perfectly logical explanations. The Right and the Left, Protestant and Roman Catholic, have all thought at one point or another (and perhaps still think) that popular religion can be educated or properly evangelized into oblivion. Historical results, after centuries of attempts, have shown how resilient and adaptable Latino popular Catholicism is indeed.

Perhaps there are two important starting points that can lead to an adequate interpretation of the people's religion and probably are the keys to discovering how to respectfully relate to and work with it. Namely, seriously to rethink the crucial distinction between *Tradition* and *traditions* made by Claude LeJay in 1546 and shared by the Reformation.[83] And to challenge the fears and ideologies that fan Euro-American cultural and ecclesiastical assumptions of what is truth.

Popular Catholicism is not an interesting vestige of the Christian past, or just a cultural symbol that can be instrumentalized for this or that agenda. It is a different way of relating to reality and of living the Christian gospel.

NOTES

1. Throughout this article I will explicitly refer to, name, and discuss numerous rites, symbols, and beliefs commonly identified with popular Catholicism among U.S. Latinos. A descriptive list of "examples" of popular Catholicism is not really necessary and can even be misleading. From the many references and discussions, it will become apparent that the symbolic and doctrinal repertoire of the people's religion is broad and varied. However, two important interpretive keys to keep in mind are the historical, developmental nature of this repertoire, and the fact that it is not mainly ritual. Even when some symbols, rites, or beliefs might be important for one generation, they might not be important (or at least not in the same manner and for the same reasons) for another generation. Nevertheless, the living fact of popular Catholicism and its crucial importance have remained constant throughout the centuries. It is my hope that this article will make this point perfectly clear.

2. In this paper the terms *Hispanic* and *Latino* will be used interchangeably. Both terms will only refer to United States populations of Latin American (or perhaps even Spanish) cultural roots. I will also use the term *Antilles* (and its adjective *Antillean*) in reference to the Spanish-speaking islands of the Caribbean. The latter term (*Caribbean*), more generic, is avoided here because it also refers to other linguistic areas.

3. It will become evident that, in this chapter, I assume Mesoamerica and the Antilles to be the cultural and historical roots of U.S.

Hispanics. This is certainly the case with the immense majority of all U.S. Latinos. There are other Hispanic communities in this country, however, that claim roots in other Latin American areas. Much of what will be said here, however, is probably applicable to these remaining populations too.

4. The expression and following insights are derived from Max Weber, with input from Renato Ortiz. See M. Weber, *Essays in Sociology* (Oxford: Oxford University Press, 1946); and R. Ortiz, *A consciência fragmentada: Ensaios de cultura popular e religião* (Rio de Janeiro: Ed. Paz e Terra, 1980).

5. See O. Espín, *Evangelización y religiones negras* (Rio de Janeiro: Ed. PUC, 1984), vol. 2.

6. See Espín, *Evangelización*, vol. 2, pp. 220–245; and A. Gramsci, *Os intelectuais e a organização da cultura* (Rio de Janeiro: Ed. Civilização Brasileira, 1979); P. Vrijhof and J. Waardenburg, eds., *Official and Popular Religion* (The Hague: Mouton, 1979).

7. See, for example, J. O'Callahan, *El cristianismo popular en el Egipto antiguo* (Madrid: Ed. Cristiandad, 1978).

8. For what follows, see, for example, Espín, *Evangelización*, esp. vols. 2 and 3; idem, "Religiosidad popular: Un aporte para su definición y hermenéutica," *Estudios Sociales* 58 (1984), pp. 41–57; L. Cabrera, *El Monte* (Miami: Ed. Universal, 1969); J. M. Murphy, *Santería: An African Religion in America* (Boston: Beacon Press, 1988); M. Cros Sandoval, *La religión afrocubana* (Madrid: Ed. Playor, 1975). Toward the end of this chapter I will mention pentecostalism and briefly discuss the possible relation between popular Catholicism and Hispanic Protestantism's own popular religion.

9. See Espín, "Irokó e Ará-Kolé: Comentário exegético a un mito iorubá-lucumí," *Perspectiva Teológica* 44 (1986), pp. 29–61.

10. See E. B. Idowu, *Olódùmaré: God in Yoruba Belief* (London: Longmans Green, 1963); and J. O. Lucas, *The Religion of the Yorubas* (Lagos: CMS, 1946).

11. See Espín, *Evangelización*, vol. 3, pp. 551–614; idem, "Ashé-Sê y lo fundamental en el Vodú," *Estudios Sociales* 59 (1985), pp. 17–30.

12. See J. J. Santiago, "The Spiritistic Doctrine of Allan Kardec: A Phenomenological Study" (doctoral dissertation, Rome, Gregorian University, 1983); and V. Crapanzano and V. Garrison, eds., *Case Studies in Spirit Possession* (New York: John Wiley and Sons, 1977).

13. I think I have shown the fundamental religious similarities among the main communities in my paper, "The Vanquished, Faithful Solidarity, and the Marian Symbol," in J. Coultas and B. Doherty, eds., *On Keeping Providence* (Terre Haute, Ind.: St. Mary of the Woods College Press, 1991), 84–101.

14. See R. S. Goizueta, "Rediscovering Praxis: The Significance of U.S. Hispanic Experience for Theological Method," in R. S. Goizueta, ed., *We are a People: Initiatives in Hispanic American Theology* (Minneapolis: Fortress Press, 1992), pp. 51–78; and O. Espín, "Grace and Humanness," in idem, pp. 133–164.

15. See a summary presentation of the more common approaches in my article, "Religiosidad popular."

16. See, for example, O. Espín, "The God of the Vanquished," in *Listening. Journal of Religion and Culture* 27, no. 1 (1992), pp. 70–83. An interesting volume not exclusively (but mainly) on religious iconography is O. Debroise, E. Sussman, and M. Teitelbaum, eds., *El corazón sangrante. The Bleeding Heart* (Seattle: University of Washington Press/Boston: Institute of Contemporary Art, 1991).

17. See the very suggestive and well-founded explanation for these assertions in G. Macy, *The Banquet's Wisdom* (Mahwah, N.J.: Paulist Press, 1992), 10–14. See also, L. Rothkrug, "Religious Practices and Collective Perceptions: Hidden Homologies in the Renaissance and Reformation," in *Historical Reflections/Réflexions Historiques* 7, no. 1 (1980), pp. 3–251; B. Hamilton, *Religion in the Medieval West* (London: Edward Arnold, 1986); K. Pennington and R. Somerville, eds., *Law, Church, and Society* (Philadelphia: University of Pennsylvania Press, 1977).

18. *Reconquista* is the usual historical term for the long period of Christian "reconquest" of the Iberian peninsula from the Muslims.

19. For what follows on medieval Iberian history, see, for example, L. P. Harvey, *Islamic Spain, 1250–1500* (Chicago: University of Chicago Press, 1990); R. García-Villoslada et al., *Historia de la Iglesia Católica: Edad Media* (Madrid: Biblioteca de Autores Cristianos, 1976), vol. 2; F. Martín Hernández, *La Iglesia en la historia* (Madrid: Atenas, 1984), vol. 2; J. C. Olin, *Catholic Reform: From Cardinal Ximenes to the Council of Trent, 1495–1563* (New York: Fordham University Press, 1990); A. Ballesteros Beretta, *Alfonso X el Sabio* (Barcelona: Ed. Laia, 1963); J. Boswell, *The Royal Treasure: Muslim Communities under the Crown of Aragon in the Fourteenth Century* (New Haven: Yale University Press, 1977); R. I. Burns, *The Crusader Kingdom of Valencia: Reconstruction on a Thirteenth-Century Frontier* (Cambridge: Harvard University Press, 1967); idem, *Moors and Crusaders in Mediterranean Spain: Collected Essays* (London: Longmans Green, 1978); idem, *The Worlds of Alfonso the Learned and James the Conqueror: Intellect and Force in the Middle Ages* (Princeton: Princeton University Press, 1985), J. N. Hillgarth, *The Spanish Kingdoms, 1250–1516* (Oxford: Oxford University Press, 1976–1978), 2 vols.

20. To the bibliography in the preceding note, add (for example) the following on medieval Iberian Christianity: J. M. Palomero Páramo, *La imaginería procesional sevillana: Misterios, nazarenos y cristos* (Seville: Publicaciones del Ayuntamiento, 1987); L. Melgar Reina and A. Marín Rújula, *Saetas, pregones y romances litúrgicos cordobeses* (Cordoba: Publicaciones del Monte de Piedad, 1987); A. Aroca Lara, *El Crucificado en la imaginería andaluza* (Cordoba: Publicaciones del Monte de Piedad, 1987); W. A. Christian, *Apparitions in Late Medieval and Renaissance Spain* (Princeton: Princeton University Press, 1981); idem, *Local Religion in Sixteenth-Century Spain* (Princeton: Princeton University Press, 1981).

21. For what follows on *traditio*, see O. Espín, "Tradition and Popular Religion: An Understanding of the *Sensus Fidelium*," in A. F. Deck, ed., *Frontiers of Hispanic Theology in the United States* (Maryknoll, N.Y.: Orbis Books, 1992), pp. 62–87, and the bibliography indicated there. See also my "Pentecostalism and Popular Catholicism: Preservers of Hispanic Catholic Tradition?" presidential address at the 1992 Colloquium of the Academy of Catholic Hispanic Theologians of the U.S., published in *ACHTUS Newsletter* 4 (1993).

22. *Autos sacramentales* were theatrical representations of biblical scenes or of Christian virtues that had to be taught to the people. Very frequently whole villages were involved in these religious plays. These dramatic representations were either complete theatrical creations (as in the case of plays on virtues and sins), or they were reenactments of the biblical stories (used as the basic script). In the latter case, however, adaptations and interpretations were frequent. Most of the peasant actors were illiterate, and so their use of the biblical texts depended heavily on memory and on fidelity to the transmitted gestures and words. This use of memory, however, may not be construed as necessarily leading to misunderstandings of the biblical text. On the contrary, the relative freedom of adaptation often allowed for very informed and correct understandings and applications of the Scriptures. The village clergy, usually not well educated (if educated at all), seems to have had little influence on the actual plays.

23. See the texts of the reports of one massive religious census in W. A. Smith, *Local Religion in Sixteenth-Century Spain*. This census, though held under Philip II, unquestionably reflects as well the local, village-type religion common during the fifteenth century.

24. See E. Vilanova, *Historia de la teología cristiana* (Barcelona: Ed. Herder, 1987–1992), 3 vols., esp. vol. 1, pp. 650–654, 856–943.

25. For what follows on LeJay, and on the theology of Trent and

the reformers, see the bibliography in note 20, above. And also, E. Vilanova, *Historia de la teología cristiana*, vol. 2, pp. 569–572; J. Delumeau, *Naissance et affirmation de la Reforme* (Paris: PUF, 1965); idem, *Le catholicisme entre Luther et Voltaire* (Paris: PUF, 1971); H. Jedin, *A History of the Council of Trent* (St. Louis: Herder Book Co., 1957), 2 vols.; J. Pelikan, *The Christian Tradition: Reformation of Church and Dogma, 1300–1700* (Chicago: University of Chicago Press, 1984).

26. On colonial evangelization and Church, see (from a vast bibliography), O. Espín, "Trinitarian Monotheism and the Birth of Popular Catholicism: The Case of Sixteenth-Century Mexico," *Missiology* 20, no. 2 (1992), pp. 177–204; L. Lopetegui and F. Zubillaga, *Historia de la Iglesia en la América española* (Madrid: Biblioteca de Autores Cristianos, 1965), 2 vols.; R. Ricard, *The Spiritual Conquest of Mexico* (Berkeley: University of California Press, 1966); E. Rull Fernández, *Autos sacramentales del Siglo de Oro* (Barcelona: Ed. Plaza y Janés, 1986); H. Goodpasture, ed., *Cross and Sword: An Eyewitness History of Christianity in Latin America* (Maryknoll, N.Y.: Orbis Books, 1989); R. De Roux, *Dos mundos enfrentados* (Bogota: CINEP, 1990); J. M. de Paiva, *Colonização e catequese* (São Paulo: Cortez Editoria, 1982); L. Rivera Pagán, *A Violent Evangelism: The Political and Religious Conquest of the Americas* (Louisville: Westminster/John Knox Press, 1992); J. F. Schwaller, *The Church and Clergy in Sixteenth-Century Mexico* (Albuquerque: University of New Mexico Press, 1987); E. Dussel, ed., *Materiales para una historia de la evangelización en América Latina* (Barcelona: Ed. Nova Terra/CEHILA, 1977).

27. This point of the inequality of the interlocutors is very well documented and explained by Luis Rivera Pagán in his *A Violent Evangelism*. This context of inequality as precondition for evangelization is of extraordinary importance, and it remains a concealed but operative reality in modern Euro-American (Catholic and Protestant) evangelizing attempts directed at U.S. Latinos.

28. One is reminded, of course, of Antonio de Montesinos, Bartolomé de Las Casas, and many others. See, for example, B. de Las Casas, *Brevísima relación de la destrucción de las Indias* (Mexico: Fondo de Cultura Económica, 1965); idem, *En defensa de los indios: Colección de documentos*, A. Larios, ed. (Seville: Editoriales Andaluzas Unidas, 1985); G. Gutiérrez, *Dios o el oro de las Indias* (Salamanca: Ed. Sígueme, 1989).

29. See, for example, J. M. Mira, *A evangelização do negro no período colonial* (São Paulo: Ed. Loyola, 1983); and also Espín, *Evangelización y religiones negras*, esp. vol. 3 and the extensive bibliography mentioned there.

30. The literature on the slave and/or native rebellions is very vast. As examples, see C. Esteban Deive, *Los guerrilleros negros* (Santo Domingo: Fundación García Arévalo, 1989); R. Price, *Sociedades cimarronas* (Mexico: Siglo XXI Editores, 1981); K. Gosner, *Soldiers of the Virgin: The Moral Economy of a Colonial Maya Rebellion* (Tucson: University of Arizona Press, 1992). Luis Rivera Pagán, in *A Violent Evangelism*, documents a number of native and slave rebellions during the early stages of the conquest. I must add that the very existence today of non-Christian religions from colonial days, as well as popular Catholicism itself, underlines the fact and degree of resistance of so many of the vanquished peoples.

31. See R. Ricard, *The Spiritual Conquest of Mexico*, pp. 83–95; J. García Icazbalceta, *Don Fray Juan de Zumárraga, primer obispo y arzobispo de México* (Mexico: n. ed., 1881), pp. 208–219. There are numerous references to native willingness to adopt Christianity in the writings of Bartolomé de Las Casas. See the collection of his writings, *En defensa de los indios*, and Antonio Larios's superb introductory essay.

32. For what follows on Amerindian and African peoples and religions, see (as examples from a very vast bibliography), I. Rouse, *The Tainos: Rise and Decline of the People Who Greeted Columbus* (New Haven: Yale University Press, 1992); J. Soustelle, *La vie quotidienne des aztéques à la veille de la conquête espagnole* (Paris: Ed. Hachette, 1955); M. León-Portilla, ed., *The Broken Spears: The Aztec Account of the Conquest of Mexico* (Boston: Beacon Press, 1962); idem, *Aztec Thought and Culture: A Study of the Ancient Nahuatl Mind* (Norman, Okla.: University of Oklahoma Press, 1963); L. Burkhart, *The Slippery Earth: Nahua-Christian Moral Dialogue in Sixteenth-Century Mexico* (Tucson: University of Arizona Press, 1989); A. Demarest and G. Conrad, *Ideology and Pre-Columbian Civilizations* (Santa Fe: School of American Research Press, 1992); R. Markman and P. Markman, *The Flayed God: The Mesoamerican Mythological Tradition* (San Francisco: Harper Collins, 1992); D. Carrasco, ed., *To Change Place: Aztec Ceremonial Landscapes* (Niwor, Colo.: University Press of Colorado, 1991); M. Moreno Fraginals, ed., *Africa en América Latina* (Mexico: Siglo XXI Editores, 1977); W. Bascom, *Sixteen Cowries: Yoruba Divination from Africa to the New World* (Bloomington: Indiana University Press, 1980).

33. See D. Carrasco, *To Change Place: Aztec Ceremonial Landscapes;* R. Ricard, *The Spiritual Conquest of Mexico*, pp. 176–193; L. Cabrera, *El Monte;* R. Markman and P. Markman, *The Flayed God*, pp. 29–62.

34. See R. Ricard, *The Spiritual Conquest of Mexico*, pp. 194–206; B. de Las Casas, "Apologética historia sumaria," in *En defensa de los indios*, pp. 63–98; J. García Icazbalceta, "Representaciones religiosas

de México en el siglo XVI," in J. García Icazbalceta, *Opúsculos varios* (Mexico: n. ed., 1896), vol. 2, pp. 307–368.

35. *Mestizaje* is the racial and/or culture mixing of Spanish and Amerindian. *Mulataje* is the mixing of Spanish and African. *Mestizo(-a)* or *mulato(-a)* is the person of mixed blood or culture. In this chapter I am using these terms mainly in their cultural connotations. I have chosen, for the sake of simplicity, to use *mestizaje* and *mestizo(-a)* only and include therein the people and processes of *mulataje*.

36. To understand the history of the implementation of Trent in the Spanish colonies, one must first understand the *patronato regio* (the royal "patronage," or almost complete control over the Church in the Americas). See E. Dussel, *Historia General de la Iglesia en América Latina* (Salamanca: Ed. Sígueme/CEHILA, 1983), vol. 1, pp. 241–251; A. de Egaña, *La teoría del Regio Vicariato español en Indias* (Rome: Pontificial Gregorian University, 1958); J. García Gutiérrez, *Apuntes para la historia del origen y desenvolvimiento del regio patronato indiano* (Mexico: Fondo de Cultura Económica, 1941). On Trent's implementation, see J. Villegas, *Aplicación del concilio de Trento en Hispanoamérica* (Montevideo: Ed. Lozada, 1975); E. Dussel, *Historia General de la Iglesia en América Latina*, vol. 1, pp. 372–396; P. de Leturia, *Perché la nascente Chiesa ispanoamericana non fu rappresentata a Trento* (Rome: Pontifical Gregorian University, 1959), pp. 495–509; idem, *Felipe II y el Pontificado en un momento culminante de la historia hispanoamericana* (Rome: Pontifical Gregorian University, 1960), pp. 59–100.

37. *Criollos* are the white descendants of the Spaniards, born in the colonies. The term can also be used in a broader sense to refer to cultural components typical of Latin America. In this chapter, however, the term refers to the descendants of the Spaniards as well as to those who are, in fact, their cultural and political (if not always racial) heirs. These often tend to be today's social elites.

38. Some bibliographical references in E. Dussel, *Historia general de la Iglesia en América Latina*, vol. 1, pp. 358–365. See also M. León-Portilla, ed., *The Broken Spears*; and L. Burkhart, *The Slippery Earth*.

39. Texts are collected in J. G. Durán, ed., *Monumenta Catechetica Hispanoamericana: Siglo XVI* (Buenos Aires: Universidad Católica Argentina, 1984). See also J. B. Glass, "A Census of Middle American Testerian Manuscripts," *Handbook of Middle American Indians* 14 (1975), pp. 281–296.

40. *Tlacuilos* were Aztec scribes.

41. O. Espín, "Trinitarian Monotheism and the Birth of Popular Catholicism: The Case of Sixteenth-Century Mexico," in *Missiology*, 20, no. 2 (1992), pp. 177–204.

42. See many of these in J. G. Durán, ed., *Monumenta Catechetica Hispanoamericana: Siglo XVI*. This series will eventually collect and publish colonial religious education texts from the sixteenth through the eighteenth centuries.

43. There are numerous examples of these other texts. For example, there are the (published) chronicles and collected writings of Bartolomé de Las Casas, Bernal Díaz del Castillo, Agustín Dávila Padilla, Toribio de Benavente (Motolinía), Bernardino de Sahagún, Ramón Pané, and many others.

44. See R. Ricard, *The Spiritual Conquest of Mexico*, pp. 176–206; O. Espín and S. García, "Lilies of the Field: A Hispanic Theology of Providence and Human Responsibility," *Proceedings of the Catholic Theological Society of America* 44 (1989), pp. 68–90; J. M. Kobayashi, *La educación como conquista. La empresa franciscana en México* (Mexico: El Colegio de México, 1974); S. Gudeman, "The *Manda* and the Mass," *Journal of Latin American Lore* 14, no. 1 (1988), pp. 17–32; F. Lizardo, *Danzas y bailes folklóricos dominicanos* (Santo Domingo: Fundación García Arévalo, 1974).

45. See, R. F. Dickey, *New Mexico Village Arts*, 3rd ed. (Albuquerque: University of New Mexico Press, 1990); E. Boyd, *Popular Arts of Spanish New Mexico* (Santa Fe: Museum of New Mexico Press, 1974); A. Cabrillo y Gariel, *Autógrafos de pintores coloniales* (Mexico: Universidad Nacional Autónoma de México, 1953); J. McAndrew, *The Open-Air Churches of Sixteenth-Century Mexico* (Cambridge: Harvard University Press, 1965); F. A. Schroeder, "Retablos mexicanos," *Artes de México* 106 (1968), pp. 11–28; E. W. Weismann, *Mexico in Sculpture, 1521–1821* (Cambridge: Harvard University Press, 1950).

46. See, J. Castellanos and I. Castellanos, *Cultura afrocubana*, 4 vols. (Miami: Ediciones Universal, 1988–1994); M. León-Portilla, ed. *The Broken Spears*; idem, "Testimonios nahuas sobre la conquista espiritual," *Estudios de Cultura Náhuatl* 11 (1974), pp. 11–36; L. Burkhart, *The Slippery Earth*; J. Klor de Alva, "Spiritual Warfare in Mexico" (doctoral dissertation, University of California at Santa Cruz, 1980).

47. Mexico (and hence, the present American Southwest) became independent from Spain in 1821, the same year of Florida's purchase. Cuba and Puerto Rico remained part of the diminished Spanish colonial empire until the Spanish-American War of 1898. That year both islands came under United States jurisdiction. Cuba became an independent republic in 1902, while Puerto Rico remains an American territory (technically an *associated state*).

48. The last five years of the fifteenth century saw the establishment of the first *ayuntamientos* in the Americas, strictly following the

Iberian model of local government. The organization of town and village life in the colonies was one of the earliest (and more urgent) political decisions of the Spanish crown. See, F. Moya Pons, *Historia colonial de Santo Domingo* (Santiago de los Caballeros: Publicaciones de la UCMM, 1976).

49. What follows on the popular hermeneutic of trinitarian doctrines is dependent on the research for my article, "Trinitarian Monotheism and the Birth of Popular Catholicism: The Case of Sixteenth-Century Mexico." The present chapter, however, further develops or specifies some items first discussed in that article.

50. Arianism and Docetism were heretical movements in Christian antiquity. Today they have become symbolic of two opposed points of view on Jesus of Nazareth—that he was only human (Arianism) or that he was only divine (Docetist). Historically, however, these two movements were not as doctrinally simplistic as might appear here. See R. C. Gregg, "Arianism," in *Westminister Dictionary of Christian Theology*, ed. A. Richardson and J. Bowden (Philadelphia: Westminister Press, 1983), pp. 40–41; and F. Young, "Docetism," ibid., p. 160.

51. O. Espín, "Trinitarian Monotheism and the Birth of Popular Catholicism: The Case of Sixteenth-Century Mexico."

52. In the article cited in the preceding note I argue these points based, mostly but not exclusively, on the evidence from the pictographic catechisms of the sixteenth century. One important example is the Testerian text called the *Libro de Oraciones*, currently in Mexico's National Museum of Anthropology (MNA 35–53), and published in limited edition by Zita Basich de Canessi (*Un catecismo del siglo XVI* [Mexico: Editorial Offset, 1963]).

53. See, for example, R. Markman and P. Markman, *The Flayed God: The Mythology of Mesoamerica*; P. F. Verger, *Orixás: Deuses iorubás na África e no Novo Mundo* (Rio de Janeiro: Corripio Editora, 1981).

54. See my article, "Vanquishment, Faithful Solidarity, and the Marian Symbol." For research that allows me to conclude that there was an interpretation of the Christian God through feminine forms of the divine in Mesoamerica, see M. León-Portilla, *Aztec Thought and Culture: A Study of the Ancient Nahuatl Mind*; A. M. Garibay, *Llave del Náhuatl. Colección de trozos clásicos, con gramática y vocabulario, para utilidad de los principiantes* (Mexico: n. ed., 1940); E. Hunt, The *Transformation of the Hummingbird: Cultural Roots of a Zinacatecan Mythical Poem* (Ithaca, N.Y.: Cornell University Press, 1977); J. I. Dávila Garibi, *Breve estudio etimológico acerca del vocablo "Guadalupe"* (Mexico: Emilio Pardo e Hijos, 1936); C. Siller Acuña, *Para comprender el mensaje de Guadalupe*, 2nd ed. (Buenos Aires: Ed. Guadalupe, 1989). This book includes the

complete text of the *Nican Mopohua*, the Nahuatl-language account of the Guadalupe story). I am indebted to Juan Alvarez Cuauhtemoc for some very suggestive interpretations of the Nahuatl tradition, and for some bibliographical indications. I do not necessarily agree with his christological conclusions.

55. A neologism meaning "right speech" or "right words." It also points to the social defense mechanisms implied by the need for "right speech."

56. *Tonantzin* is a Nahuatl word that means "our true mother." It was one of the names of the goddess Cihuacóatl, the consort of Quetzalcóatl (the "plumed serpent" god who in turn was the symbol of wisdom, creation, etc.). Tonantzin was immensely popular and revered before the Spanish conquest. One of her sanctuaries had been on the hill called Tepeyac, right outside Mexico City. Much of the external appearance and demeanor referred by the visionary Juan Diego to Guadalupe had clear roots in the appearance and demeanor of Tonantzin.

57. For example, see L. Boff, *O rosto materno de Deus. Ensaio interdisciplinar sobre o feminino e suas formas religiosas* (Petropolis, Brazil: Ed. Vozes, 1979).

58. See my articles, "God of the Vanquished" and "Trinitarian Monotheism and Birth of Popular Catholicism."

59. See J. Lafaye, *Quetzalcóatl and Guadalupe: The Formation of the Mexican National Consciousness, 1531–1813* (Chicago: University of Chicago Press, 1976); and O. Espín, "Irokó e Ará-Kolé: Comentário exegético a um mito iorubá-lucumí."

60. See the Acta and decrees of the many synods held in Spanish America during the colonial period. For example, J. García de Palacios, ed., *Sínodo de Santiago de Cuba de 1681* (Madrid/Salamanca: Instituto de Historia de la Teología, 1982); C. de Armellada, "Actas del concilio provincial de Santo Domingo (1622–23),"*Missionalia Hispanica* 27 (1970), pp. 129–252; J. A. Soria Vasco, "Concilios hispanos y latinoamericanos," in J. A. Soria Vasco, ed., *El concilio de Braga y la función de la legislación particular en la Iglesia* (Salamanca: Pontificia Universidad de Salamanca, 1975); J. T. Sawicki, ed., *Bibliographia synodorum particularium*, Monumenta Iuris Canonici, Series C, Subsidia, vol. 2 (Vatican City: Apostolic Library, 1967); and J. Gutiérrez Casillas, "Concilios provinciales mexicanos," in A. Alcalá Alvarado, ed., *Historia general de la Iglesia en América Latina, vol. 5: México* (Salamanca: Ed. Sígueme/CEHILA, 1984), pp. 61–64.

61. On late colonial reevangelization efforts, see (for example), J. de Martín Rivera, "La vida cotidiana en la cristiandad americana,"

in A. Alcalá Alvarado, ed., *Historia general de la Iglesia en América Latina*, pp. 95–164.

62. I suspect that this identification between the Virgin of Guadalupe and the Mary of Catholic devotion was never solidly established among the people (by now mostly mestizos). Even today one can see significant lacunae in this identification. The Church's attempts at making Guadalupe into the historical Mary of Nazareth in Aztec garb have, at best, touched those already involved with the ecclesiastical institutions, and few others beyond these circles. The same observation, I think, can be made in reference to the Cuban devotion to the Virgin of Charity. One should remember the mechanism of *ortholalia* before optimistically evaluating catechetical success at the popular level. Brazilian anthropologist Nina Rodrigues, describing the facts and results of the evangelization of African slaves and their descendants in Latin America, said that the Church deluded itself if it thought that these populations had ever been properly or even sufficiently evangelized (in *L'Animisme fétichiste des nègres de Bahia* [Salvador, Brazil: n.ed., 1900], 101).

63. On one side of the Church were the immense majority of Catholics, i.e., natives, African slaves, and mestizos. These still shared, substantially, in the religious worldview of the medieval *traditio*. Evidently, the mestizo population, by their very racial and culturally mixed reality, were the living link between the majority of Catholics and the dominant ecclesiastical (Spanish and criollo) elites. Mestizo Catholicism was, in itself, the result of "mixing," not in a simplistic syncretic sense, but in the same manner that the earlier Iberian Catholicism had been able to assimilate and integrate Roman, Visigothic, and Islamic elements within the Spaniards' experience of the Reconquista. Mestizos, within their experience of alienation and second-class status in colonial society, assimilated and integrated Spanish pre- and post-Tridentine Catholicism, thereby bringing forth doctrinal, ecclesiological, and sacramental reinterpretations not possible in earlier centuries. These reinterpretations made sense of Catholicism in a new way (not "modern" while not merely "traditional") and from within a new socio-historical context (different from the native and African ones, as well as from the Spanish and criollo milieux). The elites had begun, by the end of the colonial period, their march toward modernity and toward the worldview and cultural premises thereof. The nineteenth century would consolidate the *cultural* split within U.S. Hispanic (and Latin American) Catholicism—a "modern" minority that attempted to follow Trent (and, later, the First and Second Vatican Councils), and a majority that was still grounded in the worldview (and, consequently,

the practices) of pre-Tridentine Catholicism, safe in the still traditional, rural context. The twentieth century has begun to force the confrontation between *traditio* and elite Catholicisms.

64. For this section, see (for example), L. Medina Ascensio, "La Iglesia ante los nuevos estados," in A. Alcalá Alvarado, ed., *Historia General de la Iglesia en América Latina*, vol. 5, pp. 165–230; A. Alcalá Alvarado, "La reorganización de la Iglesia ante el estado liberal," in ibid., pp. 231–285; M. Figueroa Miranda, *Religión y política en la Cuba del siglo XIX* (Miami: Ed. Universal, 1975); M. Fernández Santelices, *Bibliografía del P. Félix Varela* (Miami: Saeta Ediciones, 1991); W. Moquin and C. Van Doren, *A Documentary History of the Mexican Americans* (New York: Praeger Publishers, 1971); M. Sandoval, ed. *Fronteras: A History of the Latin American Church in the U.S.A. since 1513* (San Antonio: MACC/CEHILA, 1983). Within this latter book, see especially the chapters on the nineteenth century by R. Santos ("The Age of Turmoil"), C. Tafolla ("The Church in Texas"), L. Hendren ("The Church in New York Mexico"), M. Sandoval and S. Alvarez ("The Church in California"). See also, L. Pitt, *The Decline of the Californios: A Social History of the Spanish-Speaking Californians, 1846–1890* (Berkeley: University of California Press, 1966); J. Castellanos and I. Castellanos, *Cultura Afro-Cubana*, vol. 3; and the pertinent sections in A. Morales Carrión, ed., *Puerto Rico: A Political and Cultural History* (New York: W. W. Norton, 1983).

65. For the development of popular Catholicism in the Antilles (especially during the nineteenth century), I have yet to find a better synthetic exposition than the one by J. Vidal in his "Popular Religion among the Hispanics in the General Area of the Archdiocese of Newark," in *Presencia Nueva*, Office of Research and Planning (Newark: Archdiocese of Newark, 1988, limited edition), pp. 235–352. Vidal includes an extensive bibliography.

66. See O. Espín, *Evangelización y religiones negras*, vol. 2, pp. 220–245, and the extensive bibliography cited there.

67. See J. Lafaye, *Quetzalcóatl and Guadalupe*; and M. Vizcaíno, ed., *La Virgen de la Caridad, patrona de Cuba* (Miami: SEPI, 1981).

68. Compare these two points of view, that could not be more different, concerning popular Catholicism among Cubans: M. Rodríquez Adet, "Cuba y la Virgen de la Caridad," in M. Vizcaíno, ed., *La Virgen de la Caridad*, pp. 40–44; and F. Castro, *Fidel y la religión. Conversaciones con Frei Betto* (Santo Domingo: Ed. Alfa y Omega, 1985). Instructive are: M. Fernández, *Religión y revolución en Cuba* (Miami: Saeta Editores, 1984); and R. Gómez Treto, *La Iglesia durante la construcción del socialismo en Cuba* (San José: Ediciones del DEI, 1989).

69. For Hispanic Catholicism in Florida, see M. V. Gannon, *The Cross in the Sand: The Early Catholic Church in Florida, 1513–1870,* 2nd. ed. (Gainesville, Fla.: University Presses of Florida, 1983); and M. J. McNally, *Catholicism in South Florida, 1868–1968* (Gainesville: University Presses of Florida, 1982). Both works include extensive bibliographies.

70. In northern Florida (in and around St. Augustine), the only identifiable group of Hispanic Catholics from the colonial period have usually called themselves *Minorcans* (from the Balearic island off the Mediterranean coast of the Iberian peninsula). They have assimilated into mainstream American life, with only a few noticeable vestiges of their origins remaining. It would not surprise me if their refusal to be identified as *Hispanics* came from fear of Protestant persecutions and prejudice, or from suspicion that they might not be patriotic Southerners. Northern Florida, after all, is part of the American South.

71. See the bibliographical reference in note 64, above. I think that J. Vidal's understanding of Antillean religious apathy (at worst) or growing disconnection from and disenchantment with the Church (at best), during the nineteenth century, is fundamentally correct and merits further study.

72. See M. Sandoval, ed., *Fronteras*; and L. Pitt, *The Decline of the Californios.* Other volumes in the present series include pertinent bibliography on popular Catholicism after the annexation. For Hispanic Catholicism in the Southwest during the nineteenth century, see the pertinent sections in: R. Alvarez, *Familia: Migration and Adaptation in Baja and Alta California, 1800–1975* (Berkeley: University of California Press, 1987); M. Barrera, *Race and Class in the Southwest: A Theory of Racial Inequality* (Notre Dame, Ind.: University of Notre Dame Press, 1979); L. J. Mosqueda, *Chicanos, Catholicism and Political Ideology* (Lanham, Md.: University Press of America, 1986); R. Acuna, *Occupied America: A History of Chicanos,* 2nd ed. (New York: Harper and Row, 1981); A. de León, *The Tejano Community, 1836–1900* (Albuquerque: University of New Mexico Press, 1982); A. Mirandé, *The Chicano Experience* (Notre Dame, Ind.: University of Notre Dame Press, 1985).

73. There are many *surviving* examples of this. One important case is the *Hermandad de Nuestro Padre Jesús Nazareno,* the famous Penitentes of New Mexico. See M. Weigle, *Brothers of Light, Brothers of Blood* (Albuquerque: University of New Mexico Press, 1976).

74. See P. Ribeiro de Oliveira, "Religião e dominação de classe: O caso da 'romanização,'" *Religião e Sociedade* 6 (1980), pp. 167–188.

75. See, for example, Pitt, *The Decline of the Californios,* pp. 55–61.

76. Although the home altars have older roots, their survival in the modern American Southwest seems to be due (at least in part) to the enforced transformation of public piety into private devotional expressions. See, for example, K. F. Turner, "Mexican-American Home Altars: Towards Their Interpretation," *Aztlan*, 13, nos. 1–2 (1982), pp. 318–360; T. J. Steele, *Santos and Saints: The Religious Folk Art of Hispanic New Mexico* (Santa Fe: Ancient City Press, 1982).

77. For this section, besides the vast literature from the social sciences on the impact of "modernity" on U.S. Latinos, see F. Bean and M. Tienda, *The Hispanic Population of the United States* (New York: Russell Sage Foundation, 1990); F. Schick, eds., *Statistical Handbook on U. S. Hispanics* (Phoenix: Oryx Press, 1991); and the pertinent sections in A. F. Deck, *The Second Wave: Hispanic Ministry and the Evangelization of Cultures* (Mahwah, N.J.: Paulist Press, 1989).

78. I have found Antonio Gramsci's social analysis, which takes popular Catholicism seriously into account, to be very useful when applied to U.S. Hispanic populations. The term *subaltern* is Gramscian. A good introduction to his thought on religion is H. Portelli, *Gramsci y la cuestión religiosa* (Barcelona: Ed. Laia, 1977). See also, O. Maduro, *Religión y conflicto social* (Mexico: Ediciones del CRT, 1977).

79. The Euro-American Church seems to have also assumed that incorporation into the American middle classes (and into the world of modernity and "progress," with all that these entail) will inevitably and automatically bring about the religious Euro-Americanization of Latinos. Middle-class status and overall success at joining the American economic and political mainstream can indeed play an important role in the possible religious Euro-Americanization of U.S. Latinos. However, the process of *religious* Euro-Americanization has limits today even among the successfully "mainstreamed" Latinos. There are at least three reasons for this. First, the Hispanic middle classes have begun to find ways to "negotiate" the culturally cognitive and symbolic means necessary to remain *religiously* Latino (in varying degrees of authenticity) while justifying their successful participation in American society. Second, there are sufficiently exposed doubts as to the merits of modernity and "progress," and the latter's consequences on cultures such as the Hispanic ones. And third, it is theologically and pastorally absurd for the Euro-American Church to be promoting modernity among Latinos as the preferred cultural setting for Catholicism, considering the profoundly secularizing philosophical premises of modernity and its terribly high historical and social costs.

80. For example, the *Vírgenes* of Hispanic popular Catholicism appear prominently in gatherings, publications, and even on neigh-

borhood walls, where cultural identity and pride are consciously emphasized. The United Farm Workers have proudly and frequently displayed images of the Virgin of Guadalupe and of the Virgin of San Juan de los Lagos. Cuban Americans have been emphasizing the Virgin of Charity as a unifying cultural (and political) symbol since the 1960s. Although most of the time for laudable causes and motives, I suspect that popular Catholicism is, nevertheless, being instrumentalized in most of these cases.

81. For this section, I refer the reader once more to my paper, "Pentecostalism and Popular Catholicism: Preservers of Hispanic Catholic Tradition?"

82. See, for example, F. C. Rolim, *Religião e classes populares* (Petropolis, Brazil: Ed. Vozes, 1980); B. Leers, *Catolicismo popular e mundo rural* (Petropolis, Brazil: Ed. Vozes, 1977); P. Ribeiro de Oliveira, ed., *Renovação carismática católica* (Petropolis, Brazil: Ed. Vozes, 1978). See also the very suggestive article by R. Finke and R. Stark, "How the Upstart Sects Won America: 1776–1850," *Journal for the Scientific Study of Religion* 28, no. 1 (1989), pp. 27–44.

83. See note 24, above.

10

The History of Hispanic Liturgy since 1965

Arturo J. Pérez

I don't know what made me do it. It could have been that I was feeling particularly good that morning and willing to take up a challenge. Maybe it was because saying good-bye to people at the end of Mass had become a little boring. Or maybe it was because I knew that *los viejitos* (the elders) always told the truth. The "new" liturgy was barely ten years old, and I was viciously curious about its impact on the parishioners. We had tried to implement the reform in this community and so, feeling good, or looking for a challenge, or just out of an act of trust, I asked the old woman, "¿Cómo le gusta la misa que celebramos cada domingo?" (How do you like our Sunday masses?) She responded respectfully, "Oh *Padrecito,* (translation follows) I like it very much. Now that everyone speaks Spanish I can understand all the words. I like the songs that we sing. I like to see your young face smiling at us, and the clothes that you wear, they are very beautiful. I like everything." Needless to say I was feeling affirmed, content at having done a good job, and yes, even smug, until she added after taking a long breath, "But there is one thing *Padrecito*. I cannot pray anymore. " The simplicity and starkness of her answer struck me to the heart. "Something is missing," I thought. She gently and reverently kissed my hand, crossed herself, and left me standing there. *Los viejitos* always tell the truth.[1]

Something is missing. The changes in the liturgy that occurred in the late 1960s came to pass without the interior spirit of the reform having been made more evident. Providing new liturgical experiences that were authentically reflective of people's faith and spirituality were hit and miss. In a particular way this was felt in the Hispanic community as trial and error sometimes confused reform with superficial adaptation. Sarapes on altars did not satisfy deeper yearnings. The *viejita* reveals the struggle to bring to the light of day a unity that was and is a constant strain (both in theme and tension) in the Hispanic community. This strain is mirrored in the history of Hispanic liturgy.

Chronicling Hispanic liturgy's development has not been an easy task for two reasons. First, we are living in an age concerned about the historically correct reconstruction of the past. It is common knowledge that facts and details are subjectively categorized if not personally selected for classification by the historian. This subjectivity is only enhanced when the history being remembered, in this case Hispanic liturgy (barely old enough to have a history) is curiously interwoven with the historian's own liturgical history. The duality of objective historical writing and subjective telling of the story is a strain in both senses of the word. Yet this strain is reminiscent and symbolic of Hispanic liturgy itself insofar as there is both an official tradition of prayer, the Roman rite, and a traditional way of prayer that is commonly called popular religiosity. The strain of bringing these two traditions together is centuries old. There are times when they seem opposed to one another, like two adversaries in mortal combat. The experience of five hundred years of evangelization and prayer, success and error, seem to be bringing the two rivals to face the fact that they are reflections of one another.

Secondly, I cannot help but admit that the echoes of this struggle are also present in this essay, with some issues passionately detailed while others are narrated in a more detached way. In researching this essay, it became apparent that there is a scarcity of public documentation on the subject of the history of Hispanic liturgy. Nonetheless, two major sources exist for this history. First, it can be found in published writings about liturgy from the Hispanic perspective, in people's personal notes, in the archives of the National Conference of Catholic Bishops' Committee on the Liturgy (BCL), in local diocesan liturgical offices, in the official acts of meetings of such groups as the Instituto de Liturgia Hispana (ILH) and the BCL subcommittee for Hispanic liturgy. Secondly, it is being developed and recorded within the memory of many individuals who have worked to foster, if not fight for, the reform of the liturgy within the Hispanic community. These people are living documents of all that has been accomplished. Only through their generous time and patience have I been able to document what has actually occurred. A more thorough and systematic documentation needs to be done so that this precious evolving history is not lost from the public record and so that the passion behind these events is simply narrated.

What is sought after is the relationship (worship) that a people have with God as it is expressed in their life of prayer (liturgy). When a person encounters God in and through a life event a conversion occurs, a decision is made, a response is given. "Worship expresses and mediates the divine-human relationship. . . . The possibility of worship implies both human subjects who desire relationship with God and a God who fulfills that desire."[2] Simply stated, we can say that liturgy is one of the ways a Christian people responds to God's initiative. It is an expression of their faith-filled lives. It is the format in which they deepen their relationship with God through public prayer. The official liturgy of the Roman rite refers to the Eucharist, sacraments, and the liturgy of the hours. (Implied with the hours is the principle of sanctifying time, and the liturgical year acts out the sanctification of time on a seasonal basis.) Popular religiosity refers to the prayers, devotions, symbols, gestures, and movements that also form what we can call a Hispanic liturgical tradition. How people pray reveals what people believe. In life the Hispanic community does not make categorizations or distinctions between official and popular. They both form a single category of prayer, a single garment of faith.

The theme of the liturgical reform is a struggle to weave together spirit and event, people and faith, principle and practice, life and worship into one unified experience. The reform of the liturgy was a reform in the very way that the Catholic Church in general and the Hispanic community in particular came face to face with God and one another. The liturgical reform is based on a reform of heart more than of rite. It is a call affirming the community in its gifts and talents, challenging its weaknesses and limits, discerning its spirit and direction. It is the way the community brings to life, remembers, and celebrates the paschal mystery of Christ, his life, death, and resurrection, in this God-given moment. This is the Christian struggle that gives meaning to life. It is what moves us to pray in whatever format or structure that meets our need. It is what motivates us to search for what is missing in our liturgy. I am grateful for the struggle that sheds light on the way that the Hispanic community has prayed since the promulgation of *Sacrosanctum Concilium*, the Constitution on the Sacred Liturgy (1963) which stated:

> The Church earnestly desires that all the faithful be led to that full, conscious, and active participation in liturgical celebrations called for by the very nature of the liturgy. Such participation by

the Christian people as a "chosen race, a royal priesthood, a holy nation, God's own people" (1 Pt 2:9; see 2:4-5) is their right and duty by reason of their baptism. (No. 14)

This "full, conscious, and active participation" is the norm and critique of the liturgical reform that Vatican II initiated. Like an underground stream that gives life to what is rooted above, an underlying theme throughout this essay is the history of inculturation of the liturgy from the Hispanic perspective. How the Roman rite has been articulated, appropriated, celebrated, sung, acted out in the life of the Hispanic faithful is our quest.

To give shape and form to this historical pursuit, I have structured this essay around the following themes: 1) the liturgical historical reality of popular religiosity; 2) the ecclesial documents that rooted Hispanic liturgy; 3) the weaving of Hispanic liturgy into official liturgical Church structures; 4) the development of liturgical ministerial life; 5) Hispanic liturgical music and music publishing; 6) the development of la danza as a Hispanic liturgical gesture; 7) the prophecy of social justice within Hispanic liturgy. A bibliography that lists publications on Hispanic liturgy since 1965 ends this quest and raises challenging questions for future study.

THE LITURGICAL HISTORICAL REALITY OF POPULAR RELIGIOSITY

It is interesting to note that after the Church's fourth century, liberation from persecution at the hands of the Emperor Constantine, the official Roman liturgy became severed from people lives. Devotions and popular religious practices began to be the ways the common folk worshiped while the intricate, formal rituals of prayer were left in the professional hands of the clergy and religious. This separation between official and popular would continue in the succeeding centuries. This should not be interpreted to mean that these two perspectives were always in opposition. Luis Maldonado holds that during the Middle Ages a general harmony and cross-fertilization between the official and the popular actually existed. The hierarchy even went so far as to guarantee and respect people's liberty to express their religious feelings through their devotions. This would change in the fourteenth century. Various heretical movements, Franciscan contentiousness, anticlericalism, and a rise in superstitious practices would ferment mutual suspicion and distrust. Eventually a separation, but not a complete divorce, of the popular from the official Church practices would take place.[3] Sixteenth-century Spanish *conquistadores* would bring not only the practices of an official Roman liturgy but also their own popular practices of faith. It is not possible here to detail the missionary process of evangelization and its liturgical consequences. Let us only pause for a moment to look at the attitude that was fostered in Mexico as an example of what was happening.

> It seems, nevertheless, that the main purpose of the missionaries was not to institute a new formalism, but to create an environment, in which to allow a new spirit to unfold. Before the arrival of the Spaniards, paganism had permeated the whole life of the Indians, birth to death, from the temple to the hearth, in war and peace. . . . The missionaries in Mexico transmitted to their Indians a whole Christianity, for Christianity really deserves its name only when it informs and penetrates, when it becomes all the life of a man, even in his slightest act and most fleeting thoughts.[4]

Some of the early Spanish missionaries were initially tolerant of the indigenous practices of worship they encountered, and they lived with the hope that eventually the people themselves would filter these experiences into one cohesive act with the liturgy of the Church. The foundation of Hispanic popular religiosity is based on this process of mixing official with indigenous prayer. From the beginning of the *mestizo* people, there have been these two experiences of prayer. It was through the official liturgy that the conquered people participated in the religious, cultic, and civil life of the Spanish kingdom. It was through the secretly practiced Indian and African indigenous acts of worship and devotion that the people remained free and continued to venerate the gods of their ancestors.

Many Church leaders, theologians, and liturgists have categorized the practices of popular religiosity as superstitious, magic, primitive, uninformed, and evil. Though secreted away from unbelieving eyes they ritualize the experience of God by the mestizo people. Within this volume, a more detailed account of popular religiosity is found (see Orlando Espín's essay). Suffice it to say that popular religiosity is the primary way the mestizo people of the Americas prayed, and still pray today. It is what fostered an identity for a new race of people. It made sense of a nonsensical, oppressive situation. With the light of the gospel illuminating its distortions and weaknesses, popular religiosity reveals a unique presence of God within our traditions.

Three points, like threads braided together, require our attention. We need to note the relationship between popular religiosity and: 1) the official liturgy of the Church; 2) the clergy; and 3) the liturgical movement.

Liturgy and popular religiosity

Ideally, liturgy, by definition, expresses in ritual the faith of the Church. Liturgy is how the Church acts out its identity with the life, death, and resurrection of Jesus through the Eucharist, the moments of passage that are celebrated in the seven sacraments, and in the sanctification of time through the liturgy of the hours and the liturgical year. Through these acts, the Church reveals its relationship with God through officially patterned feast days, texts, symbols, gestures, and music. The liturgy expresses outwardly what the Church inwardly believes. It can be said that the liturgy is the expression of the spiritual life of the Church. Its spirituality becomes transparent for all to see. Through liturgy, faith in Jesus is constantly recreated, regenerated, and revealed within the lives of the baptized.

Sixto J. Garcia and Orlando Espín offer a clarifying definition of popular religiosity.

> In general terms, popular religiosity can be defined as the set of experiences, beliefs and rituals which ecclesially and socially peripheral groups create and develop in their search for an access to God and salvation. Often popular religiosity is created as a response to socio-cultural contexts that make people perceive themselves as somehow distant from the "official" Church and society.[5]

Popular religiosity is the ritual expression of the spiritual life of the Hispanic people. It is an expression of how the Hispanic community belongs to the Church. In conjunction with official worship, the faith life of the community is nourished through these devotions. Within popular religiosity are contained the symbols and rituals that are accepted as the right/rite way of celebrating a birth, joining two persons in marriage, bringing our beloved dead to their final place of rest, as well as initiating young women into the community through the Quinceañera (fifteenth birthday) celebration, protecting our children from evil through blessings, and acting out our prayer through promises and processions. In many instances, these practices perform a sacramental function in the eyes of the Hispanic family. *La presentación del niño* (the presentation of a child in the church) for the Mexican community, *echar agua* (to pour water over a baby) for the Puerto Rican community, are good examples of popular rituals that occur prior to but are associated with baptism. Practices like these depict an attitude of faith that the Latin American Conference of Bishops' final document at Puebla, Mexico, called "popular Catholicism." Sacramentals link popular Catholic home practices with the liturgical Catholic actions of the institutional church. They are integrally connected with the Hispanic community's experience of prayer.

Clergy and popular religiosity.

For the Hispanic community, liturgy in the United States, Latin America, Mexico, and the Caribbean, going back to colonial times, has been guided by foreign clergy and religious. They are foreign not insofar as they themselves have immigrated from other countries to the United States (though this is often the case) but rather because they are non-Spanish speaking and non-Hispanic. There are few native Hispanic clergy in the United States. All clergy are formed and fashioned in prayer by their seminaries and institutions of formation. Their worship experiences are often based on monastic, contemplative patterns in which profound silence, great organization, and rehearsed ritual movement are the norm. Individual religious charisms play a particular role insofar as they mold a person spiritually. Clergy are brought up in not only a particular mindset but they are also shaped in a particular "heart-set". This is as it should be, since liturgy is more an expression of the heart than it is of the head. To their credit, with good will and generosity these clergy have learned to speak a new language, adapted themselves to a new culture, and opened their hearts to guide the prayer of the people they serve. On the spectrum of learning about the Hispanic people, they vary in their appreciation, feeling, and talent for integrating popular religiosity into their own spirituality and personal prayer. To the degree they are successful in this process, they are able to foster and promote Hispanic liturgy.

Popular religiosity is not dependent upon the clergy, foreign or native. The priest is needed for blessings, mainly of water, medals, and people that pertain to popular practices. There is no particular school of instruction, no ceremony of official acceptance and recognition, no assignment or placement for work. The leaders of this prayer learn from their firsthand experiences. They imitate, adapt, almost spontaneously ritualize what they have heard and seen. They are acknowledged by the people themselves as the ones who know what to do, what prayers/words to say, how to lead their people in the age-old traditions of faith. Some of these traditions, such as *limpias* (healings) may strain the liturgical relationship, yet they hold the seeds of faith so often mentioned in the ecclesial documents on liturgy and evangelization. What these leaders of prayer do is share the gifts they have been given. Some people abuse these traditions and some fraudulently take on this role, but they usually are easily identified since they tend to seek some power or economic gain for their "gifts."

The Liturgical movement and popular religiosity

"This present century has seen an extraordinary recovery and renewal by the Christian Church of its worship and the understanding of that worship as central to its life and work."[6] This recovery and renewal defines more the liturgical movement that was going on in Europe and in the United States rather than in other parts of the world. On the one hand, the reform was freeing the Church from a style and structure of liturgy that was rigid and static, while on the other, it was fostering an attitude of liturgy that was generating a new appreciation for diversity and creativity. The Church's liturgy, which led to the subsequent promulgation of the Constitution on the Sacred Liturgy, was the first point on Vatican II's agenda, primarily because the preliminary work had already been done and its focus was seen as pastorally oriented. The "full, active, and conscious participation" of the faithful in the liturgy was translated into the use of the vernacular, the development of ministries, and the promotion of cultural adaptation.

While very aware that all Hispanics are not immigrants, many who leave their native homelands, like other groups before them, are economically poor and have had limited education and even less liturgical formation and instruction. Liturgy used to be appreciated in terms of personal or communal activities and was celebrated in special ways throughout the liturgical year which instilled feelings for God, Mary, the saints, the dead, one another, and for home. The twentieth-century immigrant Hispanic crossed the border with timeless treasured religious traditions and popular practices of faith. As a Catholic people, they first sought out the church as a familiar place where they could again find peace and security. They sought to share these treasures with the new church. What they found was an intolerance not only for their traditions, symbols, and religious practices but also for their language, their culture, and essentially for themselves. In the same age that the official Church was liturgically freeing itself from four centuries of rigidity, the Church in the United States was imposing its practice of worship upon the Hispanic people. The liturgy conveyed a sense of Americanization for all ethnic groups. The American flag often prominently displayed in many sanctuaries gave a clear message for everyone who crossed the threshold of the church: Diversity was threatening. "Let them learn English!" seemed like a national slogan. Perhaps the clearest symbol of this time can be seen in the almost normative practice that relegated the Hispanic community to the Church basement, gym, or hall for Sunday worship. Popular religiosity, as always, maintained and nourished the faith of the community during this time. It never lost its initiative or original spirit of adaptation. It remained true to its nature to be a fluid, flexible living pattern of prayer. It was this pattern of prayer that would be nourished through Vatican II and in the succeeding meetings of the U.S. and Latin American bishops' conferences. Ideals and realities would mix and match, positively and negatively, yet development and growth would always occur.

ECCLESIAL DOCUMENTS THAT HAVE ROOTED HISPANIC LITURGY

The Constitution on the Sacred Liturgy was promulgated on December 4, 1963, by Pope Paul VI. Some dioceses in the United States had already set up the liturgical commissions that the constitution would promote (Sacrosanctum Concilium [SC], no. 44). These would develop in many places into full-time offices or departments of worship. Those responsible for liturgy were also to be found in chancery offices and in offices of catechetics or religious education. The latter had authority over the preparation and celebration of the sacraments of confession, first communion, and confirmation. To the extent that the constitution awakened a broader understanding of liturgy, catechetical programs would sometimes extend into the areas of baptism, the Easter triduum, liturgical music, and Sunday worship.

This Constitution provided the structure for worship, be it for eucharistic or sacramental liturgies or for the liturgy of the hours. In it are contained the general norms for the reform of the Roman rite:

The rites should be distinguished by noble simplicity; they should be short, clear, and unencumbered by useless repetitions; they should be within the people's powers of comprehension, and normally should not require much explanation. (SC, no. 34).

These norms not only provoked a change in the externals of rite and ritual but also instilled a sense of inner conversion, a change of heart of all who would gather to worship. As we have seen, the spirit of the reform would sometimes come into conflict with the reality of its implementation, and in recent times with its reinterpretation. This conflict would not diminish the emphasis or the importance of the ecclesial documents that followed.

The Roman rite is like a human skeleton that is recognizable as a unique individual only when it is embodied and comes to life within a particular culture and religious tradition. The reform held to this basic principle of inculturation when the constitution used phrases such as "the Church has no wish to impose a rigid uniformity. . . . [S]he respects and fosters the spiritual adornments and gifts of the various races and peoples. . . . Sometimes in fact she admits such things into the liturgy itself" (SC, no. 7); "the revision of liturgical books should allow for legitimate variations and adaptations to different groups" (SC, no. 38). The constitution would go on to state that popular practices needed to harmonize with the liturgy but not be uncritically accepted. (SC, no. 40).

Other Vatican II documents—The Pastoral Constitution on the Church in the Modern World, *Gaudium et Spes* (1964); the Decree on the Church's Missionary Activity, *Ad Gentes Divinitus* (1965); Pope Paul VI's *On Evangelization in the Modern World, Evangelii Nuntiandi* (1975); more currently Pope John Paul II's *The Evangelizing Work of the Apostles of the Slavs, Saints Cyril and Methodius, Slavorum Apostoli* (1985); and his *The Mission of the Redeemer, Redemptoris Missio* (1990)—further refine these principles when they foster respect for culture and diversity within the Church.

The magisterial documents of the Latin American bishops' conferences of Medellín (1968) and Puebla (1979) bring a new appreciation and awareness of the gifts that each culture inherently contains. The particular passages that refer to liturgy serve as guiding principles in the process of liturgical development for the Hispanic community of the United States. The most concise and important of these is found in the documents of Puebla:

> We must see to it that the liturgy and the common people's piety cross-fertilize each other . . . the religion of the people, with its symbolic and expressive richness, can provide the liturgy with creative dynamism. When examined with proper discernment, this dynamism can help to incarnate the universal prayer of the Church in our culture in a greater and better way. (No. 465)

The principles of "cross-fertilization" and "creative dynamism" are translated into the religious experience of the Hispanic community by those who seek to bridge the liturgical tradition of the Church and Hispanic traditions of popular religiosity. In the conclusions from the Second National Encuentro held in 1977, the bonds of faith and religiosity are seen as the Hispanic community's source of unity and enrichment of the universal Church: "With this authentic popular religiosity and these values we wish to contribute to the integral development and life of the Catholic Church in this country."[7]

In 1980, before the members of the National Conference of Catholic Bishops of the United States, Father Virgilio Elizondo stated:

> The Hispanic church has much to contribute to the entire community of believers on this point. The popular expressions of the people are concrete manifestations of the tradition of the Church as it has been interiorized in the hearts of the faithful by the Spirit and has become the most beloved treasure of the people.[8]

In the same address, he went on to emphasize more forcefully that "Today, our popular expressions of the faith should not be merely tolerated or even worse ridiculed. Rather, they should be joyously welcomed into the total life of the Church of the United States."[9]

The principles of cross-fertilization and creative dynamism between the official liturgy and popular religiosity continued to be reiterated in other documents of the National Conference of Catholic Bishops, namely, *The Hispanic Presence* (1983), *Prophetic Voices: Conclusions of the Tercer Encuentro* (1985), and *The National Pastoral Plan for Hispanic Ministry* (1987). These documents reveal an evolving awareness of the importance of diversity and affirm the gifts of the Hispanic community. Hispanic liturgy has developed from the principles of cross-fertilization and creative dynamism, diversity and affirmation. In these life-giving principles Hispanic liturgy is rooted, has flowered, and grows to harvest as an authentic shape, structure, and format of prayer within the official liturgy of the Church.

THE WEAVING OF HISPANIC LITURGY INTO OFFICIAL LITURGICAL CHURCH STRUCTURES

Nine years after the promulgation of the Constitution on the Sacred Liturgy, in 1972, the Mexican American Cultural Center

(MACC) was founded in San Antonio, Texas. Its mission and purpose were to respond to the pastoral needs of Spanish-speaking Catholics in the United States, particularly Mexican Americans. On April 7, 1974, the Bishops' Committee on the Liturgy (BCL) officially recognized MACC as one of its centers for liturgical research and study. Like other centers, MACC was to be concerned with the celebration of parish liturgy. Its unique goals were to study popular religious practices of Mexican Americans, to prepare programs of formation for those working in these communities, and to develop culturally sensitive catechetical and liturgical resource materials. Through workshops, study courses, the development of bilingual, bicultural rituals, and the production of a lectionary prepared for the Spanish speaking of the U.S. (this would be based on the lectionary approved for Spain), MACC hoped to further the adaptation of the Roman rite.[10] Father Juan Alfaro, a member of MACC's staff, began to publish in 1977 sets of homily notes (local priests had asked for Spanish resource material). This service gradually grew until 1982 when the notes were being written on a regular basis and achieved a national following with 220 personal and diocesan subscriptions. (This number may be deceiving since the notes are reduplicated on the local level). It serves not only as a homily resource but also as a biblical reflection for base community meetings and bible study groups.

Even though MACC was an official liturgical center, the BCL still did not feel the need to move too quickly. In 1980, the BCL responded to a petition from MACC's Father Ricardo Ramírez to make available bilingual rituals of the sacraments most commonly used within the Hispanic community: "it is not possible and was too soon to think about bilingual rituals."[11] MACC had already published *Bilingual Rites of Baptism and Marriage* in the mid-1970s. The BCL's attitude would later change with the official publication of an abridged version of *Pastoral Care for the Sick/Cuidado pastoral de los enfermos* (1986).

This was a time of creativity and experimentation. It was a Spirit moment within the Hispanic people. Though not officially approved, new eucharistic prayers were written that resonated with the cultural and religious reality of the Hispanic community. Pablo Sicilia asked the question "Why a Chicano liturgy?" as an introduction to a booklet containing new Chicano and Mexicano anaphoras (eucharistic prayers); some written by Manuel Martinez and Lonnie Reyes. Similarly Antonio Stevens-Arroyo and Hector Montes wrote Puerto Rican anaphoras. These helped to create an attitude that liturgy needed to reflect more faithfully the reality of Hispanic life.

Also in 1974, through its Hispanic subcommittee, headed by Bishop Rene Gracida, the BCL began to study the need for a Spanish-language lectionary. Unlike that of MACC, this one would be based on the *Biblia Latinoamericana*, the edition widely used in Latin America and that was gaining popularity in the United States. This lectionary later was published through the efforts of the Northeast Hispanic Pastoral Center of New York.

During these years there was a growing awareness on the part of other organizations that the Hispanic community needed to have official representation and recognition within the BCL. At the June 6–9, 1977, meeting of the board of directors of the Federation of Diocesan Liturgical Commissions (FDLC), two motions were passed that encouraged the Bishops' Committee on the Liturgy "to hire a competent liturgist to deal with Hispanic worship questions" and encouraged local bishops "to send for graduate studies in liturgy, competent personnel for work in the area of Hispanic worship."[12] Groups such as PADRES, a national organization of Mexican-American priests, would foster the need for making the liturgy more relevant to the Hispanic community. These ideas would continue to germinate for a number of years without any apparent success. Because of the scarcity of Hispanic priests, diocesan bishops jealously guarded their native clergy. When positions were available these priests would not be released for national service. It should also be noted that the current number of Hispanic persons in the United States who have a master's decree in theology with a specialization in liturgy number fewer than ten.

Another thread of Hispanic liturgy was woven into the official liturgical garments of the Church through the joint efforts of Father John Gallen, S.J. of the Center of Pastoral Liturgy of the University of Notre Dame, Indiana, and Pablo Sedillo of the Secretariat for Hispanic Affairs, Washington, D.C. Through their initiative a meeting was held at the Mexican American Cultural Center on January 17–20, 1979, in order to discuss the liturgical needs of the Hispanic community. The stated purpose for this gathering was to reflect upon cultural pluralism and its liturgical implications, the inculturation/adaptation of the liturgy especially among Hispanics, the role of popular piety in the liturgy, and liturgical celebrations within the struggle for liberation. It was at this meeting that the Instituto de Liturgia Hispana (ILH) was inaugurated. Its mission was to be "a national institute dedicated to study, develop, and promote the liturgical life of the Hispanic communities in the United States. It seeks the inculturation of liturgical celebrations in order to help the meaningful and complete participation of the total assembly."[13] Its first elected president was Father Robert Torres of Little Rock, Arkansas, who appointed a national board of directors representative of the Spanish-speaking community of the United States. The institute would later elect Father Arturo Pérez (Chicago) to succeed him. He would be followed by Father Juan Sosa (Miami) and then by Sister Rosa María Icaza, C.C.V.I. (San Antonio).

In the succeeding meetings the institute's mission was further defined. It sought to serve as the official liturgical advisor to the National Conference of Catholic Bishops. Through investigative study of popular religiosity, the formation of liturgical ministries in the Hispanic community, and the creation of new materials, the ILH set its future agenda. It demonstrated its liturgical competence as it participated in the BCL's 1981 national study on liturgy, *The Mystery of Faith*, by translating it into Spanish, conducting workshops, promoting the study in the Hispanic community, and later reformulating it into a liturgical catechetical instrument entitled *Tomen y coman*. In this same year the president of the institute was made ex officio advisor to the Bishops' Committee on the Liturgy and a member of the board of the National Advisory Committee (NAC) for the Secretariat of Hispanic Affairs; a year later the institute would establish an official relationship with the National Federation of Diocesan Liturgical Commissions. All this helped set a pattern of cooperation in which the ILH has ably assisted the BCL and others in the preparation of the Spanish translation of official texts, such as the *La música en culto católico* (*Music in Catholic Worship/Liturgical Music Today*, 1984), *La ambientación y el arte en el culto católico* (*Environment and Art in Catholic Worship*, 1986), and the 1991 publication of the *Rito de la iniciación cristiana de adultos* (*Rite of Christian Initiation of Adults*). Currently its members are assisting the BCL with the translation of the *Order of Christian Funerals*, a bilingual edition of *Sunday Celebrations in the Absence of a Priest*, *The Book of Blessings for the United States*, and the Spanish version of the book of *Catholic Household Blessings and Prayers*.

Under the institute's patronage the First National Hispanic Liturgical Conference was held in 1983 in New York, with an overflow crowd. Since then it has held four other national conferences and annual membership meetings. The ILH has also been the officially appointed group to prepare the liturgical celebrations at national Hispanic meetings like the Third National Encuentro in 1985 and the National Hispanic Ministry Conference, "Raices y Alas" in 1992. Throughout these years the institute has also published its own works, *Criteria for the Liturgical Celebrations in Hispanic Communities, Morning Prayer,* and *Religiosidad popular: Las imágenes de Jesu-cristo y la Virgin María en América Latina.*

The BCL established in May, 1982, a standing subcommittee for Hispanic liturgy comprises mainly institute members. Through the work of this subcommittee the U.S. bishops would petition Rome to consider Spanish as a liturgical language proper to the United States in 1984. Great satisfaction would be felt by the members of the Hispanic liturgy subcommittee in January of 1985 when Rome confirmed Spanish as a liturgical language in the United States. This action gave the National Conference of Catholic Bishops authority over its own liturgical Spanish texts and freed it from the use of the confusing array of liturgical books produced by other Spanish-speaking national bishops' conferences. From this base two significant accomplishments would be made: the development of a *sacramentary* (the book of prayers used by the priest at the Eucharist) adapted for the U.S. Hispanic community and the official Roman recognition of the United States as a Spanish-speaking country.

From the very start, the subcommittee on Hispanic liturgy was aware of the different Spanish translations in use. Unlike the English-speaking bishops' conferences which did all their work through the International Committee on English in the Liturgy, the Spanish-speaking countries were not unified. Spain, Mexico, and Colombia published the most commonly used Spanish texts. After an investigation by this subcommittee, the Mexican *Misal Romano* was chosen as the base for a new Hispanic sacramentary. Adaptations were made regarding the translations of text for uniquely United States feasts such as Thanksgiving and the Fourth of July. Other changes included the particular calendar for celebrations in the United States, and the use of *ustedes* instead of *vosotros* as is found in all other translations. (*Ustedes* is the commonly used pronoun for "you" plural form used in Mexico, the Caribbean, and most Central and Latin American countries while *vosotros* is the form used in Spanish spoken in Spain. *Vosotros* would be considered foreign to most U.S. Hispanics.) The required request for confirmation of the sacramentary project by the Congregation for Divine Worship and the Discipline of the Sacraments was made in 1989 and granted on March 12, 1990. Unfortunately, the particular question of the use of *ustedes* has proved to be a stumbling block; final approval is still pending.

Since 1984, Rome itself had been looking at the question of the diversity of Spanish translations that were commonly available. It wanted a unified translation similar to other language groups such as English, French, and German. A meeting was held in the Vatican in February of 1986. Representatives of Spanish-speaking episcopal conferences and their liturgy offices were present. The United States sent Bishop Ricardo Ramírez, then the chair of the subcommittee on Hispanic Liturgy and Father John Gurrieri, executive director of the secretariat of the Bishops' Committee on the Liturgy, as official observers. During this gathering, when votes for approval on a *texto único* (the first common Spanish text of the Eucharistic prayers, Our Father, Gloria, Creed, and other responses) were being recorded, the representative from Chile asked why the United States was not voting. The answer that was given revealed that the United States was present as an observer. The Chilean delegate noted that there existed more Spanish-speaking persons in the U.S. than in some of the countries present at this meeting. Cardinal Mayer, chair of this session, said it was up to the delegates if they wanted to change the status of the U.S. representative from observer to full voting membership. Affirmation was quickly given, and the United States was thereafter recognized as a Spanish-speaking county.[14]

The use of the *texto único* began on the first Sunday of Advent, December 3, 1989. Its use also initiated an innovative distinction from the English sacramentary. The new text would not just bind the Hispanic community of the United States liturgically to the rest of the Spanish-speaking countries of the world, but it would also include the four more pastorally oriented "Swiss Synod" eucharistic prayers. This would provide greater variety from the nine anaphoras (Eucharistic prayers I-IV, two Eucharistic prayers of reconciliation, three eucharistic prayers with children) of the English sacramentary.

The subcommittee on Hispanic liturgy was also responsible for the celebration of Our Lady of Guadalupe being raised from memorial to feast day rank throughout the United States in 1988. This in effect would make Guadalupe an obligatory celebration in all churches throughout the country.

Mario Paredes, Guillermo Ramagosa, Ken Smith, and the Northeast Catholic Pastoral Center for Hispanics (New York), as mentioned earlier, took a leadership role in liturgy. It was their determination to publish a lectionary appropriate for use by the Hispanic community. This was no simple task. Spanish-language materials were not easily marketable. Many publishers were hesitant if not completely unwilling to enter into this arena unless they were assured of economic success. The lectionary is a specialized book for worship. It contains the prescribed readings of Scripture for any given eucharistic liturgy. The production of a new translation would be a complicated and costly venture. Only through the financial help of grants, especially from the Pallotines of the Immaculate Conception Province, and advance purchase orders was the first *Leccionario Hispanoamerico* for Sundays and solemnities produced in 1982. Five years later a second volume for ferial days (weekdays) would become available. When the sanctoral and ritual Mass volume (readings for the saints' feast days and Masses for the sacraments and other occasions) is published, the complete *lectionary* will be a significant contribution in the development of liturgy for the Hispanic community.

Another thread in the weaving of Hispanic liturgy into official liturgical Church structures is identified with the attitude toward the speaking of Spanish during worship. In the melting-pot framework of mind, the use of any language in the United States other than English was perceived in some ways as being un-American. Learning the language of this new land was a high priority for any recent arrival. Yet for a time the Church, through its system of national parishes, maintained not only the language but also the ethnic customs and traditions of new immigrants. Chicago, like other big cities, had as many as eight different ethnic parishes within blocks of each other. In many Polish communities, Saturday language classes helped preserve the ways of the old country; though this system gradually fell into disuse, vestiges of it still exist in some places.

The Hispanic community, diverse even in the way Spanish is spoken, has maintained its language.

> Not only does the Spanish language enable Hispanics to understand each other across the barriers of nationality and regional peculiarities; it is also the incarnation and symbol of their whole culture and values to a much greater degree than English is to the English-speaking peoples, so that the fact that they share a common language makes them feel, at a very deep level, that they are one people—especially when dispersed among people who do not speak that language or share those values.[15]

Through language, identity, culture, and religious practices, values are not only preserved but also are handed down to succeeding generations. Having linguistically competent Spanish-speaking priests was a pastoral need for the Hispanic community.

An important decision was made in the 1950s by Cardinal Spellman in New York, where the growth of the Puerto Rican community was a major concern. The hope that they would eventually learn English led to the abandonment of national parishes for the Puerto Rican community and the endorsement of integrating them into English-language parishes. In 1956 Spellman decided to send one-half of the ordination class for summer studies in a total Spanish-language immersion program. The following year the class was held in Puerto Rico itself, thus enabling the newly ordained a more complete cultural experience. It may have been seen to be a temporary pastoral plan, since integration would eventually dictate its discontinuation. This was certainly not the case in other parts of the United States where seminary practice sometimes stumbled over parish policy.

In the Southwest the parochial situation was erratic since some pastors maintained "local rule" mandating prohibitions against speaking Spanish. In the 1950s, Virgilio Elizondo recalls, Archbishop Lucey of San Antonio requiring his seminarians to learn Spanish. Yet in San Antonio, there was not universal acceptance. In the mid 1960s, Father (later Bishop) Patricio Flores said, "When I was ordained, I was sent to a parish where I was asked not to use Spanish to communicate with people who did not understand English."[16]

In the late 1970s many seminaries would have an official requirement to the effect that seminarians needed to speak Spanish in order to minister adequately. In practice the requirement was largely ignored. Often bishops would not support their seminary faculties, and would ordain to the priesthood candidates who had not satisfactorily learned Spanish or another pastoral language. Los Angeles' St. John's Seminary in Camarillo could serve as an example of this. With the appointment of Archbishop Mahoney in the mid-1980s St. John's language requirement began to be enforced. This coincided with a national change of attitude. Minimum Spanish-language requirements for priesthood ordination would be generally instituted and supported in dioceses with large Spanish-speaking populations. Practice and policy would meet when hierarchy, faculty, and student body united in accepting the Spanish language as a pastoral need of the Hispanic

community. Though many seminaries are making attempts to provide culturally sensitive formation programs, St. Vincent de Paul
Seminary (Boynton Beach, Florida) and St. John Vianney College
Seminary (Miami, Florida) are presently the only bilingual, bicultural seminaries in the United States. The students' language
requirements are also requirements for the faculty.

As evidenced in these events this was a Spirit-filled time.
MACC's designation as a center for liturgical research in 1974 was
a starting point. Spanish becoming an official liturgical language
for the United States was a breakthrough. New texts reflecting the
reality of Hispanic life, the affirmation of Hispanic traditions of
prayer as authentic sources of spirituality, and liturgical organizations accepting Hispanic persons as advisors and consultants
on policy making communities moved Hispanic liturgy more into
the mainstream of Church life. A new liturgical institute formed
to foster and promote Hispanic liturgy solidified the movement.
Through the strain and struggle a new liturgical garment for the
Church was being woven. It would be worn by those who served
the community as liturgical ministers.

THE DEVELOPMENT OF LITURGICAL MINISTERIAL LIFE

Liturgical ministry has developed in the Hispanic community
for the following reasons. The first is found in the Constitution on
the Sacred Liturgy: "In liturgical celebrations each one, minister or
layperson, who has an office to perform, should do all of, but
only, those parts which pertain to that office by the nature of
the rite and the principles of liturgy"(no. 28). "Servers, lectors,
commentators, and members of the choir also exercise a genuine
liturgical function. They ought to discharge their office, therefore,
with the sincere devotion and decorum demanded by so exalted
a ministry and rightly expected of them by God's people" (no.
29). No longer was the liturgy seen to be a "one person show." It
was everyone's baptismal right to celebrate liturgy. Through the
particular ministries that the constitution enumerated and others
that would be later recognized, such as extraordinary ministers
of the Eucharist, ministers to the sick, ministers of hospitality,
liturgy became again a work of the people. The community took
ownership of their prayer. This was the general principle for the
entire Church.

Secondly, the use of the vernacular, the language of the people, for liturgy and the lack of native clergy presented a very particular liturgical opportunity. The priest-celebrant or the leader of prayer was usually not a native Spanish speaker. (Even today, the number of Hispanic priests who speak Spanish is still disproportionately small compared to the number of Hispanic Catholics.) Many people had been taking on emerging leadership roles within the community through their participation in such activities as Spanish Marriage Encounters, Cursillos, the charismatic renewal, Jovenes Obreros Cristianos (JOC, Young Christian Workers), Acción Católica (Catholic Action), and, more recently, through the *comunidades de base* (base communities). People were invited to come forward and lead their community in these new roles. Persons of simple educational backgrounds, people with skills-training and formal instruction, all began to stand in front of their peers. Factory workers, busboys, restaurant cooks, housewives, office managers, secretaries, and mechanics now proclaimed the Scripture, distributed communion, visited the sick, directed choirs, welcomed their neighbors, prepared the liturgy for the people of their parish, and led Scripture reflection groups. Sunday took on a definite native Hispanic presence as Spanish filled the Church in word, song, and in the faces of those who ministered. The reinstitution of the permanent diaconate moved this Hispanic presence into the circle of ordained ministry where native Spanish-speaking men could now be authorized to preach, baptize, marry, and preside at funerals. In many cases the permanent diaconate in the Spanish-speaking community became a team approach insofar as the deacons' wives stand alongside their husbands throughout their training and ministry. With the advent of priestless communities, laypersons presiding at Sunday communion services in the absence of a priest heightened the need for lay leaders.

The third factor in the development of liturgical leadership was again influenced by popular religiosity. Popular religious practices are not dependent upon the clergy. There are recognized people, through traditions and custom, who have learned the right/rite way of praying for the needs of the community. One example of these presiders are the *rezadores/rezadoras*. These are women and men, often the elderly, who know by heart the special prayers that accompany life's events, for example a patronal feast novena, the novenario (the novena following the death of a person), or the prayers for the sick when they are visited in their homes. Though not a hard-and-fast rule, it can be said also that the leadership of prayer life in the Hispanic community has traditionally been a feminine role. The main practitioners and promoters of popular religiosity are women. The first ways and words of prayer are taught by the *abuelas* (grandmothers), mothers, women religious, and catechists. It is from them that the *feeling* of prayer, the holy, the love of God, Mary, and the saints is transmitted. It has been women who lead their children to Mass and convey the meaning of Church as a special place of prayer, a home for God and for us, their little ones. The popular religious customs of men are more limited to activities such as memberships in *cofradías* (brotherhoods or confraternities) such as the Penitentes (penitents) of New Mexico, the Adoración Nocturna del Santísimo (All Night Adoration of the Blessed Sacrament), the Caballeros de San Juan (Knights of St. John the Baptist), the making of *promesas* (promises), the carrying of *andas* (portable shrines carried through the neighborhood) on special feast days, the lighting of candles, and asking for blessings. In their religious practices, men functioned in background/support roles rather than as clearly visible leaders of prayer.

Popular religious roles began to evolve into liturgical ministries. This was not a simple process for women or men. Though women were the primary transmitters of prayer in many circumstances, their active participation in the Church stopped at the altar rail. The first women lectors and extraordinary ministers of communion were truly valiant women. Men who became active by taking on liturgical roles for Sunday prayer seemed, at first, to be out of step with their peers. Again, it must be stated that the impact of the Cursillos, Spanish Marriage Encounters, the charismatic renewal, JOC, Acción Católica, and the base communities were prime factors in preparing men and women to participate more consciously in the life of their parish. There was a mutual, reciprocal, and positive effect by which the parish benefited. One of the areas of lay leadership was the liturgy. With training, preparation, and education, visits to the sick many times included the bringing of the Eucharist; novenas would incorporate Scripture and thoughtful reflections on its meanings; deacons and their wives would more frequently guide the preparation programs for baptism and marriage and celebrate these sacraments with the community; occasionally *rezadores/rezadoras* would kneel next to the priest at special feasts, praying the traditional prayers; and more often liturgical ministers would sit on parish councils, helping to direct the operation of the local church.

Fourthly, throughout these years liturgical ministries were being promoted through programs and courses that often led to granting certificates of *capacitación* (competency). The Mexican American Cultural Center (San Antonio), Northeast Hispanic Catholic Center (New York), Mundelein College's Hispanic Institute (Chicago) which is now part of Loyola University, the Southeast Pastoral Institute (Miami), the Instituto de Liturgia Hispana, and local diocesan worship offices are examples of institutions that enhanced liturgical leadership at the grassroots level. They provided the research and resources that would foster greater appreciation for liturgy. Liturgy became Hispanic when Hispanics took ownership of liturgy.

The issue of certificates was a two-edged sword. Programs and courses were only cursory introductions into specific fields of theology or liturgy. The certificates brought a sense of professionalism to the lay ministers. In some cases, these local parish people were now hired for full-time positions and given the responsibility of training and forming new ministers. In extreme cases, this meant taking on the trappings of professionalism, namely, titles, secretaries, office appointments, and business cards. The community seemed to be distanced from the grassroots staff members who were to be represented by them. Yet in the bureaucracy of the Church today, persons without title, salary, and office are volunteers and therefore are often not seen, valued, and appreciated for what they offer. For this reason they are not in decision-making roles. Instead of being bridges between parish personnel and parishioners, lay ministers in general, and lay liturgical ministers in particular, were put in a position of choosing one side over the other for their ministerial identity. This created a tension for the minister and opened her/him up to frustration. The struggle to take on an official role strained many relationships. Yet through these moments liturgical ministerial life took on the rhythm of Hispanic life. This can be seen especially in the creation of music appropriate for public prayer.

HISPANIC LITURGICAL MUSIC AND MUSIC PUBLISHING

The Music

Nothing so defines a people as its music. The sounds of diversity of the Hispanic community are easily heard. The differences of rhythm, melodies, and style reveals us to ourselves and to one another. The movements, steps, and gestures that accompany this music are also appropriate to each group. Yet even here, as in all areas of our mestizaje, there are common roots. Sacred music existed for all indigenous people of the Americas. Though the use of musical instruments varied, percussion, especially drums, and wind instruments were found among all peoples. Sung texts expressed not only the petitionary prayer of the people but also their relationship, their understanding, and their place before the gods of their time. Without venturing further, let it suffice to say that the mixing of the sacred music of the Spaniards and of the peoples they encountered did not end at the time of the conquest but has continued to our present day. This is seen in the way music written by composers from Spain has constantly been used by the Hispanic community. Three notable examples of this music today would be *Pescador de hombres*, by Cesáreo Gabaraín, Juan A. Espinosa's *Santa María del camino*, and *Un pueblo que camina*, by Emilio Vicente Mateu.

As with most Hispanic ethnic groups there existed before 1965 a musical treasury of vernacular religious and devotional hymns that were popularly known. Some hymns, though in Latin, were part of the wealth of sung prayers that were used with regularity. It could be said that most "Hispanic" music at this time did not identify any individual group. Popular rhythms and texts were not introduced into Hispanic liturgy until after Vatican II. The first attempts at developing music for the Hispanic community centered more in translating into Spanish hymns from other cultures and languages. United States and European religious music was soon being sung at Spanish Masses. In some cases, popular melodies of the day were rewritten with religious texts. In this way, the music of "Red River Valley" (appears in some areas under the title, "Junto a ti" and "Una tarde en caná"), "Michael Row Your Boat Ashore" (sometimes called "El Señor resucitó" and "Caridad y comprensión"), and "O Clementine" ("Viva Cristo Rey" appears based on this) can still be heard at Eucharist in some parishes. But I want to focus on the more positive creative efforts that were made and advanced authentic Hispanic liturgical music.

One of the most positive efforts made would be the development of Spanish *coros* (choirs). The choirs' diversity in style and make-up would be reflective of the Hispanic community. Running the risk of overgeneralization, a typical Spanish choir would be made up of guitars, percussion, and other instruments more proper to the different Hispanic ethnic groups. Examples of these instruments would be the *guitarrón* (bass guitar) of Mexico, the *cuatro* of Puerto Rico, the *flautas* (flutes) of the Andean countries, and the *tambora* (a particular kind of drum) of the Dominican Republic. Each choir would have its own history of success and failure, advancement and breakdown. The Spanish choir is a major source of spirit and life for the Hispanic community.

The Rondalla of St. Joseph's Parish of Saginaw, Michigan, serves as a good example of the Spanish choir's development and importance. Soon after Vatican II ended, Father William Frigo, O.F.M. Cap., asked for volunteers to help with the music at the Spanish Mass. Jaime Fulgencio raised his hand to help, though he could not read music but played guitar by ear. He persuaded his brother, Jorge, who played guitar in a local cantina and another friend, Salvador Gomez to join him. St. Joseph's music program then began to take shape. The group played music typical of Mexico and Texas. The changes in the Church did not seem as difficult as the challenges of living within an Anglo context and atmosphere. The Rondalla, typically a group of strolling musicians, was formed about 1970. Instead of being roving troubadours, this Rondalla would serve the liturgical assembly with their music. They extended beyond the sanctuary of the church by singing serenades at funerals, at homes for the aged, and at prisons. Eventually the Rondalla made three recordings of their music in 1977, 1978, and 1983. They have been instrumental in promoting their parish Guadalupe celebrations, in establishing *danza* groups, and in continuing to inspire and animate the Sunday liturgy at St. Joseph's.

Choirs played and sang music reflective of their particular ethnic origin. Our attention is drawn to the development of four musical styles: the New Mexican, Mexican American, the Puerto Rican, and the Cuban. Afterwards, a survey of the efforts that the major religious music publishing companies have made in fostering Hispanic music needs to be woven into the cloth that makes up Hispanic liturgy.

New-Mexican music

The New Mexican tradition is more than a geographic place or an individual state on a map. It expresses a particular perspective within the Southwest that dates back to 1598.[17] A particularly rich musical tradition was that of the *alabados* (praises). These were praises sung to God. They are popularly believed to have originated at the time of the conquest. The alabados were the Indian attempts to imitate the hymns and chants of the missionaries. Through song, the indigenous people learned Church doctrine. It is said that Fray Antonio Margil de Jesús (1657–1726) was one of its original promoters in the areas of Texas and Mexico.[18] This practice would spread to other parts of Central and Latin America.

The alabado forms a special part of the sacred music tradition of the Brothers of Our Father Jesus, commonly known as the Penitentes, a lay religious society that began sometime in the late eighteenth century and apparently was rooted in the Franciscan missionary movement. The Penitente alabados, though emphasizing the passion of our Lord also included hymns in praise of the Virgin Mary, the saints, the dead, and even sometimes the dawn. Being quite long, they would be transcribed into *cuadernos* (copybooks) for safekeeping.[19]

During the time of the 1910 Mexican Revolution, when clergy and religious were being persecuted, a Mexican seminary in exile was begun in Las Vegas, New Mexico. It would develop a choir that traveled throughout the Southwest singing popular religious and folkloric hymns. It was an unconscious step in recognizing the unity between these two styles of music. This unity would later influence the development of a Mexican musical style.

Perhaps the first hymnal for the Spanish-speaking community was published by the *Revista Católica* (Las Vegas, New Mexico) in the 1900s as a blue book called *Cánticos espirituales*.[20] It consisted mostly of music from Spain but also included popular religious hymns. This little book would be the staple of religious musical nourishment of the New Mexican family and community. *Cantos sagrados populares*, published in 1911 by a Mexican company, was in use in many areas of New Mexico until the mid-1940s. The Penitentes, a Catholic brotherhood found only in this area, used their own hymnal, *Himnos sagrados*, in 1912. In 1953, under the imprimatur of Archbishop Lucey of San Antonio, Texas, *Tesoro de cánticos sagrados* (McLaughlin and Reilly Company, Boston) would be put together by the religious order, the Oblates of Mary Immaculate. Later, in 1976, Henry J. Rael, would publish *El misalito: Canta el pueblo de Dios, dominical y festivo* by his own company, SIMCO (San Ignacio Music Co.). It was a seasonal *misalito* very similar to what is used today.

It should be noted that it is a matter of practice in the Santa Fe archdiocese for Spanish and English to be sung at all Masses. By tradition, the area has grown accustomed to the blending of languages while gathered for prayer.

Mexican-American music

One particular influence that inspired the composition of Mexican-American music was the publication of the *Misa Panamericana* (1965) by Juan Marcos Leclerc, a Chilean working at the Centro de Formación Intercultural (CIF) that was founded by Ivan Illich. This Mass, a conglomeration of melodies from different Latin American countries, is popularly called *Misa Mariachi* since it was played by mariachis and was adopted for regular Sunday use at the Cathedral in Cuernavaca, Mexico, in 1966 by Bishop Sergio Mendez Arceo. This music brought Mexican and Latin American rhythms into the celebration of the Eucharist.

Carlos Rosas, Mexican by birth, is one of the first Hispanic composers who was taken by the spirit of the Southwest. His composition, *Virgencita bendice estos dones* in 1973 propelled him into this new arena. It was first sung in San Antonio at a Mass for the Sociedades Guadalupanas with Bishop Patricio Flores presiding and with a 1000-voice choir. What makes Rosas' music popular is that it is composed not only with the religious spirituality of the Mexican American in mind but also the musical capability of the people and the untrained, unprofessional musician. It is therefore easily learned and sung. As Rosas said, "It is important that we help people express their faith with music that is adequate and appropriate in text, theology, pastoral practice, and liturgy."[21] Other contributions by Rosas were his *Misa de San Juan* (1975), and the well-known *Rosas de Tepeyac* (1976).

In the early 1970s Rosa Martha Zarate of California also promoted a particular Hispanic perspective. She sought to provide music "to convoke the Mexican community, the *campesinos* in the struggle within the Church."[22] She is well known for singing *Indio*, based on a work of Carlos Alberto Lopez Arango of Colombia that depicts *el indio* as a stranger in his own land. She feels this typifies the plight of many Mexican immigrants who might see the United States as an occupied territory. She worked on the development of music that some would judge as being liturgically inappropriate. Zarate's music reflects the prophetic dimension of the liturgy and Scripture by emphasizing biblical themes of political/religious protest. Her work with *comunidades de base* stresses this perspective. *Profetiza* (1985) was used at the Third National Encuentro and continues to be sung throughout the United States while finding favor also in Mexico and Latin America. *Cántico de la Mujer* (1987) reflects the struggle found in *mujerista theology* (this does not translate literally as "feminist theology" but rather depicts an emphasis on Hispanic women). In 1989 *Solidaridad*, which confirms the commitment of people in the struggle for freedom, was published. As she states, "music should not pacify people."[23] Her efforts would often place her at odds with Church officials and structures. Zarate's music is not generally found in major hymnals but remains popular among the base communities, refugee groups, and indigenous peoples. *Abya Yala* (*Our Mother in Full Maturity*, in the Kuna language, the name for the American continent in its totality given by the National Council of Indigenous Nations) is her latest work (1992).

Puerto Rican music

Father William Loperena, O.P., and Pedro Escabi, an Episcopalian layman and musician, both of Puerto Rico, along with Angel Pérez, a Spaniard, could perhaps be recognized as the first composers of post–Vatican II Hispanic music. (It must be remembered that Puerto Rico politically belongs to the United States but ecclesiastically is affiliated with CELAM, the Latin American Episcopal Conference. The connection and influence between Puerto Rico and the East Coast of the United States, in particular New York, is bound in blood and tradition.)

Within a year after the Constitution on the Sacred Liturgy was published, Loperena wrote *Misa Jíbara*, the Roman Mass based on the popular music rhythms of Puerto Rico. The word *jíbara* itself refers to the people of the *campo*, the rural sections of the island. This Mass found favor within the general community while it gained criticism and censorship from the hierarchical authorities of the church.[24] The local bishops upheld music from Spain as a classical standard worthy for liturgy. By nature, popular rhythms strengthen identity, in this case Puerto Rican identity. The Mass was perceived as being influenced by the political liberationist movements of the day and therefore subject to suspicion.

Angel Pérez, a Spaniard who worked in the Puerto Rican community of New York in the mid-1960s also made a contribution. As part of the Spanish-speaking Apostolate Office, whose director was Father Robert Fox, Pérez wrote *Misa Hispana*. This Mass was an attempt to represent the musical styles of the many different Hispanic ethnic groups of the area.

The Puerto Rican order of religious women, Instituto de Jesús Mediador, in the late sixties asked Pedro Escabí for a Mass set to Puerto Rican popular melodies. He wrote *Misa en la menor* (in A minor, a traditional tone for popular music) that would be played by guitar, *cuatro*, and other instruments. It was used until the early 1970s.

Cuban music

Since 1978, research on different musical styles was being done in the Miami area. Under the auspices of the Committee on Popular Piety, chaired by Father Juan Sosa, the Shrine of Our Lady of Charity, and in conjunction with the Southeast Pastoral Institute (SEPI), *Misa Cubana* was published in 1981. This would be the first of many ventures into the systematic approach of providing music in the rhythm and style of this Caribbean community. There was a growing trend to improve the quality of religious music in both its production and its execution. It was hoped that music would be more scripturally based and conform more closely to *Music in Catholic Worship*, a document published by the United States Catholic Conference. To this end, SEPI and the Office of Worship and Spiritual Life developed programs through Barry University on music and liturgy. *Sábado musical* began in 1990. It provided the theological reflection of persons like Casiano Floristán from Spain, Guillermo Fernández and Rogelio Zelada from Miami while offering the opportunity to perform new music by local composers. It was through the efforts of persons like María Pérez-Rudisill, a team of local pastoral musicians, in collaboration with the association of Hispanic priests that the music hymnal *Cantemos al Señor* (1986) would be published. But even this was seen as inadequate in providing Caribbean-style music. This led to the production of a collection of four tapes and music books, *Cuba canta al Señor*. Through the cooperation of the Office of Worship and SEPI, the original collection grew from four to seven tapes in 1992. It contains one hundred selections, representing the wide variety of Caribbean rhythms and styles.

Music was also produced for particular religious groups. These groups were unified by styles of prayer rather than ethnic origin. The Penitentes of New Mexico through the *alabados* hymns that accompanied their rites and dramas influenced the liturgy of the surrounding communities. The Cursillo hymn "De colores" is symbolic of how Cursillo music became characteristic of many Hispanic parishes but also overflowed into the English-speaking community. The charismatic renewal brought not only new music but also gestures (clapping and rhythmic moving) to the liturgy. All of this music, especially the charismatic, which is heavily dependent upon music from Spain, has influenced parish liturgy insofar as these hymns (and gestures) have been interwoven with the rest of the parish music repertoire.

Another, more recent influence of the past decade that is taking place in the United States Hispanic community stems from the publication of bilingual hymns and the practice of celebrating multicultural liturgies. Bilingual hymns are sung by the community or choir in two or more languages. This new format responds to two contemporary realities: more Hispanics are bilingual, able to speak English and Spanish; and there exists a hope, if not specific goal, within parishes that the English- and Spanish-speaking communities (as well as other language and cultural groups) would unite on feast days as one "family." Music coincides with the development, practice, and study of multicultural liturgies.

Mark Francis understands multicultural liturgies to mean "a conscious attempt at helping all members of the assembly, regardless of their culture and language, feel 'at home' at worship."[25] Under regular situations, "feeling at home " is difficult to achieve, and these kinds of celebrations may in fact be harmful to the development of liturgy in the Hispanic community. Multicultural liturgy reflects the growing trend toward multiculturalism. Bishop Enrique San Pedro of Brownsville, Texas, and chair of the U.S. Bishops' Committee for Hispanic Affairs looks upon multiculturalism negatively if Hispanics turn out to be treated as a "minority within the Catholic church" when they are not.[26] Allan Figueroa Deck criticizes multiculturalism as being devastating for the Hispanic community:

> In practice the Hispanic communities do not find secure, inviting places of worship, and ministers to go with them. . . . Even more telling is the case of Holy Week. In the multicultural context the official liturgy, which is already quite complicated and difficult to celebrate, is burdened with patches of this and that culture. . . . The result is a flat, unmoving and (for Hispanics) somewhat unrecognizable Holy Week.[27]

Hispanic liturgy carries the feeling of home when it is promoted, accepted, and valued for its own worth and not reduced to the lowest common denominator among other groups. Multicultural liturgies characterize a new pastoral opportunity for the Church that must be faced. The development of Hispanic liturgy and liturgies culturally sensitive to all racial and ethnic peoples must be fostered before everyone is gathered superficially into a liturgy in which no one is at home. This serves as a special challenge to publishers who provide the liturgical music and resources that these communities need.

Music Publishing Companies

As was stated previously, publishing for the Spanish-speaking community of the United States has been a risky business venture. Presses were hesitant to invest in an unknown and untested market. In this vacuum, scriptural texts, liturgical and homiletical aids, and music hymnals were produced on the local level. Materials were either homemade or imported from other Spanish-speaking countries. While this provided a sense of creativity, it also was frustrating in its failure to produce well-translated and appropriately sensitive cultural material for the diverse Hispanic community. Frequently it was easier to import and copy material than to write and produce new music.

In the early years, there were three notable exceptions, three very significant contributions to Hispanic liturgical music that were made by U.S. musicians and liturgists.

First, Our Sunday Visitor, Inc., based in Huntington, Indiana, took a unique approach in 1975 when they published the massive bilingual hymnal, *Cantemos al Señor/The Catholic Hymnal*, divided into separate English and Spanish sections. Each contained the ordinary of the Mass, two Latin Masses, and hymns from the respective Spanish- and English-speaking traditions. Second, Elias Isla, Sch.P., of the Bronx, New York, edited in 1977 the small red book, *Aleluya, alabad al Señor*, through the Centro Verdad y Vida. It contained the Ordinary of the Mass, a collection of 205 hymns, traditional and contemporary, from fourteen Spanish-speaking countries, and very uniquely, the format for morning and evening prayer. Third, The San Antonio Music Ministry Association released in 1981, *La familia de Dios celebra*. As the preface states, "The majority of hymns in this hymnal were composed by thirty-five Hispanic composers of San Antonio, Texas." New hymns, traditional and popular works, and the ordinary of the Mass filled the 713-page book.

Music, composed from the experience of a sensitive and talented composer, sings the soul of the community. Music, as a cultural art form, creates the religious atmosphere for a people to pray their need and their joy. Music, within the Hispanic community, is an act of self-identification. It creates the feeling of God's presence.

Those who influence its development as well as those who create it offer a great service to the Hispanic community. It could well have been with these thoughts in mind that the Southwest Liturgical Conference, the oldest liturgical conference in the United States (inaugurated in 1963), has been sponsoring a Hispanic Music Composition Competition since 1981. It has fostered the creation of new music for the Hispanic community. During the summer of 1992 and through the combined efforts of the Office of Worship of the archdiocese of Santa Fe and the National Association of Pastoral Musicians, the first Conference for Hispanic Liturgical Musicians was successfully held in Albuquerque, New Mexico, thus recognizing and affirming the important place of Hispanic liturgical musicians. These events influence what music companies will publish.

Another factor that influenced the religious music market was the lack of trained musicians within the Hispanic community. It is commonly known that many if not most Hispanic musicians play and sing by ear rather than by reading music. Few are trained in what constitutes liturgical music, and so they remain very susceptible to selecting music that is well known, can be easily learned, or is suggested by the clergy and the community. Only recently has new material been published. Yet, it must be noted that the importation of music, especially from Spain, still outweighs the composition of music and the publication of liturgical resources by local Hispanic composers and authors. The practice of photocopying music, where it still exists, bypasses not only copyright laws but also jeopardizes the livelihood of the few struggling Hispanic composers and authors who can devote full time to this work. Music publishing companies cannot foster new local music and talent unless there is a balanced economic gain for their encouragement and investment. Four particular liturgical and music companies have been gradually taking the risks necessary for providing musical/liturgical resources for the Hispanic community. The history of their support is instrumental in the development of the liturgy.

Pueblo Publishing Co./Liturgical Press

Mr. Bernard Benziger of Pueblo Publishing Company was one of the first to publish resource materials for the Hispanic community. (Remember that this company helped provide the first two volumes of the *Leccionario Hispanoamericano*.) Pueblo published the first Spanish participation aid, *Misal del pueblo*, in 1971. Within a year a very practical, but unauthorized (by the Bishops' Committee on the Liturgy) bilingual booklet for the funeral liturgy appeared. The first Spanish music published by Pueblo was *Veintiún cantos litúrgicos* by Brother Alfredo Morales, F.S.C. (a native of Cuba), in 1979, followed in 1981 by *Cantos musicales*, the musical arrangements for the *Misal del pueblo* and for Holy Week. In 1985 the firm issued the first Spanish homily preparation aid, *Homilias para el leccionario*. Pueblo Publishing was bought by the Liturgical Press in 1990. This company continues to make available Pueblo's materials besides producing their own Spanish liturgical and scriptural books and booklets. G.I.A., a Chicago-based company, followed Pueblo's lead.

G.I.A. Publications

1979 G.I.A produced *Misa San José*, by Howard Hughes, a known American composer. When unsolicited music manuscripts began arriving at their offices, G.I.A. also began to look ahead. Lorenzo Florián and Donna Peña both sent their work for review and planted the first seeds for G.I.A. Florian's *Quiero servirte mi Señor* collection was published in 1981. *Cantos de Taizé* (translations of different works from the ecumenical monastery of Taizé, France) in 1986, and *Alma Mía*, a collection of music by Donna Peña in 1988, followed. All of this came to fruition in 1991 and 1992 when seven more collections were published by Florián, Peña, José Carrera, and Cuco Chávez. Perhaps the more significant step that G.I.A. took came when they hired Lorenzo Florián as editor and member of their staff, thereby placing him in a policy- and decision-making position of the company. Paluch Publishing Company would take a more cautious step.

Paluch Publishing Company

El misalito has become a byword in the Spanish-speaking community since 1985 when it first appeared. It was Paluch's initial venture into the Hispanic market and has become a mainstay for many parishes. The music it provides is very traditional; only recently has more variety been found. *El misalito* offers Spanish popular religious hymns, music from composers of Spain, and translations of many English and French hymns. As an insert in the English missalette, it is very convenient for English- and Spanish-speaking communities. This is helpful for parishes that have only one musician/organist playing the same translated music for both language groups. The Spanish section is quite limited in its number of pages. The greatest challenge of providing a full compliment of liturgical resources designed specifically for the Hispanic community was made by Oregon Catholic Press.

Oregon Catholic Press

No publishing house has done more to influence Hispanic music than OCP. It began using a market approach with the publication of the Spanish-language insert to *Today's Missal* and has moved to inculturating its entire staff. The Spanish insert was made available in 1978 to bilingual parishes. Five years later (in 1983) this insert appeared as a separate publication, *Misal del día*. It became apparent that more Spanish music was needed than could be included in this missalette. On December 10, 1982, OCP became the exclusive licensing agents in the United States for the Spanish publishing houses of Ediciones Musicales Pax, Ediciones Paulinas, and Editorial Apostolado de la Prensa. This fostered and promoted the musical compositions of such persons as Carmelo Erodzaín, Cesareo Gabaraín, Juan Espinosa, and Emilio Mateu. The editors collected one hundred hymns, Mass ordinaries, antiphons, and acclamations into a 128-page booklet and published it under the well-known title, *Cánticos de gracias y alabanza* in 1982. Few Hispanic composers were included.

A greater commitment to the Hispanic community was made in 1989 when OCP debuted, during the Southwest Liturgical Conference, *Flor y canto*, a complete Spanish music hymnal, containing 711 titles, Mass parts, and 80 bilingual pieces. Its authors are Hispanic-American, Spaniards, and Anglo. It has found great popularity in the United States and is also exported to Nicaragua and South America. OCP employs Hispanic composers such as Mary Frances Reza, Brother Rufino Zaragosa, O.F.M., Ana Victoria Demezas, Dolores Martínez, and Rudy Vela, S.M., as part of their editorial staff. It employs other Spanish-speaking personnel and offers Spanish classes to its non-Spanish speaking employees. In 1989 OCP began publishing *Liturgia y canción*, a bilingual, quarterly liturgy planning aid. Recognizing the diversity of the Hispanic community in the United States the firm is making efforts to be sensitive to the deeper individual dimensions of Hispanic liturgy and spiritual life. Though not a music publishing company, Liturgy Training Publications provided resources that have benefited the development of Hispanic liturgy.

Liturgy Training Publications

LTP's first Spanish-language publication was *Los ministros de la comunión a los enfermos*, presented in 1985. This work sought to be handy aid for those who would visit the sick. Though LTP has translated some of its more popular materials, such as works on baptismal sponsors and a booklet celebrating lent, Holy Week, and Easter, its most notable contribution is the *Manual de procla-madores*, first published in 1989. This is a manual for lectors and gospel readers that provides a brief scriptural commentary, phonetic pronunciation, and suggestions for the proper thematic emphasis of the reading. The manual is not really a translation of its English counterpart; its comments are written from the Hispanic perspective.

Music's greatness is that it allows life's passion to be felt and embraced. This passion reflected in moments of pain and pleasure give heart to the struggle and depth to the prayer. Our music is our strength. It sings our spirituality. But we are not angels, some formless images barely here and not really there. We are people whose bodies strain to express in gesture and movement the "full, active, and conscious participation" that the liturgy calls for.

The Development of La Danza
as a Hispanic Liturgical Gesture

The use of the term *liturgical gesture and movement* serves our purpose for understanding *la danza*, which is so often misinterpreted and perhaps mistranslated as "dance". Gesture and movement help us to see such popular religious practices as processions, *posadas* (the novena commemorating Joseph and Mary's searching for an inn), pilgrimages, *parrandas* (the Puerto Rican Christmas and Epiphany custom of visiting homes of family and friends) from a clearer liturgical perspective and therefore their place within the liturgical acts of the Hispanic community. (See also in this volume Edmundo Rodriguez's essay, "The Hispanic Community and Church Movements: Schools of Leadership.")

Father Thomas Krosnicki, S.V.D., has written about the distinction between *liturgical dance* and what he believes is a more authentic clarification, *liturgical gesture and movement*.[28] Briefly stated, he offers this term as a way of showing that the liturgy is itself gesture and movement that celebrate the paschal mystery. Appropriate gestures and movements—of priest, ministers, and congregation—that occur within the liturgical act are to be at the service of the community's prayer. He goes on to state that this appropriateness must be critiqued and pastorally judged by the local churches. "As men and women born of the culture and cognizant of its ramifications, local church leaders, in union with their pastors, will be the best judges of the use of new and extended gesture-movement within the ritual patterns of a given people."[29]

Jaime Vidal refined this distinction for the Hispanic community when he described "high and low context" communications:[30]

> Generally speaking the "Northern" cultures—Germans, Scandinavians, English, American WASPS, and non-WASPS to the degree that they have successfully assimilated—are *low context* while the "Mediterranean" cultures—Italians, Spaniards, Greeks, Arabs, and Latin Americans—are high context. Low context cultures are much more interested in *content*, in what you say rather than how you say it. . . . In high context cultures, on the other hand, factors of context and feeling are essential to successful communication. The high context person or group will not assimilate the message, or be motivated to act on it, on the strength of words alone; if they are to be effective, the words must be wrapped in a matrix of tone, emphasis, gesture (facial and bodily), body contact, etc.[31]

Viewed from this framework, physical movement is very natural and important for the Hispanic community. Liturgy is meant to be not cerebral but evocative. "Full, active, and conscious participation" means to be fully human. To be fully human in any celebration is to unite mind, heart, and body. Gesture, especially in la danza, seems to help fill this need.

The specific use of la danza as a liturgical expression, has been employed by the Mexican and Mexican-American community more than by any other ethnic Hispanic group. Martha Ann Kirk's brief study, *Dancing with Creation: Mexican and Native American Dance in Christian Worship and Education*,[32] traces the origin of sacred dance in its Jewish expression, in the history of Spain, at the time of the conquest, and its catechetical use in the missions of the Southwest. She helps us to see rhythmic physical movement as a spiritual discipline and expression of prayer. Carlos and Teresa Rosas make a useful linguistic distinction between the terms *baile* and *danza*.[33] *Baile* refers to what is popularly called dance, be it rock and roll or a waltz. *La danza* carries the indigenous primitive sense of sacred movement before God. During major feasts it was performed not only by individuals but by the entire gathered community of worshipers. When we open the term *danza* to mean liturgical gesture and movement, then we can also see that it is not solely the act of a few persons but oftentimes it includes the whole community.

Within the Mexican/Mexican-American community of the United States the feast of Our Lady of Guadalupe has been the primary opportunity for la danza. This stems from the traditional celebration of Guadalupe in Mexico City, where indigenous peoples still practice their sacred dance at the entrance to the shrine. They do not enter the Church. This practice was carried over to the United States. Bishop Patricio Flores promoted the Rosas' initiative of enriching the liturgy with music and movements clearly identifiable with the local Hispanic community.

In the early 1970s Carlos and Teresa Rosas of San Antonio, Texas, began to introduce *una danza de ofertorio* (a liturgical movement during the rite of preparation of the altar and gifts) with children using music especially written for this moment. From the very outset, it was well received. At a diocesan festival celebrating the feast of Guadalupe some two hundred children participated. Since then the Rosas have successfully developed other moments for use during the Eucharist and have created a form of catechesis about la danza as prayer for both children and adults. Virgilio Elizondo recounts that Archbishop Furey of San Antonio was probably the first bishop to allow la danza to enter the Church. It is said that when the archbishop questioned the religious meaning of what was going on outside the Cathedral, he was told that through these movements the people were praying. "If they are praying then they belong inside of the Church!" he responded.

The inclusion of la danza in the liturgy was not universally accepted. In 1976, Father Robert O'Hara, a Missionary of the Holy Family and pastor of Our Lady of Victory Church, was ordered out of the diocese of Corpus Christi by Bishop Thomas Drury after the celebration of a deacon ordination liturgy that included la danza by Mexican-American children.[34]

If music creates the feeling of God's presence then liturgical gesture and movement is the Hispanic physical response to that feeling. The incarnation of liturgy into recognizable and representative prayer for the Hispanic community is never more clearly seen than when liturgy is acted out during the fiesta celebrations. In all Hispanic communities, the important times of the liturgical year, such as Christmas and Holy Week, are opportunities for the faithful to live out dramatically the events being celebrated. These may include representations of the birth of Christ as acted out in the *pastorelas* (plays based on scriptural events), the Epiphany dramas of the Three Kings, the Last Supper, the living stations of the cross through the neighborhood, and the services of *pésame* (sympathy) given to the Sorrowful Mother. Many Hispanic communities, such as those located around St. Mary's Cathedral in Miami, in Chicago's Pilsen neighborhood, or in New York's barrio (known to outsiders as Spanish Harlem), hold outdoor Good Friday processions. These are stations of the cross with funeral processions sometimes including a coffin containing a life-size statue of the dead crucified Christ. The great patronal feast days of St. John the Baptist, Our Lady of Charity, and Our Lady of Altagracia include solemn liturgies and long processions. Prayer is lived out in these moments. These great movements are orchestrated for the entire community to take an active role in the events that are being celebrated. They bring to life the mystery of God's presence. They help to weave the liturgy into one, full, conscious act.

The historical liturgical developments that we have encountered in this essay are like threads that when woven together fashion a cloth cut to fit the faith experience of the Hispanic community. There is one more thread of experience that must also be woven into this cloth. Its actual historical development is not as easily traced but rather is the very fiber of life within the Hispanic community.

THE PROPHECY OF SOCIAL JUSTICE WITHIN HISPANIC LITURGY

I have left to the end one last thematic thread that is woven throughout the fabric of this essay. This thread is Hispanic liturgy as social justice, or, better stated, the prophecy of social justice. The bishops of the United States in their pastoral letter on Hispanic ministry, *The Hispanic Presence* (1983), asked the "Hispanic peoples to raise their prophetic voices" in the Third National Encuentro (no. 18). This petition has been taken seriously not only during the encuentro but in the subsequent years as well. Prophecy strains the status quo. Hispanic liturgy symbolically acts out a call for change by its very presence on the parish Sunday Mass schedule. Hispanic liturgy asks the simple yet penetrating question "Why?" Ricardo Ramírez in 1977 was one of the first to consider this prophetic stance from a liturgical viewpoint:

> The task of questioning and asking others to question themselves is that of deabsolutizing what the dominant group has absolutized or may be in the process of absolutizing. . . . It may be said that a minority group can serve as a saving instruction of the dominant group, even saving it from itself in such pitfalls of dominance

as elitism, a sense of superiority, conformism and convention. . . .
Hispanics in the United States are searching for a new liturgical
expression of their cultural heritage and Christian experience, one
that is in keeping with their way of thinking and their way of feeling
the presence of grace in their lives.[35]

Convention is not an official principle of liturgy. Questions—
Why is the way we pray not officially more reflective of our faith?
Why is popular religiosity not affirmed more readily as integral, or-
ganic elements of our liturgical gatherings? Why are our struggles
and successes not reflected more positively in Sunday worship?
Why are we sometimes made to feel that we have to justify who
we are and how we pray?—are passionately felt. While I acknowledge a positive bias in what has been historically depicted in this
essay, controversies, such as those associated with the *Misa Jíbara*,
local bishops' unwillingness to release Hispanic priests for national
positions of influence, the initial hurt that came from the rejection
of everything Spanish (language, popular religious traditions, and
the very personhood of the Hispanic Catholic, which unfortunately
continues in many places): these and other issues just underline the
question, Why?

This question in all of its diverse forms is not so much a confrontation as an invitation to consider life from another perspective.
The question invites inclusivity and openness, a change of heart—
the very essence of the liturgical reform's purpose.

The prophecy of social justice leads us to acknowledge that the
prophet must also hear the message that is being proclaimed and
take it very much to heart. The Hispanic community must also
take greater responsibility for the way it gathers to celebrate the
presence of Christ's life, death, and resurrection within it. Liturgy
does not change the unjust situation. Liturgy brings injustice into
the light, gives spirit to ask questions, inspires decisions to make
the necessary changes in the world where we live. Liturgy models
the kingdom as it will be, inclusive of all God's people, inclusive of
their color, gender, language, customs, foods, melodies, traditions,
all that makes up the heart of their prayer. As natural as it is to
share a meal after every festive liturgy in the Hispanic community,
so it is natural that change in the status quo of our liturgical
celebrations must occur. The controversies will not disappear but
rather they call for a reconciliation that weaves them into the fabric
of the rites, rituals, traditions (official and popular) that make up
our prayer.

Hispanic liturgy leads to social action as a response to what has been heard and preached, to what has been blessed and broken, to what has been given for the growth of the community. It is prophetic liturgy when Hispanic liturgical ministers serving in the sanctuaries of our churches also give witness to what was celebrated by helping in voter registration drives. The celebration of posadas and Christ's birth among the *anawim*, the poorest of the poor, leads the assembly to open its eyes and assure that justice is achieved for newly arrived immigrants, the homeless, and the poor of the community. The liturgical embrace of peace leads the gathered believers to live in solidarity with all who are making efforts to publicize the human rights violations that daily come to light. The gesture of holding hands during the Our Father, so often found in the Hispanic community, binds a people in their purpose to build the kingdom in this parish. The voices that pray and sing in unity acknowledge the truth that *somos Iglesia* (we are Church) and not merely a tolerated part of it.

No example so eloquently reflects this social awareness that is raised in Hispanic liturgy as does the image of a priest, vested in the colors of the United Farm Workers movement of Cesar Chavez, celebrating Mass in the open grape fields of California with the farm worker strikers and their families under the protection of a banner that bears a hand-painted drawing of Our Lady of Guadalupe. This scene is repeated in diverse ways around the United States among the various Hispanic ethnic groups. The word, "Oremos . . ."(Let us pray), has not been an escape from the strains of the struggle but rather gives shape and form to our faith response to the question, Why?

We began this essay wondering with the *viejita*, "What is missing in Hispanic liturgy?" The themes treated here highlight how the Hispanic community has liturgically attempted not only to provide what is missing but also to have the liturgy come more fully alive according to the Hispanic tradition.

Though it may seem that official Roman liturgy and popular religiosity were at times in marked contrast, indications show that there is a blending going on, however slow and cautious as it may be. Examples of these indications are found in the willingness of institutions such as the Instituto de Liturgia Hispana and the Bishops' Committee on the Liturgy to work together; the inclusion of a sixteenth-century indigenous text, the *Nican Mopohua* (the transcription of Blessed Juan Diego's account of the Guadalupe apparition) in the office of readings for the feast of Our Lady of Guadalupe; the United States' being recognized as having Spanish as an official liturgical language and being included within the Spanish-speaking family of countries; la danza being an ordinary part of festive celebrations and the great processions as integral elements of Holy Week. It could well be said that the initial sixteenth-century process of blending the official and the popular has never ended. The mestizo practice of prayer continues.

In the Old Testament we read that Jacob gave his son Joseph a coat of many colors. It was a marvel to behold. Its texture, touch, and tone testified to Jacob's love. Hispanic liturgy is our coat of many colors woven from interior threads of strain, struggle, and Spirit. It has been our faith that binds each thread together. It becomes our gospel wedding garment for the fiesta of life that we celebrate with all of our brothers and sisters, each arrayed in the garments of God's goodness to them. This indeed is a historical and awesome place to be.

NOTES

1. Arturo J. Pérez, "Towards a Hispanic Rite, Quizás," *New Theology Review* 3 (November 1990), pp. 80–81.

2. Margaret Mary Kelleher, O.S.U., "Worship," *The New Dictionary of Theology*, ed. Joseph A. Komonchak et al. (Collegeville, Minn.: Liturgical Press, 1991), p. 1105.

3. Luis Maldonado, *Génesis del catolicismo popular* (Madrid: Ediciones Christiandad, 1970), p. 1.

4. Robert Ricard, *The Spiritual Conquest of Mexico* (Berkeley: University of California Press, 1966), pp. 290–291.

5. Sixto García and Orlando Espín, " 'Lilies of the Field': A Hispanic Theology of Providence and Human Responsibility," *Catholic Theological Society of America Proceedings* 44 (1989), p. 70.

6. H. Ellsworth Chandlee, "The Liturgical Movement," *Dictionary of Liturgy and Worship*, ed. J. G. Davies (Philadelphia: Westminster Press, 1986), p. 307.

7. *Proceedings of the II Encuentro Nacional Hispano de Pastoral* (Washington, D.C.: Secretariat for Hispanic Affairs, National Conference of Catholic Bishops, United States Catholic Conference, 1978), p. 82.

8. Virgilio Elizondo, "The Christian Identity and Mission of the Catholic Hispanic in the United States," in *Hispanic Catholics in the United States* (New York: Centro Católico de Pastoral para Hispanos del Nordeste, Inc., 1980), p. 64.

9. Ibid., p. 67.

10. United States Catholic Conference, National Conference of Catholic Bishops, Bishops' Committee on the Liturgy, *Newsletter* 12 (June–July 1976), p. 25. A brief history of MACC is given, along with the proposed liturgical projects.

11. Historia del Instituto de Liturgia Hispana, official notes, San Antonio, Texas.

12. United States Catholic Conference, National Conference of Catholic Bishops, Bishops' Committee on the Liturgy, *Newsletter* 13 (August 1977), p. 78.

13. A description of the Instituto de Liturgia Hispana is found in its constitution.

14. Bishop Ricardo Ramírez. Interview with the author.

15. Jaime Vidal, "Popular Religion among the Hispanics in the General Area of the Archdiocese of Newark," in *Presencia Nueva: Knowledge for Service and Hope* (Newark, N.J.: Office of Research and Planning, 1988), p. 256.

16. Moisés Sandoval, *On the Move* (Maryknoll, N.Y.: Orbis, 1990), p. 65.

17. Moisés Sandoval, ed., *Fronteras* (San Antonio: Mexican American Cultural Center, 1983), p. 197.

18. Gabriel Saldívar, *Historia de la música en México* (Mexico, D.F.: SEP/Editiones Gernila, S.A., 1987), p. 151.

19. Martha Weigle, *The Penitents of the Southwest* (Santa Fe: Ancient City Press, 1970), p. 43.

20. Mary Frances Reza, Office of Worship, archdiocese of Santa Fe, has a collection of these early hymns. She is a valuable resource in having grown up with this New Mexican tradition. She could be called one of our "living documents."

21. Carlos Rosas, interview with the author, June 10, 1992, at the Tepeyac Institute, El Paso, Texas.

22. Rosa Martha Zarate, interview with the author, October, 1992.

23. Rosa Martha Zarate, interview with the author, December 1992.

24. Ana María Díaz-Stevens, "La *Misa Jíbara* as an Ideological Battlefield," paper presented at the Fifteenth International Congress of the Latin American Studies Association, San Juan, Puerto Rico, 1989.

25. Mark Francis, C.S.V., *Liturgy in a Multicultural Community* (Collegeville, Minn.: Liturgical Press, 1991), p. 49.

26. "Hispanics Critique Multiculturalism," *National Catholic Reporter*, June 19, 1992, p. 6.

27. Allan Figueroa Deck, "The Crisis of Hispanic Ministry: Multiculturalism as an Ideology," *America* 163, no. 2 (July 14–21, 1990), p. 35.

28. Thomas A. Krosnicki, "Dance within the Liturgical Act," *Worship* 61 (July 1987), pp. 349–357.

29. Ibid.

30. Vidal, "Popular Religion among the Hispanics in the General Area of Newark," p. 258.

31. Ibid.

32. Martha Ann Kirk, C.C.V.I., *Dancing with Creation* (Saratoga: Resource Publications, 1983).

33. Teresa Rosas and Carlos Rosas, interviews with the author.

34. Rick Casey, "Parish Dances; Bishop Cuts In," *National Catholic Reporter*, March 5, 1976, p. 1.

35. Ricardo Ramírez, *Fiesta, Worship, and Family* (San Antonio: Mexican American Cultural Center, 1981), p. 15.

BIBLIOGRAPHY

How we pray as Hispanics has compelled different authors to reflect theologically on Hispanic liturgy. Their books and articles are attempts to use Hispanic liturgy as a locus for theological reflection. The authors in this bibliography describe, clarify, deepen, question, and intensify the experience that liturgy offers—an experience of the presence of God within the Hispanic world. The bibliography is representative of what has been published to date.

An overview reveals that the 106 works were written by thirty-four authors. Six persons wrote almost half of them, namely, Virgilio Elizondo, Angela Erevia, Marina Herrera, Arturo Pérez, Ricardo Ramírez, and, most significant for the sheer number of his works specifically on liturgy (20), Juan Sosa. Almost everything was written in English (only fourteen works are in Spanish) and most of the thirty-four authors are of Mexican-American descent. This gives a definite perspective to the written liturgical reflection that has taken place and draws attention to the need for other Hispanic ethnic groups to reflect from the genius of their experience.

Virgilio Elizondo is not a Hispanic liturgist but the title, "Founder of Hispanic Theology" in the United States is well earned. His numerous works often shed light on the subject of Hispanic liturgy from a broader theological viewpoint. He writes as a Mexican American,

using the cultural symbols and themes of the Southwest as his principle themes. His first major work, *Christianity and Culture*, published
in 1975, was one of the first books to validate the Hispanic cultural
experience of popular religiosity.

Angela Erevia, M.C.P.D., also a Mexican American, and Marina
Herrera, originally from the Dominican Republic, write about Hispanic liturgy, its catechetical implications, and opportunities for it
for parishes. Erevia's best-known work, *Religious Celebration for the
Quinceañera*, has seen five reprints since it first appeared in 1980.
Though initially written for young women, she has developed a program and text to include young men. The title was changed to reflect
this development: *Quince Años: Celebrating a Tradition* in 1985. It is
currently being used as a parish/diocesan program for Victoria, Texas
(since 1982), and Dallas, Texas (since 1990).

Marina Herrera, a prolific theological writer, often reflects on the
liturgy and its cathechetical implications within a parish. "Popular
Piety as a Parish Resource" (1981), "Celebrations for a Multicultural
Church" (1983), and "Religion and Culture of the Hispanic Community as a Context for Religious Education: Impact of Popular Religiosity on U.S. Hispanics" (1985) are representative of her insightful work.

Arturo Pérez, a native Mexican American of Chicago, Illinois,
began publishing in 1981 with "Baptism in the Hispanic Community."
The bilingual booklet *Popular Catholicism* (1988) pastorally treats the
relationship of popular Catholic practices and the official liturgy.

Bishop Ricardo Ramírez, born in Bay City, Texas, has written on
various subjects of Hispanic liturgy such as environment, liturgy as
prophecy, popular religiosity as an expression of Hispanic spirituality,
and the Rite of Christian Initiation of Adults. Two articles written in
1977, "Liturgy from the Mexican American Perspective" and "Is the
Prophet Speaking Spanish?" were his initial works in this area.

Juan Sosa is a Cuban-born priest of Miami, Florida, whose first
work, *Religiosidad Popular* (1979), was a reflection on the Cuban liturgical experience. Though many of his writings generally pertain to Hispanic liturgy, his references to the popular religious practice of *santería*
(an Afro-Cuban religion) and *espiritismo* (spiritism) clearly identify his
work with a Caribbean viewpoint. His writings are found in national
and international liturgical journals. The study of his work is privotal
in defining the liturgical diversity of the Hispanic community.

Jaime Vidal's two major works, "Popular Religion in the Lands
of Origin of New York's Hispanic Population" (1982) and "Popular
Religion among the Hispanics in the General Area of the Archdiocese
of Newark" (1988), are relatively unknown insofar as they are not

in any bookstore or subscription series. They were published by the research offices of the archdioceses of New York and Newark as part of larger studies of Hispanics in these regions. These essays are well-documented liturgical resources offering rich insights from the specific Puerto Rican perspective. Because of the absence of other material representative of the Puerto Rican experience, they stand alone in their importance.

Abalos, David T. *Latinos in the United States: The Sacred and the Political.* Notre Dame, Ind.: University of Notre Dame Press, 1986.

Boehm, Mike. "Musical Resources for the Hispanic Community." *Pastoral Music* 10, no. 3 (February–March 1986), pp. 24–25.

Carrasco, David. "A Perspective for a Study of Religious Dimensions in Chicano Experience: *Bless Me Ultima* as a Religious Text." *Aztlán* 13 (1982), pp. 195–221.

Díaz-Stevens, Ana María. "La *Misa Jíbara* as an Ideological Battlefield." Paper presented at the Fifteenth International Congress of the Latin American Studies Association, San Juan, Puerto Rico, 1989.

Elizondo, Virgilio, *Christianity and Culture.* Huntington, Ind.: Our Sunday Visitor, 1975.

———. "Politics, Catechetics, and Liturgy." *Religion Teacher's Journal,* November–December 1976, pp. 30–32.

———. "Our Lady of Guadalupe as Cultural Symbol: The Power of the Powerless." *Concilium* 102 (1977).

———. "Who Is the Catechumen in the Spanish Speaking Community of the U.S.A.?" In *Becoming a Catholic Christian.* New York: Sadlier, 1977.

———. "Popular Religion as Support of Identity: A Pastoral-Psychological Case-Study Based on the Mexican American Experience in the U.S.A." In *Popular Religion,* ed. Greinacher, Norbert, and Mette, pp. 34–43. Edinburgh: T. and T. Clark, 1986.

Escamilla, Roberto. "Worship in the Context of Hispanic Culture." *Worship* 51 (July 1977), pp. 290–293.

Espín, Orlando. "Religiosidad popular: Un aporte para su definición y hermenéutica." *Estudios Sociales* 58 (October-December 1984), pp. 41–56.

———. "Irokó e Ará-kolé: Commentário exegético a um mito iorubálucumí," *Perspectiva Teológica* 18, no. 44 (January–April 1986), pp. 29–61.

———. "Tradition and Popular Religion: An Understanding of the *Sensus Fidelium.*" In *Frontiers of Hispanic Theology in the United States,* pp. 62–87. Maryknoll, N.Y.: Orbis, 1992.

Everia, Angela. *A New Direction for Catechetics and Liturgy for the Mexican American*. San Antonio: Mexican American Cultural Center, 1975.

————. "Popular Religiosity and Cathechesis of the Mexican American." *PACE* 7 (1976).

————. "Cultura y fe relacionadas a educación religiosa." *El Visitante Dominical*, September 11, 1977.

————. "Death and Funerals in the Mexican American Community." *PACE* 10 (1979).

————. *Religious Celebrations for the Quniceañera*. San Antonio: Mexican American Cultural Center, 1980.

————. *Quince Años: Celebrating a Tradition*. San Antonio: Missionary Catechists of Divine Providence, 1985.

————. "Quince Años: Celebrating a Tradition." *Catechist*, March 1989, pp. 10–11.

————. "Religión Casera: The Hispanic Way." *Momentum* 22, no. 4 (November 1991), pp. 32–34.

————. *A Remembrance of My Quince Años*. [Complete liturgy for Quince Años Mass.] San Antonio: Missionary Catechists of Divine Providence, 1992.

Faith Expressions of Hispanics in the Southwest. San Antonio: Mexican American Cultural Center, 1977. New ed., 1991.

Figueroa-Deck, Allan. "Liturgy and Mexican American Culture." *Modern Liturgy* 3, no. 7 (October 1976), pp. 24–26.

————. "The Crisis of Hispanic Ministry: Multiculturalism as an Ideology." *America* 163, no. 2 (July 14–21, 1990), pp. 33–36.

————. "The Spirituality of the United States Hispanic: An Introductory Essay." *U.S. Catholic Historian* 9, no. 1 and 2 (Winter 1990), pp. 137–146.

Flores, Richard. "Mexican: Fiesta People." *Modern Liturgy* 13, no. 3 (April 1986), pp. 12–13.

Francis, Mark. *Liturgy in a Multicultural Community: American Essays in Liturgy*. Collegeville, Minn.: Liturgical Press, 1991.

————. "Hispanic Popular Piety and Liturgical Reform." *Modern Liturgy* 18 (October 1992), pp. 14–17.

————. "Is Multicultural Liturgy Possible? Reflections on the Inculturation of Worship in a Multicultural Parish." *New Theology Review* 5, no. 3 (August 1992), pp. 30–44.

Galilea, Segundo. *Religiosidad popular y pastoral hispano-americana*. New York: Northeast Catholic Pastoral Center for Hispanics, 1981.

Gonzales, Joe. "Music in the Multicultural Parish." *Liturgy 80* 17, no. 6 (August-September 1986), pp. 14–15.

Gonzalez-Wippler, Migene. *Santería: The Religion: A Legacy of Faith, Rites, and Magic*. New York: Harmony Books, 1989.

Hammond, John. "Arroz." *Modern Liturgy* 12, no. 2 (March 1985), p. 14.

Herrera, Marina. "Popular Piety as a Parish Resource." *Service* 3 (1981), pp. 93–94.

———. *Hablemos del compadrazgo en la familia Hispana*. Chicago: Claretian Publications, 1982.

———. "Celebrations for a Multicultural Church." *Momentum*, February 1983, pp. 30–32.

———. Experiencing Cross and Resurrection: Contrasting Perspectives." *Catechist*, February 1983, p. 16.

———. "Mary in Hispanic Piety." *Catechist*, April 1983, p. 18.

———. "Hispanic Dimensions of Baptism." *Catechist*, November 1985, pp. 38–39.

———. "Images Proclaim the Word." *Catechist*, April–May 1985, p. 68.

———. "Popular Devotions and Liturgical Education." *Liturgy* 5, no. 1 (1985), pp. 33–37.

———. "Religion and Culture of the Hispanic Community as a Context for Religious Education: Impact of Popular Religiosity on U.S. Hispanics." *Living Light* 21, no. 2 (January 1985), pp. 126–146.

———. "The Sacraments in Cross-Cultural Perspective." *Catechist*, September 1985, p. 47.

———. "First Communion Celebration in Hispanic Practice." *Catechist*, February 1986, pp. 14–15.

———. "Marriage: Union of Persons and Ideas." *Catechist*, April 1986, pp. 20–21.

Herrera, Marina, and Elly Murphy. "The Religious Nature of Dance." In *Focus on Dance X: Religion and Dance*, ed. Dennis J. Fallon and Mary Jane Wolbers. Reston, Va.: American Alliance for Health, Physical Education, Recreation, and Dance, 1982.

Hinojosa, Juan-Lorenzo. "Culture, Spirituality, and U.S. Hispanics." In *Frontiers of Hispanic Theology in the United States*, pp. 154–164. Maryknoll, N.Y.: Orbis, 1992.

Huitrado-Rizo, Juan José. "Hispanic Popular Religiosity: The Expression of a People Coming to Life." *New Theology Review* 3 (November 1990), pp. 43–55.

Icaza, Rosa María. "The Cross in Mexican Popular Piety." *Liturgy* 1, no. 1 (1980), pp. 27–34.

———. *Catholic Celebration: A Reflection on the Liturgical Renewal/ Celebración católica: Una reflexión sobre la renovación liturgica*. San Antonio: Mexican American Cultural Center, 1989.

————. "Spirituality of the Mexican American People." *Worship* 63 (May 1989), pp. 232–246.

Jabush, Willard. "They Sing in Tampico." *Pastoral Music* 8, no. 3 (February–March 1984), pp. 19–21.

Kirk, Martha Ann. *Dancing with Creation.* Saratoga: Resource Publications, 1983.

————. "Mexican Folk Dances for Ordinary Time." *Modern Liturgy* 11, no. 3 (April 1984), pp. 8–9.

Liturgy 80 12, no. 7 (October 1981). Bilingual ed. treating Mary, music and quinceañera.

Matovina, Tim. "Liturgy, Popular Rites, and Popular Spirituality." *Worship* 63 (July 1989), pp. 351–361.

————. "The Italian 'Problem' and the Hispanic Opportunity." *America* 165, no. 15 (November 16, 1991), pp. 362–363.

————. "Liturgy and Popular Expressions of Faith: A Look at the Works of Virgil Elizondo." *Worship* 65 (September 1991), pp. 436–444.

Mayer, Robert. "A Quinceañera Mass." *Modern Liturgy* 3, no. 7 (October 1976), pp. 28–29.

Murphy, Joseph M. "Traces of African Religiosity Came to U.S. as Santería." *Liturgy*, November–December 1979, pp. 10–12.

————. *Santería: An African Religion in America.* Boston: Beacon Press, 1988.

Pérez, Arturo J. "Baptism in the Hispanic Community." *Emmanuel* 87 (February 1981), pp. 77–86.

————. "Lent: Conversion Liturgy." *Hosana 1* 1, no. 1 (Spring 1983), pp. 31–35.

————. *Popular Catholicism.* Washington, D.C.: Pastoral Press, 1988.

————. "Signs of the Times: Towards a Hispanic Rite, Quizás." *New Theology Review* 3 (November 1990), pp. 8–88.

————. "The Fifth Centenary of Evangelization in the Americas." *Liturgy* 9, no. 4 (Fall 1991), pp. 27–33.

Pérez, Arturo, and Kevin Hays, "Worship in a Multicultural Community." *Liturgy 80*, May–June 1986, pp. 13–14.

Ramírez, Ricardo. "Is the Prophet Speaking Spanish?" *Living Worship* (1977), pp. 1–14.

————. "Liturgy from the Mexican American Perspective." *Worship* 51 (July 1977), pp. 293–298.

————. "Environment at the Service of the Ambiente." *Liturgy* (1978), pp. 21–23.

————. *Fiesta, Worship, and Family: Essays on Mexican American Perception on Liturgy and Family Life* (San Antonio: Mexican American Cultural Center, 1981).

————. "Reflections on the Hispanization of the Liturgy." *Worship* 57 (1983), pp. 26–34.

————. "Hispanic Spirituality." *Social Thought* 11 (Summer 1985), pp. 6–13.

————. "El descubrimiento del tesoro mas rico en la liturgia: El rito de la iniciación cristiana para adultos." Miami: Instituto de Liturgia Hispana, 1986.

Religiosidad popular: Las imagenes de Jesucristo y la Virgen María en América Latina. San Antonio: Instituto de Liturgia Hispana, 1990.

Reyes, Logino. "A Poco Eucharistic Prayer." *Modern Liturgy* 3, no. 7 (October 1976), p. 27.

Rodriguez-Holguín, Jeanette. "Hispanics and the Sacred." *Chicago Studies* 29 (August 1990), pp. 137–154.

Romero, C. Gilbert. *Hispanic Devotional Piety: Tracing Biblical Roots*. Maryknoll, N.Y.: Orbis, 1991.

Rosas, Carlos. "Mexican Americans Sing Because They Feel Like Singing." *Pastoral Music* 1, no. 5 (June–July 1977), pp. 14–17.

Sosa, Juan. "Santa Bárbara y San Lázaro." In *Cuba: Diaspora*, pp. 101–103. Miami: Christian Commitment Foundation, 1976.

————. "An Anglo-Hispanic Dilemma: Liturgical Piety or Popular Piety." *Liturgy* 24, no. 6 (November–December 1979), pp. 7–9.

————. "Religiosidad popular." In *Cuba: Diaspora*, pp. 27–29. Miami: Christian Commitment Foundation, 1979.

————. "Popular Piety: An Integral Element of the Conversion Process." In *Christian Initiation Resources*, vol. 1, pp. 249–254. New York: Sadlier, 1980.

————. "Liturgy in Two Languages . . . Some Principles." *Pastoral Music* 5, no. 6 (August–September 1981), pp. 36–38.

————. "El ministerio de la música litúrgica en nuestras comunidades hispanas." *Liturgy 80*, pp. 10–11. Chicago: Office for Divine Worship, 1981.

————. "Illness and Healing in Hispanic Communities. *Liturgy* 2 (1982), pp. 62–67.

————. "Let us Pray . . . *en español.*" *Liturgy* 3, no. 2 (Spring 1983), pp. 63–67.

————. "Liturgy in Three Languages." *Pastoral Music* 7, no. 3 (February–March 1983), pp. 13–15.

————. "Religiosidad popular y sincretismo religioso: Santería y espiritismo." *Documentaciones Sureste*, no. 4, pp. 1–13 (Spanish); 14–26 (English). Miami: Oficiana Regional del Sureste para Asuntos Hispanos, 1983.

————. "Liturgia hispana en los Estados Unidos. *Notitiae: Sacra Congregatio pro Culto Divino* 20 (1984), pp. 688–696.

————. "Criterios para las celebraciones litúrgicas en las comunidades hispanas." Miami: Instituto de Liturgia Hispana, 1988.

————. "Los simbolos religiosos: Una llamada a la oración." *Phase* 29, no. 173 (1989), pp. 403–410.

————. "Texto Unico: A Unified Liturgical Text for Spanish Speaking Catholics." *Liturgy 80* (May–June 1989), pp. 9–10.

————. "Renewal and Inculturation." *Liturgy* 9, no. 2 (Winter 1990), pp. 17–23.

————. "Liturgy and Culture: Tradition and Creativity." *Worship and Ministry* [magazine for the diocese of Orlando, Fla.] 2 (1991), pp. 24–25.

————. "The Fifth Centenary: A Historical Encounter with Prayer." *Liturgia y canción* 3, no. 4 (1992), pp. 8–19.

————. "Liturgia, religiosidad popular y evangelización: El ejemplo de la liturgia hispana en los Estados Unidos." *Phase* 32, no. 190 (July–August 1992), pp. 295–304.

————. "Reflections from the Hispanic Viewpoint." In *The Awakening Church: Twenty-Five Years of Liturgical Renewal*, ed. Lawrence J. Madden, S.J., pp. 121–124. Collegeville, Minn.: Liturgical Press, 1992.

————. "Bilingual Music or Bilingual Texts." *Liturgia y canción* 4, no. 2 (1992), pp. 5–6. [Also in Spanish.]

Vela, Rudy. "Hispanic *Bienvenida:* An Embrace and a Kiss." *Pastoral Music* 13, no. 5 (June–July 1989), p. 40.

Vidal, Jaime. "Popular Religion in the Lands of the Origin of New York's Hispanic Population." In *Hispanics in New York: Religious, Cultural, and Social Experiences*, vol. 2, pp. 1–48. New York: Office of Pastoral Research of the Archdiocese of New York, 1982.

————. "Popular Religion among the Hispanics in the General Area of the Archdiocese of Newark." In *Presencia Nueva: Knowledge for Service and Hope*, pp. 235–352. Newark, N.J.: Office of Research and Planning, 1988.

Zapata, Dominga. "Saints in the Hispanic Community." *Liturgy* 5 (Fall 1985), pp. 59–63.

————. "Hispanic Liturgy as Prophecy." *Liturgy* 6 (Summer 1986), pp. 59–63.

————. "The Rhythm and Prayer Life of the Poor." *Liturgy* 8 (Summer 1990), pp. 25–29.

11

The Challenge of Evangelical/Pentecostal Christianity to Hispanic Catholicism

Allan Figueroa Deck, S.J.

The churches ought to discover what is now being said "in God's laboratory in Brazil." The unexpected growth of the churches is possible only if the old missionary approaches are abandoned, only if the "cultural coldness, the systematized, privileged and secularized Christendom of North America is renounced."

William R. Read[1]

Attempting to articulate and interpret the significance of Hispanic Catholicism's encounter with evangelical Protestantism in the United States is a daunting task. Careful gathering of primary sources has yet to occur and monographs, especially of the phenomenon in the United States, are very limited. This essay is an effort to frame the question in its broadest terms, to begin the task of understanding this momentous encounter, with its implications for Hispanics in the United States, and, as I believe we will discover, for Christianity itself in both North and South America.

The first and lengthiest part of the essay stresses the need to conceive of this phenomenon in broader terms, with more sophistication than has been the case so far. The second section develops the topic of how one is to interpret the phenomenon of enthusiastic religion, a key consideration for grasping the various ways people—both mainstream thinkers and Hispanics—resist dealing with this major trend in religion. The third section brings to the surface an idea that has only recently been suggested, namely, the affinity between Hispanic popular Catholicism and evangelical/pentecostal Christianity. This view may, indeed, be a key for understanding a phenomenon infinitely more complex and subtle than commonly thought. The fourth part raises the foundational question of conversion and attempts to describe how it has come about in the past (in the gestation of popular Hispanic Catholicism)

and how it occurs today in the radically different context of modernity. In the fifth and final section a number of key issues and
insights regarding this movement toward evangelical/pentecostal
Christianity are discussed along with some of their implications
for Roman Catholic evangelization efforts among Hispanics.

FRAMING THE QUESTION:
BEYOND THE SUPERFICIAL AND ANECDOTAL

One of the more striking developments in the history of Christianity worldwide is the dramatic emergence of a flourishing pente-
costal/charismatic movement particularly in the latter half of the
twentieth century. Church demograher David Barrett estimates
the total population of pentecostal/charismatic Christians in excess
of 150 million, with more than a third of this population in Latin
America. Pentecostalism is by far the fastest-growing movement
in worldwide Christianity. Barrett projects that if current growth
rates are sustained, pentecostal Christianity will account for 21
percent of all Christians in the world by the end of the century.[2]
Latin American Catholics are flocking to pentecostalism in very
significant numbers in both Latin America and in the United States.
Two of pentecostalism's largest congregations are found in Latin
America.[3] Father Flavio Amatulli, a leading Catholic expert on
Protestantism in Mexico, estimates the number of Protestants there
in the order of 6 million, of whom 70 percent are pentecostals.[4]
      This chapter is concerned with the appeal of evangelical re-
ligion in the United States and only tangentially with the phenomenon in Latin America. A word, however, is in order regarding
the status of scholarship on Latin American evangelicalism since
the dramatic growth of that religion in Latin America and the symbiotic nature of its relationship with United States evangelicalism
are important if not key factors in understanding why this form
of Christianity is so successful on both sides of the Rio Grande.
Pablo A. Deiros, in his contribution to the first volume of the
impressive Fundamentalisms Project headed by Martin E. Marty
and R. Scott Appleby, has written one of the more comprehensive
introductions to Latin American Protestantism available. In the
conclusion to this highly researched monograph, Deiros makes a
point that may come as a surprise to mainstream Protestant and
Catholic thinkers in the United States; namely, that fundamentalist
evangelicalism is more attractive to the Latin American masses

than liberation theology and even the Christian base communities. This is so, according to Deiros, because liberation theology and the Christian base communities have not shed a certain elitist element. They have not "gone in the door" of the simple faith and common sense of the popular masses. In their effort to unmask the sources of oppression, liberation theology and the base communities have exposed the Church to the direct attack of the political oligarchies. Consequently the Church ceases to be the haven where the peoples' suffering can be dealt with, as Deiros and David Stoll call it, in a *euphemistic*, symbolic, and ritualistic way. Deiros believes that "because it is proving itself capable of responding to the immediate concerns of the lower-class masses, Protestant evangelicalism, fundamentalist-style, will continue to grow in numbers in Latin America."[5]

Turning now to evangelicalism's influence in the United States, a recent study made for the U.S. Catholic bishops in 1990 indicates that the vast majority of Protestant congregations that have attracted immigrant U.S. Hispanics are pentecostal or evangelical (mainly Baptist).[6] What are the background, the context, and possible reasons for this astonishing development?

While Protestant missionary endeavors can be traced back to the early nineteenth century in several areas inhabited by Hispanics, the astonishing growth of Hispanic Protestantism, particularly in the second half of the twentieth century, is not primarily the result of the earlier efforts. Rather, Protestant proselytism of Hispanics began a sustained period of growth only at the end of the last century, when pentecostalism was born and when evangelical Protestantism under pressure from modernist trends ceased being the principal, mainline form of American Protestantism. For the time being hegemony passed to the urban, liberal, intellectual elites in the various denominations. The 1925 Scopes trial was a watershed in this development, according to historian George Marsden.[7] The public's negative reaction to the trial was a defeat for the evangelicals who attempted to hold back the onslaught of modernism by reverting to a particularly rigid form of biblical fundamentalism.

Perhaps the subsequent success of evangelical outreach to Hispanics can be traced to evangelicalism's decline among mainstream, affluent, educated, urban Protestants. New immigrant groups, poorer and often rooted in rural experiences, would likely become a new audience for the evangelicals, the source of new vitality. Both they and the pentecostals recruited from the ranks of the poor with much more ease than the mainline churches.

The vast majority of today's Hispanic Protestants trace their origins to this period in the history of American Protestantism. Whereas the first Protestant outreach was principally in the hands of the mainline churches of the nineteenth century, the second outreach has occurred in this century and its main protagonists have been the evangelicals and pentecostals. Hispanics have generally chosen to enter into the evangelical/pentecostal current. They are thus contributing to a significant revitalization of evangelical Protestantism, the predominate, classic form of U.S. Protestantism. Modernism or, to use Paul Ricoeur's expression, "the acids of modernity," contributed much to evangelicalism's precipitous decline in the early decades of this century. Now Hispanics, more than any other U.S. minority, are contributing to its revival and making evangelicalism, particularly in its pentecostal manifestation, the fastest growing and arguably the most dynamic division of Christianity in the United States and in the world today.

One place to begin an analysis of this phenomenon is in the abundant literature of the Church Growth movement under the indefatigable leadership of Donald McGavran.[8] Fuller Theological Seminary, by far the largest theological seminary of any denomination in California, together with other institutions in the area of Pasadena have become the center of the Church Growth movement's extensive educational, missionary, charitable, and publishing efforts.[9]

The success of evangelicals and pentecostals in Hispanic ministry is also grasped through a study of the gradual flowering of this trend in several Latin American nations.[10] One of the more basic observations to make about this vast movement of evangelical and pentecostal Christians is the symbiosis between their North American and Latin American missionaries. U.S.-born Latinos and native Latin Americans have crossed the Rio Grande in both directions. The approaches eventually hammered out, so successful in many parts of Latin America, are the same ones used here in the United States.[11] Church historian Justo L. González, while speaking about the more mainline United Methodist Church, documents this in his study of Hispanic Methodists: "One characteristic of Hispanic United Methodism . . . is that its strength is in direct proportion to its connection with centers of Hispanic culture outside the United States."[12]

Despite some gains on the part of Justo L. González's United Methodists, however, it is not they who are attracting impressive numbers of Hispanics. This is part of a larger picture: The historic

decline of mainline Protestantism in general and the vigorous upsurge of more marginalized denominations and independent congregations of either an evangelical or pentecostal stripe.[13] Today
when one speaks of Hispanic Protestantism one is not usually
talking about the "historical" churches at all but, rather, about
some strain of evangelicalism and especially pentecostalism. These
are churches which exhibit some of the classic features of the *sect*.
They are headed by gifted, winning, charismatic leaders and are
often independent of hierarchies or higher church governments.
They enjoy, moreover, the benefit of not being perceived as institutions and escape or are somewhat untainted by the postmodern
disenchantment with institutional religion.[14] Donald W. Dayton
has gone farther and called this charismatic Christianity a kind of
"third force": "I am often inclined to suggest that churches like my
own, in the holiness movement, or those of Pentecostalism, are so
different from magisterial Protestantism that they constitute some
new strand in the church—a sort of 'third force' that is neither
Catholic nor Protestant."[15]

Before discussing the history of the more recent outreach of
Protestants to Hispanic Catholics, however, let us consider past
missionary efforts in more detail.

In one of the few monographs of its kind, Edwin Sylvest, Jr.,
provided an example of the process by which Hispanic Catholics
in the Southwest first became involved with mainline Protestant
denominations, especially Presbyterians and Methodists, in the period immediately after the Mexican-American War.[16] David Maldonado gave a summary of the historical experience of Hispanic
Protestants from a mainline perspective and emphasized the nineteenth century.[17] R. Douglas Brackenridge and Francisco O. García-
Treto wrote the most complete and current history of Presbyterians
and Mexican Americans in the Southwest currently available.[18]
Clifton L. Holland presented a more detailed analysis in his study
of Protestantism among Hispanics in Los Angeles.[19] Holland's
study demonstrates that the churches that eventually succeeded in
attracting Hispanics were virtually all evangelical or pentecostal.
He showed how the lack of allowing Hispanics to organize, fund,
and control their own churches led to the decline of mainstream
Protestant outreaches. The reasons mainstream efforts did not
thrive, while those of evangelicals and Pentecostals did, were, according to Holland: 1) they had informal "on-the job" training
programs for ministers, 2) they established relatively small communities in the barrios where the people were to be found, 3) they

identified ministers from the community itself, 4) they empowered them to function, and 5) they seldom if ever questioned the need to use Spanish in the ministry. These are the features of successful evangelization of Hispanics that are detected more in the outreach of nonmainline churches than in that of the more established ones, whether Protestant or Catholic.

Justo L. González, in his history of Hispanic Methodism, sheds light on some of the reasons for the reluctance of mainline churches to allow Hispanics their own space and their own way of doing things. It was assumed that Hispanics would simply adapt to the preexisting patterns of ministry, church government, organization, and funding. This assumption neglected the concrete social class and cultural location of Hispanics and led to failure after failure.[20] Those assumptions in the United States are driven by the middle-class horizon of most church leaders and the increasingly strong pragmatic, managerial, and technological orientation of planners who get the attention of bishops and church administrators. In this regard it can be noted that evangelical/pentecostal efforts have been characterized by a *respect* for some important idiosyncracies of the local community and its natural, indigenous leaders. Today we might call that respect a feature of a dialogical, inculturating mode, that is, the ability to rethink ministry as insiders from within the culture to be evangelized instead of imposing preconceived ideas and inappropriate approaches on benighted outsiders.

Thomas H. Groome, a leading pastoral theologian, gives a possible explanation for this failure to engage in meaningful dialogue on the part of mainline (both Protestant and Roman Catholic) churches. He refers to an attitude underlying much of mainstream, contemporary religious education and church leadership. Following Max Horkheimer, Groome calls it *instrumental reasoning* or *technical rationality:*

> Technical rationality is moved by an instrumental interest in "what works" to produce "results." It does not engage knowers as "think-ing-persons-in-relationship" with reality but functions as an adversarial stance toward nature, society and other people; it obliterates the dialectical relationship that should exist between knower and known if knowledge is to be life-giving and historically responsible. . . . [I]t employs the mind in a one-dimensional, utilitarian logic that excludes memory and imagination and concentrates only on what it claims are objective and empirical "facts" in order to promote commodity production and bureaucratic management. . . .

[I]t results in a refusal to think of outcomes beyond what "works for control" and demands a suspension of imagination.[21]

Most Catholic commentaries on evangelical/pentecostal proselytism have not pursued these more serious and perhaps subtle explanations of the nature of this development. They have not sought to frame the issue in its deeper social, cultural, and historical underpinnings. Catholic reflections on this trend have tended, rather, to be argumentative, to be a form of latter-day apologetics.[22] For decades Roman Catholic writers have been bemoaning the proselytism of what they disdainfully call *the sects*. They note the inroads made with Hispanics.[23] This is an issue repeatedly mentioned by Catholic clerical authorities from the local parish priest to the pope himself, but serious self-evaluation and soul searching has usually not characterized their reflections.

There has been some change, however, as revealed by the 1986 conference sponsored by the Vatican on sects and new religious movements which issued a document, one of the first of its kind, framing the question in more serious and intellectually engaging terms.[24] The report, for instance, suggests that the word *sect* not be used since it is somewhat derogatory. It acknowledges many of the positive contributions of these new religious movements and admits that their success has something to do with their ability to respond to the real needs of people, the need, for example, of community, of affective prayer and worship, and of access to the Bible. More recently the Latin American bishops devoted several pages to the issue in the preparatory document for their fourth general conference that took place in Santo Domingo in October 1992.[25] Recent scholarly works like those of David Martin, David Stoll, and Florencio Galindo have begun to treat this phenomenon with the seriousness it deserves.[26] They have analyzed the reality of evangelical/pentecostal religion within the Latin American context. Mexican journalist Juan Castaingts Teillery writing in the influential Mexico City daily *Excelsior* offered these reflections on evangelical proselytism in Mexico and by extension in all of Latin America:

> From now on all the churches will compete in a "marketplace of beliefs." The church with the better "marketing" will have more clients. Everything points to the fact that the Protestant churches have better "marketing...." We believe that in the coming years Mexico will undergo a profound cultural revolution consisting in the notable increase in Protestantism. In a few decades we will have

a Mexico that is 20 or more percent Protestant. This fact implies one of the most powerful changes ever registered in our history.[27]

One of the implications of Castaingts Teillery's remarks is that the Catholic church now competes with other churches for the religious soul of Mexico. As Roger Finke and Rodney Stark point out in their provocative analysis of the social history of religion in the United States, *The Churching of America: 1776—1990*, competition among the churches is a blessing. For where churches have had a monopolistic control over a people's or nation's religion, they have often tended toward corruption, abuse, and lethargy.[28] Unfortunately there are still no comparable works dealing with the issue as it has unfolded among United States Hispanics.[29]

The available data on the appeal of evangelical Protestantism to U.S. Hispanics indicate that appreciable numbers of them are indeed either joining these churches or at least flirting with them. Andrew Greeley maintains that more than a million have left the Roman Catholic Church in the fifteen-year period between 1973 and 1988 and that the larger percentage of these are joining either evangelical or pentecostal churches.[30] Gerardo Marín and Raymond J. Gamba found that only 72.9 percent of Hispanics in the San Francisco area identified themselves as Roman Catholics.[31] This is down from projections of twenty years ago in which 92 percent considered themselves Catholic. The 1985 survey of Roberto Gonzalez and Michael La Velle showed that more than half of all U.S. Hispanics have been contacted by one of these evangelical or pentecostal groups.[32] The data included in Martin's and Stoll's works reveal that the largest and fastest growing type of Protestantism in Latin America is precisely evangelical/pentecostal.[33] The study recently completed for the United States bishops' Ad Hoc Committee on Proselytism confirms the seriousness of the challenge these groups are posing for immigrant Catholics in general in the United States and especially for Hispanics.[34]

Before proceeding any further, however, it may be helpful to focus briefly on the nature of evangelical and pentecostal Christianity. In a general overview of Hispanic Catholic "defections" to these churches it is impossible always to make the relevant distinctions between these two related but quite distinct trends in contemporary Christianity. What, then, does one mean by evangelical and pentecostal? For the purposes of this discussion I refer the reader to the writings of George M. Marsden. This prolific student of evangelical religion in the United States has demonstrated that evangelical Christianity is an extremely influential form of American Protestantism, perhaps *the* most influential form. Marsden outlines its salient features:

> The essential evangelical beliefs include (1) the Reformation doctrine of the final authority of the Bible, (2) the real historical character of God's saving work recorded in the Scripture, (3) salvation to eternal life based on the redemptive work of Christ, (4) the importance of evangelism and missions, and (5) the importance of a spiritually transformed life.[35]

In an earlier work Marsden provides a richly textured account of evangelicalism at one of the decisive moments in its gestation in the United States, the period between 1870 and 1925.[36] For the purposes of our study he makes four points that are quite relevant. The first is that evangelical Protestantism is intimately linked to certain features of the Anglo-American cultural ethos with its orientation toward individual responsibility, work, civic pride, egalitarianism. It grew out of Calvinism and Puritanism. Second, it has a great appeal for ordinary people, since from an early stage evangelicalism adopted a popular philosophy of life called *Scottish Common Sense Realism*. Third (as mentioned above), evangelicalism gave rise to fundamentalism in the heat of Protestantism's struggle with modernism and liberalism. Fourth, pentecostalism, while being distinct in terms of its practical, less fundamentalist, use of the Bible, is an outgrowth of the holiness movement in evangelical Protestantism, specifically Methodism.[37] In very simple terms, pentecostalism gives much greater importance to the doctrine of the Holy Spirit and to the outward manifestation of the Spirit in power. It is also worth noting that African Americans have played a substantial role in both evangelical and pentecostal Christianity. They have had a strong presence in both but especially in pentecostalism where the spontaneous expression of feeling has been a hallmark. Baptists, who are evangelicals, generally eschew the emotion. But this distinction becomes blurred in the case of the black Baptists.

Perhaps the most important lesson to be learned from the impressive cultural history woven by Marsden in his works on evangelicalism is that this topic is an extremely complex and substantial one. It has to do with some of the most profound issues in American cultural history, such as the impact of modernity on life, on attitudes toward science and technology, and on moral values. The study of evangelical religion in the United States is, moreover, a basic requirement for understanding contemporary liberal-conservative cultural conflicts. James Davidson Hunter tells us in his *Culture Wars* that those conflicts have blossomed into full-scale combat. Peter Steinfels, reviewing Hunter's book in the *New York Times*, states:

> Professor Hunter labels the opposing camps as the "orthodox" and the "progressivist".... Where once religious groups fought one another over matters of doctrine and ritual observance, today, according to Professor Hunter, the fault line between orthodox and progressivists runs right through the major faiths, dividing them internally over conflicting conceptions of moral authority.... The orthodox view moral authority as based on something external to the self, whether as a sacred text or a law of nature; moral truths are clearly definable, permanent, universal and "transcendent." The "progressivists" view moral authority as an evolving blend of historic faith and traditional wisdom modified by contemporary circumstances.[38]

Hunter's concept of *culture wars* may provide a key for grasping, at least partially, the nature and ongoing success of evangelical/pentecostal proselytism of today's Hispanic.

INTERPRETING THE PHENOMENON

Perhaps the single most important issue affecting the critical analysis of the challenge of evangelical Protestantism for Hispanic Catholics or for mainline Christians of any cultural background is the failure to take the phenomenon seriously. Everyday experience seems to demonstrate that those who find this issue of interest or are even alarmed by it do little more than bemoan it, wring their hands, or dismiss it with a simplistic explanation. When discussing the movement of significant numbers of Latin Americans to these religions it has been quite common to ascribe it to a plot by the C.I.A. Or it is understood as another example of how ignorant, superstitious people can be manipulated into preposterous religious beliefs by crafty agents of well-financed fringe denominations. Stoll and others have documented real C.I.A. and evangelical church efforts of this kind.[39] Thoughtful analyses of the phenomena, nevertheless, reveal that the massive movement of Hispanic Catholics away from their ancient Church both in Latin America and the United States is a much more complex and subtle reality than many would like to believe. How do we explain the resistance even on the part of often well-informed Catholics and others to a more nuanced understanding of these facts?

Ronald A. Knox alludes to the problem of interpretive posture or stance in his now classic study of what he called *enthusiasm* or *ultrasupernaturalism* in the history of Christianity. As a fiercely committed English Roman Catholic he tells us in the foreword that he planned to line up all the "rogues," that is, demonstrate the nature of the error involved in the various enthusiastic expressions of Christianity that did not remain in union with Rome. He wanted to create a "rogues' gallery" he tells us. But as he got deeper into the topic he came to respect the underlying experiences and concerns of those who over the centuries had promoted this enthusiastic Christianity: "somehow in the writing, my whole treatment of the subject became different; the more you got to know the men, the more human did they become, for better or worse; you were more concerned to find out why they thought as they did than to prove it was wrong."[40]

A similar experience is reported in a more recent study of evangelical religion in the U.S. by historian Randall Balmer. He was raised in a narrow, evangelical Christian home that, as is common, tended toward being fundamentalist as well. He rejected all of that and became an Episcopalian. Later in life he returned to his roots with his book *Mine Eyes Have Seen the Glory: A Journey into the Evangelical Subculture in America*. In the epilogue he tells us:

> Evangelicalism will also persist, I think, because of its timeless appeal. It promises intimacy with God, a support community, an unambiguous morality, and answers to the riddles of eternity. . . . Evangelicalism simply will not go away. In the 1920's H. L. Mencken, no friend of evangelicals, remarked that if you tossed an egg out of a Pullman window almost anywhere in the country, you would hit a fundamentalist. Pullman cars are obsolete in America today. Fundamentalists are still around.[41]

Both Knox and Balmer are dealing with a critical issue, namely, the hermeneutic or the interpretive perspective taken toward this reality. My contention is that most mainline Christian writers, be they Roman Catholic or Protestant, have approached the topic with suspicion and even prejudice. It is my contention that the relevance and import of the phenomenon called evangelical religion among Hispanics or any other people cannot be assessed as long as the attitude is basically condescending, patronizing, or outright hostile (as has been especially the case among Catholic Hispanics).

The question then emerges, Why so much negativity toward evangelical and especially pentecostal Christianity? Surely there are good, even excellent, reasons for this resistance. Among mainline Catholics and Protestants in the U.S. it has to do with the perception—often true, no doubt, but also exaggerated or even unfounded—that evangelicals oversimplify the Christian tradition, tend toward excessive emotionalism and a fractious sectarianism, are sometimes linked with nationalistic and even racist elements of society. Clifton L. Holland in the study of Hispanic Protestantism in Los Angeles, confirming an earlier conclusion of researchers Leo Grebler, Joan Moore, and Ralph Guzman,[42] discovered that it tended to flourish among rather introverted, conservative Hispanics who were clinging together in a kind of fortress mentality:

> Much of recent Hispanic church growth has taken place among conservative Hispanic churches which represent various degrees of introversion, rather than among the so-called "liberal" Hispanic churches related to the mainline Protestant denominations.[43]

Another source of negativity toward evangelical Protestantism and especially toward its pentecostal expression, however, is its historic identification with the popular classes, the poor and less educated members of society. The style of prayer and socialization typical of rural or blue-collar communities where evangelicalism thrives the most are usually problematic for the more educated classes. Learned discussions of the phenomenon of evangelical religion are often led by the academicians at university, seminary, and theologate. They often view these matters from the perspective of the class that dominates in their institutions and churches. Usually this is the middle and upper middle classes with which they themselves are identified in terms of vital interests and tastes.

For Hispanics the principle source of resistance to evangelical Protestantism has to do with its intimate connection with the North American ethos, especially its perceived individualism and consumerism. Hispanics in this regard view evangelical Protestantism as the quintessential expression of U.S. religion and culture, an interpretation masterfully developed by George Marsden in *Fundamentalism and American Culture*. Given the need to resist the onslaught of Americanization and certain forms of modernization, the thoughtful Hispanic will view evangelical efforts to convert Hispanics as a particularly vicious attack on his or her cultural identity. Even though the Hispanic American may not be active in practicing the Catholic faith, he or she perceives that the culture is permeated by a kind of Catholic ethos that revolves around a rich collection of rites and symbols. Many of those rites and symbols are imbued with a certain Catholic spirit. The evangelical penchant for reducing the mediation between God and humanity to the Scriptures is antithetical to the Hispanic Catholic tendency to multiply mediations. Not only the Church but the saints, angels, and especially the Virgin Mary are viewed as mediators in addition to Jesus Christ himself. The more democratic, egalitarian ethos of evangelicalism is somehow foreign to the hierarchical configuration of both the Hispanic family and society. Hispanics have often experienced serious family divisions when a member becomes a Protestant. In Hispanic culture this is not just a religious matter. It is a profound cultural, social, and familial rupture.

These are only some of the reasons for the suspicion and lack of openness toward the evangelical phenomena. They are certainly appreciable. In the effort to fairly assess the reality one must ask, however, Upon what grounds may one approach the issue with openness and generosity in the effort to shed greater light on the reality and better grasp its significance? The resistance to evangelical/pentecostal Christianity is quite intense. For Hispanics, however, and despite the many serious reasons they have to resist this trend, there appears to be a way to overcome the barriers. The key to overcoming these seeming contradictions is what I call the *unanalyzed affinity*.

THE UNANALYZED AFFINITY: POPULAR RELIGIOSITY AND EVANGELICALISM

Scholarly efforts to compare and contrast evangelical Protestantism with Hispanic Catholicism will be well advised to take Hispanic popular Catholicism, not the standard, textbook version, as the norm. As I have argued in my book *The Second Wave*, this is the lived religion of most Hispanics.[44] It is important to acknowledge the distinctive character of the existential Catholicism of most Hispanics. Their Catholicism is hardly the reflection of a rigorous religious formation based upon accepted catechetical texts. Rather, theirs is a popular faith mediated especially by grandmother, mother, and women in general. Its standards and practices are not articulated in books or in any other form of print medium.

This deeply rooted form of Catholicism is communicated orally, from person to person, within the context of family, rancho, town, or barrio. It almost totally lacks rational articulation but is not for that less convincing and motivating. For this simple faith is quite captivating and graphic, dramatic and emotive. It eschews the cognitive in its effort to appeal to the senses and the feelings. It does this through symbol and rite. Its main qualities are a concern for an immediate experience of God, a strong orientation toward the transcendent, an implicit belief in miracles, a practical orientation toward healing, and a tendency to personalize or individualize one's relationship with the divine. These qualities, Peter W. Williams tells us, are also present in normative Catholicism, but they are much more present in Hispanic popular religiosity. They are notably absent in mainline Protestantism, however, which, unlike Catholicism, tended to succumb to modernity's programmatic leveling of belief through relentless inquiries into the historicity of every Christian doctrine and practice.[45]

The point I want to make here is that the movement from popular Catholicism to some form of evangelical or pentecostal Protestantism is not as strange and drastic as it may seem. In a certain sense the movement of Hispanics to evangelical religion is a way to maintain a continuity with their popular Catholic faith which in the period both before and after the Second Vatican Council has been disparaged, opposed, dismissed, or ignored by many official teachers of the Church.[46] This is the point that Harvey Cox makes in *Religion in the Secular City:* "The history of the antagonism [between modern rationality and popular religion] makes it hard for the modern theological enterprise to recognize and draw on people's religion as a key source in the building of a postmodern theology."[47]

What Cox affirms about theologians may also be applicable to pastoral agents, mainline priests, and religious educators who tend to see popular religiosity as a problem to be uprooted, not a strength upon which to build. The period after the Second Vatican Council has been an "age of the theologian," a time of serious efforts to adapt their concepts to the everyday life of the Church. The effort, however, has not always been informed by knowledge of other cultures and social classes, or by respect for the somewhat anomalous religion of ordinary people.

The tension between normative and popular faith has been one of the main features of Hispanic Catholicism since the first evangelization of the sixteenth century. The powerful presence of pre-Columbian religious forms and sensibilities in the Catholicism of the first indigenous converts and the absence of native, indigenous priests throughout the colonial period created a permanent suspicion among the clergy and other learned Catholics about the syncretic religion of the natives and of their progeny, the *mestizos*.[48] This tension was magnified by migration to the United States where Catholicism had achieved an extraordinary level of coherence among the faithful masses through the Catholic school system and well-organized religious education programs for Catholic children in the public schools. This remarkable cohesiveness between the normative faith of the official Church and that of the ordinary faithful was achieved through many means, but the famous Baltimore catechism is the example that readily comes to mind.

In the period after the Second Vatican Council, U.S. Catholics have generally pursued a course of renewal which once again gave emphasis to the cognitive, rational articulation of the new norms of the Council. Hispanic Catholicism can seem anomalous and even heterodox to the confirmed Anglo-American Catholic whether one looks at it from the pre– or post–Vatican II perspective.

Another factor that helps explain the distance between mainstream U.S. Catholicism and popular Hispanic Catholicism is social class location. In a certain sense it was easier for U.S. Catholics of a century ago to receive Hispanics. Both groups tended to be outsiders to the American way of life. Traditional U.S. Catholic ethnic groups—Irish, German, Italian, or Slavic—were uniformly working class. The style of their faith, manners, and experiences were not as separate as the distinct languages they spoke. Today's Catholic immigrants, Hispanics, for instance, find their U.S. Catholic counterparts much more affluent, more educated, and, as a result, more distant from them socially and culturally than was the case a century or even half a century ago.[49]

Needless to say, U.S. Hispanics, especially the recent immigrants among them, find mainline Protestants equally or even more distant than their U.S. Catholic contemporaries. There are some Protestants, however, who have overcome this distance—the evangelicals and especially the pentecostals. For that is the branch of Protestantism that historically, especially in the last hundred years, has appealed to the working class, the poor, and the marginated in U.S. society. Consequently one will find evangelical and pentecostal churches in the barrios or on Main Street inner-city storefronts. In these urban neighborhoods small, inviting congregations of a hundred or so Hispanics have emerged; almost invariably they are led by a Hispanic who reaches out to them in Spanish without hesitation. These are all circumstances that render the evangelization quite effective.

From Cultural to Personal Conversion

The winning ways of these small Protestant congregations, their communitarian flavor, and their accessibility are features which help the Hispanic overcome some strong resistances. Mexican Catholics, for example, natives of the Catholic heartland of Mexico—the states of Jalisco, Michoacán, Guanajuato, and Zacatecas—often have a horror of Protestants. They are afraid that conversion to Protestantism on the part of a family member will tear apart the entire family. Do not the Protestants denigrate and disdain Mary, the Mother of Jesus? Do they not attack veneration of the saints, one of the hallmarks of Mexican Catholicism? These Catholic Mexicans may also still prize the memory of the Cristero Rebellion, a war their grandparents fought precisely in defense of the Church and against an anti-Catholic government in the 1920s. Are they now to walk away from this heritage and change religion the way one would change clothes?

Yet evangelical/pentecostal Protestants are breaking down these historic resistances. Perhaps the contemporary ability of Hispanic Catholics to convert to some form of Protestantism can be explained to some extent by Hispanic Catholicism's penchant for syncretism. It should be recalled that many, if not most, Third World cultures manifest a remarkable ability to combine diverse religious beliefs and traditions. Western Christianity, with its strong philosophical orientation, is sensitive to what it views as inconsistencies in religious theory and practice. Not so for the native peoples of the Americas and for the Africans who populated the Caribbean islands and the coasts of Central and South America. Their religious beliefs are expressed through symbol and therefore enjoy a kind of openendedness that at different times has scandalized the European Christian. In the encounters of today's Catholic Hispanic with diverse and even antithetical strands of Christianity perhaps a similar syncretic tendency is still at work.[50]

In addition, evangelical and pentecostal churches stress something that Hispanic Catholics intuit to be of great importance today, specifically within the context of their confrontation with the culture of modernity. Their ancient Catholicism came about as the result of the conversion of a people, of an entire culture. The method used by the mendicant orders was one of the last great flowerings of Constantinianism. What mattered was not the individual, personal transformation of the Indian, but rather the transformation of the collective symbols and rituals of their culture. This distinction is difficult for modern people to grasp given the highly personal and individual horizon of modern cultures. The concept of personal conversion would have been foreign to Aztecs, Mayans, or any other indigenous and African peoples. It was also rather foreign to the sixteenth-century friars whose mindset was still imbued with the ideology of Christendom and the principle *cujus regio, ejus religio*. Hispanics today, however, are at various stages of modernization. They sense that their communal orientation to religion is inadequate. They seek a more self-conscious, individualized faith. The subjection to forces outside themselves, the heteronomy of their traditional Catholic worldview, becomes increasingly dysfunctional. They sense the need to move beyond their collective, ancestral conversion of centuries ago. For it is not adequate to the challenges of the modern world with its stress on human autonomy, mobility, personal freedom, and human rights.

Consequently today's Hispanic in the United States, in contrast to what was possible or even thinkable at other times, seeks to appropriate *personally* his or her faith. But the large, impersonal, Catholic parish is simply not the most likely place for this to occur. The smaller assembly favored by the evangelicals and pentecostals is ideally suited for the modern context. Yet they do not destroy the communitarianism of the earlier conversion. Being relatively small, these evangelical/pentecostal congregations come closer to the rural, small community context that is most familiar to the people.

Hispanic Catholicism flourished in the premodern context characterized by a belief in hierarchy, respect for elders, and an orientation toward the collectivity and the common good. Hispanic Catholicism enters into crisis when confronted with the drastically different order of modernity, its emphasis on individual rights and equality. In the shift from premodern to modern society the vital psychological space goes from family and significant others to oneself, from the well-being of the collectivity to one's own personal fulfillment. Hispanic Catholicism is simply identified with the premodern, the more ancient way of life, while Protestantism is actually the form of Christianity that arose with modernity itself.

For Protestantism emphasized the possibility of entering into a personal, direct relationship with God by diminishing many of the mediations (sacraments, images, saints, visible Church) that seemed to stand in the place of such a direct friendship. Consequently, Hispanics attracted to evangelical religion are looking for something they realize has been lacking if not denied them in the past: personal conversion. Yet they do not desire to abandon completely their communitarian ethos. Nor do they have to in order to become Protestants. To the contrary, the small faith-sharing orientation of many evangelical churches affirms the communal thrust of Hispanic popular Catholicism while at the same time orienting the people toward more self-determination.

In a similar way, the popularity of cursillos and the charismatic renewal among Hispanic Catholics in the past thirty years is due in large measure to the way that these movements satisfy the need for a more personally appropriated faith.[51] Something of the same dynamic may be the case in the Hispanic people's attraction for evangelical and pentecostal religion. In addition to strong conversion experiences, these churches also provide a vigorous community setting. These two features (personal conversion and community) appear to be the ones most sought by Hispanics in their search for a deeper spirituality, as reported by the 1986 Vatican study.[52] By providing those experiences the evangelical/pentecostals become an effective bridge for Latin American Christianity shaken to its core by the challenges of modernity.

Theologian Avery Dulles detects an evangelizing turn in the thought and ecclesial vision of recent popes. Pope Paul VI's *On Evangelization in the Modern World* is considered one of the most important church documents of the post–Vatican II era.[53] Pope John Paul II has taken up the theme of evangelization with characteristic vigor. In some measure the pope's emphasis on evangelization is due to the extraordinary success and dynamism of evangelical and pentecostal Christianity. He is very aware of this trend and mentions "the challenge of the sects" frequently. Dulles describes this shift to an evangelizing, missionary mentality as "one of the most surprising and important developments in the Catholic Church since Vatican II." The phrase *new evangelization*, which is the name given this emerging ecclesial orientation, has received a great deal of attention in Europe and Latin America. It is only now being taken seriously in the United States.[54]

The emphasis given evangelization in today's Roman Catholic Church is due to many factors. It is not unreasonable to suggest that one of them is the Catholic Church's recognition of the dramatic success of evangelical/pentecostal efforts to promote personal conversion and appropriation of the faith. The so-called cultural Catholicism of traditional Catholic peoples must somehow be transformed into a more responsible, mature faith suitable to a modern, secularized world given to various forms of practical atheism. In this respect evangelical/pentecostal evangelization efforts reflect a successful response to the challenges modernity poses for Christianity. In turn, evangelicalism and pentecostalism pose several challenges to mainline Christianity and to Catholicism in particular. These challenges include but go beyond the context of Catholicism's confrontation and tensions with modernity.

The Major Challenges

Perhaps the underlying appeal of evangelical religion resides in the fact that it is a way of standing up to a kind of elitism that arises in the mainline churches, both Roman Catholic and Protestant. Much of the literature cited above suggests that the main characteristic of evangelical and pentecostal Christianity is not its conservatism but rather its populism. It has a certain down home flavor, a simpler appeal, and greater accessibility to those with limited educational backgrounds. In the Latin American world the resistance to elite religion took the form of *religiosidad popular*. In the United States among Protestants it takes the form of evangelicalism and pentecostalism. The mainline religious thinkers of the United States, unaware, perhaps, of their social class location and its powerful affect on their attitudes, have tended to conceive of evangelicalism in terms of conservative-liberal antagonisms. What really is at stake, however, is the search of ordinary people for a faith that is characterized by an explicit affirmation of God's transcendence, strong convictions about God's will in certain matters of morality founded on biblical teaching, a confidence in God's power to work miracles and especially to heal, and the possibility of establishing a personal relationship with God appropriate for the highly individualized modern world. For Hispanics these needs were in some sense met by their popular Catholicism. Evangelical religion, as mentioned above, may seem more suitable for the modern world given that religion's strong emphasis on personal relationship with Christ.

Bishop Roberto 0. González pursues this thought and summarizes the challenge of the so-called sects in these words:

. . . . part of the success of the sects is their evangelical rootedness in the Gospel—that they seem to present Christ in all his power as the foundation of a new life, of conversion, of forgiveness of sins. Their preaching seems to be based solely upon the person and power of Christ.[55]

Further on in the same article Bishop Gonzalez provides a trenchant description of evangelical religion. The points he highlights are expressive of the nature of the challenge posed by the evangelical trend:

What are they [the sects] saying? That the heart of Christianity is a personal relationship with Jesus Christ, as Saviour and Lord, in whom I find forgiveness of sins and newness of life. That Christ is everything! Then everything else that the Church stands for, in terms of faith and morals, comes out of the relation with that center of universal history, which is the person of Jesus Christ. He has the power to grant me radically new existence, to free me from all imperfections, to purify me from my sins and to free me from all limitations that the world and the law and custom seem to impose on me.[56]

Bishop González's observation about freedom from the law and custom is relevant to another challenge posed by evangelical religion, namely, its relevance to the encounter of Hispanics with the culture of modernity. More and more attention is being focused upon this encounter which is perhaps the single most dramatic process currently underway in Latin America and among Latin Americans in the United States. The analyses of David Martin and other students of modernity in Latin America reveal that evangelical/pentecostal Christianity provides a new orientation for ordinary people seeking to deal with the stresses involved in the rapid changes brought about by urbanization, secularization, and immigration. The movement away from traditional Catholicism accordingly has something to do with finding a new religious organizing principal. Conversion to evangelical religion allows Hispanics (gives them permission, as it were) to free themselves from the hierarchical, strongly communal, rural, traditional social and family structure, a system that seems more and more dysfunctional in the new circumstances of immigrant life in the United States or, for that matter, in the huge Latin American metropolis. This shift has elements of continuity as well as change. On the one hand, the affectivity of traditional religion is sustained as is the strong orientation toward transcendence. Yet a new personal freedom is experienced, one founded on the strong catharsis, the conversion experience of the born-again Christian.[57]

The mainstreaming of United States Catholicism, its strong middle-class orientation today, the increasing professionalization of its ministers both clerical and lay are the source of considerable discomfort for Hispanics. The horizon of Church leaders unwittingly absolutizes the middle-class norm. This leads to parish situations, approaches to prayer, worship, and preaching, styles of architecture, church administration, and fund raising that clash with Hispanic sensibilities. In the face of this discomfort evangelical/pentecostal churches provide a most attractive alternative.

The arrival of so many diverse ethnic groups to the United States in the last twenty-five years and the consequent emergence of multicultural ministries is a challenge related to the previous one. Outreach specifically targeted on Hispanics is sometimes combined with outreach to other groups. Pastors justify not doing more for Hispanics on the grounds that they have a responsibility to all. Thus services for Hispanics are watered down. Directions and orientations for the church, parish councils, diocesan pastoral councils, diaconate programs may move away from particular groups like Hispanics and develop somewhat amorphous, nondescript programs that offer "something for everybody."[58]

Contrasting with the multicultural ideology that appears to be endemic to a growing number of U.S. Catholic Church leaders is the remarkably successful approach of the evangelicals and pentecostals formulated by the church growth movement of Donald McGavran: "If people preferred to become Christians as part of social groups, without having to cross racial, linguistic, or class barriers, then the most successful, fastest growing churches would be socially homogeneous."[59]

In the United States, particularly in the period after the civil rights movement of the 1960s and 1970s, such an approach, predicated on what seems to be a "separate but equal" principle, is problematic. The challenge consists, then, in programmatically gearing the outreach and the church context to integration of the various ethnic and social class communities while respecting their often urgent need for their own turf. Historically, the Catholic Church pursued a policy not unlike the one championed by McGavran: the national parish. When Hispanic ministry became a larger piece

of the Church's overall ministry in the period after the Second
World War, however, this policy was already being abandoned.
Jay Dolan demonstrates the importance of both the national parish
and enthusiastic religion, revivalism, for ethnic Catholics of other
times in his groundbreaking work entitled *Catholic Revivalism:*

> Historians have always considered revivalism as a major force in
> American religious history. Yet, they have consistently limited their
> vision to the Protestant phase of this phenomenon, believing that
> Roman Catholics were not so evangelically oriented. This study cor-
> rects that limited view and suggests that the religion of revivalism
> not only found a home among Catholics, but indeed was a major
> force in forming their piety and building up the church.[60]

Hispanic Catholics are challenged by an evangelical Protestantism
that continues to practice the "wisdom" of nineteenth-century
American Catholicism by affirming the national parish approach,
that is, having congregations established just for the Spanish-
speaking and promoting among them an enthusiastic, highly affective religiosity.

    The Hispanic Catholic response to these challenges is taking
various forms. One of them is expressed through the concept mentioned above and presently gaining currency among Hispanic ministry leaders: the "new evangelization." Pope John Paul II gave the
impetus for this concept in his 1983 allocution opening the novena,
the years of preparation for the fifth centenary of the coming of
the gospel to the Americas in 1992. Bishop Roberto González has
formulated what this concept might mean for Hispanic Catholics
struggling to lead better lives and attracted to some of the features
of evangelical/pentecostal Christianity. He stresses the need to
acknowledge the positive values in much of what the evangelicals
are saying and doing. At the same time he suggests that a fuller,
more challenging and rooted Christian life can still be discovered in
Catholicism. The challenges he sees facing United States Hispanics
are secularism, consumerism, and sectarianism. He believes that
the Catholic tradition has something to offer in response to these
challenges. While respecting and even learning from the insights
and faith tradition of evangelicals, González believes that ultimately the greatest challenge to Hispanic Catholics does not come
from the sects but, rather, from what he calls "radical secularism
and the concomitant consumerism that tend to exclude all forms of
transcendence and religiosity from the dominant culture and from
the public and civic life."[61]

The Latin American bishops seem to suggest something similar in their treatment of the appeal of evangelical religion in their preparatory document for Santo Domingo. In general they have taken the "high road" and responded to the phenomenon not by condemning the evangelical/pentecostal churches but by showing how the phenomenon relates to deeper trends in the culture, especially to the challenges of modernity. Among the factors contributing to the rise of evangelical Protestantism in Latin America is the ongoing search for meaning, especially for ultimate meaning and transcendence, among the youthful masses of Latin Americans.[62] In the context of dramatic changes taking place in their societies, politics, and culture, people continue to seek God and not just earthly solutions. Perhaps this insight relates as well to Hispanics in the United States who face similar upheavals. The explicit faith orientation of evangelical religion responds directly to the need for religious orientation of a people who historically have been extremely faith oriented.

The stress on God's transcendence is enhanced by three typical features of evangelical Christianity that clearly appeal to Hispanics: 1) the emphasis on feelings expressed in music; 2) the stress on the accessibility of the Bible to the ordinary believer (not just to the exegete and the *savant*);[63] and 3) the small faith community orientation which creates an atmosphere where peer witnessing and reinforcement can occur. These elements are often absent in the religious milieu of the more affluent and educated.

Mainline religion—Protestantism going back to nineteenth-century liberalism, and Roman Catholicism more recently in Europe and the United States—has tended toward elitism, has often distanced itself from the concerns of ordinary people becoming the refined religion of those in the know. It has made its peace with the anonymity and mobility of the city and modern life. The future vitality of the churches, then, depends upon their ability to immerse themselves again in the human experience of a faithful for whom middle-class ways and full-fledged modernity are still an illusive possibility, not the unquestioned norm. Evangelical religion and pentecostalism are leading the way in this as the dramatic data on the growth of worldwide pentecostalism indicate.

It must be noted, however, that the basic ecclesial communities constitute another, perhaps not totally unrelated, response to the challenges outlined here. Their path has been traced in several studies, most recently by Marcello Azevedo.[64] Their importance for ministry among Hispanic Catholics in the United States has been repeatedly underscored by both the bishops and the Hispanic Catholic leadership itself. Certainly some of the same qualities found in evangelical Christianity can be found in these small Christian faith communities: a sense of community, less anonymity, and a more affective style. The basic ecclesial communities also promote a clear, direct sense of social commitment, something that evangelical religion does not, at least initially, seem to stress.[65] David Stoll, as mentioned earlier, has noted that the base communities have not been as successful among the poor as the evangelical/pentecostal congregations because the base communities have sometimes lost sight of the euphemistic, symbolic, and ritual way popular religion deals with oppression.[66] These base communities, however, have not lost sight of the communal thrust of Hispanic cultures. Roberto S. Goizueta calls this the intrinsic communal character of praxis and links it to the principle of solidarity in Catholic social teaching. He believes that "in the praxis of U.S. Hispanics community has ontological priority, for it gives birth to subjectivity." Goizueta quotes Virgilio Elizondo: "For our native forefathers, . . . it was the community that called forth the individuality of the person."[67]

Putting together David Stoll's critique of liberation theology and the base communities with the observations of Roberto Goizueta and Virgilio Elizondo, one might conclude that a future path for Christianity in Latin America and among United States Hispanics can be found in a dialectical relationship, a dialogue, a give-and-take between the insights of liberation theology and the experiences of the base ecclesial communities on the one hand and, interesting enough, the evangelical/pentecostal communities on the other. This path will perhaps be the fruit of a mature analysis and evaluation of the complex religious, social, economic, political, and cultural ferment experienced by Hispanics in North and South America. The path may become a new, vital form of ecumenism.

Finally, the quotation from William R. Read at the beginning of this chapter captures the essence of the long-range issue raised for Hispanic Catholics in the United States by evangelical and pentecostal Christianity. The evangelization of U.S. Hispanic Catholics demands that one "abandon the cultural coldness, the systematized, privileged and secularized Christendom" of the mainline religions of North America. That means promoting a countercultural gospel message. Interestingly enough, then, Hispanic Catholicism with both its popular religiosity and zeal for social justice on the one hand and evangelical Protestantism on the other may have more in common than is usually thought. Donald Dayton was attempting to articulate the basis for this surprising confluence in these words:

> As these movements (Pentecostalism and liberation theology) come more and more into dialogue, they may discover that they have more in common than they think. A central feature of Pentecostalism is its doctrine of "divine healing" which to my mind asserts very fundamentally the salvific intention of God to save and transform the body and this world—an assumption that the movement shares in some sense with the theology of liberation and social transformation.[68]

Dayton goes on to note that liberation theologians like Gustavo Gutiérrez are becoming more aware of the need to develop a deeper spirituality; while pentecostals and evangelicals are speaking more and more of the need for a social ethic. A recent work by pentecostal Hispanic theologian Eldin Villafañe, *The Liberating Spirit: Toward an Hispanic American Pentecostal Social Ethic*, is an example of this trend that may come as a surprise to mainline Christians unfamiliar with the work of pentecostal thinkers.[69]

The subtle and often perplexing reality of evangelical religion's appeal to Hispanic Catholics is, consequently, an issue that involves some of the weightier questions regarding how Hispanics will change and live their Christian faith in the context of U. S. culture as it too changes and moves toward the next millennium. In the interplay between seemingly disparate religious traditions—the evangelical/pentecostal and the Catholic—a vision of Christianity, its possible future tone and texture, emerges to our surprise and wonderment. That battle is being fought in the minds and hearts of today's Hispanic Americans. As they go, so goes the Christianity and religion of the Americas, both North and South.

NOTES

1. William R. Read, *Brazil 1980: The Protestant Handbook*, (Monrovia, Calif.: Mission Advanced Research and Communications Center, 1973), p. xxix.

2. See Vinson Synan, "Varieties and Contributions," *Pneuma* 9, no. 1 (Spring 1987), pp. 31–49.

3. See David Barrett, *World Christian Encyclopedia* (New York: Oxford University Press, 1982), pp. 815–848.

4. Flavio Amatulli, *El sectarismo nos cuestiona* (Mexico, D.F.: Apóstoles de la Palabra, 1988), p. 12.

5. See Pablo A. Derios, "Protestant Fundamentalism in Latin America," in *Fundamentalisms Observed*, ed. Martin E. Marty and R. Scott Appleby. (Chicago: University of Chicago Press, 1991), p. 181. David Stoll explains the dilemma of liberation theology and the base Christian communities in "A Protestant Reformation in Latin America?" *Christian Century* 107, no. 2 (January 17, 1990), p. 45.

6. Eleace King, I.H.M. *Proselytism and Evangelization: An Exploratory Study* (Georgetown: CARA/Georgetown University, 1991), p. 40.

7. George M. Marsden, *Fundamentalism and American Culture* (New York: Oxford University Press, 1980), p. 184.

8. Hans-Jurgen Prien discusses the Church Growth movement in considerable detail in *La historia del cristianismo en América Latina* (Salamanca: Ediciones Sígueme, 1985), pp. 1094–1102.

9. Synan, "Varieties and Contributions," provides an extensive bibliography on pentecostalism in the notes, pp. 46–49. Many of the authors and institutions involved with worldwide pentecostalism are centered in Southern California in the area of Fuller Theological Seminary. The journal of the society for Pentecostal Studies called *Pneuma*, for example, is published at Fuller.

10. David Stoll outlines the history and salient features of contemporary evangelical and pentecostal missionary outreach to Latin America in chapter 4 of *Is Latin America Going Protestant?*, (Berkeley: University of California, 1990), pp. 68–98.

11. The fall 1986 issue of *Pneuma* has two articles on Latin American pentecostalism especially in light of its ecumenical relations. The first is by Everett A. Wilson, "Latin American Pentecostals: Their Potential for Ecumenical Dialogue"; the second, by Carmelo E. Alvarez, "Latin American Pentecostals: Ecumenical and Evangelical." These articles tend to support the notion that pentecostalism on both sides of the Rio Grande is a complex movement with similar challenges and difficulites (see pp. 85–95). Pablo A. Derios summarizes the current status of evangelicalism in Latin America in "Protestant Fundamentalism in Latin America."

12. Justo L. González, *Each in Our Own Tongue* (Nashville, Tenn.: Abingdon, 1991), p. 30.

13. See James Davidson Hunter, *The Coming Generation* (Chicago: University of Chicago Press, 1987).

14. Another trend worth noting here is that growing numbers of mainline Protestant Hispanic congregations are becoming "evangelical" or "charismatic," that is, they subscribe to the styles and theological emphases of evangelicalism and/or pentecostalism but

remain within the mainline Church. A similar observation may be made regarding Roman Catholic charismatics.

15. Donald W. Dayton, "Is Latin America Turning Pentecostal? The Ecumenical Significance of a Religious Revolution," unpublished paper given at National Academy of Ecumenism (NAAE) annual meeting, St. Louis, Mo., September 28, 1991, pp. 17–18.

16. Edwin Sylvest, Jr., "The Protestant Presence (1845 to the present)," in *Fronteras*, ed. Moisés Sandoval (San Antonio: MACC Bookstore, 1983), pp. 277–338. Sylvest gives a more recent overview of Hispanic Protestantism including the movement toward evangelicalism in "Hispanic American Protestantism in the United States," in *On the Move: A History of the Hispanic Church in the Unites States*, ed. Moisés Sandoval (Maryknoll, N.Y.: Orbis, 1991), pp. 115–130.

17. David Maldonado, "Hispanic Protestantism: Historical Reflections," *Apuntes* 11, (Spring 1991), pp. 3–16.

18. R. Douglas Brackenridge and Francisco O. García-Treto, *Iglesia Presbiteriana: A History of Presbyterians and Mexican Americans in the Southwest* (San Antonio: Trinity University Press, 1987).

19. Clifton L. Holland, *The Religious Dimension in Hispanic Los Angeles* (South Pasadena, Calif.: William Carey Library, 1974).

20. González, *Each in Our Own Tongue*, pp. 35–37.

21. Thomas H. Groome, *Sharing Faith* (San Francisco: Harper, 1991), pp. 81–82.

22. The work of Father Flavio Amatulli, an Italian missionary in Mexico, is an excellent example of an approach taken by the Church in Latin America. See Flavio Amatulli, *Catolicismo y Protestantismo* (Acayucan, Veracruz: Apóstoles de la Palabra, 1985).

23. See Carlos Martínez García, "Secta: Un concepto inadecuado para explicar el protestantismo mexicano," *Boletín Teológico*, 23, no. 41 (March 1991), 55–72. He objects to the uncritical use of the term *sects* to refer to evangelical and pentecostal religious groups in Mexico and, by inference, in Latin America. He suggests that the term reflects a prejudice not only on the part of Roman Catholic church leadership but also on the part of social scientists, journalists, and other writers who insist on viewing the growth of this form of Protestantism over so many decades of the twentieth century with disdain and fear.

24. *Vatican Report on Sects, Cults, and New Religious Movements*, in *Origins*, 16, no. 1 (May 22, 1986), pp. 1–10.

25. *Documento de consulta: Nueva evangelización, promoción humana, cultura cristiana* (Santo Domingo, D.R.: CELAM, 1992), pp. 138–142.

26. Stoll, *Is Latin America Going Protestant?* David Martin, *Tongues of Fire* (Oxford: Basil Blackwell, 1990); Florencio Galindo, C.M. *El protestantismo fundamentalista: Una experiencia ambigua para América Latina* (Estella, Navarra: Editorial Verbo Divino, 1992).

27. Juan Castaingts Teillery, "Las iglesias ante el mercado de creencias," *Excelsior*, April 10, 1993, pp. 1–F and 7–F. My translation.

28. See Roger Finke and Rodney Stark for their concept of *religious economy* in *The Churching of America: 1776–1990* (New Brunswick, N.J.: Rutgers University Press, 1992), pp. 17–21.

29. The lucid, pioneering, and still not outdated analysis of sociologists Renato Poblete, S.J., and Thomas F. O'Dea in their article of more than three decades past deserves mention here: "Anomie and the 'Quest for Community': The Formation of Sects among Puerto Ricans of New York," *American Catholic Sociological Review* 21, no. 1 (Spring 1960), pp. 18–36. In addition, there are recent journalistic efforts to address this question: See Mark Christensen, "Coming to Grips with the Losses: The Migration of Catholics into Conservative Protestantism," *America*, January 26, 1991, pp. 58–59; Andrés Tapia, "Viva los evangélicos," *Christianity Today*, October 21, 1991, pp. 16–22; Richard Rodríguez, "A Continental Shift," Los Angeles *Times*, August 13, 1989, Sunday part 5, p. 1; Vicki Larson, "The Flight of the Faithful," *Hispanic*, November 1990, pp. 18–24; Edward L. Cleary, "John Paul Cries Wolf: Misreading the Pentecostals," *Commonweal*, November 20, 1992, pp. 7–8.

30. Andrew Greeley, "Defection among Hispanics," *America*, July 30, 1988, pp. 61–62.

31. Gerardo Marín and Raymond J. Gamba, *Expectations and Experiences of Hispanic Catholics and Converts to Protestant Churches* (San Francisco: University of San Francisco, Social Psychology Laboratory, Technical Report no. 2, February 1990), p. 4.

32. Roberto O. González and Michael LaVelle, *The Hispanic Catholic in the United States: A Socio-Cultural and Religious Profile* (New York: Northeast Hispanic Pastoral Center, 1985), p. 134.

33. Martin, *Tongues of Fire*; and Stoll, *Is Latin America Turning Protestant?*

34. Eleace King, *Proselytism and Evangelization*.

35. George M. Marsden, *Understanding Fundamentalism and Evangelicalism* (Grand Rapids, Mich.: Eerdsmans, 1991), pp. 4–5.

36. See Marsden, *Fundamentalism and American Culture*.

37. Ibid., pp. 3–8.

38. Peter Steinfels, "Beliefs," in the *New York Times*, Saturday, December 7, 1991.

39. Stoll, *Is Latin America Turning Protestant?* pp. 250–251.

40. Ronald A. Knox, *Enthusiasm* (Westminster, Md.: Christian Classics, 1951), p. vi.

41. Randall Balmer, *Mine Eyes Have Seen the Glory: A Journey into the Evangelical Subculture in America* (New York: Oxford University Press, 1989), pp. 233–234.

42. Leo Grebler, Joan Moore, and Ralph Guzman, *The Mexican American People: The Nation's Second Largest Minority* (New York: Free Press, 1970), pp. 494–507.

43. Holland, *Religious Dimension in Hispanic Los Angeles,* p. 444. Also see Grebler, Moore, and Guzman, *Mexican American People,* pp. 498–499.

44. Allan Figueroa Deck, *The Second Wave* (Mahweh, N.J.: Paulist Press, 1989), pp. 56–57.

45. Peter W. Williams, *Popular Religion in America* (Chicago: University of Illinois Press, 1989), pp. 9–14.

46. The negativity toward popular religion in the period after Vatican II has not been as strong among the bishops who have generally insisted on the need to respect it. See John Eagleson and Philip Scharper, eds., in *Puebla and Beyond* (Maryknoll, N.Y.: Orbis, 1979), pp. 184–188. Papal pronouncements on popular religion since Pope Paul VI's period have been generally positive. See Pope Paul VI, *On Evangelization in the Modern World* (Washington, D.C.: USCC Publications, 1976), no. 48.

47. Harvey Cox, *Religion in the Secular City* (New York: Simon and Schuster, 1984), p. 241.

48. This is exactly the point made by Robert Ricard in *La conquista espiritual de México* (México, D.F.: Fondo de Cultura Económica, 1986), p. 23, where he stresses one of the major findings of his lifelong study of the evangelization of Mexico: " . . . he tratado de mostrar que la debilidad principal de la obra evangelizadora de los religiosos españoles estribaba en el fracaso del Seminario de Tlaltelolco y en la enorme laguna que representaba la ausencia de un clero indígena completo. . . . La iglesia de México resultó una fundación incompleta. O mejor dicho, no se fundó una Iglesia mexicana, y apenas se sentaron las bases de una iglesia criolla; lo que se fundó, ante todo y sobre todo, fue una Iglesia española . . . donde los fieles indígenas hacían un poco el papel de cristianos de segunda catelgoría."

49. Sociologists Roger Finke and Rodney Stark have studied the affect of middle-class mores and mindsets on evangelism, the outreach of mainline churches to immigrants, in "The Upstart Sects Win America—1776–1850," in*The Churching of America, 1776–1990,* pp. 54–108. They discuss Catholic outreach to immigrants and compare it to

that of the evangelical/pentecostal denominations in "The Coming of the Catholics, 1850–1926," in the same book, pp.109–144. Sociologist Joseph P. Fitzpatrick explains the relevance of social class distance for contemporary Catholic approaches to Hispanic ministry in "The Hispanic Poor in the American Catholic Middle-Class Church," *Thought* 63, no. 249 (Spring 1988), pp.189–200.

50. Andrew Greeley, following the lead of David Tracy, sheds light on the way Catholics develop their faith. Catholics have an *analogical* imagination, while Protestants seem to have a *dialectical* one. One of the characteristics of Catholics, then, is the ability to hold contradictions in tension. This is what makes the Church "catholic." Perhaps this tendency is at work with Hispanics who even when they become Protestants do not cease being Catholic in a certain sense, that is, a Catholic ethos continues to inspire them. See Andrew Greeley, *The Catholic Myth* (New York: Charles Scribner's Sons, 1990), pp. 34–47. Hence Hispanics in evangelical and pentecostal churches may be "Trojan horses" on behalf of Catholicism. Eleace King found, for example, several pentecostal and other Protestant Hispanic churches with images of the Virgin Mary (Our Lady of Guadalupe) and other Catholic symbols (*Proselytism and Evangelization*, p. 53).

51. Deck, *Second Wave*, pp. 67–69.

52. *Vatican Report on Sects, Cults, and New Religious Movements*, pp. 4–5.

53. See Kenneth Boyack, C.S.P., *Catholic Evangelization Today*, (Mahwah, N.J.: Paulist Press, 1987), pp. 5–7.

54. Avery Dulles, "Pope John Paul II and the New Evangelization," *America*, February 1, 1992, p. 70.

55. Roberto O. González, "The New Evangelization and Hispanics in the United States," *America*, October 19, 1991, p. 268.

56. Ibid., p. 269.

57. In addition to David Martin's treatment of the move to evangelical Christianity as a moment in the modernization of Latin America (*Tongues of Fire*, pp. 284–285), Marcello Azevedo also treats of the effectiveness of the sects in dealing with the reality of Latin America's intense urbanization in *Basic Ecclesial Communities in Brazil* (Washington, D.C.: Georgetown University Press, 1987), pp. 125–126. My thesis is that an analogous situation obtains in the United States.

58. Allan Figueroa Deck, "The Crisis of Hispanic Ministry: Multiculturalism as an Ideology," *America*, July 21, 1990, pp. 33–36.

59. David Stoll, *Is Latin America Turning Protestant?* p. 75.

60. Jay P. Dolan reviews the salient features of the Church's historic, nineteenth-century outreach to Catholic ethnics including the national parish experience in *Catholic Revivalism* (Notre Dame, Ind.: University of Notre Dame Press, 1978), p. xix.

61. R. González, "New Evangelization and Hispanics," p. 268.

62. *Documento de consulta*, p. 139.

63. In this connection C. Gilbert Romero develops the relationship between popular Hispanic religiosity and the Bible. He shows how biblical symbolism and imagery are constitutive elements of Hispanic religiosity. See his *Hispanic Devotional Piety: Tracing the Biblical Roots* (Maryknoll, N.Y.: Orbis, 1991), p. 19–20ff.; and by the same author, "Tradition and Symbol as Biblical Keys for a U.S. Hispanic Theology," in Alan Figueroa Deck, ed., *Frontiers of Hispanic Theology in the United States*, (Maryknoll, N.Y.: Orbis, 1992), pp. 41–61.

64. M. Azevedo, *Basic Ecclesial Communities in Brazil*.

65. The bishops speak encouragingly of the small faith communities in the pastoral letter on Hispanic ministry, *The Hispanic Presence: Challenge and Commitment* (Washington, D.C.: USCC Publications, 1983), p. 27. The more than 1200 Hispanic Catholic leaders assembled in Washington, D.C., for the Third National Pastoral Encuentro in 1985 produced a document, the *National Pastoral Plan for Hispanic Ministry* (Washington, D.C.: USCC Publications, 1987). In this document the basic ecclesial community is singled out as an especially apt tool for effective evangelization (see, p. 10).

66. See note 5.

67. Roberto S. Goizueta, "Rediscovering Praxis," in *We are a People*, ed. Roberto S. Goizueta, (Minneapolis: Fortress Press, 1992), pp. 64–65. For Hispanic culture's affinity with the Catholic concept of solidarity, see Roberto S. Goizueta, "The Church and Hispanics in the United States: From Empowerment to Solidarity," in *That They Might Live*, ed. Michael Downey (New York: Crossroad, 1991), pp. 168–169.

68. Dayton, "Is Latin America Turning Protestant?" pp. 22-23.

69. Eldin Villafañe, *The Liberating Spirit* (Lanham, Md.: University Press of America, 1992).

Conclusion

Jay P. Dolan

On the first day of class in my American history course I write three dates on the blackboard—1607, 1608, 1610. Then I ask the students to identify the significance of each date. Someone always knows that 1607 represents the founding of Jamestown, but seldom does anyone know the significance of the other two dates— the founding of Quebec in 1608 and the founding of Santa Fe in 1610. The reasoning behind my pedagogical cunning is to impress upon the students the French and Spanish dimension of American history as well as the more familiar English aspect. While English settlers were struggling to establish a colony along the Chesapeake, Spanish settlers were attempting to do the same in New Mexico, a remote corner of Spain's colonial empire. The Spanish had already established settlements in Florida during the sixteenth century and founded the historic town of St. Augustine in 1565. The settlement of the Texas region took place in the early eighteenth century, and shortly thereafter the Spanish settled in the area we now call Arizona. Then came the colonization of the Pacific coast region and the Hispanic presence in that area has given California a distinctive heritage. The history of Spanish America changed drastically in the early nineteenth century when Mexico took over the territories from Spain; even more drastic was the American conquest of these regions in the mid-nineteenth century. The American takeover marginalized the Hispanics and they became the forgotten people. But Hispanics are no longer forgotten. Their growth in the twentieth century, most especially in the period since the 1950s, has transformed them into a major force in American society.

In 1950 and 1960 the U.S. Census did not even have a category for Hispanics. That changed in 1970, and since then a fairly accurate demographic profile of Hispanics has become available. Clearly one of the most remarkable aspects of this profile is the rapid growth of the population. Since 1970 the number of Hispanics in the U.S. has more than doubled, and according to the 1990

440

census 22.4 million Hispanics now live in the U.S. A conservative estimate that represents 9 percent of the U.S. population, it makes them the second largest minority group in the nation; African Americans represent the largest minority group with a population of approximately 30 million in 1990.

Like other immigrant groups, Hispanic newcomers have settled in certain regions of the country, generally those areas that have a long history of a Hispanic presence. The Southwest is clearly the cultural and political capital for Mexican Americans. In Texas, one out of five people (19 percent) is Hispanic and in some cities like Laredo (93 percent), El Paso (69 percent) and San Antonio (56 percent) Hispanics make up the majority of the population. Florida has claimed a Cuban population since the nineteenth century, and today two out of three people in Miami are Hispanic, most of them Cuban. New York is the capital of the Puerto Rican people, with over half a million Puerto Ricans living in the city in 1990.

The remarkable growth of the Hispanic population since the 1960s is certainly one of the most striking conclusions that emerges from this study of Hispanic America since World War II. The reasons for this growth are twofold: immigration and a high birth rate. One study estimates that about half of the increase in the Hispanic population in the 1980s can be attributed to the high birth rate and the other half to immigration.[1] With Cubans being the one exception because of their high median age, the Hispanic birth rate far exceeds that of the non-Hispanic; in fact, the birth rate of Hispanics from Central and South America, a more recent immigrant group, is more than double the birth rate of non-Hispanics in the U.S. Such a high birth rate helps to account for the age structure of the Hispanic population, which has a median age of 25.5 compared to 32.2 for the U.S. population as a whole. Such a young population clearly suggests that there will be significant growth in the future and the challenges of the present will pale in comparison to the challenges that the twenty-first century will present to both Church and nation.

Another important point to be made is that the immigrants of the 1980s and 1990s confront many of the same problems that immigrants of all ages have encountered. Joan Moore put this very well in her essay:

> Most Hispanic communities include large numbers of people who face problems of adjustment to a new society. No other large minority community has such a serious problem. The Cuban success

story in Miami shows clearly that large-scale government help can make a major difference, but the message has not been generalized. The latest wave of Latino immigration coincides with serious fiscal problems in federal, state, and local governments; public help for Hispanic arrivals and their children will not be forthcoming. For their part, immigrants strain existing institutions, and in major centers of immigration (like Los Angeles and Houston) public schools and government-operated health facilities have occasionally done their best to reject their undocumented immigrant clients. Even when some immigrants—like the Puerto Ricans—are eligible for public assistance, the economic crisis in cities like New York has caused such a cutback of government services that the Hispanic population finds itself at the very bottom of the economic pile.

Though the people themselves, like all immigrants, will take up some of the slack through their own networks, the church must also step in and respond to the call for social and economic justice that comes forth from these immigrant communities. Undoubtedly the call will grow louder with each new wave of Hispanic immigration.

Another major consequence of large scale population growth is the growing chasm between Hispanic newcomers and a Church whose leadership is overwhelmingly non-Hispanic. This is not a new problem, but it has become much more serious because of the large-scale increase in the Hispanic population. In the not too distant future Hispanic Catholics may very well outnumber all other Catholics in the U.S. combined. Yet, the decision makers in the Church, both at the local and national level, are overwhelmingly non-Hispanic. This situation is somewhat reminiscent of the Italian experience in the late nineteenth and early twentieth centuries. Italians did not feel at home in a Church run by the Irish, and this alienation was carried over to the twentieth century. Like the Italians of the nineteenth century, Latinos are outsiders in their own Church and will remain so until some creative solution is arrived at that will provide for more Hispanic leaders and decision makers at both the local and national level. If such a solution is not achieved, then the chasm between what has been called the church of *el pueblo* and the institutional Church will undoubtedly grow wider as the alienation of the people intensifies. Moreover, it is clear that any effort to bridge the gap between *el pueblo* and the official institutional Church must take into consideration the importance of Latina women in the religious life of the people. Traditionally women have assumed important roles in the religious life of the community. Without their involvement in the future no attempt to narrow the chasm will be terribly effective. This certainly will be a major challenge for a Church that has been firmly wedded to the patriarchal model of religion for centuries.

Another important theme that emerges from these essays is the diversity of the people whom we label *Hispanic* or *Latino*. Simply put, they are not all alike. Though they share a common language and other cultural traits, the diversity among them is most pronounced. To lump them together and treat them as one people because of a shared language might be effective for marketing purposes, but it overlooks the very different cultures that make up the Latino population in the United States. First of all they come from eighteen different Latin American republics as well as Spain and Puerto Rico. Each of these countries has its own particular history and culture. Mexican-Americans are very conscious of being a conquered people who were marginalized by the conquering Americans during the course of the nineteenth century. Cubans are welcomed in the United States as political refugees, victims of Castro and communism. Few immigrant groups have had such a welcome mat awaiting them when they arrived in this country. Puerto Ricans, on the other hand, have had a very ambivalent relationship with the United States. Living under the Spanish flag for centuries, Puerto Rico came under American control after the Spanish American War. The desired Americanization of Puerto Rico never totally took place, and many Puerto Ricans are not satisfied with their Commonwealth status in relation to the United States. Dominicans, on the other hand, cannot wait until they come to the United States. As Marina Herrera noted in her essay: "The Dominican attitude to this country is best exemplified in a graffito that appeared in 1964, at the height of the American occupation of Santo Domingo ordered by President Lyndon B. Johnson: 'Yankee, go home *y llévame contigo*' (and take me with you!)" The Dominicans and the Cubans love baseball whereas soccer is the favorite pastime of the Mexicans. War and political repression have driven many people from Central American countries to the United States. Many of these migrants have entered the country illegally, and they live a clandestine life in the barrio. El Salvador is one example where political repression forced emigration. In fact, it is estimated that possibly as much as one-tenth of El Salvador's total population is now residing illegally in the United States.[2]

One constant in immigration history is the motivating force that persuades people to leave hearth and home and journey to a strange new land. *Panis et libertas*, bread and freedom, inspired millions of Europeans to leave their homeland in the nineteenth century and similar dreams of political freedom and economic opportunity have persuaded millions of people from Latin America to migrate to the United States. For some groups, such as the Cubans and the Salvadorans, political freedom was the main motivating force, whereas for Mexicans and Puerto Ricans economic opportunity has been the principal reason for emigrating to this country.

The patterns of settlement also underscore the diversity of the Hispanic peoples. Cubans have always had close ties with Florida and after the Cuban revolution in 1959 Cuban emigrés have flocked to South Florida; they now make up about one-half of Miami's population. Most Salvadoran refugees live in California in the urban areas of Los Angeles and San Francisco; Nicaraguans have found a home in Miami; and immigrants from the Dominican Republic are one of the fastest-growing communities in New York City.

The Southwest United States has long been the political and cultural capital for Mexican Americans, but even within this region there is significant diversity. As Joan Moore commented, "The Mexican-American population in the United States is so old and so diverse that it defies almost all generalities." A good part of this diversity stems from the diverse subregions of the Southwest. The border cities that stretch along the Texas border are some of the poorest parts of the country. Close ties are maintained with relatives across the border and in a city like El Paso there is a continuous flow of traffic back and forth across the border. Los Angeles is another Mexican-American stronghold and its status as a global city offers economic opportunities not found in the border cities of Texas. The size of the Mexican-American community in Los Angeles is so large that it defies easy generalizations. Some Mexican Americans are well assimilated into the American lifestyle; others are much more resistant and strive to maintain their Latino heritage, and as a result they have become politically active on behalf of their Latino community. The third type of lifestyle that Moore described was that of the Hispanos of New Mexico and southern Colorado. Descendants from the Spanish settlers of the seventeenth and eighteenth centuries, they proudly claim an identity distinct from the more recently arrived Mexicans.

Add the ingredient of class or economic status and the diversity among Hispanics becomes even more apparent. The Cubans are better educated and more prosperous as a group than other Hispanics. That is partially explained by the type of people, the so-called Golden Exiles who emigrated immediately after the 1959 revolution. Another reason was the vast amount of public funds, nearly $1 billion between 1965 and 1976, that was spent to provide relief and assistance to the Cuban refugees. As a result they have helped to turn Miami into a major financial and commercial center for all of Latin America. At the other end of the spectrum are the Puerto Ricans. They are not only the poorest Hispanic subgroup, they are perhaps the "worst-off ethnic group in the United States."[3] Such poverty is most visible in New York City where more than a third of all Puerto Ricans on the mainland live. In 1992, as Joan Moore noted, "more than half (55 percent) of all Puerto Ricans in the city fell below the poverty line." Moreover, "black median family income is substantially higher than Puerto Rican, and is rising more rapidly. The black home-ownership rate is more than double the Puerto Rican rate. Puerto Rican families are more than twice as likely as black families to be on welfare, and are about 50 percent more likely to be poor."[4] At a national level, more Puerto Rican families, roughly 50 percent, are headed by a single parent than any other Hispanic group, roughly 50 percent, and the poverty rate among female-headed families is 65 percent. Such statistics can scarcely convey the grimness of the Puerto Rican situation on the mainland. Among the Mexicans diversity is once again the pattern. In a region like New Mexico some Mexicans belong to the elite class of U.S. senators, business leaders, and state politicians. In cities like San Antonio and Los Angeles a distinct middle class exists. But among the Mexican born in this country 28 percent fell below the poverty line in 1991, and along the Texas border, as Moore notes, "an estimated quarter of a million people live in some 1,000 *colonias*—new rural slum communities that often lack basic utilities, water, and sewers."

Given the historical and cultural differences of each Hispanic subgroup, their diverse patterns of settlement, and their divergent economic situations, the idea of a Latino unity remains, in David Badillo's words, "largely a speculative concept." A single Hispanic experience simply does not exist. This has important consequences for the institutional Church and its leaders who strive to minister to this large and diverse people. Marina Herrera commented on this point in her essay in the following manner:

> It is extremely difficult and even perilous to speak, for the sake of academic purity, religious unity, or expediency, of Hispanics as one ethnic group with one voice. It is difficult because if one finds broad

enough parameters that encompass the variety of communities that comprise the Hispanic population, then most policies are rendered inoperative and next to useless in the programming of services and programs to serve them. All Hispanics are not Spanish speaking, all are not Catholic, all are not of a particular racial makeup, all are not poor, all are not outside the mainstream culture, all are not without the best education, all are not politically powerless, all have not experienced racial or cultural discrimination at the hands of the dominant society. It is perilous also because false expectations of unity from both Hispanics and non-Hispanic leaders causes serious divisions and unnecessary hostilities in communities where Hispanics are struggling to make inroads into the controlling structures, discovering who they are and the contributions they can make.

Although the diversity of Latinos has been most emphasized in the 1990s, there have been periods when a pan-Latino identity was stressed. This was noticeable in the pre–World War II era when political events in Mexico and Puerto Rico mobilized opinion among Hispanics on the mainland and created an awareness of a common identity among diverse Spanish-speaking groups. This pan-Latino awareness was, as Anthony Stevens-Arroyo noted, "immensely aided by the emergence of Latino newspapers and radio programs in urban centers such as New York, Los Angeles, Chicago, Tampa, and Philadelphia." Music and movies strengthened this awareness as larger and larger numbers of Latinos were communicating with one another across regional and national boundaries. A common religion, Catholicism, also helped to shape this identity. In the 1950s and 1960s this sense of a common identity as Hispanics or Latinos began to intensify. The 1960s and early 1970s was an especially key period in this development. The War on Poverty mobilized people at the neighborhood level and unleashed an activism that cut across national or cultural boundaries. The civil rights movement stressed the mobilization of minority groups and fostered a group consciousness among Hispanics of different cultural traditions. Cesar Chavez and his struggle to organize the farmworkers became a national symbol for Hispanics, and this served to emphasize the commonality rather than the diversity of the Latinos in the United States.

Developments within Catholicism also reinforced the move toward a pan-Latino identity. Imported to the United States from Spain in 1957 the *cursillo*, an intense weekend experience of spiritual renewal, became very popular in the 1960s and 1970s among

Hispanic Catholics. As Stevens-Arroyo noted, "the Cursillo" movement "played a role in creating a Latino Catholic identity. In some places, such as New York, to be Catholic was virtually synonymous with being a cursillista." Another important step toward strengthening the sense of a pan-Latino identity was the relocation of the Office for the Spanish-Speaking from Texas to Washington, D.C., in 1970 where it became part of the complex of national Catholic offices now known as the United States Catholic Conference. This relocation and upgrading in importance of the Office for the Spanish-Speaking suggested that Hispanics were taking on a new identity within the church; the Spanish-speaking apostolate was no longer to be limited to the Southwest and the needs of the Mexican-American farm workers. It was a national apostolate that crossed regional and cultural boundaries. Another key development was the 1972 national pastoral meeting (*encuentro*) of Hispanic Catholics. About 250 leaders of the Hispanic Catholic community gathered in Washington, D.C., to discuss the situation of Hispanic Catholics. They were no longer willing to accept a second-class status in the Church and they drew up a list of seventy-eight resolutions that demanded action from Church leaders.

By the early seventies, then, it was clear that Hispanic Catholics were becoming more organized on a national level and more militant in seeking their demands. This sense of a common cause intensified throughout the 1970s and resulted in the convocation in 1977 of the second national pastoral meeting. This time twelve hundred people gathered in Washington, D.C., to discuss the needs of Hispanic Catholics in the U.S. Representing Hispanics across the country, the delegates published a document that eloquently stated what it meant to be Catholic and Hispanic in the United States. Then in 1983 the National Conference of Catholic Bishops published a letter on Hispanic ministry, *The Hispanic Presence: Challenge and Commitment*. This represented the high point of pan-Latino identity since in the 1980s conflict began to develop among Hispanics and the sense of diversity among Hispanic groups emerged as a dominant theme.

Clearly, conflict had frequently been present whenever Hispanics of diverse backgrounds with different agendas came together, but it seemed to become more intense as the 1980s progressed. Stevens-Arroyo, a Puerto Rican, attributes this to the creation of a Latino identity within Catholicism that was modeled on the Mexican-American experience. This model is not applicable to the

Puerto Rican experience, according to Stevens-Arroyo. Even more divisive was the conflict that emerged over the type of ministry to be encouraged in the Hispanic community. One approach, which Stevens-Arroyo labels *pastoralist*, focuses on change "within the Church and its structures as a more important sphere of activity than direct action for social change." Others wanted a more activist approach and have "directly applied the goals of liberation theology to U.S. society so as to advocate a radical economic and political change in the direction of socialism." For the pastoralist, the chosen sphere of activity is the Church; for the liberationist, the secular community is where the action should take place. Such conflict has led Stevens-Arroyo to conclude that pan-Latino "identity had been fragmented both ideologically and among various nationality groups." Without a doubt, a national commitment on the part of Church leaders to Hispanic Catholics as a single group within the Church is also weakening. With an emphasis on diversity and the weakening of a pan-Latino identity, the focus of institutional Church activity and commitment has clearly shifted to the local and regional area.

The one and the many, the common and the diverse; this is a paradox that is not only very American but is also very Hispanic. Hispanics do indeed share some important traits. Spanish is the dominant language; Catholicism is the prevailing religion; and the traditional family structure is highly valued and still prevalent. Yet, within this unity is such striking diversity that it precludes anyone from speaking and acting as if there was a common Latino experience in the United States.

The same forces that inspired the desire for a pan-Latino identity were also instrumental in forming an Hispanic Church within the larger American Catholic Church. Gradually over the course of the last fifty years, most especially since the 1960s, Hispanic Catholics have created a Church within the Church. This development is similar to the German Catholic experience in the United States in the late nineteenth century. In the late 1880s and early 1890s German Catholics organized annual national meetings where they addressed their particular needs within the context of the United States. The clergy formed a national organization that sought to promote the cause of German Catholicism; they lobbied for more episcopal appointments, championed the use of the German language, the value of the parochial school, and the national parish. There clearly was a self-awareness among Germans that they were not only different from the rest of American Catholics but also had special needs and concerns that had to be addressed. Polish immigrant Catholics also organized nationally in order to promote the cause of Polish Catholicism in the United States. In the twentieth century the one group that has succeeded in forming a national Church within the larger Church are the Hispanics, and what they have accomplished far surpasses in scope and permanence what the Germans or Polish did.

The new self-awareness among Hispanics became most visible in the 1960s when, according to Moisés Sandoval, they "had finally found a secure identity as a people, without which they could not organize in the Church and preach their own unique message." Rejecting the ideal of assimilation "they decided that their destiny was to remain distinct from mainstream society. They realized as well that they had much to contribute because of their religiosity and values as Hispanic Catholics." Buoyed by their new self awareness and confident about the importance of their place in the church and society Hispanic Catholics began to build a Church within the Church. The establishment of a national office for the Spanish speaking in 1964 and its relocation to Washington, D.C., in 1970 was a major step in this development. From this flowed the founding of numerous regional offices across the country; these local offices for Hispanic ministry have become the vital centers for evangelization within Hispanic communities. Three national pastoral meetings, encuentros, have taken place since 1972, and each gathering has produced a blueprint for action among Hispanic Catholics. The regional offices and the encuentros have served as training grounds for developing lay leadership and as Sandoval emphasizes time and again without such lay leadership the formation of an Hispanic church would never have occurred.

Between 1970 and 1992 twenty-three Hispanic priests have been promoted to the hierarchy. The first was Patricio Flores who was ordained a bishop in 1970; he soon became the shepherd and bishop for Hispanics across the country, most especially Mexican Americans. As more Hispanic priests became bishops, Flores limited his work to his own diocese in San Antonio, Texas. The training of priests for the Hispanic church has taken on new dimensions in recent years. No longer are Hispanic seminarians forced to give up their culture and language in order to survive in the seminary. Their culture and language is respected and in some dioceses candidates for the priesthood are required to study Spanish; in a few seminaries even the course of instruction is bilingual and bicultural. This was unheard of in the 1950s and 1960s. A major reason for this development is the recognition by Church leaders that "pluralism, not assimilation and uniformity, is the guiding principle in the life of communities in both the ecclesial and secular societies."[5]

Given the small number of Hispanic priests, about two hundred American born and fifteen hundred foreign born, and the declining number of priests in general, ministry in the Hispanic church has come in large part from laypeople and one of the most significant developments in this regard has been the establishment of centers or institutes for developing lay ministers. One of the more notable centers was the Mexican American Cultural Center (MACC) established in San Antonio, Texas, in 1971. Other important centers include the Southeast Pastoral Institute (SEPI) in Miami and the Tepeyac Institute in El Paso. Like the Germans and Polish before them, Hispanic clergy organized their own association, PADRES, in 1969 to promote the cause of Hispanic Catholics within the larger American Catholic church. Hispanic women religious did the same two years later when they formed Las Hermanas. Finally, reflecting the liturgical awakening that had taken place within Catholicism since World War II, Hispanics established an Institute of Hispanic Liturgy, and this organization has successfully led the movement to produce Spanish-language liturgical texts as well as hymnals that were officially recognized by Church authorities. Hispanic theologians have also formed their own scholarly organization, the Academy of Catholic Hispanic Theologians of the U.S. (ACHTUS); just recently a new journal, *Journal of Hispanic/Latino Theology*, was established.

What all of this activity over the past quarter century suggests is that a very vibrant Hispanic Church has developed within the larger Catholic Church in the United States. The Mexican-American influence in the development of this Church has been most decisive. The primary reason for this is that the Mexican Americans are the largest Hispanic group in the United States comprising almost two thirds (62 percent) of the total U.S. Hispanic population. Because of their size, as well as their centuries-long presence in the U.S., they have become a dominant force in the Hispanic Church. This Church has all the characteristics of an institution with the bureaucratic trademarks of national organizations, offices, conventions, and institutes. It is not centrally organized or controlled but is informally linked together by a common concern—the welfare of Hispanic Catholics. It is a Church within a Church, and its position within the Catholic Church somewhat resembles that of the Black Church within the Protestant ecclesiastical establishment.

A major influence on this Hispanic Catholic awakening was the renewal of Catholicism that was taking place in Latin America in the post–Vatican II era. The first signs of this became noticeable with the organization in the United States of CICOP (Catholic Inter-American Cooperation Program) in 1964. This organization promoted conversations and discussions among Latin American and North American clergy and laity. Much more significant was the 1968 meeting of the Latin American hierarchy at Medellín, Columbia. This historic meeting sought to apply the insights of Vatican II to the Church in Latin America. From this gathering emerged a new understanding of the Church in Latin America and the ideas that surfaced at Medellín were soon transplanted to the United States. Chief among these ideas was the theology of liberation; the concept of small Christian base communities (*comunidades eclesiales de base*) was another idea that has become popular in Hispanic communities in the United States. Born "among the struggling poor of Latin America" these comunidades, according to Edmondo Rodríquez, represent "a different way of thinking and of being Church which resurrects an intimate sense of community, trims the modern urban neighborhoods down to size, and affords ordinary people an opportunity to do ministry." The idea of the encuentro also came directly from Latin America in the person of Edgard Beltrán, a Columbian priest active in Church renewal, and this would have an enormous impact on Hispanic Catholicism north of the border. In addition, some of the key people in the Latin American renewal, such as the Brazilian pastoralist, José Marins, spent a great deal of time in the U.S. lecturing and teaching Americans about the new ideas surfacing in Latin America. The Mexican American Cultural Center in San Antonio was a key center where much of this cross fertilization of ideas initially took place. The Latin American influence was also noticeable in the music and spirituality that was emerging among Hispanics in the United States. Not to be forgotten was the Spanish influence in these years. The Cursillo, an experience that was so central to the Hispanic Catholic community, was imported from Spain as was marriage encounter, a spiritual renewal program for married couples that has become quite popular in the United States. The Spanish influence is also visible in the liturgical life of Hispanic parishes, especially in the area of sacred music.

The link with Latin America and Spain underscores a very important point—Hispanic Catholicism has a different history and a different heritage from the rest of the American Catholic community. For this reason the Hispanic way of being Catholic is very different from what Orlando Espín calls the *Euro-American* way of being Catholic. Contemporary Hispanic Catholicism can trace its roots back to medieval Spain; as Espín notes in his essay, this religion took shape before the sixteenth-century Council of Trent, and it was this religion that was transplanted to Latin America and those regions that would eventually become part of the United States. The Catholicism that the immigrants from Europe brought with them in the nineteenth century was a religion formed in great part by the Council of Trent. This was the religion of the immigrant Church that spread throughout much of the United States in the nineteenth and twentieth centuries; it was a Mass-and-sacraments style of Catholicism where a person's religious commitment was measured by regular attendance at Sunday Mass and frequent reception of the sacraments. This was not the Catholicism that Mexicans, either American born or Mexican born, practiced.

Hispanic Catholicism is, as Allan Figueroa Deck, S.J., describes it,

> hardly the reflection of a rigorous religious formation based upon accepted catechetical texts. Rather, theirs is a popular faith mediated especially by grandmother, mother, and women in general. Its standards and practices are not articulated in books or in any other form of print medium. This deeply rooted form of Catholicism is communicated orally, from person to person, within the context of family, rancho, town, or barrio. It almost totally lacks rational articulation but is not for that less convincing and motivating. . . . Its main qualities are a concern for an immediate experience of God, a strong orientation toward the transcendent, an implicit belief in miracles, a practical orientation toward healing, and a tendency to personalize or individualize one's relationship with the divine.

As the religion of the Council of Trent, known as Tridentine Catholicism, took hold in Latin America long after the conquest of the region, it came into conflict with the pre-Tridentine Iberian Catholicism transplanted from Spain in the sixteenth century. They were two different ways "of relating to reality and of living the Christian gospel." This resulted in a division within Latino Catholicism between the official, Tridentine style of being Catholic and what has become known as "popular" Catholicism; between a mass-and-sacraments Catholicism and a popular religion practiced by the majority of the people. This division was carried over to the United States where Latino popular Catholicism came into conflict with the official Tridentine Catholicism of the Euro-American Church. Euro-American Catholics, both clergy and laity, looked upon the popular Catholicism of Hispanics as a superstitious holdover from the Middle Ages. This mentality has persisted to the present day to the point where, in the opinion of Orlando Espín and indeed many others,

> the alternatives offered by official Catholicism (progressive or conservative) to U.S. Latinos seem clear and are certainly not new—either leave the pre-Tridentine style of Catholicism behind by becoming religiously Euro-Americanized, or face the continued onslaught of accusations of ignorance and superstition, followed by pastoral activity geared to educate correctly in "real" Roman Christianity. The American Church's attempts at understanding Hispanic popular Catholicism seem all too frequently motivated by the hope for the latter's early and definitive demise.

Certainly, many Hispanics participate in the official type of Catholicism that is normative for the Euro-American Church and a certain blending of the two traditions is noticeable in the Hispanic Catholic liturgy. Nonetheless, popular Catholicism is, as Deck put it, "the lived religion of most Hispanics." It is not only the way in which most Latinos practice religion, but Orlando Espín would argue that it is also "a key matrix of all Hispanic cultures." Moreover, Hispanic popular Catholicism has a very strong matriarchal dimension to it as Ana María Díaz-Stevens and others have noted. This places it at odds with the patriarchal tradition of Tridentine Catholicism and serves to heighten the differences between the two styles of Catholicism.

Another theme that runs throughout several of these essays is the recognition of a two-tiered Church. Catholicism in the United States is divided into a white, suburban, middle-class Church and an urban, lower-class Church made up of people of color. These two Churches go their own way, seldom interacting, and this serves to widen the chasm that divides Hispanic Catholicism from Euro-American Catholicism. Moreover, the poverty that is so prevalent in Puerto Rican barrios and Mexican colonias has forced many Hispanic Church leaders to focus their attention on issues of social

justice. The idea for organizations such as PADRES and Las Hermanas was born amid the barrios of San Antonio where hunger,
unemployment, malnutrition, and inadequate schools underscored
the need for social justice; in many parishes the Cursillo centers on
similar social justice issues; and certainly the poverty of much of
the Hispanic Church accounts for the popularity among Hispanics of liberation theology, a theology born in the barrios of Latin
America that seeks to apply the Christian gospel to the social reality
experienced by the poor.

The pronounced middle-class orientation of Euro-American
Catholicism is also a "source of considerable discomfort for Hispanics," according to Deck. "The horizon of Church leaders," he
writes, "unwittingly absolutizes the middle-class norm. This leads
to parish situations, approaches to prayer, worship, and preaching,
styles of architecture, church administration, and fund raising that
clash with Hispanic sensibilities. In the face of this discomfort,"
argues Deck, "evangelical/pentecostal churches provide a most
attractive alternative."

The challenges that Hispanic Catholicism pose for Church leaders in the United States are formidable. Over the course of the
twentieth century and most especially since the 1960s Hispanic
Catholics have fashioned a Church within a Church. In some respects this is similar to what happened with German Catholics in
the United States in the late nineteenth century. But the Hispanic
church has become much more developed and more enduring than
the German model. A more accurate comparison would be with
the Black Protestant Church. African-Americans have fashioned a
unique institution, a Church within a Church that was born in the
days of slavery and has grown and prospered long after slavery
was abolished. The Black Protestant religious experience is clearly
different from that of its white counterpart be it Methodist, Baptist,
or Pentecostal. Moreover, the Black Church provides a network of
institutions that seeks to meet not just the religious needs of the
people but their educational, social, and political needs as well.
What is taking place within Hispanic Catholicism today is very
similar to what has happened in the African-American Protestant Church over the course of the twentieth century. Catholics
in the Euro-American Church must realize this and seek to understand more fully the Hispanic Catholic experience. They must
understand the unique histories and respect the diverse cultures
of Hispanics in the United States. As the Catholic hierarchy said
in its pastoral letter on Hispanic ministry, "the Church shows its

esteem for this dignity by working to ensure that pluralism, not assimilation and uniformity, is the guiding principle in the life of communities in both the ecclesial and secular societies. All of us in the Church should broaden the embrace with which we greet our Hispanic brothers and sisters and deepen our commitment to them." If we do not, then it is certain that the number of Hispanic Catholics will dwindle in the years ahead.

NOTES

1. Che-Fu Lee and Rev. Raymond H. Potvin, "A Demographic Profile of U.S. Hispanics," in *Strangers and Aliens No Longer: The Hispanic Presence in the Church of the United States* (Washington, D.C.: United States Catholic Conference, 1993), p. 39.

2. Kevin J. Christiano, "The Church and the New Immigrants," *Religion and the Social Order* 2, p. 179.

3. Nicholas Lemann, "The Other Underclass," *Atlantic Monthly*, Dec. 1991, p. 96. Many Puerto Ricans do not agree with the conclusions that Lemann made regarding their culture.

4. Ibid., p. 97.

5. *The Hispanic Presence: Challenge and Commitment: A Pastoral Letter on Hispanic Ministry* (Washington, D.C.: National Conference of Catholic Bishops, 1983), p. 5.

CONTRIBUTORS

David Badillo is an urban historian specializing in comparative Latino Studies and Assistant Professor of Latin American Studies at the University of Illinois at Chicago.

Allan Figueroa Deck, S.J., is Associate Professor of Theological Studies and Coordinator of Hispanic Pastoral Programs at Loyola Marymount University in Los Angeles.

Ana María Díaz-Stevens is Associate Professor of Church and Society at Union Theological Seminary.

Jay P. Dolan is Professor of History at the University of Notre Dame and former Director of the Cushwa Center for the Study of American Catholicism.

Orlando O. Espín is Associate Professor of Theology and of Latino Studies at the University of San Diego.

Marina Herrera is a writer, lecturer, and consultant on pastoral and ministry education issues that arise from the multicultural Church.

Joan Moore is Professor of Sociology at the University of Wisconsin-Milwaukee.

Arturo J. Pérez is a priest of the archdiocese of Chicago who writes and lectures on the topics of Hispanic liturgy and spirituality.

Edmundo Rodríguez, S.J., is the Director of the Jesuit Spirituality Center at Grand Coteau, Louisiana, former Provincial Superior of the Jesuits of the South, and former pastor of Our Lady of Guadalupe Church in San Antonio, Texas.

Moisés Sandoval is the editor-at-large of *Maryknoll Magazine* and the editor of *Revista Maryknoll*.

Anthony Stevens-Arroyo is professor of Puerto Rican Studies at Brooklyn College, C.U.N.Y.